Ø BIP 1984+

The Collector's Guide
to Antiquarian Bookstores

The Collector's Guide to Antiquarian Bookstores

COMPILED BY

Modoc Press, Inc.

With an Introduction by

Leona Rostenberg and Madeleine B. Stern

MACMILLAN PUBLISHING COMPANY
A Division of Macmillan, Inc.
NEW YORK

Collier Macmillan Publishers
LONDON

Macmillian Publishing Company
866 Third Avenue
New York, NY 10022

Collier Macmillan Canada, Inc.

Library of Congress Catalog Card Number: 84-21289

Printed in the United States of America

printing number
1   2   3   4   5   6   7   8   9   10

Library of Congress Cataloging in Publication Data
Main entry under title:

The Collector's guide to antiquarian bookstores.

  Bibliography: p.
  Includes index.
  1. Antiquarian booksellers—United States—Directories.
2. Antiquarian booksellers—Canada—Directories.   I. Modoc
Press.
Z475.C65   1984   070.5'025'73   84-21289
ISBN 0-02-903750-6

Acknowledgment

  The compilers of this *Guide* extend their sincerest appreciation to the bookstores and dealers throughout the United States and Canada who so promptly and courteously responded to the request for information. Their support of the project is further evidence of the enthusiasm and love of books that is shared by booksellers and book collectors everywhere.

CONTENTS

Contents

Contents

INTRODUCTION

"Books" were collected long before there were books. When "books" were scrolls of papyri, the Egyptian monarch Ramses II amassed a splendid library of them. When "books" were wax tablets containing the inscriptions of ancient writers, those great Romans Cicero and Pliny the Younger assembled significant collections of such materials. In the Middle Ages, when "books" existed in the form of illuminated vellum leaves and monastic scrolls, they too were collected, and during the fourteenth century the incomparable Italian poet Petrarch filled his house at Verona with letters and documents containing the records of early scholarship.

With Johann Gutenberg's invention of printing by movable type in 1455, books became books more or less as we know them today, and an enormous impetus was naturally given to the field of collecting. Now multiple copies of a book became available and could be distributed among a far larger readership. By the early sixteenth century, our version of the so-called pocket book was improvised, thanks to the imaginative publications program of the great Venetian House of Aldus Manutius. For a few *scudi,* a student could purchase a copy of Catullus or Ovid in a small enough format to slip into the saddlebag as he rode off to the university. The manufacture of books had begun its snowballing progress which would augment that species of man- and womankind known as collectors.*

With the development of the early printing press, the collector could buy in a fairly limited field: the classics, some lay literature, legal texts, religious tomes, and the glosses of the schoolmen. An early sixteenth-century bibliophile, Willibald Pirckheimer of Nuremberg, stationed book scouts throughout Germany, the Lowlands, and Italy. In a short time he could boast that he owned nearly every book published in Italy. From Venice, his agent, the great artist Albrecht Dürer, wrote rather disconsolately that he had been unable to acquire a truly rare book for the Nuremberg patrician. As the century progressed, it

---

*The use of the masculine pronoun in reference to the collector more or less throughout is a shortcut in semantics, certainly not an antifeminism. Portions of this introduction are based upon the authors' *Between Boards: New Thoughts on Old Books* (Montclair and London, 1978).

produced one of the great collectors of all time, the Frenchman Jean Grolier, whose superb inlaid bindings bear the motto: "Grolierii et amicorum."

Book collecting in seventeenth-century England was to some extent contagious. Members of the Royal Society developed libraries within their specific fields. Synonymous with the names of Pepys and Evelyn are their great libraries, while their mutual friend, the distinguished scientist Robert Hooke, assembled a working library of over 3,000 items. Today collecting is no mere hobby but a serious pursuit, and a group of "modern firsters" animatedly discuss in their particular patter mint copies of Betjeman, Updike, and Oates.

Why does this particular breed of *genus humanum* flourish? Has the collector been stimulated by acquisitive instincts for books more beautiful, more impressive, rarer than those owned by a rival collector? Perhaps. But the true bibliophile is an individual of knowledge and discernment.

Many book collectors suffer from book-buying compulsion. The psychiatrist interprets this drive as an inherited malady or a sickness stemming from a disturbed childhood, but the collector views his so-called illness with joy and rapture. He cannot wait until his next purchase; he is impatient to read the next good catalogue. There is no physical pain associated with his disease—except to his purse—and the true collector never worries about funds. There is always his bookseller, whom the collector metamorphoses upon occasion into his banker, a banker unacquainted with "interest" or "payment due." The bibliophile buys with undiminished joy. Did not the great Wilberforce Eames hoist a hammock between towering columns of books? There he slept. A bed would have occupied space essential for new acquisitions. The English collector James Edwards went a step further: he stipulated that his coffin be constructed from the shelves of his library!

The enthusiastic collector regards his books as an extension of himself. Many collectors buy those books that relate to their professions. A lawyer infected with the collecting bug will search for a copy of Littleton's *Tenures* or a neat little Elzevier edition of the *Justinian Code,* and once his shelves begin to bulge he probably will seek bigger fish. His bookseller recommends the first edition of Grotius' *On International Law* (Paris 1625) or Blackstone's *Commentaries.* And why not acquire a copy of Montesquieu's *Spirit of the Laws* whose philosophy influenced our own Founding Fathers?

Physicians outrank lawyers as collectors. The field of medicine is extremely broad, and hence the true medical bibliophile will buy within his own specialty. The ophthalmologist will leap with joy if a copy of the first work on the opthalmoscope of Bartisch becomes his property, and there is not a collecting cardiologist who would not forfeit a portion of his practice for the first edition of Harvey's *On the Circulation of the Blood* (1628). Just so, the gastroenterologist yearns for a copy of William Beaumont's *Experiments and Observations on the Gastric Juice, and the Physiology of Digestion* (1833), one of the earliest works to describe the digestive process.

And so it goes. Artists and architects, once confirmed collectors, will acquire

Introduction

Vasari's *Lives of the Painters,* Leonardo da Vinci's *Treatise on Painting,* the texts of Vitruvius, Serlio, and Wren, the books illustrated by Peter Paul Rubens, Hogarth, Blake, Manet, and others.

Tradesmen, fired by their calling, have become collectors. A partner in Chubb & Company, a firm of locksmiths, acquired a large collection of books and prints relating to his trade, and, speaking of locksmiths, we are quite certain that the royal locksmith Louis XIV studied with admiration the plates of locks and bolts in the *Encyclopédie* of Diderot and Alembert. A few decades ago, within the Concourse of Rockefeller Center in New York City, the firm of Charles de Zemler, gentlemen's hair dressers, featured in their windows a dazzling array of books on male coiffure, mustaches and mustachios, and hair styles of the past, along with shaving mugs and Roman salvers.

The latent instinct for collecting is surely stimulated by travel. What visitor to Florence will not be spurred to acquire books associated with its manifold marvels, its art and architecture, its history and literature? Will he not beseech his bookseller to obtain treatises on the careers of Michelangelo or Cellini, on the Duomo and the Baptistery, on the history of Santa Croce? Infused with the spirit and influence of the Medicis, the collector will buy the Lives of Lorenzo the Magnificent and his successors, the Grand Dukes of Tuscany. The collector of belles-lettres will happily invest in a copy of the Aldine Dante or poems by the literati of the Cinquecento.

The visitor to Paris is enthralled with the narrow streets of the Left Bank, the gardens, and the boutiques. And so he adds to his library *L'Etat de Paris* (1650) which describes in detail the great metropolis of yesteryear. It is not impossible to buy a description of Les Invalides written long before the Emperor Napoleon came to rest in that great vaulted crypt. How beguiling are the gardens and grottoes of Versailles, its fountains and parks, the Hermitage where Marie Antoinette played shepherdess! And so the traveler immerses himself in books on landscape gardening, architecture, and tracts about the fairy queen who was to become the tragic Widow Capet.

Some individuals become collectors by mere accident. A customer fascinated by the history of Mary of Scotland told us the source of his infatuation. Having come to New York with his wife on a buying spree, he became bored with her dawdling in a 57th Street shop, left her, and began to wander about. In the window of an antique shop he saw a rather dark picture in a broken frame. Upon closer examination he discovered it to be a portrait of another tragic queen, Mary of Scotland. Enamored of the painting, he purchased it immediately, and now is the collector, not only of paintings and engravings but of books and tracts all relating to Mary Stuart. He remains one of her most faithful suitors.

Once the collector is "hooked," he pursues all possibilities for his buying mania. Various media serve the collector. The outstanding source of specialist books is the antiquarian bookseller, ready to serve his specialist customer. The Antiquarian Booksellers Association of America, Inc., a group of the most prestigious rare book and autograph dealers, includes individuals in the fields of the American Indian, botany, Egyptology, gardening, illustrated books, mathematics, science fiction, the stock market, and gambling.

There is no gamble in the purchase of a book from a member of the ABAA. The collector browses in the rooms of a knowledgeable enthusiast who shows off his books with delight and discusses their significance with intelligence. The visitor may view freely, and will usually find titles for which he has long searched or others equally provocative with which he is unfamiliar. Often a friendship develops between collector and dealer that helps build the collection.

The collector—whether on the scent of the Stuart monarch James I, the eighteenth-century biographer James Boswell, the great nineteenth-century novelist Henry James, or the twentieth-century author of *Ulysses,* James Joyce—will study diligently the catalogues that relate to his subject. And as he studies them, he will begin to see connections where he had failed to see them before. The collector of James I will be thrilled to discover a little-known life of the monarch's favorite, the Duke of Buckingham, and will emit a barbaric yawp if he locates a volume printed at the Pilgrim Press in Leyden where future voyagers to the New World published their invectives against Stuart policy. Just so the Boswell collector may unearth from a dull-looking catalogue the prospectus of a book by Boswell's great subject, the lexicographer Samuel Johnson; the Henry James collector may spy out a letter written to the author of *The Ambassadors* by Edith Wharton; the pursuer of James Joyce may snatch from an unsuspecting catalogue a delectable history of early twentieth-century Dublin and its taverns.

But if the recent catalogues, foreign or domestic, have not proved fertile for such collectors, they can always attend the auction houses, many of which issue specialized catalogues. These may include just those titles for which they have been searching in New York, Boston, San Francisco, London, Bath, or South Berwick, Maine. Auctions have a varied character. They may be boring, frustrating, or intolerably exciting.

The Henry James collector, for example, now extremely knowledgeable after his perusal of many catalogues and his visits to several bookshops, is nervously awaiting the bidding on No. 101. This item happens to be an indistinguished-looking ephemeral newspaper of 1871 published in six issues only "in Aid of the Destitute People of France." But our collector by this time knows that in it appeared a little-known creation by Henry James, "Still Waters," and so, to round out his holdings, he must have it. The bidding begins quietly, and the collector is overcome with the prospective thrill of ownership. Suddenly, from the rear of the room, his bid is topped. From then on he is caught in the web of competition from which he at length emerges triumphant, but afflicted forever with the incurable malady of auction fever.

Once the collector has amassed a tidy library he is prepared to enlarge his holdings in calf and boards, morocco and cloth. Books have a habit of invading the home, creeping past the so-called library into the dining room, the dinette, the bedrooms, onto couches, stools, and the baby's high chair. An effort should be made to house books carefully, with consideration for their health. They may be arranged by subject, or author, or even imprint. They should be arranged in glass-enclosed cases within a humidified area. There is, of course, a problem with small books. They are somewhat bashful and tend to hide, slip into dark corners, or retreat behind quartos and folios. The collector Hooke created gliders for his small books—in all likelihood supports to keep them in place—and Pepys placed blocks under his small volumes. What joy for the bibliophile to introduce a new quarto to his proud folios. What delight for the collector to view his books standing up smartly in bright array—those delegates from a world of the past, transmitting to the present the pain and joy of yesteryear.

Of all the joys that accrue from antiquarian book collecting, perhaps none is more gratifying than the joy of studying individual acquisitions, for that joy sometimes results in serendipity. When the collector of twentieth-century first editions or press books, for example, starts leafing through a recent purchase, perhaps he may find, laid into a copy of Hemingway's *Across the River and into the Trees* an unexpected leaflet containing advance reviews and solicited endorsements. The serendipity will be increased if such a leaflet turns out to be previously unrecorded. Thanks to his attention to his Hemingway acquisition, the buyer finds that he has literally purchased a twofer. Just so a modern press enthusiast may find, tucked into a copy of a Black Sun imprint, a prospectus announcing past and forthcoming press issues.

As we go back over the centuries, with book in one hand, magnifying glass in the other, and deerstalker atop, we can cry other "Eurekas." A collector of nineteenth-century Americana, for instance, stumbling upon a commonplace-looking cloth-bound study on crime and its phrenological treatment, will be enriched in more than one way by noting that the portraits of criminals illustrating the book were engraved from daguerreotypes by none other than the great Mathew Brady. Moreover, since the *Rationale of Crime* was published in New York in 1846 when Brady was in his early twenties, those portraits represent the artist's earliest book illustrations. A pile of *Frank Leslie's Weeklies* might turn up a bonanza for the knowing collector if he discovers among the folio newssheets two issues of January 1863 containing Louisa May Alcott's first published anonymous thriller, "Pauline's Passion and Punishment." The Sherlockian book collector of eighteenth-century imprints may find, as he browses through a pile of unexciting French Revolutionary pamphlets, the Decree of 3 October 1793 that ordered the execution of the Widow Capet, otherwise known as Marie Antoinette. Or perhaps, in a lot of eighteenth-century English broadsides he may stumble upon one printed for James Woodmason in 1780 describing his invention of a copying apparatus that surely was the great-great-grandfather of the Xerox machine.

The seventeenth century yields up its prizes too: a small work on the properties of butter that hints at concern about cholesterol (in 1664!), a French treatise on sleep discussing the relation of dreams to illness, including a frontispiece showing a psychiatrist tending a patient who reclines on a couch (in 1670!), or even a seventeenth-century edition of the works of the great physician-alchemist Paracelsus bearing the handwritten inscription, "Robt Browning from his father"—a gift that bore loving testimony to the young poet's own early poem "Paracelsus." Capping many seventeenth-century prizes, we recall a Latin Declaration of War by the English Commonwealth against the States of Holland printed in 1652 that turned out to be a product of John Milton's mighty pen when the great poet was Latin Secretary to the Council of State. The sixteenth century discloses its treasures too to the patient Sherlockian—a neo-Latin poem, for example, that describes a mugging that occurred in 1576; a dull-looking treatise of 1598 that turns out to contain previously unrecorded accounts of that great Elizabethan world-traveler Sir Francis Drake.

Such serendipitous finds, such joys, are to be had from books of all ages. But they are not to be from the mere acquisition of such books. Books that are acquired must be cherished not only as physical objects but as sources of knowledge, as treasures to be mined. In other words, to attain the optimal pleasure and excitement from his books, the collector must browse through them, study them, connect them one with another. If he fails to do this, he may as well collect matchboxes. Books are meant not only to stand upon shelves but to be opened and explored.

Where there are joys, there are pitfalls, and perhaps the greatest pitfall that confronts the eager collector is the temptation to buy everything, to spread himself thin, to generalize his collection. For a collection to hang together, to make sense, it must be a specialist collection. Choosing a specialty that he can learn to master, the collector can wander like Magellan through the cloth- or calfbound volumes of his choice and become explorer and discoverer. Fortunately, of the making of specialties, as of the making of books, there seems to be no end. And so, in that extension of his personality that is an appropriate collection of books, doctor, lawyer, Indian Chief must come to certain terms regarding its nature. The doctor pursues medical works; the lawyer, legal tomes; the Indian Chief, treatises and treaties relating to the American Indian. But in truth there are as many subjects to form the basis of a specialized book collection as there are in life itself. The bird-watching enthusiast may hit upon ornithology as a suitable theme for pursuit; the historian may alight upon the French Revolution or the Spanish Inquisition. From chemistry to witchcraft, from goldmining to pottery, from cabbages to kings, there are unifying bases for specialist book collections.

There are other unifying bases as well. In place of theme or topic as connecting link, an author may be used. Extraordinary collections have been assembled consisting of books by and about William Shakespeare and Francis Bacon, Sir Walter Scott and George Eliot, Henry James and Edith Wharton, Ernest Hemingway and James Joyce. To each his taste. Some will reach out for Louisa May Alcott, others for Gertrude Stein. Many collectors of modern firsts use the author as the pivotal point of their specialist collection, seeking not only books and pamphlets by the author of their choice, but works about that author, and even books that have been in the library of that author.

A third unifying basis for a specialist collection is neither theme nor author but genre: French novels or Italian sonnets, Scandinavian plays or American sermons. Still another is imprint or publisher: books published in sixteenth-century Venice by Aldus Manutius and his family; books published by the House of Elzevier in seventeenth-century Leyden; books issued by Mathew Carey in Philadelphia or Isaiah Thomas in Boston during the eighteenth and nineteenth centuries. Still another theme is format: miniature books for some, elephant folios for others. We would not go so far as to suggest a collection of books selected to fit a designated shelfspace, or books selected to harmonize with the colors of rugs and draperies, but collectors have been known to assemble such libraries. There are unifying themes everywhere. In the fields of ephemera, autographs and manuscripts, maps and prints, other specialist collections suggest themselves. Once his specialty has been determined, the collector's life in books will revolve about Judaica or Mormonism, space travel or imaginary voyages, mining or gardening, a prolific author, a romance cycle, an exciting imprint. Henceforth he will be in hot pursuit of his specialty. For, once the basis of his collection has been established, it serves as a catalyst. The collector has found his "connection."

Yet even then, to avoid the pitfalls and to intensify the joys of collecting, the collector must use restraint and exercise judgment. He will find, as he accumulates books in his specialty, that he must address himself to certain questions so that his collection will be crafted to reality. First of all, the base upon which he is building must not be too broad or too narrow. If witchcraft is his chosen specialty, he will find that its scope is far too wide, and if he persists he will probably either immolate himself out of desperation or drown himself, inundated by auguries and demonologies from the time of ancient Greece through merry old England to the days of the Salem delusions and on to *Rosemary's Baby*. Such a subject, in other words, will eventually have to be cut down to the realms of possibility, limited to witchcraft in a particular place or at a particular time or in a particular manifestation. On the other hand, if he restricts his theme too narrowly, he may end up with a so-called collection long before he has satisfied his urge to collect.

Similarly, a genre collection of books of translations would be so extensive as to be unmanageable. Limit the genre to eighteenth-century English translations of the classics, and you have an absorbing and feasible project. Limit it to French translations of *Gone with the Wind* between 1936 and 1956, and you have narrowed the interest along with the possibilities. In the same way, if the imprints of a particular publisher form the basis of a collection, the publisher chosen should be neither one whose output consists of thousands of titles nor one whose productions were extremely limited.

In short, after the unifying base has been selected it must be assessed for attainability. Some magnificent themes are simply impossible to apply to a collection of books. Who, for example, would not wish to assemble in one bookcase the first work that issued from the press of each State or Territory of the Union?But unless the collector has found an unknown copy of *The Freeman's Oath* which rolled from the Widow Glover's press in Cambridge, Massachusetts, in 1638, he might as well abandon the idea—unless he can substitute for *The Freeman's Oath* a copy of the *Bay Psalm Book* of 1640. Such caviar, however, is not for the general.

Few collections are ever complete. Yet, if only for the joy of the chase, the collector should *aim* at completeness. The concept of completeness will of course vary with the nature of the collector and of his collection. Some collectors will stick closely, even rigidly, to their theme or genre or author or publisher. Others, gifted perhaps with more imagination, will want to flesh out their collections with related background materials that bring the whole to life. Such collectors will see connections where more intractable bibliophiles will not. In a collection relating to the Medici family, for example, they will include the books and pamphlets that trace not only the political fortunes of Tuscany but also the literary and artistic, scientific and intellectual attainments that developed under Medici patronage. To the obvious will be added the less obvious, from guidebooks of Florence to the writings of the Italian humanists of the time.

The collector must be emotionally as well as intellectually fortified to achieve his ends. If he loses a hoped-for item at auction, or a gem that he spies too late in a bookseller's catalogue, he must not wallow in a slough of despond. Such frustrations will surely be compensated by the acquisition of unexpected prizes. Books have a way of disappearing, it is true, but they also have a way of resurfacing.

A major restriction confronting the collector is the restriction imposed by his own pursestrings. The media habitually blow up as newsworthy sales of astronomically priced manuscripts and printed books, but would-be collectors should be reminded that libraries can be assembled for far more modest fees. The collector who is willing to wait and to watch, to stalk his prey with deliberation, will eventually be able to build up a library without impoverishing himself and his family. In this connection, we should also like to emphasize that the motive force for any collector should never be the investment angle alone. It is true that the passage of time usually imparts the patina of gold upon most book collections, but this is by no means always the case. Modern firsts, for instance, are always speculative, since no one can know which of our contemporary greats will remain great a century from now. Moreover, the tides of taste are always in flux. There was a time when Shakespeare was considered dull! Therefore, caveat emptor: do not buy a book because you think it will be transmuted into gold. In concentrating upon such alchemy, you will miss all the fun of the acquisition.

A final—or rather, the final—question which the collector must consider is the disposition of his books after death. There are several alternatives. Titans among collectors—Henry E. Huntington, J. Pierpont Morgan, Henry Clay Folger, the Beineckes—immortalized their names by laying the foundations for great libraries housed in palatial edifices. While today's collectors can no longer conceive, much less realize, such grandiose collections, there are still collectors who will prefer to keep their collections intact. Those collectors will probably bequeath their books to an institution. If they do so, they should be advised to bequeath, along with the collection, funds to add to the collection; otherwise it may not continue to grow. Still other collectors, wishing either to accrue funds for their heirs or to impart joy to succeeding generations of collectors, may sell their libraries to a bookseller or place them on the auction block. The great library of Robert Hoe, "one of the finest private libraries in the world," was sold in a series of auctions starting in 1911, bringing a then unprecedented $1,932,000. The Jerome Kern sale of rare first editions, held in 1929, totaled slightly less, $1,729,000. More recently, the Thomas W. Streeter sale of Americana held between 1966 and 1969 fetched a grand total of $3,104,982. With the democratization of collecting the few titan book collectors of the past have given way to the many lesser collectors of the present. Lesser collections, realizing more modest prices, can also be auctioned either *en bloc* or piecemeal, and in opting for the auction block the collector, dispersing the books he has assembled with joy, disperses that joy along with his books.

To experience the joy of the chase, the joy of building a library, and even the joy of dismantling a library, the collector must be endowed with certain properties. He must be, first of all, either educated or self-educated. His education will increase with every book he purchases, but only if he brings to it some background of curiosity, learning, and taste. The good collector must learn to "case" with intelligence the book fairs he attends, and to read catalogues promptly, quickly, but carefully. He must not neglect the small print that informs the would-be purchaser about condition or edition. In this connection, he must have some knowledge about editions. He will doubtless prefer the first edition in most cases as the edition most closely associated with the author, but there are instances where he should learn to prefer later editions, as in the case of Leopold Mozart's study of *Violin Method,* or William Wollaston's *Nature of Religion Delineated.* Mozart's work is interesting in first edition, but far more interesting in second edition because that edition happens to contain the first mention in a book of Leopold's illustrious son Wolfgang Amadeus Mozart. As for the Wollaston tome, the first edition is of little interest, but the third is interesting indeed because it was set up in London by a young compositor employed in Palmer's printing house whose name was Benjamin Franklin. Such matters the eager collector will learn, not from experience, but from the use of reference books. He should acquire and study the bibliographical reference books in his field of collecting, for those "books about books" are the guides that will illuminate his mind and enrich his collection. The good collector should learn, too, how to collate his books for completeness and how to care for them physically once they are on his shelves.

Primarily, however, the good collector must learn to select, doubtless after trial and error, disappointment and frustration, those specialist booksellers who can best supply and even suggest his wants. The collector should limit the number of dealers from whom he habitually buys; else he will spread himself too thin and see the prices of his desiderata rise dramatically as a multitude of suppliers inundate him with offers and "quotes." In short, the collector should rely upon the integrity and ability of the specialist dealer of his choice, for it is indeed true that the good specialist bookseller can serve a creative function in the building of a library.

After all, are not bookseller and collector shaped from the same mold? Their basic motivation—the love of books—is the same. The bookseller loses through his mistakes and the collector usually has to live with his, and in this, too, specialist collector and specialist bookseller have much in common. Exercising patience and imagination, both have experienced the joys of the chase; both have turned detective in studying their acquisitions; both have beheld with rising exhilaration the structures they have wrought, the structures built of calf or vellum, paper, boards or cloth, that house the human spirit.

LEONA ROSTENBERG
MADELEINE B. STERN

SCOPE

The term "antiquarian bookstore" defies definition. It may well connote a bookstore that deals in very old, very rare, and very expensive books. However, it is used throughout the United States and Canada as a term meaning the availability of old, scarce, and used books regardless of the date of demarcation a bookseller may use in determining the status of the books for sale. *The Collector's Guide to Antiquarian Bookstores* by no means includes every such bookstore in the United States and Canada. It does, however, describe over 1,000 dealers and includes bookstores that have responded to questionnaires as well as some that have been otherwise recommended.

The majority of bookstores described in this *Guide* are open shops where customers are welcome to browse through the displayed stock. These stores have regular business hours, buy and sell books, maintain want lists, conduct search services, and very often have appraisal services.

Some booksellers in this *Guide* maintain a sizable stock in specialized areas and welcome the collector by appointment only. The reason for "appointment only" may be because bookselling is an avocation and some owners may have other pursuits that keep them busy during regular business hours. Other booksellers may have a thriving mail order business and require appointments to allocate their time properly. Most important, many specialized booksellers prefer to know the customers' wants beforehand, thereby giving the dealers the opportunity to gather together those books that they know will be of interest.

There are very few "mail order only" dealers included in this *Guide*. It has been estimated that there are over 3,000 such dealers in the United States alone. Those listed in this *Guide* are included because they specialize in unique antiquarian fields that may be of interest to the collector. Most publish catalogues and many advertise in the *American Book Collector* and *AB Bookman's Weekly*, major publications for the specialist book collector and bookseller. Although some booksellers may be classified as "mail order only," one should not hesitate to contact them. They share a common trait with the buyer—a love of books. They are delighted to share their expertise and most will take the time to see a collector if informed of a prospective visit.

The *Guide* is primarily for the individual who wants to browse and for the book collector who experiences a joy in books that comes from the serendipity of finding a treasure in a book shop or in the building of a collection by frequent forays into the antiquarian and used bookstores throughout the United States and Canada.

Entries in the *Guide* are as complete and accurate as possible. Bookstores, however, are enterprises subject to the whims of the economy and some disappear quickly during a recession. Bookstores often meet their demise by the wrecker's ball, terminated leases, or competition in the marketplace. All of the bookstores in this *Guide* are independently owned and operated, and sometimes their locations force them to compete with larger, franchised booksellers. However, the antiquarian booksellers as well as the used and out-of-print dealers are permanent fixtures of our society and will continue to be nourished by the enthusiastic pursuits of book collectors everywhere.

ORGANIZATION

Entries in this *Guide* are arranged alphabetically by state and province. Each entry has been given a number which appears on the line immediately above the name of the bookstore/dealer. This entry number also appears in the Subject Index. If the user of the *Guide* is interested in a particular subject, say, archaeology, the best point of entry into the *Guide* is via the Subject Index. Under archaeology the user will find all bookstores/dealers who handle material on archaeology listed by entry number.

The main entry for each bookstore has been designed for browsing. The entries attempt to create the atmosphere of the bookstore and do so by a general description, a brief biography of the owner(s) when available, a history of the business, and other pertinent facts. The types of material and subject areas handled by the firm are also listed for "browsing," very much like the category signs which many used bookstores display for the benefit of browsing patrons.

A brief Glossary following these introductory comments lists those terms that have been used in the *Guide*. Not an all-inclusive listing of terms pertinent to the field of book arts, it is intended solely to clarify for the reader any term encountered herein whose meaning may not be clear.

ANTIQUARIAN BOOKSELLERS ASSOCIATIONS

Several organizations in the United States and Canada are associated with the antiquarian book trade. Bookstores/dealers who have identified themselves as being members of such organizations have been so noted with the complete name of the association.

The major organization in the United States is the Antiquarian Booksellers Association of America (ABAA) which was founded in 1949 to encourage interest in rare books and manuscripts and to maintain the highest standards in the antiquarian book trade. Members of the ABAA often display black on white decals in a prominent location on their premises. A counterpart organization in Canada is the Antiquarian Booksellers Association of Canada.

Many booksellers in both Canada and the United States belong to the International League of Antiquarian Booksellers as well as the Antiquarian Booksellers Association, which has its headquarters in England.

REFERENCE MATERIALS

There are many books, monographs, magazine articles, and other reference materials devoted to book collecting. For the collector desiring to know more about the book arts, bookselling, or any aspect of the book—from its creation to its ultimate resting place on the shelf of the owner—the local public library is the primary resource. Librarians are collectors, too, and will be more than happy to assist anyone in finding the reference sources of interest.

Five references are included below because they are excellent treatments of the topic of book collecting and can be recommended for both the novice and the advanced collector. Three of the references are books and two are periodical publications.

Books:

ABC for Book-Collectors. John Carter. Alfred A. Knopf, New York, 1963. Revised Edition.
  No book collector should be without this excellent treatment of the technical terms of book collecting and bibliography. It is actually a glossary of terms and is highly entertaining reading because of the wit and informal manner of the author. This is a true gem of a book.

Modern Book Collecting. A Guide for the Beginner Who Is Buying First Editions for the First Time. Robert A. Wilson. Alfred A. Knopf, New York, 1980.
  Mr. Wilson is both a collector and a bookseller. He is the owner of the Phoenix Bookstore in New York City and his experience gives this work "the touch of the poet." The book is illustrated, gives sources for modern first editions, and includes Mr. Wilson's list of the fifty most important books of American literature published since the end of World War II.

The Pleasures of Book Collecting. Salvatore J. Iacone, Harper & Row, New York, 1976.

This book is of the "how-to" sort and is exciting for anyone who wants to know about acquiring valuable books. Mr. Iacone shares his joy of books and recommends plans for collecting. He covers all aspects of the subject from the collector's point of view. Thirty-six excellent photographs are included.

Periodicals:

AB Bookman's Weekly including *Antiquarian Bookman* (in two parts). P.O. Box AB, Clifton, New Jersey 07015.
This publication is used by just about every bookseller in the United States and has worldwide distribution. Each issue includes articles that are concerned with specialist book collecting and these articles are eventually gathered into the *Antiquarian Bookman,* an annual publication in two parts. The *AB Bookman's Weekly* is used not only by the bookseller/dealer but also by librarians and individual collectors. A feature of the weekly is the list of books wanted and books for sale arranged under the name of the buyer or seller. If one is searching for an elusive title, there is every possibility that it will be found here.

American Book Collector. Bi-monthly (January, March, May, July, September, November). The Moretus Press, Inc., 274 Madison Avenue, New York, New York 10016.
The *American Book Collector* should be the prized magazine subscription of all book collectors. The articles and illustrations are superb and display that "touch of the connoisseur." This bi-monthly publication will keep one abreast of antiquarian book events and the availability of dealers' catalogues. Book reviews are also included.

GLOSSARY

AMERICANA any book about America, usually the United States; books relating to America or individual Americans; subcategories of the term are Western Americana, Southwest Americana, etc.

−ANA a suffix attached to a word to describe any kind of book or material related to that subject; specifically it refers to the subject of the material and not the author; sometimes it is not easily attachable and creates strange-looking and -sounding words.

APPRAISAL an expert or official evaluation of an individual book or a collection of books.

ASSOCIATION COPY a book or ephemeral material that belonged to the author, usually carrying the author's annotations or perhaps the signature of a person upon whom a character in the book was based; there can be many ways in which material is associated with the author, e.g., a book from his/her personal library, a Presidential citation to the author, a theater playbill signed by the author of the book on which the drama was based.

BELLES LETTRES literature that is regarded for its aesthetic value rather than its didactic or informative content.

BROADSIDE a large sheet of paper printed on one side; often used for poetry.

CALLIGRAPHY the art of fine handwriting.

CASEBOUND used to describe a hardbound book as opposed to one that is bound in paper (paperback).

CHAPBOOK a term not in common use today but referring to a pamphlet or a cheaply printed book that was "hawked" by street vendors in the eighteenth and nineteenth centuries.

CLOTH used to describe the material most often used for the binding of books; when used in booksellers' catalogues it indicates that the book described does not have a book jacket whether or not it ever had one.

COLOR PLATE BOOK any book with plates in color, either aquatinted or hand-colored.

DEDICATION COPY a copy signed by the author and presented to the person to whom the book is dedicated; the copy should bear not only the author's name but some form of annotation such as "to . . . in appreciation of twenty years of friendship."

DUST JACKET the paper jacket that is placed around most books to protect the cloth covers.

EPHEMERA a term applied to material not easily classifiable under any other heading; it can include magazine articles, reviews, photographs, personal possessions, calling cards; often a catch-all term used to classify items in a bookstore that are not books, maps, prints, or works of art.

FACSIMILE applied to describe a new edition of a rare work long out-of-print that has been "faithfully" reproduced, including adherence to the original typeface and design.

FINE BINDING a term expressing the high quality and excellence of the bookbinder's art.

FINE PRINTING a term expressing high-quality printing usually accomplished on a small press and often utilizing a specially designed typeface and composed in metal to produce the excellence of the final product.

FIRST EDITION the first appearance of a work as a book in its first printing.

FOLIO a large book with the dimensions of 12 by 15 inches; also refers to the page numbers of a book.

FORE-EDGE PAINTING refers to painted decoration on the fore-edges of the leaves of a book; the technique was used in England during the late eighteenth and nineteenth centuries; painting was accomplished by slightly fanning out the pages and then applying the decoration; when the book is closed the painting is concealed but when the pages are fanned out the painting reappears.

GRAPHICS a broad term used to describe prints, maps, posters, reproductions; original graphics are the direct result of the artist's effort and often bear his signature and the unique number of the impression out of the total number of impressions made from the original plate, e.g., 41/100.

HARDBOUND a book that has been bound in boards (usually cardboard) which have been covered in various kinds of material.

HIGH SPOT a method of collecting books whereby only those titles are sought that have appeared on a list compiled by a literary critic, literary periodical, newspaper book review supplement, or other media; it also applies to the collecting of Pulitzer Prize, Nobel Prize, or Hugo Award winners, or of titles in a category that accumulate over the years (e.g., books made into movies that win Academy Awards as Best Picture).

HORN BOOK an early primer consisting of a single page mounted on a tablet, usually of wood, and protected by a transparent sheet of horn; used to teach children to read; prevalent during the sixteenth, seventeenth, and early eighteenth centuries.

ILLUMINATED MANUSCRIPT a book or manuscript that has text, page, or initial letters decorated with ornamental designs, miniatures, or lettering.

ILLUSTRATED BOOKS books containing drawings, photographs, graphics, etchings, and sketches often reproduced from original works of art which depict scenes from the work or any aspect of the subject of the work; prevalent in children's literature and early works in botany, anatomy, travel, and exploration.

INCUNABULA books printed before the year 1501; the rarest of all books and truly deserving the adjective "antiquarian."

INSCRIBED COPY a book containing a handwritten annotation by the author.

JUVENILES books written for children; often applied to books written for older children.

JUVENILIA applies to works written when an author was a young child.

KEY BOOK a book that is considered one of the most important and significant works in its field.

LIMITED EDITION an edition of a work that is limited to a specific number of copies.

Glossary

MANUSCRIPT a work written by hand; however, it is often used to refer to the original text of a work, whether written by hand or typewritten.

MINIATURE BOOK a book of very small size, usually measuring 3" or less along the spine.

MINT CONDITION a book as good as new.

MODERN FIRST EDITION usually applied to the first appearance and first printing of a book in the twentieth century; the cut-off date may vary depending upon the authority using the term.

OCTAVO refers to the most common size of a book, 6 × 9 inches.

OUT-OF-PRINT a book no longer in stock in the publisher's warehouse.

PAPERBACK a book bound in paper, usually of a coated stock; although pamphlets and other types of works are often bound in paper, the term "paperback" has become synonymous with the editions of a work that have been previously published in hardbound editions and have been reissued in this format for the mass market.

PRESENTATION COPY a book presented by the author (sometimes by the publisher) to another person and usually bearing an inscription that gives some indication of the reason for the presentation.

PRESS BOOKS books produced by a small press and in small quantities of excellent quality.

PRIVATE PRESS a small organization (as opposed to a major publisher) that produces books of superior quality in small numbers; many specialize in some aspect of the literary world, e.g., poetry, history, sporting arts, and fine printing.

PROVENANCE the history of the ownership of a book; often found on the inside of a book opposite the title page as a signature and date, bookplate, or coat of arms; further evidence of the book's ownership can be in the form of the bookseller's marks and other annotations.

QUARTO refers to the size of a book measuring 9 × 12 inches.

RARE often used to describe the stock of an antiquarian dealer, usually in the phrase "old, rare, and out-of-print"; a rare book is one which is hard to find, of which only one copy is extant, or which belongs to a group of books of which there are few copies available anywhere.

READING COPY often used to describe a book available in a used bookstore to which there is no intrinsic value other than the fact that it is in a condition that it can be read.

REMAINDER a copy of a book that has been part of a publisher's overstock and is sold in quantity to a distributor who in turn releases the books to bookstores; remaindered items are sold at considerably less than the original retail price and their condition is as good as new; many collectors scan remainder lists for first editions of their specialties; remaindered items can also be inexpensively bound copies of the original sheets which were not bound as part of the original stock.

REVIEW COPY a book used by a book reviewer or critic, often before publication, for evaluating the work.

SCHOLARLY pertaining to works of scholarship, often published by university presses or specialist publishing houses.

SEARCH SERVICE a service provided by many bookstores whereby the bookseller will seek a copy of the book(s) desired by the patron; the art of "searching" may sometimes require the techniques of the detective.

SECOND HAND COPY a book that has no true value to the serious collector; synonymous with "reading copy."

SIGNED COPY a book bearing the signature of the author.

VINTAGE PAPERBACK a paperback title characterized by excellence and enduring appeal; classic.

WRAPPERS the paper covers of a book or pamphlet, not to be confused with "dust jacket" or "dust wrapper."

United States

ALABAMA

1
Book Legger
522 Jordan Lane, NW
Huntsville, Alabama 35805   (205) 539-5547

The Book Legger is a general used and out-of-print bookstore and carries significant works in all areas. The store occupies 1,200 square feet of space.
How to Get There: The bookstore is located in the Preston Building just south of Holmes Avenue.
Owner/Biography: David L. Stone. Mr. Stone is a former teacher and librarian.
Year Founded/History of Bookstore: 1976. The present owner purchased the business in 1982 and has expanded the out-of-print selection by some 10,000 volumes.
Number of Volumes: 30,000.
Types/Classifications: Hardbound, paperback, National Geographic magazines.
General Subject Areas: General.
Mail/Telephone Orders; Credit Cards: Both. Payment due prior to shipping. No credit cards.
Business Hours: Monday through Friday 10:00 AM - 6:00 PM; Sunday 1:00 PM - 6:00 PM.
Parking Facilities: Business parking lot.
Special Features: Search service.
Collections/Individual Items Purchased: Both.

2
Gary Wayner
Route 3, Box 18
Fort Payne, Alabama 35967   (205) 845-5866

Gary Wayner is a dealer in scholarly antiquarian material. His business is mostly by mail order.
How to Get There: The business is located at the intersection of Highway 35 and I-59.
Owner/Biography: Gary Wayner.
Year Founded/History of Bookstore: 1975.
Number of Volumes: 2,000.
Types/Classifications: Hardbound, out-of-print, signed copies, color plate books.
General Subject Areas: Bibliographies, Biography, Birds, Botany, Herpetology, Horticulture, Natural History.
Author Specialties: William Hamilton Gibson, Charles Darwin, Alfred Russell Wallace.
Mail/Telephone Orders; Credit Cards: Both. Visa and Mastercard accepted.
Business Hours: By chance.
Catalogue: Published 4 times per year.
Collections/Individual Items Purchased: Both.

ALASKA

3
Alaskana Bookshop
4617 Arctic Boulevard
Anchorage, Alaska 99503   (907) 561-1340

The bookstore is the "little green house on the corner" of 47th Avenue and Arctic in Anchorage. It is a five room house with an old fashioned, homey atmosphere, and every room contains bookshelves filled with books. Specializing in Alaska materials, rare, out-of-print, and new, the bookstore also features supplies for hunting and fishing, mountain climbing, geoscience, and Arctic exploration. The first Friday of each month is Open House. The bookstore contains 800 square feet of space.

How to Get There: The shop is located at the corner of-47th Avenue and Arctic Boulevard.

Owner/Biography: Eugene F. Short, D.Ed., is a former president of the Anchorage Community College. He has been a dealer in out-of-print Alaskana since 1969.

Year Founded/History of Bookstore: Dr. Short founded the business in 1969, operating it out of his home. He opened the shop in 1976 next door to his residence, and it has remained at the same location since. In 1980 he acquired the geoscience library and stock formerly operated by Bruce Canady in Lebanon, Oregon.

Number of Volumes: 30,000.

Types/Classifications: Hardbound, paperback, magazines, ephemera, first editions, out-of-print, signed copies, limited editions, exploration supplies.

General Subject Areas: Alaskana, Arctic and Antarctic Exploration, Children's Literature, Fishing, Geoscience, History, Hunting, Mountain Climbing.

Mail/Telephone Orders; Credit Cards: Both; no credit cards.

Business Hours: Tuesday through Saturday 1:00 PM - 6:00 PM, and by appointment.

Parking Facilities: Parking lot for business.

Special Features: Search service, bibliography.

Collections/Individual Items Purchased: Both.

4
Observatory
212 Katlian Street
P.O. Box 1770
Sitka, Alaska 99835   (907) 747-3033

The bookstore is in a former Indian dwelling in downtown Sitka, Alaska. The owner describes it as a "small, inconvenient, and very much out of space bookstore......the democratic antiquarian bookstore." The stock includes 2,500 titles on Alaska and Canada, 8,000 general used books on all subjects, and 400-500 maps and prints on the Arctic. The shop contains 460 square feet of space.

How to Get There: The shop is located on the channel in Sitka Bay, across from the ANB boat harbor. Sitka is on Baranof Island, seventy miles from the mainland.

Owner/Biography: Dee Longenbaugh, owner, has been an Alaskan since 1963; she is a writer, researcher, historian, and dealer in anything pertaining to books, maps, and prints.

Year Founded/History of Bookstore: This bookstore was founded in 1977, and the owner has just added a branch called "The Observatory North," at 4608 Lake Spenard Drive, Anchorage, Alaska 99503, telephone (907) 248-5796, dealing only in antiquarian maps and prints. Currently, the branch bookstore is by appointment only, but "great plans are afoot."

Number of Volumes: 12,500.

Types/Classifications: Most all general types and classifications of material.

General Subject Areas: Alaskana, Canadiana, General.

2

Specific Specialties: Within the fields of Canadiana and Alaskana: Exploration, Voyages, Aviation, Flora, Fauna, Biography, Technical, Anthropology, Geology, and almost any type of Non-Fiction.

Mail/Telephone Orders; Credit Cards: Both; personal check with order; the store will hold the order for two weeks after quoting; order returnable for nearly any reason. An additional telephone number is (907) 747-3457.

Business Hours: May - September: Monday through Saturday 10:00 AM - 5:30 PM; October - April: Monday through Saturday 1:00 PM - 5:30 PM.

Parking Facilities: Street.

Special Features: Search service, research on any Arctic subject; international quotes and sales especially invited.

Catalogue: Once a year.

Collections/Individual Items Purchased: Both.

Booksellers' Memberships: Book Club of Washington.

5
Old Harbor Books
210 Lincoln Street
Sitka, Alaska 99835   (907) 747-8808

This is a general bookstore in downtown Sitka, Alaska, dealing primarily in new books, but stocking out-of-print and Alaskana, and providing a search service. The shop contains 1,500 square feet of space.

How to Get There: The shop is located in the middle of downtown Sitka.

Owner/Biography: A Corporation.

Year Founded/History of Bookstore: Founded in 1976, the shop's original location was 2 blocks from the present one. In 1982 the Corporation purchased its own building, and hopes to remain there permanently.

Number of Volumes: 10,000.

Types/Classifications: Hardbound.

General Subject Areas: Alaska, General.

Mail/Telephone Orders; Credit Cards: Both. No credit cards.

Business Hours: Monday through Friday 10:00 AM - 6:00 PM; Saturday 10:00 AM - 5:00 PM.

Parking Facilities: Street.

ARIZONA

6
Baseball Books Only
5672 East Scarlett Street
Tucson, Arizona 85711   (602) 747-5394

This specialized dealer operates his business from a private residence and deals in one subject only - baseball.
How to Get There: Call for directions.
Owner/Biography: J. C. Percell. Mr. Percell started collecting books about baseball as a hobby 25 years ago.
Year Founded/History of Bookstore: 1977.
Number of Volumes: 5,000.
Types/Classifications: Hardbound, out-of-print.
General Subject Areas: Baseball.
Mail/Telephone Orders; Credit Cards: Both. No credit cards.
Business Hours: Daylight hours.
Parking Facilities: Street parking.
Special Features: Search service.
Collections/Individual Items Purchased: Both.
Booksellers' Memberships: Society for American Baseball Research.

7
Beachcomber Book Shop
5763 West Potvin Lane
Tucson, Arizona 85742   (602) 744-1619

This bookstore is nestled among the saguaro cactus in the rolling foothills near Tucson in an area of small horse ranches. The shop is in a large white building filled with 20th Century aviation, military and naval history, and literature. This has been the Beachcomber's special interest since 1959. When the shop was moved from the shores of Birch Bay, Washington in 1976, the Beachcomber name moved too. The shop occupies 3,000 square feet of space.
How to Get There: Take the Cortaro Road exit from Freeway I-10. Go east to Frontage Road beside railroad track. Go left, north on Frontage Road to Camino de Manana. Go east about two miles to Decker Road, turn left on Decker and follow signs one mile to mailbox sign on left.
Owner/Biography: Beachcomber of Arizona, Inc. The book shop was founded in 1959 by Paul Gaudette at Birch Bay, Washington. He is a veteran of the Third Army in World War II. The business was incorporated in 1983 with James Thorvardson.
Year Founded/History of Bookstore: 1959.
Number of Volumes: 25,000.
Types/Classifications: Hardbound, paperback, magazines, broadsides, autographs, ephemera, out-of-print, first editions.
General Subject Areas: Aviation History, Aviation (20th Century), Military History, Military Literature, Naval History.
Specific Specialties: U.S. Marine Corps, Airships, Third Reich, Military Elite Units, Military Unit Histories.
Other Specialties: Foreign publications; large holdings of German and Polish titles.
Mail/Telephone Orders; Credit Cards: Both. Visa and Mastercard accepted.
Business Hours: Monday through Saturday 9:00 AM to 5:00 PM.
Parking Facilities: Parking available.

Special Features: Large number of ducks and cats to be viewed, depending upon local hawk activity. Horses may be petted.
Catalogue: Published monthly.
Collections/Individual Items Purchased: Both.

8
Bonita Porter - Books
2011 West Bethany Home Road
Phoenix, Arizona 85015   (602) 242-9442

This is an intimate, comfortable bookshop dedicated to purveying fine books to fellow bibliophiles. The shop occupies 960 square feet of space.
Owner/Biography: Bonita and Paul Porter.
Year Founded/History of Bookstore: 1965. The bookstore was founded in Las Vegas, Nevada and moved to Phoenix in 1975.
Number of Volumes: 6,500.
Types/Classifications: Hardbound, first editions, fine bindings, out-of-print, signed copies, limited editions, illustrated books.
General Subject Areas: Arizona History, Juvenile Literature, Literary Classics, Southwest Americana.
Author Specialties: W. Somerset Maugham.
Other Specialties: Scholarly works prior to 1900.
Mail/Telephone Orders; Credit Cards: Both. Payment must accompany order unless customer is known by the owners. No credit cards.
Business Hours: Tuesday through Saturday 9:30 AM - 5:30 PM.
Parking Facilities: Public parking lot.
Catalogue: Published intermittently.
Collections/Individual Items Purchased: Both.

9
Book Stop
2504 North Campbell
Tucson, Arizona 85719   (602) 326-6661

The Book Stop is probably the oldest used bookstore in Tucson. The store carries all varieties of books from Western Americana to science fiction, cookbooks, and literature. The store is comfortably situated next to an ice cream store and browsing with an ice cream cone is permitted. The Book Stop occupies 3,500 square feet of space.
How to Get There: The shop is located in central Tucson, north of the University of Arizona. From the Grant Road exit of Freeway 90 go east to Campbell then 2 blocks north.
Owner/Biography: Laurie Allen.
Year Founded/History of Bookstore: 1967.
Number of Volumes: 100,000.
Types/Classifications: Hardbound, paperback, scholarly out-of-print, first editions.
General Subject Areas: Biography, General, History, Western Americana.
Specific Specialties: Arizona, Southwest Indians.
Mail/Telephone Orders; Credit Cards: Both. No credit cards.
Business Hours: Monday through Saturday 10:00 AM - 11:00 PM; Sundays 12:00 Noon - 11:00 PM.
Parking Facilities: Business parking lot.
Special Features: Search service; appraisals.
Collections/Individual Items Purchased: Both.

10
Bookman's Used Books
18 North Tucson Boulevard
Tucson, Arizona 85716   (602) 325-5767

Bookman's Used Books is a general bookshop with extensive stock in all areas. The store is well lit and very well organized. Personal service is provided by knowledgeable people. The shop occupies 7,000 square feet of space.

How to Get There: The bookstore is conveniently located at the northeast corner of Tucson Boulevard and Broadway.

Owner/Biography: Robert Schlesinger.

Year Founded/History of Bookstore: 1974.

Number of Volumes: 500,000.

Types/Classifications: Hardbound, paperback, magazines, records, sheet music, comics, out-of-print, modern first editions, association copies.

General Subject Areas: Automotive, Books About Books, Detective Fiction, Mysteries, Southwestern Americana, 20th Century First Editions.

Specific Specialties: Bisbee (Arizona), Tucson (Arizona), Northland Press.

Author Specialties: J. Frank Dobie, Ross Santee, Thomas Merton, G.K. Chesterton, C.S. Lewis, William Eastlake, Donald Wetzel, Edward Abbey.

Mail/Telephone Orders; Credit Cards: Both. American Express, Visa, Mastercard accepted.

Business Hours: Monday through Saturday 10:00 AM - 9:00 PM; Sunday 1:00 PM - 5:00 PM.

Parking Facilities: Business parking lot.

Special Features: Seach service; record store.

Collections/Individual Items Purchased: Both.

Miscellaneous: Phonograph records and magazines bought and sold.

11
Duck's Books
1800 South Milton
Flagstaff, Arizona 86001   (602) 779-5365

Duck's Books is the largest used bookstore in Flagstaff. It is a general purpose used and rare bookstore with books of all types, arranged so that titles can be found quickly. The store occupies 1,265 square feet of space.

How to Get There: The shop is located in the Greentree Village Center which is the first shopping center on the right coming in to town on I-17. If coming east or west on I-40, go north from the Northern Arizona University exit.

Owner/Biography: John C. Duck. Mr. Duck is a retired Naval Officer.

Year Founded/History of Bookstore: 1981. Duck's Books was originally in downtown Flagstaff but expansion necessitated a move to the present location.

Number of Volumes: 20,000.

Types/Classifications: Hardbound, paperback, autographed material, out-of-print, rare.

General Subject Areas: Children's Literature, Cookbooks, Fantasy, Literature, Mysteries, Natural History, Occult, Philosophy, Religion, Science Fiction, Sports, Western Americana.

Specific Specialties: Grand Canyon.

Mail/Telephone Orders; Credit Cards: Mail orders, no telephone orders. Cash with order. No credit cards.

Business Hours: Monday through Saturday 10:30 AM - 7:30 PM.

Parking Facilities: Shopping center parking.

Special Features: Search service.

Collections/Individual Items Purchased: Both.

12
Haunted Book Shop

7211 N. Northern
Tucson, Arizona 85704   (602) 297-4843

This is a large bookstore that sells new books and which has a concessionaire department that features a selection of used, rare, and out-of-print books.

How to Get There: The shop is located in the Casas Adobes Shopping area in the northwest section of Tucson about 9 miles due north of the center of town.

Year Founded/History of Bookstore: 1977.

Number of Volumes: 10,000 (on a rotating basis).

Types/Classifications: Hardbound, some magazines, out-of-print.

General Subject Areas: Biography, Children's Literature, Fiction, Southwest Americana, Travel.

Mail/Telephone Orders; Credit Cards: Both. Visa and Mastercard accepted.

Business Hours: Monday through Saturday 9:30 AM - 5:30 PM; Sundays 11:00 AM - 4:00 PM.

Parking Facilities: Ample parking space provided adjacent to bookstore.

Special Features: Search service; free parking and proximity to a 20-acre park located in an unspoiled desert area owned and maintained by the bookstore.

Collections/Individual Items Purchased: Both.

13
Joan Robles at the Haunted Book Shop

7211 N. Northern
Tucson, Arizona 85704   (602) 297-4843

Joan Robles is an antiquarian concessionaire in a large book store that sells new books of all kinds. Ms. Robles has a general stock of hardbound books of all types but specializes in Southwestern Americana.

How to Get There: The Haunted Book Shop is located in the northwest section of Tucson near the intersection of Ina and Oracle Roads.

Owner/Biography: Joan Robles.

Year Founded/History of Bookstore: 1975.

Number of Volumes: Approximately 10,000 volumes that are featured in the store on a rotating display.

Types/Classifications: Hardbound.

General Subject Areas: Southwestern Americana.

Mail/Telephone Orders; Credit Cards: Both. Visa and Mastercard accepted.

Business Hours: Monday through Saturday 9:30 AM - 5:30 PM, Sunday 11:00 AM - 4:00 PM.

Parking Facilities: Business parking lot.

Special Features: Regular search service.

Collections/Individual Items Purchased: Both.

14
John W. Kuehn, Bookseller

8 Brewery Gulch
P.O. Box 73
Bisbee, Arizona 85603   (602) 432-4249

The bookstore is in the historic Medigovich Building built in 1902 on Brewery Gulch which, according to the owner, was once "one of the wildest streets in the West, with scores of saloons, whorehouses, and hop joints servicing the miners in the fabulously wealthy Copper Queen Mine and other mines here." The bookstore is also known as the Bisbee Bookstall, and contains 1,000 square feet of space.

How to Get There: Bisbee is approximately 100 miles southeast of Tucson on Highway 80. Situated at 5300 feet in the Mule Mountains, it is the county seat of Cochise County, and is reached by passing through a tunnel (the Time Tunnel) into the canyon which runs the length of the town. Twenty-five miles south of Tombstone, Bisbee is on the Mexican border.

Owner/Biography: John W. and Grace Kuehn. John Kuehn, owner, has been in the antiquarian book business since 1946 with a few interruptions, such as the Korean War. Until 1950 he operated the Manor Book Store founded by his father in Chicago. Then from 1953 to 1978, The Book Stall in Rockford, Illinois. At the end of 1978 he moved to Bisbee, Arizona.

Year Founded/History of Bookstore: 1946.

Number of Volumes: 10,000.

Types/Classifications: Hardbound, ephemera, first editions, out-of-print, fine bindings.

General Subject Areas: American Literature, Americana, Arizona, Detective, English Literature, Mexico, Military, Mystery, New Mexico, Travel.

Author Specialties: William Eastlake.

Mail/Telephone Orders; Credit Cards: Both. Visa, Mastercard.

Business Hours: Daily 9:00 AM - 5:00 PM.

Parking Facilities: Street and nearby lot.

Special Features: Search service.

Catalogue: Lists, several times a year.

Collections/Individual Items Purchased: Both.

15
Readex Book Exchange
P.O. Box 1125
Carefree, Arizona 85377   (602) 488-3304

The name of the residence is ARIBIOME. The studio, library, stacks, and displays are in a separate portion of the building from the private living quarters. The building was designed by the owner, Mr. Marion Cox. The Readex Book Exchange specializes in material that shows originality and creativity in the field of art and science.

How to Get There: To reach the Readex Book Exchange, travel north on either Scottsdale Road or Cave Creek Road (from the Phoenix area) to Scopa Trail.

Owner/Biography: Marion Cox and Nellie Oliver. Mr. Cox has been in the book and other objects of art exchange since 1937.

Year Founded/History of Bookstore: 1937. The business was established in Salem, Ohio and had two previous locations.

Number of Volumes: 8,000.

Types/Classifications: Hardbound, magazines, manuscripts, reports, documents, objets d'art.

General Subject Areas: Art and Science.

Author Specialties: Ray Bradbury.

Other Specialties: Scholarly Works.

Mail/Telephone Orders; Credit Cards: Both. Cash with order. No credit cards.

Business Hours: Daily 9:00 AM - 5:00 PM.

Parking Facilities: Business parking lot.

Special Features: Research undertaken; student, author, and corporation assistance with papers, reports, documentation, and authentication.

Catalogue: Catalogue published.

Collections/Individual Items Purchased: Both.

16
Rose Tree Inn Books
4th and Toughnut
P.O. Box 7
Tombstone, Arizona 85638   (602) 457-3326

This bookstore is operated in connection with the Rose Tree Museum and "The World's Largest Rosebush." The store carries Western Americana only and occupies 400 square feet of space.

Owner/Biography: Burton J. Devere.

Year Founded/History of Bookstore: 1940.
Number of Volumes: 5,000.
Types/Classifications: Hardbound, paperback, magazines, first editions, out-of-print, signed copies.
General Subject Areas: Western Americana.
Mail/Telephone Orders; Credit Cards: Both. Visa and Mastercard accepted.
Business Hours: Seven days per week 9:00 AM - 5:00 PM.
Parking Facilities: Street parking.
Catalogue: Published 3 times per year.
Collections/Individual Items Purchased: Both.

17
Russ Todd Books
28605 North 63rd Street
Cave Creek, Arizona 85331   (602) 585-0070

The shop is located in the owner's home in the desert, 10 miles north of Scottsdale. Visitors are welcome but should call ahead to be sure someone is there. The shop specializes in Western Americana, particularly Arizona and New Mexico.
Owner/Biography: Russ Todd.
Year Founded/History of Bookstore: 1978.
Number of Volumes: 10,000.
Types/Classifications: Hardbound, ephemera, photographs, first editions, out-of-print, scarce, rare.
General Subject Areas: Western Americana.
Specific Specialties: History, Archaeology, Indian Arts and Crafts, Cattle, Outlaws, Mining, Arizona, New Mexico.
Author Specialties: Southwest Authors.
Mail/Telephone Orders; Credit Cards: Both. No credit cards.
Business Hours: By chance or appointment.
Collections/Individual Items Purchased: Both.

18
Those Were The Days !
516 South Mill Avenue
Tempe, Arizona 85281   (602) 967-4729

The store is in the heart of Old Town Tempe, in a 70 year old building, just a few blocks from Arizona State University. The shop is a marvelous melange of out-of-print and new books, antiques, and collectibles. The upstairs loft provides a leisurely atmosphere for bowsing and perusing.
How to Get There: Tempe, a Phoenix suburb, is easily reached via I-10 to the 48th Street North offramp, then a quarter of a mile north to University Drive. From there, east on University Drive about 2 miles to Mill Avenue, then north 2.5 blocks.
Year Founded/History of Bookstore: 1972.
Number of Volumes: 1,000.
Types/Classifications: Hardbound, magazines, ephemera, new, used, out-of-print.
General Subject Areas: Americana, Antiques, Catalogues, Children's Books, Collectibles, Cookbooks, Medical, Photography, Sheet Music.
Mail/Telephone Orders; Credit Cards: Both. Visa, Mastercard.
Business Hours: Monday through Friday 9:30 AM - 6:00 PM; Thursday until 9:00 PM; Saturday 10:00 AM - 6:00 PM; Sunday 12:00 Noon - 5:00 PM.
Parking Facilities: Ample free off-street parking at the rear of the store.
Collections/Individual Items Purchased: Individual items.

19
Van Allen Bradley
P.O. Box 4130, Hopi Station
Scottsdale, Arizona 85261 (602) 991-8633

The stock of the bookstore is in the owner's home. The business is entirely mail order or by appointment.

How to Get There: Telephone for directions.

Owner/Biography: Van Allen Bradley, owner, was born in Albertville, Alabama. Graduated from the University of Missouri, he spent most of his career as a newspaper writer and editor. His last professional newspaper post was that of literary editor of the Chicago Daily News from 1948 to 1971. He resigned in 1971 to become a full-time rare book and manuscript dealer. He is the author of several books including "The Book Collector's Handbook of Values" (Putnam), first published in 1972 and now in its fourth edition; it is a standard reference work in the field. Mr. Bradley has been located in Scottsdale since 1978.

Year Founded/History of Bookstore: The business was started in 1964 by Van Allen Bradley as a part time endeavor under the name Heritage Book Shop. It was then located in Lake Zurich, Illinois. It has been full time since 1971.

Number of Volumes: 3,000.

Types/Classifications: Hardbound, paperback, autographs, manuscripts, ephemera, first editions.

General Subject Areas: Americana, Literature.

Mail/Telephone Orders; Credit Cards: Both. Credit references required from new customers; shipping charges are extra. No credit cards.

Business Hours: Twenty-four hours a day; call for an appointment.

Parking Facilities: Ample space in the driveway.

Special Features: Search service. The owner says: " always a drink for the thirsty, a hamburger for the hungry, and better fare for the big spender."

Catalogue: Four to six times a year.

Collections/Individual Items Purchased: Both.

Booksellers' Memberships: Antiquarian Booksellers Association of America.

ARKANSAS

20
Dickson Street Bookshop
318 West Dickson
Fayetteville, Arkansas 72701   (501) 442-8182

The Dickson Street Bookshop is a general out-of-print shop offering titles in just about any subject. The shop occupies 1,200 square feet of space.

How to Get There: The shop is located off Highway 71-B.
Owner/Biography: Choffel & O'Donnell.
Year Founded/History of Bookstore: 1978. The store was founded by two northerners opting for the beautiful Ozarks. They have 25 years combined experience in the out-of-print book trade.
Number of Volumes: 15,000 plus 30,000 in warehouse.
Types/Classifications: Hardbound, paperback, autographs, ephemera, first editions, signed copies, out-of-print, limited editions, color plate books.
General Subject Areas: General.
Specific Specialties: Arkansas, Oklahoma, Americana, Philosophy, Nature, Folklore, Poetry.
Author Specialties: William Butler Yeats, John Gould Fletcher, Vance Randolph, John Clellon Holmes.
Mail/Telephone Orders; Credit Cards: Both. Cash with order. No credit cards.
Business Hours: Monday through Saturday 11:00 AM - 9:00 PM.
Parking Facilities: Ample parking available.
Special Features: Search service, card index of customer wants maintained.
Collections/Individual Items Purchased: Both.

21
Yesterday's Books, Etc.
258 Whittington Avenue
Hot Springs, Arkansas 71901   (501) 624-6300

The owner describes the bookstore as a "small, cozy, old fashioned bookshop on the corner, where customers always feel free to sit down on the carpet to see what is on the lower shelves, and discussions of authors and ideas flow freely." Subjects are separated on the shelves, and fiction is in order by authors. The stock is mostly from local homes, mainly large estates of books.

How to Get There: In Hot Springs one should drive north on Central Avenue to the Fountain, then left onto Whittington Avenue and proceed four blocks.
Owner/Biography: Rose Lee Edwards, owner, describes herself as being an antiquarian booklady for about nine years, but having been born with a love of books. When there is time she does a little oil painting of birds and landscapes of "beautiful Arkansas."
Year Founded/History of Bookstore: Founded in 1974, the bookstore is still at its original site.
Types/Classifications: Hardbound, magazines, postcards, broadsides, stereo views, paperbacks, ephemera, old collectible paperbacks, scrapbooks, photograph albums, first editions, fine bindings, out-of-print, color plate books, limited editions.
General Subject Areas: Architecture, Art, Biography, Children's Books, Fiction, Games, History, Medicine, Music, Nature, Occult, Philosophy, Religion, Science Fiction and Fantasy, Sports, Travel.
Specific Specialties: Americana, Arkansas, Cookbooks.
Mail/Telephone Orders; Credit Cards: Both. Stamped, self addressed envelope must accompany requests if a reply is desired. Cash with order on all books. Telephone orders will hold a book for one week. No credit cards. Mailing address: P.O. Box 1728 (rest of address same as above).
Business Hours: Daily 9:30 AM - 4:30 PM.

Parking Facilities: Street.
Special Features: Search service.
Catalogue: Three to six times per year.
Collections/Individual Items Purchased: Both.
Booksellers' Memberships: Associated Antique Dealers of Hot Springs, Arkansas.

CALIFORNIA

22
A B I Books
Post Office Box 30564
Santa Barbara, California 93130   (805) 682-9686

The bookstore combines an interest in the traditional fields of private press publications and illustrated books of the last 100 years with the shop's expertise in the art of the book as a beautiful object, in a broader than usual sense: original art of book illustrators, fine bindings, the Modern Movement in Europe, America, and England, and its relationship to book production, graphic art, typography, and related book arts. Visits are by appointment only.

How to Get There: Telephone for directions.
Owner/Biography: Jeffrey Akard, Nancy Isakson.
Year Founded/History of Bookstore: 1980. Contains 800 square feet of space.
Number of Volumes: 2,000.
Types/Classifications: Books, prints, drawings, paintings, sculpture, ceramics; fine bindings, press books, illustrated books.
General Subject Areas: Illustrated Books, Private Press Publications.
Specific Specialties: Historical and/or scholarly importance in the history of Typography, Illustration, and Fine or Commercial Book Production. English Avant-Garde (1890-1940), Illustrators of the Curwen Press, Art Theory in English in the 20th Century, Processes of Graphic Reproduction, Original Art of Book Illustrators, Art "Objects" related to Fine Book Production: Sculpture, Print Making, Glassware and Ceramics, Printing Presses, Posters.
Author Specialties: Paul Nash, Eric Gill, Eric Ravilious, Herbert Bayer, Edward Wadsworth, Ben Nicholson, John Piper, Christopher Dresser, Robert Delauney, C.R.W. Nevinson, Charles Ricketts, William Morris, and individuals related either ideologically or artistically to any of the above.
Mail/Telephone Orders; Credit Cards: Both; supply trade references. No credit cards.
Business Hours: Monday through Saturday 10:00 AM - 5:00 PM by appointment only.
Parking Facilities: Street.
Catalogue: Four times a year.
Collections/Individual Items Purchased: Both.
Booksellers' Memberships: Antiquarian Booksellers Association of America.

23
A Change Of Hobbit
1853 Lincoln Boulevard
Santa Monica, California 90404   (213) 473-2873

The bookstore believes it is the world's oldest science fiction store. It has paperback science fiction and fantasy organized alphabetically by author in the large front room, with special cases for new titles, newly reissued titles, anthologies, science non-fiction, and books of science fiction and fantasy criticism and commentary. Walking through the rainbow archway into the even larger rainbow-walled rear room, one will discover new, current, and some older hardbacks. Here, too, is the art wall, holding original science fiction paintings displayed for sale. Science fiction and fantasy art books, illustrated editions, trade-sized science books, and remaindered hardbacks can also be found in the rainbow room. Every three weeks or so, the full-sized gazebo in the rainbow room is the site of author autographings. An alcove off the rainbow room is the home of back-issue magazines, books for younger readers, and the film- and media-related books. The bookstore contains 4,800 square feet of space.

How to Get There: Santa Monica is 4 to 5 miles west of West Los Angeles; the bookstore is 1 1/2 blocks south of Highway 10 (Santa Monica Freeway), at the Lincoln exit, and two doors north of Pico Boulevard.

The shop is about one mile inland from the coast.

Owner/Biography: Sherry M. Gottlieb, owner, received her BA in dramatic arts (playwriting) from the University of California (Berkeley) in 1969. She opened the bookstore in 1972 because she "was sick of being a college educated secretary and couldn't find enough science fiction to read."

Year Founded/History of Bookstore: In 1972 the bookstore was originally opened in a 12' by 12' room over a laundromat. In 1974 it was moved to a ground floor store of 960 square feet of space in Westwood. In 1981 it again expanded by a factor of five to the current size and location. Ms. Gottleib's "franchise" is The Other Change Of Hobbit, 2433 Channing Way, Berkeley, California, 94704 (separately owned and operated).

Number of Volumes: 75,000.

Types/Classifications: Hardbound, paperback, magazines, posters, calendars, cards, original artwork and jewelry, games (new and used), out-of-print, first editions, limited and signed editions, rare paperbacks, rare magazines, pulps.

General Subject Areas: Children's Science Fiction Literature, Critical Works on Speculative Fiction, Horror, Science Books, Science Fiction and Fantasy, Science Fiction Reference.

Specific Specialties: Hugo Award winners, Nebula Award winners, Ray Bradbury, Stephen King, Harlan Ellison, Frank Herbert, Philip Jose Farmer, Jack Vance, Time Travel, Vampires, Post-Holocaust (Atomic or Cataclysmic), New Physics, Dragons, and Unicorns.

Author Specialties: Ray Bradbury, Stephen King, Harlan Ellison, Frank Herbert, Philip Jose Farmer, Philip K. Dick, Jack Vance, Samuel R. Delany, Piers Anthony, Isaac Asimov, Robert Heinlein, Arthur C. Clarke, Douglas Adams, Fritz Leiber, J. R. R. Tolkien, Andre Norton, Robert Silverberg.

Mail/Telephone Orders; Credit Cards: Both; send want lists for new, used, or out-of-print paperbacks, hardbounds, magazines; free search service for paperbacks and magazines; world wide mail orders: Visa, Mastercard. An easy way to remember the telephone number is "GREAT SF" (473-2873).

Business Hours: Monday through Friday 10:30 AM - 8:00 PM; Saturday and Sunday 10:30 AM - 6:00 PM.

Parking Facilities: The bookstore has a parking lot in the rear and there is free street parking in the front.

Special Features: Free search service, monthly autograph parties, rumor control, science fiction news dispensing, movie consulting service, and other special events. A monthly newsletter is available for self-addressed stamped envelopes, or for pickup at the shop. The bookstore is also expert at identifying science fiction novels and stories by a plot description. It is also pleased to recommend reading based on individual customers' tastes, and is happy to give advice to those new to collecting science fiction. Appraisals available for a fee.

Collections/Individual Items Purchased: Both.

Miscellaneous: The bookstore does its best to keep its customers' loyalty by attempting to carry everything in the field of speculative fiction (science fiction, fantasy, and horror).

24
Aardvark Books
237 Church Street
San Francisco, California 94114   (415) 552-6733

A general used bookstore with extensive collections in many subjects; it contains approximately 1,700 square feet of space.

How to Get There: The bookstore is near the intersection of Church and Market Streets in downtown San Francisco.

Owner/Biography: J. Hadreas.

Year Founded/History of Bookstore: 1978.

Number of Volumes: 30,000.

Types/Classifications: Hardbound, paperback.

General Subject Areas: General.

Mail/Telephone Orders; Credit Cards: Both. Visa and Mastercard accepted.

Business Hours: Monday through Saturday 10:30 AM - 10:30 PM; Sunday 9:30 AM - 9:30 PM.

Parking Facilities: Street.

Special Features: Search service.

Collections/Individual Items Purchased: Both.

25
About Books
13330 Paseo Del Verano Norte
San Diego, California 92128   (619) 487-5121

The bookstore is located at the Bernardo Winery in North San Diego County, on the outskirts of Rancho Bernardo. The winery was established in 1889. About Books is one of eleven specialty shops at the winery, and contains about 375 square feet of space. Over sixty categories of non-fiction books are featured.

How to Get There: Approximately 25 miles north of the city of San Diego, from highway I-15, take the Bernardo Drive offramp east to Pomerado Road, north to the first traffic light which is Paseo Del Verano Norte. The Bernardo Winery is about a mile from the traffic light.

Owner/Biography: E. J. Weathers.

Year Founded/History of Bookstore: 1981.

Number of Volumes: 8,000.

Types/Classifications: Hardbound, magazines, postcards, photographs, ephemera, first editions, out-of-print, color plate books.

General Subject Areas: Aeronautics, American Government, American History, American Indians, American Presidents, Anthropology, Archaeology, Architecture, Art, Atlases, Automotive, Biography, Business, California History, Carpentry, Children's Books, Cinema, Cooking, Crafts, Dictionaries, Exploration, Foreign Languages, Furniture, Games, Geography, Graphics, History, Hobbies, Humor, Law, Marine, Medical, Metaphysics, Military, Music, Natural History, Philosophy, Photography, Plumbing, Poetry, Radio, Railroads, Religion, San Diego (California) History, Science, Sports, Television, Theater, Travel, Wine.

Mail/Telephone Orders; Credit Cards: Both; the bookstore pays shipping charges. Visa and Mastercard accepted.

Business Hours: Wednesday through Sunday 11:00 AM - 5:00 PM.

Parking Facilities: Ample parking in the courtyard of the winery and in front of the shop.

Special Features: Search service, book repairs (not rebinding).

Collections/Individual Items Purchased: Both.

26
About Music
357 Grove Street
San Francisco, California 94102   (415) 621-1634

This is a small bookstore specializing in books about music and musicians. It contains approximately 530 square feet of space.

How to Get There: The bookstore is located 1/2 block from the San Francisco Opera House, across from the Performing Arts Center garage.

Owner/Biography: Owners Susan Albrecht and Gerald Skeels both hold music degrees and are active in music performance in the San Francisco Bay area.

Year Founded/History of Bookstore: 1979.

Number of Volumes: 2,300.

Types/Classifications: Hardbound, paperback, some out-of-print magazines (there are no new magazines), first editions, out-of-print, some association copies, press books, signed copies, presentation copies, limited editions.

General Subject Areas: Biography, Children's Books, Dance, Jazz, Opera, Technical.

Specific Specialties: Music and musicians (some material is in Foreign Languages).

Mail/Telephone Orders; Credit Cards: Both; mail orders: cash or credit card number with order; Visa and Mastercard accepted.

Business Hours: Hours vary; call first.

Parking Facilities: Public parking garage.

Special Features: Searches: $2.00 each title.

Catalogue: Four times a year.

Collections/Individual Items Purchased: Both.

27
Abreyde Books
4500 Soquel Drive
Soquel, California 95073   (408) 475-9061

Abreyde Books deals in out-of-print books in the fields of theology and religion, both East and West. It is not open as a retail outlet but will make appointments if one calls at any "reasonable hour." Catalogues are issued and want lists are answered.
Owner/Biography: Jesse W. Case-Gabbard.
Year Founded/History of Bookstore: 1976.
Number of Volumes: 25,000.
Types/Classifications: Hardbound, paperback, some periodicals, broadsides, autographs, ephemera, out-of-print.
General Subject Areas: Literary Criticism, Philosophy, Religion (Eastern and Western), Theology.
Mail/Telephone Orders; Credit Cards: Both. No credit cards.
Business Hours: By appointment only; call at any "reasonable hour."
Catalogue: Published 4 or 5 times per year.
Collections/Individual Items Purchased: Both.

28
Acorn Books
510 O'Farrell Street
San Francisco, California 94102   (415) 563-1736

The bookstore has grown rapidly in its three years of existence, squeezing many thousands of books into its 500 square feet of space. These books, both hardbound and paperback, are organized by subject, and alphabetically by author, so that a customer's specific wants can be met quickly. Most of the books are in all areas of non-fiction, although there is a small literary section as well.
How to Get There: The shop is located in the downtown area, easily reached by foot from all of the major hotels as well as by the city bus system.
Owner/Biography: Mr. and Mrs. Joel M. Chapman. Mr. Chapman has been in the out-of-print and used book business for the better part of twenty years, having previously been a partner in the Albatross Book Store, also located in San Francisco.
Year Founded/History of Bookstore: 1980.
Number of Volumes: Hardbound 15,000; paperback 20,000.
Types/Classifications: Out-of-print hardbound, paperback, pre-1950 magazines, autographs, postcards, photographs; good quality books in all fields.
General Subject Areas: California, Children's Books, Cinema, Dance, Illustrated Books, Maritime, Modern First Editions, Music, Theater.
Author Specialties: Jack London, John Steinbeck, William Saroyan, Robinson Jeffers, P.G. Wodehouse.
Other Specialties: California, San Francisco.
Mail/Telephone Orders; Credit Cards: Both. Visa and Mastercard accepted.
Business Hours: Monday through Saturday 11:00 AM - 7:00 PM.
Parking Facilities: Street parking, parking lots within one block.
Special Features: Search service.
Collections/Individual Items Purchased: Both.

29
Acres of Books
240 Long Beach Boulevard
Long Beach, California 90802   (213) 437-6980

Acres of Books is a mecca for book collectors in the Los Angeles area. There are literally acres of books. A classification scheme is posted at the entrance to assist in locating the desired subject area. A separate fiction section, very extensive, is located in the back portion of the store. Sales personnel are knowledgeable bookpersons and very helpful (patrons are never disturbed). Browsing is encouraged.

How to Get There: The bookstore can be reached via the Long Beach Freeway exiting on Broadway and proceeding three blocks east to Long Beach Boulevard. The store stands in the midst of a massive renovation of downtown Long Beach. The block on which it stands has been spared demolition temporarily and plans to move the bookstore to another location have been shelved until needed.

Year Founded/History of Bookstore: 1933.

Number of Volumes: "Acres."

Types/Classifications: Hardbound, paperback, first editions, out-of-print, reading copies, sheet music, magazines.

General Subject Areas: General.

Mail/Telephone Orders; Credit Cards: Mail orders.

Business Hours: Tuesday through Saturday 9:15 AM - 5:30 PM.

Parking Facilities: Ample parking in public lots nearby, metered street parking.

30
Ada's
1624 West Lewis Street
San Diego, California 92103   (619) 291-4736

The bookstore specializes in out-of-print and new children's books. The bookstore contains 600 square feet of space.

Owner/Biography: Ada Greer.

Year Founded/History of Bookstore: 1975.

Number of Volumes: 2,000.

General Subject Areas: Children's Books.

Specific Specialties: Color Plate Books, Jessie Wilcox Smith Illustrations.

Mail/Telephone Orders; Credit Cards: Telephone orders.

Business Hours: Tuesday through Saturday 9:00 AM - 5:00 PM.

Parking Facilities: Street.

Special Features: Imported Cards, Note Papers, Search Service.

Collections/Individual Items Purchased: Both.

Booksellers' Memberships: San Diego Booksellers Association.

31
Adams Avenue Book Store
3502 Adams Avenue
San Diego, California 92116   (619) 281-3330

This is a general bookstore featuring out-of-print fiction and collectibles.

How to Get There: Traveling on either Route 805 or 15, take first exit (Adams) south of Route 8.

Owner/Biography: Laura and Irvin Weiss.

Year Founded/History of Bookstore: The bookstore changed to its present ownership in March 1983.

Types/Classifications: General, out-of-print fiction, collectibles, first editions, fine bindings, signed copies, limited editions.

General Subject Areas: Mysteries, Western Americana.

Mail/Telephone Orders; Credit Cards: Both; no credit cards.

Business Hours: Monday through Saturday 11:00 AM - 4:30 PM; Friday to 7:00 PM.

Parking Facilities: Street.

Collections/Individual Items Purchased: Both.

Booksellers' Memberships: San Diego Booksellers Association.

32
Aladdin Books and Memorabilia
122 West Commonwealth Avenue
Fullerton, California 92632   (714) 738-6115

The bookstore has one of California's largest selections of new and used conjuring books, journals, and apparatus, as well as one of the largest collections of movie memorabilia. In addition, it maintains a large stock of first edition fiction and collectible books in many subject areas. It contains 1,300 square feet of space.

How to Get There: Fullerton is approximately 30 miles south of Los Angeles, and five miles north of Disneyland in Orange County. From the Riverside Freeway (91) exit north to Fullerton via Harbor Boulevard. The bookstore is located 3 minutes north of the Freeway, on Commonwealth, 1/2 block west of Harbor.

Owner/Biography: John T. Cannon.

Year Founded/History of Bookstore: 1982.

Number of Volumes: 8,000.

Types/Classifications: Hardbound, paperback, conjuring apparatus, magazines, photographs, posters, first editions, out-of-print, signed copies, limited editions, original filmscripts.

General Subject Areas: Art, Chess, Children's Literature, Cinema, Circus, Conjuring, Cooking, Crafts, Detective Fiction, Disneyana, Gambling, Games, Golf, Horror, Magic, Modern Fiction, Music, Mystery, Nature, Oziana, Popular Culture, Science Fiction and Fantasy, Television, Theater, Transportation, Western Americana, Western Fiction.

Specific Specialties: Current and Vintage Movie Material (Disney, Hitchcock, Science Fiction and Fantasy).

Author Specialties: Harlan Ellison, Professor Hoffman (Magic and Games).

Mail/Telephone Orders; Credit Cards: Both; cash with order; no credit cards.

Business Hours: Monday through Saturday 10:00 AM - 6:00 PM; Sunday by appointment.

Parking Facilities: Street, and at rear of shop.

Special Features: Search service; want lists accepted.

Collections/Individual Items Purchased: Both.

33
Alan Wofsy Fine Arts
401 China Basin Street
San Francisco, California 94107   (415) 986-3030

The bookstore features original graphics from all periods, original posters and decorative printed matter, books with original graphics, art reference books, fine press books.

How to Get There: The shop is situated at Pier 50, near the intersection of 3rd and 4th Streets just south of the large blue China Basin Building.

Owner/Biography: Alan Wofsy.

Year Founded/History of Bookstore: The bookstore was located in the north waterfront area for 12 years, then moved to the south waterfront area during 1983.

Types/Classifications: Art books, limited edition art books, autographs, ephemera, posters, prints, bibliographies, art reference books, fine bindings, press books, signed books.

General Subject Areas: Architecture, Art, Children's Books, Facsimiles of 16th and 17th Century Art Books, Foreign Language Art Books, Monographs on Artists, Print Reference Books.

Specific Specialties: Georges Rouault, Aristide Maillol, William Rothstein, James McNeill Whistler, Cervantes, School of Paris Posters, Zoophilia, Philately, German Artists, French Artists, Impressionists, Contemporary Glass Art, Autographs, Postcards, Frank Lloyd Wright.

Other Specialties: Publishes art reference, art books, and bibliographies.

Mail/Telephone Orders; Credit Cards: Both; mail address: P.O.Box 2210, San Francisco, CA 94126; no credit cards.

Business Hours: By appointment only.

Parking Facilities: Free on-site parking.

Special Features: Publishing.

Catalogue: Annually.

Collections/Individual Items Purchased: Both.

34
Albatross Book Store
166 Eddy Street
San Francisco, California 94102 (415) 885-6501

This is a large general bookstore with an impressive assortment of over 200,000 items. It is well organized, has good lighting, clean aisles, and a staff that remembers the definition of service to the customer, "who always comes first."

How to Get There: The bookstore is in the heart of San Francisco, just two blocks up Eddy Street from where the Powell Street Cable Car turnaround is located and two blocks from the city's newest luxury hotel, The Ramada Renaissance. It is also one short block down Taylor Street from the Hilton Hotel Tower. The Bay Area Rapid Transit (BART), Muni Metro, Greyhound, and San Francisco Airporter are all within 4 blocks of the shop.

Owner/Biography: Donald W. and Rose H. Sharp. Don Sharp started in the book business 30 years ago with a mail order service specializing in Western Americana. In 1963 he bought the Albatross and has operated and expanded it to two full floors, a mezzanine, and a newly opened garret. In addition, a new shop was opened this year in the charming village of Tiburon just north of the Golden Gate Bridge in lovely Marin County. Rose Sharp, an aviation enthusiast, runs the Tiburon shop and specializes in searching for the out-of-print and hard-to-find items.

Year Founded/History of Bookstore: The bookstore was founded in 1952 and has been under the present owner since 1963.

Number of Volumes: 200,000.

Types/Classifications: Hardbound, paperback, magazines, pulps, first editions, out-of-print, leather bindings, illustrated books, limited editions, fine press, autographed, presentation copies.

General Subject Areas: Animals, Architecture, Aviation, Belles Lettres, Black Literature, Children's Books, Dance, Foreign Countries, History, Judaica, Nature, Occult, Philosophy, Plays, Science, Science Fiction and Fantasy, Self-Help, Shakespeare, Theater, War.

Specific Specialties: Sewing, Crafts, Archaeology, Anthropology, Business, Folklore, Genealogy, Psychology, Travel, Religion, Christian Religion, Eastern Religions, Reference.

Author Specialties: Jack London, John Steinbeck, Ernest Hemingway, Walt Kelly, Henry Miller, Jack Kerouac, Amelia Earhart, Richard Bach.

Mail/Telephone Orders; Credit Cards: Both; payment with order. Visa and Mastercard accepted.

Business Hours: Monday through Friday 10:00 AM - 6:00 PM; Saturday 11:00 AM - 6:00 PM.

Parking Facilities: Parking lot adjacent to shop; pay by the hour.

Special Features: An especially active free search service with a high rate of success. The bookstore ships books in carefully-wrapped packages anywhere in the world.

Collections/Individual Items Purchased: Both.

Booksellers' Memberships: Antiquarian Booksellers Association of America.

Miscellaneous: The city of San Francisco is proud of its old bookstores and works hard to protect them from high rents. San Francisco is filled with avid readers and people who love the presence of books around them. This bookstore encourages browsers, buyers, sellers, and those who enjoy trading.

35
Albatross II Book Shop
100 Main Street
Tiburon, California 94920 (415) 435-1506

The bookstore is a small, well planned shop, in clean, bright condition, featuring fine oak shelving and display cases, all in a warm, cheerful atmosphere. The shop is part of the famous Ark Row of Tiburon. The shelves, cases, and counters were hand built by one man specifically for the shop. In addition to books the shop offers fine glass paperweights from Scotland.

How to Get There: Tiburon is north of the Golden Gate Bridge, San Francisco, in Marin County. One should take Highway 101 to the Tiburon (No.131) offramp, then four miles to the heart of the town. Tiburon is also served by the Red & White Fleet ferryboat out of San Francisco, and by Golden Gate Transit buses. It is a short walk from boat or bus to the shop.

Owner/Biography: Donald W. and Rose H. Sharp, owners, also own the Albatross Book Store in San Francisco.

Year Founded/History of Bookstore: September, 1983.

Number of Volumes: 4,000.

Types/Classifications: Hardbound, leather bound, prints, first editions, out-of-print, signed copies, presentation copies, fine press.

General Subject Areas: Americana, Animals, Architecture, Art, Automobiles, Aviation, Belles Lettres, Biography, California, Cooking, Early West (U.S.), Entertainment, Fiction, Firefighting, Foreign Language Books, Games, Gardening, Health and Beauty, Illustrated Children's Books, Marine, Military, Mining, Mysteries, Occult, Plays, Poetry, Railroads, Ranching, Reference Material, San Francisco, Science Fiction and Fantasy, Sports, World History.

Author Specialties: Jack London, Henry Miller, Jack Kerouac, Ernest Hemingway, John Steinbeck.

Mail/Telephone Orders; Credit Cards: Both; check or charge card number with expiration date; postage is extra. Visa and Mastercard accepted.

Business Hours: Tuesday through Sunday 11:00 AM - 6:00 PM; closed Monday.

Parking Facilities: Validated parking; ask at entrance.

Special Features: Free search service; the store will ship anywhere in well packed, carefully wrapped packages; gift certificates and gift wrapping available the year 'round.

Catalogue: Is published.

Collections/Individual Items Purchased: Both.

Booksellers' Memberships: Antiquarian Booksellers Association of America.

Miscellaneous: The owners welcome browsers and vow to present a warm, friendly, well lighted, and clean atmosphere.

36
Alphabooks
18046 Ventura Boulevard
Encino, California 91316   (818) 344-6365

The bookstore features neatness, organization, and special attention to the customer. It is a general antiquarian bookstore and contains 2,020 square feet of space.

How to Get There: From the Ventura Freeway, north of Los Angeles, take the Reseda Boulevard offramp, south to Ventura Boulevard (2 blocks), left turn onto Ventura Boulevard (east), to the third light (Lindley), then 1/4 block further. The bookstore is on the south side, and is well marked on the side of the building.

Owner/Biography: Ray and Betty Vasin. Betty, a bookseller by profession, has been with Alphabooks for 18 years. Prior to that, she had three years of experience with other bookstores. Ray is a professional writer.

Year Founded/History of Bookstore: The Vasins purchased the bookstore in 1965 from its previous owner who had owned and operated the shop under another name for five years.

Number of Volumes: 25,000 hardbound, 30,000 paperback, 10,000 magazines.

Types/Classifications: Hardbound, paperback, back issue magazines, ephemera, sheet music, prints, collectibles.

General Subject Areas: Americana, Arts, Aviation, Children's Literature, Cookbooks, Crafts, Fiction, Fishing, Gardening, Guns, History, Hobbies, Hunting, Literature, Marine, Metaphysics, Mysteries, Natural History, Sailing, Science Fiction and Fantasy, Westerns.

Specific Specialties: Self-Help (How-To) in all categories.

Other Specialties: Art Periodicals in English language only.

Mail/Telephone Orders; Credit Cards: Both; prepaid by credit card or check. Visa and Mastercard accepted.

Business Hours: Monday through Thursday 11:00 AM - 6:00 PM; Friday 11:00 AM - 7:00 PM; Saturday 11:00 AM - 6:00 PM; Sunday 12:00 Noon - 5:00 PM.

Parking Facilities: Business lot and street.

Special Features: Search service; personalized service; low key selling approach.

Collections/Individual Items Purchased: Both.

Miscellaneous: Excellent lighting, tiled floors, and well arranged stock where customers can discover their books while browsing in a pleasant atmosphere.

37
Anacapa Books
3090 Claremont Avenue
Berkeley, California 94705   (415) 654-3517

This is a general stock bookstore with 1,800 square feet of space in the shop and 2,000 square feet in the warehouse.

Owner/Biography: David S. Wirshup.
Year Founded/History of Bookstore: The bookstore was founded in 1975 in Santa Barbara, California.
Number of Volumes: 30,000.
Types/Classifications: First Editions.
General Subject Areas: American Fiction, American Poetry, British Fiction, British Poetry.
Specific Specialties: Expatriates, Women Authors.
Mail/Telephone Orders; Credit Cards: Both.
Business Hours: Monday through Friday 9:00 AM - 5:00 PM.
Parking Facilities: Street.
Catalogue: Six to eight times a year.
Collections/Individual Items Purchased: Both.

38
Antiquus Bibliopole
4147 24th Street
San Francisco, California 94114   (415) 285-2322

The bookstore is located in an old Victorian house situated in the Noe Valley. Upon entering, one will see rows of shelves in the hallway, then three more rooms with shelves that reach to the high ceilings, where books are arranged by subject. There are many antique bookcases. The closets are filled with books, and some books are to be found on tables. The bookshop contains 630 square feet of space.

How to Get There: The shop is located fifteen minutes from downtown San Francisco. If driving west on Market Street, one should make a left turn on Castro to 24th Street, then a right on 24th, proceed past Bud's Icecream. The shop has signs on the steps of the bookstore.

Owner/Biography: Pauline A. Grosch, owner, is originally from Canada and worked in insurance companies for many years; she enjoys traveling, especially to buy books. She is a past president of the Antiquarian Booksellers Association of America. Constantly rearranging the store to give it a new look, Ms. Grosch lives in back of the bookstore.

Year Founded/History of Bookstore: Started in 1973 with a small inventory, the bookstore relocated one year later to its present building in order to have room for more stock. The name for the store was derived from H. Jackson's book "Anatomy of Bibliomania." Antiquus means lover of old things; bibliopole means seller of books. Ms. Grosch believes that the shop is the only antiquarian bookstore in the Noe Valley.

Number of Volumes: 15,000.
Types/Classifications: Hardbound books, framed prints relating to bookselling, maps, and framed posters of Virginia Woolf and Willa Cather. There are also modern first editions, signed copies, fine bindings, color plate books, out-of-print.

General Subject Areas: Art, Biography, Books About Books, California History, Children's Books, Cooking, Philosophy, Travel.

Author Specialties: Willa Cather, Virginia Woolf, Kay Boyle, Colin Wilson, John Fowles, D.H. Lawrence, Aldous Huxley.

Mail/Telephone Orders; Credit Cards: Both. A deposit is not required with inquiries, but payment must be sent with a firm order. No credit cards.

Business Hours: Wednesday through Saturday 11:00 AM - 5:00 PM.
Parking Facilities: Street, public parking lot a half block from the shop.
Special Features: Search service; new books will be ordered.
Catalogue: Lists will be sent on a special subject or author.
Collections/Individual Items Purchased: Both.
Booksellers' Memberships: Antiquarian Booksellers Association of America, American Booksellers Association, Merchants Association.
Miscellaneous: The bookstore will put books on hold for a period of ten days for a 50 percent deposit.

39
Argonaut Book Shop
786-792 Sutter Street
San Francisco, California 94109 (415) 474-9067

The bookstore occupies two large rooms open to the public. One enters first into a large, well lit room with oak flooring and antique bookcases filled with fine and rare books, mostly dealing with the history of the American West. This room is also where are kept the fine press books and other rare subject matter. The second room is devoted to good books in varied subject areas. The two rooms contain a total of 1,500 square feet of space.

How to Get There: The bookstore is located just three blocks from Union Square in downtown San Francisco.

Owner/Biography: Robert D. Haines, Jr.

Year Founded/History of Bookstore: The bookstore was founded in 1941 on Kearny Street in the middle of the financial district of San Francisco by Robert D. Haines. The Argonaut was a founding member of the Antiquarian Booksellers Association of America and has been a member in good standing ever since. The shop has always been "family run," and is now owned by Robert D. Haines, Jr. The shop moved its location in 1969.

Number of Volumes: 10,000.

Types/Classifications: Fine and rare hardbound books, autographs, manuscripts, and related material, authentic primitive art from Africa, Oceania, and the Americas, first editions, press books, signed books, inscribed books, limited editions, rare association copies, cartographic material.

General Subject Areas: West (U.S.).

Specific Specialties: Exploration Voyages to America or the South Pacific, Western Americana, California, Southwest (U.S.), Civil War (U.S.), Art, Fine Press Books of Western American Presses.

Other Specialties: California Spanish Period, Early San Francisco, Spanish Southwest, Western American Presses including Grabhorn, John Henry Nash, Allen Press, Russell, California Private Press Books, Lewis & Clark, Captain James Cook, George Vancouver.

Mail/Telephone Orders; Credit Cards: Both; cash with order, returnable; established credit due in 30 days; personal check, money order, Visa, Mastercard.

Business Hours: Monday through Friday 9:00 AM - 5:00 PM; Saturday 9:00 AM - 4:00 PM.

Parking Facilities: Street, and a public parking garage 1/2 block away.

Catalogue: Three to six times a year.

Collections/Individual Items Purchased: Both.

Booksellers' Memberships: Antiquarian Booksellers Association of America, International League of Antiquarian Booksellers.

40
Ark Bookshop
1703 University Avenue
Berkeley, California 94703 (415) 841-2853

The bookstore consists of two rooms lined with bookshelves on the walls and in the center of the store. Oftentimes there are books stacked on the floor, against the sides. The shop carries quality books in several scientific disciplines and social areas, and is known as a place where people love to browse and often discover books they have long searched for. It contains 1,000 square feet of space.

How to Get There: If driving, one should take the University Avenue exit of the Freeway, go east to the corner of McGee.

Owner/Biography: Louis Laub.

Year Founded/History of Bookstore: Founded in January of 1965, the bookstore is still in the original location, and with the original owner.

Number of Volumes: 20,000.

Types/Classifications: Hardbound, paperback, ephemera, autographs, first editions, rare and very scarce books, out-of-print, and limited editions.

General Subject Areas: American West, Americana, Californiana, Children's Books, Engineering, Literature, Marine, Ships, Technology.

Other Specialties: Scholarly Works in several areas.

Mail/Telephone Orders; Credit Cards: Both; cash with order; libraries billed; order will be held until payment arrives. Visa and Mastercard accepted.
Business Hours: Tuesday through Friday 11:00 AM - 5:30 PM; Saturday 10:00 AM - 5:00 PM.
Parking Facilities: Street.
Special Features: Search service, appraisals; Mr. Laub is a senior member of the American Society of Appraisers.
Catalogue: Once a year.
Collections/Individual Items Purchased: Both.

41
Arthur H. Clark Company
1264 South Central Avenue
Glendale, California 91204   (213) 245-9119

Visiting this bookstore is like visiting a bookshop in the 19th Century. Surrounded by oak bookcases and furniture, the booklover may browse through thousands of volumes dealing with Western American History. Hidden within the corners of the building lie the operations of a fine press publisher, as well. The bookstore contains 1,000 square feet of space.
How to Get There: The driver should take the Ventura Freeway (Route 134) to Glendale, off at Central Avenue, and south to the bookstore.
Owner/Biography: Arthur H. Clark.
Year Founded/History of Bookstore: Originally founded in 1902 in Cleveland, the business was moved to Glendale in 1930, and has been there since.
Number of Volumes: 30,000.
Types/Classifications: Hardbound, ephemera, broadsides, first editions, press books, limited editions.
General Subject Areas: Non-Fiction, Western Americana.
Mail/Telephone Orders; Credit Cards: Both; Visa, Mastercard.
Business Hours: Daily 8:15 AM - 4:45 PM.
Parking Facilities: Limited.
Special Features: Search service, publishing, appraisals.
Catalogue: Seven times a year.
Collections/Individual Items Purchased: Both.

42
B & L Rootenberg Rare Books
P.O. Box 5049
Sherman Oaks, California 91403   (213) 788-7765

This is a specialized bookstore dealing in the rare works in the history of science and medicine and works that have made an impact on western civilization.
How to Get There: Sherman Oaks is located ten minutes from Westwood and the UCLA campus via the San Diego Freeway. Please telephone for an appointment and precise directions will be given.
Owner/Biography: Barbara Rootenberg.
Year Founded/History of Bookstore: 1970.
Number of Volumes: Approximately 3,000.
Types/Classifications: Rare books, manuscripts, original materials.
General Subject Areas: Economics, History of Ideas, History of Science, Medicine, Philosophy, Technology.
Specific Specialties: 15th through 20th centuries (including the Nobel Laureates).
Mail/Telephone Orders; Credit Cards: Both. Mail orders should be based on catalogue listings or telephone/mail inquiry. No credit cards.
Business Hours: By appointment only.
Special Features: Appraisals of personal and university libraries.
Catalogue: Published once per year.

Collections/Individual Items Purchased: Both.
Booksellers' Memberships: Antiquarian Booksellers Association of America, International League of Antiquarian Booksellers, American Library Association, Manuscript Society, Bibliographic Society, Society of American Archivists, History of Science Society, History of Medicine Society, International Science Information Service.

43
Bargain Bookshop
3325 South Street
Long Beach, California 90805   (213) 531-6909

Bargain Bookshop is a husband-wife run shop and deals in all types of used books. The shop occupies 2,000 square feet of space.
How to Get There: From the Los Angeles area take the Long Beach Freeway south to the 91 Freeway (often referred to as the Artesia Freeway) east to Downey off ramp; go south to South Street, and turn right.
Owner/Biography: Dolores and Lee Martin.
Year Founded/History of Bookstore: 1967. This is the third store operated by the Martins.
Number of Volumes: 75,000.
Types/Classifications: Hardbound, paperback, back issue magazines, comic books, out-of-print, first editions, signed copies.
General Subject Areas: Americana, Biography, Cinema, Cookbooks, Gambling, Gardening, Juvenile, Magic, Metaphysics, Poetry, Religion, World History, World War II.
Specific Specialties: Victorian Architecture, Old Children's Books (1910 to 1940), California History, Cleveland (Ohio); American Indian Pottery, Silver, Baskets.
Author Specialties: Ray Bradbury, Ted DeGrazia, Walt Disney, Jack London, Robert Service.
Mail/Telephone Orders; Credit Cards: No telephone orders. Personal check or cashier's check with mail orders. No credit cards.
Business Hours: Tuesday through Friday 12:00 Noon - 6:00 PM; Saturday 11:00 AM to 5:00 PM; closed Sunday and Monday.
Parking Facilities: Public parking lot.
Special Features: Search service; paperback trade.
Collections/Individual Items Purchased: Both.

44
Bargain Bookstore
1053 Eighth Avenue
San Diego, California 92101   (619) 234-5380

This bookstore is one of San Diego's oldest and largest\dealers in used, out-of-print, hardbound and paperback stock. The store occupies 2,200 square feet of space.
How to Get There: Downtown San Diego location, one block north of the Public Library.
Owner/Biography: Jim and Nancy Lindstrom.
Year Founded/History of Bookstore: 1952. The bookstore had a downtown location at 936 Broadway dating back to 1922 under different ownership. The present location was founded by Lafayette Young in 1952. The present owners have maintained the bookstore since 1952.
Number of Volumes: 100,000.
Types/Classifications: Hardbound, paperback, magazines, broadsides, **drawings**, graphics, prints, paintings, first editions, fine bindings, out-of-print, association copies, press books, signed copies, presentation copies, limited editions, color plate books.
General Subject Areas: Architecture, Art, Cinema, Classics, Computers, Information Theory, Linguistics, Mathematics, Metaphysics, Military, Music, Mythology, Natural History, Philosophy, Photography, Physics, Private Presses, Southwestern Americana, Stock Market, Theater, Typography.
Specific Specialties: American Small Presses, Typography 1890 - 1940; Bandar Log Press.
Author Specialties: Frank Holme, Fred Goudy, Henry Miller, Jane Austen, Mark Twain, Ernest Hemingway, Thomas Wolfe, John Steinbeck, Erskine Caldwell, Theodore Dreiser, Sherwood Anderson, Vardis

Fisher, William Faulkner.
Other Specialties: Bandar Log Press.
Mail/Telephone Orders; Credit Cards: Both. Visa and Mastercard accepted.
Business Hours: Monday through Saturday 10:00 AM to 5:00 PM.
Parking Facilities: Public parking lots, street parking.
Collections/Individual Items Purchased: Both.
Booksellers' Memberships: San Diego Booksellers Association.

45
Barry Cassidy Rare Books
2003 T Street
Sacramento, California 95814   (916) 456-6307

Barry Cassidy Rare Books has a specialty in northern California fine presses, including Grabhorn, Nash, etc. The store occupies 750 square feet of space.
How to Get There: The bookstore is located about one mile southeast of the newly restored State Capitol Building.
Owner/Biography: Barry Cassidy.
Year Founded/History of Bookstore: 1975.
Number of Volumes: 4,000.
Types/Classifications: Hardbound, paperback, magazines, broadsides, autographs, ephemera, first editions, fine bindings, out-of-print, association copies, press books, signed copies, presentation copies, limited editions, color plate books.
General Subject Areas: Literary First Editions, Western Americana.
Specific Specialties: Northern California Fine Presses.
Mail/Telephone Orders; Credit Cards: Both. No credit cards.
Business Hours: Monday through Friday 9:30 AM - 4:00 PM. Weekends by appointment.
Parking Facilities: Store parking lot in back.
Catalogue: Published irregularly.
Collections/Individual Items Purchased: Both.

46
Bart's Corner
302 West Matilija Street
Ojai, California 93023   (805) 646-3755

Bart's is unique among bookstores because most of its books are on outside shelves arranged around patios under huge oaks. The booktore also has a "Bookhouse" containing better books, including first editions, cookbooks, and art books. The bookstore occupies approximately 10,000 square feet of space.
How to Get There: Ojai is 15 miles north of Ventura via Highways 33 and 150. Bart's Corner is one block north of the main street at the corner of Canada and Matilija Streets.
Owner/Biography: Gary Schlichter. Gary has owned Bart's Corner for seven years.
Year Founded/History of Bookstore: 1964. The "Bookhouse" was originally a honeymoon cottage built in 1935. It was transformed by Richard Bartindale into an outdoor bookstore. The site has also had a restaurant and antique store.
Number of Volumes: 100,000.
Types/Classifications: Hardbound, paperback, magazines, show biz photos, some prints.
General Subject Areas: General.
Specific Specialties: Religion, Metaphysics.
Author Specialties: Krishnamurti.
Mail/Telephone Orders; Credit Cards: Both. Visa and Mastercard accepted.
Business Hours: Tuesday through Sunday 10:00 AM to 5:30 PM.
Parking Facilities: Street parking.
Special Features: Flower shop adjoining.

Collections/Individual Items Purchased: Both.

47
Bay City Books
629 State Street
Suite 215
Santa Barbara, California 93101   (805) 962-4411

Bay City Books issues catalogues of first edition detective fiction and modern literature. Collectors are welcome by appointment, usually on Mondays. Phone and mail inquiries regarding specific authors will receive a computerized response listing items from stock which may be of interest. The shop occupies 770 square feet of space.

How to Get There: The location is upstairs in the Fithian Building, above Gallager's restaurant and next to the offices of Capra Press.

Owner/Biography: Charles Johnson and Eric Kelley. Charles Johnson is a southern Californian who came to Santa Barbara to attend the University of California - Santa Barbara and returned to further his career in bookselling. He has worked for B. Dalton-Pickwick and manages the used book room of the Earthling Bookshop. Eric Kelley came from Germany at the age of fifteen and studied at UCLA. He was a store-level buyer for Brentano's and owns The Book Den, a general used bookstore in Santa Barbara.

Year Founded/History of Bookstore: 1983. Bay City Books is just beginning. The owners hope to issue several catalogues a year and attend antiquarian book fairs. They are interested in purchasing collections of detective fiction and modern literature and will be using the latest in computer technology to respond to collector inquiries.

Number of Volumes: 1,000.

Types/Classifications: First editions, signed copies, association copies, first periodical appearances, broadsides, fine printing.

General Subject Areas: California, Detective Fiction, Modern Literature, West (U.S.).

Author Specialties: Charles Bukowski, Raymond Chandler, Dashiell Hammett, Jack Kerouac, Dennis Lynds, Ross MacDonald, Henry Miller.

Mail/Telephone Orders; Credit Cards: Both. Prepaid credit card charges accepted. Visa and Mastercard accepted.

Business Hours: By appointment only. Mondays are best.

Parking Facilities: Public parking across the street; 90 minutes free.

Catalogue: Published 3 to 4 times per year.

Collections/Individual Items Purchased: Both.

48
Bennett & Marshall Rare Books
8205 Melrose Avenue
Los Angeles, California 90046   (213) 653-7040

Bennett & Marshall Rare Books is a general antiquarian bookshop specializing in both the scholarly book of the 19th and 20th Centuries and the rare book from the 15th Century on. It specializes primarily in art books, European and English history, history of science, medicine and mathematics as well as early printed books. The establishment occupies 1,000 square feet of space.

How to Get There: The bookshop is located in the West Hollywood/Beverly Hills area in the center of the greater Los Angeles metropolitan region.

Owner/Biography: George S. Allen, Daniel E. Guice, Yvonne S. Guice.

Year Founded/History of Bookstore: 1941.

Number of Volumes: 5,000.

Types/Classifications: Hardbound, out-of-print scholarly, first editions, rare.

General Subject Areas: American History, Americana, British History, Mathematics, Medicine, Natural History, Science, Travels and Voyages.

Mail/Telephone Orders; Credit Cards: Both. No credit cards.

Business Hours: Tuesday through Saturday 9:00 AM - 5:00 PM.
Parking Facilities: Street parking.
Catalogue: Published 3 times per year.
Collections/Individual Items Purchased: Both.
Booksellers' Memberships: Antiquarian Booksellers Association of America.

49
Bernard M. Rosenthal, Inc.
251 Post Street
San Francisco, California 94108   (415) 982-2219

Bernard M. Rosenthal, Inc. specializes in antiquarian books, chiefly before 1650, including medieval manuscripts and incunabula. It is located on the second floor at the above address and occupies 1,500 square feet of space.

Owner/Biography: Bernard M. Rosenthal and Ruth Rosenthal.
Year Founded/History of Bookstore: 1953. The business was begun in New York City in March of 1953 at 19 East 71st Street. It subsequently moved to 120 East 85th Street and in the summer of 1970 relocated to San Francisco.
Types/Classifications: Antiquarian books before 1650, medieval manuscripts, incunabula.
General Subject Areas: Bibliography, Early Printing, History of Scholarship, Paleography, Scholarly Texts in the Humanities.
Mail/Telephone Orders; Credit Cards: Mail order customers must give proper references or send payment with order. Telephone orders accepted only from people known to the owners. No credit cards.
Business Hours: Irregular hours; appointment essential.
Parking Facilities: Public parking garages nearby.
Catalogue: Published irregularly.
Collections/Individual Items Purchased: Both.
Booksellers' Memberships: Antiquarian Booksellers Association of America including Northern California Chapter.

50
Biblioctopus
Box 309
Idyllwild, California 92349   (714) 659-5188

Biblioctopus carries to the extreme the idea of quality over quantity. The specialty is fiction and always stocked are some of the best in the marketplace. The owners state that serious collectors of first editions and rare books "should prepare for a feast."

How to Get There: Idyllwild is an isolated spot in a large national forest at 5500 feet in altitude. It can be reached from Palm Springs via highway. Communication must be by mail or telephone. Visitors by written appointment only.
Owner/Biography: Melissa and Mark Hime, A. Hime, J. Hime.
Year Founded/History of Bookstore: 1980.
Types/Classifications: Rare, first editions, presentation copies, autographs, manuscripts.
General Subject Areas: The finest in fiction.
Mail/Telephone Orders; Credit Cards: Both. No credit cards.
Business Hours: By written appointment only.
Special Features: Biblioctopus consistently stocks a respectable percentage of the very best items for sale in the United States; collections built for sophisticated collectors.
Catalogue: Published frequently.
Collections/Individual Items Purchased: Both.
Booksellers' Memberships: Antiquarian Booksellers Association of America, Manuscript Society.
Miscellaneous: The owners state that Biblioctopus represents "an oasis for the serious collector weary of less than the best."

51
Book Attic
10239 Fair Oaks Boulevard
Fair Oaks, California 95628 (916) 961-3703

The Book Attic is a general stock used bookstore with over 50 categories of hardbound books. Californiana, military history, religion, and natural science are the largest sections, but a little bit of everything is available. An added attraction is live music provided by a canary and a singing finch with occasional comment by a cocatiel named Cecil. The store occupies 1,200 square feet of space.

How to Get There: The bookstore is located in quaint Fair Oaks Village, along with antique and specialty shops. It is 20 miles north of Sacramento. Take Highway 50 to Sunrise North. Turn right at Fair Oaks Boulevard, right after crossing the American River, take the first left turn and the bookstore is 3 blocks further on the left.

Owner/Biography: Carolyn J. Garrison. Carolyn was raised in four different states from coast to coast, but has spent the last 30 years in the Sacramento area. A graduate of California State University - Sacramento and holder of a California teaching credential, she found herself unemployable after 15 years of raising children. She therefore made her own job and even after seven years still feels she is living her only fantasy. She has the only store in town with architect-designed shelves, thanks to her husband Jim.

Year Founded/History of Bookstore: 1976. The store began with 500 square feet but moved to a larger space one block away after two years.

Number of Volumes: 30,000.

Types/Classifications: Hardbound, general used stock.

General Subject Areas: Americana, Art, Biography, Business, California, Children's Literature, Classics, Crafts, Crime, Do-It-Yourself, Drama, Fiction, Foreign Language, Geography, History, Humor, Language, Medicine, Metaphysics, Military, Music, Occult, Photography, Poetry, Psychology, Religion, Science, Science Fiction, Show Business, Sociology, Sports, Travel, Western Americana.

Mail/Telephone Orders; Credit Cards: Both. No credit cards.

Business Hours: Monday through Thursday 10:00 AM to 6:00 PM; Friday and Saturday 10:00 AM to 5:00 PM. Sunday by whim.

Parking Facilities: Business parking lot.

Special Features: Search service.

Catalogue: Projected for summer of 1984.

Collections/Individual Items Purchased: Both.

52
Book Attic
555 West Base Line
San Bernardino, California 92410 (714) 883-6908

The Book Attic is located in an old fashioned building with a brick front and 12-foot ceilings. Most of the books are on easily accessed shelves located along the wall and are organized by subject and author. The stock has been selected with quality and condition in mind. Acquisitions are pursued actively so that customers may always find a new tempting tidbit on the shelves.

How to Get There: San Bernardino is 60 miles east of Los Angeles. Take the Base Line off-ramp from Interstate 215, go east 2-1/2 blocks.

Owner/Biography: Dick and Kathy Thompson, Steve and June Case.

Year Founded/History of Bookstore: 1979. The Book Attic began as a mail order business. In August of the following year the retail store opened at its present location with under 500 square feet of floor space. The area was doubled to 1000 square feet in November 1983.

Number of Volumes: 7,500.

Types/Classifications: Hardbound, some western magazines, some ephemera, California Presses.

General Subject Areas: American Indians, Americana, Biography, Books About Books, Californiana, Civil War (U.S.), Cookbooks, Hollywood, Poetry, Railroads, Sailing, Western Americana, World War II.

Mail/Telephone Orders; Credit Cards: Both. Cash with order. No credit cards.

Business Hours: Wednesday through Friday 10:00 AM - 5:30 PM; Saturday 10:00 AM - 3:00 PM.

Parking Facilities: Street parking.

Special Features: Search service. The Book Attic has published "Black Origins in the Inland Empire," (1983) a book on local history, and plans to publish additonal titles in the future.
Catalogue: Published 2 times per year.
Collections/Individual Items Purchased: Both.

53
Book Baron
1236 South Magnolia Avenue
Anaheim, California 92804   (714) 527-7022

This is a large general bookstore occupying 8,600 square feet and featuring new, used, and rare books. The shop has wide aisles and carpeting. The fiction room alone stocks over 8,000 titles.
How to Get There: The bookstore is located at Ball and Magnolia in an Alpha Beta Shopping Center, 2 miles south of the intersection of Highways 5 and 91, within 2 miles of Disneyland and Knott's Berry Farm.
Owner/Biography: Bob Weinstein. Mr. Weinstein has 10 years of bookselling experience.
Year Founded/History of Bookstore: 1980.
Number of Volumes: 100,000.
Types/Classifications: Hardbound, paperback, magazines, broadsides, autographs, first editions, fine bindings, out-of-print, association copies, press books, signed copies, presentation copies, limited editions, color plate books.
General Subject Areas: General.
Mail/Telephone Orders; Credit Cards: Both. Visa and Mastercard accepted.
Business Hours: Monday through Saturday 10:00 AM - 6:00 PM; Sunday 12:00 Noon - 5:00 PM.
Parking Facilities: Public parking lot.
Special Features: Search service.
Collections/Individual Items Purchased: Both.
Booksellers' Memberships: Orange County Book Society.

54
Book Carnival
840 North Tustin Avenue
Orange, California 92667   (714) 538-3210

The Book Carnival is one of Orange County's finest used and out-of-print bookstores specializing in first editions, modern literature, science fiction, detective fiction, with comics and paperbacks rounding out the inventory. The stock occupies 2,400 square feet of space.
How to Get There: The bookstore can be reached from Los Angeles via the 91 Freeway east to the 55 Freeway and exit on Katella to Tustin Avenue. From the south beach communities via the 5 Freeway north to the 55 Freeway north and exiting on Chapman, west to Tustin Avenue.
Owner/Biography: Ed and Pat Thomas. Ed Thomas is a bookaholic and Pat has lived with his condition for 29 years. Book Carnival is a dream come true for them both.
Year Founded/History of Bookstore: 1981.
Number of Volumes: 20,000.
Types/Classifications: Hardbound, paperback, broadsides, first editions, fine bindings, out-of-print, association copies, press books, signed copies, presentation copies, limited editions, color plate books, comic books, comic art.
General Subject Areas: General.
Mail/Telephone Orders; Credit Cards: Both. Cash with order. Visa and Mastercard accepted.
Business Hours: Monday through Thursday 11:00 AM - 6:00 PM; Friday 11:00 AM - 6:00 PM; Saturday 10:00 AM - 5:00 PM.
Parking Facilities: Public parking lot.
Collections/Individual Items Purchased: Both.

55
Book Cellar
124 Orangefair Mall
Fullerton, California 92632   (714) 879-9420

The Book Cellar contains two floors (4,200 square feet) of books from five centuries, shelving up to the twelve-foot ceiling, and with rolling library ladders. There is a massive 100-year old roll-top desk, ceiling fans, a 1910 brass hand-crank cash register, and classical music. The better stock is displayed in 16 lighted glass cases and on an entire wall of shelving behind sliding glass panels. Each of these books is fully described on individual catalog cards. The store is decorated with posters from international rare book fairs and 35 individually framed quotes about books, booksellers, and book collecting by famous people throughout history.

How to Get There: Twenty-five minutes southeast of Los Angeles and 3 miles north of Disneyland, the store is in a mall at the corner of Harbor Boulevard and Orangethorpe, 1 block north of the 91 Freeway.

Owner/Biography: David Cormany. After several years designing and building the race cars he drove on the Grand Prix circuit, Mr. Cormany abandoned his second successful career as a business executive and began his antiquarian book business at age 31, "escaping the politics and hypocrisy of the corporate rat race." He has had his writing and photography published, is a marathon runner, and gourmet cook. His personal library of 11,000 titles includes 813 cookbooks.

Year Founded/History of Bookstore: 1975. The Book Cellar was founded by Mr. Cormany at the current address.

Number of Volumes: 104,000.

Types/Classifications: Hardbound, paperback, broadsides, original manuscripts, photographs, autographed material, first editions, limited editions, signed copies, association copies, presentation copies, illustrated books, fine bindings, out-of-print.

General Subject Areas: Americana, Ancient History, Archaeology, Architecture, Art, Books About Books, Cookery and Wine, Erotica and Curiosa, General, History of Ideas, Literary Criticism, Literature, Metaphysics, Occult, Philosophy, Photography, Rare and Distinctive Bibles, Religion, Theology, Voyages and Exploration, Women Authors, Women's Biography.

Specific Specialties: Civil War (U.S.), American Revolution, Beat Generation, General Custer, Cars and Racing, American Indians, Decadence and Deviance, Egypt and Pyramids, Franklin Library, Freemasonry, Secret Societies, Limited Editions Club, Mormonism, Heritage Press, Cults, Utopianism and Alternate Lifestyles, Entomology, Rubaiyats.

Author Specialties: Henry Miller, Alan Watts, Thomas McGuane, Kenneth Patchen, Tom Robbins, Mark Twain, Jack Kerouac, John Garnder, M.F.K. Fisher, Frank Frazetta, Frank Lloyd Wright, Pablo Picasso, Salvador Dali, Marc Chagall, Joan Miro, Arthur Rackham, Edmund Dulac, Nielsen, Maxfield Parrish, John Muir, Oscar Wilde, T.E. Lawrence, Thomas Paine, Ayn Rand, Anais Nin, James Joyce.

Other Specialties: Influential Books, Scholarly Works, Nostalgia, Banned and Suppressed Works, Bizarre and Controversial Subjects, Iconoclastic Works, Esoterica, Book Trade Catalogues.

Mail/Telephone Orders; Credit Cards: Both. The Book Cellar pays the postage on all orders. Visa and Mastercard accepted.

Business Hours: Monday through Friday 10:00 AM - 9:00 PM; Saturday and Sunday 10:00 AM - 6:00 PM.

Parking Facilities: Acres of free parking.

Special Features: Free search service. David Cormany is an accredited appraiser for insurance, tax, and probate purposes.

Catalogue: Published twice yearly.

Collections/Individual Items Purchased: Both.

Booksellers' Memberships: Antiquarian Booksellers Association of America.

Miscellaneous: The Book Cellar is featured in Brady and Lawless' "Favorite Bookstores" (1978). A Western Union cable address (RAREBOOKS) is maintained. Mr. Cormany encourages browsing and sherry is served.

56
Book Den
15 East Anapamu Street
Santa Barbara, California 93101   (805) 962-3321

The bookstore refers to itself as Santa Barbara's oldest and largest used bookstore. It has served the community for more than fifty years. It is located downtown, directly across from the main public library with convenient public parking off Anacapa Street. It carries a large general stock plus back-issue magazines, comics, note cards, and calendars. The store occupies 4,500 square feet of space.

Owner/Biography: Eric Kelley, owner, was born in Germany, and came to the United States at age fifteen with his family. After obtaining his BA at UCLA, he worked at Brentano's in the San Francisco Bay Area as a store-level buyer and assistant manager. He came to Santa Barbara in 1979 to purchase the Book Den with a partner. He assumed full ownership at the beginning of 1984.

Year Founded/History of Bookstore: The bookstore was founded in 1928 in Oakland, California by Max Richter. He moved the store to Santa Barbara and its present location in 1933. After his death the store was run by his son who sold it to Richard and Susan Phelps. They oversaw its expansion into the neighboring storefront and sold the store to the present owner in 1979.

Number of Volumes: 20,000.

Types/Classifications: General used books, hardbound and paperback, back issue magazines, note cards, used and collector's comic books, ephemera, local histories, postcards, first editions, leather bindings, remainders.

General Subject Areas: Accounting, American Indians, Americana, Anthropology, Antiques, Architecture, Art, Astronomy, Auto Repair, Aviation, Biography, Biology, Black Studies, Business, California, Chicano Studies, Children's Books, Children's Illustrators, Cinema, Computers, Crafts, Creative Writing, Crime, Dance, Drama, Education, Fiction, Foreign Languages, Gardening, Geology, Graphic Arts, History, Home Repair, Horses, Humor, Journalism, Law, Literary Criticism, Mathematics, Metaphysics, Music, Mysteries, Mythology, Natural Science, Pets, Philosophy, Photography, Poetry, Political Science, Psychology, Railroads, References, Religion, Sailing, Santa Barbara History, Science Fiction and Fantasy, Secretarial Skills, Sociology, Sports, Television, Travel, Women's Studies.

Specific Specialties: Children's Illustrators, Spanish Architecture, Mediterranean Architecture, Santa Barbara (California) Authors, Santa Barbara (California) History.

Mail/Telephone Orders; Credit Cards: Both; prepayment required. Visa and Mastercard accepted.

Business Hours: Monday through Saturday 9:30 AM - 5:30 PM; Sunday 12:00 Noon - 5:00 PM.

Parking Facilities: Public parking lot adjacent to the bookstore; the first 90 minutes are free.

Special Features: Search service, friendly assistance.

Collections/Individual Items Purchased: Both.

57
Book End
245 Pearl Street
Monterey, California 93940   (408) 373-4046

The Book End is a general subject bookstore comprised of approximately 70 percent hardbound and 30 percent paperback stock. The store specializes in foreign language books. In addition to the wide selection of French, German, and Spanish books are Russian, Italian, Polish, and Chinese. Located in the Old Monterey section of town, the Book End also features children's books and poetry.

How to Get There: The shop is located near Fisherman's Wharf in the old section of Monterey.

Owner/Biography: The Andersons - Doc, Sylvia, and John.

Year Founded/History of Bookstore: 1977.

Number of Volumes: 15,000.

Types/Classifications: Hardbound, paperback, first editions, out-of-print, signed copies, limited editions.

General Subject Areas: Americana, Biography, Children's Books, Cookbooks, Drama, Foreign Language, Poetry, Presidents (U.S.), Religion, Sports.

Mail/Telephone Orders; Credit Cards: Both. No credit cards.

Business Hours: Monday through Saturday 10:30 AM - 5:30 PM; Sunday 12:00 Noon - 4:00 PM.

Collections/Individual Items Purchased: Individual items only.

58
Book Harbor
201 North Harbor Boulevard
Fullerton, California 92632   (714) 738-1941

Book Harbor is a large out-of-print and used bookstore with over 250 categories of books. It also carries new books. The store occupies 3,000 square feet of space.
How to Get There: Located in downtown Fullerton at the corner of Harbor and Amerige.
Owner/Biography: Al Ralston and Jerome Joseph.
Year Founded/History of Bookstore: 1978.
Number of Volumes: 65,000 hardbound; thousands of paperback.
Types/Classifications: Hardbound, paperback, magazines, broadsides, autographs, ephemera, out-of-print, first editions, fine bindings, association copies, press books, signed copies, presentation copies, limited editions, color plate books.
General Subject Areas: General.
Mail/Telephone Orders; Credit Cards: Both. Add $1.50 per book for postage and handling costs; California residents add 6 percent sales tax. Visa and Mastercard accepted.
Business Hours: Monday through Friday 11:00 AM - 9:00 PM; Saturday 10:00 AM - 6:00 PM; Sunday 12:00 Noon - 5:00 PM.
Parking Facilities: Large parking lot behind building.
Special Features: Search service, appraisals.
Miscellaneous: Owners have 7,000 modern first editions, fine to mint condition in dust jackets. These items may.be seen by appointment. Call for details. Items are priced individually, not as a collection.

59
Book Land
1025 B Street
Hayward, California 94541   (415) 582-2606

Book Land is a large bookstore occupying 5,880 square feet of space and featuring paperbacks new and old, plus new and used hardbound books. The shop specializes in auto repair, romance, and science fiction.
How to Get There: The bookstore is located in downtown Hayward and can be reached by taking the A Street off ramp from Highway 17 or by taking the Hayward exit from Highway 580.
Owner/Biography: Ed and Margaret Lustig.
Year Founded/History of Bookstore: 1967. Book Land originally opened in a small store just 2 blocks away from its present location and outgrew it in just 5 years. The present store opened in 1972 and is six times the size of the original store.
Number of Volumes: 250,000.
Types/Classifications: Hardbound, paperback, back issue magazines (National Geographic, Fortune, Playboy, etc.), out-of-print, first editions, signed copies.
General Subject Areas: Applied Science, Art, Auto Repair, Biography, Business, Dictionaries, Economics, How-To-Do-It, Music, Mysteries, Novels, Photography, Political Science, Romances, Science Fiction, Self-Help, Westerns.
Mail/Telephone Orders; Credit Cards: Both. Cash with order. Visa and Mastercard accepted.
Business Hours: Daily 10:00 AM - 5:30 PM.
Collections/Individual Items Purchased: Both.
Booksellers' Memberships: American Booksellers Association, Northern California Booksellers Association.

60
Book Nest
366 Second Street
Los Altos, California 94022   (415) 948-4724

The Book Nest is located in a charming New England Cape Cod style house. The rooms are attractively decorated and each room has a chair or two for reading. The stock is comprehensive and leans toward classics and out-of-print books. Modern first editions are featured.

How to Get There: The store is situated between San Jose and San Francisco. Take 280 north or south to El Monte East exit; proceed to Foothill Expressway, left to Main Street, right on Main to Second, turn right.

Owner/Biography: Edwin F. Schmitz.

Year Founded/History of Bookstore: 1978.

Types/Classifications: Hardbound, out-of-print, first editions.

General Subject Areas: General.

Author Specialties: John Steinbeck.

Mail/Telephone Orders; Credit Cards: Both. No credit cards.

Business Hours: Tuesday through Saturday 10:00 AM - 5:30 PM.

Parking Facilities: Public parking lot.

Special Features: Search service ($2 per search request).

Collections/Individual Items Purchased: Both.

Booksellers' Memberships: Central California Antiquarian Booksellers.

61
Book Peddler - Used Books
842 Main Street
Morro Bay, California 93442 (805) 772-3810

The Book Peddler is the only used bookstore in the small coastal town of Morro Bay. Bibliophiles are welcome. If the store is closed upon arrival, call the emergency number on the front door and the owner will be glad to open up. The shop occupies 900 square feet of space.

How to Get There: Morro Bay is 15 miles west of San Luis Obispo off Highway 1. The town is about half-way between Los Angeles and San Francisco.

Owner/Biography: Kathleen Muhs.

Year Founded/History of Bookstore: 1981.

Number of Volumes: 15,000.

Types/Classifications: Hardbound, paperback, memorabilia, movie and television photos.

General Subject Areas: General.

Specific Specialties: Sailing, Boating.

Mail/Telephone Orders; Credit Cards: Both. Check with order. No credit cards.

Business Hours: Monday through Saturday 10:00 AM - 5:00 PM.

Parking Facilities: Street parking.

Special Features: Search service.

Collections/Individual Items Purchased: Both.

62
Book Sail
1186 North Tustin Street
Orange, California 92667 (714) 997-9511

The Book Sail has recently ceased its retail walk-in operation to devote full attention to mail order operations. It issues one large catalogue per year, supplemented by numerous lists. Customer want lists in areas of the Book Sail's specialization are solicited and are actively quoted. The establishment occupies 9,000 square feet of space. Visits may be arranged by appointment.

How to Get There: The bookstore is 35 minutes from downtown Los Angeles via the Golden State Freeway (5) south to the Riverside Freeway (9) and east to the Costa Mesa Freeway (55), south to the Katella exit. Take Katella right to Tustin, then left one block.

Owner/Biography: John McLaughlin.

Year Founded/History of Bookstore: 1966.

Number of Volumes: Over 100,000.

Types/Classifications: Hardbound, paperback, uncommon and unusual magazines, autographed books and documents, pulps, comics and comic art, Hollywood autographs and ephemera, early and collectible toys, literary first editions, illustrated books, film scripts, fine bindings, original art.

General Subject Areas: Popular Culture.

Specific Specialties: Emphasis on 19th and 20th century popular culture including all subjects commonly associated with such a category: Science Fiction and Fantasy, Horror in all fields; popular illustrators including books and original art; pulps and pulp artwork; Detective and Mystery first editions and autographs; film and related ephemera including other areas of the Performing Arts; manuscripts and other unique material in all of the above fields.

Other Specialties: Stephen King first editions, manuscripts, ephemera; Ray Bradbury; Margaret Brundage Weird Tales artwork; Disney Studios and other original art; Ian Fleming first editions, manuscripts, etc.; original illustrations including Pogany, Rackham, Clarke, Dulac, etc.; original art from paperbacks, science fiction and fantasy, comic art, and magazine art, dust wrapper art, etc.

Mail/Telephone Orders; Credit Cards: Both. Standard mail order procedure. Visa and Mastercard accepted.

Business Hours: Tuesday through Saturday 9:30 AM - 5:30 PM.

Parking Facilities: Free adjacent parking facilities.

Catalogue: Published annually with supplemental lists. Yearly subscription to lists $7.50.

Collections/Individual Items Purchased: Both.

Booksellers' Memberships: Antiquarian Booksellers Association of America.

63
Book Stop
3369 Mt. Diablo Boulevard
Lafayette, California 94549   (415) 284-2665

The Book Stop carries general stock with a specialty in literary biography and letters. The establishment occupies 1,000 square feet of space.

Owner/Biography: Larry Kimmich.

Year Founded/History of Bookstore: 1979.

Number of Volumes: 20,000.

Types/Classifications: Hardbound, paperback.

General Subject Areas: General.

Specific Specialties: Literary Biography, Letters.

Mail/Telephone Orders; Credit Cards: Both. Cash with order. No credit cards.

Business Hours: Tuesday through Saturday 12:00 Noon - 6:00 PM.

Collections/Individual Items Purchased: Both.

64
Book Vault
3682 A South Bristol Street
Santa Ana, California 92704   (714) 549-9548

The Book Vault carries general stock with 95 percent hardbound and 5 percent paperback. The shop occupies 1,050 square feet of space.

How to Get There: Santa Ana is 25 minutes southeast of Los Angeles via the Santa Ana Freeway. The store is 2 blocks north of the San Diego Freeway in Santa Ana.

Owner/Biography: Ron Greenwood.

Year Founded/History of Bookstore: 1976.

Number of Volumes: 11,000.

Types/Classifications: Hardbound, paperback.

General Subject Areas: General.

Mail/Telephone Orders; Credit Cards: Both. Visa and Mastercard accepted.

Business Hours: Monday through Friday 12:00 Noon - 5:30 PM; Saturday 11:00 AM - 6:00 PM.

Parking Facilities: Business parking lot in front.

Special Features: Search service.
Collections/Individual Items Purchased: Both.

65
Bookery
316 Main Street
Placerville, California 95667

(916) 626-6454

Located in one of the older buildings on Main Street in old "Hangtown." The owners have maintained a rustic appearance and a warm friendly atmosphere inside as well as outside the bookstore. Fiction and non-fiction, current and older books are all categorized for selective browsing. Mother Lode information and books about the Mother Lode area are also available. The shop occupies 1,000 square feet of space.

How to Get There: The bookstore is located one block off Highway 50 in downtown Placerville.

Owner/Biography: Celia Baxter and Nancy Dunk.

Year Founded/History of Bookstore: 1980. The building housing The Bookery was built in the mid-1800's. It has been a haven for readers for the past decade. The shop opened in the spring of 1980 and succeeded two "new" bookstores which were in the same location. The new owners, Celia Baxter and Nancy Dunk, bought the business in September 1983.

Number of Volumes: Over 15,000.

Types/Classifications: Hardbound, paperback, out-of-print.

General Subject Areas: Animals, Anthropology, Arts, Automobiles, Biography, Business, Children's Books, Classics, Cookbooks, Crafts, Diet and Nutrition, Drama, Economics, Education, Fitness and Health, Foreign Countries, Games, History, Hobbies, Marriage, Mathematics, Medical, Metaphysics, Mysteries, Philosophy, Plants, Poetry, Political Science, Psychology, Reference, Religion, Science, Science Fiction and Fantasy, Self-Help, Sex, Short Stories, Sociology, Sports, War, Westerns, Women/Men.

Mail/Telephone Orders; Credit Cards: Both. Prepaid with order. No credit cards.

Business Hours: Monday through Friday 10:00 AM - 5:30 PM; Saturday 10:00 AM - 4:30 PM.

Parking Facilities: Public parking lot, street parking.

Special Features: Search service.

Collections/Individual Items Purchased: Both.

66
Bookstall
708 Sutter Street
San Francisco, California 94109

(415) 673-5446

The Bookstall is a small shop where each volume is handpicked by the owners and displayed for comfortable and easy browsing. Glass cases hold highlights from specialites. The good condition of books is a feature at this store.

How to Get There: The bookstore is located within walking distance from the central shopping area of San Francisco and near two BART stations.

Owner/Biography: Henry and Louise Moises. The Moises met while attending San Jose State University. A mutual interest in books led them into the book business. Henry's background in mathematics and physics and Louise's interest in children's literature gave them natural areas of specialization.

Year Founded/History of Bookstore: 1974. The Bookstall began originally across the Bay in Oakland and in 1981 moved to San Francisco.

Number of Volumes: 10,000.

Types/Classifications: Hardbound, some ephemera and pamphlets, first editions, signed copies, presentation copies, out-of-print.

General Subject Areas: Aviation, California, Children's Literature, Cookbooks, Gardening, History of Science, Literature, Mathematics, Mountaineering, Physics, Printing, Typography, West (U.S.), World War I, World War II.

Specific Specialties: Alice in Wonderland, Night Before Christmas, Children's Illustrators, Himalayas, Andes, Alps, Canadian Rockies, Sierras, Scientific Classics and Monographs.

Mail/Telephone Orders; Credit Cards: Both. Cash with order. American Express, Visa, Mastercard accepted.

Business Hours: Monday through Saturday 11:00 AM - 5:30 PM.

Parking Facilities: Public parking, street parking, nearby parking lots.

Special Features: Search service; specialties filed and collectors notified when appropriate books come in; book talks at clubs and libraries.

Catalogue: Published 6 times per year.

Collections/Individual Items Purchased: Both.

Booksellers' Memberships: Antiquarian Booksellers Association of America including Northern California Chapter.

67
Brick Row Book Shop
278 Post Street No. 303
San Francisco, California 94108
(415) 398-0414

The Brick Row Book Shop carries first editions and important early editions. It specializes in 18th, 19th, and early 20th century English and American literature, books about books, bilbiography, and fine printing. The shop occupies 1,200 square feet of space.

How to Get There: The shop is located at the corner of Post and Stockton Streets on Union Square.

Owner/Biography: John Crichton and Matt Lowman.

Year Founded/History of Bookstore: 1915. The original store was founded by E. Byrne Hackett in New Haven, Connecticut and later was moved to New York City. Franklin Gilliam purchased the business in 1954. In that year he moved to Austin, Texas and in 1971 a further move was made to San Francisco. The present owners purchased the shop in 1983.

Number of Volumes: 10,000.

Types/Classifications: Hardbound, ephemera, autographs, first editions, fine printing.

General Subject Areas: American Literature (18th, 19th, and Early 20th Centuries), Bibliography, Books About Books, English Literature (18th, 19th, and Early 20th Centuries), Fine Printing.

Mail/Telephone Orders; Credit Cards: Both. Visa and Mastercard accepted.

Business Hours: Monday through Friday 9:30 AM - 5:30 PM; Saturday 11:00 AM - 4:30 PM.

Parking Facilities: Parking nearby at Sutter-Stockton or Union Square garages.

Catalogue: Published 3 times per year.

Collections/Individual Items Purchased: Both.

68
Bruno's
1220 Polk Street
San Francisco, California 94109
(415) 441-2929

Bruno's is an intimate used bookstore specializing in current review of fine art, photography, cookbooks and bestsellers. Books are usually at one half of publishers' price or less and the stock changes almost daily. The store occupies 300 square feet of space.

How to Get There: The shop is four stores up from Sutter Street on the east side of Polk, next to the No. 19 bus stop, going north on Polk.

Owner/Biography: Tom Isenberg.

Year Founded/History of Bookstore: 1970. Originally known as the Lion Bookstore, it was started in the late 1940's by Bruno Lowenberg who later moved the store to its current location and renamed it Bruno's. Mr. Isenberg took over the business from the founder.

Number of Volumes: 100,000 items.

Types/Classifications: Hardbound, paperback, select magazines, used "current" first editions, out-of-print art, select limited editions and used best sellers.

General Subject Areas: Antiques, Art, Commercial Art, Cookbooks, English Literature, Gay Literature, History, Occult, Photography, San Francisco, Women's Literature.

Mail/Telephone Orders; Credit Cards: No mail orders. Telephone orders accepted. Visa and Mastercard accepted.

Business Hours: Monday, Tuesday, Thursday, Friday 11:00 AM - 6:30 PM; Wednesday 11:00 AM - 9:00 PM; Saturday and Sunday 12:00 Noon - 6:00 PM.
Parking Facilities: Public parking lot 1 block away on Bush Street between Polk and Larkin.
Collections/Individual Items Purchased: Both.

69
Buckabest Books and Bindery
247 Fulton Street
Palo Alto, California 94301   (415) 325-2965

This bookstore specializes in theater and ballet as well as Celtic literature. The store also provides book restoration and preservations services. Visitors are welcome by appointment only.
How to Get There: Call for directions.
Owner/Biography: Margaret A. Simmons.
Year Founded/History of Bookstore: 1972. Ms. Simmons had the store as a walk-in establishment when she returned to the United States from Anglesey, North Wales. The shop was moved to her home, where it is now with herself and Charlie the bulldog in attendance. Bucka Best was Ms. Simmons Irish grandfather.
Number of Volumes: 7,500.
Types/Classifications: Hardbound, dance posters, out-of-print, rare.
General Subject Areas: Dance, Theater.
Specific Specialties: E.G. Craig, Duke of Saxe Meiningen and the Meiningen Theatre, German Theatre, Isadora Duncan, Bookbinding, Book Restoration.
Mail/Telephone Orders; Credit Cards: Both. No credit cards.
Business Hours: By appointment only.
Parking Facilities: Street parking.
Catalogue: Published randomly.
Collections/Individual Items Purchased: Both.
Miscellaneous: Buckabest Books and Bindery has published four books, including "The Textbook of Unicorns" and "Coming Across" (Robert Conquest).

70
California Book Auction Galleries, Inc.
358 Golden Gate Avenue
San Francisco, California 94102   (415) 775-0424

The California Book Auction Galleries has a 2,000 square feet showroom where once a month for a week, rare and fine books of all descriptions are exhibited. Books are sold by catalogue only, with a one-day sale participated in by both those who attend and an average of about 100 absentee bidders from all over America. Prices are reported to "American Book Prices Current" where they are published annually. Books are consigned from collectors, booksellers, or institutions with a commission charged by the Galleries for their services.
How to Get There: Offices are located in San Francisco's Civic Center, one block from the Federal Building.
Owner/Biography: California Book Auction Galleries is a corporation owned by 3 stockholders at present; chief stockholder and founder is Maurice F. Powers.
Year Founded/History of Bookstore: 1956. The Galleries sell about $600,000 worth of fine and rare books each year and have subscribers to their monthly catalogues scattered throughout America and a few in Europe and other continents.
Number of Volumes: A permanent stock is not maintained; the Galleries handle and sell approximately 10,000 lots of books each year.
Types/Classifications: Autographs, manuscripts, maps, photographs, rare and fine books (all with a minimum value of $25).
General Subject Areas: General.
Other Specialties: Art and Art Reference.
Mail/Telephone Orders; Credit Cards: Both. Visa and Mastercard accepted.

Business Hours: Monday through Friday 9:00 AM - 5:00 PM.
Parking Facilities: Parking lots in close proximity.
Special Features: An auction house exclusively.
Catalogue: Published monthly. Generally, each of the Galleries' catalogs has a theme or subject.
Collections/Individual Items Purchased: Both; individual items if of sufficient value.
Booksellers' Memberships: Antiquarian Booksellers Association of America, American Society of Appraisers.

71
Campbell Book Shoppe
428 East Campbell Avenue
Campbell, California 95008   (408) 374-3880

The bookstore carries out-of-print books in all subjects in both hardbound and paperback. The coffee pot is always hot and free to anyone who comes in. The shop occupies 680 square feet of space.
How to Get There: Located 1 block east of Cross Street and Central, the bookstore is 3 doors down from the famous Rock Shop.
Owner/Biography: Larry Pool. Mr. Pool is the former owner of Tompkins Square Books in New York City.
Year Founded/History of Bookstore: 1975.
Number of Volumes: 4,000.
Types/Classifications: Hardbound, paperback.
General Subject Areas: Biography, History, Military, Mysteries, Philosophy, Science Fiction, Technical, Westerns.
Mail/Telephone Orders; Credit Cards: Mail orders only. No credit cards.
Business Hours: Monday through Saturday 10:30 AM - 5:30 PM; Sunday 12:00 Noon - 5:00 PM.
Parking Facilities: Public parking lot, street parking.
Special Features: Search service.
Collections/Individual Items Purchased: Both.

72
Caravan Book Store
550 South Grand Avenue
Los Angeles, California 90071   (213) 626-9944

The only antiquarian book store in downtown Los Angeles, Caravan is in its 30th year on the same street. It specializes in old, rare, out-of-print, and curious books; in pamphlets, maps, prints, original oil paintings, and bronzes.
How to Get There: The bookstore is in the central downtown area of Los Angeles with all the freeways coming into the area, as well as all the major surface streets converging downtown. It is at the intersection of 6th Street and Grand Avenue in the heart of the new financial district, and adjacent, by about a half a block, to the distinctive Los Angeles Main Library.
Owner/Biography: Mrs. Lillian E. Bernstein, owner, has been involved in the book business for more than 30 years, having worked closely with her husband, Morris Bernstein, who established the business. Her son, Leonard, has been with the firm for more than 15 years. Both are knowledgeable in the select specialties featured in the bookstore.
Year Founded/History of Bookstore: Founded in 1954, the bookstore was in its original location across the street for the first 27 years. Having been at the present address for three years, the owner plans to stay in the downtown area for many more years. Over the years, the bookstore has expanded several times and acquisitions are still being made. Its present location contains 1,200 square feet of space.
Number of Volumes: 50,000.
Types/Classifications: Books, original oil paintings and watercolors, bronzes, woodcarvings, maps, ship models, photographs, prints, signed and limited editions, first editions, broadsides, paper ephemera, leather bindings, books signed by the artist/illustrator, books signed by the author, books with fine engravings, ephemeral material relating to these kinds of books, first editions.
General Subject Areas: American Military History, Americana, California, California City Directories and

County Histories (prior to 1890), Chess, Domestic Arts (Cooking and Wine), Early Aviation and Ballooning, Expansion of the West, Maritime History, Political Memorabilia (Campaign Buttons and Pamphlets), Railroad History, Voyages and Discovery, West (U.S.), Western (U.S.) Art and Artists, Whaling, Yosemite Views (Photographs and Stereo Slides).

Author Specialties: John Steinbeck, M.F.K. Fisher, J. Ross Brown, George Catlin, individuals associated with the expansion and development of the West.

Other Specialties: Original Overland Narratives, Ships' Logs, Manuscripts, Illuminated Manuscripts.

Mail/Telephone Orders; Credit Cards: Both, but cash with mail order. No credit cards.

Business Hours: Monday through Friday 10:30 AM - 6:00 PM; Saturday 11:00 AM - 5:00 PM.

Parking Facilities: There are many parking facilities in the general area, on all sides of the bookstore (in most of the high-rise buildings, in Pershing Square, and at small adjacent lots).

Special Features: An international search service for specific titles. As specialists in Western American History and Cooking, the bookstore can help with acquisitions of rare, out-of-print, or unusual items in these and collateral fields.

Catalogue: No catalogue, but the store does issue lists of appropriate titles to collectors of special material.

Collections/Individual Items Purchased: Both.

Booksellers' Memberships: Antiquarian Booksellers Association of America including the Southern California Chapter, International League of Antiquarian Booksellers.

73
Carlos Canterbury Book Store
1107-17 San Carlos Avenue
San Carlos, California 94070 (415) 593-3392

The bookstore features general and special books, old sheet music, carvings, and chess sets.

How to Get There: The driver should take Route 101 to the Holly overpass, go one block south to San Carlos Avenue; the shop is three doors from the corner of El Camino and San Carlos.

Owner/Biography: Donna Houtchens took over ownership of the bookstore in 1981 from her parents, who had owned and operated the shop for more than 30 years.

Year Founded/History of Bookstore: Ms. Houtchens' parents founded the shop in 1951 in Redwood City, California and operated it there until 1958 when it was moved to its present location.

Number of Volumes: 45,000.

Types/Classifications: Hardbound, paperback, magazines, autographs, ephemera, broadsides, first editions, fine bindings, out-of-print, signed copies, presentation copies, color plate books.

General Subject Areas: Americana, Biography, Illustrated Children's Books, Old Sheet Music, Paintings.

Specific Specialties: Western Americana.

Other Specialties: Foreign Language Titles.

Mail/Telephone Orders; Credit Cards: Both. Visa and Mastercard accepted.

Business Hours: Tuesday through Thursday 11:00 AM - 7:00 PM; Friday and Saturday 11:00 AM - 5:00 PM; closed Sunday and Monday.

Parking Facilities: Street and parking lot.

Special Features: Free search service.

Collections/Individual Items Purchased: Both.

Booksellers' Memberships: Antiquarian Booksellers Association of America, Northern California Booksellers Association.

Miscellaneous: Prints.

74
Carol Docheff - Bookseller
1605 Spruce Street
Berkeley, California 94709 (415) 841-0770

Carol Docheff has a stock of quality children's and illustrated books that are sold directly from her home and through mail order. The books and items of original art are displayed throughout her home and the coffee pot is always on for visiting customers and dealers. Ms. Docheff offers a large stock of top quality first edition and out-of-print titles in top condition. Condition and service are the hallmarks of her business.

How to Get There: Located in North Berkeley, 3 blocks above Shattuck Avenue and 3 blocks north of the University of California campus at Spruce and Cedar. It can be reached by AC Transit and BART.

Owner/Biography: Carol Docheff.

Year Founded/History of Bookstore: 1979.

Number of Volumes: 7,500.

Types/Classifications: Hardbound, ephemera, first editions, out-of-print, signed copies, presentation copies, color plate books (English and American).

General Subject Areas: Books About Children's Books (Authors and Illustrators), Caldecott and Newbery Award Titles, Children's Books, Juvenile Science Fiction and Fantasy, Reference, Young Adult Fiction and Non-Fiction.

Author Specialties: Maurice Sendak, Robert Lawson, Dorothy Lathrop, Leo Politi, Randolph Caldecott, Edward Ardizzone.

Other Specialties: Foreign language children's books, original art by children's book illustrators.

Mail/Telephone Orders; Credit Cards: Both. Postage and insurance extra. No credit cards.

Business Hours: By appointment.

Parking Facilities: Street parking.

Special Features: Search service; for holiday shopping convenience, drop shipment and gift wrapping available; collection development.

Catalogue: Published 3 to 4 times annually.

Collections/Individual Items Purchased: Both.

75
Cartesian Bookstore
2445 Dwight Way
Berkeley, California 94704 (415) 549-3973

Cartesian Bookstore handles used books exclusively. It is located in a popular book browsing area of Berkeley; there are eight other stores within one block.

How to Get There: The store is located just off Telegraph.

Owner/Biography: Wayne Brougham.

Year Founded/History of Bookstore: 1977.

Number of Volumes: 6,500.

Types/Classifications: Hardbound, paperback, first editions, out-of-print.

General Subject Areas: Ancient and Medieval History, Church History, Classics, Philosophy, Religion, Science and Mathematics.

Other Specialties: Scholarly Works in Psychology and Literature.

Mail/Telephone Orders; Credit Cards: Mail orders require cash with order. Visa and Mastercard accepted.

Business Hours: Tuesday through Saturday 11:00 AM - 5:30 PM.

Collections/Individual Items Purchased: Both.

76
Celestial Books
P.O. Box 1066
La Canada, California 91011 (213) 790-4984

Celestial Books is a mail order business specializing in out-of-print and rare volumes in Science and Astronomy. Visits can be arranged by appointment.

Owner/Biography: Donald K. Yeomans. Dr. Yeomans is a professional astronomer.

Year Founded/History of Bookstore: 1974.

Types/Classifications: Hardbound, out-of-print, rare.

General Subject Areas: Science.

Specific Specialties: Astronomy, History of Science.

Mail/Telephone Orders; Credit Cards: Both. No credit cards.

Business Hours: By appointment.
Special Features: Search service.
Catalogue: Published once per year.
Collections/Individual Items Purchased: Both.

77
Charing Cross Road - Booksellers
1687 Haight Street
San Francisco, California 94117   (415) 552-4122

The owners state that "Charing Cross Road is a haven for an endangered species - the reader." They provide clean reading copies of books in most categories. The shop occupies 1,100 square feet of space.
How to Get There: The bookstore is near the corner of Cole, not far from Golden Gate Park.
Owner/Biography: George and Diane Moore. Both are former English teachers in San Francisco public high schools. Diane resigned after 10 years to open the bookstore. George retired in 1983 after 31 years of teaching.
Year Founded/History of Bookstore: 1977. The shop was at 944 Cole Street until 1980 when it was moved to its present location.
Number of Volumes: 7,000.
Types/Classifications: Hardbound in non-fiction, paperback, magazines, newspapers, reading copies with the occasional modern first edition.
General Subject Areas: Anthropology, Art, Child Development, Children's Books, Classics, Crafts, Drama, Economics, Education, Film, Foods, Foreign Language, Geography, Geology, History, How-To, Humor, Literary Criticism, Media, Mysteries, Mythology, Philosophy, Poetry, Political, Psychology, Religion, Science, Science Fiction and Fantasy, Theory, Travel, Wine.
Specific Specialties: Dover Design and Source Books (new), San Francisco and California, Dover Paper Doll and Coloring Books (new).
Mail/Telephone Orders; Credit Cards: Telephone orders only. No credit cards.
Business Hours: Daily 11:00 AM - 6:00 PM except Thanksgiving, Christmas, Yom Kippur.
Parking Facilities: Street parking.
Collections/Individual Items Purchased: Individual items only.
Booksellers' Memberships: Northern California Booksellers Association.
Miscellaneous: Customers have told the owners that the bookstore "is very selective and unusually well organized."

78
Chimera
405 Kipling
Palo Alto, California 94301   (415) 329-9217

Chimera is situated in a large Victorian house near the Stanford University campus with three floors full of the "world's most worthwhile books," in and out-of-print, new and used.
How to Get There: The shop is situated 1 block off University Avenue in downtown Palo Alto (exit west off Highway 101 - Bayshore Freeway).
Owner/Biography: Walter Martin.
Year Founded/History of Bookstore: 1970. Founded by Raphael Cristy, John Siscoe, and Walter Martin.
Number of Volumes: Over 100,000.
Types/Classifications: Hardbound, paperback, magazines, broadsides, autographs, ephemera, first editions, fine bindings, out-of-print, association copies, press books, signed copies, presentation copies, limited editions, color plate books, phonograph records (particularly classical and jazz).
General Subject Areas: Anthropology, Art and Architecture, Cooking and Gourmet Magazines, Drama, Golf, History, Literary Classics, Music and Dance, Philosophy, Poetry, Social Science, Sporting Books, Technical, Theology.
Other Specialties: Foreign Languages, Reference, Early Paperbacks, Anchor Books, Printing, Typography, Books About Books.

Mail/Telephone Orders; Credit Cards: No mail or telephone orders. Visa and Mastercard accepted.
Business Hours: Monday through Friday 10:00 AM - 8:00 PM; Saturday 10:30 AM - 6:30 PM; Sunday 12:00 Noon - 5:00 PM.
Parking Facilities: Very easy parking.
Special Features: Chimera publishes fine limited edition poetry, broadsides, and books in conjunction with Matrix Press.
Collections/Individual Items Purchased: Both.

79
Chimney Sweep Books
220-A Mt. Hermon Road
Scotts Valley, California 95066   (408) 438-1379

Chimney Sweep Books is located in a charming A-Frame building in King's Village Shopping Center on the way to Big Basin and Henry Cowell State Parks. The general antiquarian stock occupies 1,200 square feet of space.
How to Get There: The shopping center is 4 miles north of Santa Cruz off Route 17.
Owner/Biography: Lillian S. Kaiser.
Year Founded/History of Bookstore: 1975.
Number of Volumes: 50,000.
Types/Classifications: Hardbound, paperback, fine prints.
General Subject Areas: Children's Literature, Gardening, Irish History and Literature, Religion, Western Americana.
Specific Specialties: Pre-Vatican II, Catholica, Biblical Studies.
Mail/Telephone Orders; Credit Cards: Both. Visa and Mastercard accepted.
Business Hours: Monday through Friday 11:00 AM- 5:00 PM; Saturday 10:00 AM - 4:00 PM.
Parking Facilities: Parking in shopping center parking area.
Special Features: Free search service; appraisal service for insurance or estate valuation.
Catalogue: Published 4 times per year.
Collections/Individual Items Purchased: Both.
Booksellers' Memberships: Central California Antiquarian Booksellers Association.
Miscellaneous: A poster, designed and printed by Gene Holtan at Green Gables Press, is available. It shows a chimney sweep perched on a housetop reading a book.

80
Connolly & Wade, Books
777 West Vista Way
Vista, California 92083   (619) 758-2488

A general stock bookstore catering to all needs, Connolly & Wade's is probably the largest used, scarce, and out-of-print bookstore in San Diego's North County. There are two floors in the spacious building and clever arrangement of the shelving permits storage of over 150,000 pieces of stock. The atmosphere is relaxed and informal in keeping with the suburban yet easily accessible location. The bookstore occupies 3,000 square feet of space.
How to Get There: The bookstore is located between Los Angeles and San Diego, just a few miles east of Interstate 5 on Highway 78. Take the Melrose exit. The bookstore is the next building west of Bob's Big Boy restaurant.
Owner/Biography: Glory Wade and Daniel Connolly. Glory Wade is a native of Texas and a resident of San Diego County since 1955. She specializes in the classics and poetry. Daniel is a native of Pennsylvania and a resident of the county since 1976. He is highly knowledgeable in the fields of recent fiction and literature. They both have an encyclopedic command of facts and authors and a grand sense of humor.
Year Founded/History of Bookstore: 1981.
Number of Volumes: Over 150,000.
Types/Classifications: Hardbound, paperback, magazines, ephemera, out-of-print.

General Subject Areas: General.
Mail/Telephone Orders; Credit Cards: Both. Cash with order, postage prepaid; libraries billed. No credit cards.
Business Hours: Seven days a week 10:00 AM - 6:00 PM.
Parking Facilities: Business parking lot on three sides.
Special Features: Search service; agents for expediting sale of large collections; appraisals; reading room and meeting room available.
Collections/Individual Items Purchased: Both.
Booksellers' Memberships: San Diego Booksellers Association.
Miscellaneous: Coffee is always available. Dealers warmly welcomed.

81
Cosmopolitan Bookshop
7007 Melrose Avenue
Los Angeles, California 90038   (213) 938-7119

This bookshop prides itself on having a very large selection covering all subject categories at very reasonable prices. It gives especially attentive service to collectors, institutions, set designers, and interior decorators. Browsers are always most welcome.
How to Get There: The shop is located a half a block east of La Brea Avenue in Hollywood.
Owner/Biography: Eli Goodman.
Year Founded/History of Bookstore: 1958. The shop was located at 1071 North Western Avenue from 1958-1971 and has been at the present address since 1971.
Number of Volumes: Approximately 500,000 books, paperbacks, magazines, and records.
Types/Classifications: Hardbound, paperback, magazines, LP records, out-of-print, first editions, fine bindings, association copies, press books, signed copies, presentation copies, limited editions, color plate books.
General Subject Areas: General.
Specific Specialties: Show Business, Cinema, Theater, Plays, TV, Show Biz Biographies, Psychology, Occult, Cookbooks, Literature.
Mail/Telephone Orders; Credit Cards: Both. Payment with order. No credit cards.
Business Hours: Monday through Saturday 11:30 AM - 6:00 PM.
Parking Facilities: Street parking.
Special Features: Search service.

82
Creekside Books
751 Sir Francis Drake Boulevard
San Anselmo, California 94960   (415) 456-8501

All books at this shop are neatly arranged in alphabetical order by author on individual stacks. Books are housed in what was once a residence. The shop carries a general stock of books in excellent condition and specializes in out-of-print books, old children's books and collector's books. The shop occupies 1,000 square feet of space.
How to Get There: The bookstore is located 20 miles from downtown San Francisco over the Golden Gate Bridge into the Ross Valley to the small suburban town of San Anselmo.
Owner/Biography: E.M. Scott.
Year Founded/History of Bookstore: 1977.
Number of Volumes: 18,000.
Types/Classifications: Hardbound, paperback, out-of-print, first editions.
General Subject Areas: Art, Biography, Birds, Books About Books, Business, Californiana, Cats, Cookbooks, Crafts, Dance, Dogs, Foreign Language, Gardening, Grammar, Health, History, How-To Books, Literature, Mathematics, Metaphysics, Music, Mysteries, Mythology, Nature, Philosophy, Photography, Plays, Poetry, Psychology, Reference, Religion, Science, Science Fiction, Show Business, Sociology, Sports, Travel, Western Americana, Westerns, Wine.
Specific Specialties: Old Children's Books, Collector's Books.

Mail/Telephone Orders; Credit Cards: Both. Payment with order. No credit cards.
Business Hours: Tuesday through Saturday 12:00 Noon - 5:00 PM.
Parking Facilities: Street and off-street parking.
Special Features: Search service.
Collections/Individual Items Purchased: Both.

83
Curious Book Shoppe
198 West Main Street
Los Gatos, California 95030   (408) 354-5560

The Curious Book Shoppe is a general bookstore with fifty categories of books.
How to Get There: Los Gatos is 10 miles from San Jose. Take Highway 17 South to the second Los Gatos exit, turn left on Santa Cruz Avenue to the next light (Main Street). The shop is on the corner of Main and Santa Cruz; turn left to parking lot.
Owner/Biography: Richard P. and Dorothy R. Balch.
Year Founded/History of Bookstore: 1973.
Number of Volumes: 50,000.
Types/Classifications: Hardbound, paperback, first editions, fine bindings, out-of-print, association copies, press books, signed copies, presentation copies, limited editions, color plate books.
General Subject Areas: General.
Mail/Telephone Orders; Credit Cards: Both. Personal checks accepted; no credit cards.
Business Hours: Monday through Saturday 9:30 AM - 6:00 PM; Sunday 12:00 Noon - 5:00 PM.
Parking Facilities: Public parking lot.
Collections/Individual Items Purchased: Both.

84
D. G. Wills Books
7527 La Jolla Boulevard
La Jolla, California 92037   (619) 456-1800

D.G. Wills Books is a combination indoor/outdoor bookstore and coffeehouse filled with barber chairs, school desks, a pot belly stove, and a Victrola. It features an expresso machine, poetry readings, lectures, and music recitals.
How to Get There: La Jolla is a coastal paradise just north of San Diego.
Owner/Biography: Dennis G. Wills. Mr. Wills was schooled in Philosophy and Soviet Studies at Oxford University and Columbia University.
Year Founded/History of Bookstore: 1979.
Number of Volumes: 20,000.
Types/Classifications: Hardbound, paperback, autographs, ephemera, first editions, scholarly remainders, trade stock.
General Subject Areas: Literature, Military, Philosophy, Politics, Science.
Mail/Telephone Orders; Credit Cards: No mail orders. No credit cards.
Business Hours: Daily 10:00 AM - 10:00 PM.
Parking Facilities: Business parking lot, street parking.
Special Features: Coffee house; unusual collection of Americana folklore as store props.
Collections/Individual Items Purchased: Both.
Booksellers' Memberships: San Diego Booksellers Association.

85
Daisy Books
3878 Van Dyke Avenue
San Diego, California 92105   (619) 281-4528

Daisy Books is a retirement project. The store is a glassed-in porch and an adjoining room of the owner's home.

How to Get There: The bookstore is in east San Diego; Van Dyke Avenue is between 42nd and 43rd Streets and the bookstore is a few doors south of Unviersity Avenue.

Owner/Biography: Daisy Lamberti. Mrs. Lamberti is a retired Certified Public Accountant. She is a member of the Rosicrucian Fellowship of Oceanside, California and a student of astrology and occult philosophies.

Year Founded/History of Bookstore: 1970.

Number of Volumes: 1,000.

Types/Classifications: Hardbound, paperback, magazines, astrology data.

General Subject Areas: Astrology, Health, Metaphysics, Mysteries, Religion, Rosicrucian Philosophy, Theosophy.

Author Specialties: Max Heindel, Manley P. Hall, Corinne Heline, Geoffrey Hodson, Alan Leo, Marc Edmund Jones.

Other Specialties: Spanish translations of books by Max Heindel.

Mail/Telephone Orders; Credit Cards: Both. Cash with order including postage. No credit cards.

Business Hours: Usually open afternoons; call for appointment.

Parking Facilities: Street parking.

Special Features: Classes in astrology and philosophy.

Collections/Individual Items Purchased: Individual items only.

Booksellers' Memberships: San Diego Booksellers Association.

Miscellaneous: Daisy Lamberti also carries tapes on astrology and Rosicrucian philosophy.

86
Danville Books
176 South Hartz Avenue
Danville, California 94526   (415) 837-4200

The bookstore is located on the main street in the center of the old town part of Danville, across the street from the historic old Danville Hotel, in an area of specialty and antique shops. It occupies part of an older dwelling purchased some years ago by the bookstore owners.

How to Get There: In the old part of Danville the main street is Hartz Avenue; to the south it becomes San Ramon Road; to the north it is Danville Boulevard. At present the bookstore is in the rear of 176 Hartz Avenue, as the bookstore owners have rented the front to Heritage Photography. The bookstore occupies 700 square feet of space.

Owner/Biography: James and Eleanor Sherriff. Upon James' retirement from the FBI after more than 30 years of investigative service, the Sherriffs purchased and operated a bookstore in Monterey, California. Finding that too far from their home, they sold that business, bought an old house in Danville, restored it, and converted it to commercial use.

Year Founded/History of Bookstore: In 1977 the Sherriffs opened the bookstore in a restored dwelling converted for commercial use.

Number of Volumes: 5,000.

Types/Classifications: Hardbound, magazines of historical or literary interest, first editions, collectibles, fine bindings, illustrated.

General Subject Areas: American and British Authors (First Editions), American History, American Revolution, American West, Americana, Birds, California, China, Chinese in America, Civil War (U.S.), Natural History, Trees.

Specific Specialties: Classics, Fiction Dealing With the U.S. Civil War, Illustrated Juvenile Books, Biographies of U.S. Civil War Federal and Confederate Leaders, Gold Rush in California, Espionage, Children's Books.

Author Specialties: John Muir, Eugene O'Neill, John Steinbeck, Jack London, Mark Twain, Kenneth Roberts, Booth Tarkington, Robert Louis Stevenson, Bret Harte, George R. Stewart, H.M. Tomlinson, Willa Cather, O'Henry, Charles Dickens, Walter Edmonds. Illustrators: N.C. Wyeth, Jessie Wilcox Smith, Frederick Remington.

Other Specialties: Chinese Linguistics, including Character Writing.

Mail/Telephone Orders; Credit Cards: Mail orders; no credit cards.

Business Hours: Friday and Saturday 11:00 AM - 5:00 PM, and by appointment. It is strongly suggested that the customer should call the bookstore first (see telephone above), or the home at (415) 939-6709.
Parking Facilities: Business parking lot in back of the store.
Special Features: Search service; appraisal service for collections and individual books; books brought to the store are appraised free of charge unless a written appraisal is wanted.
Collections/Individual Items Purchased: Both.
Miscellaneous: The owners feature customer browsing and conversation over coffee.

87
Davis & Schorr Art Books
1547 Westwood Boulevard
Los Angeles, California 90024   (213) 477-6636

As art specialists, Davis & Schorr caters to individuals who collect art and want to build their libraries and artists who wish to expand their visual knowledge. They help guide the novice who wishes to know and learn. The collection reflects an orientation to collectors, art dealers, artists, and other interested individuals.
How to Get There: Located south of Wilshire Boulevard (south of Westwood Village) and 1 1/2 blocks north of Santa Monica Boulevard, the store is on the west side of the street, 5 doors south of Ohio Avenue.
Owner/Biography: L. Clarice "Cal" Davis and Elissa Schorr. Ms. Davis earned a BA in Fine Arts, an MA in Art History, and a Master of Library Science Degree. She had been head of the Art Research Library at both the Los Angeles County Museum of Art and the UCLA Art Library. She has also taught Art History. Elissa Schorr earned her BA degree in Anthropology with minor studies in Art History and Botany.
Year Founded/History of Bookstore: 1972. The business began as mail order only and in 1975 a store was opened. Ms. Schorr became a full partner in 1979.
Number of Volumes: 12,000.
Types/Classifications: Hardbound, paperback, ephemera, exhibition catalogues, livres d'artiste, original prints and drawings, signed editions, out-of-print, some limited editions, signed copies.
General Subject Areas: American and European Art.
Specific Specialties: Fine and Applied Art: Monographs of artists, general art histories in specific subject areas - ancient through modern - with emphasis on material from the 18th through the 20th Centuries; includes decorative arts, architecture, sculpture, painting, prints, drawings, photography, aesthetics, museology, collection catalogues; all periods in English, French, German, Italian, and other languages.
Mail/Telephone Orders; Credit Cards: Both. Mail orders should be sent to 14755 Ventura Boulevard No. 1-747, Sherman Oaks, California 91403; prepayment required (pro forma invoices sent). Visa and Mastercard accepted.
Business Hours: Tuesday through Friday 11:00 AM - 5:00 PM; Saturday 11:00 AM - 4:00 PM; closed Sunday and Monday.
Parking Facilities: Metered street parking.
Special Features: Search services; fees charged for appraisals, consultation, and bibliographies prepared for publications (books and exhibitions catalogues); special lists free of charge made up of books in stock on request from individuals and libraries.
Catalogue: Published 4 times per year.
Collections/Individual Items Purchased: Both.
Booksellers' Memberships: Antiquarian Booksellers Association of America including Southern California Chapter.
Miscellaneous: Also members of College Art Association of America, Art Librarians Society, American Booksellers Association.

88
Dawson's Book Shop
535 North Larchmont Boulevard
Los Angeles, California 90004   (213) 469-2186

The shop is housed in a building specially designed and built for the business. It occupies 4,000 square feet of space.

Owner/Biography: Glen and Muir Dawson. Both of the owners have devoted all of their working years to the business and they are sons of the founder - Ernest Dawson.
Year Founded/History of Bookstore: 1905. The present location is the fifth location since the founding of the business.
Number of Volumes: 30,000.
Types/Classifications: Hardbound, paperback, magazines, broadsides, autographs, ephemera, first editions, fine bindings, out-of-print, association copies, press books, signed copies, presentation copies, limited editions, color plate books.
General Subject Areas: Books About Books, Miniature Books, Mountaineering, North Americana, Oriental Art.
Mail/Telephone Orders; Credit Cards: Both. Visa and Mastercard accepted.
Business Hours: Monday through Saturday 9:00 AM - 5:00 PM.
Parking Facilities: Parking lot.
Special Features: Dawson's publishes books in its fields of interest.
Catalogue: Catalogue published.
Collections/Individual Items Purchased: Both.
Booksellers' Memberships: Antiquarian Booksellers Association of America.

89
Diva Books
P.O. Box 2503
San Anselmo, California 94960   (415) 456-0632

Diva Books specializes in American Novels 1895 - 1915. The stock occupies 600 square feet of space. Visitors are welcome by appointment.
How to Get There: Call or write for directions.
Owner/Biography: James R. Soladay.
Year Founded/History of Bookstore: 1975.
Number of Volumes: 5,000.
Types/Classifications: Hardbound, magazines (1850-1950's), out-of-print, illustrated books.
General Subject Areas: American Fiction (1895-1915).
Mail/Telephone Orders; Credit Cards: Mail orders only. No credit cards.
Business Hours: By appointment only.
Parking Facilities: Business parking lot.
Catalogue: Published quarterly.

90
Donald J. Weinstock Books
P.O. Box 2051
Huntington Beach, California 92647   (714) 848-1128

Mr. Weinstock is a dealer accepting mail orders only. He deals in out-of-print titles with heaviest holdings in 20th Century works.
Owner/Biography: Donald J. Weinstock. Mr. Weinstock is a Professor of English at California State University, Long Beach.
Year Founded/History of Bookstore: 1971.
Number of Volumes: Over 25,000.
Types/Classifications: Hardbound, some paperback, out-of-print.
General Subject Areas: Art, Biography, British and American Literature, Children's Literature, Exploration, Foreign Literature in Translation, Government, History, Juveniles, Literary Criticism, Medicine, Military, Mysteries, Philosophy, Religion, Science, Science Fiction, Show Business, Social and Behavioral Sciences, Technology, Travel, Women's Studies.
Other Specialties: Some foreign language titles.
Mail/Telephone Orders; Credit Cards: Mail orders only. No credit cards.

Special Features: Attention given to want lists.
Catalogue: Catalogues issued by subject areas on variable dates.
Collections/Individual Items Purchased: Both.

91
Doris Harris Autographs
5410 Wilshire Boulevard
Los Angeles, California 90036 (213) 939-4500

Doris Harris deals in autographs exclusively and mainly American material. Her office is in a high-rise building and on a clear day one can see the Pacific Ocean.

How to Get There: The business is located in the third block west of La Brea between Cochran and Cloverdale; near the Los Angeles County Museum of Art.

Owner/Biography: Doris Harris. Ms. Harris has been in the field of autographs since 1954 and in the Los Angeles area since 1966. She was previously in New York City (1954-1965).

Year Founded/History of Bookstore: 1966. The business was located in San Pedro from 1966-1970, on Hollywood Boulevard from 1970-1975, and in the present location since 1975.

Types/Classifications: Autographed letters and documents, association copies, presentation copies, books signed by Presidents of the United States.

General Subject Areas: American Autographed Material.

Specific Specialties: Historical, Literary, Scientific, Musical, Presidents (U.S.).

Mail/Telephone Orders; Credit Cards: Both. Payment prior to shipment until credit is established. No credit cards.

Business Hours: Monday through Friday 9:00 AM - 12:00 Noon and 2:00 PM - 5:00 PM; Saturday by appointment.

Parking Facilities: Street parking.

Catalogue: Published 2 times per year.

Collections/Individual Items Purchased: Both.

Booksellers' Memberships: Antiquarian Booksellers Association of America.

92
Douglas Books
1 H Main Street
Jackson, California 95642 (209) 223-3780

Douglas Books specializes in California and general Western Americana and carries fine books in all subjects. Many fine antiques are also found in the store.

How to Get There: Jackson is on Highway 49, the "golden chain." The argonauts took the route from one gold camp on to the next. Douglas Books is on the main floor of the 2-story red building at the end of Main Street.

Owner/Biography: Bonnie Douglas.

Year Founded/History of Bookstore: 1969.

Number of Volumes: 6,000.

Types/Classifications: Hardbound, first editions, out-of-print.

General Subject Areas: General, Photography, Western Americana.

Mail/Telephone Orders; Credit Cards: Both. Visa and Mastercard accepted.

Business Hours: Tuesday through Sunday 10:00 AM - 5:00 PM.

Parking Facilities: City parking lot and private lot next to building.

Collections/Individual Items Purchased: Both.

93
Drama Books
511 Geary
San Francisco, California 94102 (415) 441-5343

Drama Books is a small specialty store dealing in film, theater, and dance located in the heart of San Francisco's theater district. The shop caters to an international clientele. Every square inch is used to store and display books and ephemera - Sarony photographs of New York stage personalities in the 1880's or Clarence Bull and Ruth Harriet Louise portraits of Hollywood stars in the 1930's. Fourteen foot ceilings permit towering shelves and a raised balcony for film books.

How to Get There: The shop is located a little over 2 blocks west of Union Square in the block immediately west of the Curran and Geary Theatres.

Owner/Biography: Andrew DeShong. Mr. DeShong was graduated from Harvard College and received a Ph.D. in Theatre History from Yale University. He is the author of "The Theatrical Designs of George Grosz," (UMI Research Press) and has designed for various university and public theaters in the Bay Area. He received the Dramalogue award for one of his designs for the Berkeley Repertory Theatre.

Year Founded/History of Bookstore: 1975. Founded in 1975 as Castro Drama Books, the store changed its name to Drama Books in 1978 when it moved to the theater district.

Number of Volumes: 10,000.

Types/Classifications: Hardbound, paperback, magazines, some autographs, original stage and costume designs, prints, posters, first editions, out-of-print, signed copies, limited editions, color plate books.

General Subject Areas: Dance, Film, Theater.

Specific Specialties: Set and Costume Design, History of Fashion, History of Film/Theater, Acting and Directing, Dramatic Literature and Criticism, Ballet, Folk Dance, Modern and Jazz Dance, Published Film Scripts.

Author Specialties: American Playwrights (O'Neill, Williams, Shepard, Odets, Kaufman, etc.)

Other Specialties: Some foreign language material, particularly in the area of design.

Mail/Telephone Orders; Credit Cards: Both. Visa and Mastercard accepted.

Business Hours: Monday through Saturday 11:00 AM - 6:00 PM. Hours vary somewhat according to season; closed Monday January to May; open at least one night of the week during summer.

Parking Facilities: Street parking, parking lot across the street.

Special Features: Want lists maintained; customers interested in designs, prints, or posters should make an appointment in advance and describe the type of material being sought.

Catalogue: Specialized lists in several subject areas; usually 8 issued per year.

Collections/Individual Items Purchased: Both.

Miscellaneous: An important part of the store is the availability of new material, including reprints as well as used and out-of-print material; this includes acting editions of plays which may be out of print in all other forms.

94
Drew's Book Shop
31 East Canon Perdido
Santa Barbara, California 93101 (805) 966-3311

Drew's Book Shop deals in general antiquarian material and covers most all subject areas. It occupies 1,100 square feet of space.

How to Get There: The shop is located in downtown Santa Barbara.

Owner/Biography: Warren E. and Mary A. Drew.

Year Founded/History of Bookstore: 1957. The original store opened in Santa Barbara but was later moved to Boston. The Drews returned to Santa Barbara in 1972.

Number of Volumes: 15,000.

Types/Classifications: Hardbound, prints, autographs, documents, ephemera, maps, first editions, fine bindings, out-of-print, association copies, press books, signed copies, presentation copies, limited editions, color plate books.

General Subject Areas: General.

Mail/Telephone Orders; Credit Cards: Both. No credit cards.

Business Hours: Monday through Saturday 11:00 AM - 5:00 PM.
Parking Facilities: Ample parking in city lot at rear of store, first 90 minutes free.
Special Features: Appraisals of libraries, collections, rare items, etc.
Catalogue: Published occasionally.
Collections/Individual Items Purchased: Both.
Booksellers' Memberships: Antiquarian Booksellers Association of America.

95
Eclectic Gallery
1031 Trillium Lane
Mill Valley, California 94941   (415) 383-1125

Originally located on Union Street in San Francisco, The Eclectic Gallery has been in the home of its owners since 1976. Visitors are welcome by appointment to relax and browse through the illustrated books featured by the store.
How to Get There: Call for directions at the time of making an appointment to visit.
Owner/Biography: Dick Rykken and Robert Scull.
Year Founded/History of Bookstore: 1974. The Gallery originally featured more art than books. After relocating from San Francisco, the emphasis was placed on illustrated books.
Number of Volumes: 1,000.
Types/Classifications: Hardbound, first editions, ephemera, illustrated books, press books, photogravures.
General Subject Areas: Big Little Books, Disneyana, Edward S. Curtis Photogravures, Oziana, Pochoir Books and Portfolios.
Mail/Telephone Orders; Credit Cards: Both. Visa and Mastercard accepted.
Business Hours: By appointment.
Parking Facilities: Street parking.
Catalogue: Published 2 to 3 times per year.
Collections/Individual Items Purchased: Both.
Booksellers' Memberships: Antiquarian Booksellers Association of America.

96
Encyclopedias Bought and Sold
14071 Windsor Place
Santa Ana, California 92705   (714) 838-3643

Encyclopedias Bought and Sold is a small in-home shop. The books are on display in a comfortable library within a grey and white Cape Cod house. The shelves are lined with current and late general encyclopedias, well-bound classics, histories, and miscellaneous 19th Century books.
How to Get There: Santa Ana is in Orange County, 35 miles south of Los Angeles. Windsor Place is 1 1/4 miles east of the Newport 55 Freeway at the 17th Street Tustin off-ramp.
Owner/Biography: Frank and Kathleen Italiane.
Year Founded/History of Bookstore: 1965.
Types/Classifications: Hardbound, fine bindings, leatherbound books.
General Subject Areas: Encyclopedias.
Specific Specialties: Encyclopedias (Nineteenth and Twentieth Centuries); sets of classics such as the "Great Books of the Western World," Harvard Classics, complete works of an author; sets of Children's Literature, Ninth and Eleventh Editions of "Encyclopaedia Brittanica," Bible Encyclopedias, Commentaries.
Mail/Telephone Orders; Credit Cards: Both. No credit cards.
Business Hours: By appointment 10:00 AM - 10:00 PM.
Collections/Individual Items Purchased: Both.

97
Fantasy Illustrated
12531 Harbor Boulevard Suite D
Garden Grove, California 92640 (714) 537-0087

The bookstore features rare comic books and science fiction material, pulp novels from the 1940's, and Disney memorabilia. Also featured are ephemera and collectible items such as baseball cards and autographed sports photographs and autographed baseballs. The shop also contains a very complete selection of new comic books.

How to Get There: The bookstore is located 1 1/2 miles south of Disneyland between the Santa Ana (I-5) and Garden Grove (22) Freeways.

Owner/Biography: Dave Smith, owner and senior partner, and Tony Galovich, partner, grew up "reading tons of comic books and collecting hundreds of baseball cards." Now they have turned their hobbies into a business.

Year Founded/History of Bookstore: Founded in 1979 in Garden Grove, California, the shop contains 900 square feet of space. The partners plan to enlarge this soon into 2,000 square feet. They opened a branch shop in Costa Mesa, California in mid-1983 which has 325 square feet, but plans are already underway to relocate it to larger quarters in the same area. It is presently located at 1826 Newport Boulevard.

Number of Volumes: 100,000.

Types/Classifications: Comic books, out-of-print science fiction, vintage paperbacks, ephemera, toys, illustrated books.

General Subject Areas: Magic, Science Fiction and Fantasy.

Mail/Telephone Orders; Credit Cards: Both. Visa and Mastercard accepted.

Business Hours: Monday through Friday 12:00 Noon - 6:00 PM; Saturday 11:00 AM - 5:00 PM; Sunday 12:00 Noon - 4:00 PM.

Parking Facilities: Parking lot.

Catalogue: Two to four times a year; customers may order the following catalogues by enclosing $1 for each: comic books, vintage paperbacks, pulp magazines.

Collections/Individual Items Purchased: Both.

Booksellers' Memberships: Antiquarian Booksellers Association of America.

98
Ferndale Books
405 Main Street
Ferndale, California 95536 (707) 786-9135

The owner offers this quote from Christopher Morley's "Haunted Bookshop" as descriptive of Ferndale Books: "Our Shop is haunted by the ghosts/ Of all great literature, in hosts;/ We sell no fakes or trashes/ Lovers of books are welcome here,/ No clerks will babble in your ear,/ Please smoke - but don't drop ashes." The bookstore is also known as Carlos E. Benemann - Bookseller.

How to Get There: Located in Ferndale which is probably the only intact Victorian town in California, the bookstore is on Main Street. Ferndale is in Northern California, 15 miles south of Eureka and 5 miles west of Highway 101, the north-south California coastal highway.

Owner/Biography: Carlos E. Benemann.

Year Founded/History of Bookstore: 1981.

Number of Volumes: 10,000 in general stock; 15,000 Latin Americana.

Types/Classifications: Hardbound, out-of-print.

General Subject Areas: Art, Biography, California, Cooking, Crafts, History, Hunting, Military, Music, Natural History, Occult, Poetry, Psychology, Religion, Science, Science Fiction, Sports, Travel, Wine.

Specific Specialties: Latin Americana, Limited Editions Club.

Other Specialties: Archaeology, Geography, History - Scholarly Works on Latin America; works in Spanish by Latin Americans.

Mail/Telephone Orders; Credit Cards: Both. No credit cards.

Business Hours: Seven days per week 10:00 AM - 5:00 PM and by appointment.

Parking Facilities: Street parking, parking lot.

Special Features: Search service.

Catalogue: Published occasionally.
Collections/Individual Items Purchased: Both.

99
Fields Bookstore

1419 Polk Street
San Francisco, California 94109 (415) 673-2027

Fields Bookstore has a general stock of out-of-print and new books. The store has been in this location since 1931. As the story goes, George Fields bought the store from Old Man Johnson who came to San Francisco's Polk Street to open the shop after reading Frank Norris' "McTeague." Fields sold the shop in 1964 to Ruth Cooke.
How to Get There: The cross streets are California and Pine.
Owner/Biography: Ruth Cooke and Richard Hackney.
Year Founded/History of Bookstore: 1931.
Number of Volumes: 15,000.
Types/Classifications: Hardbound, rare, new, paperback, tarot decks.
General Subject Areas: Alchemy, Astrology, Bacon-Shakespeare Controversy, Children's Illustrated Books, Gardening, Hermetics, Hinduism, Islam, Kabbalah, Magic, Music, Mysticism, Parapsychology, Psychology, Rosicruciana, Tarot, Theosophy.
Specific Specialties: Ancient Near East, Egypt.
Mail/Telephone Orders; Credit Cards: Both. No credit cards.
Business Hours: Tuesday through Saturday 11:00 AM - 6:00 PM.
Collections/Individual Items Purchased: Both.

100
Frontier-Pioneer Books

1357 1/2 East Colorado Street
Glendale, California 91205 (818) 243-0221

This bookstore has a general stock of hardbound and paperback used books plus many back issues of photo magazines, National Geographics, some postcards and prints. The store occupies 690 square feet of space.
How to Get There: The store is located 6 blocks west of the Glendale Freeway and 7 blocks south of Ventura Freeway near Verdugo and Colorado.
Owner/Biography: Philip O. and Mary A. Davidson.
Year Founded/History of Bookstore: 1980.
Number of Volumes: 80,000.
Types/Classifications: Hardbound, paperback, magazines, first editions, out-of-print, signed copies.
General Subject Areas: Alaska, Arctic, Art, Automotive, Aviation, Back Packing and Camping, Canada, Children's Books, Cookbooks, Fishing, How-To Books, Hunting, Ships, War.
Author Specialties: Louis L'Amour.
Mail/Telephone Orders; Credit Cards: Both. Libraries billed; others cash with order until credit is established; postage and insurance extra.
Business Hours: Monday through Friday 10:00 AM - 5:30 PM; Saturday 10:00 AM - 5:00 PM.
Parking Facilities: Business parking lot in rear of store; street parking.
Special Features: Want lists maintained.
Catalogue: Published 1 to 2 times per year.
Collections/Individual Items Purchased: Both.

101
G. F. Gustin, Jr. Books

56 East Colorado Boulevard
Pasadena, California 91105 (818) 795-8528

This bookdealer carries a general stock including Western Americana and Literary Criticism.
Owner/Biography: G.F. Gustin, Jr.
Year Founded/History of Bookstore: 1974.
Types/Classifications: Hardbound, first editions, out-of-print.
General Subject Areas: General.
Specific Specialties: Western Americana, Literary Criticism.
Mail/Telephone Orders; Credit Cards: Call for instructions.
Parking Facilities: Street parking.

102
Gail Klemm - Books
P.O. Box 518
Apple Valley, California 92307   (619) 242-5921

Gail Klemm - Books is an antiquarian book business conducted by mail and appointment. Customers are welcome to browse through the stock of 18th to 20th Century children's books, Western Americana, typography, and miscellaneous antiquarian stock by appointment.
How to Get There: Apple Valley is located in the high desert approximately 2 hours' driving time from Los Angeles. It is easily reached by either the Antelope Valley or San Bernardino Freeways. Call for appointment and specific directions.
Owner/Biography: Gail E. Klemm. She has been an antiquarian bookseller for 17 years and presently is engaged with her husband, W.A. Klemm, in compiling a bibliography of Randolph Caldecott, 19th Century illustrator.
Year Founded/History of Bookstore: 1967. Mrs. Klemm began her business in California and moved several times due to family moves. She moved back to California in 1983 after 8 years in Ellicott City, Maryland.
Number of Volumes: 5,000.
Types/Classifications: Hardbound, out-of-print, ephemera, first editions, signed copies, color plate books.
General Subject Areas: Children's Books, Papermaking, Typography, Western Americana.
Specific Specialties: Randolph Caldecott (Books, Art, Letters, Ephemera).
Other Specialties: Foreign language children's literature (19th and 20th Centuries); early scarce political pamphlets, broadsides (Eastern states).
Mail/Telephone Orders; Credit Cards: Both. Payment in advance by new customers. No credit cards.
Business Hours: By appointment only.
Parking Facilities: Off-street private parking.
Special Features: Collection development advice; personalized service and quotes for specific customer wants; active card file/mailing list for customers.
Catalogue: Published occasionally.
Collections/Individual Items Purchased: Both.
Booksellers' Memberships: Antiquarian Booksellers Association of America including Southern California Chapter, International League of Antiquarian Booksellers.

103
Garcia-Garst, Booksellers
334 North Center, Suite L
Turlock, California 95380   (209) 632-5054

Garcia-Garst, Booksellers has a large, airy, and well-organized shop of general and out-of-print stock. It occupies 2,000 square feet of space.
How to Get There: Turlock is in California's central valley about 70 miles north of Fresno off Highway 99 and about 10 miles south of Modesto. The shop is in the North Center Plaza which can be reached from Highway 99 at the West Main Street Exit to North Center Street.
Owner/Biography: Kenneth and Beverly Garst.
Year Founded/History of Bookstore: 1978.
Number of Volumes: 60,000.

Types/Classifications: Hardbound, paperback, out-of-print, first editions, signed editions, limited editions, fine bindings, color plate books.

General Subject Areas: Art, Automobiles, Automotive Repair, Biography, Business, Californiana, Children's Books, Classics, Cookbooks, Drama, Firearms, Gardening, History, Home Improvement, Mathematics, Military, Music, Mysteries, Nature, Nautical, Needlecrafts, Orientalia, Oz Books, Philosophy, Photography, Poetry, Psychology, Railroads, Reference, Religion, Science, Science Fiction and Fantasy, Scribners Classics, Self-Help, Sporting, Travel, Western Americana, Women's Studies.

Author Specialties: John Steinbeck, Gene Stratton Porter, Jessie Wilcox Smith, Maxfield Parrish, Kay Nielsen, William Shakespeare.

Mail/Telephone Orders; Credit Cards: Both. Cash with order including postage. No credit cards.

Business Hours: Seven days per week 10:00 AM - 5:30 PM.

Parking Facilities: Business parking lot.

Special Features: Search service.

Collections/Individual Items Purchased: Both.

Booksellers' Memberships: Central California Antiquarian Booksellers Association.

104

Gene de Chene - Booksellers

11556 Santa Monica Boulevard

Los Angeles, California 90025 (213) 477-8734

This bookshop carries general used stock with a specific specialty in psychology and psychiatry. It occupies 900 square feet of space. The shop has aisles of shelving and the hardbound books are alphabetized. There is a paperbacks only section.

How to Get There: The shop is located 6 blocks west of the San Diego Freeway.

Owner/Biography: Eugene de Chene.

Year Founded/History of Bookstore: 1968.

Number of Volumes: 50,000.

Types/Classifications: Hardbound, paperback, out-of-print.

General Subject Areas: General.

Specific Specialties: Psychology, Psychiatry.

Mail/Telephone Orders; Credit Cards: Both. Cash with order. No credit cards.

Business Hours: Monday through Friday 10:00 AM - 8:00 PM; Saturday 10:00 AM - 5:00 PM; closed Sunday.

Parking Facilities: Public metered parking in rear of store.

Collections/Individual Items Purchased: Individual items only.

105

George Frederick Kolbe/Fine Numismatic Books

P.O. Drawer 1610A

Crestline, California 92325 (714) 338-6527

Over 25,000 books on numismatics are housed in a large home built in the 1920's by MGM Studios while filming in the picturesque mountain area adjacent to Lake Arrowhead.

How to Get There: Appointment suggested at which time directions will be given.

Owner/Biography: G.F. Kolbe.

Year Founded/History of Bookstore: 1967. The original shop was in Santa Ana, then in Mission Viejo. A move was made to Crestline in 1983.

Number of Volumes: 25,000.

Types/Classifications: New, rare, out-of-print, coin auction catalogues, scholarly periodicals.

General Subject Areas: Numismatics.

Mail/Telephone Orders; Credit Cards: Both. Cash with order or established credit. No credit cards.

Business Hours: By appointment 9:00 AM - 5:00 PM.

Parking Facilities: Parking available.

Special Features: Publishing sideline of new books on numismatics and also conducting public and mail auctions.

Catalogue: Published bi-monthly.

Collections/Individual Items Purchased: Both.

Booksellers' Memberships: Antiquarian Booksellers Association of America, International League of Antiquarian Booksellers.

Miscellaneous: Crestline is a rural community and there is no home mail delivery service. Visitors should call first so that the type and range of books available can be fully explained.

106
George Houle - Rare Books & Autographs
2277 Westwood Boulevard
Los Angeles, California 90064 (213) 474-1539

This specialized antiquarian bookstore has a select stock of 18th to 20th Century first editions by English and American authors, art reference works, books on the decorative arts and antiques, leather bindings, library sets, and autographs of famous people.

How to Get There: The bookstore is located south of UCLA and Westwood Village on Westwood Boulevard between Pico and Olympic Boulevards.

Owner/Biography: George Houle. Mr. Houle was formerly head of the book and manuscript department of Sotheby Park Bernet in Los Angeles and has lectured at UCLA Extension on Book Collecting.

Year Founded/History of Bookstore: 1975.

Number of Volumes: 6,000.

Types/Classifications: First editions, signed and association copies, leather bindings, original art, illustrated books, autographs (framed and unframed).

General Subject Areas: Art Monographs, Autographs, Fishing, Western Americana.

Author Specialties: Zane Grey, Vita Sackville-West, D.H. Lawrence, G.K. Chesterton, Hilaire Belloc.

Mail/Telephone Orders; Credit Cards: Both. American Express, Visa, Mastercard accepted.

Business Hours: Monday through Friday 11:00 AM - 6:00 PM; Saturday 11:00 AM - 4:00 PM; always best to phone first as hours may vary.

Parking Facilities: Metered street parking and in rear of store.

Special Features: Framed autographs; a leading dealer in the works and manuscripts of Zane Grey.

Catalogue: Published 4 to 6 times per year; $4 each or subscriptions of 4 issues $12.

Collections/Individual Items Purchased: Both.

Booksellers' Memberships: Antiquarian Booksellers Association of America, Manuscript Society, American Booksellers Association.

107
George K. Oppenheim
Rare and Foreign Language Books and Fine Prints
51 Vallejo Street
Berkeley, California 94707 (415) 527-5169

George K. Oppenheim operates his business from his private residence in the North Berkeley Hills. Visits may be arranged by appointment.

How to Get There: Directions will be given when calling for an appointment.

Owner/Biography: George K. Oppenheim.

Year Founded/History of Bookstore: 1968. Mr. Oppenheim previously operated an open store on Post Street in San Francisco.

Number of Volumes: 2,000.

Types/Classifications: Hardbound, color plate books, rare, first editions, books illustrated by modern artists (especially French).

General Subject Areas: Archaeology, Architecture, Art, Natural History, Travel.

Other Specialties: German and French books of all periods and in all fields.

Mail/Telephone Orders; Credit Cards: Both. Check with order (individuals); dealers and institutions will be billed. No credit cards.
Business Hours: By appointment only.
Parking Facilities: Street parking.
Catalogue: Published irregularly.
Collections/Individual Items Purchased: Both.
Booksellers' Memberships: Antiquarian Booksellers Association of America.

108
George Robert Kane Books
252 Third Avenue
Santa Cruz, California 95062   (408) 426-4133

This book dealer carries rare and antiquarian books and some ephemera, mostly Californiana and literary. The stock occupies 800 square feet of space.
How to Get There: From Highway 1 or 17, take Ocean Street to end, then left on East Cliff to Seabright, right on Seabright to Marine Parade, and finally left to Third Avenue.
Owner/Biography: George Robert Kane. Mr. Kane is a former newspaper publisher.
Year Founded/History of Bookstore: 1977. Originally in Los Gatos; moved to Santa Cruz in 1978.
Number of Volumes: 4,000.
Types/Classifications: Hardbound, first editions, fine bindings, press books, color plate books, illustrated books.
General Subject Areas: Californiana, English Books of Aesthetic Period, Literature, Stone and Kimball.
Specific Specialties: Margaret Armstrong bindings.
Author Specialties: Jessie Wilcox Smith, Jessie M. King, Arthur Rackham.
Other Specialties: Illustrated books using pochoir method as well as hand coloring, Cambridge Christmas Books.
Mail/Telephone Orders; Credit Cards: Both. Send check with first order; any book returnable for any reason. Visa and Mastercard accepted.
Business Hours: By appointment.
Parking Facilities: Street parking.
Catalogue: Published 2 times per year.
Collections/Individual Items Purchased: Both.
Booksellers' Memberships: Antiquarian Booksellers Association of America; Central California Antiquarian Booksellers (President).

109
Geoscience Books & Prints
P.O. Box 487-MP
Yucaipa, California 92399   (714) 797-1650

This is a specialized dealer in prints of mining, minerals, gems, and fossils, and out-of-print, scarce, and rare hardbound books on the same subjects. It is a mail order business only.
Owner/Biography: Russell and Alexandra Filer.
Year Founded/History of Bookstore: 1980.
Types/Classifications: Hardbound, out-of-print, prints.
General Subject Areas: Fossils, Gems, Minerals, Mining.
Mail/Telephone Orders; Credit Cards: Both. No credit cards.
Business Hours: Mail order: 8:00 AM - 6:00 PM.
Catalogue: Published annually.
Collections/Individual Items Purchased: Individual items only.

110
German & International Bookstore
1767 North Vermont Avenue
Los Angeles, California 90027   (213) 660-0313

This is a general bookstore with a good selection of new and used books in English and specializing in both new and used books in the German language. The store will special order titles from Germany and language tapes; many foreign dictionaries are available. The shop occupies 5,500 square feet of space.

How to Get There: Located in the Griffith Park area (Los Feliz) of Los Angeles; take Vermont Exit from Hollywood Freeway and go north of Hollywood Boulevard one block.

Owner/Biography: Dora Posner Belvin and Dave Posner.

Year Founded/History of Bookstore: 1974.

Types/Classifications: Hardbound, paperback, magazines, newspapers, out-of-print, first editions.

General Subject Areas: Art, Aviation, Business, Childbirth, Children's Books, Cinema, Cookbooks, Drama, Fiction, Gardening, Health, Humor, Nature, Photography, Psychology, Science, Science Fiction, Sociology, Technical.

Specific Specialties: All German subjects and titles.

Other Specialties: Foreign language dictionaries, German and other language tapes.

Mail/Telephone Orders; Credit Cards: Both. Check, money order, or charge card as prepayment including postage and handling. Visa and Mastercard accepted.

Business Hours: Monday through Saturday 10:00 AM - 11:00 PM; Sunday 12:00 Noon - 9:00 PM.

Parking Facilities: Street parking, lot in rear of store.

Special Features: Special ordering.

Collections/Individual Items Purchased: Both.

111
Golden Hill Antiquarian Books
2456 Broadway
San Diego, California 92102   (619) 236-9883

Golden Hill Antiquarian Books is located in an old Victorian home built in 1896. The house is still owned by the family that built it and it is in one of the first sub-divisions of San Diego, 12 blocks from the heart of downtown.

Owner/Biography: Robert L. and Margaret J. Summers.

Year Founded/History of Bookstore: 1977. The original stock of 15,000 books was purchased from the widow of a friend who was a book collector in San Diego for many years.

Number of Volumes: 15,000.

Types/Classifications: Hardbound, ephemera, first editions, out-of-print, press books, signed copies, limited editions, color plate books.

General Subject Areas: Americana, Autobiography, Biography, Children's Books.

Specific Specialties: California, Western Americana.

Mail/Telephone Orders; Credit Cards: Both. No credit cards.

Business Hours: Wednesday, Friday, Saturday 10:00 AM - 5:30 PM; other times by appointment.

Parking Facilities: Street parking.

Special Features: Search service.

Collections/Individual Items Purchased: Both.

Booksellers' Memberships: San Diego Booksellers Association.

112
Golden Horse Shoe
415 First Street
Benicia, California 94510   (707) 745-2255

The Golden Horse Shoe is basically an old-time antique shop located in a former hotel. It deals in interesting old books and a broad spectrum of ephemeral material. The business is connected with a private (circa 1890) letterpress printery, "The Liberty Tree Press." It is a major source of wood type.

How to Get There: Benicia is situated near the intersection of I-780 and I-680 about fifteen miles north of Oakland.

Owner/Biography: Bill Maccoun.

Year Founded/History of Bookstore: 1964.

Number of Volumes: 1,000.

Types/Classifications: Hardbound, magazines, broadsides, ephemera.

General Subject Areas: Americana, Californiana, Children's Books, Printing.

Mail/Telephone Orders; Credit Cards: Neither. Visa and Mastercard accepted.

Business Hours: Weekends and some afternoons; it is best to phone first.

Parking Facilities: Business parking lot, street parking.

Collections/Individual Items Purchased: Both.

113
Grounds for Murder, A Mystery Book Store
2707 Congress Street
San Diego, California 92110 (619) 294-9497

Grounds for Murder deals exclusively in mystery and mystery-related items. It carries adult and juvenile mystery and detective fiction, espionage, suspense, some true crime, some horror stories, romantic suspense, books about mysteries and mystery writing, biographies and autobiographies of mystery writers, reference books and bibliographies on mysteries, mystery games, records, magazines, and miscellaneous gift items relating to mystery. The store deals in new and used books and stocks many out-of-print items.

How to Get There: From Highway 8 take the exit for Old Town/Taylor Street or from Highway 5 take the Old Town Avenue exit; the store is upstairs in the Old Town Mercado, an open courtyard building at the corner of Congress and Mason Streets.

Owner/Biography: Phyllis Brown.

Year Founded/History of Bookstore: 1981.

Number of Volumes: 30,000.

Types/Classifications: Hardbound, paperback, magazines, records, games, calendars, Sherlock Holmes jewelry, miscellaneous gift items, some first editions, many out-of-print, some signed books, some limited editions, many British imports.

General Subject Areas: Biography and Autobiography of Mystery Writers, Books About Mysteries, Classical Whodunits, Crime Detection, Espionage, Hard-Boiled Detective Novels, Horror, Mystery Bibliography, Romantic Suspense, Suspense Stories, True Crime.

Mail/Telephone Orders; Credit Cards: Both. Payment before shipping. Visa and Mastercard accepted.

Business Hours: Monday through Saturday 10:00 AM - 6:00 PM; Sunday 11:00 AM - 6:00 PM.

Parking Facilities: Private parking lot behind building.

Special Features: Search service; want lists accepted and kept on file.

Catalogue: Newsletter published every 2 or 3 months listing some new titles.

Collections/Individual Items Purchased: Both.

114
H. N. Miller Books/Aviation Bookmobile/Mil-Air Books
901 West Alondra Boulevard
Hangars D9, M9, Q5 - Compton Airport
Compton, California 90220 (213) 632-8081

Harry "The Aviation Bookie" Miller has been collecting aviation books since 1927. In 1960 he started the Aviation Bookmobile selling books at airshows, gun shows, paper shows, and swap meets. In 1965 he rented 3 hangars at Compton Airport and piled them full of books and magazines. Mil-Air Books now stocks 10,000 titles of new, used, and hard to find out-of-print books and 80,000 back issue magazines. An alternate phone number is (213) 863-5028.

How to Get There: The Compton Airport is located on Alondra Boulevard between Central and Wilmington Avenues just north of the Artesia Freeway; take Wilmington north five traffic lights to Alondra; turn left and get in right lane and then turn right alongside a Shell Gas Station into airport. Drive down taxiway (not over 15 mph) to hangars which are lettered D9, M9, Q5. Entrance to D9 on east side of hangar; entrance to M9 and Q5 on west side of hangars (doors by fence).

Owner/Biography: Harold N. and Phyllis A. Miller. Harold Norman (Harry) Miller was born in Oregon and learned to fly in 1935. He served in the U.S. Navy and has worked for various aircraft companies. Phyllis is from Chicago and she accompanies Mr. Miller to the airshows in the bookmobile and acts as cashier.

Year Founded/History of Bookstore: 1960. The business began by selling duplicates from Mr. Miller's collection at various aviation meetings. He purchased Armed Forces Book Co. of Valley Stream, New York in 1980 and moved the stock to Compton.

Number of Volumes: 10,000.

Types/Classifications: Hardbound, paperback, brochures, autographs, airline time tables, airshow and air race photos and posters, aviation ephemera, rare, out-of-print, remainders, unbound, first editions, association copies, signed copies, presentation copies, limited editions, color plate books, manuscripts.

General Subject Areas: Air Racing, Aircraft Engines, Aircraft Mechanics, Airlines, Antiques, Army, Automobiles, Aviation, Aviation Cinema, Aviators, Balloons, Biography, Boats, Boer War, Civil War (U.S.), Electronics, Falkland Islands War, Farm Machinery, Flight Schools, Flight Training, Flying Boats, Gliders, Helicopters, Hydraulics, Internal Combustion Engines, Korean War, Lighter Than Air Craft, Military, Newspapers, Parachutes, Photography, Printing, Racecars, Railroads, RevolutionaryWar(U.S.) World War I, Rockets, Sailplanes, Science, Science Fiction, Seaplanes, Ships, Space, Stamp Collecting, Steam Engines, Tanks, UFO's, Vietman War, World War II.

Author Specialties: Ball, Ernest Gann, Nevil Chute, Serling, G. Robb Wilson, Pete Bowers, Roger Freeman, K.D. Wood, Bruhn.

Other Specialties: Foreign titles in aviation, military, and space; boys' and girls' titles in aviation specialties.

Mail/Telephone Orders; Credit Cards: Both. Check or money order with order; ten day return privilege if not as represented. Mail Order address: P.O. Box U, Norwalk, CA 90650. Visa and Mastercard accepted.

Business Hours: Weekdays 1:00 PM - 5:00 PM; Saturday (if no airshow) 10:00 AM - 5:00 PM; Sunday by appointment; also earlier or later than scheduled hours by appointment.

Parking Facilities: Beside hangar or lot at Pilot's Lounge.

Special Features: Search service; research library on premises; book and magazine publishing.

Catalogue: Lists published occasionally.

Collections/Individual Items Purchased: Both.

Miscellaneous: Research for authors, script writers, films, publishers; over 50,000 photos on file, 30,000 magazines, 10,000 titles, and 7,000 NACA/NASA reports in research library; one of the largest aviation research sources on the West Coast.

115
Hammon's Archives
1115 Front Street
Sacramento, California 95814 (916) 446-1782

Hammon's Archives specializes in books on mining, geology, Californiana, Nevada, railroadiana, and Japan. It has an extensive selection of ephemera. The shop occupies 542 square feet of space.

How to Get There: The shop is located in Old Sacramento.

Owner/Biography: Wendell P. Hammon.

Year Founded/History of Bookstore: 1975.

Number of Volumes: Over 2,000.

Types/Classifications: Hardbound, broadsides, ephemera, first editions, out-of-print.

General Subject Areas: Californiana, Geology, Mining, Nevada, Railroadiana.

Specific Specialties: California Divison of Mines publications.

Other Specialties: Japan, prints, postcards, photographs.

Mail/Telephone Orders; Credit Cards: Both. Visa and Mastercard accepted.

Business Hours: Daily 12:00 Noon - 8:00 PM and by appointment.

Parking Facilities: Available.

Special Features: Friendly atmosphere.

Catalogue: Published annually.

Collections/Individual Items Purchased: Both.

116
Harry A. Levinson - Rare Books
P.O. Box 534
Beverly Hills, California 90213   (213) 276-9311

Harry A. Levinson - Rare Books is a dealer in antiquarian materials including incunabula, English and continental literature, and early manuscripts. Visits may be arranged by appointment only.
How to Get There: Directions will be given when making an appointment.
Owner/Biography: Harry A. Levinson.
Year Founded/History of Bookstore: 1929. Mr. Levinson was originally in New York until 1948. In 1949 he relocated his business to Beverly Hills.
Number of Volumes: 6,000.
Types/Classifications: Hardbound, first editions, association copies, rare, early manuscripts.
General Subject Areas: Bibliography, Early Illustrated Books (16th through 18 Centuries), Early Science and Medicine, English and Continental Literature, Incunabula, Reference.
Specific Specialties: Elizabethan Literature.
Other Specialties: Scholarly Works, Foreign Language Titles.
Mail/Telephone Orders; Credit Cards: Both. No credit cards.
Business Hours: By appointment only.
Parking Facilities: Available.
Catalogue: Published occasionally.
Booksellers' Memberships: Antiquarian Booksellers Association of America (Founding Member), Antiquarian Booksellers Association (International), Manuscript Society.
Miscellaneous: Rare books and manuscripts appraised.

117
Helan Halbach, Books
116 East De La Guerra Street
Studio 3
Santa Barbara, California 93101   (805) 965-6432

This bookstore is a small separate studio set amid others in a Mediterranean courtyard. Books are displayed outdoors, weather permitting. The interior features skillfully arranged books, prints, and ephemera.
How to Get There: The bookstore is located between Anacapa and Santa Barbara Streets in historic Old Town.
Owner/Biography: Helan Halbach. Ms. Halbach retired to bookselling a few years ago.
Year Founded/History of Bookstore: 1967.
Number of Volumes: 2,500.
Types/Classifications: Hardbound, paperback, magazines, ephemera, vintage playing cards, games, curios, stamps, bookmarks, first editions, fine bindings, out-of-print, association copies, press books, signed copies, presentation copies, limited editions, color plate books, phonograph records.
General Subject Areas: Art, Californiana, Detective Fiction, Dictionaries, Humor, Mysteries, Napoleon III, True Crime.
Specific Specialties: Victoriana, Edwardian Period, Sherlock Holmes, Christmas Books, Blue Willow Design, Movie Memorabilia, Bookplates, Rubaiyat of Omar Khayyam.
Author Specialties: Arthur Conan Doyle, Elizabeth Daly, Mary Roberts Rinehart.
Mail/Telephone Orders; Credit Cards: Both. Payment with order; telephone orders will hold title until purchase order/payment is received. No credit cards.
Business Hours: Monday through Saturday 12:00 Noon - 5:00 PM and by special appointment.
Parking Facilities: Public parking lots.
Special Features: Search service; publishing sideline; preparation of bibliographies.
Catalogue: Published occasionally.
Collections/Individual Items Purchased: Both.

118
Hennessey & Ingalls, Inc.
1254 Santa Monica Mall
Santa Monica, California 90401   (213) 458-9074

This bookstore is a large, well-lighted, and well-organized store that has "everything in the visual arts." Wide aisles and clever shelving make for easy browsing. Poster art is displayed on the walls above the shelves.
How to Get There: Located on the pedestrians-only Santa Monica Mall, the bookstore is three blocks from the Pacific Ocean and one block south of Wilshire Boulevard.
Types/Classifications: Hardbound, paperback, out-of-print, new, imported, first editions.
General Subject Areas: Visual Arts.
Mail/Telephone Orders; Credit Cards: Mail orders. Visa and Mastercard accepted.
Business Hours: Monday through Saturday 9:30 AM - 6:00 PM; Sunday 12:00 Noon - 5:00 PM.
Parking Facilities: Parking is available in municipal parking lot behind the store; enter parking lot from 2nd Street.
Collections/Individual Items Purchased: Both.

119
Heritage Book Shop, Inc.
847 North La Cienega Boulevard
Los Angeles, California 90069   (213) 659-3674

The Heritage Book Shop carries a general antiquarian stock of rare books, first editions, and manuscripts. The shop occupies 1,600 square feet of space. An additional telephone number is (213) 659-5738.
How to Get There: The shop is situated on La Cienega Boulevard between Melrose and Santa Monica Boulevard on the west side of the street.
Owner/Biography: Ben and Lou Weinstein.
Year Founded/History of Bookstore: 1963. The shop has been at the present location for nine years and before that was on Hollywood Boulevard.
Number of Volumes: 10,000.
Types/Classifications: First editions, fine bindings, color plate books, illustrated books, high spots, fine printing, sets and bindings.
General Subject Areas: Americana, Early Printed Books, Early Voyages and Travels, Literature, Natural History.
Author Specialties: Charles Dickens, Mark Twain.
Mail/Telephone Orders; Credit Cards: Both. Check with order unless customer is known or provides acceptable trade references; libraries and institutions billed. American Express, Visa, Mastercard accepted.
Business Hours: Monday through Friday 9:30 AM - 5:30 PM; Saturday 10:00 AM - 4:30 PM.
Parking Facilities: Street parking.
Catalogue: Published approximately 6 times per year, plus numerous short lists.
Collections/Individual Items Purchased: Both.
Booksellers' Memberships: Antiquarian Booksellers Association of America.

120
Heritage Books
52 South Washington Street
Sonora, California 95370   (209) 532-6261

Heritage Books is located deep in the heart of California's Mother Lode country. It specializes in Californiana and Western Americana. In the tradition of Mark Twain and Bret Harte who walked the streets of Sonora, the bookstore serves the bibliophile with American authors. Other extensive lines include history, biography, and religions.
How to Get There: The bookstore is located on scenic Highway 49, just 8 miles from the Yosemite Park junction.
Owner/Biography: Robert M. Vance.

Year Founded/History of Bookstore: 1976.

Number of Volumes: 20,500.

Types/Classifications: Hardbound, paperback, first editions, some fine bindings and sets, maps, out-of-print, signed copies, limited editions.

General Subject Areas: Americana, Biography, Californiana, Classic Fiction, Drama, History, Military History, Mysteries, Poetry, Raildroadiana, Religion, Science Fiction.

Specific Specialties: Western Americana, World War II, Theology.

Author Specialties: Mark Twain, John Steinbeck, Ernest Hemingway, Jack London, Willa Cather, Bret Harte, John Galsworthy, Edna Ferber, Sinclair Lewis, Upton Sinclair, Booth Tarkington, Edith Wharton, William Makepeace Thackeray.

Mail/Telephone Orders; Credit Cards: Both. Cash with order. American Express, Visa, Mastercard accepted.

Business Hours: Monday through Saturday 9:30 AM - 5:30 PM.

Parking Facilities: Business parking lot, public parking lot, street parking.

Special Features: Search service; espresso bar.

Catalogue: Catalogue in progress.

Collections/Individual Items Purchased: Both.

Miscellaneous: New books also carried.

121

Holmes Book Company, Inc.

274 14th Street

Oakland, California 94612   (415) 893-6860

The Holmes Book Company has three floors of new and used books including a comfortable, carpeted California history room with large, overstuffed chairs. There is a large rare book room with a special annex filled with vintage magazines, paperbacks, postcards, and photographs. The entire second floor (or mezzanine) is packed with used and out-of-print fiction and children's books.

How to Get There: Take the Oakland Bay Bridge or BART if coming from San Francisco.

Year Founded/History of Bookstore: 1894.

Number of Volumes: 400,000.

Types/Classifications: Hardbound, paperback, sheet music, magazines, ephemera, photographs, sets, encyclopedias, first editions, out-of-print, press books, limited editions, signed and presentation copies, fine bindings, illustrated books.

General Subject Areas: Californiana, General.

Specific Specialties: Railroads, Native Americans, Missions, Mining, Women in the West, Gold Rush, San Francisciana, Oakland History, Southwest Americana, Hawaii, Alaska, WPA Guides.

Author Specialties: Jack London, John Muir, John Steinbeck, Robert Louis Stevenson.

Other Specialties: USGS Publications, California Historical Quarterlies, Historical Journals, Academy of Pacific Coast History.

Mail/Telephone Orders; Credit Cards: Both. Send mail orders to P.O. Box 858, Oakland, CA 94604. Visa and Mastercard accepted.

Business Hours: Monday through Saturday 9:30 AM - 5:30 PM; Sunday 11:00 AM - 5:00 PM.

Parking Facilities: Street parking, public parking lot next door.

Special Features: Search service; advertising service; publishers of Western Americana; monthly newsletter of new acquisitions in the field of Western Americana and local interest.

Catalogue: Published 2 times per year.

Collections/Individual Items Purchased: Both.

Booksellers' Memberships: Antiquarian Booksellers Association of America.

Miscellaneous: There is a second location in San Francisco at 22 Third Street; telephone (415) 362-3283.

122
Holmes Book Company, Inc.
22 Third Street
San Francisco, California 94103   (415) 362-3283

See HOLMES BOOK COMPANY, INC., Oakland, California.

123
Hooked on Books/The Rare Book Room
1366 North Main Street
Walnut Creek, California 94596   (415) 933-1025

Hooked on Books is the only used bookstore in Walnut Creek and specializes in fine books and prints. The Rare Book Room, located at the rear, features used books and records. The shops occupy 3,000 square feet of space.

How to Get There: Take Highway 680 to Main Street.
Owner/Biography: Rosemary McVey and Mari Cyphers.
Year Founded/History of Bookstore: Hooked on Books was established in 1975; the Rare Book Room in 1982.
Number of Volumes: 60,000.
Types/Classifications: Hardbound, paperback, magazines, first editions, signed copies, press books.
General Subject Areas: General.
Mail/Telephone Orders; Credit Cards: Both. Cash with order including postage. Visa and Mastercard accepted.
Business Hours: Daily.
Parking Facilities: Business parking lot, public parking lot, street parking.
Special Features: Search service.
Catalogue: Published bi-annually.
Collections/Individual Items Purchased: Both.
Booksellers' Memberships: American Booksellers Association.

124
House of Books
1758 Gardenaire Lane
Anaheim, California 92804   (714) 778-6406

House of Books is an in-home business consisting of one bookroom/office. It deals exclusively in Scottish, Irish, and Welsh books and those related to these categories. The books are arranged on the shelves as follows: Borders, Clans, Tartans, Family History, Cookbooks, Highlands and Islands, Scotland - Historical Biography and Fiction, History and Military, etc. Ireland and Wales categories are each shelved in separate groups.

How to Get There: Call for directions.
Owner/Biography: Mrs. Marilyn L. Bennett.
Year Founded/History of Bookstore: 1971.
Number of Volumes: 400.
Types/Classifications: Hardbound, paperback, some maps.
General Subject Areas: Ireland, Scotland, Wales.
Mail/Telephone Orders; Credit Cards: Both. Telephone requests will be held 10 days. No credit cards.
Business Hours: By appointment.
Parking Facilities: Street parking.
Special Features: Search service for the specialized categories.
Catalogue: Published twice yearly.
Collections/Individual Items Purchased: Both, if in specialty.

125
Howard Karno Books
1703 Ocean Front Walk
Santa Monica, California 90401 (213) 458-1619

Howard Karno Books is located on the beach near the world famous Santa Monica Pier. The two-story house is stocked with South American folk art, prehispanic ceramics, and Latin Americana of most subject areas. There is an emphasis on the archaeology and art of prehispanic Meso-America, Contemporary Mexican Art, and Latin American Judaica.

How to Get There: Take the Santa Monica Freeway west to 4th Street off ramp in Santa Monica, south to Pico Boulevard, west to beach, turn right on Appian Way to Pacific Terrace; house is on corner of Pacific Terrace and Appian Way.

Owner/Biography: Howard L. Karno. Mr. Karno began his book business in 1973 specializing in Latin Americana. He has a Ph.D. in Latin American History from UCLA.

Year Founded/History of Bookstore: 1973. The name of the original business was Libros Latinos owned exclusively by Mr. Karno. In 1975 George Elmendorf and Howard Madden became partners and in 1977 Mr. Karno left to form Howard Karno Books.

Number of Volumes: 15,000.

Types/Classifications: Hardbound, paperback, magazines, broadsides, ephemera, out-of-print, some color plate books.

General Subject Areas: Latin Americana.

Specific Specialties: Latin America: History, Women, Literature, Dance, Theatre, Music, Judaica, Cinema, Travel, Art (Prehispanic and Contemporary), Manuscript Materials, Natural History, Genealogy, Mexican Americans, Biographical Dictionaries, Mexican Contemporary Art, Meso-American Archaeology and Art (Prehispanic).

Mail/Telephone Orders; Credit Cards: Both. No credit cards.

Business Hours: Daily 10:00 AM - 5:00 PM.

Parking Facilities: Parking lot nearby.

Special Features: Search service; appraisals; collection development.

Catalogue: Catalogue published.

Collections/Individual Items Purchased: Both.

Booksellers' Memberships: Antiquarian Booksellers Association of America.

126
Hungry Eye Books
219 East Florida Avenue
Hemet, California 92383 (714) 658-1412

This is a general trade store stocking an integrated supply of new and used books of lasting value. The shop occupies 1,200 square feet of space.

How to Get There: The store is located in the main business block of old downtown Hemet.

Owner/Biography: Anne and Bill Jennings with Helen and Steve Fairfield.

Year Founded/History of Bookstore: 1968.

Number of Volumes: 15,000.

Types/Classifications: Hardbound, paperback, magazines, first editions, out-of-print.

General Subject Areas: Automotive, Aviation, Biography, Californiana, Indians, Western Americana.

Mail/Telephone Orders; Credit Cards: Both. No credit cards.

Business Hours: Monday through Friday 9:00 AM - 5:15 PM; Saturday 9:00 AM - 4:00 PM.

Parking Facilities: Street parking.

Special Features: Publishing sideline (local history of the Hemet area).

Collections/Individual Items Purchased: Both.

Booksellers' Memberships: Antiquarian Booksellers Association of America, San Diego Booksellers Association.

127
J & J House Booksellers
5694 Bounty Street
San Diego, California 92120   (619) 265-1113

The bookstore is an antiquarian dealership in rare and scholarly books, located within the city limits of San Diego in the vicinity of San Diego State University. Four rooms of antiquarian books hold collections of voyages and travels, first editions, children's illustrated books, philosophy, the history of science, color plate books, and private press books. The business is open by appointment only and issues monthly lists of new arrivals of collector books in addition to four to six specialty catalogues each year. The shop contains 1,500 square feet of space.

How to Get There: The shop is just north of San Diego State University and can be reached by car by exiting Interstate 8 north on College Avenue (marked exit) to Lance Street (left) and to Bounty Street (right).

Owner/Biography: Jon and Joann House.

Year Founded/History of Bookstore: 1978.

Number of Volumes: 6,000.

Types/Classifications: Antiquarian hardbound and out-of-print books, autographs, antiquarian prints and graphics, first editions, fine bindings, limited editions, private press books, fine printing, color plate (including hand colored) books, signed editions, and view books.

General Subject Areas: American Literature, Ancient History, Book Arts, Bookbinding, British Literature, Children's Illustrated Books, Ethnology, Exploration, Illustrators, Natural History, Philosophy, Science, Science Fiction and Fantasy, Sporting, Travel, Typography, Voyages, Western Americana.

Specific Specialties: Private Presses, Printing, Book History, Art Nouveau, Pre-Raphaelites, Natural History Color Plates, Sporting Art, View Books, Land Expeditions, Sea Expeditions, Alaska, Polar, Oceania, Tibet, California, Southwest (U.S.), Mountaineering, North American Big Game Hunting, Darwin, Sporting Expeditions, Naturalists' Travels, Early Science, History of the Machine, Trades and Professions, History of Science, Philosophy of Science, Logical Foundations of Mathematics, Scientific Method, Philosophy of Logic and Mathematics, History of Philosophy, British Empiricism, Nietzsche, History of Medicine, Pre-Columbian Art, Ancient Southwest (U.S.) Archaelogy, American Indians, Egyptology, Peru, Mexico, Baja California, Mythology, Antiquity, Cowboy, Range and Cattle, Outlaws and Gunmen, Western (U.S.) Art.

Author Specialties: Charles S. Pierce, Friedrich Nietzsche, Mark Twain, William Faulkner, Bertrand Russell, John Steinbeck, Robinson Jeffers, H. P. Lovecraft, Clark Ashton Smith.

Mail/Telephone Orders; Credit Cards: Both; payment by check should accompany orders confirmed in writing by customers unknown to the bookstore; Visa, Mastercard.

Business Hours: Monday through Saturday 10:00 AM - 5:30 PM by appointment only.

Special Features: Antiquarian Prints.

Catalogue: Four to six specialty catalogues a year plus 12 monthly lists.

Collections/Individual Items Purchased: Both.

Booksellers' Memberships: San Diego Booksellers Association.

128
J. B. Muns, Fine Arts Books
1162 Shattuck Avenue
Berkeley, California 94707   (415) 525-2420

The bookstore is in the renovated basement of a residence. The room, 500 square feet, is in knotty pine; there is a fireplace and a view through the double doors of a garden. Visits are by appointment only.

How to Get There: Directions will be given by phone.

Owner/Biography: Joyce Muns, owner, worked in the Acquisitions Department of the University of Southern California Library and the Music Library.

Year Founded/History of Bookstore: In 1974 the bookstore was opened in Los Angeles, then moved to the San Francisco Bay Area, next for a year in Eugene, Oregon, and for the past seven years in Berkeley.

Number of Volumes: 1,500.

Types/Classifications: Music autographs, art catalogues, general out-of-print and used books in the arts; books, ephemera, photographs, furniture, drawings, and windows about and by Frank Lloyd Wright.

General Subject Areas: Architecture, Art, Music, Photography.

Specific Specialties: 20th Century specialties and scholarly books about Art; Frank Lloyd Wright.
Mail/Telephone Orders; Credit Cards: Both; no credit cards.
Business Hours: By appointment only.
Parking Facilities: Street.
Special Features: Search service.
Catalogue: Once a year plus lists as material is acquired.
Collections/Individual Items Purchased: Both.
Booksellers' Memberships: Antiquarian Booksellers Association of America.

129
J. S. Edgren
8214 Melrose Avenue
Los Angeles, California 90046 (213) 653-2665

The bookstore features scholarly material on the Orient, including paintings and calligraphy scrolls. The shop contains 1,200 square feet of space.
Owner/Biography: Soren Edgren.
Year Founded/History of Bookstore: The office and shop were originally opened in 1977 in Carmel, California, where cataloguing is still done (J.S. Edgren, P.O. Box 326, Carmel, CA 93921); the retail bookshop was opened in Los Angeles in March 1983.
Number of Volumes: 15,000.
Types/Classifications: Scholarly books, periodicals, out-of-print, rare books in any language.
General Subject Areas: Asian Cultures, China, Far East, Japan, Korea.
Specific Specialties: Art, Archaeology.
Mail/Telephone Orders; Credit Cards: Both; no credit cards.
Business Hours: Tuesday through Saturday 10:00 AM - 5:00 PM.
Parking Facilities: Street.
Catalogue: Published irregularly.
Collections/Individual Items Purchased: Both.
Booksellers' Memberships: Antiquarian Booksellers Association of America.
Miscellaneous: The bookstore sells original works, including painting and calligraphy of the Far East.

130
Jack London Bookstore
14300 Arnold Drive
P.O. Box 337
Glen Ellen, California 95442 (707) 996-2888

A general antiquarian bookstore featuring literature by and about Jack London. The bookstore contains 4,000 square feet of space.
Owner/Biography: Russ and Winnie Kingman.
Year Founded/History of Bookstore: 1971.
Number of Volumes: 12,000.
Types/Classifications: General hardbound antiquarian stock plus everything by or about Jack London; no paperbacks other than Jack London; first editions, fine bindings, out-of-print, association copies, press books, signed copies, presentation copies, limited editions, color plate books.
General Subject Areas: Alaska, California, Hawaii, Jack London, Turn-of-the-Century Western Authors, Western Americana.
Author Specialties: Jack London, George Sterling, Arnold Genthe, John Muir, Joaquin Miller.
Other Specialties: The shop will "buy any good book that befits a Northern California antiquarian bookstore."
Mail/Telephone Orders; Credit Cards: Both; Visa, Mastercard.
Business Hours: Daily 9:30 AM - 5:00 PM.
Parking Facilities: Ample space in the store's own lot.

Special Features: A Jack London Research Center is housed in the rear room of the bookstore.
Collections/Individual Items Purchased: Both.

131
Jeremy Norman & Co., Inc.
442 Post Street
San Francisco, California 94102   (415) 781-6402

The bookstore features rare books, manuscripts, autographs, and fine bindings in a shop area of 2,200 square feet.
How to Get There: The shop is located near Union Square in downtown San Francisco, on the second floor.
Owner/Biography: Jeremy M. Norman.
Year Founded/History of Bookstore: 1970.
Number of Volumes: 5,000.
Types/Classifications: Rare books, manuscripts, autographs, fine bindings.
General Subject Areas: Economics, History of Medicine, Natural History, Science, Technology, Travel.
Mail/Telephone Orders; Credit Cards: Both; Visa, Mastercard.
Business Hours: Monday through Friday 10:00 AM - 6:00 PM; Saturday by appointment.
Catalogue: Two or three times a year.
Collections/Individual Items Purchased: Both.
Booksellers' Memberships: Antiquarian Booksellers Association of America, both National and Northern California Chapters; International Association of Antiquarian Booksellers.

132
Jerrold G. Stanoff
Rare Oriental Book Co.
P.O. Box 1599
Aptos, California 95003   (408) 724-4911

This antiquarian bookman deals in rare items on Japan and China, Orientals in America, Japanese and Chinese Arts, Natural History, and Buddhism. Visits can be arranged by appointment only.
How to Get There: Directions will be given when making an appointment.
Owner/Biography: Jerrold G. Stanoff.
Types/Classifications: Rare, out-of-print, first editions, illustrated books.
General Subject Areas: Buddhism, China, Chinese Arts, Japan, Japanese Arts, Japanese Woodblock Printed Books/Maps/Prints, Korea, Missionaries in China and Japan, Orientals in America, Travels in the Far East Pre-1900.
Author Specialties: Lafcadio Hearn.
Mail/Telephone Orders; Credit Cards: Mail orders.
Business Hours: By appointment only.
Parking Facilities: Available.
Special Features: Search service, appraisals.
Catalogue: Catalogues published.
Collections/Individual Items Purchased: Both.
Booksellers' Memberships: Antiquarian Booksellers Association of America, International League of Antiquarian Booksellers.

133
Jim Hansen Books
3514 Highland Drive
Carlsbad, California 92008   (619) 729-3383

The bookstore operates out of the owner's home in coastal Carlsbad, California. Collectors may browse, by appointment only, through a houseful of 19th and 20th Century literary first editions and out-of-print non-fiction. The shop contains 2,000 square feet of space.

How to Get There: Carlsbad is on the north coast of San Diego County, 90 miles south of Los Angeles. If driving, one should take the Elm Avenue exit from Interstate 5, go east 2 blocks to Highland Drive, and south 4 blocks.

Owner/Biography: Jim Hansen.

Year Founded/History of Bookstore: 1978.

Number of Volumes: 15,000.

Types/Classifications: Hardbound, signed copies, paperback, magazines, ephemera, postcards, sheet music, first editions, out-of-print, press books, pamphlets.

General Subject Areas: Art, Books About Books, California, Children's Books, Detective, Illustrated Books, Juveniles, Magazine First Appearances, Modern American Literature, Mystery, Nineteenth Century Literature, Science Fiction and Fantasy, Southwest (U.S.), Travel.

Specific Specialties: San Diego City History, San Diego County History, Radical Literature, Proletarian Literature.

Author Specialties: Mary Austin, Richard Armour, John Steinbeck, Jack London, Upton Sinclair, Gertrude Atherton, Ernest Hemingway, D.H. Lawrence, John Gardner, Norman Mailer, Saul Bellow, Philip Roth, Tim O'Brien, California Authors.

Mail/Telephone Orders; Credit Cards: Both; no credit cards.

Business Hours: By appointment only.

Parking Facilities: Street.

Catalogue: Once a year.

Collections/Individual Items Purchased: Both.

Booksellers' Memberships: San Diego Booksellers Association.

Miscellaneous: Furnishes libraries with general stock books, scholarly, out-of-print, and rare books.

134
Joe Herweg, Bookseller
958 Fifth Avenue
San Diego, California 92101   (619) 233-0880

The bookstore consists of three floors of clean, well lighted front and premises.

Owner/Biography: Patricia Bosvay, Lani Marnane, Joe Herweg.

Year Founded/History of Bookstore: 1960.

Number of Volumes: 150,000.

Types/Classifications: Hardbound, fine bindings, first editions, out-of-print, association copies, press books, signed copies, presentation copies, limited editions, color plate books.

General Subject Areas: Aeronautics, Americana, Animals, Ballet, Biography, Birds, China, Cinema, Drama, European Countries, General Fiction, General Science, Great Britain, History, Japan, Juveniles, Latin America, Military, Music, Mysteries, Nautical, Science Fiction and Fantasy, Travel, United States, Westerns.

Mail/Telephone Orders; Credit Cards: Both; no credit cards.

Business Hours: Monday through Saturday 10:00 AM - 5:00 PM.

Parking Facilities: Street and public parking lot.

Special Features: Search service.

Collections/Individual Items Purchased: Both.

Booksellers' Memberships: San Diego Booksellers Association.

135
Joel L. Malter & Co. Inc.
No. 518
16661 Ventura Boulevard
Encino, California 91316   (213) 784-7772

In this unique bookstore the bookcases offering literature on ancient coins and archaeology are surrounded by display cases with such artifacts for sale. This combination of rare books with rare coins and archaeological collectibles makes this a most unusual gallery/bookstore. The shop contains 1,500 square feet of space.

How to Get There: Ventura Boulevard is just off the Ventura Freeway (U.S. 101), northwest of downtown Los Angeles. From U.S. 101 take the Balboa Boulevard offramp if coming from the west, or Hayvenhurst Avenue offramp if coming from the east; proceed south to Ventura Boulevard.

Owner/Biography: Joel L. Malter.

Year Founded/History of Bookstore: The business began in 1960 in the owner's home in Venice, California. It outgrew those quarters and moved into an office building in Santa Monica in the 1960's. In late 1967 quarters for the gallery were established in the present hi-rise in Encino.

Number of Volumes: 5,000.

Types/Classifications: Hardbound, prints; some unusual items with early printing such as cuneiform tablets, hieroglyphics; art books on archaeology and numismatics.

General Subject Areas: Archaeology, Art Books, Cuneiform, Hieroglyphics, Numismatics, Scrimshaw, Weights and Measures, Whaling.

Specific Specialties: Greek and Roman Numismatic Subjects, Seal Books, Whaling Prints, Antique Maps, Documents, Scientific Instruments, Antique Scales.

Mail/Telephone Orders; Credit Cards: Both; personal check with order; Visa, Mastercard.

Business Hours: Monday through Friday 9:00 AM - 5:00 PM; Saturday by appointment.

Parking Facilities: Street, public parking lot.

Special Features: Search service, art gallery featuring items from the ancient world.

Catalogue: Quarterly.

Collections/Individual Items Purchased: Both.

Booksellers' Memberships: Friends of UCLA Library Book Fairs.

136
John Cole's Book Shop
780 Prospect
La Jolla, California 92037 (619) 454-4766

This is a general, personal service bookstore. The stock is mostly new, but there are selected out-of-print books. The shop specializes in Art and Mexico.

Owner/Biography: Barbara T. Cole, owner, has been in the book business since 1932.

Year Founded/History of Bookstore: The bookstore was founded in 1946 and was in one location for 20 years; it has been at the present location for 17.

Number of Volumes: 50,000.

Types/Classifications: Hardbound, out-of-print, new.

General Subject Areas: Biography, Children's Books, Travel.

Specific Specialties: Art, Mexico, Baja California.

Mail/Telephone Orders; Credit Cards: Both; no credit cards.

Business Hours: Monday through Saturday 9:30 AM - 5:30 PM; closed Sunday.

Special Features: Search Service.

Collections/Individual Items Purchased: Both.

137
John Howell — Books
434 Post Street
San Francisco, California 94102 (415) 781-7795

The bookstore has been in operation since 1912, furnishing fine and rare books in all fields as well as manuscripts and fine art. Its third location, the present one, was occupied in 1924, and was designed to reflect "a gentleman's library set down on a city street." From medieval illuminated manuscripts to the fine printed books of the 20th Century, individual collectors and institutions have been provided the opportunity to acquire here the finest works available. Under the direction of the founder's son, Warren Howell, the company has achieved international recognition, specializing in a number of fields, among them Western Americana and Californiana, voyages and travels, cartography, English and American literature, science and medicine, natural history, fine printing, Bibles, photography, and fine prints and paintings of the West. The store contains 3,500 square feet of space.

How to Get There: The bookstore is located in the heart of downtown San Francisco, one half block west of Union Square.

Owner/Biography: Warren R. Howell, owner, joined his father in the bookstore in 1932 and took over its operation in 1950. Among the numerous important transactions in which Mr. Howell has been involved was the purchase at auction in 1979 of the Hack Atlas for $285,000. Only a few weeks earlier Mr. Howell had handled the sale of the most costly book ever sold, with the exception of the Gutenberg Bible, a set of Audubon's "Birds of America" for $435,000. In 1960 he purchased at auction in London the log and journal of Captain Cook's voyages in the Pacific Ocean from 1768 to 1775. These two volumes, comprising the only Cook log not in institutional hands, were bought for $148,000. Among the many associations of a literary or historical nature to which Mr. Howell has been elected to the presidency are the Antiquarian Booksellers Association of America, the Booksellers' Association of America, and the Book Club of California. He has served as Secretary and Trustee of the California Historical Society. Mr. Howell has written numerous articles and contributions to books.

Year Founded/History of Bookstore: The bookstore was founded in 1912 by John Howell, stating his intention to specialize in fine and rare books. The shop has moved twice since then, assuming its present location in 1924. Warren R. Howell, John Howell's son, became head of the firm in 1950.

Types/Classifications: Fine and rare books, manuscripts, autographs, fine prints and paintings, important maps and atlases, fine photography, color plate books, illustrated books, fine bindings, incunabula, manuscripts, autograph letters, paintings, prints, photography, press books, maps, atlases.

General Subject Areas: Alaska, American Literature, Americana, Bibles, Californiana, English Literature, Hawaii, Medicine, Mexico, Natural History, Pacific Northwest, San Francisco, Science, Spanish Southwest, Sporting Books, Travels, Voyages, Western Americana.

Specific Specialties: Christian Science, San Francisco, Ornithology, Mormonism, Books About Books, California Literature, Philippines, Currier & Ives, John James Audubon, English Sporting Prints, Western Paintings.

Author Specialties: Mark Twain, Jack London, John Steinbeck, Bret Harte, Ernest Hemingway, William Faulkner, Robinson Jeffers, Oscar Wilde, Robert Louis Stevenson, Frank Norris, Rudyard Kipling, Ambrose Bierce.

Mail/Telephone Orders; Credit Cards: Both; Visa, Mastercard.

Business Hours: Monday through Friday 10:00 AM - 4:30 PM; Saturday by appointment.

Special Features: Publishers of fine limited editions of Western Americana and Californiana, especially history and art; reference works.

Catalogue: The rare book catalogues being published by the bookstore quickly become collector items, being noted for their content and fine typographical design.

Collections/Individual Items Purchased: Both.

Booksellers' Memberships: Antiquarian Booksellers Association of America (National and Northern California Chapters), Manuscript Society, International League of Antiquarian Booksellers, Book Club of California.

138
John Makarewich, Books
P.O. Box 7032
Van Nuys, California 91409

This is a mail order only shop.

Owner/Biography: John Makarewich.

Year Founded/History of Bookstore: 1946.

Number of Volumes: 30,000.

Types/Classifications: Hardbound, paperback, magazines, first editions, fine bindings, out-of-print, association copies, press books, signed copies, presentation copies, limited editions, color plate books.

General Subject Areas: Adventure, Americana, Architecture, Art, Belles Lettres, Biography, Books About Books, California, Cinema, Dance, Drama, Essays, History, History of Medicine, History of Science, Homosexuality, Horror, Illustrators, Literature, Martial Arts, Memoirs, Mountaineering, Music, Nature, Pacifica, Parapsychology, Performing Arts, Philosophy, Photography, Physical Culture, Poetry, Psychology, Science, Science Fiction and Fantasy, Sea, Sexology, Ships, Sociology, Speculative Fiction, Spies, Suspense, Technology, Theater, Travels, Treasure Hunting, True Crime, Voyages, West (U.S.).

Specific Specialties: Twentieth Century First Editions of British and American Authors, Literary Criticism,

Visual Arts, Unarmed Oriental Self-Defense Systems, Reference.
Author Specialties: More than 200 American and British Author collections.
Mail/Telephone Orders; Credit Cards: Mail order only. No credit cards.
Business Hours: No business hours; mail order only.
Catalogue: Six to eight times a year.
Collections/Individual Items Purchased: Individual items only.

139
John R. Butterworth
724 West 11th Street
Claremont, California 91711   (714) 626-0763

The businees operates from extensive library holdings in a private residence, and is by appointment only.
How to Get There: To reach Claremont Village, leave the San Bernadino Freeway at the Indian Hill Exit, go north to 11th Street, turn left four blocks.
Owner/Biography: John R. Butterworth, owner, is retired from the United States Air Force and California State University.
Year Founded/History of Bookstore: Mr. Butterworth began issuing catalogues in 1977.
Number of Volumes: 1,500 First Editions.
Types/Classifications: Hardbound first editions in British and American fiction, in fine to mint condition; signed copies, association items.
General Subject Areas: General.
Author Specialties: Ernest Hemingway, Norman Mailer, John O'Hara, Gore Vidal, John Updike, Thomas Wolfe.
Mail/Telephone Orders; Credit Cards: Both. No credit cards.
Business Hours: By appointment only.
Catalogue: Two times a year.
Collections/Individual Items Purchased: Both.

140
John Roby
3703 Nassau Drive
San Diego, California 92115   (619) 583-4263

The shop is located in a private residence with a stock room, and features a mail order business. Visits are by appointment only.
How to Get There: Call for directions.
Owner/Biography: Frances B. Roby. John Roby is a retired aeronautical engineer/pilot, and has had a lifetime of involvement in aeronautics.
Year Founded/History of Bookstore: 1960.
Number of Volumes: 7,000.
Types/Classifications: Hardbound, paperback, out-of-print.
General Subject Areas: Aerospace, Nautical, Technical.
Specific Specialties: All aspects of the specialties can be found in most all languages.
Mail/Telephone Orders; Credit Cards: Both. Cash with order. No credit cards.
Business Hours: Monday through Saturday 9:00 AM - 6:00 PM.
Parking Facilities: Private.
Special Features: Search service.
Catalogue: Occasional supplements.
Collections/Individual Items Purchased: Both.

141
John Scopazzi, Fine & Rare Books - Antique Maps
278 Post Street
Suite 305
San Francisco, California 94108   (415) 362-5708

The bookstore is centrally located in the downtown area of San Francisco, across the street from the Hyatt House on Union Square. The owner describes his shop as "a world all its own, more reminiscent of a fine private library than a book shop." Here one will find books in many fields including illustrated books, livres d'artistes, private press, fine bindings, art books, and antique maps by famous cartographers; the latter are finely matted and displayed. The shop contains 1,200 square feet of space.

Owner/Biography: John Scopazzi, owner, is one of the oldest booksellers in San Francisco, and former manager of the once famous The Newbegin's Book Shop.

Year Founded/History of Bookstore: Opened in 1970 by Mr. Scopazzi, the shop was first located at 340 Post Street, San Francisco. It has been at its present address since 1973.

Number of Volumes: 2,000.

Types/Classifications: Hardbound, illustrated books, livres d'artistes, private press, fine bindings, art books, antique maps.

General Subject Areas: Art, General.

Mail/Telephone Orders; Credit Cards: Both. No credit cards.

Business Hours: Regular business hours; Saturday by appointment.

Catalogue: Irregularly.

Collections/Individual Items Purchased: Both.

Booksellers' Memberships: Antiquarian Booksellers Association of America.

142
John Slattery, Books & Prints
352 Stanford Avenue
Palo Alto, California 94306   (415) 323-9775

This is a mail order only bookstore. Its specialties include Baedeker Guides, Russia travel before 1917, 20th Century novels, detective, and humor. The shop contains 2,700 square feet of space.

Owner/Biography: John Slattery.

Year Founded/History of Bookstore: 1970.

Number of Volumes: 10,000.

Types/Classifications: Hardbound, prints, ephemera, out-of-print.

General Subject Areas: Detective, Humor, Russia (Pre-1917 Illustrated), Twentieth Century Fiction.

Specific Specialties: Baedeker Travel Guides.

Author Specialties: Karl Baedeker, Arthur Conan Doyle.

Mail/Telephone Orders; Credit Cards: Both. No credit cards.

Business Hours: Daily 8:00 AM - 8:00 PM.

Catalogue: Four times per year.

Collections/Individual Items Purchased: Both.

143
Johnson's
Country Antique Fair Mall, Space F-7
21546 Golden Triangle Road
Saugus, California 91350   (805) 254-1474

The bookstore offers a general line of collectible books and antiques. The books occupy approximately one-half of the space in the small shop. The stock is primarily books and magazines related to early radio, but also includes a general line of collectible books. The shop is located in a modern building which houses approximately 100 antique dealers.

How to Get There: Saugus is located a short distance north of Los Angeles and can be reached easily from

Interstate 5 by exiting one mile south of Magic Mountain. Drive east on Valencia Boulevard to Soledad Canyon Road, east to Golden Triangle Road, then a right turn into the parking lot.

Owner/Biography: Delton Lee and Margaret Johnson. Dr. Johnson is a teacher who has collected antique radios and literature about early radio over many years. The Johnsons share an interest in history, politics, philosophical religious thought, technology, and a broad range of topics. They are both licensed radio amateurs. These interests are reflected in the content of their stock.

Year Founded/History of Bookstore: Started in 1984, this is a new business, and according to the owners, the stock is growing rapidly.

Number of Volumes: 1,000.

Types/Classifications: Hardbound, paperback, magazines, old sheet music.

General Subject Areas: Early Radio, Technical.

Mail/Telephone Orders; Credit Cards: Neither mail nor telephone orders accepted. Visa, Mastercard.

Business Hours: Daily 10:00 AM - 5:00 PM; Friday 10:00 AM - 9:00 PM.

Collections/Individual Items Purchased: Both.

144
Joseph The Provider
903 State Street
Suite 201
Santa Barbara, California 93101   (805) 962-6862

Joseph The Provider offers fine first editions, limited editions, signed editions, presentation and association copies, letters, and manuscripts.

How to Get There: The business is located in downtown Santa Barbara.

Owner/Biography: Ralph B. Sipper.

Types/Classifications: Hardbound, first editions, limited editions, signed copies, presentation copies, association copies, letters, manuscripts.

General Subject Areas: Modern Literature.

Mail/Telephone Orders; Credit Cards: Mail orders.

Business Hours: Call for information.

Parking Facilities: Municipal parking lot (first 90 minutes free).

Catalogue: Published regularly.

Booksellers' Memberships: Antiquarian Booksellers Association of America.

145
Kenneth Karmiole, Bookseller, Inc.
2255 Westwood Boulevard
Los Angeles, California 90064   (213) 474-7305

Kenneth Karmiole carries out-of-print and rare books on all subjects and is particularly strong in pre-1800 antiquarian items on the history of printing, art, and travel.

How to Get There: The bookstore is located between Olympic and West Pico Boulevards on Westwood Boulevard.

Owner/Biography: Kenneth Karmiole.

Year Founded/History of Bookstore: 1976.

Number of Volumes: 15,000 (including warehouse).

Types/Classifications: Rare books and manuscripts, first editions, fine bindings, out-of-print, association copies, press books, signed copies, presentation copies, limited editions, color plate books.

General Subject Areas: Americana, Art, Fine Printing, Literature, Travel.

Mail/Telephone Orders; Credit Cards: Both. American Express, Visa, Mastercard accepted.

Business Hours: Monday through Saturday 10:00 AM - 5:00 PM.

Parking Facilities: Business parking lot, street parking.

Catalogue: Published monthly.

Collections/Individual Items Purchased: Both.

Booksellers' Memberships: Antiquarian Booksellers Association of America, American Library Association.

146
Kenneth Starosciak
117 Wilmot
San Francisco, California 94115   (415) 346-0650

Located in a private residence, Kenneth Starosciak specializes in the Arts and has over 7,000 out-of-print items available. Visits can be arranged by appointment.
How to Get There: Directions will be provided when making an appointment.
Owner/Biography: Kenneth Starosciak.
Year Founded/History of Bookstore: 1974.
Number of Volumes: 7,000.
Types/Classifications: Art books, catalogues of exhibitions, first editions, rare, out-of-print.
General Subject Areas: American Studies, Antiques, Architecture, Art, Books About Books, Oriental Rugs, Photography, Textiles and Weaving.
Specific Specialties: American Art, 19th Century American Painting.
Author Specialties: Frank Lloyd Wright.
Mail/Telephone Orders; Credit Cards: Both. No credit cards.
Business Hours: Daily by appointment.
Parking Facilities: Street parking.
Catalogue: Published 3 to 4 times per year.
Collections/Individual Items Purchased: Both.
Booksellers' Memberships: Antiquarian Booksellers Association of America.

147
Kestrel Books
1 West Carmel Valley Road
Carmel Valley, California   (408) 659-4534

Kestrel Books feature rare and out-of-print books with a specialty in Western Americana.
How to Get There: The business is located in Carmel Valley, a small community located on the Carmel River, 15 miles southeast of the Carmel and Monterey coastal cities. The stock occupies 950 square feet of space.
Owner/Biography: Michael E. Clark.
Year Founded/History of Bookstore: 1976.
Number of Volumes: 9,000.
Types/Classifications: Hardbound, rare, old, out-of-print, press books, fine printing.
General Subject Areas: Western Americana.
Mail/Telephone Orders; Credit Cards: Both.
Business Hours: Call for information.
Parking Facilities: Available.
Special Features: Appraisals; search service.
Catalogue: Published 3 times per year.
Collections/Individual Items Purchased: Both.

148
Krown & Spellman, Booksellers
2283 (Rear) Westwood Boulevard
Los Angeles, California 90064 (213) 474-1745

Krown & Spellman, Booksellers specializes in books on classical antiquity, the Middle Ages, and the Renaissance. It has old, rare, out-of-print, and some new material. All aspects from Philosophy to Theology are covered with both manuscripts and printed books available. Some prints, maps, old documents, and artifacts are also for sale.
How to Get There: Turn west on Tennessee Avenue from Westwood Boulevard and then north up the alley.
Owner/Biography: Elizabeth Krown Spellman and Franklin V. Spellman.
Year Founded/History of Bookstore: 1977.
Number of Volumes: 10,000.
Types/Classifications: Hardbound, out-of-print, manuscripts, prints, old documents.
General Subject Areas: Ancient Egypt, Ancient Greece, Ancient Rome, Middle Ages, Renaissance.
Mail/Telephone Orders; Credit Cards: Both. Visa and Mastercard accepted.
Business Hours: Tuesday through Friday 1:00 PM - 5:00 PM; Saturday 10:00 AM - 5:00 PM.
Parking Facilities: Street parking.
Catalogue: Published 2 times per year.
Collections/Individual Items Purchased: Both.
Booksellers' Memberships: Westwood Bookdealers Association.

149
Lake Law Books
142 McAllister Street
San Francisco, California 94102 (415) 863-2900

The bookstore was established over 50 years ago and is still owned and operated by the Lake family. Specializing in law-related books and sets, the shop is virtually one of a kind. Although the primary focus in the store is on material for law students and attorneys, many new and used books have been added which relate to legal history, biography, and current trends in the law. It contains 2,000 square feet of space.
How to Get There: The shop is located in the Civic Center area of San Francisco, next door to Hastings College of the Law.
Owner/Biography: Lawrence Lake.
Year Founded/History of Bookstore: Founded in the 1920's by the Lake family, the bookstore is still owned by them.
Number of Volumes: 50,000.
Types/Classifications: Hardbound, paperback, new and used law books and sets.
General Subject Areas: How-To (Legal), Law Biography, Law History.
Mail/Telephone Orders; Credit Cards: Both; Visa, Mastercard.
Business Hours: Monday through Friday 9:00 AM - 5:30 PM; Saturday 10:00 AM - 5:00 PM.
Parking Facilities: Street, and parking lot one block away.
Special Features: Appraisals of law libraries.
Collections/Individual Items Purchased: Both.

150
Laurence & Geraldine McGilvery
P.O. Box 852
La Jolla, California 92038 (619) 454-4443

This shop operates by appointment only, from an upstairs office in the center of La Jolla, California. The stock of art books, art exhibition catalogues, and art periodicals is crammed into floor-to-ceiling shelves in four rooms, with a total of 1,250 square feet of space in addition to storage.

How to Get There: Visitors are welcome, but they must call for an appointment. The telephone number listed above rings at both the office and the McGilvery's home. The shop is easily reached by car or public transportation from San Diego or Los Angeles. La Jolla is about 20 minutes by car from downtown San Diego and 2 hours from Los Angeles.

Owner/Biography: Laurence and Geraldine Malloy McGilvery. Laurence was born and raised in Los Angeles and was an engineer for six years. He has beeen a book dealer since 1960. He is also an editor of and contributor to several reference works in the fields of art and literature.

Year Founded/History of Bookstore: The business was founded in 1960; the McGilverys originally entered the book business as owners of the Nexus Book Shop in La Jolla, specializing in paperbacks, and art gallery, and occasional readings and lectures. The store operated until 1964, when the owners began dealing in antiquarian art books; they have been doing so now exclusively since 1967.

Number of Volumes: 1,000 out-of-print art books; 10,000 exhibition catalogues; 75,000 art periodicals.

Types/Classifications: Hardbound, catalogues, ephemera, and periodicals in all languages, out-of-print art books, books with original prints, portfolios, facsimiles, catalogues raisonees, exhibition catalogues.

General Subject Areas: American Art, Architecture, Art, Art Collecting, Art Collectors, Art Ephemera, Art Exhibition, Art Periodicals, Art Reference, Artists' Monographs, Contemporary Art, Fine Arts, Galleries, Little Magazines, Modern Art, Museums, Oriental Art, Photography, Prints.

Other Specialties: Art Works in Foreign Languages, particularly French and German.

Mail/Telephone Orders; Credit Cards: Both; cash with order in most instances, but institutions will be billed; pro forma invoices will be sent when necessary; no credit cards.

Business Hours: Usually weekdays 11:00 AM - 5:00 PM, but appointments must be made first; visitors can be accommodated evenings and weekends.

Parking Facilities: Nearby street parking and public lots.

Special Features: The shop publishes several reference books in art and literature, and has more in progress; it will fill in missing issues of art periodicals; there is no search service for books.

Catalogue: Catalogue published irregularly.

Collections/Individual Items Purchased: Both.

Booksellers' Memberships: Both National and Southern California Chapters of the Antiquarian Booksellers Association of America, San Diego Booksellers Association (currently President).

151

Larry Edmunds Cinema and Theatre Book Shop, Inc.
6658 Hollywood Boulevard
Los Angeles, California 90028   (213) 463-3273

This book shop deals in theatre and film books exclusively. It is located appropriately in Hollywood.

How to Get There: Watch for the Capitol Records tower off the Hollywood Freeway—that's Hollywood.

Owner/Biography: G. Luboviski, President.

Year Founded/History of Bookstore: 1948.

Number of Volumes: 40,000.

Types/Classifications: Hardbound, old and rare, out-of-print, paperback, remainders, autographs, theatre lobby cards, movie magazines, stills.

General Subject Areas: Motion Pictures, Television, Theatre.

Mail/Telephone Orders; Credit Cards: Both.

Business Hours: Monday through Saturday 10:00 AM - 6:00 PM.

Parking Facilities: Street parking; commercial parking lots.

Special Features: Plays, both old and new.

Collections/Individual Items Purchased: Both.

152
Lemon Grove Bookstore
7905 Broadway
Lemon Grove, California 92045   (619) 463-2503

The bookstore carries most all subjects, and specializes in literature, both contemporary and older, and Americana.

How to Get There: Lemon Grove is northeast of San Diego. Take the Lemon Grove Avenue turnoff from Highway 94. The bookstore is in the heart of Lemon Grove.
Owner/Biography: Bill Burgett.
Year Founded/History of Bookstore: 1980.
Number of Volumes: 100,000.
Types/Classifications: Hardbound, paperback, magazines, first editions, out-of-print, signed copies.
General Subject Areas: Americana, Biography, British History, Children's Books, General, Science Fiction and Fantasy.
Mail/Telephone Orders; Credit Cards: Both; Visa.
Business Hours: Monday through Friday 11:00 AM - 6:00 PM; Saturday 10:00 AM - 5:00 PM; closed Sunday.
Parking Facilities: Business parking lot.
Collections/Individual Items Purchased: Both.
Booksellers' Memberships: San Diego Booksellers Asssociation.

153
Libra Books
18563 Sherman Way
Reseda, California 91335   (818) 344-5400

This bookstore stocks a small but varied inventory, specializing in contemporary fiction, but with interesting and often unusual finds in literature, literary criticism, drama, and film. It has a large selection of paperbacks, with an especially strong science fiction and fantasy section, all priced below market. The shop contains 1,200 square feet of space.

How to Get There: The shop is located on Sherman Way in Reseda, California, 1.5 blocks west of Reseda Boulevard.
Owner/Biography: Leo Frumkin.
Year Founded/History of Bookstore: The store was opened in 1972 on Coldwater Canyon near Victory Boulevard in North Hollywood, California. It was moved to its present location in 1975.
Number of Volumes: 10,000 hardbound, 20,000 paperback.
Types/Classifications: Hardbound, paperback, used, out-of-print.
General Subject Areas: Biography, Cinema, Drama, Fiction, General, Literary Criticism, Literature, Science Fiction and Fantasy.
Specific Specialties: Large selection of Science Fiction and Fantasy paperbacks.
Mail/Telephone Orders; Credit Cards: Both; personal check with order; no credit cards.
Business Hours: Tuesday through Saturday 10:00 AM - 6:00 PM.
Parking Facilities: Business lot, public parking one block away, metered street parking.
Special Features: Search service.
Collections/Individual Items Purchased: Both.
Miscellaneous: The bookstore features friendly, courteous, personal service, all at lowest possible prices.

154
Logos
1117 Pacific Avenue
Santa Cruz, California 95060   (408) 426-2106

The bookstore is probably the largest and longest-established used bookstore in Santa Cruz County. It has a full range of hardbound and paperback books including out-of-print and antiquarian items. The best books

are kept in a separate room open only Friday through Monday. The shop contains 3,000 square feet of space.
How to Get There: Santa Cruz is most easily accessible from San Francisco and San Jose via Highway 17.
Owner/Biography: John Livingston.
Year Founded/History of Bookstore: 1969.
Number of Volumes: 25,000.
Types/Classifications: Hardbound, paperback, out-of-print, antiquarian.
General Subject Areas: General.
Mail/Telephone Orders; Credit Cards: Mail and telephone orders not accepted; Visa, Mastercard.
Business Hours: Daily 10:00 AM - 10:00 PM.
Parking Facilities: Free public lot and metered street parking.
Collections/Individual Items Purchased: Both.
Booksellers' Memberships: Central California Antiquarian Booksellers.

155
Lorson's Books & Prints
Suite A-9
305 North Harbor Boulevard
Fullerton, California 92632   (714) 526-2523

The bookstore features a select stock of general antiquarian material; it contains 1,000 square feet of space.
Owner/Biography: James E. and Joan Lorson.
Year Founded/History of Bookstore: 1977.
Number of Volumes: 7,000.
Types/Classifications: All general types and classifications.
General Subject Areas: General.
Specific Specialties: Miniature books under 3 inches.
Mail/Telephone Orders; Credit Cards: Both; the store ships and invoices; Visa, Mastercard.
Business Hours: Monday through Saturday 10:00 AM - 5:30 PM.
Parking Facilities: Free parking at back of business complex.
Catalogue: Ten times a year.
Collections/Individual Items Purchased: Both.

156
Louis Collins Books
2nd Floor
1083 Mission Street
San Francisco, California 94103   (415) 431-5134

The bookstore consists of a large loft of 3,000 square feet of space with shelving along the walls. The stock of 10,000 volumes of out-of-print scholarly books is predominantly anthropology and the social sciences, but with select fine books in all fields.
How to Get There: The shop is located at Seventh and Missions Streets in downtown San Francisco.
Owner/Biography: Louis Collins.
Year Founded/History of Bookstore: Founded in 1969, the business has had three various mail order locations.
Number of Volumes: 10,000.
Types/Classifications: Hardbound, broadsides, ephemera, first editions, out-of-print, presentation copies, scholarly.
General Subject Areas: General.
Specific Specialties: Anthropology (Africa, Asia, North America, South America), American Indian Studies, Extrasensory Perception (ESP), Bohemian American Literature (first editions of writers central to America's Bohemians, such as Greenwich Village, Carmel, Chicago Renaissance).
Mail/Telephone Orders; Credit Cards: Both; no credit cards.
Business Hours: By appointment only.

Special Features: Search service.
Catalogue: Quarterly.
Collections/Individual Items Purchased: Both.
Booksellers' Memberships: Antiquarian Booksellers Association of America.

157
Maelstrom
572 Valencia Street
San Francisco, California 94110   (415) 863-9933

This is a general bookstore, serving readers as well as collectors with a preference for unusual items in all fields. The stock is carefully selected and attractively arranged. The store is spacious, well lit, and uncluttered. Comfortable seating areas are provided for reading or discussions. Soft music eliminates street noises. Fresh coffee is available by the mug. On request, customers will gladly be assisted, otherwise browsers won't be disturbed. The shop contains 1,300 square feet of space.

How to Get There: The bookstore is located between 16th and 17th Streets in the Northern Mission area of San Francisco, southwest of downtown, where Valencia runs parallel to Mission Street. It is easily reached by bus or car from nearby downtown and all major thoroughfares. Call for directions.

Owner/Biography: Christine Bogosian, owner, was born in Germany in 1952 and came to California in 1974. She gave up her studies and job when the unexpected opportunity presented itself to open and operate a used bookstore in San Francisco.

Year Founded/History of Bookstore: Founded in 1979, the bookstore is still in the same location and has the same owner; the original stock, purchased from another bookstore, has been continuously expanded and upgraded.

Number of Volumes: 12,000.

Types/Classifications: Hardbound, paperback, old magazines, notecards, review copies, limited editions, out-of-print, illustrated books, color plate books, first editions, press books, rare.

General Subject Areas: Africa, Americana, Anthologies, Anthropology, Archaeology, Architecture, Art, Asia, Astrology, Astronomy, Biography, Black Studies, California, Capitalism, Children's Illustrated Books, Cinema, Classical Music, Cookbooks, Crime, Criticism, Drama, Drugs, Eastern Religion, Ecology, Education, European History, Fiction, Foreign Language Instruction, Games, Geology, Health, Home Improvement, Humor, Language, Mathematics, Medicine, Mysteries, Mysticism, Nature, Naval, Near East, Nutrition, Occult, Oceania, Philosophy, Photography, Poetry, Psychology, Railroads, Reference, Religions, Rock and Roll, San Francisco, Science Fiction and Fantasy, Sex, Socialism, Sociology, South America, Sports, Technical Books, The Sixties, Travel, War, Women.

Other Specialties: Books in German and French, European Authors in English Translation.

Mail/Telephone Orders; Credit Cards: Both; cash with order; no credit cards.

Business Hours: Monday through Saturday 11:00 AM - 6:00 PM.

Parking Facilities: Two-hour free parking on 17th Street, meters on Valencia; usually no problem.

Special Features: Search service; wall space available for monthly-changed exhibits of local artists' recent works, including paintings, drawings, collages, and photographs; coffee available.

Collections/Individual Items Purchased: Both.

158
Magazine
839 Larkin Street
San Francisco, California 94109   (415) 441-7737

This is a shop specializing in back-dated magazines, ephemera, posters, prints, and paper collectibles. In addition to the more recent titles in magazines, there is an extensive stock of popular periodicals dating from 1850 to 1950. Also stocked is a large selection of men's magazines and erotica, both old and new. The staff is knowledgeable and helpful, and the shop is always neat and well organized in an area of 1,000 square feet.

How to Get There: The shop is conveniently located in central San Francisco on Larkin Street just off Geary.

Owner/Biography: Trent R. Dunphy.

Year Founded/History of Bookstore: Founded in 1973, the shop has remained in the same location with the same staff.

Number of Volumes: One-half million magazines; no books.

Types/Classifications: Magazines, broadsides, ephemera.

Mail/Telephone Orders; Credit Cards: Both; mail order inquiries should specify titles and dates and must include a self addressed stamped envelope. Each order has a $11.50 minimum ($10 purchase and $1.50 shipping charge).

Business Hours: Monday through Saturday 12:00 Noon - 7:00 PM; closed Sunday.

Parking Facilities: Street, and public garage within 1 block.

Collections/Individual Items Purchased: Both.

159
Manning's Books
1255 Post Number 625
San Francisco, California 94109   (415) 621-3565

This is a general bookstore.

How to Get There: The shop is located in the Market - Castro area of San Francisco.

Owner/Biography: Kathleen Manning.

Year Founded/History of Bookstore: 1970.

Types/Classifications: Hardbound, ephemera, fine bindings, color plate books.

General Subject Areas: Americana, Exploration, Travel.

Mail/Telephone Orders; Credit Cards: Both; no credit cards.

Business Hours: Monday through Saturday 9:00 AM - 5:00 PM.

Parking Facilities: Street.

Collections/Individual Items Purchased: Both.

Booksellers' Memberships: Antiquarian Booksellers Association of America including Northern California Chapter.

160
Marian L. Gore, Bookseller
Box 433
San Gabriel, California 91778   (818) 287-2946

Marian L. Gore is a catalogue dealer primarily, but she also does book fairs in California. The large international book fairs are of special interest to her and she does two of those, one each year alternating between San Francisco and Los Angeles. She is highly specialized, dealing in books and ephemera relative to food and drink. This specialty includes wine, beverages, cookbooks, menus, inns, and hotels.

How to Get There: Ms. Gore does not have a bookstore as such, but she will make appointments with collectors and all interested parties. For those wishing to see the collection, call Ms. Gore for directions.

Owner/Biography: Marian L. Gore.

Year Founded/History of Bookstore: 1967. Ms. Gore has been the owner from the beginning with no partners and the location has been the same since the inception.

Number of Volumes: 4,000 books plus menus and various ephemera.

Types/Classifications: Hardbound, some paperback, ephemera.

General Subject Areas: Food and Drink.

Specific Specialties: Wine, Beverages, Cookbooks, Menus, Inns, Hotels.

Author Specialties: Writers on Food and Drink, such as M.F.K. Fisher; a variety of chefs (both contemporary and historical); chefs of vast fame such as the Frenchman Careme and others more contemporary, i.e. Pellaprat, Oliver, Elizabeth David, etc.

Other Specialties: Books in French, Italian, and a few German, within the specialty of Food and Drink.

Mail/Telephone Orders; Credit Cards: Both. No credit cards.

Business Hours: Variable; call for appointment.

Catalogue: Lists or Catalogues published 2 times per year.

Collections/Individual Items Purchased: Both.
Booksellers' Memberships: Antiquarian Booksellers Association of America, International League of Antiquarian Booksellers.

161
Maurice F. Neville Rare Books
835 Laguna Street
Santa Barbara, California 93101 (805) 963-1908

This bookseller deals in 19th and 20th Century literature and mystery and detective fiction. The shop occupies 2,800 square feet of space.
Owner/Biography: Maurice F. Neville.
Year Founded/History of Bookstore: 1977.
Number of Volumes: 15,000.
Types/Classifications: First editions, inscribed books, autograph letters, and manuscripts.
General Subject Areas: Detective Fiction, Mysteries, Nineteenth Century Literature, Twentieth Century Literature.
Mail/Telephone Orders; Credit Cards: Both. Visa and Mastercard accepted.
Business Hours: Monday through Friday 9:30 AM - 5:30 PM; Saturday 10:00 AM - 2:00 PM.
Parking Facilities: Business parking lot.
Catalogue: Catalogue published.
Collections/Individual Items Purchased: Both.
Booksellers' Memberships: Antiquarian Booksellers Association of America.

162
Maxwell's Bookmark
2103 Pacific Avenue
Stockton, California 95204 (209) 466-0194

A long tradition of selling quality books is now combined with the added dimension of offering antiquarian books. In both new and old books the emphasis is on quality cloth bound books and an active interest in customer service and satisfaction. The bookstore contains 1,800 square feet of space.
How to Get There: The driver should take Interstate 5 north to the Pershing offramp, Pershing north to Harding, Harding east to Pacific, north on Pacific 6 blocks; the shop is on the corner of Pacific and Dorris.
Owner/Biography: William and Wendi Maxwell. William graduated from the University of California at Santa Cruz (UCSC) and went immediately into the book business as manager of a used bookstore. After four years he opened his own shop which he closed in 1981 to take the Bookmark location. Wendi graduated from Raymond College and is employed full time as the Training Director at the Stockton Developmental Center.
Year Founded/History of Bookstore: The bookstore was founded in 1939 and has continued in the same location. It was sold in 1971 to an employee who in turn sold it to the current owners in 1981.
Number of Volumes: 10,000.
Types/Classifications: Hardbound, paperback, ephemera, first editions, press books, general antiquarian.
General Subject Areas: Children's Books, Cookbooks, Golf, Western Americana, Wine.
Specific Specialties: California, Central Valley (California).
Author Specialties: Robinson Jeffers, Roald Dahl, Kurt Vonnegut, Walter Miller, Joan Didion.
Mail/Telephone Orders; Credit Cards: Both; Visa, Mastercard.
Business Hours: Monday through Saturday 9:30 AM - 6:00 PM.
Parking Facilities: Street, and private lot in the rear.
Special Features: Search service, keepsakes.
Catalogue: Annually.
Collections/Individual Items Purchased: Both.

163
Merlin's Bookshop
6543 Pardall Road
Isla Vista, California 93117 (805) 968-7946

The bookstore is located adjacent to the University of California at Santa Barbara and specializes in science fiction and fantasy with a stock of more than 1,800 first editions, 2,000 non-first hardbound, and 2,000 paperbacks. Its second specialty is higher mathematics with a stock exceeding 750 titles. General literature is also stocked. The shop contains 850 square feet of space.

How to Get There: Isla Vista is located 10 miles north of Santa Barbara and may be reached by taking the Los Carneros offramp from Highway 101. Proceed south toward the ocean on Los Carneros to El Collegio, left to Embarcadero Del Mar, right to Pardall Road.

Owner/Biography: Merlin D. and Flora G. Schwegman. Merlin Schwegman spent nearly 30 years as an industrial engineer prior to opening the bookstore in 1975.

Year Founded/History of Bookstore: 1975.

Number of Volumes: 20,000.

Types/Classifications: Hardbound, paperback, first editions (primarily of science fiction and fantasy).

General Subject Areas: American Indians, Anthropology, Art, Aviation, Biography, Biology, Black Studies, Children's Books, Cinema, Comics, Cookbooks, Crafts, Drama, Engineering, Fiction, Genetics, Health, History, Humor, Literature, Mathematics, Music, Mystery, Natural Science, Nautical, Nutrition, Occult, Philosophy, Physics, Poetry, Political Science, Psychology, Religion, Science Fiction and Fantasy, Sociology, Sports, Western Americana, Women's Studies.

Specific Specialties: Thomas Paine, Heritage Press Books, First Editions of Science Fiction and Fantasy, Higher Mathematics.

Author Specialties: Thomas Paine.

Mail/Telephone Orders; Credit Cards: Both; cash in advance; no credit cards.

Business Hours: Monday 1:00 PM - 6:00 PM; Tuesday through Saturday 12:00 Noon - 7:00 PM.

Parking Facilities: Street.

Special Features: Search service, building collections, binding, repair service, gold stamping.

Catalogue: Once or twice a year.

Collections/Individual Items Purchased: Both.

164
Meyer Boswell Books
982 Hayes Street
San Francisco, California 94117 (415) 346-1839

This is perhaps the only bookstore in North America specializing exclusively in rare and scholarly law. Its stock of some 4,000 volumes contains works from the 14th to the 20th Centuries, primarily pertaining to English and American law, but with significant works about other law as well. The store contains 600 square feet of space.

How to Get There: The bookstore is close to the downtown area of San Francisco, near the Civic Center. The No. 21 bus line runs on Hayes Street.

Owner/Biography: Jordan D. Luttrell is the founder and sole owner of the bookstore. He is a graduate of the University of Michigan Law School, where he was on the Law Review, and is a member of the California Bar and various legal history societies including the Selden Society and the American Society for Legal History.

Year Founded/History of Bookstore: Founded in 1976 by Jordan D. Luttrell, the bookstore has always been in the same location.

Number of Volumes: 4,000.

Types/Classifications: Hardbound, antiquarian, out-of-print, new, manuscripts, autograph letters, documents, prints, rare, scholarly, first editions, presentation copies, association copies, limited editions.

General Subject Areas: American Law, Constitutional History, Early Law of All Nations and Areas, English Law, Law, Legal History.

Specific Specialties: Pre-1600 English Law, Pre-1800 English Law, Pre-1800 American Law, Scholarly Law from university presses, United States Supreme Court, Famous Judges and Lawyers, Trials, Collected Editions of the works of lawyers and judges, Legal Autographs, Manuscripts, Documents, Prints. Blackstone's Commentaries on the Laws of England.

Author Specialties: Sir William Blackstone, James Kent, Joseph Story, Oliver Wendell Holmes, Jr., William O. Douglas, Sir Edward Coke, Clarence Darrow, Henry Bracton, Ranulf Glanville, Sir Thomas Littleton, Christopher St. Germain.

Mail/Telephone Orders; Credit Cards: Both; the shop may ask for payment in advance, at their discretion; Visa, Mastercard.

Business Hours: Monday through Friday 9:00 AM - 4:00 PM, and by appointment.

Parking Facilities: Easy street parking.

Catalogue: Twice a year plus occasional lists.

Collections/Individual Items Purchased: Both.

Booksellers' Memberships: Antiquarian Booksellers Association of America, International League of Booksellers.

165
Michael R. Thompson Rare Books
8320 Melrose Avenue
Los Angeles, California 90069 (213) 852-0252

Fine, antiquarian, scholarly books, primarily in the humanities; the bookshop contains 11,000 square feet of space.

Owner/Biography: Michael R. Thompson.

Year Founded/History of Bookstore: 1972.

Number of Volumes: 10,000.

Types/Classifications: Hardbound, first editions, out-of-print, association copies, signed copies, presentation copies.

General Subject Areas: American History, Anthropology, British History, Continental History, Economics, History of Science, Literary Biography, Literary Criticism, Mathematics, Military History, Political Science, Psychology, Sociology, Western Philosophy.

Author Specialties: Bertrand Russell.

Other Specialties: Scholarly works, foreign language titles.

Mail/Telephone Orders; Credit Cards: Mail orders. Visa and Mastercard accepted.

Business Hours: Monday through Saturday 10:00 AM - 6:00 PM.

Parking Facilities: Business parking lot, street.

Collections/Individual Items Purchased: Both.

166
Milton Hammer Books
125 El Paseo
Santa Barbara, California 93101 (805) 965-8901

The bookstore is located in historic El Paseo, the hub of downtown Santa Barbara, in a studio on the old balcony overlooking the Central Court and the beautiful Outdoor Cafe. Only antiquarian books are in stock, principally collectors' types; most are rare. All fields are covered. The ambiance is antique. The shop contains 500 square feet of space.

How to Get There: Ask for "El Paseo," which has three different entrances: State Street, De La Guerra Street, and Anacapa Street; they all lead to the Center Court (El Paseo Outdoor Cafe). The shop is one flight up, on the balcony.

Owner/Biography: Milton and Jessica Hammer.

Year Founded/History of Bookstore: Founded in 1969 on Anacapa Street, the bookstore was an antiquarian and used book shop. Three years ago it was moved to its present location and changed to dealing in rare books only.

Number of Volumes: 1,500.

Types/Classifications: Antiquarian rare books, maps, prints, autographs, letters, first editions, out-of-print, association copies, press books, signed copies, limited editions, presentation copies, color plate and illustrated books.

General Subject Areas: Americana, Art, California, Literature, Natural History, Travel.
Mail/Telephone Orders; Credit Cards: Both; cash with order; no credit cards.
Business Hours: Saturday 10:00 AM - 4:00 PM; other times by appointment.
Parking Facilities: Public parking on Canon Perdido Street; private parking with validation.
Catalogue: Twice a year.
Collections/Individual Items Purchased: Both.
Booksellers' Memberships: Antiquarian Booksellers Association of America.

167
Mitchell Books
1395 East Washington Boulevard
Pasadena, California 91104 (213) 798-4438

The bookstore is a family owned business which reaches out to the collector and to those who wish to find a good reading copy. The shop contains 1,300 square feet of space.

How to Get There: The shop is located near the corner of Hill and Washington.

Owner/Biography: John and Janet Mitchell. John started as a personal collector of American literature while Janet collected mystery fiction. During their six years of collecting they found pleasure in helping others build collections. This pleasure brought about the opening of the present bookstore.

Year Founded/History of Bookstore: The Mitchells started in 1978 by dealing by appointment from their home, then to a small shop (half the size of the present one), and from there to the current location.

Number of Volumes: 10,000.

Types/Classifications: Hardbound, first editions, limited editions, signed copies.

General Subject Areas: American History, Biography, California, Children's Books, Humor, Literature, Mystery Fiction, Plays, World War II.

Specific Specialties: Detective Fiction, Modern First Editions, John Steinbeck, Southern California History.

Author Specialties: John Steinbeck, Agatha Christie, Erle Stanley Gardner, Ernest Hemingway, S.S. Van Dine.

Mail/Telephone Orders; Credit Cards: Both; mail orders must be from the catalogue; no credit cards.

Business Hours: Tuesday through Saturday 11:00 AM - 6:00 PM.

Parking Facilities: Business parking lot at the end of the building.

Special Features: Search service.

Catalogue: One or twice a year.

Collections/Individual Items Purchased: Both.

Booksellers' Memberships: Pasadena Bookdealers Association.

168
Moe's Books
2476 Telegraph Avenue
Berkeley, California 94704 (415) 849-2087

Comprising four floors and nearly 15,000 square feet of space, the bookstore is one of the largest bookshops west of the Mississippi. Though primarily a used shop, it deals in everything from remainders to rare books. A Berkeley institution for 24 years, Moe's proudly states that it is generally regarded as one of the great bookshops in the United States.

Owner/Biography: Morris Moskowitz.

Year Founded/History of Bookstore: 1959.

Number of Volumes: 200,000.

Types/Classifications: Hardbound, paperbacks, first editions, out-of-print, limited editions.

General Subject Areas: Architecture, Art, General, Photography.

Specific Specialties: Rare and out-of-print Art, Architecture, and Photography books.

Mail/Telephone Orders; Credit Cards: Both; Visa, Mastercard.

Business Hours: Daily 10:00 AM - 11:00 PM; Friday and Saturday until Midnight.

Parking Facilities: Public parking, validated.

Special Features: Search service.
Catalogue: Published irregularly.
Collections/Individual Items Purchased: Both.

169
Mt. Eden Books & Bindery
2315 Bermuda Lane
Hayward, California 94545 (415) 782-7723

Mt. Eden Books and Bindery is primarily a mail order bookstore. People are permitted to vist on an appointment-only basis. Also offered is book restoration and book binding - all hand work. The bindery is located on the premises. Mail order address is: P.O. Box 421, Mt. Eden, California 94557.

How to Get There: When making an appointment, precise directions will be given.
Owner/Biography: Jerome Pressler.
Year Founded/History of Bookstore: 1980.
Number of Volumes: 3,000.
Types/Classifications: Hardbound, government documents in wraps, broadsides, maps, out-of-print, antiquarian, atlases.
General Subject Areas: Alaskana, California State Publications (Bulletins, Special Reports, County Reports), Californiana, Canadiana, Environment, Exploration, Geography, Geology, Mineralogy, Mining, Mining Law, Paleontology, Travel, U.S. Geological Survey Bulletins, U.S. Geological Survey Folio Atlases, U.S. Geological Survey Professional Papers, U.S. Geological Survey Water Supply Papers, Water Law, Water Problems, Western Americana.
Specific Specialties: All aspects of Geography - Soils, Water, Weather, Cultural; all sub-areas of Geology.
Mail/Telephone Orders; Credit Cards: Both. Cash with order and postpaid. No credit cards. See above for mail address.
Business Hours: By appointment only.
Special Features: Search service (free), hand bookbinding, book restoration, book repair.
Catalogue: Catalog published.
Collections/Individual Items Purchased: Both.

170
Northwest Books
3814 Lyon Avenue
Oakland, California 94601 (415) 532-5227

Northwest Books is located in a private residence. Visitors are welcome by appointment only or by chance.
How to Get There: Call for directions.
Owner/Biography: Donald McKinney.
Year Founded/History of Bookstore: 1956.
Number of Volumes: 800.
Types/Classifications: Hardbound, color plate books, antique prints, lithographs, etchings, aquatints, mezzotints.
General Subject Areas: Americana, Art, Western Americana.
Specific Specialties: Pacific Northwest, Southwestern Americana.
Mail/Telephone Orders; Credit Cards: Both. Cash with order. No credit cards.
Business Hours: By appointment or by chance.
Parking Facilities: Street parking.
Collections/Individual Items Purchased: Both.
Booksellers' Memberships: Antiquarian Booksellers Association of America.

171
Novel Experience
778 Marsh Street
San Luis Obispo, California 93401   (805) 544-1549

This is a general used bookstore with 300 square feet of space.
How to Get There: The shop is located in the downtown business area.
Owner/Biography: Margaret Nybak.
Year Founded/History of Bookstore: Founded in 1975, the shop has not changed since its opening; the quality of stock fluctuates.
Number of Volumes: 6,500.
Types/Classifications: Hardbound, paperback, magazines, ephemera, first editions, fine bindings, out-of-print, association copies, press books.
General Subject Areas: Americana, Biography, Fiction, Literary Biography.
Author Specialties: Graham Greene, Rose Macaulay, T.F. Powys.
Mail/Telephone Orders; Credit Cards: Both; no credit cards.
Business Hours: Tuesday through Saturday 2:00 PM - 5:00 PM.
Parking Facilities: Public parking lot directly across the street.
Special Features: Search service, author collections, Pre-Columbian descriptive literature.
Collections/Individual Items Purchased: Both.
Booksellers' Memberships: American Booksellers Association, Central Coast Antiquarian Book Sellers Association.

172
Old Monterey Book Company
136 Bonifacio Place
Monterey, California 93940   (408) 372-3111

This shop has a general stock with books in most categories. It also carries prints and maps. The shop occupies 750 square feet of space.
Owner/Biography: Cecil Wahle and Charles Wahle.
Year Founded/History of Bookstore: 1976.
Number of Volumes: 10,000.
Types/Classifications: Hardbound, prints, maps, first editions, out-of-print, old and rare, fine bindings, association copies, press books, signed copies, presentation copies, limited editions, color plate books.
General Subject Areas: General.
Author Specialties: John Steinbeck, Robinson Jeffers.
Mail/Telephone Orders; Credit Cards: Both. Visa and Mastercard accepted.
Business Hours: Tuesday through Saturday 11:30 AM - 5:30 PM.
Parking Facilities: Public parking lots and garages, street parking.
Special Features: Appraisals.
Collections/Individual Items Purchased: Both.
Booksellers' Memberships: Antiquarian Booksellers Association of America, Central California Booksellers Association.

173
Oriental Book Store
630 East Colorado Boulevard
Pasadena, California 91030   (213) 577-2413

This bookstore has books covering all aspects of the Orient from the Middle East to the Far East, mostly in the English language. This is one of the largest bookstores dealing in Oriental material in the United States.
How to Get There: Located on Colorado Boulevard, site of the annual "Tournament of Roses Parade," the bookstore is between El Molino and Madison.
Owner/Biography: Frank Mosher. Mr. Mosher has travelled extensively throughout the Orient.

Year Founded/History of Bookstore: 1937.
Number of Volumes: 25,000.
Types/Classifications: Hardbound, paperback, new, out-of-print.
General Subject Areas: Art, Dictionaries and Grammars, Fiction, History, Martial Arts, Medicine, Oriental Languages, Religions, Sociology.
Specific Specialties: Middle East, India, Southeast Asia, China, Korea, Japan, South Seas, Australia, New Zealand, Hawaii, Oriental Americans, Children's Books (on and about the Orient).
Mail/Telephone Orders; Credit Cards: Both. No credit cards.
Business Hours: Monday through Friday 3:30 PM - 5:30 PM; Saturday 11:00 AM - 5:30 PM.
Parking Facilities: Street parking.
Collections/Individual Items Purchased: Both.
Booksellers' Memberships: Pasadena Booksellers Association.

174
Otento Books
3817 Fifth Avenue
San Diego, California 92103   (619) 296-1424

"Otento" Books has a distinct European flavor due to the fact that the owner has tried to incorporate the best features of the many bookstores he visited in his native city The Hague in Holland. In addition, a large part of the stock is the result of yearly trips to the United Kingdom buying books. One will find more Victorian juveniles and books in foreign languages than might be expected.
How to Get There: "Otento" is located in Hillcrest, close to Interstate 5 (Washington Street off-ramp) and Interstates 8 and 163 (6th Avenue downtown off-ramp).
Owner/Biography: Robert J. Gelink. Mr. Gelink was born in The Hague, Holland. He left his native country in 1960 and became a U.S. citizen in 1976.
Year Founded/History of Bookstore: 1963.
Number of Volumes: 35,000.
Types/Classifications: Hardbound, paperback, fine bindings, antiquarian, fore-edge paintings, general out-of-print.
General Subject Areas: American History, Art, British History, Classics, Costume, Fiction, Fishing, French History, Humor, Hunting, Music, Nature, Religion, Science Fiction and Fantasy, Sea and Ships, Show Business, Theater, Victorian Juveniles, War, Western Americana.
Specific Specialties: Hakluyt Society Books, Chess, Bridge, Turn-of-the-Century Fiction, Jardine (Natural History).
Mail/Telephone Orders; Credit Cards: Both. Visa and Mastercard accepted (when amount is over $20).
Business Hours: Monday through Saturday 11:00 AM - 5:00 PM.
Parking Facilities: Street parking.
Special Features: Search service.
Catalogue: Published infrequently.
Collections/Individual Items Purchased: Both.
Booksellers' Memberships: Antiquarian Booksellers Association of America including Southern California Chapter, San Diego Booksellers Association.

175
P. F. Mullins Books
109 Beechtree Drive
Encinitas, California 92024   (619) 436-7810

P.F. Mullins is a family run business in the home. Customers make appointments to browse or buy. A stock of 7,500 books covers most subject areas with strong emphasis on John Steinbeck, James Michener, Ernest Hemingway, and such subjects as jazz, biography, and the Far East. The shop occupies 750 square feet of space.
How to Get There: The business is located 30 miles north of San Diego; from I-5 take Encinitas Boulevard east toward Rancho Santa Fe, one block before El Camino Real turn right onto Beechtree Drive.

Owner/Biography: Paul and Roslyn Mullins.
Year Founded/History of Bookstore: 1979.
Number of Volumes: 7,500.
Types/Classifications: Hardbound, paperback, magazines, first editions, out-of-print, signed copies.
General Subject Areas: Automotive Repair Manuals, Biography, Black Literature, Books About Books, Caribbean Studies, Chess, China, Civil War (U.S.), Far East, Jazz, Modern Literature, Surfing.
Author Specialties: John Steinbeck, James Baldwin, Ernest Hemingway, James Michener.
Mail/Telephone Orders; Credit Cards: Both. No credit cards.
Business Hours: By appointment.
Parking Facilities: Street parking.
Special Features: Search service.
Catalogue: Published 2 times annually; lists also published.
Collections/Individual Items Purchased: Both.
Booksellers' Memberships: San Diego Booksellers Association.

176
Pacific Beach Book Store
1972 Garnet Avenue
San Diego, California 92109   (619) 273-9082

This store carries used books and magazines of all types. It occupies 400 square feet of space.
Owner/Biography: Mrs. Doreen E. Murphy.
Year Founded/History of Bookstore: 1953.
Number of Volumes: 10,000.
Types/Classifications: Hardbound, paperback, magazines, first editions, out-of-print.
General Subject Areas: General.
Mail/Telephone Orders; Credit Cards: No mail or phone orders.
Business Hours: Monday through Saturday 10:00 AM - 5:30 PM.
Parking Facilities: Street parking.
Collections/Individual Items Purchased: Individual items only.

177
Paperback Alley
5840 Hollister Avenue
Goleta, California 93117   (805) 967-1051

This bookstore carries popular, current, and out-of-print paperbacks.
Owner/Biography: Shannon Rose.
Year Founded/History of Bookstore: 1978.
Number of Volumes: 20,000.
Types/Classifications: Paperpacks, out-of-print.
General Subject Areas: Classics, History, Mysteries, Romance, Science Fiction and Fantasy, Suspense.
Mail/Telephone Orders; Credit Cards: No mail or phone orders. No credit cards.
Business Hours: Monday through Saturday 10:30 AM - 5:30 PM.
Parking Facilities: Street parking.
Collections/Individual Items Purchased: Individual items only.

178
Pepper & Stern - Rare Books, Inc.
P.O. Box 2711
Santa Barbara, California 93120   (805) 569-0735

Pepper & Stern does most of its business by catalogues but visitors are always welcome by appointment. It maintains a very large stock emphasizing material that is rare or unique.

How to Get There: Directions will be given when phoning for an appointment.
Owner/Biography: James Pepper, Deborah Sanford, Peter L. Stern.
Number of Volumes: 20,000.
Types/Classifications: First editions, association copies, signed copies, presentation copies, limited editions, autograph letters, original manuscripts.
General Subject Areas: American and English Literature, Detective Fiction, Mysteries, Rare Cinema Material, Science Fiction.
Author Specialties: Aldous Huxley, Ring Lardner, John Le Carre, Ross MacDonald, H.L. Mencken, George Orwell, Ellery Queen, Agatha Christie, Bram Stoker, Rex Stout, James Thurber, S.J. Perelman, John Updike, Larry McMurtry, S.S. Van Dine, Nathanael West, Paul Bowles, Robert Van Gulik, H.G. Wells, Eric Ambler, Len Deighton, Zane Grey, Thomas Wolfe, Ray Bradbury, Jack London, Ernest Hemingway, F. Scott Fitzgerald, Dashiell Hammett, Raymond Chandler, John Dickson Carr, Arthur Conan Doyle, Cornell Woolrich, P.G. Wodehouse, Edgar Rice Burroughs, Mark Twain, John Steinbeck, William Faulkner, W. Somerset Maugham, Kurt Vonnegut, Ross MacDonald, Earl Derr Biggers, Sax Rohmer, C.S. Forester, Dick Francis, R. Austin Freeman, Graham Greene, Stephen King, Willa Cather, D.H. Lawrence.
Mail/Telephone Orders; Credit Cards: Both. Visa and Mastercard accepted.
Business Hours: Anytime by prior appointment Monday through Friday 10:00 AM - 5:00 PM.
Catalogue: Published 8 times per year.
Collections/Individual Items Purchased: Both.
Booksellers' Memberships: Antiquarian Booksellers Association of America.
Miscellaneous: Pepper & Stern - Rare Books, Inc. also has an office in Sharon, Massachusetts.

179
Peri Lithon Books
5372 Van Nuys Court
San Diego, California 92109   (619) 488-6904

Peri Lithon Books is located in a private residence. It reflects the interests of one of its proprietors, Captain John Sinkankas, U.S. Navy (Retired), Ph.D., who is a well-known earth sciences author and writer on gemological/lapidary subjects as well as mineralogy and prospecting. His experience in the earth science field dates back to early childhood but the active collection of books on gemstones, etc. began in the late 1950's. Visits may be arranged by appointment only.
How to Get There: The bookstore is located in the Pacific Beach section of San Diego. Call for directions.
Owner/Biography: John and Marjorie J. Sinkankas.
Year Founded/History of Bookstore: 1971. The business started as an offshoot of the owner's collecting interests in earth sciences literature, and also to supply such literature to other collectors. It has always operated from the owner's home.
Number of Volumes: 7,500.
Types/Classifications: All types including ephemera, art work, etc. but very largely hardbound books and paperbound geoscience; out-of-print, very small stock of owner's own works and certain imports.
General Subject Areas: Earth Sciences.
Specific Specialties: Geology, Mineralogy, Petrology, Economic Geology, Mining, Paleontology, Earth Science and Chemistry Histories, Chemistry (especially inorganic applied to earth sciences and mining), Biographies of Geologists/Mineralogists, Gemology and Precious Stones, Jewels, Jewelry, Jewelry Making, Precious Metals, Metallurgy.
Other Specialties: Subject areas above also handled in foreign languages.
Mail/Telephone Orders; Credit Cards: Both. Prepayment or established credit. No credit cards.
Business Hours: By appointment only.
Parking Facilities: Street parking.
Special Features: Peri Lithon Books handles many smaller items of ephemeral nature which are not normally handled by any other earth science dealers.
Catalogue: Published 5 to 6 times annually.
Collections/Individual Items Purchased: Both.
Booksellers' Memberships: Antiquarian Booksellers Association of America including Southern California Chapter, San Diego Booksellers Association.

180
Perry's Antiques & Books
1863 West San Carlos
San Jose, California 95128   (408) 286-0426

In addition to antiques, Perry's carries an extensive stock of hardbound books. The store occupies 4,000 square feet of space.

Owner/Biography: Frank Perry.

Year Founded/History of Bookstore: 1947. The business began in Campbell, California as a combination bookshop and antique store. It continued to grow and moved to San Jose in 1957 and in 1973 occupied its current location.

Number of Volumes: 100,000.

Types/Classifications: Hardbound, magazines, autographs, ephemera, first editions, limited editions, out-of-print, color plate books, signed copies, illustrated books.

General Subject Areas: Americana, Biography, Children's Literature, Occult, Poetry, Religion, Science Fiction, Sports, Western Americana.

Specific Specialties: Oziana.

Author Specialties: Edgar Rice Burroughs, Jack London, H. Rider Haggard.

Mail/Telephone Orders; Credit Cards: Both. Visa and Mastercard accepted.

Business Hours: Tuesday through Saturday 10:30 AM - 5:00 PM.

Parking Facilities: Street parking.

Special Features: Search service.

Catalogue: Published once per year.

Collections/Individual Items Purchased: Both.

181
Pettler & Lieberman, Booksellers
7970 Melrose Avenue
Los Angeles, California 90046   (213) 651-1568

Pettler & Lieberman, Booksellers is a small bookstore with definite tastes. It was established as a place where good, recent books could be kept alive through the stocking of those titles worthy of note and reading but no longer readily available. The shop occupies 1,000 square feet of space.

How to Get There: The store is situated in a section of Los Angeles that lies between the cities of West Hollywood and Beverly Hills. Melrose Avenue runs just south of Santa Monica Boulevard and the shop is between the major cross streets of Fairfax Avenue and La Cienega Boulevard.

Owner/Biography: Robert Pettler and Victor Lieberman.

Year Founded/History of Bookstore: 1978.

Number of Volumes: 8,000.

Types/Classifications: Hardbound in dust jackets plus selected paperbacks, magazines, manuscripts and literary-related film posters, first editions, out-of-print, signed copies, limited editions, presentation copies, association copies.

General Subject Areas: Books Made Into Films, Contemporary American Fiction, Film, Humor, Literary Anthologies, Literary Biography, Movie Screenplays, Mystery and Detective Fiction, Plays, Poetry.

Specific Specialties: Within the field of Contemporary American Fiction, the stock tends to specialize in post war authors, many of whom are still active today.

Author Specialties: Edward Abbey, Jerome Charyn, John Cheever, Harry Crews, Don Delillo, Joan Didion, William Eastlake, Frederick Exley, William Faulkner, F. Scott Fitzgerald, John Fowles, John Gardner, Barry Hannah, Jim Harrison, William Harrison, Joseph Heller, John Irving, William Hjortsberg, Stephen King, William Kotzwinkle, Joseph McElroy, Ian McEwan, Thomas McGuane, Larry McMurtry, John McPhee, Norman Mailer, Bernard Malamud, Peter Matthiessen, Vladimir Nabokov, Tim O'Brien, John O'Hara, Craig Nova, Walker Percy, Daryl Ponicsan, Tom Robbins, Judith Rossner, Philip Roth, Irwin Shaw, Terry Southern, Robert Stone, Hunter Thompson, John Updike, Kurt Vonnegut, Gore Vidal, Paul West, Jorge Amado, Julio Cortazar, Jose Donoso, Juan Goytisolo, Mario Vargas Llosa, Gabriel Garcia Marquez, James M. Cain, Raymond Chandler, James Crumley, Len Deighton, Ian Fleming, Dick Francis, Dashiell Hammett, George V. Higgins, Elmore Leonard, John Le Carre, John D. MacDonald, Robert B. Parker, Dell Shannon, Georges Simenon, Jonathan Valin, Donald Westlake.

Mail/Telephone Orders; Credit Cards: Both. Visa and Mastercard accepted.
Business Hours: Monday through Saturday 11:00 AM - 6:00 PM.
Parking Facilities: Ample street parking.
Special Features: Search service.
Catalogue: Published infrequently.
Collections/Individual Items Purchased: Both.

182
Phoenix Bookstore
514 Santa Monica Boulevard
Santa Monica, California 90401   (213) 395-9516

The Phoenix Bookstore is one of Los Angeles' newest bookstores specializing in metaphysics and related subjects, both new and used. The new stock is displayed on the main floor, a spacious room with floor to ceiling shelving and moveable library ladders. The ambience is further enhanced by classical music. Rare items are displayed in glass cases and on the balcony. Used books are shelved in the downstairs area which is also used for occasional poetry readings and author-attended events.

How to Get There: The store is conveniently located on Santa Monica Boulevard, five blocks from the Pacific Ocean between Fifth and Sixth Streets. The Santa Monica Public Library is one block away.

Owner/Biography: Jamie O'Toole and Michael Goth. Both Ms. O'Toole and Mr. Goth were previously at the Westwood Bookstore which met its demise upon the demolition of the block on which it stood for many years (a subsequent move to a location nearby but out of the mainstream of the walk-in traffic was not successful). Jamie has 11 years' experience in book buying and Michael is an antiquarian bookman specializing in metaphysics.

Year Founded/History of Bookstore: 1983.

Types/Classifications: Hardbound, paperback, magazines, first editions, out-of-print, association copies, fine bindings, magazines, broadsides, ephemera.

General Subject Areas: Comparative Religions, Metaphysics, Occultiana, Traditional Studies.

Mail/Telephone Orders; Credit Cards: Mail orders only. Cash with order. Visa and Mastercard accepted.

Business Hours: Monday through Saturday 10:00 AM - 7:00 PM; Sunday 12:00 Noon - 5:00 PM.

Parking Facilities: Street parking, municipal parking lot (3 hours free) on Fourth Street between Arizona Avenue and Santa Monica Boulevard.

Special Features: If not in stock, books can be ordered from all publishers.

Catalogue: Published once per year.

Collections/Individual Items Purchased: Both.

Booksellers' Memberships: Antiquarian Booksellers Association of America including Southern California Chapter.

183
Phoenix Rising
732 Main Street
Susanville, California 96130   (916) 257-9262

The Phoenix Rising is located in a turn-of-the-century building. It carries a general used and out-of-print stock. The shop occupies 1,800 square feet of space.

How to Get There: Susanville is a popular stopping point for people travelling to and from Oregon and Washington.

Owner/Biography: Gini Segedi and Isytaya.

Year Founded/History of Bookstore: 1983.

Types/Classifications: Hardbound, paperback, magazines, ephemera, first editions, out-of-print.

General Subject Areas: Americana, Art Books, Automotive, Aviation, Children's Books, Cookbooks, Foreign Language, Gardening, Humor, Medical, Metaphysics, Movies, Music, Mysteries, Natural History, Nautical, Philosophy, Psychology, Railroads, Religion, Science Fiction, Sciences, Sports, Theater, World Wars I and II.

Mail/Telephone Orders; Credit Cards: Both. Cash with order including postage. Visa and Mastercard accepted.

Business Hours: Monday through Saturday 10:00 AM - 5:00 PM.

Parking Facilities: Street parking.

Special Features: Search service; appraisals; New Age study groups and classes; reading room for metaphysical students.

Collections/Individual Items Purchased: Both.

Miscellaneous: Gini Segedi is also the owner of Book Stop III in Las Vegas, Nevada. He is also a member of the San Diego Booksellers Association.

184
Printers' Shop
4047 Transport
Palo Alto, California 94303 (415) 494-6802

The Printers' Shop specializes in books on the book arts including typography, type specimens, calligraphy, lithography, engraving, illumination, etching, hobby printing, private presses, collecting, and bibliography. From the fine printed books and rare collectors' editions to practical manuals and "how-to" books, The Printers' Shop offers a very specialized stock for the novice or experienced book person.

How to Get There: Travel Bayshore (101) to San Antonio Road; then south towards Los Altos; left at Charleston, left at Commercial (one short block); Commercial is one block long and Transport Street is at the end. The shop is almost opposite the intersection with a big "TPS" on the top of the building.

Owner/Biography: Frederica Postman. Ms. Postman was a hobby printer for many years and opened the shop in 1974 to sell letterpress equipment for small press printers. Books were added in 1975 and in 1982 the equipment portion of the business was liquidated leaving this unique specialist collection.

Year Founded/History of Bookstore: 1974.

Number of Volumes: 1,000.

Types/Classifications: Hardbound, paperback, periodicals, broadsides, ephemera, posters, first editions, out-of-print, limited editions.

General Subject Areas: Book Arts.

Mail/Telephone Orders; Credit Cards: Both. Mail orders from known customers or pro forma invoice. No credit cards.

Business Hours: Monday through Friday (generally) 9:00 AM - 5:00 PM; best to call ahead.

Parking Facilities: Ample street parking.

Special Features: Search service; select private press distribution.

Catalogue: Published infrequently.

Collections/Individual Items Purchased: Both.

Booksellers' Memberships: Central California Antiquarian Booksellers Association.

185
Prometheus Paperbound
3189 16th Street
San Francisco, California 94103 (415) 552-7470

This shop carries a general stock of used books. It occupies 1,600 square feet of space.

How to Get There: The shop is located on 16th Street near Guerrero.

Owner/Biography: N. Healey and K. Ridinger.

Year Founded/History of Bookstore: 1975.

Number of Volumes: 30,000.

Types/Classifications: Hardbound, paperback, general used.

General Subject Areas: Biographies, Criticism, Fiction, History, Literature, Mysteries, Philosophy, Poetry, Psychology, Religion, Science, Social Sciences.

Mail/Telephone Orders; Credit Cards: No mail or phone orders. Visa and Mastercard accepted.

Business Hours: Tuesday through Saturday 11:00 AM - 6:00 PM.

Parking Facilities: Street parking.

186
R. Sorsky, Bookseller
3845 North Blackstone
Fresno, California 93726   (209) 227-2901

R. Sorsky operates a mail order business specializing in materials related to woodworking only. Stock can be viewed by appointment.
How to Get There: Call for directions.
Owner/Biography: R. Sorsky.
Year Founded/History of Bookstore: 1977.
Number of Volumes: 800.
Types/Classifications: Hardbound, paperback, new, used.
General Subject Areas: Cabinetmaking, Timber, Woodworking.
Mail/Telephone Orders; Credit Cards: Both. Visa and Mastercard accepted.
Business Hours: Monday through Friday 9:30 AM - 5:30 PM; Sunday 12:00 Noon - 5:00 PM; closed Saturday.
Parking Facilities: Parking lot.
Catalogue: Published 3 to 4 times per year.
Collections/Individual Items Purchased: Both.

187
R. F. "Dick" Webb Auto Books
3043 East Tulare Street
Fresno, California 93721   (209) 683-8513

Dick Webb is a specialist in automotive literature and automobile racing material. His shop is open by appointment only.
How to Get There: The shop is located in the southeastern part of Fresno.
Owner/Biography: Richard F. Webb.
Types/Classifications: Hardbound, magazines, manuals, catalogs, emphemera.
General Subject Areas: Automotive Literature.
Specific Specialties: Anything automotive published in the U.S. from 1895 to 1941; historical, biographical, and technical automotive items; car owner's manuals, repair manuals for individual models, auto sales catalogs 1895 - 1941; all types and classes of auto racing published in the U.S. 1895 - 1959, histories of auto racing and track histories, driver autobiographies and biographies, auto racing ephemera, out-of-print auto racing titles published in U.S. after 1959.
Mail/Telephone Orders; Credit Cards: Mail orders. Mailing address: P.O. Box 891, Fresno, CA 93714.
Business Hours: By appointment only.
Parking Facilities: Ample parking.
Collections/Individual Items Purchased: Both.

188
Rancho Books
1431 Ocean Avenue
Suite 800
Santa Monica, California 90401   (213) 396-9567

Rancho Books specializes in Western Americana, particularly California and the early West. Visits may be arranged by appointment.
How to Get There: Near the Santa Monica Pier.
Owner/Biography: Stan Dahl and John Jones.
Year Founded/History of Bookstore: 1967.
Number of Volumes: 10,000.
Types/Classifications: Hardbound, broadsides, autographs, ephemera, first editions, fine bindings, out-of-print, association copies, press books, signed copies, presentation copies, limited editions, color plate books.

General Subject Areas: Western Americana.
Specific Specialties: California and the Early West.
Mail/Telephone Orders; Credit Cards: Both. Cash with order. No credit cards.
Business Hours: By appointment only.
Parking Facilities: Street parking.
Catalogue: Published occasionally.
Collections/Individual Items Purchased: Both.

189
Randall House
185 Post Street
San Francisco, California 94108   (415) 781-2218

Randall House is an antiquarian bookstore handling Americana, literary first editions, press books and fine printing, and rare books in all fields. The store occupies 1,600 square feet of space.
How to Get There: The bookstore is located in downtown San Francisco not far from Union Square.
Owner/Biography: Ronald R. Randall.
Year Founded/History of Bookstore: 1975.
Types/Classifications: Hardbound, autographs, prints, paintings, first editions, fine bindings, out-of-print, association copies, press books, signed copies, presentation copies, limited editions.
General Subject Areas: General.
Specific Specialties: Americana, Vogages, Travels, Exploration.
Mail/Telephone Orders; Credit Cards: Both. Visa and Mastercard accepted.
Business Hours: Monday through Friday 9:00 AM - 5:00 PM; Saturday 10:00 AM - 4:00 PM.
Parking Facilities: Public parking lot nearby, street parking.
Special Features: Collection development; appraisals.
Catalogue: Catalogue published.
Collections/Individual Items Purchased: Both.

190
Rare Book Room
1367 North Broadway
Walnut Creek, California 94596   (415) 933-1025

See HOOKED ON BOOKS, Walnut Creek, California.

191
Regent Street Books
2747 Regent Street
Berkeley, California 94705   (415) 548-8459

This is a small shop based in a converted garage near the Berkeley campus of the University of California.
Owner/Biography: Mark B. Weiman.
Year Founded/History of Bookstore: 1979.
Number of Volumes: 500.
Types/Classifications: Hardbound, out-of-print scholarly books.
General Subject Areas: Analytical Psychology, Dreams, Psychiatry, Psychoanalysis, Sleep.
Other Specialties: Scholarly Works.
Mail/Telephone Orders; Credit Cards: Both. No credit cards.
Business Hours: By appointment only.
Parking Facilities: Street parking.
Special Features: Search service; publishing sideline; typesetting and graphic design.
Catalogue: Published once per year.

Collections/Individual Items Purchased: Individual items only.

192
Ricamar Books
3808 Rosecrans Street
Suite 418
San Diego, California 92110   (619) 291-6094

Ricamar Books carries mostly non-fiction titles, especially unusual and sometimes controversial books not usually found in the best seller mass market mainstreams. The business is by mail or telephone order only.
Owner/Biography: Richard H. Rongstad. The owner is a retired Navy man.
Year Founded/History of Bookstore: 1980.
Number of Volumes: 100.
Types/Classifications: Hardbound, paperback, monographs.
General Subject Areas: Behavioral Science, Controversial Books and Subjects, Health and Fitness, Paranormal Phenomena, Politics, Psychology, Warfare.
Specific Specialties: UFO's, Psychic Healing, Possessions, Exorcism, Deception and War, Terrorism, Parapsychology, Self-Help, Holistic Health.
Author Specialties: Raymond Fowler, Cynthia Hind.
Mail/Telephone Orders; Credit Cards: Both. Cash or money order in U.S. funds; personal checks showing U.S. zip code (items held 21 days before shipping).
Business Hours: 24 hour answering service.
Catalogue: Published randomly.
Collections/Individual Items Purchased: Individual items only.
Booksellers' Memberships: San Diego Booksellers Association.

193
Richard Hansen Californiana
11245 Dry Creek Road
Auburn, California 95603   (916) 885-4878

Richard Hansen has a compact selection of over 5,000 items relating to the history of California and the American West including books, ephemera, and cartography.
How to Get There: Call for an appointment and directions.
Owner/Biography: Richard Hansen. Mr. Hansen has 20 years' experience as a part-time dealer in Californiana.
Year Founded/History of Bookstore: 1964.
Number of Volumes: 5,000.
Types/Classifications: Hardbound, ephemera, maps, out-of-print.
General Subject Areas: Californiana.
Other Specialties: Old deeds, broadsides, letter sheets, bill heads, sight drafts, town view reprints.
Mail/Telephone Orders; Credit Cards: Both. Visa and Mastercard accepted.
Business Hours: By appointment.
Parking Facilities: Large area can accommodate campers.
Special Features: Established Historic California Press in 1983; reprint works of value to California history.
Catalogue: Catalogues available at $1 per single issue, $5 per year.
Collections/Individual Items Purchased: Both.

194
Richard L. Press - Fine and Scholarly Books
1228 North Street No. 2
Sacramento, California 95814   (916) 447-3413

The bookstore is located in the center of Sacramento across the street from the magnificently restored State Capitol and park. The shop is to be found on the first floor of a lovely Arts and Crafts building, and contains approximately 800 square feet of space.

How to Get There: From Highway 80 exit at 15th or 16th Street and go four blocks to 12th Street.

Owner/Biography: Richard L. Press, owner, holds the BA, MLS, and PhD degrees, the latter in Middle East Anthropology.

Year Founded/History of Bookstore: Founded in 1980, the bookstore is at its original site and under the same ownership.

Number of Volumes: 2,500.

Types/Classifications: Hardbound, broadsides, ephemera, out-of-print, fine bindings, press books, limited editions.

General Subject Areas: Architecture, Art, Cooking, Dance, Design, Islam, Judaica, Middle East, North Africa, Photography, Wine.

Specific Specialties: Modern Art, Modern Architecture, English Book Illustrators of the 1920's and 1930's.

Mail/Telephone Orders; Credit Cards: Both. Visa and Mastercard accepted.

Business Hours: Tuesday through Saturday 10:00 AM - 6:00 PM.

Parking Facilities: Street.

Catalogue: Two times a year.

Collections/Individual Items Purchased: Both.

195
Robert Allen/Books
P.O. Box 582
Altadena, California 91001   (213) 794-4210

Robert Allen/Books carries antiquarian and choice books including first and noteworthy editions.

How to Get There: Write or phone for exact directions.

Owner/Biography: Robert and Priscilla Allen.

Year Founded/History of Bookstore: 1977.

Number of Volumes: 5,500.

Types/Classifications: Antiquarian, some prints, maps, and ephemera; first editions.

General Subject Areas: History of Ideas (Before 1801), Literature (Before 1801).

Specific Specialties: The Odd and Interesting After 1801; Classical, Renaissance, and Enlightenment Literature; Children's Literature (19th Century); Women's Studies, Racial History, Poetry (19th and 20th Centuries).

Author Specialties: Ovid, Gelli, Erasmus, Samuel Johnson.

Other Specialties: Italian books, neo-Latin books, French books.

Mail/Telephone Orders; Credit Cards: Both. No credit cards.

Business Hours: By appointment.

Parking Facilities: Ample street parking.

Special Features: Appraisals, search service.

Catalogue: Published 4 times per year.

Collections/Individual Items Purchased: Both.

Booksellers' Memberships: Pasadena Booksellers Association.

196
Robert Perata - Books
3170 Robinson Drive
Oakland, California 94602   (415) 482-0101

This is an in-home business which deals in antiquarian books, particularly Western Americana. Visits can be arranged by appointment.

How to Get There: The business is located 1 mile off Highway 13 in the Oakland Hills.

Owner/Biography: Robert and Mary Ann Perata.

Year Founded/History of Bookstore: 1969.
Number of Volumes: 900.
Types/Classifications: Fine printing, press books, fine bindings, illustrated books.
General Subject Areas: Western Americana.
Mail/Telephone Orders; Credit Cards: Both. No credit cards.
Business Hours: By appointment.
Catalogue: Published 4 times per year.
Collections/Individual Items Purchased: Both.
Booksellers' Memberships: Antiquarian Booksellers Association of America including Northern California Chapter.

197
Robert Ross & Co.
6101 El Escorpion Road
Woodland Hills, California 91367 (213) 346-6152

Robert Ross is an antiquarian dealer in old historical maps, prints, and related books. He conducts his business by mail order and appointment only.

How to Get There: Call the above telephone number evenings and weekends for an appointment. Directions to Woodland Hills will be given.
Owner/Biography: Robert Ross.
Types/Classifications: Hardbound, out-of-print, first editions, maps, prints.
Mail/Telephone Orders; Credit Cards: Mail orders.
Business Hours: By appointment only.
Collections/Individual Items Purchased: Both.

198
Ross Valley Book Company, Inc.
1407 Solano Avenue
Albany, California 94706 (415) 526-6400

This store is devoted solely to materials on the American Far West with new, used, and rare books, maps, western art, pamphlets, and ephemeral materials. Frequent catalogues and newsletters are issued. The store holds autographing parties for significant books on the West by local authors.

How to Get There: Albany is immediately north of Berkeley, California.
Owner/Biography: Robert L. Hawley.
Year Founded/History of Bookstore: 1978.
Number of Volumes: 6,000.
Types/Classifications: Hardbound, paperback, broadsides, autographs, ephemera, maps, original western art, out-of-print, new, rare, press books.
General Subject Areas: Far West (U.S.).
Specific Specialties: Fur Trade, Cattle Trade, Spain in the New World, Women in the West.
Author Specialties: Ramon Adams, J. Evetts Haley, Herbert E. Bolton.
Mail/Telephone Orders; Credit Cards: Both. From new customers, payment in advance or local credit references; credit extended to institutions and known customers. No credit cards.
Business Hours: Tuesday through Saturday 10:00 AM - 6:00 PM.
Parking Facilities: Ample street parking.
Special Features: Search service; appraisals; collection development advice.
Catalogue: Published 5 to 8 times yearly.
Collections/Individual Items Purchased: Both.

199
Rudolph Wm. Sabbot - Natural History Books
5239 Tendilla Avenue
Woodland Hills, California 91364   (818) 346-7164

A special room in a private residence has been converted to house the stock offered by this bookseller. He deals exclusively in Natural History books. Visitors are welcome to browse but an appointment must be made in advance.

How to Get There: Located 5 blocks off the Ventura Freeway in the city of Woodland Hills which is in the western part of the San Fernando Valley of Los Angeles. Specific instructions will be furnished either by telephone or mail.

Owner/Biography: Rudolph Wm. and Irene M. Sabbot.

Year Founded/History of Bookstore: 1965. In 1977 the Sabbot's were appointed as North American agents to handle the publications (Natural History) of the British Museum.

Number of Volumes: 10,000.

Types/Classifications: Hardbound, paperback (institutional publications), first editions, out-of-print, fine bindings, limited editions, color plate books.

General Subject Areas: Natural History.

Specific Specialties: Mammalogy, Ornithology, Herpetology, Ichthyology, Entomology, Paleontology, Botany, Zoology.

Other Specialties: Travels and explorations devoted primarily to natural history surveys and collections; biographies and bibliographies of noted naturalists; natural history books in all disciplines, antiquarian and current, in their language of origin.

Mail/Telephone Orders; Credit Cards: Both. Prepaid, except for established customers and institutional libraries. No credit cards.

Business Hours: By appointment daily 9:00 AM - 7:00 PM.

Parking Facilities: Street and driveway parking.

Special Features: Appraisals; search service.

Catalogue: Published 3 times yearly.

Collections/Individual Items Purchased: Both.

Booksellers' Memberships: Antiquarian Booksellers Association of America including Southern California Chapter, International League of Antiquarian Booksellers.

200
Sagebrush Press
P.O. Box 87
Morongo Valley, California 92256   (619) 363-7398

Sagebrush Press deals mainly through catalogues and specializes in Western Americana. Visitors are welcome by appointment.

How to Get There: Call or write for directions.

Owner/Biography: Dan and Janet Cronkhite.

Types/Classifications: Hardbound, emphemera, out-of-print.

General Subject Areas: Western Americana.

Specific Specialties: California and Nevada Deserts, Death Valley.

Mail/Telephone Orders; Credit Cards: Mail order only. No credit cards.

Business Hours: By appointment.

Special Features: Publishing and printing sideline business.

Catalogue: Published twice per year.

Collections/Individual Items Purchased: Both.

201
Sam: Johnson's Bookshop
11552 Santa Monica Boulevard
Los Angeles, California 90025   (213) 477-9247

Sam: Johnson's Bookshop has only very good books in very fine condition. The stock is general with strength in classic fiction and scholarly books. Music enhances browsing. The shop occupies 950 square feet of space.

How to Get There: Located 1/2 mile west of the San Diego Freeway, the shop is on the south side of Santa Monica Boulevard near the corner of Colby.

Owner/Biography: Robert E. Klein and Lawrence D. Myers. Both are writers and Mr. Klein teaches English at Santa Monica College.

Year Founded/History of Bookstore: 1977.

Number of Volumes: 25,000.

Types/Classifications: Hardbound, some paperbacks, first editions, leather bindings, old and rare, out-of-print.

General Subject Areas: Art, Books About Books, Classic (Greece and Rome), Cookbooks, Eighteenth Century ("Sam: Johnson & Friends"), Fantasy, History, Literature, Medieval, Movies, Mysteries, Reference, Religion, Renaissance, Technical.

Author Specialties: Samuel Johnson, G.K. Chesterton, C.S. Lewis, George MacDonald, Charles Williams, Lord Dunsany, Algernon Blackwood.

Other Specialties: Scholarly books, especially in literature and history.

Mail/Telephone Orders; Credit Cards: No mail orders. Visa and Mastercard accepted.

Business Hours: Monday through Saturday 11:00 AM - 6:00 PM.

Parking Facilities: Street parking, metered public parking lot behind shop.

Special Features: Good music and good talk.

Collections/Individual Items Purchased: Both.

Miscellaneous: Fine stereo system playing classical music.

202
San Fancisciana
1090 Pt. Lobos
Cliff House
San Francisco, California 94121   (415) 751-7222

San Francisciana carries San Francisco posters, photographs and cards, movie stills, and reproductions of early San Francisco photographs. The shop specializes in fruit crate labels - oranges, lemons, apples, pears, vegetables, grapes, and grapefruit.

How to Get There: The shop is located in the Cliff House by Seal Rocks and Ocean Beach near the end of Golden Gate Park. Drive to the end of Geary or the end of Fulton if coming from central San Francisco.

Owner/Biography: Marilyn Blaisdell.

Year Founded/History of Bookstore: 1970.

Types/Classifications: Ephemera.

General Subject Areas: Fruit Crate Labels, Movie Stills, San Francisco Posters.

Mail/Telephone Orders; Credit Cards: Daily 11:00 AM - 5:00 PM.

Business Hours: Mail orders only. Cash with order. No credit cards.

Parking Facilities: Street parking.

Collections/Individual Items Purchased: Both.

Booksellers' Memberships: Antiquarian Booksellers Association of America.

203
San Francisco Mystery Bookstore
746 Diamond Street
San Francisco, California 94114   (415) 282-7444

This is a small and well stocked store dealing exclusively in mystery and detective fiction, both in-print and out-of-print. It occupies 500 square feet of space.

Owner/Biography: Bruce Taylor.
Year Founded/History of Bookstore: 1976. The shop was previously known as Murder, Inc.
Number of Volumes: 10,000.
Types/Classifications: Hardbound, paperback, first editions, out-of-print, association copies, signed copies, limited editions.
General Subject Areas: Detective Fiction, Mysteries.
Mail/Telephone Orders; Credit Cards: Both. No credit cards.
Business Hours: Monday through Friday 12:00 Noon - 6:00 PM; Saturday 10:00 AM - 6:00 PM.
Parking Facilities: Street parking.
Collections/Individual Items Purchased: Both.

204
San Jose Book Shop
1231 E Kentwood Avenue
San Jose, California 95129   (408) 446-0590

The San Jose Book Shop deals exclusively in the subject of metaphysics.
Owner/Biography: Heather Buckley Neville.
General Subject Areas: Metaphysics.
Business Hours: Monday through Saturday 10:00 AM - 6:00 PM.

205
Santa Monica Book Bazaar
131 Broadway
Santa Monica, California 90401   (213) 451-2710

The Book Bazaar is a small corner bookstore which carries out-of-print hardbound and paperback stock plus magazines. A special interest is in Western Americana.
How to Get There: The store is within one block of the Pacific Ocean in downtown Santa Monica.
Year Founded/History of Bookstore: 1961.
Types/Classifications: Hardbound, paperback, out-of-print, magazines.
General Subject Areas: General.
Specific Specialties: Western Americana.
Mail/Telephone Orders; Credit Cards: Neither. No credit cards.
Business Hours: Monday through Saturday 9:30 AM - 6:00 PM. (Owner may be out to lunch around the noon hour.)
Parking Facilities: Free 3-hour parking is available in the municipal lot on Second Street between Broadway and Arizona Avenue.

206
Second Debut Books
P.O. Box 30268
Santa Barbara, California 93130   (805) 687-2781

Second Debut Books carries a general stock of hardbound books. Visits can be arranged by appointment.
How to Get There: Call for directions when making an appointment.
Owner/Biography: Mildred Miller. Mrs. Miller is from Ohio and has a career in writing, proofreading, and editing.
Year Founded/History of Bookstore: 1979.
Number of Volumes: "Thousands."
Types/Classifications: Hardbound, out-of-print, first editions.

General Subject Areas: General.
Specific Specialties: Biography, Metaphysics.
Mail/Telephone Orders; Credit Cards: Both. Check or money order (include a self addressed stamped envelope). No credit cards.
Business Hours: By appointment.
Special Features: Search service.
Catalogue: Catalogue published.
Collections/Individual Items Purchased: Individual items only.

207
Second Time Around Bookshop
391 East Main Street
Ventura, California 93001

(805) 643-3154

This shop is probably one of the largest used and out-of-print bookstores in Southern California. It stocks books in all general subject areas and also sells back-issue magazines and used recordings. The shop contains 6,000 square feet of space.
How to Get There: The bookstore is located on the main street in downtown (OldTown) Ventura.
Owner/Biography: James Staley, Manager.
Year Founded/History of Bookstore: 1975.
Number of Volumes: 40,000.
Types/Classifications: Hardbound, magazines, paperback, recordings, modern first editions.
General Subject Areas: Agriculture, Americana, Animals, Anthroplogy, Art, Automotive, Aviation, Biography, Children's Books, Cinema, Drama, Eastern Studies, Ecology, Economics, Education, Erotica, Ethnic Studies, Fishing, Gardening, Health, Heritage Press, History, How-To Books, Humor, Hunting, Languages, Modern Library, Music, Nature, Navigation, Philosophy, Poetry, Political Science, Psychology, Reference, Religion, Science, Sociology, Travels, War, Women, World War II.
Specific Specialties: American History, European History, World History, African History, Asian History, Latin American History, Occult.
Mail/Telephone Orders; Credit Cards: Both. Visa, Mastercard.
Business Hours: Winter: Daily except Tuesday 10:00 AM - 5:00 PM; Summer: Daily 9:00 AM - 6:00 PM.
Special Features: Search service.
Collections/Individual Items Purchased: Both.

208
Silver Door
901 Hermosa Avenue
Hermosa Beach, California 90254

(213) 379-6005

The shop is probably the only bookstore in Southern California to carry nothing but Detective/Mystery Fiction, Adventure/Spy/Thriller Fiction, and related items. The owners describe it as "a tiny den of iniquity located steps away from the Hermosa Pier," and just 20 minutes south of the Los Angeles Airport. It contains 500 square feet of space.
How to Get There: The bookstore can be reached from the 405 (San Diego) Freeway, using the Rosecrans (Manhattan Beach) offramp west to Sepulveda, then south to Pier Avenue, then west to Hermosa Avenue, then south two blocks to the shop.
Owner/Biography: Karen and Dick La Porte.
Year Founded/History of Bookstore: The shop was founded in 1977 as a mail order business. It still does the mail order business but also opened the shop in 1980.
Number of Volumes: 10,000.
Types/Classifications: Hardbound, paperback, magazines, ephemera, first editions, association copies, out-of-print, signed copies, presentation copies, limited editions.
General Subject Areas: Adventure, Detective Fiction, Mysteries, Spy, Thriller.
Mail/Telephone Orders; Credit Cards: Both. Prepayment unless customer is known to the store; postage additional; sales tax where applicable. No credit cards.

Business Hours: Thursday, Friday, Saturday 1:00 PM - 5:00 PM, or any time by appointment.
Parking Facilities: Street.
Special Features: Search service, library appraisal.
Catalogue: Two times per year.
Collections/Individual Items Purchased: Both.

209
Sun Dance Books
1520 North Crescent Heights
Hollywood, California 90046   (213) 654-2383

Sun Dance Books is open by appointment only. In addition to offering hardbound, out-of-print rare books, it accomplishes collection development and appraisals.
How to Get There: Directions will be given when calling for an appointment.
Owner/Biography: Allan Adrian.
Year Founded/History of Bookstore: 1972.
Number of Volumes: 7,000.
Types/Classifications: Hardbound, pamphlets, ephemera, out-of-print.
General Subject Areas: Imaginary Voyages and Travels, Indians of the Americas, Mexico and Latin Americana, Pacific Ocean Voyages, Southwest and Far West Americana.
Specific Specialties: Filibusters (William Walker, Col. Henry Crabb, etc.)
Other Specialties: All subject areas purchased in any language; Spanish Inquisition, Pyrotechnia, Orientals in the Americas, Japanese-American Relocation Camps.
Mail/Telephone Orders; Credit Cards: Both. No credit cards.
Business Hours: By appointment.
Special Features: Collection development; appraisals.
Catalogue: Published irregularly.
Collections/Individual Items Purchased: Both.
Booksellers' Memberships: Antiquarian Booksellers Association of America.

210
Sylvester & Orphanos Booksellers
2484 Cheremoya Avenue
P.O. Box 2567
Los Angeles, California 90078   (213) 461-1194

Sylvester & Orphanos Booksellers operates a mail order business only and offers out-of-print first editions of American and English literature. The shop occupies 780 square feet of space.
Owner/Biography: Ralph Sylvester and Stathis Orphanos.
Year Founded/History of Bookstore: 1970.
Number of Volumes: 25,000.
Types/Classifications: Hardbound, first editions, fine bindings, out-of-print, association copies, press books, presentation copies, limited editions.
General Subject Areas: American and English Literature.
Specific Specialties: Modern 20th Century Authors.
Mail/Telephone Orders; Credit Cards: Both. No credit cards.
Business Hours: Monday through Friday 9:00 AM - 7:00 PM.
Special Features: Publishing.
Catalogue: Published 4 times per year.
Collections/Individual Items Purchased: Both.

211
This Old House Bookshop
5399 West Holt Boulevard
Montclair, California 91763   (714) 624-5144

The bookstore is in a painted stucco building erected in 1960, with shelves and bins containing over 35,000 general interest items, sorted by price and by interest. The bookstore contains 1,700 square feet of space.

How to Get There: Montclair is 33 miles east of Los Angeles. To reach the bookstore take either the Riverside Freeway (US 60) or the San Bernardino Freeway (US 10); the bookstore is between the two freeways, so take the Central Avenue offramp from either.

Owner/Biography: Thomas H. Guthormsen, owner, is a veteran of World War II and studied books as a G.I. student. At first he had a book mail order business and later sold books from his front porch as a sideline. Since relocating to the present address in 1958 he has been active in developing the shop. He is especially interested in research in books.

Year Founded/History of Bookstore: 1956.

Number of Volumes: 35,000.

Types/Classifications: Hardbound, paperback, magazines, first editions, autographed books, association copies, remainders.

General Subject Areas: Fiction, General, Non-fiction.

Specific Specialties: Juvenile, Scholarly, Mystery.

Other Specialties: Gone With The Wind, Remembrance of Things Past, Winston Churchill.

Mail/Telephone Orders; Credit Cards: Both; cash with order. No credit cards.

Business Hours: Daily and by appointment.

Parking Facilities: Business parking lot.

Special Features: Search service.

Collections/Individual Items Purchased: Individual items only.

212
Tolliver's Books
1634 South Stearns Drive
Los Angeles, California 90035   (213) 939-6054

The bookstore is located on the second floor of a duplex in a large (8,000 square foot) Spanish style apartment converted into a bookshop. The store offers books in the science fields only.

How to Get There: The shop is located in the Pico Boulevard/La Cienega area of Los Angeles, two to three blocks west of Fairfax, off Pico Boulevard.

Owner/Biography: James D. and Evelyn C. Tolliver, owners, have been natural history and science booksellers since 1964.

Year Founded/History of Bookstore: 1970.

Number of Volumes: 40,000.

Types/Classifications: Hardbound, paperback, magazines, first editions, fine bindings, out-of-print, association copies, press books, signed copies, presentation copies, limited editions.

General Subject Areas: Birds, Computer Science, Electronics, Engineering, Fish, Land Mammals, Latin America, Marine Biology, Mathematics, Mexico, Oceanography, Physics, Reptiles, Sea Mammals, Space Technology.

Other Specialties: Science titles in all languages.

Mail/Telephone Orders; Credit Cards: Both. No credit cards.

Business Hours: By appointment only.

Parking Facilities: Street.

Special Features: Search service.

Catalogue: Two times a year.

Collections/Individual Items Purchased: Both.

213
Transition Books
445 Stockton Street
San Francisco, California 94108   (415) 391-5161

The bookstore is a small street-level shop in the heart of downtown San Francisco. It has a large stock of surrealist and Dada material (including autographs) and French artist books. The shop contains 450 square feet of space.

How to Get There: The shop is located 1.5 blocks north of Union Square.

Owner/Biography: Richard Q. and Michele G. Praeger.

Year Founded/History of Bookstore: 1979.

Number of Volumes: 4,000.

Types/Classifications: Hardbound, magazines, broadsides, autographs, ephemera, modern first editions including review copies, association copies, signed copies, presentation copies, limited editions, art books, illustrated books.

General Subject Areas: Literary Criticism, Modern Literature, Twentieth Century Architecture, Twentieth Century Art Books, Twentieth Century Photography.

Specific Specialties: Modern American and European Authors in First Editions, Little Magazines, First Editions of Translations of American and British Authors, Dadaism, Surrealism, French Artists, French Books.

Author Specialties: James Joyce, William Faulkner, John Steinbeck, Jack London, Ernest Hemingway, Gertrude Stein, American Expatriates in London, A. Breton.

Other Specialties: First Editions of French, Spanish, and South American Authors in the Original or in Translation.

Mail/Telephone Orders; Credit Cards: Both. Visa, Mastercard.

Business Hours: Tuesday through Saturday 12:00 Noon - 5:30 PM; other times by appointment. An additional telephone listing: (415) 346-2619.

Parking Facilities: Sutter-Stockton Municipal Garage.

Catalogue: Published irregularly.

Collections/Individual Items Purchased: Both.

Booksellers' Memberships: Antiquarian Booksellers Association of America.

214
Treehorn Books
522 Wilson Street
Santa Rosa, California 95401   (707) 525-1782

The owners describe their bookstore as an old-fashioned general used bookstore which is likely to have something for everyone. They welcome collectors, and give discounts to dealers. The bookstore contains 1,250 square feet of space.

How to Get There: The bookstore is located in Santa Rosa, California, one block west of Highway 101, in Old Railroad Square.

Owner/Biography: Keith Hotaling and Michael Stephens.

Year Founded/History of Bookstore: 1978.

Number of Volumes: 20,000.

Types/Classifications: Hardbound, paperback, magazines, records, ephemera, first editions, illustrated books, out-of-print.

General Subject Areas: Art, Biography, Children's Books, Cooking, History, Literature, Military, Religion, Western Americana.

Specific Specialties: Illustrated Children's Books, Old Cookbooks, World War II, Sonoma County (California), Socialism, Communism.

Author Specialties: Jack London, Luther Burbank, M.F.K. Fisher.

Mail/Telephone Orders; Credit Cards: Both. No credit cards.

Business Hours: Monday through Saturday 11:00 AM - 5:00 PM.

Parking Facilities: Street.

Special Features: Search service, appraisals.

Collections/Individual Items Purchased: Both.

215
Trophy Room Books
4858 Dempsey Avenue
Encino, California 91436   (213) 784-3801

The bookstore features big game hunting in Africa, Asia, and North America. It also stocks African travel and exploration and has some volumes on early Central Asian mountain travel and exploration. The shop is a mail order operation and open by appointment only to regular customers.
How to Get There: Call for directions. The shop is close to two major freeways.
Owner/Biography: Ellen and Jim Herring.
Year Founded/History of Bookstore: Founded in 1974, the shop grew out of the owners' own collection of books. It is in the original location, with the original owners.
Number of Volumes: 2,500.
Types/Classifications: Hardbound only. The stock is almost entirely out-of-print; there are some association copies and presentation copies as well as related color plate items.
General Subject Areas: African Exploration, Big Game Animals, Big Game Hunting, Central Asia Mountain Travel and Exploration, Natural History.
Specific Specialties: Big Game Hunting in Africa, Asia, North America.
Mail/Telephone Orders; Credit Cards: Both. Payment with order; foreign orders must be paid with U.S. dollars. Visa, Mastercard.
Business Hours: By appointment only: Monday through Friday 9:00 AM - 5:00 PM. Business telephone also rings at owners' home.
Parking Facilities: Street (free).
Special Features: Search service.
Catalogue: Four times per year.
Collections/Individual Items Purchased: Both.
Booksellers' Memberships: Antiquarian Booksellers Association of America.

216
Vagabond Books
2076 Westwood Boulevard
Los Angeles, California 90025   (213) 475-2700

The bookstore specializes in rare and hard-to-obtain books in its specialty fields. It contains 1,000 square feet of space.
How to Get There: The shop is 1.5 miles south of the University of California at Los Angeles (UCLA), between Santa Monica and Olympic Boulevards.
Owner/Biography: Craig and Patricia Graham, owners, are college graduates and dedicated readers.
Year Founded/History of Bookstore: The bookstore was first opened by its present owners in Santa Monica, California in 1976 and was relocated to its present address in 1978.
Number of Volumes: 30,000.
Types/Classifications: Hardbound mainly, autographs, paperback originals, first editions, fine bindings, out-of-print, association copies, press books, signed copies, presentation copies, limited editions, color plate books.
General Subject Areas: Art, Cinema, Detective, Fiction, History, Jazz, Literature, Modern Art, Music, Photography, Poetry.
Specific Specialties: Expatriate Literature of the 1920's (Paris).
Author Specialties: Raymond Chandler, Vladimir Nabokov, Virginia Woolf, Graham Greene, James Joyce, John Gardner, Rex Stout, John Updike, Jorge Borges, Ernest Hemingway, Anthony Burgess, Cornell Woolrich.
Other Specialties: The bookstore specializes in rare and hard-to-obtain books in its specialty fields.
Mail/Telephone Orders; Credit Cards: Both. Cash with order. Visa, Mastercard.

Business Hours: Monday through Saturday 11:00 AM - 6:00 PM.
Parking Facilities: Ample street parking and large parking lot in back of the store.
Special Features: Search service, appraisals.
Catalogue: A mysteries catalogue is currently under preparation.
Collections/Individual Items Purchased: Both.
Booksellers' Memberships: Antiquarian Booksellers Association of America.

217
Valley Book Store
132 East Main Street
El Cajon, California 92020 (619) 447-9068

This is a general bookstore with stock in most categories; it contains 700 square feet of space.
How to Get There: If driving, take Route 8 east to El Cajon Boulevard in El Cajon, turn on Main Street to East Main; the cross street is Magnolia Avenue.
Owner/Biography: Clifford Lloyd Trittipo.
Year Founded/History of Bookstore: 1973.
Number of Volumes: 30,000.
Types/Classifications: Hardbound, paperback.
General Subject Areas: Biography, Children's Books, General, Literature, Science Fiction and Fantasy.
Specific Specialties: Mystery.
Mail/Telephone Orders; Credit Cards: No credit cards.
Business Hours: Monday through Saturday 9:00 AM - 5:00 PM; Sunday 11:00 AM - 5:00 PM.
Parking Facilities: Street.
Collections/Individual Items Purchased: Both.
Booksellers' Memberships: San Diego Booksellers Association.

218
Van Norman - Booksellers
4047 Bay View Court
San Diego, California 92103 (619) 296-6451

Van Norman - Booksellers specializes in fine books and prints by mail order only. The stock occupies 1,200 square feet of space.
Owner/Biography: Allen and Grace H. Van Norman. The Van Normans are avid collectors and participants in the various specialities listed below.
Year Founded/History of Bookstore: 1979. The Van Normans are the original founders at the present location.
Number of Volumes: 14,000.
Types/Classifications: Hardbound, ephemera, prints, posters, maps, first editions, out-of-print, signed copies, illustrators.
General Subject Areas: Aeronautics, Alaska, Antarctic, Archaeology, Architecture, Arctic, Astronautics, Astronomy, Automobiles, Biography, Books About Books, Cats, Children's Literature (Illustrated), Cookbooks, Crafts, Dance (Ballet), Dogs, Finance and Wall Street, Geology, History of American Business and Industry, Hollywood, Horses, Hunting and Fishing, Journalism, Law, Lincoln, Magic, Maritime, Medicine, Meteorology, Mexico, Mountaineering, Nautical, Numismatics, Photography, South America, Sports, Technical, Theater, Trains, Travel, U.S. Civil War, Western Americana.
Specific Specialties: San Diego History, California History, Indians, Southwest, Birds, Animals, Plants, Trees, Naturalists, Aquatic Animals and Fishes, Baja California (Mexico).
Author Specialties: Louis Bromfield, Ernest Hemingway, Sinclair Lewis, Max Miller, Upton Sinclair, Somerset Maugham, John Steinbeck, Irving Stone.
Mail/Telephone Orders; Credit Cards: Both. Personal check with order; ten day return privilege. No credit cards.
Business Hours: Monday through Friday 8:00 AM - 8:00 PM.

Special Features: Search service with specialization in listed fields.
Collections/Individual Items Purchased: Both.
Booksellers' Memberships: San Diego Booksellers Association.

219
Vernon & Zona Braun - Booksellers
9004 Rosewood Drive
Sacramento, California 95826   (916) 363-3862

This bookstore is primarily a mail order business; special customers may visit by appointment only.
How to Get There: Call first for an appointment and directions.
Owner/Biography: Vernon and Zona Braun. Vernon is retired from the Air Force, and is a collector of Western Americana and a seller of duplicated items, ephemera, and natural history.
Year Founded/History of Bookstore: 1960.
Number of Volumes: 15,000.
Types/Classifications: Hardbound, paperback, magazines, broadsides, ephemera, photographs, first editions, fine binding, out-of-print, press books, signed copies, limited editions, color plate books.
General Subject Areas: Americana, Local Histories, Natural History, State Histories, Western Americana.
Specific Specialties: Pacific Northwest (U.S.), Colorado, Montana, Idaho, Washington, Oregon, Nevada, California, Arizona, New Mexico, Texas, Alaska, South Seas, North Dakota, South Dakota, WPA State Guides, Rivers of America Series.
Author Specialties: Willa Cather, Ernest Hemingway, Ross Santee, Dan Cushman, A.B. Guthrie, J. Frank Dobie, Ann Zwinger.
Mail/Telephone Orders; Credit Cards: Both. Personal check or cash with order; postage and insurance extra. No credit cards.
Business Hours: Weekdays 8:00 AM - 5:00 PM.
Parking Facilities: Street.
Collections/Individual Items Purchased: Both.

220
Vernon Howard - Books / Gamut Book Shop
723 California Drive
Burlingame, California 94010   (415) 343-7428

This is a large general stock antiquarian bookstore with several specialties well represented. The shop contains 1,200 square feet of space.
How to Get There: The bookstore is located three miles south of the San Francisco airport. From San Francisco, take the Bayshore Freeway south, exit at Broadway (which is the second turnoff after the airport), go west across the tracks, turn left on California Drive. From San Jose, drive north on the Bayshore Freeway, take the Peninsula Avenue Exit, go west across the tracks, turn right on California Drive.
Owner/Biography: Vernon Howard, owner, was in the University of California at Berkeley when he was bitten by the love of books.
Year Founded/History of Bookstore: Founded in 1940, the business was mail order from the owner's home in San Francisco until 1970. In that year the store was founded in Burlingame.
Number of Volumes: 50,000.
Types/Classifications: Hardbound.
General Subject Areas: General.
Specific Specialties: Mountaineering, Western Americana, American History, Literature, World Travel, World History, Sciences, Humanities, Music, Medicine, Law, Art, Cookbooks, Sea, Military, Biography, Belles Lettres, Poetry, Children's Books, Foreign Literature, Semantics, Sociology, Psychology.
Mail/Telephone Orders; Credit Cards: Both. Personal checks. No credit cards.
Business Hours: Saturday 1:00 PM - 5:30 PM, and by appointment. The owner is generally in the store most mornings 9:30 AM - 12:30 PM, but the visitor should call first.
Parking Facilities: Good street parking available.

Collections/Individual Items Purchased: Both.

221
Volume One Used Books
1405 Second Street
Napa, California 94559   (707) 252-1466

The bookstore is on a corner lot. It is a well lit, clean, spacious, uncluttered shop. All books are shelved; the majority, in alphabetical order. The business is family owned and run. Fifty percent of the business is paperback exchange. The shop contains 1,000 square feet of space.

How to Get There: The shop is located in the city of Napa, just one hour's drive north of the San Francisco Bay area. It is just off Route 121-29; take the First Street Exit east to Second Street, follow to the corner of Second and Franklin Streets.

Owner/Biography: Judith H. Philbrick, Scott C. Stephenson. Judith has always loved books, so when the opportunity arose to buy the bookstore in 1977 she happily did so. In early 1982 her son Scott became a partner. Scott had worked in the store in its early years, but had recently been managing a shoe store in the Bay Area, and was more than happy to get back in the book business.

Year Founded/History of Bookstore: Founded in 1975, the store was purchased by its present owner in 1977. It is still on its original site.

Number of Volumes: 10,000 paperback, 5,000 hardbound.

Types/Classifications: Hardbound, paperback, National Geographics, postcards, maps, tour guides for the wine country, some first editions, out-of-print, remainders.

General Subject Areas: General.

Mail/Telephone Orders; Credit Cards: No mail or telephone orders. No credit cards.

Business Hours: Monday through Friday 9:30 AM - 5:30 PM; Saturday 10:00 AM - 4:00 PM.

Parking Facilities: Street.

Special Features: Paperback trade-in policy, paperback exchange.

Collections/Individual Items Purchased: Both.

222
W. Graham Arader III
560 Sutter Street
San Francisco, California 94102

See: W. GRAHAM ARADER III, King of Prussia, Pennsylvania.

223
W. R. Slater - Books
1639 Humphrey Drive
Concord, California 94519   (415) 825-2617

This is a mail order operation specializing in science fiction and fantasy first editions, digest magazines, paperback first editions and first printings, all at reasonable prices. The shop contains 400 square feet of space. Visitors should call first for an appointment.

How to Get There: If driving from San Francisco take Highway 680 east to Highway 4 at Pleasant Hill, then to Willow Pass in Concord, then east 2 miles.

Owner/Biography: William and Kathleen Slater.

Number of Volumes: 3,000.

Types/Classifications: Hardbound, paperback, magazines, first editions, signed copies, limited editions.

General Subject Areas: Science Fiction and Fantasy.

Specific Specialties: Fantasy-related Children's Books like Tom Swift.

Mail/Telephone Orders; Credit Cards: Both. No credit cards.

Business Hours: Evenings and weekends by appointment.

Parking Facilities: Street.
Special Features: Limited search service; want lists invited.
Catalogue: Sporadic.
Collections/Individual Items Purchased: Both.

224
Wahrenbrock's Book House
726 Broadway
San Diego, California 92101   (619) 232-0132

The bookstore describes itself as San Diego's oldest and largest bookstore. It is housed on three floors and contains high-demand nonfiction both new and used, new clothbound fiction, military history, world history, and a few other specialized areas along with a large literature room containing used clothbound as well as new and used paperbacks. The total space is 7,200 square feet.

How to Get There: The shop is in the middle of downtown San Diego, California, between 7th and 8th Avenues on the city's main street, Broadway.

Owner/Biography: C.A. Valverde, Manager; Jan Tonnesen, Assistant Manager.

Year Founded/History of Bookstore: The bookstore was founded in 1935 selling used books and magazines. In 1944 it moved to 7th and Broadway and was purchased by its present owners in 1965. The rare book department was started in 1969. The last move, to its present location, was in 1983.

Number of Volumes: 250,000.

Types/Classifications: Hardbound, paperback. The stock is 60 percent general antiquarian, 10 percent rare, 20 percent new, and 10 percent ephemera. There are also signed letters, maps, pressbooks, autographed material.

General Subject Areas: Baja California, California, Children's Books, County Histories, Genealogy, Mexico, Music, Nautical, Occult, Travels, Voyages.

Other Specialties: Books in Spanish.

Mail/Telephone Orders; Credit Cards: Both. The store will ship with a bill to established customers; others require cash with order; personal check accepted; charge card orders shipped same day. Visa, Mastercard.

Business Hours: Monday through Friday 9:30 AM - 5:30 PM; Saturday 9:00 AM - 5:00 PM; closed Sunday.

Parking Facilities: Public parking lot, street.

Special Features: General stock of good antiquarian books at reasonable prices; specialty catalogues issued; rare book room open by appointment only.

Catalogue: Published usually in conjuction with book fairs, but a quarterly is planned.

Collections/Individual Items Purchased: Both.

Booksellers' Memberships: Antiquarian Booksellers Association of America; San Diego Booksellers Association.

225
Wessex Books & Records
1083 El Camino Real
Menlo Park, California 94025   (415) 321-1333

The bookstore is a general shop with a highly selective stock, emphasizing quality and scholarly books, mostly in hardcover. Fiction and literary criticism account for more than half of the stock. The store believes that it maintains one of the best general hardcover collections of literary fiction in the United States in addition to scholarly and university press books in most subjects. It also carries an extensive stock of LP records. The shop contains 1,200 square feet of space.

How to Get There: The store is located 1.5 miles north of Stanford University on El Camino Real, 2 doors south of Santa Cruz Avenue. It is between the exits for Willow Road and Marsh Road of U.S. 101, and between the exits for Sandhill Road and Woodside Road of Highway 280. Menlo Park is 35 minutes south of San Francisco.

Owner/Biography: Thomas Haydon.

Year Founded/History of Bookstore: Founded in 1975, the bookstore is on the original site, and with the original owner.

Number of Volumes: 25,000 books, 8,000 LP records.

Types/Classifications: Hardbound, quality paperbacks, LP records, first editions, scholarly books, modern first editions, university press books.

General Subject Areas: Blues Music, Books About Books, History, Literary Criticism, Music, Mysteries, Philosophy, Prose, Psychology, Twentieth Century Fiction.

Author Specialties: Thomas Hardy, Georges Simenon, P.G. Wodehouse.

Other Specialties: Scholarly books in most subjects. Classical LP Records, Blues LP Records, Jazz LP Records.

Mail/Telephone Orders; Credit Cards: Both. Prepaid. No credit cards.

Business Hours: Monday through Saturday 11:00 AM - 6:00 PM; Sunday 12:00 Noon - 5:00 PM.

Parking Facilities: Street, public lots, private lot in the rear.

Collections/Individual Items Purchased: Both.

Booksellers' Memberships: Antiquarian Booksellers Association of America.

226
West L.A. Book Center
1650 Sawtelle Boulevard
Los Angeles, California 90025   (213) 473-4442

The bookstore is located in what was formerly the West Los Angeles American Legion Post. The main display area is fully carpeted with five comfortable and uncluttered aisles. The books are grouped and the shelves are labeled by subject matter. In many cases the books are also alphabetized for further convenience. The shop contains 1,300 square feet of space.

How to Get There: The shop is located one-half block south of Santa Monica Boulevard and one block west of the San Diego Freeway.

Owner/Biography: Kenneth M. Hyre.

Year Founded/History of Bookstore: 1959.

Number of Volumes: 25,000.

Types/Classifications: Hardbound, paperback, select magazines, fine bindings in singles and in sets.

General Subject Areas: American History, American Literature, Americana, Architecture, Art, Baedeker Guides, Biography, Children's Books, Cinema, Crafts, English History, English Literature, European History, European Literature, Foreign Literature in Translation, Gardening, Literary Criticism, Military History, Music, Mysteries, National Geographics, Occult, Photography, Poetry, Science Fiction and Fantasy, Selective Magazines, Theater, Travel.

Mail/Telephone Orders; Credit Cards: Both; terms for individuals and institutions stated in the catalogue; no credit cards.

Business Hours: Monday through Friday 12:00 Noon - 7:00 PM; Saturday 12:00 Noon - 6:00 PM; Sunday 1:00 PM - 5:00 PM.

Parking Facilities: Business parking lot.

Catalogue: One or two per year.

Collections/Individual Items Purchased: Both.

227
William & Victoria Dailey, Ltd.
8216 Melrose Avenue
Los Angeles, California 90046   (213) 658-8515

The bookstore is located in a lovely Art-Deco building on Melrose Avenue where antique stores, art galleries, and fashion establishments are joined by several rare book shops. Its selective stock of books and prints is beautifully displayed on premises designed and built to the owners' specifications. The shop contains 1,650 square feet of space. Private collectors, institutional representatives, and accredited dealers are always welcome.

How to Get There: The store is located in West Hollywood on Melrose Avenue between La Cienega and Crescent Heights.

Owner/Biography: William and Victoria Dailey.

Year Founded/History of Bookstore: 1974.

Number of Volumes: 6,000 books, 2,000 prints.

Types/Classifications: Rare books, illustrated books, fine prints.

General Subject Areas: Applied Arts, Bibliography, Fine Arts, Literature, Medicine, Printing, Private Presses, Science.

Specific Specialties: Graphic Processes, History of Lithography, Catalogues Raisonnes, 19th Century French Prints (especially the influence of Japanese art on French art), History of Printing.

Mail/Telephone Orders; Credit Cards: Both. Visa, Mastercard, American Express.

Business Hours: Tuesday through Friday 10:00 AM - 6:00 PM; Saturday 11:00 AM - 5:00 PM.

Parking Facilities: Street.

Catalogue: Three times a year.

Collections/Individual Items Purchased: Both.

Booksellers' Memberships: Antiquarian Booksellers Association of America.

Miscellaneous: The bookstore maintains a private press, The Press of the Pegacycle Lady, under which it publishes various works of art, poetry, and aesthetics.

228

William P. Wreden, Books & Manuscripts

200 Hamilton Avenue

P.O. Box 56

Palo Alto, California 94302 (415) 325-6851

The bookstore is a spacious (4,000 square feet of space) old general antiquarian bookstore in downtown Palo Alto, California. The stock, which ranges from art to zoology, and from a few dollars to several hundred, is organized by subject and alphabetically by author within subject areas. Of particular interest are sections of English and American literature, Western Americana, Californiana, trade catalogues, bibliography, book arts, fine press books. A limited selection of autograph letters, ephemera, maps, and prints is also available. Catalogues are issued once a year and will be sent upon request. Catalogue books may be seen at the shop. The store has a continuing interest in purchasing both individual books and collections of a fine or unusual nature.

Owner/Biography: William P. Wreden, Sr., Owner; William P. Wreden, Jr., Manager. Mr. Wreden, Sr., with extensive experience in the field, does appraisals for a fee. A founding member of the Antiquarian Booksellers Association of America, Mr. Wreden, Sr. has been in the business for over forty years.

Year Founded/History of Bookstore: William P. Wreden, Sr. started the business on Howard Avenue in Burlingame, California in 1937. The store occupied three different locations there before moving to Palo Alto in 1953 after a disastrous fire. During the 1960's his son William managed a branch shop in San Francisco. In 1970 the business was consolidated at its present location.

Number of Volumes: 15,000.

Types/Classifications: Hardbound, broadsides, autographs, ephemera, first editions, press books, out-of-print, signed copies, limited editions, manuscripts.

General Subject Areas: American Literature, English Literature, General, Printing, Western Americana.

Specific Specialties: California, Trade Catalogues.

Mail/Telephone Orders; Credit Cards: Both. Visa, Mastercard.

Business Hours: Tuesday through Saturday 10:00 AM - 5:00 PM.

Parking Facilities: Street and nearby off street public parking lots.

Special Features: The bookstore occasionally publishes limited editions in the fields of bibliography and Western Americana.

Catalogue: Published annually.

Collections/Individual Items Purchased: Both.

Booksellers' Memberships: Antiquarian Booksellers Association of America (founding member), Antiquarian Booksellers Association International.

229
Wilshire Books
3018 Wilshire Boulevard
Santa Monica, California 90403   (213) 828-3115

This is a general bookstore occupying 800 square feet of space.
Owner/Biography: Leigh D. Peffer.
Year Founded/History of Bookstore: 1968.
Types/Classifications: Hardbound, paperback, used, out-of-print.
General Subject Areas: General.
Business Hours: Monday through Saturday 11:00 AM - 6:00 PM; Sunday 12:00 Noon - 5:00 PM.
Collections/Individual Items Purchased: Both.

230
Woodruff & Thush "Twice Read Books"
81 East San Fernando
San Jose, California 95113   (408) 294-3768

The bookstore contains a million used books, paperbacks, and magazines on all subjects. The store is a city
block long.
Owner/Biography: Morris Thush, Craig Thush.
Year Founded/History of Bookstore: The bookstore was founded in 1928 by the present owners.
Number of Volumes: One million.
Types/Classifications: Hardbound, paperback, magazines.
General Subject Areas: General.
Mail/Telephone Orders; Credit Cards: Both. Visa, Mastercard.
Business Hours: Monday through Saturday 10:30 AM - 5:30 PM.
Parking Facilities: Street.
Collections/Individual Items Purchased: Both.

231
Xanadu Galleries
212 North Orange
Glendale, California 91203   (213) 244-0828

The bookstore features an extensive collection of out-of-print and first editions, children's books, art,
religious and literary works. Two specialties are 1800's leather bound books and a widespread collection of
Western Americana. The bookstore contains 7,500 square feet of space.
Owner/Biography: Evelyn Schneirsohn.
Year Founded/History of Bookstore: 1952.
Number of Volumes: 100,000.
Types/Classifications: Hardbound, manuscript materials, first editions, limited editions.
General Subject Areas: American Literature, Art, Biography, Children's Books, English Literature, Herit-
age Press, Poetry, Western Americana.
Author Specialties: Ernest Hemingway, D.H. Lawrence, Carl Sandburg, Upton Sinclair.
Mail/Telephone Orders; Credit Cards: Both. Visa, Mastercard.
Business Hours: Monday through Friday 10:00 AM - 6:00 PM; Saturday 11:00 AM - 4:00 PM.
Parking Facilities: Public parking lot.
Special Features: The bookstore also includes antiques for sale and a fine art gallery.
Collections/Individual Items Purchased: Both.

232
Yesterday's Books
2859 University Avenue
San Diego, California 92104 (619) 298-4503

This is a general bookstore, with 700 square feet of space.
Owner/Biography: Kenneth E. Baker.
Year Founded/History of Bookstore: 1976.
Number of Volumes: 12,000.
Types/Classifications: Hardbound, paperback, magazines.
General Subject Areas: General stock.
Mail/Telephone Orders; Credit Cards: Mail orders only; money order must accompany mail order. No credit cards.
Business Hours: Daily 10:00 AM - 6:00 PM.
Parking Facilities: Street.
Collections/Individual Items Purchased: Both.
Booksellers' Memberships: San Diego Book Sellers Association.

233
Zeitlin & Ver Brugge Booksellers, Ltd.
815 North La Cienega Boulevard
Los Angeles, California 90069 (213) 655-7581

The only large red barn on "Restaurant Row," the bookstore has been in business for more than 50 years. Internationally known dealers in old and rare books in the history of science and medicine, the shop also handles examples of early printing, Western Americana, Californiana, and art. A gallery upstairs carries old master prints and works by 20th Century Western and Californian artists. An additional telephone is (213) 652-0784.
How to Get There: From the San Diego Freeway take Sunset Boulevard east, turn right (south) on La Cienega. From the Hollywood Freeway take Highland to Sunset, then west to La Cienega, and south. The store is on the west side of the street south of Santa Monica Boulevard.
Owner/Biography: Jacob I. Zeitlin and Josephine Ver Brugge Zeitlin. Jake Zeitlin, poet, raconteur, and self-proclaimed wheeler-dealer, though past 80 still presides over the sales floor. His wife Josephine handles a flourishing technical books department.
Year Founded/History of Bookstore: The bookstore has been in business for more than 50 years.
Types/Classifications: Hardbound, prints, art.
General Subject Areas: Art, Californiana, History of Medicine, History of Science, Old Master Prints, Western Americana, Works of 20th Century Western and California Artists.

234
Zeitlin Periodicals Co. Inc.
817 South La Brea Avenue
Los Angeles, California 90036 (213) 933-7175

The bookstore features extensive stocks in books and journals in the fields of science, medicine, liberal arts, and earth sciences. Its special fields are in professional and learned society publications, as well as out-of-print geological publications.
How to Get There: The bookstore is located on La Brea Avenue in Los Angeles between Wilshire Boulevard and Olympic Boulevard, and contains approximately 10,000 square feet of space.
Owner/Biography: Stanley L. Zeitlin, President.
Year Founded/History of Bookstore: Founded in 1925 as Zeitlin & Ver Brugge, Books. The Periodical Division was established in 1960.
Number of Volumes: 10,000.
Types/Classifications: Hardbound, periodicals, sets of back-issue journals and periodicals available in complete sets, single volumes, or single issues, in all fields.

General Subject Areas: Journals, Periodicals.

Specific Specialties: Technical, Scientific, Medical, Liberal Arts, Professional and Learned Society Publications; the foregoing featured in both American and Foreign publications.

Other Specialties: U.S. Geological Survey publications, various state geological publications.

Mail/Telephone Orders; Credit Cards: Both; no credit cards.

Business Hours: Monday through Friday 9:00 AM - 5:00 PM.

Parking Facilities: Business parking lot.

Catalogue: Catalogue published semi-annually.

Collections/Individual Items Purchased: Collections.

Booksellers' Memberships: Antiquarian Booksellers Association of America.

COLORADO

235
Bargain Book Shop
600 East Abriendo
Pueblo, Colorado 81004 (303) 543-5101

Bargain Book Shop of Pueblo carries mostly paperback novels, fiction and non-fiction trade books, comics. Used books are sold for half the original price and new paperbacks are offered at 20 percent discount. The shop occupies 2,000 square feet of space.

How to Get There: Conveniently located off Highway I-25. Take Abriendo Exit; second building to right off this exit.

Owner/Biography: Nancy Catalano.

Year Founded/History of Bookstore: 1968. The original site of the store was 413 West Northern in Pueblo; moved to present location in 1978.

Number of Volumes: 150,000.

Types/Classifications: Paperback, some magazines and hardbound books, comics.

General Subject Areas: Biography, Children's Books, Gothic Novels, Historical Romance, Science Fiction and Fantasy, Westerns.

Specific Specialties: Harlequin Romance.

Other Specialties: Comics.

Mail/Telephone Orders; Credit Cards: Both. Mail orders must be prepaid. No credit cards.

Business Hours: Monday through Saturday 10:00 AM to 5:00 PM; closed Sundays.

Parking Facilities: Business parking lot; street parking.

Collections/Individual Items Purchased: Individual items only.

236
The Cache!
7157 West U.S. 34
Loveland, Colorado 80537 (303) 667-1081

Used books occupy about one third of "The Cache!" The shop also carries antiques, crafts, collectibles, and metal location equipment. The book section occupies about 400 square feet of space.

How to Get There: The shop is located west of the Loveland city limits about 4 miles on U.S. 34, north side of road.

Owner/Biography: Martha P. Anderson and Edward T. Anderson.

Year Founded/History of Bookstore: 1973. The business began in the basement of the Anderson home and eventually was located in the old town section of Fort Collins. It was moved to the present location in 1977.

Number of Volumes: 20,000.

Types/Classifications: Hardbound, paperbacks, magazines, miscellaneous paper ephemera, first editions, out-of-print, signed copies.

General Subject Areas: General.

Specific Specialties: Colorado.

Author Specialties: Zane Grey.

Mail/Telephone Orders; Credit Cards: Both. No credit cards.

Business Hours: Fall and Winter Daily 10:00 AM - 4:00 PM; Spring and Summer Daily 9:00 AM - 6:00 PM.

Parking Facilities: Parking in front of building.

Special Features: Search service.

Collections/Individual Items Purchased: Individual items only.

237
Collectors' Center
609 Corona Street
Denver, Colorado 80218   (303) 831-7237

The Collectors' Center is probably Denver's oldest antiquarian bookstore. It occupies 7,500 square feet of space.

Owner/Biography: Don Bloch.
Year Founded/History of Bookstore: 1952.
Number of Volumes: 18,000.
Types/Classifications: Hardbound, first editions, fine bindings, out-of-print, association copies, press books, signed copies, presentation copies, limited editions, color plate books, maps, old postcards, rare newspapers and periodicals, rare historical pamphlets, rare paperbacks, rare phonograph records (jazz, classical), sets, prints, ephemera.
General Subject Areas: Americana, Architecture, Art, Biography, Crafts, Criminology, Essays, Gardening, Hobbies, Metaphysics, Military, Music, Natural History, Occult, Poetry, Presidents (U.S.), Religion, Sea and Ships, Social Sciences, Sports and Games, Transportation, Travel and Adventure.
Mail/Telephone Orders; Credit Cards: Both. No credit cards.
Business Hours: Monday through Friday 10:00 AM - 12:00 Noon, 1:00 PM - 5:00 PM; Saturday 9:00 AM - 1:00 PM.
Parking Facilities: Business parking lot, street parking.
Collections/Individual Items Purchased: Both.

238
Court Place Antiquarian Bookshop
3827 West 32nd Avenue
Denver, Colorado 80211   (303) 455-0317

This bookshop is the "largest of its kind in the Rocky Mountain West." It is located in 4,500 square feet of shop space behind an old Victorian mansion about 4 minutes from downtown Denver. Apart from 75,000 rare, scarce, and used books are original works of art by American artists and a variety of prints. Among the more unusual categories available are incunabula and fore-edge paintings.

How to Get There: Take Speer Boulevard North to 32nd Avenue, turn left and go 8 blocks to the corner of 32nd and Osceola. The number 32 bus goes right in front of the store from downtown Denver.
Owner/Biography: Alan and Marcy Culpin. The Culpins started the bookshop as a side line. Alan teaches at a local college and Marcy is an historian with the National Park Service.
Year Founded/History of Bookstore: 1976. Beginning in a corner of the Nepenthes Coffeehouse, the bookshop moved after two years to a second story location. It moved to its present location in 1982.
Number of Volumes: 75,000.
Types/Classifications: Hardbound, some early periodicals, leather bindings, decorative cloth bindings, first editions, fine bindings, out-of-print, association copies, press books, signed copies, presentation copies, limited editions, color plate books, incunabula.
General Subject Areas: Americana, Anthologies, Anthropology, Archaeology, Art, Aviation, Bibliography, Biography, Books About Books, Chess, Children's Books, Civil War, Engineering, Exploration, Fore-Edge Paintings, Geology, History, Humor, Hunting and Fishing, Law, Literary Criticism, Medical, Military, Mining, Mountaineering, Music, Mysteries, Natural History, Philosophy, Poetry, Psychology, Railroads, Religion, Science, Sociology, Sports, Technical, Theatre, Topography, Travel, Western Americana.
Specific Specialties: Colorado, New Mexico, Utah, Mormonism, Wyoming, Arizona, California, Texas, Northwest, Great Plains, Western Art, American Indians, Fur Trade, Cowboys and Cattlemen, Westerns, Europe, China, Southeast Asia, Australia, Pacific Islands, India, Africa, Arctic, Antarctic, Canada, Alaska, Birds, Gardening, Reptiles, Animals, Horses, Dogs.
Author Specialties: Mark Twain, Ernest Hemingway, John Steinbeck, D.H. Lawrence, Graham Greene.
Mail/Telephone Orders; Credit Cards: Both. Shipped via U.S. Postal Service only. American Express and Visa accepted. An additional telephone number is (303) 455-5477.
Business Hours: Monday through Thursday 10:30 AM - 5:30 PM; Friday and Saturday 10:00 AM - 2:00 PM; Sunday 12:00 Noon - 4:00 PM.
Parking Facilities: Street parking.

Special Features: Search service; publishing.
Catalogue: Published 3 to 4 times per year.
Collections/Individual Items Purchased: Both.
Miscellaneous: The shop also carries works of Western Art (oils, water colors, and prints).

239
Hermitage Antiquarian Bookshop
2817 East 3rd Avenue
Denver, Colorado 80206   (303) 388-6811

The Hermitage Antiquarian Bookshop carries hardbound scholarly, rare, out-of-print, first editions, limited editions, and press books. The shop occupies 1,000 square feet of space.
Owner/Biography: Robert W. Topp.
Year Founded/History of Bookstore: 1973.
Number of Volumes: 25,000.
General Subject Areas: Scholarly Fields.
Specific Specialties: Western Americana, Modern First Editions.
Mail/Telephone Orders; Credit Cards: Both. American Express, Visa, Mastercard accepted.
Business Hours: Seven days per week 10:00 AM - 5:30 PM.
Parking Facilities: Free parking behind building.
Catalogue: Published yearly.
Collections/Individual Items Purchased: Both.
Booksellers' Memberships: Antiquarian Booksellers Association of America.

240
King's Market - Booksellers
1021 Pearl Street
Suite D
Boulder, Colorado 80302   (303) 444-8484

The King's Market is an antiquarian and modern book shop dealing in out-of-print and hard-to-find books of a scholarly nature. The shop occupies 1,000 square feet of space.
Owner/Biography: Robert Wayne.
Year Founded/History of Bookstore: 1981.
Types/Classifications: Hardbound, paperback, out-of-print, first editions, fine bindings, reading copies.
General Subject Areas: Alaska, Colorado, Exploration, Geology, Mathematics, Mountaineering, Philosophy, Science, Western Americana.
Mail/Telephone Orders; Credit Cards: Both. Visa and Mastercard accepted.
Business Hours: Monday through Saturday 11:00 AM - 4:30 PM and by appointment.
Parking Facilities: Public parking lot.
Special Features: Search service.
Catalogue: Published 2 times per year.
Collections/Individual Items Purchased: Both.
Miscellaneous: The King's Market has a computer bulletin board for telecommunications.

241
Kugelman & Bent Books
5924 East Colfax Avenue
Denver, Colorado 80220   (303) 333-1269

This bookstore specializes in modern literature, "lost fiction," and poetry. It occupies 1,000 square feet of space.
Owner/Biography: Michael Grano and Steve Wilson.

Year Founded/History of Bookstore: 1981.
Number of Volumes: 20,000.
Types/Classifications: Hardbound, broadsides, autographs, ephemera, first editions, out-of-print, association copies, signed copies, presentation copies, limited editions.
General Subject Areas: Literature, Philosophy, Poetry, Regional American Literature.
Mail/Telephone Orders; Credit Cards: Both. Visa and Mastercard accepted.
Business Hours: Monday through Saturday 9:00 AM - 6:00 PM.
Parking Facilities: Street parking.
Catalogue: Catalogue published.
Collections/Individual Items Purchased: Both.

242
Mt. Falcon Books
926 9th Avenue
Greeley, Colorado 80631 (303) 356-9211

This is an antiquarian bookstore dealing in out-of-print and used books of a general nature. Some rare items are included in the stock. The shop contains 1,400 square feet of space.
How to Get There: Greeley is located at the junction of U.S. Highways 85 and 34, midway between Denver, Colorado and Cheyenne, Wyoming, and about 50 miles east of Rocky Mountain National Park.
Owner/Biography: Ron Stump and Sandra Bower.
Year Founded/History of Bookstore: 1979.
Number of Volumes: 14,000.
Types/Classifications: Hardbound, paperback, magazines, broadsides, ephemera.
General Subject Areas: General.
Specific Specialties: Western Americana, Jack Kerouac and the "Beats."
Author Specialties: Jack Kerouac.
Other Specialties: Hot Air Ballooning.
Mail/Telephone Orders; Credit Cards: Both; cash with order; Visa, Mastercard.
Business Hours: Monday through Saturday 9:30 AM - 5:30 PM.
Special Features: Search Service.
Collections/Individual Items Purchased: Both.

243
Prospector
2505 West Alamo Avenue
Littleton, Colorado 80120 (303) 798-5552

This is a small walk-in shop specializing in Modern Library, illustrated classics, hunting, fishing, nautical, railroads, mining, agriculture, and Western Americana. The shop occupies 415 square feet of space.
How to Get There: Littleton is south of Denver. The shop is in the same building as the Trailways Package Express Depot. Alamo Avenue is a one way (west) street.
Owner/Biography: Melville L. Moore. Mr. Moore is a former arts and crafts instructor, museum curator, and technical art and technical publications editor.
Year Founded/History of Bookstore: 1972.
Number of Volumes: 12,500.
Types/Classifications: Hardbound, out-of-print, first editions, press books, signed copies, color plate books.
General Subject Areas: American Indians, Arizona, Boy Scouts, California, Colorado, Contemporary Authors, Explorers and Settlers, Flora and Fauna, Mines and Mining Men, Montana, Mountain Men, Natural History, Nevada, New Mexico, Spanish Southwest, Texas, Utah, Wyoming.
Author Specialties: Baden Powell, William Hillcourt, Dan Beard, John Muir, Enos Mills, Ernest Thompson Seton.
Other Specialties: Handbooks for engineers, architects, and contractors.
Mail/Telephone Orders; Credit Cards: Both. Cash with order; returnable within 10 days of mailing date. Visa and Mastercard accepted.

Business Hours: Tuesday through Saturday 10:00 AM - 5:00 PM.
Parking Facilities: Free parking lot.
Collections/Individual Items Purchased: Individual items only; collections sometimes.
Miscellaneous: The owner states that he is "good at letting browser's alone or can be talkative as heck when encouraged."

244
Rosenstock Arts
1228 East Colfax Avenue
Denver, Colorado 80218   (303) 832-7190

Rosenstock Arts stocks a wide selection of new and out-of-print Western Americana with a special emphasis on the fur trade and early Colorado. There is also a good selection of titles about American art and artists to complement the extensive collection of paintings.

How to Get There: Located on Denver's main east-west avenue, the bookstore is about one mile east of the State Capitol Building.
Owner/Biography: Fred A. Rosenstock. Mr. Rosenstock is known as one of the most knowledgeable dealers in Western Americana with experience dating back to the 1920's. At one time he owned one of the largest private collections of paintings by and printed material relating to Charles M. Russell, the cowboy artist.
Year Founded/History of Bookstore: 1928. For decades Mr. Rosenstock operated the Bargain Bookstore in downtown Denver, moving several miles away in 1962 to open a strictly antiquarian shop. He decided to retire in 1976 at the age of 80 but after a few weeks reopened his store as Rosenstock Arts.
Number of Volumes: 10,000.
Types/Classifications: Hardbound, some early photographs and albums, many original paintings and etchings, first editions, color plate books.
General Subject Areas: American Artists, American Indians, Early Colorado, Fur Trade, Southwest, Western Americana, Western Railroading.
Other Specialties: Sets of Bodmer, Catlin, and McKenney-Hall documentaries on the American Indian.
Mail/Telephone Orders; Credit Cards: Both. Payment in advance if customer is not known to the store. No credit cards.
Business Hours: Monday through Friday 10:00 AM - 5:00 PM; Saturday 10:00 AM - 3:00 PM.
Parking Facilities: Street parking.
Special Features: Publishing sideline - Old West Publishing Co.
Collections/Individual Items Purchased: Both.

245
Rue Morgue Bookshop
956 Pearl
Boulder, Colorado 80302   (303) 443-8346

The Rue Morgue Bookshop takes its name from Edgar Allan Poe's "The Murders in the Rue Morgue," the first detective story ever written. It is an all-mystery bookstore carrying some new books with an emphasis on used, rare, and out-of-print. A wide range of reference works in the field is available to customers who wish to look up favorite authors.

How to Get There: The shop is located in a courtyard 1 block west of the downtown Boulder Mall at 10th and Pearl. Boulder is about 30 miles northwest of Denver and is reached by U.S. 36; exit on Pearl Street and travel west 18 blocks, following the downtown traffic loop at the Mall.
Owner/Biography: Tom and Enid Schantz. Both have contributed articles, interviews, and book reviews relating to mystery fiction to various publications including "The Armchair Detective" and "The Bloomsbury Review" and have done introductions for books from their own and other publishing houses. In addition to cataloging rare and out-of-print mysteries, the Schantz' publish a newsletter, "The Purloined Letter," describing new books in the field. It is issued about 10 times yearly to customers.
Year Founded/History of Bookstore: 1969.
Number of Volumes: 10,000.

Types/Classifications: Hardbound, paperback, back issue magazines, first editions, rare, scarce, out-of-print, reading copies.

General Subject Areas: Detective Fiction, Mysteries.

Specific Specialties: Sherlock Homes, Victorian Detective Fiction, Droodiana, English Mysteries, Private Eye Fiction.

Author Specialties: Arthur Conan Doyle, R. Austin Freeman, John Dickson Carr, Dashiell Hammett, Raymond Chandler, Ellery Queen, Agatha Christie, Ngaio Marsh, Michael Innes, Freeman Wills Crofts, John Rhode, Sax Rohmer.

Mail/Telephone Orders; Credit Cards: Both. New customers are asked to pay in advance if not using credit card; postage etc. charged at cost. Visa and Mastercard accepted.

Business Hours: Monday through Saturday 10:00 AM - 5:30 PM, Sunday 12:30 PM - 4:30 PM; also by appointment.

Parking Facilities: Street parking, nearby public parking lots.

Special Features: Publishing sideline - Rue Morgue Press (name changed in 1980 from Aspen Press).

Catalogue: Published 6 to 8 times per year.

Collections/Individual Items Purchased: Both.

Booksellers' Memberships: West End Booksellers.

CONNECTICUT

246
Alton Ketchum
333 Cognewaug Road
Cos Cob, Connecticut 06807 (203) 869-1070

Alton Ketchum operates his business from his private home. He is a specialist in newspapers and deals in direct mail orders only.

How to Get There: If it is extremely urgent that you visit Mr. Ketchum, please call for an appointment.

Owner/Biography: Alton Ketchum. Mr. Ketchum is a retired advertising executive and has been listed in "Who's Who in America."

Year Founded/History of Bookstore: 1970. The business has been operated from the same site with the same owner and activity.

Number of Volumes: 200,000 historic newspapers.

Types/Classifications: Historic newspapers, magazines, broadsides.

General Subject Areas: British and American Newspapers.

Specific Specialties: Especially strong on the U.S. Revolutionary and Civil War Periods.

Mail/Telephone Orders; Credit Cards: Both. Cash with order. Telephone orders are accepted from established customers. No credit cards.

Business Hours: Afternoons and evenings.

Catalogue: Catalogue published.

Collections/Individual Items Purchased: Collections only.

247
Angler's and Shooter's Bookshelf
Goshen, Connecticut 06756 (203) 491-2500

This unique book dealer specializes in the literature of angling, hunting (shooting), and the sporting art. The business is primarily mail order. The stock represents what may well be the largest inventory of sporting books in the world.

How to Get There: Should a visit be necessary, call for appointment and directions.

Owner/Biography: Colonel Henry A. Siegel.

Year Founded/History of Bookstore: 1967. The business was originally located in New York City and moved to its present location in 1968.

Number of Volumes: 75,000.

Types/Classifications: Hardbound, rare, out-of-print, selected new titles.

General Subject Areas: Angling, Hunting (Shooting), Sporting Art.

Specific Specialties: Sporting Literature.

Other Specialties: Derrydale Press Books.

Mail/Telephone Orders; Credit Cards: Both. No credit cards.

Business Hours: None. Phone between 6:00 AM and 11:00 PM.

Special Features: The business includes The Angler's and Shooters Press. The latest publication is "The Derrydale Press: A Bibliography."

Catalogue: Published in two parts annually. There is a $5 charge for catalogue which includes over 5,000 items.

Collections/Individual Items Purchased: Both.

Booksellers' Memberships: Antiquarian Booksellers Association of America including Middle Atlantic and Northeast Chapters.

248
Antiquarium
66 Humiston Drive
Bethany, Connecticut 06525 (203) 393-2723

The Antiquarium specializes in antiquarian, scholarly, out-of-the-way unusual books, manuscripts, prints, maps, and paper ephemera. There is no open stock. Visits may be arranged by appointment only.

How to Get There: Call for directions.

Owner/Biography: Lee and Marian Ash. Mr. Ash is a professional librarian and library consultant. He owns a very large reference collection and desires to help dealers or collectors, by mail or telephone, who may need reference help (within reason and not too frequently) at no charge whenever he can. Mr. Ash states that "book people" are a friendly lot to know and are generally mutually helpful. He has compiled and edited "Subject Collections: A Guide to Special Collections and Subject Emphases in United States and Canadian Libraries," (Bowker, 1984). He is the compiler and publisher of "Serial Publications Containing Medical Classics," (Antiquarium, 1979) and is the editor and book review editor of "Special Collections: A Quarterly Survey of Subject Collections in Libraries, with Reviews of the Reference Literature, Bibliographic Controls, and Directories of Collections of Related Interest," (Haworth Press, 1981-date).

Year Founded/History of Bookstore: 1959.

Number of Volumes: 30,000 (including ephemera).

Types/Classifications: Hardbound, broadsides, autographs, ephemera, first editions, fine bindings, out-of-print, association copies, press books, signed copies, presentation copies, limited editions, color plate books.

General Subject Areas: Art, Bibliography, Books About Books, Description and Travel, History, Librarianship, Natural History, Psychiatry, Reference Books, Scholarship, Wild Animal Training.

Specific Specialties: Arctic, Antarctica, Australia, Cats, China, Connecticut Local History, Demonology, Discovery and Exploration, Homosexuality, Icelandica (History and Travel Only), Japan, Korea, Medical History and Historic Medicine, Training the Big Cats, Maritime History, Museology, Pacific Rim and Islands of the Pacific, Polar Regions, Witchcraft, Satanism, Tibet.

Author Specialties: Baron Corvo, Rupert Brooke, Edward Gorey, Gavin Maxwell, Edna St. Vincent Millay, Eleanor Roosevelt, Frederic Rolfe, Adlai Stevenson, Mervyn Peake, Gore Vidal, Sir Arthur Quiller-Couch.

Mail/Telephone Orders; Credit Cards: Both. Cash with order except for established clients. No credit cards.

Business Hours: By appointment only.

Special Features: Appraisals of books, manuscripts, prints and maps for estate, gift, or insurance purposes (collections or individual pieces). Standard fees and expenses. Mr. Ash will travel anywhere to evaluate library or private collections.

Catalogue: Published irregularly.

Collections/Individual Items Purchased: Both.

Booksellers' Memberships: Connecticut Antiquarian Booksellers Association, New England Appraisers Association, American Society of Professional Consultants, Grolier Club, Players Club.

249
Antique Books
3651 Whitney Avenue
Hamden, Connecticut 06518 (203) 281-6606

Antique Books is located in a large home plus two additional buildings. Hardbound books of early Americana are featured and most are over 100 years old. The stock occupies 3200 square feet of space. Visitation is by appointment or chance.

How to Get There: The shop is located on Whitney Avenue (Highway 10) between New Haven and Hartford. If traveling by Highway 91, take exit 10 to deadend, turn right on Whitney.

Owner/Biography: Willis O. Underwood. Mr. Underwood has been a collector of early Americana for over thirty years. He is now in semi-retirement and has operated as a business for eight years.

Year Founded/History of Bookstore: 1975.

Number of Volumes: 30,000.

Types/Classifications: Hardbound, first editions, out-of-print, limited editions.

General Subject Areas: Agriculture, Biography, Children's Literature, Early Americana, Education, History, Literature, Medicine, Music, Natural History, Nautical, School Books, Science, Travel.

Specific Specialties: Civil War (U.S.), Revolutionary War (U.S.), State Histories.

Other Specialties: Early American school books in Spanish, French, German, Greek, and Latin.
Mail/Telephone Orders; Credit Cards: Both. Instructions specified in catalogue. No credit cards.
Business Hours: By appointment only.
Parking Facilities: In circular driveway.
Catalogue: Published 10 times per year.
Collections/Individual Items Purchased: Both.

250
Bancroft Book Mews
86 Sugar Lane
Newtown, Connecticut 06470   (203) 426-6338

Bancroft Book Mews is conducted from the owner's home and visits can be arranged by appointment. The specialty of the house includes books about music, musicians, composers. Scores, librettos, sheet music, and old programs are also available plus a small number of records. Theater and dance are subjects of interest and books in these categories are accumulating gradually.

How to Get There: Phone for directions. Newtown is near Danbury, Connecticut and easily accessible from Route 84.

Owner/Biography: Eleanor C. Bancroft. Ms. Bancroft is a former manager of bookstores and owner of her own retail bookstore (new) for ten years.

Year Founded/History of Bookstore: 1981.

Number of Volumes: 2,500.

Types/Classifications: Anything of interest in the music field, first editions, fine bindings, out-of-print, association copies, press books, signed copies, limited editions, presentation copies, color plate books.

General Subject Areas: Biography, Cinema, Fiction, Humor, Music, Poetry, Regional Books, Travel.

Mail/Telephone Orders; Credit Cards: Both. Telephone orders to known customers only. Mail orders require payment in advance except for libraries. No credit cards.

Business Hours: By appointment only.

Catalogue: Catalogue is expected to be published in the near future.

Collections/Individual Items Purchased: Both.

Booksellers' Memberships: Fairfield Country Antiquarian Booksellers Association.

251
Bibliolatree
Route 66
East Hampton, Connecticut 06424   (203) 267-8222

Bibliolatree occupies half the basement of the "Country Store" with its yarn shop, Indian curios, and miscellaneous furniture. The books try to stay on their shelves neatly, if precariously; they are arranged in the usual categories, the fundamental division being between American literature and history and all others. The shop occupies 2,500 square feet of space.

How to Get There: The shop is about midway between East Hampton and Marlborough (Connecticut) on Route 66. From Hartford take Route 2 to Marlborough; exit at the 66 ramp; turn right. From Middletown go east on 66. From New Haven go to Middletown and east on 66.

Owner/Biography: Paul O. Clark.

Year Founded/History of Bookstore: 1977.

Number of Volumes: 25,000.

Types/Classifications: Hardbound, some magazines, first editions, signed copies, illustrated books.

General Subject Areas: American and English Literature, Arts and Crafts, Children's Literature, Economics, General History, Law, Literary Criticism, Music, Nature, Philosophy, Photography, Psychology, Travel.

Mail/Telephone Orders; Credit Cards: Both. No credit cards.

Business Hours: Saturday and Sunday 1:00 PM on; other days occasionally (call).

Parking Facilities: Ample parking lot right in front.

Collections/Individual Items Purchased: Both.

252
Book Block
8 Loughlin Avenue
Cos Cob, Connecticut 06807   (203) 629-2990

The Book Block occupies 1,000 square feet of space. This antiquarian bookdealer specializes in literature, fine printing, private press pooks, voyages, and travels. Customers are welcome by appointment.

How to Get There: 2nd exit in Connecticut of I-95 after the Westchester line (if traveling from New York). Call for precise directions.

Owner/Biography: David Block. Mr. Block has been an antiquarian bookseller for the past five years and was previously an editor and publisher.

Year Founded/History of Bookstore: 1978. The Book Block moved from a retail shop in downtown Greenwich to an office location.

Number of Volumes: 2,500.

Types/Classifications: Broadsides, autographs, first editions, fine bindings, association copies, press books, signed copies, presentation copies, limited editions, color plate books, fine printing.

General Subject Areas: Americana, Literature, Private Press Books, Voyages and Travels.

Mail/Telephone Orders; Credit Cards: Both. Personal checks should include postage and insurance. Visa and Mastercard accepted.

Business Hours: By appointment only.

Parking Facilities: Ample parking available.

Catalogue: Published 5 times per year.

Collections/Individual Items Purchased: Both.

Booksellers' Memberships: Antiquarian Booksellers Association of America, International League of Antiquarian Booksellers, Connecticut Antiquarian Booksellers Association.

253
Books & Birds
Mason Street
Coventry, Connecticut 06238   (203) 742-8976

Books & Birds is located in an old woolen mill which now houses a variety of entreprenurial businesses, crafts people, and flea marketers. The books are sorted by categories, but there are also piles of "to-be-sorted" volumes. The building is unheated, so winter visitors should dress warmly. The shop occupies about 1,500 square feet of space.

How to Get There: Mason Street is off Main Street (Route 31) in the center of Coventry, opposite the town's library. The factory building housing the store is the driveway on the right. Coventry is in eastern Connecticut, close to the University of Connecticut and I-86.

Owner/Biography: Gil Salk. Mr. Salk operates Books & Birds as a part-time labor of love. He is an active birdwatcher, fisherman, and photographer, a member of MENSA, and a single parent of a young daughter.

Year Founded/History of Bookstore: 1980. The store was begun originally as a hobby.

Number of Volumes: 15,000.

Types/Classifications: Hardbound, some paperbacks, occasional magazines, records, ephemera, bird-related prints and decoys, illustrated books.

General Subject Areas: Adventure, Americana, Antiques, Art, Biography, Bird Books, Books About Books, Business, Children's Books, Cooking, Crafts, Drama, Education, Erotica, Gardening, History, Hobbies, Law, Military, Music, Mysteries, Nature, Nautical, Performing Arts, Poetry, Psychology, Reference, Religon, Science Fiction, Sexuality, Sociology, Sports, Technical, Travel, Women, Writing.

Specific Specialties: Books and art relating to birds.

Mail/Telephone Orders; Credit Cards: Both. Cash or check with order (institutions billed), insurance extra.

Business Hours: Friday and Saturday 12:00 Noon - 4:00 PM; hours to be expanded.

Parking Facilities: Business parking lot with ample room.

Special Features: Search service.

Collections/Individual Items Purchased: Both.

Booksellers' Memberships: Connecticut Booksellers Association.

254
Branford Rare Book & Art Gallery
221 Montowese Street
Branford, Connecticut 06405 (203) 488-5882

Branford Rare Book & Art Gallery is located on the central square of the shoreline town of Branford, 10 minutes from New Haven. It stocks Americana and travel and is housed in an art deco building. The shop occupies 600 square feet of space.
How to Get There: Take exit 54 from Route 95 (Connecticut Turnpike).
Owner/Biography: John R. Elliott.
Year Founded/History of Bookstore: 1978.
Number of Volumes: 15,000 in shop and warehouse.
Types/Classifications: Hardbound, ephemera, maps, out-of-print.
General Subject Areas: American Letters, Americana, Travel.
Mail/Telephone Orders; Credit Cards: Both. Visa and Mastercard accepted.
Business Hours: Tuesday through Saturday 10:00 AM - 4:30 PM.
Parking Facilities: Business parking lot.
Catalogue: Published 4 times per year.
Collections/Individual Items Purchased: Both.
Booksellers' Memberships: Connecticut Antiquarian Booksellers Association, Ephemera Society of America.

255
Bryn Mawr Bookshop
56 1/2 Whitney Avenue
New Haven, Connecticut 06510 (203) 562-4217

This bookshop sells used and rare books in all categories from Art to Zoology for the benefit of Bryn Mawr College. The shop occupies 2,500 square feet of space.
How to Get There: The bookstore is located in central New Haven, 1 block from Yale University.
Owner/Biography: Bryn Mawr College Alumnae Association of New Haven.
Year Founded/History of Bookstore: 1972. The shop grew out of the annual 3-day sale held for about 20 years to raise money for Bryn Mawr College scholarships.
Number of Volumes: 25,000.
Types/Classifications: Hardbound, paperback, magazines, broadsides, autographs, ephemera, first editions, out-of-print.
General Subject Areas: General.
Mail/Telephone Orders; Credit Cards: Both. No credit cards.
Business Hours: Wednesday through Friday 12:00 Noon - 3:00 PM; Saturday 10:00 AM - 1 PM.
Parking Facilities: Public parking lots, metered street parking.
Special Features: Card file of "wants" kept for regular customers.
Collections/Individual Items Purchased: All stock is donated.
Miscellaneous: Tax credits are given for donations over $25.

256
Chuck's Books
530 Newfield Street
Route 72
Middletown, Connecticut 06457 (203) 346-1637

Chuck's Books is a very pleasant, well organized store that has a good selection at all times of approximately 20,000 used books in many categories. It has a back-up stock of more than 30,000 volumes. New and used comics and fine gifts are also available as well as a search service. The stock occupies 600 square feet of space.
How to Get There: The bookstore is located on Route 72 just 1.3 miles north of the junction of Routes 66 and 72 in Middletown on right hand side or 3 miles south of Cromwell on left hand side of Route 72.

Owner/Biography: Chuck James. Chuck has pursued careers in the fields of engineering and psychology with a BA from Central Connecticut State University. He has been professionally active in the bookselling trade for the past six years.

Year Founded/History of Bookstore: 1983.

Number of Volumes: 20,000 (30,000 in storage).

Types/Classifications: Hardbound, paperback, magazines, comics, gifts, first editions, out-of-print.

General Subject Areas: General.

Mail/Telephone Orders; Credit Cards: Both. No credit cards.

Business Hours: Tuesday through Thursday 10:00 AM - 6:00 PM; Friday 10:00 AM - 9:00 PM; Saturday 10:00 AM - 6:00 PM; Sunday 11:00 AM - 4:00 PM.

Parking Facilities: Ample free parking.

Special Features: Limited search service; personalized service; customers are invited to spend time and chat.

Collections/Individual Items Purchased: Both.

Booksellers' Memberships: New England Booksellers Association, Connecticut Antiquarian Booksellers Association.

257
Clipper Ship Bookshop
12 North Main Street
Essex, Connecticut 06426   (203) 767-1666

Located in an 18th century riverport village, the bookstore is in a house built circa 1820. The first floor is devoted to general trade and current books covering all subjects with a specialty in nautical and maritime books. The second floor is devoted entirely to antiquarian and out-of-print books with a very large nautical and and maritime section.

How to Get There: Take exit 69 North off I-95 (Connecticut Turnpike) then Exit 3 (Essex) at bottom of exit ramp make a left then a right at the traffic light, follow this road (West Avenue) into town; at traffic circle make a left and the bookshop is on the right hand side of the street.

Owner/Biography: Frank T. Crohn, Jr.

Year Founded/History of Bookstore: 1946. The Clipper Ship has had four different locations in Essex since 1946, moving into larger space each time. The present owner is the fourth to own the bookshop.

Number of Volumes: Antiquarian 3,500; general trade 15,000.

Types/Classifications: Hardcover, some ephemera, first editions, signed copies, some limited editions.

General Subject Areas: Art, Autobiography, Biography, Children's Literature, History, Hunting and Fishing, Nature, Nautical and Maritime, New England, Travel.

Mail/Telephone Orders; Credit Cards: Both. Postage $1.50 for first book and $.50 for each additional book (shipped via UPS). Visa and Mastercard accepted.

Business Hours: May 31st to September 7th and November/December: Monday through Saturday 9:00 AM - 6:00 PM; Sunday 11:00 AM - 5:00 PM.

Parking Facilities: Street parking.

Special Features: Search service.

Collections/Individual Items Purchased: Both.

Booksellers' Memberships: New England Booksellers Association.

258
Colebrook Book Barn
Route 183, North
Colebrook, Connecticut 06021   (203) 379-3185

The stock at the Colebrook Book Barn is general, representing old, used, and rare in most fields. It is located in an old New England barn.

How to Get There: Colebrook is in northwest Connecticut, approximately 30 miles northwest of Hartford. The Book Barn is 1 mile north of the center of Colebrook on Route 183.

Owner/Biography: Robert S. Seymour.

Year Founded/History of Bookstore: 1955.
Number of Volumes: 15,000.
Types/Classifications: Hardbound, rare, ephemera, out-of-print.
General Subject Areas: Americana, Children's Books, English and American Literature.
Mail/Telephone Orders; Credit Cards: Both. Cash with order unless an established customer. Visa and Mastercard accepted.
Business Hours: Daily including Sunday 10:00 AM - 5:00 PM; appointment advised; evenings by appointment only.
Parking Facilities: Parking in front of shop.
Catalogue: Published 1 to 3 times per year.
Collections/Individual Items Purchased: Both.
Booksellers' Memberships: Antiquarian Booksellers Association of America, Ephemera Society.
Miscellaneous: The Book Barn is unheated, and although visitors are welcome by appointment in the winter, browsing is uncomfortable except on the warmest days.

259
Deborah Benson Bookseller
River Road
West Cornwall, Connecticut 06796   (203) 672-6614

Deborah Benson Bookseller deals in out-of-print and rare books with specialties in modern first editions, fore-edge paintings, and inscribed books.
How to Get There: Call for directions.
Owner/Biography: Deborah Covington. Ms. Covington has been in the book business for 38 years; her father was a well known bookseller.
Year Founded/History of Bookstore: 1956.
Number of Volumes: 12,000.
Types/Classifications: Out-of-print, rare, first editions, fore-edge paintings, inscribed books.
General Subject Areas: General.
Author Specialties: Dorothy Parsons Lathrop, John Steinbeck.
Mail/Telephone Orders; Credit Cards: Both. Cash with order. No credit cards.
Business Hours: "24 hours a day."
Parking Facilities: Plenty of parking space available.
Special Features: Search service.
Collections/Individual Items Purchased: Both.
Miscellaneous: Appraisals.

260
Flynn's Printer's Devil Bookstore
1660 Meriden-Waterbury Turnpike
Milldale, Connecticut 06467   (203) 628-5424

See FLYNN'S PRINTER'S DEVIL BOOKSTORE, Middletown, Connecticut.

261
Flynn's Printer's Devil Bookstore
20 Riverview Center
Middletown, Connecticut 06457   (203) 344-0022

The Printer's Devil Bookstores aim to be interesting and well organized used book havens. Their specialty is metaphysics and science fiction with a great many collectible magazines, paperbacks, and comics. The second store is located in Milldale, Connecticut.
How to Get There: The Middletown store is located next to Sears. The Milldale store is on Route 66 in the Milldale Plaza.

Owner/Biography: Andreia J. Flynn.
Year Founded/History of Bookstore: 1969. The Milldale store is the original store; the Middletown store opened in 1975.
Number of Volumes: 100,000.
Types/Classifications: Hardbound, paperback, magazines, comics.
General Subject Areas: General.
Mail/Telephone Orders; Credit Cards: Neither. No credit cards.
Business Hours: Middletown: Monday through Saturday 9:30 AM - 5:30 PM; Thursday and Friday until 8:00 PM; Milldale: Monday through Saturday 9:30 AM to 6:00 PM; Friday until 9:00 PM; Sunday 12:00 Noon - 5:00 PM.
Parking Facilities: Business parking lot in Milldale; public parking lot in Middletown.
Catalogue: Published monthly.
Collections/Individual Items Purchased: Both.

262
John Steele Book Shop
385 Capitol Avenue
Hartford, Connecticut 06106   (203) 522-8126

The bookstore carries a large stock of used, out-of-print, and antiquarian books. The shop contains 1,100 square feet of space; the storage area is an additonal 1,000 square feet.
How to Get There: If driving, take the Capitol Avenue Exit from I-84. The shop is two blocks west of the State Capitol.
Owner/Biography: William W. Keifer.
Year Founded/History of Bookstore: 1983.
Number of Volumes: 50,000.
Types/Classifications: Hardbound, paperback, magazines, ephemera, first editions, out-of-print, color plate books.
General Subject Areas: General.
Specific Specialties: Connecticut History, New England.
Other Specialties: Older Technical Books, Wireless, Carpentry.
Mail/Telephone Orders; Credit Cards: Both. No credit cards; personal checks accepted.
Business Hours: Tuesday through Saturday 11:30 AM - 5:00 PM; Sunday and Monday by appointment.
Collections/Individual Items Purchased: Both.

263
Jumping Frog
161 South Whitney Street
Hartford, Connecticut 06105   (203) 523-1622

The bookstore is in a storefront of a 1920's apartment building, situated in a quiet neighborhood less than a mile from the Mark Twain Memorial and the Harriet Beecher Stowe House. The shop contains 725 square feet of space.
How to Get There: From Interstate 84 take Exit 46, turn right at the second light. The shop is on the left, halfway down the first block.
Owner/Biography: William M. McBride and Deidre Whitlock McBride. Mr. McBride operated McBride First Editions, a mail order business specializing in first editions of modern literature, for six years before opening the shop. Mrs. McBride previously worked in her father's book business, Whitlock Farm Books, of Bethany, Connecticut. Mr. Mc Bride is the author of several books on book collecting including "A Pocket Guide to the Identification of First Editions," "Points of Issue," and "Mark Twain: A Bibliography of the Collection of the Mark Twain Memorial and the Stowe-Day Foundation." Mrs. McBride is the compiler of "A Traveler's Directory of Old Book Stores in New England, New York, New Jersey, and Pennsylvania."
Year Founded/History of Bookstore: 1983.
Number of Volumes: 8,500.

Types/Classifications: Hardbound, selected paperbacks, original magazine advertising for American and foreign automobiles, trucks, railroads, and aircraft; autographed literary material; illustrated books; 99 percent of the stock is first editions.

General Subject Areas: Advertising, Aircraft, Art, Automobiles, Children's Books, Detective, Drama, History, Humor, Jazz, Literary Biography, Music, Poetry, Railroads, Transportation, Trucks.

Specific Specialties: American First Editions, British First Editions, First Editions in English of Foreign Language Works including Russian, Japanese, French, Spanish.

Author Specialties: Mark Twain, William Styron.

Mail/Telephone Orders; Credit Cards: Both. No credit cards. Want lists accepted for first editions of literary material only. The shop will quote first editions by telephone from the ready stock.

Business Hours: Wednesday 11:00 AM - 5:30 PM; Thursday 11:00 AM - 9:00 PM; Friday 11:00 AM - 5:30 PM; Saturday 10:00 AM - 5:30 PM; Sunday 1:00 PM - 5:30 PM; Monday and Tuesday by appointment; a second telephone number is (203) 523-7707.

Parking Facilities: Street, with no meters.

Special Features: The bookstore is also headquarters for McBride/Publisher which provides material for collectors (see Owner/Biography above); new titles are added yearly.

Collections/Individual Items Purchased: Both.

264
Kingsmill Bookshop
Route 32, Hall Complex
South Willington, Connecticut 06265 (203) 429-1970

The shop is located in the former blacksmith's shop of a 19th Century mill now used to house a few small businesses and a post office. The shop occupies 700 square feet of space and spans a small stream, the run off of the town pond.

How to Get There: Willington is 25 miles northeast of Hartford and can easily be reached from Exit 100 of I-86; from this exit take Route 74 for 1 mile to Route 32 and then 2 miles to the bookshop.

Owner/Biography: William and Eleanor Peters. William was a librarian for 20 years and for the last 15 years was Acquisitions Librarian at nearby University of Connecticut.

Year Founded/History of Bookstore: 1980.

Number of Volumes: 6,000.

Types/Classifications: Hardbound, out-of-print, first editions.

General Subject Areas: Fiction, Literary Criticism, Philosophy, Poetry, Religion.

Specific Specialties: University Press Publications.

Mail/Telephone Orders; Credit Cards: Mail orders only. Payment with order. No credit cards.

Business Hours: Thursday and Friday 1:00 PM - 5:00 PM; Saturday 10:00 AM - 4:00 PM; Sunday by chance.

Parking Facilities: Business parking lot.

Special Features: Search service.

Catalogue: Published occasionally.

Collections/Individual Items Purchased: Both.

265
Laurence Witten Rare Books
181 Old Post Road
P.O. Box 490
Southport, Connecticut 06490 (203) 255-3474

The bookstore is situated in a beautiful Victorian house in historic Southport, Connecticut; the shop contains 2,500 square feet of space.

How to Get There: The shop is near Southport Center, one minute's drive from Exit 19 of the Connecticut Turnpike, U.S. Interstate I-95.

Owner/Biography: Laurence Witten.

Year Founded/History of Bookstore: Founded in 1951, the bookstore has always been in Connecticut, first in Bethany, then in New Haven, next in Easton, and finally in Southport since 1976.

Number of Volumes: 2,000.

Types/Classifications: Early printed and early illustrated books; Medieval books and manuscripts, early bindings, incunabula, illuminated manuscripts.

General Subject Areas: Medieval, Middle Ages, Renaissance.

Specific Specialties: Original Materials of the Middle Ages and Renaissance.

Other Specialties: Most of the books and manuscripts are in Continental European languages.

Mail/Telephone Orders; Credit Cards: Both; no credit cards.

Business Hours: Monday through Friday 9:00 AM - 5:00 PM.

Parking Facilities: The shop's own parking lot.

Catalogue: Twice a year.

Collections/Individual Items Purchased: Both.

Booksellers' Memberships: Antiquarian Booksellers Association of America, Antiquarian Booksellers Association (England), Verband Deutscher Antiquare.

266
Mark V. Ziesing, Bookseller
768 Main Street
Willimantic, Connecticut 06226 (203) 423-5836

The shop is located above 768 Main Street on the second floor and contains 400 square feet of space.

How to Get There: Willimantic is about 40 miles east of Hartford.

Owner/Biography: Mark V. Ziesing.

Year Founded/History of Bookstore: 1973.

Number of Volumes: 30,000.

Types/Classifications: Hardbound, paperback, magazines; new, used, and vintage books; first editions, signed copies, ephemera.

General Subject Areas: Horror, Science Fiction and Fantasy, Weird.

Author Specialties: Gene Wolf, Philip K. Dick.

Mail/Telephone Orders; Credit Cards: Both; payment required with order along with postage unless prior arrangements are made. Visa and Mastercard accepted. Mail address: P.O. Box 806, Willimantic, CT 06226. Second phone: (203) 423-3867.

Business Hours: Tuesday through Saturday 10:00 AM - 5:00 PM; and by appointment.

Parking Facilities: Municipal lot and street parking.

Special Features: Search service; publishing sideline.

Catalogue: Bimonthly.

Collections/Individual Items Purchased: Both.

Booksellers' Memberships: Antiquarian Booksellers Association of America.

267
Museum Gallery Book Shop
360 Mine Hill Road
Fairfield, Connecticut 06430 (203) 259-7114

The bookstore specializes in books about the Fine and Decorative Arts. It contains approximately 2,500 square feet of space. Visitors are urged to call ahead to make an appointment as the owner may be off book hunting himself.

How to Get There: Fairfield, Connecticut is some 52 miles east of New York City. The bookstore is located about midway between Interstate 95 and the Merritt Parkway.

Owner/Biography: Henry B. Caldwell.

Year Founded/History of Bookstore: The shop opened its doors in June 1977 in a one-room establishment just off the Old Post Road in Southport, Connecticut. The shop was moved in the summer of 1982 to the Greenfield Hill section of Fairfield.

Number of Volumes: 10,000.

Types/Classifications: Hardbound, monographs, out-of-print.
General Subject Areas: Architecture, Artists, Decorative Arts, Fine Arts, Sculpture.
Mail/Telephone Orders; Credit Cards: Both; no credit cards; personal checks accepted.
Business Hours: By appointment only.
Parking Facilities: Ample.
Special Features: Search service on books related to Fine Arts.
Catalogue: Published infrequently.
Collections/Individual Items Purchased: Both.
Booksellers' Memberships: Fairfield County Antiquarian Booksellers.

268
Nutmeg Books
354 New Litchfield Street (Rt. 202)
Torrington, Connecticut 06790

(203) 482-9696

The bookshop occupies two floors of an outbuilding behind the owners' house. Books of all categories in a wide variety of price ranges fill two large rooms downstairs. The upstairs room contains additional books as well as prints, maps, and ephemera. The shop contains 1,000 square feet of space.
How to Get There: Torrington is in the northwestern corner of Connecticut, bordering the Litchfield Hills. A hardworking industrial city, it is easily reached via Route 8 or Route 202. The bookstore is to the rear of a large blue house on Route 202 midway between central Torrington and colonial Litchfield.
Owner/Biography: Bill and Debbie Goring.
Year Founded/History of Bookstore: 1977.
Number of Volumes: 15,000.
Types/Classifications: Used, out-of-print, rare, some maps, graphics, and ephemera.
General Subject Areas: General.
Mail/Telephone Orders; Credit Cards: Both; Mastercard.
Business Hours: Tuesday through Sunday 12:00 Noon - 5:00 PM; other times by appointment.
Parking Facilities: Parking in rear.
Special Features: Search service.
Catalogue: Publishes bi-monthly lists.
Collections/Individual Items Purchased: Both.
Booksellers' Memberships: Northwestern Connecticut Antiquarian Booksellers Association, Fairfield County Antiquarian Booksellers Association.

269
O'Connell's Yesteryear
828 Orange Street
New Haven, Connecticut 06511

Mr. O'Connell describes his bookstore as "a great big pile of books." He requests that visits be made by appointment only and these should be arranged by mail.
Owner/Biography: Peter J. O'Connell. Mr. O'Connell holds a B.A. from Johns Hopkins University and an M.A. from Yale University. He is a writer, editor, researcher, and lecturer.
Year Founded/History of Bookstore: 1976. O'Connell's Yesteryear was formerly located at 970 State Street in the historic district of New Haven.
Number of Volumes: 10,000.
Types/Classifications: Hardbound, paperback, magazines, broadsides, autographs, ephemera, first editions, fine bindings, out-of-print, association copies, press books, signed copies, presentation copies, limited editions, color plate books.
General Subject Areas: General.
Mail/Telephone Orders; Credit Cards: No telephone orders. Mail orders must include price of book plus $.50 per volume for postage. No credit cards.
Business Hours: By appointment or mail order only.

Parking Facilities: Street parking.
Special Features: "Knowledgeable conversation."

270
R & D Emerson
The Old Church, Main Street
Falls Village, Connecticut 06031 (203) 824-0442

R & D Emerson deals in old and rare books in all fields. The shop occupies 3,000 square feet.
How to Get There: Call for directions.
Owner/Biography: Robert and Dorothy Emerson.
Year Founded/History of Bookstore: 1948. The business was founded in New York City and moved to Connecticut in 1961.
Number of Volumes: 50,000.
Types/Classifications: Hardbound, rare, first editions, out-of-print.
General Subject Areas: General.
Mail/Telephone Orders; Credit Cards: Both. Visa and Mastercard accepted.
Business Hours: Seven days a week (closed January, February, March) 12:00 Noon - 7:00 PM.
Parking Facilities: Street parking.
Catalogue: Published occasionally.
Collections/Individual Items Purchased: Both.
Booksellers' Memberships: Antiquarian Booksellers Association of America.

271
Raven Metaphysical Book Shop
40 West Broad Street
Pawcatuck, Connecticut 06379 (203) 599-3535

The book shop carries both used and new books on astrology, metaphysics, occult, and meditation. It occupies 2,000 square feet of space.
How to Get There: The shop is located in downtown Pawcatuck near the resort area of Watch Hill, Rhode Island.
Owner/Biography: James A. Faiella and June White.
Year Founded/History of Bookstore: 1974.
Number of Volumes: 3,000.
Types/Classifications: Hardbound, paperback, new, out-of-print, gems, stones.
General Subject Areas: Astrology, Metaphysics, Mysticism, Occult, Psychic Phenomena.
Author Specialties: Edgar Cayce, Rudolph Steiner, Jess Stern.
Mail/Telephone Orders; Credit Cards: No mail orders; telephone orders accepted. No credit cards.
Business Hours: Wednesday through Sunday 10:00 AM - 2:00 PM.
Parking Facilities: Public parking in rear of store.
Collections/Individual Items Purchased: Both.
Miscellaneous: Special speakers and workshops.

272
Walter E. Hallberg, Bookseller
16 Hawthorn Street
Hartford, Connecticut 06105 (203) 524-1618

The bookstore, featuring paperback Americana, is presently open by appointment only.
Owner/Biography: Walter E. Hallberg.
Year Founded/History of Bookstore: 1935.
Number of Volumes: 5,000.

Types/Classifications: Paperback, imprints, photographs, lithographs, autographs, maps, documents, ephemera.

General Subject Areas: Americana.

Specific Specialties: Connecticut.

Mail/Telephone Orders; Credit Cards: Both.

Business Hours: By appointment only (presently).

Collections/Individual Items Purchased: Both.

273
Whitlock Farm Booksellers

20 Sperry Road

Bethany, Connecticut 06525 (203) 393-1240

The bookstore consists of four barns on what was once a large farm. Now besides books only turkeys, some beef cattle, and horses remain. The two barns open to the public are the sheep barn and the turkey brooding house. Books priced over $5.00 are in the Turkey House, with those over $25.00 in five tall glass-front locked cases. The books on the current Whitlock catalogue (about 1,000) are in the "Morgue." The Sheep Barn houses books priced under $5.00. In total, there is in excess of 5,000 square feet of space.

How to Get There: Take Route 69 four miles north of the Wilbur Cross Parkway at New Haven, or twelve miles south of Route 84 at Waterbury. Watch for the bookstore's sign at the boundary of Woodbridge and Bethany. Follow Morris Road (short and winding) to the end.

Owner/Biography: Gilbert Whitlock, owner; Everett Whitlock, manager.

Year Founded/History of Bookstore: The current business was founded in 1948, but the owner is continuing the father's business begun in 1899. The owner ran the farm from 1932 but started filling farm buildings with books after World War II when farming in the area was no longer feasible. Sales the first year were only a few hundred dollars but increased dramatically every year thereafter. The business has never moved except to expand across the street.

Number of Volumes: 50,000.

Types/Classifications: Hardbound, paperback, magazines, broadsides, autographs, ephemera, small antiques, prints, maps, rare books, color plate books, early printing, incunabula, first editions, fine bindings, out-of-print, association copies, press books, signed copies, presentation copies, limited editions, fore-edge paintings, manuscripts, letters, diaries.

General Subject Areas: General.

Specific Specialties: The store specializes mainly in uncommon books in every field, especially early and illustrated, fine bindings, curious books. Children's Books, Toys, Games, Connecticut History, Early Medicine and Science.

Other Specialties: Natural History, Farming, Country Life, Outdoor Life, Husbandry, Gardening, Horticulture, Cooking, Hunting, Fishing, Animals, Birds, Snakes, Insects, Fish, Homecrafts, Carpentry, Trades.

Mail/Telephone Orders; Credit Cards: Both; cash with order unless credit has been established with the store; Visa, Mastercard.

Business Hours: Tuesday through Sunday 9:00 AM - 5:00 PM; closed Monday.

Parking Facilities: Large parking lot.

Special Features: Picnic tables, tennis court, country roads for walks, kitchen, bathroom, cosy print loft, matting service.

Catalogue: Every two or three weeks.

Collections/Individual Items Purchased: Both.

Booksellers' Memberships: Antiquarian Booksellers Association of America.

Miscellaneous: The shop strives to be a friendly, helpful store with a staff of 9.

274
Whitlock's Inc.

17 Broadway

New Haven, Connecticut 06511 (203) 562-9841

The bookstore carries a large general and diversified stock.

How to Get There: The store is located in the Yale University area, one block from the Sterling Memorial Library.

Owner/Biography: Reverdy Whitlock.

Year Founded/History of Bookstore: The store has existed continuously since 1900 as a part of the New Haven community.

Number of Volumes: 25,000.

Types/Classifications: Hardbound, paperback, magazines, broadsides, autographs, ephemera, first editions, fine bindings, out-of-print, association copies, press books, signed copies, presentation copies, limited editions, color plate books.

General Subject Areas: Connecticut, General, Yale University.

Other Specialties: Scholarly Works, Classics.

Mail/Telephone Orders; Credit Cards: Both. Personal check or money order with order. Visa, Mastercard.

Business Hours: Monday through Saturday 9:30 - 5:30.

Parking Facilities: Street, parking lot.

Special Features: Search service.

Collections/Individual Items Purchased: Both.

275
William Reese Co.
409 Temple Street
New Haven, Connecticut 06511 (203) 789-8081

The bookstore is located in a town house just two blocks from the Yale University's rare book library, the Beinecke. The store contains 2,500 square feet of space.

How to Get There: From Interstate 91 take the Trumbull Street Exit (No. 3), proceed past the first traffic light one block where there are two sets of lights spaced about 20 yards apart. Turn left at the second light, onto Temple. The house is halfway up the block in a row of townhouses.

Owner/Biography: William S. Reese, owner, is a Yale University graduate and assistant curator of Western Americana. He has been actively involved in rare books since being a teenager. He is the author of numerous articles on American bibliography and Western Americana.

Year Founded/History of Bookstore: 1979.

Number of Volumes: 5,000.

Types/Classifications: Hardbound, pamphlets, broadsides, color plate books, press books.

General Subject Areas: Americana, Classic Works in the History of Science, Classics, Colonial America, Early Exploration, Early Travel, Eighteenth Century Literature, English Literature, French Literature, History of Fine Printing, History of Philosophy, History of Technology, Literature, Natural History (American), Nineteenth Century Literature, Revolutionary America, Russian Literature, Western Americana.

Specific Specialties: Pre-1700 American Imprints, Pre-1550 Americana.

Mail/Telephone Orders; Credit Cards: Both. Pro-forma invoices sent to new customers, otherwise will bill with order, net 30 days; discounts to dealers who reciprocate. No credit cards.

Business Hours: By appointment only. Generally available Monday through Friday 10:00 AM to 6:00 PM.

Parking Facilities: Metered street parking.

Special Features: The bookstore states that it has one of the best stocks of Americana in the country. Want lists, especially literary ones, are solicited.

Catalogue: Eight time a year.

Collections/Individual Items Purchased: Both.

Booksellers' Memberships: Antiquarian Booksellers Association of America, Grolier Club, Club of Odd Volumes (Boston).

276
Wm & Lois Pinkney Antiquarian Books
240 North Granby Road (Route 189)
Granby, Connecticut 06035 (203) 653-7710

The bookshop is contained in two large finished rooms in an old red barn built in 1800. The shop contains over 1,000 square feet of space.

How to Get There: Granby is 19 miles north of the city of Hartford, Connecticut. If driving, take Route 20 off Interstate 91 at the Bradley Field Exit. At Granby Center go 2 miles north on Route 189 (North Granby Road). The barn is near the large white house with a pickett fence.

Owner/Biography: William and Lois Pinkney.

Year Founded/History of Bookstore: Founded in 1960, the bookstore was moved from Watertown, New York, to its present location in 1976.

Number of Volumes: 15,000.

Types/Classifications: Hardbound books, prints, souvenir view books from all states, first editions, fine bindings, out-of-print, association copies, press books, signed copies, presentation copies, limited editions, color plate books.

General Subject Areas: Americana, Children's Books, Cookbooks, Natural History, New England, New York State, Travel, Western Americana.

Mail/Telephone Orders; Credit Cards: Mail orders. Cash with order. Visa, Mastercard.

Business Hours: By appointment only.

Parking Facilities: Small lot in the rear.

Collections/Individual Items Purchased: Both.

Booksellers' Memberships: Antiquarian Booksellers Association of America, International League of Antiquarian Booksellers.

277

Wolfgang Schiefer Books About Brazil

23 Church Street

Georgetown, Connecticut 06829   (203) 544-9046

The bookstore is located in a 100-year old gate house that has changed little from its original condition. It contains 200 square feet of space. The business is primarily mail order.

How to Get There: Church street is located off Route 107, one street east of the intersection of Routes 7 and 107.

Owner/Biography: Wolfgang Schiefer.

Year Founded/History of Bookstore: Started in 1979 in New Haven as a full-range bookstore, the shop is now probably the only U.S. bookstore specializing solely in Braziliana.

Number of Volumes: 3,000.

Types/Classifications: Rare and out-of-print books, vintage photographs, first editions, fine bindings, association copies, press books, signed copies, presentation copies, limited editions, color plate books.

General Subject Areas: Brazil.

Specific Specialties: Amazon River.

Other Specialties: Braziliana in many languages.

Mail/Telephone Orders; Credit Cards: Both. Mail order requests must be listed in the shop's catalogue. No credit cards.

Business Hours: By appointment only.

Special Features: Will search Braziliana.

Catalogue: Once per year.

Collections/Individual Items Purchased: Both.

Miscellaneous: Mail order represents 95 percent of the business.

DELAWARE

278
Attic Books
1175 Pleasant Hill Road
Newark, Delaware 19711   (302) 738-7477

Attic Books is operated only on a hobby basis and is open by appointment only. The shop, a 20' x 30' remodeled stable, holds a general stock of first editions and Americana.

How to Get There: Telephone or write for directions.

Owner/Biography: C. W. Mortenson. Mr. Mortenson is a Ph.D. chemist turned lawyer and is retired from private practice.

Year Founded/History of Bookstore: 1947.

Number of Volumes: 20,000.

Types/Classifications: Hardbound, autographs, first editions, out-of-print, association copies, signed copies, presentation copies, limited editions.

General Subject Areas: Americana.

Specific Specialties: Pre-Columbian Discovery of America, Delaware.

Author Specialties: William Faulkner, Ernest Hemingway, Frederic Remington.

Mail/Telephone Orders; Credit Cards: Both. Cash with order. No credit cards.

Business Hours: By appointment only.

Parking Facilities: No problem with parking as the location is in the countryside.

Special Features: Mr. Mortenson states that he operates Attic Books "for the fun of it."

Collections/Individual Items Purchased: Both.

279
Hollyoak Book Shop
306 West 7th Street
Wilmington, Delaware 19801   (302) 429-0894

The Hollyoak Book Shop occupies 1,800 square feet of space and has an "old book store flavor." The stock is very general with an accent on travel. An additional telephone number is (302) 798-2708.

How to Get There: The shop is only minutes from I-95 in Wilmington.

Owner/Biography: Morton Rosenblatt.

Year Founded/History of Bookstore: 1964.

Number of Volumes: 50,000.

Types/Classifications: Hardbound, paperback, magazines, broadsides, autographs, ephemera, first editions, out-of-print.

General Subject Areas: General.

Specific Specialties: Travel, Military.

Mail/Telephone Orders; Credit Cards: Both. Cash with order.

Business Hours: Monday through Friday 9:00 AM - 4:00 PM; Saturday 9:00 AM - 2:00 PM.

Parking Facilities: Street parking.

Catalogue: Published sporadically.

Collections/Individual Items Purchased: Both.

280
Horseshoe Lane Books
436 New London Road
Newark, Delaware 19711

(302) 731-9445

Horseshoe Lane Books has a small, select stock of general antiquarian books. The stock is normally sold by mail and at bookfairs, but visits may be arranged by appointment.

How to Get There: New London Road is Route 896.

Owner/Biography: Robert M. Eisenberg.

Year Founded/History of Bookstore: 1975.

Number of Volumes: 3,500.

Types/Classifications: Hardbound, some paperback, first editions, out-of-print.

General Subject Areas: Delawariana, Detective Fiction, Horticulture, Natural History.

Mail/Telephone Orders; Credit Cards: Both. Cash with order if not an established customer. No credit cards.

Business Hours: Monday through Friday after 5:00 PM; sometimes Saturday and Sunday.

Parking Facilities: Street parking.

Catalogue: Published periodically.

Collections/Individual Items Purchased: Both.

281
Oak Knoll Books
414 Delaware Street
New Castle, Delaware 19720

(302) 328-7232

Oak Knoll Books specializes in antiquarian books on the history of the book including printing, bookbinding, papermaking, book collecting, bookselling, and book illustration. The shop occupies 1,000 square feet of space.

How to Get There: The bookstore is located in historic New Castle.

Owner/Biography: Robert D. Fleck.

Year Founded/History of Bookstore: 1976.

Number of Volumes: 20,000.

Types/Classifications: Rare, out-of-print.

General Subject Areas: Book Arts.

Mail/Telephone Orders; Credit Cards: Both. Cash with order or suitable references. Visa and Mastercard accepted.

Business Hours: Monday through Friday 10:00 AM - 5:00 PM.

Parking Facilities: Street parking with no time limit.

Catalogue: Catalogue published 10 times per year; newsletter 4 times per year.

Collections/Individual Items Purchased: Both.

Booksellers' Memberships: Antiquarian Booksellers Association of America including Middle Atlantic Chapter.

DISTRICT OF COLUMBIA

282
Columbia Bookshop
3506 Connecticut Avenue, NW
Washington, District of Columbia 20008   (202) 337-8333

The Columbia Bookshop is on the second floor of an older building. There are three rooms of books occupying 650 square feet of space.

How to Get There: From Interstate 495 (Capital Beltway) take the exit for Connecticut Avenue South, from Maryland Avenue proceed southbound on Connecticut into D.C. The bookshop is on the right hand side of the street just below Potter Street in a neighborhood known as Cleveland Park. It can also be reached by Metro subway from downtown to the Cleveland Park station.

Owner/Biography: George W. Pollen and Joel D. Simon. Mr. Pollen is well-known in the Washington area used and out-of-print book trade. He worked for various booksellers over a period of years before opening the bookshop on MacArthur Boulevard. Mr. Simon is also employed by Vitro Industries.

Year Founded/History of Bookstore: 1980. The original site was 4816 MacArthur Boulevard, NW, just west of Georgetown. The move to the present location occured in 1982.

Number of Volumes: 7,000.

Types/Classifications: Hardbound, paperback, first editions, fine bindings, out-of-print.

General Subject Areas: American Biography, American History, American Military History, Ancient and Medieval History, Art, Criminology, English and American Literature, History and Philosophy of Law, Literary Criticism, Music, Philosophy, Poetry, Psychiatry, Psychology, Sociology, U.S. Supreme Court.

Author Specialties: All major English and American authors, 19th and 20th Centuries, anything by and about; especially criticism published by university presses.

Mail/Telephone Orders; Credit Cards: Both. Personal check is welcomed; customer is billed for postage.

Business Hours: Seven days a week 11:00 AM to 7:00 PM.

Parking Facilities: Street parking.

Collections/Individual Items Purchased: Both.

283
Estate Book Sales
2824 Pennsylvania Avenue, N.W.
Washington, District of Columbia 20007   (202) 965-4274

Estate Book Sales deals in select books from estate libraries in the nation's capital.

Owner/Biography: Howard Wilcox and Christopher Cooper.

Year Founded/History of Bookstore: 1948.

Number of Volumes: 40,000.

Types/Classifications: Hardbound, paperback, first editions, fine bindings, out-of-print, association copies, press books, signed copies, presentation copies, limited editions, color plate books.

General Subject Areas: General.

Mail/Telephone Orders; Credit Cards: Both. No credit cards.

Business Hours: Seven days per week 1:00 PM - 6:00 PM.

Parking Facilities: Street parking.

Collections/Individual Items Purchased: Both.

284
Folger Shakespeare Library Museum Shop and Bookstore
201 East Capitol Street, S.E.
Washington, District of Columbia 20003 (202) 546-2626

The focus of the bookstore is on the Renaissance and Eighteenth Century with other emphases varying according to the plays being presented in the Museum's connected theater, public programs, etc. Shakespeare is primary and the shop has books, posters, original prints, and museum gift items. The bookstore is located inside the Folger Library which houses some of the world's most impressive and important titles on Shakespeare, the Renaissance, and the Eighteenth Century. The exterior of the building is white marble and the building contains a Tudor-inspired Great Hall and Theatre.

How to Get There: Located at the corner of East Capitol and 2nd Street, S.E., the shop is just one block east of the U.S. Capitol. The store is easily reached by Metro (exit at Capitol South or Union Station). The building is across the street from the Library of Congress (Thomas Jefferson Building) and next door to the Library of Congress Annex.

Owner/Biography: Administered by Amherst College; Judy M. Edelhoff, Sales Manager.

Year Founded/History of Bookstore: 1932. The Folger was founded by Henry Clay Folger. The bookstore has been in operation approximately 10 years.

Number of Volumes: Several hundred.

Types/Classifications: Hardbound, paperback, original prints, some autographed copies of books/booklets, out-of-print, some limited editions, color plate books.

General Subject Areas: Eighteenth Century, Medieval Titles, Renaissance, Shakespeare, Theatre.

Author Specialties: William Shakespeare, Renaissance Playwrights and Authors, Eighteenth Century Authors.

Other Specialties: Scholarly Works, Facsimiles, Renaissance Foreign Language Titles (French, Italian).

Mail/Telephone Orders; Credit Cards: Both; telephone orders with credit card. Shipping, insurance, and handling charge; all orders must be prepaid; allow 30 days for delivery; special orders accepted. American Express, Visa, Mastercard accepted.

Business Hours: Monday through Saturday 10:00 AM - 4:00 PM; occasional evening hours during special events (not advertised, but phone for information).

Parking Facilities: Street parking.

Special Features: Occasional book parties; some in-house titles published; product development of exclusive items for Museum Shop.

Catalogue: Discontinued in 1983; may continue as newsletter and/or direct mail pieces.

Booksellers' Memberships: American Booksellers Association, Mid-Atlantic Booksellers Association, American Library Association.

Miscellaneous: This bookstore is a delight. The space is small, but titles are select and may be hard to find elsewhere. After seeing the store, one should be sure to browse through the changing exhibition of rare books in the Great Hall of the Folger.

285
Lambda Rising, Inc.
2012 S Street, NW
Washington, District of Columbia 20009 (202) 462-6969

The owners of the bookstore state that it is the world's leading gay and lesbian bookstore. Though primarily a new book outlet, the shop also stocks nearly 5,000 rare, out-of-print, and collectible books written by, for, or about gays and lesbians. It includes many classics by Walt Whitman, Gertrude Stein, Oscar Wilde, William Burroughs, and Edward Carpenter. The bookstore contains 800 square feet of space.

How to Get There: The store is easy to find at the intersection of Connecticut Avenue and S Street, two blocks north of the Dupont Circle Metro (subway) stop.

Owner/Biography: L. Page Maccubbin and James M. Bennett, owners, are both active in the gay community. Mr. Maccubbin is an elected Advisory Neighborhood Commissioner and participates in numerous boards of non-profit organizations that serve the gay community. Together the owners founded the local Gay Pride Day Festival which now boasts 25,000 participants each year. They were also the co-founders of the Gay Caucus of the American Booksellers Association.

Year Founded/History of Bookstore: Founded in 1974, the bookstore has posted a 36 percent growth rate in each of the years since.

Number of Volumes: 50,000.

Types/Classifications: Hardbound, paperback, magazines, autographs, ephemera, rare, collectible, out-of-print, gift items, recordings, greeting cards, jewelry.

General Subject Areas: Gay, General, Lesbian.

Specific Specialties: Virtually everything in print related to Gay, Lesbian, Transgenderism, Transvestism categories.

Author Specialties: All Gay and Lesbian Authors.

Mail/Telephone Orders; Credit Cards: Both; Visa, Mastercard, American Express; (see also Special Features below).

Business Hours: Daily 10:00 AM - 8:00 PM.

Parking Facilities: Street, plus paid parking lot across the street.

Special Features: The shop can handle mail orders for any gay or lesbian title in print, and will accept want lists for out-of-print and collectible titles in this field. Orders for currently in-print titles can be placed only by phone, toll free at (800) 621-6969, with a major credit card.

Catalogue: Annually; the mail order catalogue of 2,000 currently in-print titles is available for $2.

Collections/Individual Items Purchased: Both.

Booksellers' Memberships: American Booksellers Association.

286
Lantern — A Bryn Mawr Bookshop
2803 M Street
Washington, District of Columbia 20007   (202) 333-2803

The bookstore sells used and rare books donated by Washington collectors benefitting Bryn Mawr College Scholarship Fund. The bookstore recently moved to larger quarters which contain 1,800 square feet of space. It is in the picturesque basement of an historic Georgetown house.

Owner/Biography: Bryn Mawr Club of Washington, composed of alumnae of Bryn Mawr College. The alumnae also staff the shop as volunteers.

Year Founded/History of Bookstore: The shop was founded in 1977 and moved to larger quarters in 1980.

Number of Volumes: 12,000.

Types/Classifications: All general classifications.

General Subject Areas: General.

Mail/Telephone Orders; Credit Cards: Mail orders accepted; no credit cards.

Business Hours: Tuesday through Thursday 11:00 AM - 3:00 PM; Friday, Saturday 11:00 AM - 5:00 PM.

Parking Facilities: Street, public parking lot.

287
Lloyd Books
Suite 719
1346 Connecticut Avenue N.W.
Washington, District of Columbia 20036   (202) 785-3826

The bookstore features a small, select collection of fine rare books from the 18th, 19th, and 20th Centuries. Located on the seventh floor of the Old Dupont Circle building in Washington, D.C., the shop specializes in sporting (including numerous Derrydale Press books), exploration, travel, maritime, and Americana. It contains 700 square feet of space.

Owner/Biography: Stacy B. Lloyd III.

Year Founded/History of Bookstore: 1981.

Number of Volumes: 1,000.

Types/Classifications: Hardbound, fine bindings, first editions, out-of-print, signed copies, limited editions, color plate books.

General Subject Areas: Americana, Canada, Exploration, Fur Trade, Maritime, Sporting, Travel.

Mail/Telephone Orders; Credit Cards: Both; no credit cards.

Business Hours: Monday through Friday 10:00 AM - 5:00 PM.
Special Features: In-depth catalogues, books well researched.
Catalogue: Catalogue published.
Collections/Individual Items Purchased: Both.

288
Old Print Gallery
1220 31st Street N.W.
Washington, District of Columbia 20007 (202) 965-1818

This is one of the most comprehensive antique print and map shops in the United States. It contains 2,000 square feet of space.
How to Get There: The shop is located in historic Georgetown, directly across from the Georgetown Post Office on 31st Street, one block east of Wisconsin and M Streets.
Owner/Biography: James C. Blakely, Judith Blakely, James von Ruster.
Year Founded/History of Bookstore: 1971.
Types/Classifications: Antique prints and maps.
General Subject Areas: Americana, European Topography, Historical Prints, Maps, Military Prints, Natural History, Nautical Scenes, Political Cartoons, Town Views.
Mail/Telephone Orders; Credit Cards: Both. Visa and Mastercard accepted.
Business Hours: Monday through Saturday 10:00 AM - 6:00 PM.
Parking Facilities: Street.
Special Features: Search service, paper conservation, appraisals, custom framing.
Catalogue: Five times a year.
Collections/Individual Items Purchased: Both.
Booksellers' Memberships: Antiquarian Booksellers Association of America, Appraisers Association of America, International League of Antiquarian Booksellers.

289
Second Story Books
2000 P Street NW
Washington, District of Columbia 20036 (202) 659-8884

See SECOND STORY BOOKS, 3236 P Street NW, Washington, DC.

290
Second Story Books
3236 P Street NW
Washington, District of Columbia 20007 (202) 338-6860

The bookstore features four locations in the Washington-Baltimore metropolitan area: two in Washington, one in Baltimore, and one in Bethesda. All carry comprehensive stocks of used, rare, and out-of-print books as well as recordings. Together, they contain 40,000 square feet of space.
Owner/Biography: Allan Stypeck.
Year Founded/History of Bookstore: 1974.
Number of Volumes: 750,000 in the four locations.
Types/Classifications: Hardbound, paperback, magazines, broadsides, autographs, ephemera, first editions, fine bindings, out-of-print, association copies, press books, signed copies, presentation copies, limited editions, color plate books.
General Subject Areas: Comprehensive.
Specific Specialties: Washington, DC.
Mail/Telephone Orders; Credit Cards: Both. American Express, Visa, and Mastercard accepted.
Business Hours: Daily 10:00 AM - 10:00 PM.

Parking Facilities: Street; Bethesda location has its own parking lot.
Special Features: Search service, custom binding, appraisals, recordings.
Catalogue: Infrequently; special collections.
Collections/Individual Items Purchased: Both.
Booksellers' Memberships: Antiquarian Booksellers Association of America.

291
Wayward Books
1002-B Pennsylvania Avenue SE
Washington, District of Columbia 20003   (202) 546-2719

The bookstore is located in the basement of an historic building on Pennsylvania Avenue eight blocks from the Library of Congress on Capitol Hill. Despite the crowded quarters browsers are always made more comfortable on chairs or hassocks scattered throughout the rooms. The shop contains 750 square feet of space.
How to Get There: The store is located less than 3 blocks from the Eastern Metro (subway) station, and ten blocks east of the U.S. Capitol going out Pennsylvania Avenue.
Owner/Biography: Sybil H. Pike and Doris Grumbach. Sybil Pike is a professional librarian who is happiest reading and buying books. She finds it hard sometimes to part with them. Doris Grumbach is a novelist and critic who is similarly passionate about collecting books.
Year Founded/History of Bookstore: The bookstore began life in 1975 in the basement of the Pike-Grumbach residence, operating by appointment, mail order, and book fairs until 1981. It has been at its open-shop location since then and has grown from three thousand to eight thousand volumes.
Number of Volumes: 8,000.
Types/Classifications: Principally hardbound with occasional prints, maps, periodicals. Choice old and medium rare out-of-print books including first editions, press books, limited signed editions, modern first editions.
General Subject Areas: Architecture, Art, Ballet, Black Fiction, Black Poetry, Blacks, Books About Books, Civil Liberties, Cooking, Politics, Psychology.
Author Specialties: Blacks Authors, Black Poets.
Mail/Telephone Orders; Credit Cards: Both. No credit cards at present.
Business Hours: Tuesday through Friday 11:30 AM - 6:30 PM; Wednesday to 8:00 PM; Saturday and Sunday 12:00 Noon - 5:00 PM.
Parking Facilities: Street.
Catalogue: Infrequently published.
Collections/Individual Items Purchased: Both.

292
Yesterday's Books
4702 Wisconsin Avenue
Washington, District of Columbia 20016   (202) 363-0581

The bookstore is a large, general used bookstore housed on two floors of an old building, with a total of 2,500 square feet of space. It contains most all categories, from the 50 cent paperbacks to the antiquarian collector's corner.
How to Get There: Located in northwest Washington, D.C., the store is six blocks from the D.C.-Maryland border. The Tenley Metro Line (subway) is 1.5 blocks away; the store is also on the Friendship bus line or near any 30-35 numbered buses.
Owner/Biography: Lisa Harry.
Year Founded/History of Bookstore: The bookstore has been in the same location since its founding in 1974. It started as a one-room paperback "shack" and has grown to an entire two floors and a collection of great diversity.
Number of Volumes: 40,000.
Types/Classifications: All general types, classifications, and subject areas in over 200 categories.
General Subject Areas: Architecture, John Steinbeck First Editions, Washington (D.C.).

Author Specialties: John Steinbeck.
Other Specialties: French Language, Spanish Language, Italian Language.
Mail/Telephone Orders; Credit Cards: Both. Visa, Mastercard, American Express.
Business Hours: Monday, Thursday, Friday, Saturday 11:00 AM - 9:00 PM; Tuesday, Wednesday 11:00 AM - 7:00 PM; Sunday 1:00 PM - 7:00 PM.
Parking Facilities: Street.
Special Features: Search service.
Collections/Individual Items Purchased: Both.

FLORIDA

293
All Books & Prints Store
4329 South West 8th Street
Miami, Florida 33134   (305) 444-5001

A general stock bookstore, the shop contains 1,000 square feet of space.

How to Get There: If coming from Miami Beach, take any causeway west to Le Jeune Road, south to SW 8th St., also known as the Tamiami Trail or State Road 41. From all points north, take I-95 into Miami. Miami International Airport on Le Jeune Road is just three miles north of the shop.

Owner/Biography: Albert and Marian Ledoux, owners, are two bibliophiles who spend much time expounding the qualities of authors and books, who know the categories of books, and what is notable concerning them.

Year Founded/History of Bookstore: The business was founded in 1949 on 4th Avenue in New York City near 8th Street and the old Wanamaker Building. Demolishing and converting of the entire area into low rent housing forced the closing of the bookstore in 1957, and enabled the transfer of the shop "from the giant rock to the Florida sands."

Number of Volumes: Over 100 tons of books, maps, magazines, etc.

Types/Classifications: Hardbound, paperback, magazines, fine bindings, fine covers, illustrated books, first editions.

General Subject Areas: Airplanes, Americana, Architecture, Art, Astrology, Astronomy, Automobiles, Bibles, Biography, Biology, Botany, Chemistry, Chess, Children's Literature, Economics, Encyclopedias, Fishing, Games, History, Languages, Mathematics, Metaphysics, Occult, Philosophy, Psychology, Radio, Religion, Science Fiction and Fantasy, Stamps, Technical, Theology, Theosophy.

Specific Specialties: Arctic, Antarctic, Travel, South America.

Mail/Telephone Orders; Credit Cards: Both; for mail orders send a return addressed, stamped envelope, with the specific name, author, title, date of publication; no credit cards; certified check, money order.

Business Hours: Monday through Saturday 11:00 AM - 3:30 PM; other times by appointment.

Parking Facilities: Parking lots on both sides of the shop.

Special Features: Search service.

Collections/Individual Items Purchased: Both.

294
Alla T. Ford, Rare Books
114 South Palmway
Lake Worth, Florida 33460   (305) 585-1442

This book business is operated from the owner's home and 90 percent of sales are by mail. Visitors may browse by appointment only.

Owner/Biography: Mrs. Alla T. Ford. Mrs. Ford was listed in "Who's Who of American Women" in 1974 and in "Southern Personalities" in 1971.

Year Founded/History of Bookstore: 1956.

Number of Volumes: 10,000.

Types/Classifications: First editions, fine bindings, association copies, press books, signed copies, limited editions, color plate books.

General Subject Areas: Americana, Astronomy, Aviation, Biography, Children's Literature, Magic, Metaphysics, Miniature Books - Ford Press, Science Fiction and Fantasy.

Author Specialties: Arthur Conan Doyle, Edgar Rice Burroughs, John F. Kennedy, Albert Schweitzer, L. Frank Baum.

Other Specialties: Foreign Language Books.

Mail/Telephone Orders; Credit Cards: Both. Cash with order, postage extra. No credit cards.
Business Hours: No regular hours. Call for appointment.
Parking Facilities: Street parking.
Catalogue: A few lists are published each year.
Collections/Individual Items Purchased: Individual items only.

295
Book Gallery
1150 Main Street
Gainesville, Florida 32601   (904) 378-9117

The Book Gallery is one of the largest used bookstores in Florida with floor to ceiling (12 feet) books in a 3,000 square foot area. Titles are divided into over 50 categories with larger sections arranged alphabetically by author.
How to Get There: The bookstore is in the Gainesville Shopping Center.
Owner/Biography: Dan Morgan and Kaye Henderson.
Year Founded/History of Bookstore: 1973.
Number of Volumes: 100,000.
Types/Classifications: Hardbound, paperback, new and collectible comics.
General Subject Areas: Comic Books, Cookbooks, Metaphysics, Science Fiction, Self-Help.
Specific Specialties: Floridiana.
Author Specialties: Marjorie Kinnan Rawlings, Harry Crews.
Mail/Telephone Orders; Credit Cards: Both. Payment in advance except to trade; personal checks accepted as well as Visa and Mastercard.
Business Hours: Monday through Saturday 10:00 AM - 6:00 PM; Friday 10:00 AM - 8:00 PM.
Parking Facilities: Parking in front of store.
Special Features: Search service.
Collections/Individual Items Purchased: Both.
Booksellers' Memberships: Florida Antiquarian Booksellers Association.

296
Book Gallery West Inc.
4121 NW 16th Boulevard
Gainesville, Florida 32601   (904) 371-1234

This bookstore stocks used books in a wide variety of categories plus a full line of new books and magazines. The bookstore occupies 2,500 square feet of space.
How to Get There: Book Gallery West is located in the Millhopper Shopping Center.
Owner/Biography: Anne Morgan, Dan Morgan, Bill Landis.
Year Founded/History of Bookstore: 1983.
Number of Volumes: 75,000.
Types/Classifications: Hardbound, paperback, magazines.
General Subject Areas: Cookbooks, Science Fiction and Fantasy, Self-Help.
Specific Specialties: Floridiana.
Author Specialties: Marjorie Kinnan Rawlings, Harry Crews.
Mail/Telephone Orders; Credit Cards: Both. Personal check with order except for dealers. Visa and Mastercard accepted.
Business Hours: Monday through Saturday 10:00 AM - 7:00 PM; Sunday 1:00 PM - 5:00 PM.
Parking Facilities: Shopping center parking lot.
Special Features: Search service.
Collections/Individual Items Purchased: Both.
Booksellers' Memberships: Florida Antiquarian Booksellers Association.

297
Books & Things
473 N.E. 20th Street
Boca Raton, Florida 33431   (305) 395-2227

All books are shelved for easy browsing and card catlogued by author for quick reference. The shop occupies 850 square feet of space with an additional warehouse.

How to Get There: The bookstore is situated halfway between Palm Beach and Fort Lauderdale. It is one block off US 1 and 2 miles from I-95 using either Yamato or Glades Road exits.

Owner/Biography: Jean and Ed SeGall.

Year Founded/History of Bookstore: 1971.

Number of Volumes: 20,000.

Types/Classifications: Hardbound, paperback.

General Subject Areas: Architecture, Art, Biography, Cookbooks, Decorative Arts, Drama, History (All Countries), Juveniles.

Mail/Telephone Orders; Credit Cards: No mail or phone orders. American Express, Visa, and Mastercard accepted.

Business Hours: Monday through Saturday 9:30 AM - 5:00 PM.

Parking Facilities: Shopping center parking lot.

Collections/Individual Items Purchased: Collections only.

Booksellers' Memberships: Florida Antiquarian Booksellers Association.

298
Brasser's Used Books
8701 Seminole Boulevard
Seminole, Florida 33542   (813) 393-6707

Brasser's Books has 60,000 used paperbacks and antiquarian books. It specializes in Floridiana, sports, military, and juveniles with a large selection of American literature from 1830 to 1970. The store occupies 4,000 square feet of space.

How to Get There: Seminole is located between St. Petersburg and Clearwater and near the Gulf of Mexico beaches of Madeira Beach and Indian Rocks Beach. From Tampa the store is exactly 3 miles from Route 688 which is the Indian Rocks Beach-Largo cut off from I-75 South.

Owner/Biography: Thomas Brasser.

Year Founded/History of Bookstore: 1972. Originally at 6400 Seminole Boulevard.

Number of Volumes: 60,000.

Types/Classifications: Hardbound, paperback, pre-1960 magazines,   ephemera, limited editions, out-of-print, first editions.

General Subject Areas: General.

Specific Specialties: Floridiana, Football, Baseball, Golf, Tennis, Spanish-American War, World War I, World War II, Juveniles.

Author Specialties: Mark Twain, John Steinbeck, Ernest Hemingway, James Michener, Gene Stratton Porter, Elbert Hubbard.

Other Specialties: Rare Archaeology, Geology, Anthropology.

Mail/Telephone Orders; Credit Cards: Both. $1.09 per book postage charge. Personal checks accepted.

Business Hours: Monday through Friday 9:00 AM - 5:00 PM; Saturday 9:00 AM - 4:00 PM.

Parking Facilities: Parking lot accommodating 25 cars.

Special Features: Search service.

Catalogue: Published infrequently (on subjects only).

Collections/Individual Items Purchased: Both.

Booksellers' Memberships: Florida Antiquarian Booksellers Association (Charter Member).

299
Farley's Old & Rare Books
5855 Tippin Avenue
Pensacola, Florida 32504

(904) 477-8282

Farley's is located in an old 4-room house which has been restored. It occupies 800 square feet of space.
How to Get There: Proceed north on 9th Avenue to College Boulevard, turn right at tennis courts, turn left onto Tippin Avenue and in the 2nd block on the left is the store.
Owner/Biography: Owen and Moonean Farley.
Year Founded/History of Bookstore: 1975.
Number of Volumes: 6,000.
Types/Classifications: Hardbound, paperback, magazines, sheet music, some postcards and photographs, out-of-print.
General Subject Areas: Americana, Biography, Children's Books, Civil War (U.S.), Foreign Language, Mysteries, Occult, Poetry, Religion, Science Fiction and Fantasy, Technical, Westerns.
Author Specialties: Ernest Hemingway, Gene Stratton Porter.
Mail/Telephone Orders; Credit Cards: Both. Visa and Mastercard accepted.
Business Hours: Tuesday through Saturday 10:00 AM - 5:00 PM.
Parking Facilities: Business parking lot.
Special Features: Search service; minor book repairs; appraisals.
Collections/Individual Items Purchased: Both.

300
Galvez Books and Silver, Inc.
208 South Florida Blanca Street
Pensacola, Florida 32501

(904) 432-2874

The bookstore is located in the historical district of downtown Pensacola. The shop takes its name from Bernardo de Galvez, the Spanish field marshall who defeated the British in the siege of Pensacola in the Spring of 1791. It occupies 3,260 square feet of space in a house built in the middle 1890's. Pine floors, high ceilings, and fireplaces make a cozy setting for the stock of books, maps, and prints.
How to Get There: Highway 98 from the east, or I-110 spur from the north will bring one to Pensacola's Historical District. The bookstore is a half a block north of Government Street and one block east of Alcaniz, easy walking distance from Seville Square.
Owner/Biography: Mr. and Mrs. David Halfen.
Year Founded/History of Bookstore: 1979.
Number of Volumes: 15,000.
Types/Classifications: Hardbound antiquarian and out-of-print books, maps, and prints.
General Subject Areas: American History, Aviation, Biography, Business, Cinema, Cookbooks, Crafts, Crime, Economics, Education, Environment, Florida History, Games, Gardening, Hobbies, Journalism, Language, Law, Literature, Medicine, Military, Military Arms, Music, Mystery, Nature, Philosophy, Poetry, Politics, Psychology, Religion, Science, Science Fiction and Fantasy, Sea, Social Science, Sports, Technology, Television, Theater, World History, World War I, World War II.
Specific Specialties: Floridiana, Pensacola, Gulf Coast, Alabama, Louisiana, the South.
Author Specialties: Southern Authors, Florida Authors.
Mail/Telephone Orders; Credit Cards: Both. Cash with order and include a self addressed stamped envelope. Visa and Mastercard accepted.
Business Hours: Tuesday through Saturday 10:00 AM - 5:00 PM.
Parking Facilities: Street.
Special Features: Search service.
Collections/Individual Items Purchased: Both.

301
Harbar Book Exchange
916 East Semoran Boulevard (Highway 436)
Casselberry, Florida 32707 (305) 834-0153

Harbar Book Exchange strives to present a clean, comfortable, relaxed atmosphere for browsers, complete with music, seating, and good lighting. Books are placed alphabetically by author in an appropriate category. The shop occupies 850 square feet of display space.

How to Get There: The bookstore is located in the Casselberry Square Shopping Center in the greater Orlando area; Route 436, 4 1/2 miles east of I-4 near the Junction of Red Bug Road.

Owner/Biography: Harry and Barbara Oldford (thus the Harbar).

Year Founded/History of Bookstore: 1980.

Number of Volumes: 27,750.

Types/Classifications: Hardbound, paperback, out-of-print, some new books, old prints, maps, comic books.

General Subject Areas: General.

Specific Specialties: Militaria, War, Cinema, Entertainment, Cooking.

Mail/Telephone Orders; Credit Cards: Both. Call to determine availability, price, tax, and postage charges; books mailed on receipt of payment. No credit cards.

Business Hours: Monday 10:00 AM - 7:00 PM; Tuesday through Saturday 10:00 AM - 5:00 PM; closed Sunday.

Parking Facilities: Shopping center parking area.

Special Features: Referral to those offering related services, i.e. bookbinding, restoration, auction services, specialty dealers, and book search; University Products available for book preservation and restoration and library supplies; local libraries refer inquiries concerning reference information and appraisals to Harbar; serves as agent for a text-book buying company and has supplied collectible material for Price Guide illustrations.

Collections/Individual Items Purchased: Both.

Booksellers' Memberships: Florida Antiquarian Booksellers Association.

302
Haslam's Book Store
2025 Central Avenue
St. Petersburg, Florida 33713 (813) 822-8616

Haslam's is one of the southeast's largest new and used bookstores. Located on Florida's West Coast in downtown St. Petersburg, it offers over 13,000 square feet of retail space for new, used, and antiquarian books. The stock is arranged carefully for easy browsing and has a large service-dedicated staff. Haslam's is considered one of Florida's greatest rainy day attractions.

How to Get There: The shop is located on Central Avenue at 20th Street just off Exit 11 of Interstate 275 South; 20 minutes from Tampa, Clearwater; 1 1/2 hour drive from Orlando.

Owner/Biography: Haslam Family.

Year Founded/History of Bookstore: 1933.

Number of Volumes: 300,000.

Types/Classifications: Hardbound, paperback, comics, first editions, fine bindings, out-of-print, association copies, press books, signed copies, presentation copies, limited editions, color plate books.

General Subject Areas: Americana, Art, Biography, Floridiana, Juvenile, Metaphysics, Religion, Science Fiction and Fantasy, U.S. History.

Mail/Telephone Orders; Credit Cards: Both. American Express, Visa, Mastercard, Diners, Carte Blanche accepted.

Business Hours: Monday through Saturday 1:00 AM - 5:30 PM; Friday Night until 9:00 PM.

Parking Facilities: Ample business parking in 3 lots.

Collections/Individual Items Purchased: Both.

Booksellers' Memberships: Florida Antiquarian Booksellers Association.

303
Jack Owen Old Book Shop
113 North Country Road
Palm Beach, Florida 33480   (305) 833-3920

The bookstore is located in a Spanish-arched Addison Mizner building which is listed by the Historical Preservation Society. The small shop (400 square feet) is crammed to its 12-foot high ceiling with 8,000 books, a computer, and its self-proclaimed "cranky" owner who "welcomes buyers, tolerates browsers, and discourages children."

How to Get There: If driving, exit I-95 at Okeechobee Boulevard, drive east across the Intracoastal Waterway, turn left at the 2nd traffic light (South Country Road), drive north one mile past The Breakers hotel. The shop is one block north of the hotel, on the same side of the street.

Owner/Biography: Jack Owen, owner, is an English journalist, and has resided in Palm Beach since 1963. He is a life-long "accumulator," and a bibliophile since 1977.

Year Founded/History of Bookstore: The bookstore was founded in 1965; the location started as a liquor store in the 1920's, then became a jeweller's. After that, it was used as a store room for the collected books of a "retired State Department employee" (Owen), and evolved into a business over the years.

Number of Volumes: 9,000.

Types/Classifications: Hardbound, first editions, fine bindings, out-of-print, press books, signed copies, reading copies.

General Subject Areas: Antiques, Biography, First Edition Fiction, General, Golf, History, Maritime, Tennis.

Mail/Telephone Orders; Credit Cards: Both; no credit cards.

Business Hours: Mid November - June: Monday through Saturday 11:00 AM - 5:30 PM, or by appointment.

Parking Facilities: Street.

Special Features: Search service, appraisals for estates.

Catalogue: Published irregularly.

Collections/Individual Items Purchased: Both.

Booksellers' Memberships: Florida Antiquarian Booksellers Association.

304
Lighthouse Books
1735 First Avenue North
St. Petersburg, Florida 33713   (813) 822-3278

Previously located near the St. Petersburg Yacht Club, giving it its name, the bookstore moved in 1984 to a new location. Now in a 1920's bungalow painted marine blue with white trim, it has the ever present bookseller's bow window. Increasing its floor space by 50 percent to 1,500 square feet, the new shop has four rooms of books and related antiques for sale. There is a sitting area by the fireplace for reading or resting. The new shop is recognizable by the sign with a handpainted lighthouse; the entrance is under the sign.

How to Get There: If driving Interstate 4 or 75 take the 5th Avenue North Exit, continue straight on 20th Street to Central Avenue , then left (east) to 16th Street; head back west on 1st Avenue North which is one way west.

Owner/Biography: Michael and Cathie Slicker, owners, are both involved in historic preservation. Mike, a Florida native, founded the Florida Antiquarian Bookdealers Association and was chairman of its annual bookfair for 1983-84. Cathie is on the board of trustees of the local historical museum, and is a former chairperson of the Pinellas City Historical Commission. Mike is the book dealer, Cathie is the office manager.

Year Founded/History of Bookstore: Before 1977 when the Slickers purchased the bookstore it was known as Dorothy Beil Books. It was located near the Yacht Club until mid-1984 when it was moved to an old house which the owners converted into a bookstore.

Number of Volumes: 10,000.

Types/Classifications: Hardbound, prints, broadsides, first editions, fine bindings, association copies, out-of-print, press books, signed copies, presentation copies, limited editions, color plate books, postcards, pamphlets, ephemera, early detective paperbacks, fore-edge paintings, prints, chromos, sheet music, tract books, dime novels, engravings, hand colored engravings, rare books, unusual books.

General Subject Areas: Americana, Antiques, Art, Aviation, Black History, Books About Books, British

Isles, Caribbean History, Children's Books, Cookbooks, Detective, Early Automobiles, Early Spanish Explorations, Europe, Far East, Florida, Natural History, Railroads, Sailing, Ships, South (U.S.), Southern (U.S.) Literature, Steamboats, Topography, Travel, Women's Movement.

Specific Specialties: Sheet Music.

Author Specialties: First Editions of 20th Century Writers, Marjorie Kinnan Rawlings, Tennessee Williams, Kirk Munroe, Ernest Hemingway, William Faulkner, Carson McCullers, Charles Dickens, Southern (U.S.) Writers, Eudora Welty, Marjorie Stoneham Douglas, Rex Beach, John D. MacDonald, Rider Haggard, Vladimir Nabokov, John O'Hara, Mark Twain.

Mail/Telephone Orders; Credit Cards: Both; Visa, Mastercard.

Business Hours: Monday through Friday 10:00 AM - 5:00 PM; Saturday 10:00 AM - 4:00 PM.

Parking Facilities: Street.

Special Features: Free search service; book-related antiques. Under the name Little Bayou Press the owners publish original works having to do with Florida and its history.

Catalogue: Four times a year.

Collections/Individual Items Purchased: Both.

Booksellers' Memberships: International League of Antiquarian Booksellers, Antiquarian Booksellers Association of America, Florida Antiquarian Booksellers Association.

305
San Marco Book Store

1971 San Marco Boulevard
Jacksonville, Florida 32207   (904) 396-7597

This book store carries a general stock of used and out-of-print hardbound books.

How to Get There: Heading south on I-95, cross the St. Johns River and take the first exit to San Marco Boulevard; go right 1 mile.

Owner/Biography: The Blauers: John, Laura, Mike.

Year Founded/History of Bookstore: 1978.

Number of Volumes: 7,000.

Types/Classifications: Hardbound, first editions, out-of-print.

General Subject Areas: General.

Author Specialties: Ernest Hemingway, Marjorie Kinnan Rawlings, Eugenia Price, Robert Ruark, John Lennon.

Other Specialties: Signed materials by The Beatles, B.B. King, Rolling Stones, Buddy Holly, Chuck Berry, Bill Hailey.

Mail/Telephone Orders; Credit Cards: Mail orders only. Cash with order, prepaid postage; libraries billed. Visa and Mastercard accepted.

Business Hours: Monday through Friday 10:00 AM - 5:30 PM; Saturday 10:00 AM - 4:00 PM.

Parking Facilities: Public parking lot, street parking.

Special Features: Search service; appraisals.

Catalogue: Published sporadically.

Collections/Individual Items Purchased: Both.

Booksellers' Memberships: Florida Antiquarian Booksellers Association.

306
Tappin Book Mine, Inc.

705 Atlantic Boulevard (A1A)
Atlantic Beach, Florida 32233   (904) 246-1388

This is a general antiquarian bookstore, clean, orderly, well lighted, well organized, and staffed by book people who are customer oriented. It is a high volume shop with everything priced to cater to the reader and collector. The shop contains 1,700 square feet of space.

Owner/Biography: F. Donald Tappin, Owner; Douglas C. Tappin, General Manager. The original owners, father and son, are still working at the trade full time.

Year Founded/History of Bookstore: 1974.

Number of Volumes: 30,000.

Types/Classifications: Hardbound, paperback, broadsides, autographs, ephemera, first editions, out-of-print, signed copies, limited editions.

General Subject Areas: General.

Specific Specialties: Military History, All Wars, Nautical Items, Pre-Civil War (U.S.) Maps, Literature, Engineering, How-To Books, Science Fiction and Fantasy, Florida History, Florida Maps.

Other Specialties: Scholarly works.

Mail/Telephone Orders; Credit Cards: Both. Mail orders must be pre-paid. Visa, Mastercard.

Business Hours: Monday through Saturday 10:00 AM - 6:00 PM; Thursday and Friday until 7:30 PM.

Parking Facilities: In front and at the rear of the shop.

Special Features: Search service.

Collections/Individual Items Purchased: Both.

Booksellers' Memberships: Florida Antiquarian Booksellers Association.

GEORGIA

307
Book Dispensary
Service Merchandise Plaza
4588 Memorial Drive at I-285
Decatur (Atlanta), Georgia 30032   (404) 296-2186

The bookstore features four retail store branches offering general categories of out-of-print and collectible books, both hardback and paperback, to the general public. Branch locations are in Decatur, Georgia and Columbia, South Carolina. This branch contains 2,700 square feet of space.

Owner/Biography: The Book Dispensary, Inc.

Year Founded/History of Bookstore: From one small store and a few hundred books in 1975, to four large stores and over 150,000 books today.

Number of Volumes: 150,000 in the four branches.

Types/Classifications: Hardbound, paperback, out-of-print, collectible books, first editions, fine bindings. Sells only books.

General Subject Areas: General.

Specific Specialties: South Carolina and Georgia Regional Subjects.

Author Specialties: South Carolina and Georgia Regional Authors.

Mail/Telephone Orders; Credit Cards: Both. Visa and Mastercard accepted.

Business Hours: Monday through Saturday 10:00 AM - 9:00 PM; Sunday 11:00 AM - 9:00 PM.

Parking Facilities: All locations are in shopping centers or free standing stores.

Special Features: All locations offer a search service.

Collections/Individual Items Purchased: Both.

308
Book Lady
414 Bull Street
Savannah, Georgia 31401   (912) 233-3628

Customers have told the owners of this bookstore that it is "charming, cozy, inviting, well-arranged." This is what they strive for and they are gratified to have it appreciated. The store occupies 800 square feet of space laid out in four small "specialty" rooms.

How to Get There: The Book Lady is in the heart of the beautiful downtown historic district of Savannah.

Owner/Biography: Anita L. Raskin, assisted by Lonnie Evans.

Year Founded/History of Bookstore: 1979. The owner made the quite logical progression from reader to collector to book scout to bookstore owner. Years and years of walking into thrift shops and estate sales and overhearing people say "here comes the book lady" made it clear to Anita Raskin what the name of her eventual shop would have to be.

Number of Volumes: 4,500.

Types/Classifications: Hardbound, paperback, first editions, fine bindings, out-of-print, association copies, signed copies, rare.

General Subject Areas: Americana, Art, Biography, Black Culture, British History, Children's Literature, Cinema, Classics, Cooking, Dance, Fishing, Humor, Hunting, Journalism, Juveniles, Literature, Military, Music, Natural History, Nautical, Politics, Psychology, Theater, Travel, Women's Interest.

Specific Specialties: Americana, especially books dealing with the coastal region of Georgia and South Carolina, its history and culture, art and occupations (such as rice planting), the heritage of its people (on the mainland and the off-shore islands).

Mail/Telephone Orders; Credit Cards: Both. Cash with order. No credit cards.

Business Hours: Monday through Friday 10:00 AM - 5:00 PM; Saturday 10:00 AM - 3:00 PM.
Parking Facilities: Plenty of parking along attractive streets and surrounding parks.
Special Features: Search service.
Collections/Individual Items Purchased: Both.

309
Bookman of Arcady
206 Jones Avenue
Tybee Island, Georgia 31328 (912) 786-5842

The Bookman of Arcady is situated in the library and study of a private cottage and specializes in used books. The stock occupies 1,200 square feet of space.
How to Get There: Take Route 80 east from Savannah to Tybee Island, then right on Jones Avenue. The house is on the left between 2nd and 3rd Streets.
Owner/Biography: Mary Zeller. Mrs. Zeller was a book clerk, bookstore manager, and book buyer for many years. She and her late husband were small collectors but often sold their best items. When Mrs. Zeller retired, she decided to sell used and rare books by mail order and run a search service. She scouts for books in New England every summer.
Year Founded/History of Bookstore: 1979. Mrs. Zeller has removed her fine press books to Stoddard, New Hampshire where she spends her summers. She also has a small stock of used books there. She states that the "climate in New England is better for books."
Number of Volumes: 1,200.
Types/Classifications: Hardbound, many poetry broadsides, first editions, out-of-print press books.
General Subject Areas: Biography, Fiction, Literature, Nature, Poetry, Sociology, Travel.
Author Specialties: Conrad Aiken, William Ferguson, Marcel Proust, John Wieners.
Other Specialties: Penmaen Press, Burning Deck Press.
Mail/Telephone Orders; Credit Cards: Both. Cash with order except university libraries. No credit cards.
Business Hours: By appointment only.
Special Features: Search service.
Collections/Individual Items Purchased: Individual items only.

310
Bookshop
Miller Hills Shopping Center
Warner Robins, Georgia 31093 (912) 922-7231

The Bookshop is roomy and comfortable with three seating areas for serious browsers, a fireplace, and rocking chairs. The shop occupies 2,800 square feet of space.
How to Get There: Take Warner Robins exit off I-75 and go 7 miles on connector route which becomes Watson Boulevard; the shop is in the second shopping center on the right opposite the theater. Warner Robins is 15 miles south of Macon.
Owner/Biography: Hulda S. Robuck.
Year Founded/History of Bookstore: 1970.
Number of Volumes: Over 30,000.
Types/Classifications: Hardbound, out-of-print, rare.
General Subject Areas: Children's Literature, General.
Specific Specialties: Georgiana, Southern History, Cherokee and Creek Indian History, Southern Cookbooks.
Other Specialties: Art gallery selling original paintings by well-known Georgia artists; limited prints.
Mail/Telephone Orders; Credit Cards: Both. Postal money order. Visa and Mastercard accepted.
Business Hours: Monday through Saturday 10:00 AM - 6:00 PM.
Parking Facilities: Business parking lot.
Special Features: Search service.
Collections/Individual Items Purchased: Both.

311
Coopers Books and Stamps
2403 Lawrenceville Highway
Decatur, Georgia 30033   (404) 636-1690

Coopers Books is located in what was formerly a residence. The books are moderately priced and in very good condition. Classics are a specialty.

How to Get There: Take I-285 to Lawrenceville Highway; the store is inside the perimeter about 1 mile.
Owner/Biography: Emily Cooper.
Year Founded/History of Bookstore: 1979.
Number of Volumes: 50,000.
Types/Classifications: Hardbound, paperback, out-of-print.
General Subject Areas: Biography, Children's Literature, Classics, History, Psychology, Religion, Science Fiction and Fantasy.
Mail/Telephone Orders; Credit Cards: Both. Add postage. No credit cards.
Business Hours: Monday through Saturday 9:30 AM - 6:00 PM.
Parking Facilities: Public parking lot.

312
Harvey Dan Abrams Bookseller
3703 Peachtree Road, N.E.
Suite L 1
Atlanta, Georgia 30319   (404) 233-6763

Harvey Dan Abrams has been an antiquarian bookseller for 20 years. Visits may be arranged by appointment only. See below for mail address.

Owner/Biography: Harvey Dan Abrams, owner, has been in the antiquarian book business for 20 years.
Year Founded/History of Bookstore: 1963.
Number of Volumes: 30,000.
Types/Classifications: Hardbound, broadsides, autographs, ephemera, first editions, fine bindings, out-of-print, association copies, press books, signed copies, presentation copies, limited editions, color plate books, maps.
General Subject Areas: Americana, Cherokee Indians, Confederate Imprints, Southern Americana, Southern Poets, War Between the States.
Specific Specialties: Gone With the Wind.
Author Specialties: Margaret Mitchell, Joel Chandler Harris, Abraham Lincoln, John and Charles Wesley, George Whitfield, Sidney Lanier, Flannery O'Connor.
Mail/Telephone Orders; Credit Cards: Both. No credit cards. Mail address: P.O. Box 13763, Atlanta, Georgia 30324.
Business Hours: By appointment only.
Parking Facilities: Available.
Collections/Individual Items Purchased: Both.
Booksellers' Memberships: Antiquarian Booksellers Association of America.

313
Jacqueline Levine
107 East Oglethorpe Avenue
Savannah, Georgia 31401   (912) 233-8519

Business is conducted by appointment and mail order only. The books are shelved in the garden apartment of an 1820 townhouse in the heart of Savannah's historic district.

How to Get There: Call for directions.
Owner/Biography: Stanley and Jacqueline Levine.
Year Founded/History of Bookstore: 1938.

Number of Volumes: 5,000.
Types/Classifications: Hardbound, limited editions.
General Subject Areas: Americana, Antiques, Books About Books, Fore-Edge Paintings, Limited Editions Club, Ships and the Sea.
Mail/Telephone Orders; Credit Cards: Both. No credit cards.
Business Hours: By appointment.
Parking Facilities: Street parking.
Catalogue: Published 2 times per year.
Collections/Individual Items Purchased: Both.
Booksellers' Memberships: Antiquarian Booksellers Association of America, International League of Antiquarian Booksellers.

314
Memorable Books
5380 Manor Drive
Stone Mountain, Georgia 30083   (404) 469-5911

This is a general out-of-print bookstore serving the community, collectors, and scholars. It contains 1,000 square feet of space.
How to Get There: The shop is just off Main Street opposite the City Hall (the old RR depot) in the heart of the village of Stone Mountain. Ponce de Leon Avenue in Atlanta becomes Main Street in Stone Mountain. From Athens and Monroe on US 78, exit at East Ponce de Leon and turn left. The shop is located in the building addition at the rear of a two story red brick building on the corner of Main Street and Manor Drive.
Owner/Biography: Ella and George Hoak.
Year Founded/History of Bookstore: The bookstore was founded in 1979 in the Buckhead section of Atlanta, but after operating at that site for three years the building was scheduled for demolition. The owners sought a developing setting of arts and crafts shops and found it in Stone Mountain.
Number of Volumes: 12,000.
Types/Classifications: Hardbound, scholarly, paperback, magazines, maps, prints, ephemera, out-of-print, first editions, signed copies, fine bindings, sets, and scholarly reference books and paperbacks not otherwise readily available.
General Subject Areas: Americana, Architecture, Art, Behavioral Sciences, Biography, Books About Books, Civil War (U.S.), Classics, Collecting, Cookbooks, Crafts, Drama, Economics, Essays, Fiction, French, Gardening, German, Government, History, Life Sciences, Literary Criticism, Military, Mystery, Occult, Philosophy, Photography, Physical Sciences, Poetry, Politics, Religion, Research Methods, Science Fiction and Fantasy, Short Stories, South (U.S.), Spanish, Sports, Technology, Urbanization.
Other Specialties: Many foreign language titles and scholarly works.
Mail/Telephone Orders; Credit Cards: Both; no credit cards.
Business Hours: Tuesday through Saturday 11:00 AM - 5:00 PM.
Parking Facilities: Street, and business parking lot.
Special Features: Search service, repair, rebinding.
Collections/Individual Items Purchased: Both.

315
Old New York Book Store
1069 Juniper Street, N.E.
Atlanta, Georgia 30309   (404) 881-1285

This is a general out-of-print bookstore specializing in first editions. The stock includes about 30,000 titles including a small stock of rare books.
How to Get There: Located in the heart of midtown Atlanta, the bookstore is one block east of Peachtree Street between 11th and 12th Streets; exit from I-75-85 at 14th Street or 10th Street and travel east.
Owner/Biography: Cliff Graubart and Howard McAbee.
Number of Volumes: 30,000.

Types/Classifications: Hardbound, first editions, out-of-print, signed copies, presentation copies, limited editions.
General Subject Areas: General.
Mail/Telephone Orders; Credit Cards: Both. American Express, Visa, and Mastercard accepted.
. *Business Hours:* Monday through Saturday 11:00 AM - 6:00 PM; Sunday 1:00 PM - 6:00 PM.
Parking Facilities: Business parking lot.
Catalogue: Published annually.
Collections/Individual Items Purchased: Both.

316
Oxford Book Store
2345 Peachtree Road, N.E.
Atlanta, Georgia 30305   (404) 262-3332

This bookstore is one of the largest general bookstores in the southeastern United States. It carries new hardcover titles and has a large collection of used paperbacks and comics. The store occupies 9,000 square feet of space.
Year Founded/History of Bookstore: 1970.
Number of Volumes: 50,000 used; 250,000 new.
Types/Classifications: New hardbound, paperback, magazines, out-of-print.
General Subject Areas: General.
Mail/Telephone Orders; Credit Cards: Both. Visa and Mastercard accepted.
Business Hours: Sunday through Wednesday 9:00 AM - 10:00 PM; Thursday through Saturday 9:00 AM - Midnight.
Parking Facilities: Public parking lot.
Special Features: Search service, coffee house.
Collections/Individual Items Purchased: Both.

317
W. Graham Arader III
1317 Berwick Avenue
Atlanta, Georgia 30306

See: W. GRAHAM ARADER III, King of Prussia, Pennsylvania.

318
Yesteryear Book Shop, Inc.
256 East Paces Ferry Road, N.E.
Atlanta, Georgia 30305   (404) 237-0163

The bookstore has been located for the past twelve years in the old established shopping district of Buckhead, north of downtown Atlanta. Books are arranged by subject matter in turn-of-the-century book-cases, with antique book and printing presses, portrait busts, and literary prints featured throughout the two large rooms of the shop. The shop contains 1,400 square feet of space, with an additional 1,000 in storage space. Prints and maps are in a separate area.
How to Get There: The store is 6.5 miles north of downtown Atlanta, one-half block off Peachtree Road in the Buckhead shopping district. It is also easily accessible from I-75 (West Paces Ferry Road, 3 miles), and I-85 (Piedmont Road Exit, 2.5 miles).
Owner/Biography: Frank O. Walsh, III; Polly G. Fraser. Frank Walsh was born in Atlanta, received his B.A. from University of Virginia, and has spent 12 years in the antiquarian book trade. Polly Fraser was born in Birmingham, attended Garland Junior College, Boston and Rhode Island School of Design, and has been in the antiquarian book trade for 7 years.
Year Founded/History of Bookstore: Founded in 1971, the bookstore is still in its original location, with the same ownership. There has been one expansion incorporating a second storefront in the building. The shop

opened as a general used and out-of-print stock operation, but has changed over the years to become specialized in scarce and rare books, fine editions, and old maps and prints.

Number of Volumes: 16,000 (includes storage).

Types/Classifications: Hardbound books, old prints, old maps, documents, autographs, paper ephemera, first editions, fine bindings, out-of-print, signed copies, limited editions, illustrated books, fine sets.

General Subject Areas: Biography, Civil War (U.S.), Classic Fiction, Decorative Arts, Eighteenth Century Prints, General History, Georgia History, Maps of Georgia and the Southeastern U.S., Marine History, Military, Naval History, Nineteenth Century Prints, Southeastern U.S. History, World War I, World War II.

Specific Specialties: County and Local (Georgia) History, Children's Book Illustrators, Architecture, Antiques, Early American Newspapers, Obsolete Stocks and Bonds, Western Americana, Western American Indians, Bibliography.

Author Specialties: Joel Chandler Harris, Carson McCullers, Flannery O'Connor, N.C. Wyeth, Maxfield Parrish, Arthur Rackham, Edmund Dulac, Charles C. Jones, Jr., Sidney Lanier.

Mail/Telephone Orders; Credit Cards: Both. Personal checks and cash only; no credit cards.

Business Hours: Monday through Friday 10:00 AM - 5:30 PM; Saturday 10:30 AM - 5:00 PM.

Parking Facilities: Street and public parking lot.

Special Features: Specialized search service; appraisals on individual items and entire collections.

Catalogue: Published occasionally.

Collections/Individual Items Purchased: Both.

Booksellers' Memberships: Antiquarian Booksellers Association of America.

HAWAII

319
Pacific Book House
Kilohana Square
1016 Kapahulu Avenue
Honolulu, Hawaii 96816   (808) 737-3475

The store is open for browsing in two rooms with a connecting arch. The general stock is on open shelves in organized categories around the walls with rare books in glass-fronted cases and in low glass-topped cases. The decor is Spanish Mission with heavy beams and plaster. The shop opens into a pleasant courtyard with antique and other shops opening into it. Walk-in traffic is light and there is usually time for the owner to discuss books with customers and give personalized service. The literature and poetry sections are especially good and the Hawaiiana stock is possibly the largest in the world.

How to Get There: Kilohana Square is a small shopping complex of 20 stores of which the majority are antique stores or other specialty shops; it is about 1 1/4 miles from Waikiki (Kapahulu Avenue is perpendicular to Kalakaua Avenue at the Diamond Head end); drive or take a taxicab because bus service is poor.

Owner/Biography: Gay N. Slavsky. Mrs. Slavsky is a native of Texas who has been in Honolulu since 1946.

Year Founded/History of Bookstore: 1963.

Number of Volumes: 6,000.

Types/Classifications: Rare, out-of-print, manuscripts, documents, autographs, ephemera, first editions, fine bindings, association and signed copies, limited editions, prints and engravings, illustrated books.

General Subject Areas: Americana, Art and Antiques, Children's Books, Cookbooks, European and Asian History, Geology, Hawaii and Pacific History and Exploration, Literature (18th and 19th Century), Military History, Natural History, Philosophy, Poetry, Religion.

Specific Specialties: Hawaiian Language.

Mail/Telephone Orders; Credit Cards: Both. Cash with order except to institutions and established accounts; all books returnable within 10 days of receipt. No credit cards.

Business Hours: Monday through Friday 10:00 AM - 5:00 PM; Saturday 10:00 AM - 4:00 PM.

Parking Facilities: Business parking lot in courtyard at Kilohana Square.

Special Features: Appraisal business in rare books, business archives, autographs and manuscripts for estate, charitable gift, and insurance purposes.

Catalogue: Published several times per year.

Collections/Individual Items Purchased: Both.

Booksellers' Memberships: Antiquarian Booksellers Association of America, Hawaii Antique Dealers Association.

320
Pacific Prints
RR 1, Box 276
Wailuku, Maui, Hawaii 96793   (808) 244-9787

Pacific Prints specializes in Hawaii and the Pacific, offering fine photography, books, maps, and prints. Visitors are welcome by appointment.

How to Get There: The bookstore is located on the Island of Maui.

Types/Classifications: Out-of-print, maps, prints, photographs.

General Subject Areas: Hawaii, Pacific Islands.

Mail/Telephone Orders; Credit Cards: Mail orders.

Business Hours: By appointment.

Catalogue: Catalogues published ($1 each domestic, $3 foreign).

321
Tusitala Bookshop
116 Hekili Street
Kailua, Hawaii 96734   (808) 262-6343

The bookstore is on two carpeted floors; the first floor has 750 square feet of space, and the second floor 2,000 square feet. The shop features Hawaii and South Pacific material.

How to Get There: The small town of Kailua is on the windward side of the Island of Oahu in the Hawaiian Islands chain. A lovely mountain drive from Honolulu takes one across the pali (cliff), with its spectacular view. Kailua is on the seashore. The owner invites the bookhunter to "come browse, then spend the day on one of the finest beaches in Hawaii."

Owner/Biography: B. Lee Reeve.
Year Founded/History of Bookstore: 1976.
Number of Volumes: 75,000.
Types/Classifications: Hardbound, paperback, prints, autographs, ephemera, first editions, fine bindings, press books, signed copies, engravings, sets.
General Subject Areas: American History, Americana, Antiques, Art, Australia, Biography, Business, Children's Books, China, Cinema, Civil War (U.S.), Classics, Cookbooks, Crafts, Crime, Drama, Gardening, Health, History, Humor, Japan, Korean War, Law, Literature, Medicine, Men, Music, Mysteries, Nature, New Zealand, Occult, Parents, Philippines, Philosophy, Plays, Poetry, Psychology, Religion, Science, Science Fiction and Fantasy, Southeast Asia, Sports, Travel, Vietnam War, Voyages, Westerns, Women, World War II.
Specific Specialties: Hawaii, South Pacific, Aviation, Sea.
Author Specialties: Robert Louis Stevenson.
Mail/Telephone Orders; Credit Cards: Both; Visa, Mastercard.
Business Hours: Monday through Saturday 10:00 AM - 5:30 PM; closed Sunday.
Parking Facilities: Business parking lot.
Special Features: Search service.
Collections/Individual Items Purchased: Both.

IDAHO

322
Boise Book Farm
5600 Hill Road
Boise, Idaho 83703   (208) 344-9265

The Boise Book Farm has what is probably Boise's largest collection of old, scarce, rare, and out-of-print, vintage and like-new books, records, magazines, comics, and sheet music. The store has a selection of quality books on numerous subjects and is located in the unlived-in portions of a two-level residence. Non-fiction and records are found in what once were garage areas. Children's literature, poetry, and classics, oversized books, mysteries, and sheet music are in the walk-in basement. Another separate building houses fiction (alphabetized by author), paperback books, and other books which are in one stage or another of being proceed. Change and rearrangement are a constant at the Boise Book Farm and the owners consider it a continuous challenge to better utilize the space and display more books. The store occupies 2,800 square feet of space. Picnic grounds, tables, and restrooms are available.

How to Get There: The bookstore is 6-1/2 miles from downtown Boise and can be reached by going west on State Street to the Collister Shopping Center (4600 West), turn right on Collister Street, left on Hill Road and stay on Hill Road until signs direct you to the Boise Book Farm.

Owner/Biography: Ethel Ficks. Ms. Ficks holds a BA in Psychology and a Masters Degree in Elementary Education with a reading specialty. She has been actively involved in selling used books since 1975 and has attended the ABA Bookseller's School.

Year Founded/History of Bookstore: 1975.

Number of Volumes: 200,000.

Types/Classifications: Hardbound, paperback, magazines, comic books, sheet music, maps, postcards, art prints, rare, out-of-print, vintage.

General Subject Areas: Americana, Automotive, Biography, British History, Business, Children's Literature, Classics, Drama, Economics, History, Medical, Music, Natural Science, Poetry, Psychology, Religion, Science Fiction and Fantasy, Self-Help, Theater, Travel.

Mail/Telephone Orders; Credit Cards: Both. Include price of book plus postage. Visa and Mastercard accepted.

Business Hours: Browsing hours Monday through Friday 9:00 AM to 4:00 PM.

Parking Facilities: Ample parking in large yard.

Special Features: Search service, special ordering, classes in book collecting, assistance in customer awareness of books in special subjects.

Collections/Individual Items Purchased: Both.

323
Book Shop
908 Main Street
Boise, Idaho 83702   (208) 342-2659

The Book Shop is a general trade bookstore specializing in western materials, primarily Idaho and the Pacific Northwest. The shop occupies 3,753 square feet of space.

Owner/Biography: Jean B. Wilson.

Year Founded/History of Bookstore: 1889.

Number of Volumes: 80,000.

Types/Classifications: Hardbound, paperback, first editions, fine bindings, out-of-print, signed copies, limited editions.

General Subject Areas: Biography, Children's Books, Cookbooks, Literature, Western Americana.

Specific Specialties: Idaho, Pacific Northwest, Basque, Nez Perce Indians, Caxton Imprints.
Author Specialties: Vardis Fisher.
Mail/Telephone Orders; Credit Cards: Both. Visa and Mastercard accepted.
Business Hours: Monday through Saturday 8:30 AM - 5:30 PM.
Parking Facilities: Public parking lot, street parking.
Special Features: Search service; quarterly newsletter reviewing books of interest to the Western collector.
Catalogue: Published sporadically.
Collections/Individual Items Purchased: Both.

ILLINOIS

324
A & A Prosser, Booksellers
3118 North Keating Avenue
Chicago, Illinois 60641 (312) 685-7680

The bookstore contains approximately 15,000 volumes which are displayed in sectional bookcases and in stacks of old-fashioned apple boxes.

How to Get There: The store is located about 9 miles from Chicago's "Loop," near the corner of street numbers 3200 north and 4800 west. If arriving by auto: Kennedy Expressway north to Belmont Avenue then west on Belmont to Keating Avenue, then 1/2 block south on Keating.

Owner/Biography: Andrew and Antoinette Prosser.

Year Founded/History of Bookstore: Founded in 1947; the present location, containing 2,500 square feet, has been occupied since 1954.

Number of Volumes: 15,000.

Types/Classifications: Hardbound; out-of-print Catholic books from Pre-Vatican II.

General Subject Areas: Biography, Essays, Fiction, Religion.

Author Specialties: G.K. Chesterton, Hilaire Belloc, Cardinal Newman, Ronald Knox, Robert Hugh Benson, Maurice Baring, Graham Greene, Evelyn Waugh, Catholic Authors of Pre-Vatican II.

Mail/Telephone Orders; Credit Cards: Both. No credit cards.

Business Hours: Weekdays 9:00 AM - 6:00 PM.

Parking Facilities: Street.

Special Features: Search service within their specialities of Pre-Vatican II and out-of-print Catholic books.

Catalogue: Semi-annually.

Collections/Individual Items Purchased: Both.

325
Abraham Lincoln Book Shop
18 East Chestnut Street
Chicago, Illinois 60611 (312) 944-3035

Located in a brownstone on Chicago's near North side, the bookstore, containing 1,500 square feet of space, has the warmth and qualities one would wish for in a home library: all-wood paneling, sliding wood and glass shelf doors, sliding mahogany doors, and fireplace. Outside is Centennial Park, dedicated during the Civil War Centennial.

How to Get There: The bookstore is located one block west of Michigan Avenue, Water Tower Place, and the Hancock Building.

Owner/Biography: Daniel R. Weinberg.

Year Founded/History of Bookstore: Established in 1933, this is the 36th year at the present location in a brownstone on Chicago's near North side. Founded by Lincoln scholar Ralph Newman, the bookstore is now solely owned by his associate, Daniel Weinberg, who took over 12 years ago.

Number of Volumes: 10,000.

Types/Classifications: Hardbound, rare, new, used books, autographs, letters, documents, broadsides, pamphlets, engravings, drawings, prints, photographs, first editions, limited editions, fine bindings, out-of-print, signed copies, presentation copies.

General Subject Areas: Abraham Lincoln, American Biography, American Political History, Americana, Chicago History, Civil War (U.S.), Illinois History, U.S. Presidency and Presidents.

Mail/Telephone Orders; Credit Cards: Both. Visa and Mastercard accepted.

Business Hours: Monday through Saturday 9:00 AM - 5:00 PM; or by appointment.

Parking Facilities: There are numerous public parking lots in the area.

Special Features: Appraisals (for gift, tax, insurance, and estate purposes), search service (within their fields), representation at auctions (for individuals or institutions).

Catalogue: Three times a year.

Collections/Individual Items Purchased: Both.

326
Articles of War Ltd.
7101 North Ashland Boulevard
Chicago, Illinois 60626   (312) 338-7171

This bookstore is primarily a mail order operation. They do have facilities for the visitor but as the stock is not at the Ashland Avenue address, prior appointment must be made to browse.

How to Get There: Directions will be given when calling to make an appointment.

Owner/Biography: Bob Ruman and Mike Cobb.

Year Founded/History of Bookstore: 1971.

Number of Volumes: 5,000.

Types/Classifications: Hardbound, paperbacks, magazines.

General Subject Areas: Military.

Specific Specialties: Strictly military history, all branches of service, from ancient Greek and Roman through all wars and periods including modern military history. Weapons, tanks, aircraft, ships, military modeling, and model soldier painting reference books are all carried.

Mail/Telephone Orders; Credit Cards: Both. Visa and Mastercard accepted.

Business Hours: Appointments can be made for Saturdays only; phone (312) 282-6321.

Catalogue: Published 2 to 4 times per year.

Collections/Individual Items Purchased: Both.

327
Bank Lane Books
782 North Bank Lane
Lake Forest, Illinois 60045   (312) 234-2912

Bank Lane Books handles general out-of-print and first editions. The shop also offers a free book search service.

How to Get There: Two blocks north of Market Square.

Owner/Biography: Doris J. Flynn.

Year Founded/History of Bookstore: 1979.

Number of Volumes: 20,000.

Types/Classifications: Hardbound, out-of-print, first editions.

General Subject Areas: General.

Mail/Telephone Orders; Credit Cards: Both. Cash with order. No credit cards.

Business Hours: Monday, Thursday, Friday, Saturday 10:00 AM - 5:00 PM; Tuesday 12:00 Noon - 5:00 PM. Closed Wednesdays.

Special Features: Free book search service.

Collections/Individual Items Purchased: Both.

Booksellers' Memberships: Midwest Bookhunters Association.

328
Beasley Books
1533 West Oakdale
2nd Floor
Chicago, Illinois 60657   (312) 472-4528

163

Beasley Books is operated from a private residence. The stock occupies 400 square feet of space.
How to Get There: Located on the near North Side of Chicago, a few miles east of Interstate 90/94 (Fullerton exit), 3 blocks north of Diversey at Ashland.
Owner/Biography: Paul and Elizabeth Garon.
Year Founded/History of Bookstore: 1979.
Number of Volumes: Over 4,000.
Types/Classifications: Hardbound, paperback, broadsides, ephemera, literary magazines, manuscripts, first editions, signed copies, unusual editions.
General Subject Areas: American Literature (20th Century), Detective Fiction, English Literature (20th Century), Radical Literature, Science Fiction and Fantasy.
Specific Specialties: American Left Movement (Fiction, Poetry, Plays), Black Literature, Beat Literature.
Author Specialties: Nelson Algren, Guy Davenport.
Other Specialties: First editions of books published by the Charles H. Kerr Company.
Mail/Telephone Orders; Credit Cards: Both. No credit cards.
Business Hours: By appointment only.
Parking Facilities: Street parking.
Catalogue: Published 6 times yearly.
Collections/Individual Items Purchased: Both.
Booksellers' Memberships: Antiquarian Booksellers Association of America, Midwest Bookhunters.

329
Blue Dahlia Bookshop

124 East Beaufort Street
Normal, Illinois 61761   (309) 452-6014

The bookstore consists of two shops: one open and one closed. The open shop is a small, 400-square foot store, selling books to the public and engaging in local searching of out-of-print books. The closed shop is much larger, 8 rooms and 3,430 square feet of space, and is devoted to selling exclusively by mail and engaging in nation-wide searches.
How to Get There: The open shop is in the primary downdown area; the mail shop is closed to the public.
Owner/Biography: Thomas Paul Blanco.
Year Founded/History of Bookstore: Founded in 1974, the bookstore assumed its present name in 1980.
Number of Volumes: Open shop: 7,000; closed shop: 65,000.
Types/Classifications: Hardbound, vintage paperbacks, paperbacks of detective and science fiction; first editions, scholarly, scarce, out-of-print.
General Subject Areas: Art, Children's Fiction (Old and Illustrated), Detective Fiction, General Americana, History, Literary Criticism, Literature, Science Fiction, Theater, True Crime.
Specific Specialties: Crime Fiction; London Slums and Related Fiction (1835-1945).
Author Specialties: D.H. Lawrence, Thomas Burke, Arthur Morrison, Ross MacDonald, Cornell Woolrich, William Irish, George Hopley, F. Scott Fitzgerald, Ford Maddox Ford, Djuna Barnes, P.G. Wodehouse, Edgar Allen Poe, Nathanael West, Thomas Hardy, Robert Browning, William Faulkner, Robert Louis Stevenson, Raymond Chandler, Dashiell Hammett, John Dickson Carr, Carter Dickson, Arthur Conan Doyle, Agatha Christie, Patricia Highsmith.
Mail/Telephone Orders; Credit Cards: Both; no credit cards.
Business Hours: Monday through Saturday 11:00 AM - 5:30 PM; call first if from out of town.
Parking Facilities: Street.
Special Features: Nation-wide searches; collections formed; appraisals.
Catalogue: Six to twelve times a year.
Collections/Individual Items Purchased: Both.

330
Booksellers Row Inc.

2445 North Lincoln Avenue
Chicago, Illinois 60614   (312) 348-1170

The bookstore offers a general collection of used and out-of-print books in a location containing 2,200 square feet of space.

Year Founded/History of Bookstore: 1978.
Number of Volumes: 30,000.
Types/Classifications: Hardbound, paperbacks, general used, out-of-print, review copies, antiquarian, and fine.
General Subject Areas: General.
Other Specialties: The bookstore does not specialize, but stocks a wide range of scholarly titles.
Mail/Telephone Orders; Credit Cards: No mail or telephone orders; Visa and Mastercard.
Business Hours: Daily 12:00 Noon - 10:30 PM.
Parking Facilities: Street.
Collections/Individual Items Purchased: Both.

331
Bookstall of Rockford
606 Gregory Street
Rockford, Illinois 61108   (815) 963-1671

The Bookstall of Rockford occupies a 10-room old house. It contains 1,500 square feet of space and features a general stock plus some old magazines, bound periodicals, and pamphlets.

How to Get There: Gregory Street is at the 900 block of Kishwaukee Street.
Owner/Biography: Karl Moehling and John Peterson.
Year Founded/History of Bookstore: 1980.
Number of Volumes: 10,000.
Types/Classifications: Hardbound, first editions, out-of-print.
General Subject Areas: Agriculture, Americana, Art, Biography, Literary Criticism, Literature, Local History, Military History, Natural History, Religion, Technology.
Mail/Telephone Orders; Credit Cards: Both. No credit cards.
Business Hours: Saturdays 10:00 AM - 5:00 PM or by appointment.
Parking Facilities: Street parking.
Collections/Individual Items Purchased: Both.
Booksellers' Memberships: Midwest Bookhunters.

332
Cassity Book Store
105 North Vermilion Street
Danville, Illinois 61832   (217) 446-7415

This is a general used and antiquarian bookshop, which contains 3,000 square feet of space.

Owner/Biography: Dale T. Cassity.
Year Founded/History of Bookstore: Since its founding in 1957 the bookstore has undergone three moves and one consolidation of two stores.
Number of Volumes: 50,000.
Types/Classifications: Hardbound, paperback, autographs, ephemera, prints; first editions, fine bindings, out-of-print, signed copies, color plate books.
General Subject Areas: General.
Other Specialties: Subject dictionaries.
Mail/Telephone Orders; Credit Cards: Mail orders: cash with order or established credit; telephone orders accepted. No credit cards.
Business Hours: Weekdays 9:30 AM - 4:30 PM.
Parking Facilities: Public parking lot, street.
Special Features: Search service.
Collections/Individual Items Purchased: Both.
Miscellaneous: The bookstore will buy any non-fiction book it does not have.

333
Cogitator Books
344 McKinley
Libertyville, Illinois 60048　　　　　　　　　　　　　　　　　　　(312) 362-4676

Cogitator Books is now operating out of the owner's residence after being a bookstore for many years. It sells primarily by appointment only plus mail order and Book Fairs.

Owner/Biography: Donald V. Vento.

Year Founded/History of Bookstore: 1964. The business began in Evanston at three different locations, then moved to Wilmette before moving the better stock to the residence.

Number of Volumes: 25,000.

Types/Classifications: Hardbound, paperback, broadsides, a few autographs and letters, first editions, fine bindings, out-of-print, association copies, press books, signed copies, presentations copies, limited editions, color plate books.

General Subject Areas: Children's Books, Detective Fiction, First Editions (19th Century), Modern First Editions, Political Science.

Mail/Telephone Orders; Credit Cards: Both. Payment with order unless an established customer; if inquiry only send self addressed stamped envelope.

Business Hours: Calls between 9:00 AM - 5:00 PM.

Catalogue: Published occasionally.

Collections/Individual Items Purchased: Both.

Booksellers' Memberships: Antiquarian Booksellers Association of America, International League of Antiquarian Booksellers, Midwest Bookhunters Association.

334
Edenrock Books
42720 North Hunt Club Road
Antioch, Illinois 60002　　　　　　　　　　　　　　　　　　　(312) 395-7069

This book warehouse is open by appointment only. It contains books in every category and attempts to live up to its name, Edenrock Books, "a little bit of everything." All books are grouped by subject for easy searching and priced for easy resale or for the avid collector. The coffee is always hot on weekends and evenings.

How to Get There: Take I-294 to I-94 out of Chicago, go past Great America and through the Toll Plaza; exit Route 173 and go west to Hunt Club Road; then go north 1 1/3 miles to a driveway with a large sign announcing Edenrock Irish Setters.

Owner/Biography: John E. Swan. Mr. Swan has been a collector of books for 25 years.

Year Founded/History of Bookstore: 1981.

Number of Volumes: 15,000.

Types/Classifications: Hardbound, ephemera, first editions, out-of-print, association copies, press books, signed copies.

General Subject Areas: General.

Specific Specialties: Aldous Huxley, C.S. Lewis, Dorothy Sayers, G.K. Chesterton, Willa Cather, Christopher Morley.

Other Specialties: Far East books.

Mail/Telephone Orders; Credit Cards: Both. Cash with first order and until credit is established. No credit cards.

Business Hours: By appointment.

Parking Facilities: Ample parking.

Special Features: Search service; free coffee; animals for animal lovers to pet and feed.

Catalogue: Published frequently.

Collections/Individual Items Purchased: Both.

Booksellers' Memberships: Midwest Bookhunters.

Miscellaneous: Dealer discounts offered.

335
First Impressions
26 W 580 Butterfield Road
Wheaton, Illinois 60187   (312) 668-9418

First Impressions is a one-woman, in-home operation. Visitors are welcome by appointment.
How to Get There: The bookstore is on Illinois Route 56 between Naperville Road and Herrick/Weesbrook Road; phone for more specific directions.
Owner/Biography: Jean Jacklin. Ms. Jacklin is a happy retiree from a publishing company.
Year Founded/History of Bookstore: 1972.
Number of Volumes: 5,000.
Types/Classifications: Hardbound, some paperbacks, magazines, ephemera, first editions, out-of-print.
General Subject Areas: Children's Illustrated Books, Children's Series, Detective Fiction, General, Mysteries.
Mail/Telephone Orders; Credit Cards: Both. Cash with order except for known customers or libraries. No credit cards.
Business Hours: By appointment.
Catalogue: Published 3 to 4 times per year and for sale.
Collections/Individual Items Purchased: Both.
Booksellers' Memberships: Midwest Booksellers Association.

336
Hamill & Barker
400 North Michigan Avenue
Chicago, Illinois 60611   (312) 644-5933

Hamill & Barker is an antiquarian bookseller of rare books and first editions.
Owner/Biography: Frances Hamill and Terence A. Tanner.
Year Founded/History of Bookstore: 1928.
Types/Classifications: Hardbound, first editions, rare, autographs, manuscripts, fine bindings, sets, illustrated books.
General Subject Areas: Americana, Architecture, Bibliographies, Books About Books, Early Printed Books, Incunabula, Literature, Medicine, Mountaineering, Natural History, Science, Travel.
Specific Specialties: Illinois, Midwest (U.S.)
Mail/Telephone Orders; Credit Cards: Both. No credit cards.
Business Hours: Monday through Friday 9:00 AM - 4:30 PM; closed July and August.
Parking Facilities: Three nearby parking lots on Rush Street.
Collections/Individual Items Purchased: Both.
Booksellers' Memberships: Antiquarian Booksellers Association of America, Antiquarian Booksellers Association (England), International League of Antiquarian Booksellers.

337
Harry L. Stern Ltd.
One North Wacker Drive
Suite 206
Chicago, Illinois 60606   (312) 372-0388

Harry L. Stern Ltd. deals in antiquarian books and maps, particularly Americana and Classical Civilization.
How to Get There: The business is located 1 block east of the Northwestern Railroad Station.
Owner/Biography: Harry L. Stern.
Year Founded/History of Bookstore: 1976.
Types/Classifications: Hardbound, maps, first editions, fine bindings, out-of-print, association copies, press books, signed copies, presentation copies, limited editions, color plate books, atlases.
General Subject Areas: Americana, Classical Civilization, Science.

Specific Specialties: American Revolution, Canada Before 1800.
Mail/Telephone Orders; Credit Cards: Both. No credit cards.
Business Hours: By appointment only.
Catalogue: Published once per year.
Collections/Individual Items Purchased: Both.
Booksellers' Memberships: Antiquarian Booksellers Association of America.

338
Historical Newspapers & Journals
9850 Kedvale
Skokie, Illinois 60076   (312) 676-9850

This dealer specializes in 18th to 20th Century newspapers, maps, manuscripts, and magazines. It is located in a cedar building in Skokie. Visits can be arranged by appointment only.

Owner/Biography: Steve and Linda Alsberg.
Year Founded/History of Bookstore: 1973.
Number of Volumes: 8,000 issues.
Types/Classifications: Newspapers, Periodicals, Manuscripts, Maps.
General Subject Areas: General.
Specific Specialties: Civil War (U.S.), Revolutionary War (U.S.), Chicago, Illinoisiana.
Mail/Telephone Orders; Credit Cards: Both. No credit cards.
Business Hours: By appointment only.
Parking Facilities: Street parking.
Special Features: Search service.
Catalogue: Published 3 times per year.
Collections/Individual Items Purchased: Both.

339
Jacks Used Books
718 East Northwest Highway
Mt. Prospect, Illinois 60056   (312) 398-7767

The owner of this bookstore prides himself in offering "one of the neatest, most pleasant bookstores anywhere." The shop contains 1,000 square feet of space.

How to Get There: The bookstore is located 7 blocks southeast of Route 83, and 10 minutes from O'Hare Field.
Owner/Biography: Jack Huggard, owner, is "finally doing what he really wants to do: be an antiquarian book dealer."
Year Founded/History of Bookstore: Founded in 1975, the bookstore is in its original site, and has its original owner.
Number of Volumes: 20,000.
Types/Classifications: Harbound, paperback, first editions, out-of-print, signed copies, illustrated art books.
General Subject Areas: Adventure, Americana, Antiques, Aviation, Biography, Children's Books, Cinema, Cooking, Crime, English History, French History, History, Modern Fiction, Mystery, Nature, Nostalgia, Poetry, Railroads, Science Fiction and Fantasy, Sports, Suspense, Transportation, Westerns, World War I, World War II.
Specific Specialties: Modern First Editions.
Mail/Telephone Orders; Credit Cards: Both; for mail orders, personal check or cash is required; no credit cards.
Business Hours: Monday, Wednesday, Friday 9:00 AM - 5:00 PM; Tuesday, Thursday 9:00 AM - 9:00 PM; Saturday 9:00 AM - 5:00 PM.
Parking Facilities: Business parking lot.
Special Features: Search service, want lists accepted.
Collections/Individual Items Purchased: Both.

340
James Dowd - Bookseller
38 W 281 Toms Trail Drive
St. Charles, Illinois 60174   (312) 584-1930

This bookstore is mainly a mail order business from a private residence. The hours are by appointment only. The shop contains 2,000 square feet of space.

How to Get There: The shop is 35 miles west of the Chicago Loop off Route 64; the visitor is advised to call for directions.

Owner/Biography: James and Frances Dowd. James is the author of two books and a contributor to others; he works elsewhere full time as an Assistant Manager, but has been in the book trade for 20 years. Frances assisted in the operation of the previous Dowd's Bookshop in St. Charles in 1979-80; she is a professional secretary.

Year Founded/History of Bookstore: Founded in 1964, the bookstore operated from the owners' home in Naperville, Illinois until 1971, when it was moved to Hinckley, Illinois. It operated as a full service bookstore in 1979 and 1980.

Number of Volumes: 5,000.

Types/Classifications: Hardbound, ephemera, out-of-print, press books, first editions.

General Subject Areas: Americana, Catholic Americana, General George A. Custer, Pacific Northwest (U.S.), Plains Indians, West (U.S.).

Author Specialties: Thomas Merton.

Mail/Telephone Orders; Credit Cards: Both; personal check with order; Illinois state sales tax to residents; reciprocal discounts to accredited dealers; no credit cards.

Business Hours: By appointment only.

Parking Facilities: Street.

Special Features: Search service; distributor for Ye Galleon Press books, and stock has on hand numerous of its new and out-of-print titles.

Catalogue: Two times a year.

Collections/Individual Items Purchased: Both.

Booksellers' Memberships: Midwest Bookhunters.

341
James M. W. Borg, Inc.
No. 1500
8 South Michigan Avenue
Chicago, Illinois 60603   (312) 236-5911

The bookstore contains rare and fine examples of 19th and 20th Century English and American literature, natural science, inscribed books, autographs, and art. The shop has 1,000 square feet of space. By appointment only.

How to Get There: Because much of the stock is located off premises, appointments are essential. The shop is located one block north of The Art Institute.

Owner/Biography: Dr. James Borg, PhD., owner, has a background which includes the founding of a game corporation, teaching both high school and college, publishing (Chiron Press), and film making. Dr. Borg's special areas of interest encompass psychoanalysis, anthropology, and the history of religions. The principal trade of the bookstore, however, is literature.

Year Founded/History of Bookstore: 1977.

Number of Volumes: 4,000.

Types/Classifications: Hardbound, proofs, autographs, watercolors, drawings, first editions, association copies, press books, signed copies, presentation copies.

General Subject Areas: American Literature, Americana, English Literature, Medicine, Natural Science, Western (U.S.) Fiction, Women's Literature.

Specific Specialties: Victorian Period, 19th Century Literature, Edwardians, 20th Century Literature.

Author Specialties: Charles Dickens, Jack Lindsay, Women Authors, Robert Browning, Elizabeth Barrett Browning.

Mail/Telephone Orders; Credit Cards: Both; Visa, Mastercard.

169

Business Hours: Monday through Friday 9:00 AM - 5:00 PM by appointment only.
Parking Facilities: Public parking lot.
Special Features: Publishing sideline.
Catalogue: Six times a year.
Collections/Individual Items Purchased: Both.
Booksellers' Memberships: National and Midwest Chapters of the Antiquarian Booksellers Association of America.
Miscellaneous: Computer-assisted appraisals, collection building and promotional assistance for institutions and corporations.

342
John Wm. Martin - Bookseller
436 South 7th Avenue
La Grange, Illinois 60525   (312) 352-8115

While this is primarily a mail order antiquarian bookstore, collectors and dealers who have specific wants or areas of interest are welcome. An appointment is essential. The stock is all priced and well organized. The shop contains 1,000 square feet of space.

How to Get There: The bookstore is in the historic village of La Grange, Illinois, two blocks east of La Grange Road between the Stevenson (155) and Eisenhower (1290) Expressways. Either Expressway may be taken to La Grange Road from downtown Chicago. The shop is but a few blocks from the Burlington train station, a 30-minute trip from Chicago's Loop.

Owner/Biography: John Wm. Martin, owner, received his B.A. in English from the University of Minnesota, and both his M.A. and Ph.D. in English from the University of Oregon.

Year Founded/History of Bookstore: 1973.

Number of Volumes: 5,000.

Types/Classifications: Hardbound, leatherbound, first editions, important editions, association copies, press books, signed copies, limited editions, fine bindings, sets.

General Subject Areas: American Literature, Drama, English Literature, Fiction, Literary Criticism, Poetry.

Specific Specialties: 18th Century English Literature, 19th Century English Literature, 18th Century American Literature, 19th Century American Literature, Early 20th Century Literature.

Author Specialties: Hans Christian Andersen, Charles Dickens, Alfred Lord Tennyson, William Thackeray, Robert Browning, Elizabeth Barrett Browning, William Morris, Algernon Charles Swinburne, J.M. Barrie, Joseph Addison, Johnathan Swift, Alexander Pope, William Blake, Lord Byron, Rudyard Kipling, Henry Wadsworth Longfellow, George Meredith, Sir Walter Scott, Burton Stevenson, John Dryden, Samuel Johnson, Nicholas Rowe, Hugh Walpole, George Bernard Shaw, H.G. Wells, Robert Bridges, T.S. Eliot, Robert Frost, John Galsworthy, D.H. Lawrence, John Masefield.

Other Specialties: Books About Books, Literary Biography, Literary Criticism.

Mail/Telephone Orders; Credit Cards: Both. Payment must accompany initial orders. No credit cards.

Business Hours: Daily 7:00 AM - 9:00 PM by appointment only.

Parking Facilities: Street.

Special Features: Appraisals; catalogues issued free if interests are indicated.

Catalogue: Four times per year.

Collections/Individual Items Purchased: Both.

Miscellaneous: Appraisals; collection development for institutions and individuals; the owner bids at all of the major British and American auction houses.

343
Joyce Klein Bookseller
177 South Oak Park Avenue
Oak Park, Illinois 60302   (312) 386-6564

This book shop carries a general stock of used and rare books with an emphasis on first edition children's illustrated books and cooking.

How to Get There: The shop is located in a suburban Chicago area.
Owner/Biography: Joyce Klein.
Types/Classifications: Rare, out-of-print, first editions, limited editions.
General Subject Areas: Adventure, Americana, Art, Biography, Catholicism, Children's Illustrated Books, Cooking, Detective Fiction, Illinois, Ireland, Music, Mysteries, Mysticism, Occult, Poetry, Travel, Victorian Juvenile.
Specific Specialties: Chicago.
Mail/Telephone Orders; Credit Cards: Mail orders.
Business Hours: Monday through Saturday 10:00 AM - 6:30 PM; Sunday 11:00 AM - 3:00 PM.
Parking Facilities: Ample parking.
Collections/Individual Items Purchased: Both.

344
Kennedy's Bookshop
1911 Central Street
P.O. Box 191
Evanston, Illinois 60204   (312) 864-4449

Kennedy's Bookshop carries a stock of standard, scholarly, and out-of-print antiquarian books.
How to Get There: The shop is located on the Chicago area's North Shore.
Owner/Biography: Ashley Kennedy III.
Types/Classifications: Out-of-print, rare, first editions, limited editions.
General Subject Areas: General.
Specific Specialties: Scholarly Works.
Mail/Telephone Orders; Credit Cards: Mail orders. Address for mail orders: P.O. Box 191, Evanston, Illinois 60204. Telephone for mail orders: (312) 475-2481.
Business Hours: Tuesday through Friday 10:00 AM - 6:00 PM; Saturday 10:00 AM - 5:30 PM.
Parking Facilities: Ample parking.
Collections/Individual Items Purchased: Both.
Booksellers' Memberships: Antiquarian Booksellers Association of America.

345
Kenneth Nebenzahl, Inc.
333 North Michigan Avenue
28th Floor
Chicago, Illinois 60601   (312) 641-2711

This attractive bookstore, located in the tower of a Chicago art-deco skyscraper, specializes in fine books, manuscripts, maps, and prints. There is usually an exhibition available for viewing.
How to Get There: The bookstore is located in the skyscraper at the corner of Michigan Avenue and Wacker Drive, where Michigan Avenue crosses over the Chicago River.
Owner/Biography: Kenneth Nebenzahl and Jocelyn Spitz Nebenzahl. Mr. Nebenzahl is an author and lecturer on the subjects of rare books and the history of cartography. He and Mrs. Nebenzahl sponsor the annual Kenneth Nebenzahl, Jr. lecture series in the history of cartography at the Newberry Library in Chicago.
Year Founded/History of Bookstore: 1957.
Number of Volumes: 12,000.
Types/Classifications: First editions, fine bindings, press books, color plate books, atlases, illustrated books.
General Subject Areas: Americana, Early Printing, Natural History, Science, Voyages.
Specific Specialties: Discovery, Exploration, Colonial Period, French and Indian War, American Revolution, Federal Period, Jacksonian Era, Westward Movement, Civil War (U.S.), Government Exploration, Transmississippi West.
Mail/Telephone Orders; Credit Cards: Both. Until a regular account is established, customers are requested to send remittance with order or supply three trade references. Visa and Mastercard accepted.
Business Hours: Monday through Friday 9:00 AM - 5:00 PM.

Parking Facilities: Public parking lot.
Special Features: An annual exhibition of fine maps about the first of December.
Catalogue: Published 2 times per year (both map and book catalogues are issued).
Collections/Individual Items Purchased: Both.
Booksellers' Memberships: Antiquarian Booksellers Association of America, International League of Antiquarian Booksellers.

346
Left Bank Bookstall
104 South Oak Park
Oak Park, Illinois 60302   (312) 383-4700

The Left Bank Bookstall offers a select and varied stock of used and rare books in most areas.
How to Get There: The bookstore is located in a suburb of Chicago.
Owner/Biography: Zientek & Goodwin, Booksellers.
Types/Classifications: Rare, out-of-print, first editions.
General Subject Areas: General, Lake Michigan, Old Chicago, Prairie Architecture.
Author Specialties: Edgar Rice Burroughs, Ernest Hemingway, Frank Lloyd Wright.
Mail/Telephone Orders; Credit Cards: Mail orders.
Business Hours: Normal business hours; best to phone first.
Parking Facilities: Available.
Collections/Individual Items Purchased: Both.

347
Old Book Barn
RR 1
Argenta, Illinois 62501   (217) 795-2087

The bookstore is housed in a large old barn converted to hold books. There are approximately 80,000 volumes of used and out-of-print, low priced stock on three floors. The shop contains 3,000 square feet of space plus additional for storage.
How to Get There: If driving, one should take I-72 to the Argenta exit (south), then 300 feet to a side road with the "Old Book Barn" sign.
Owner/Biography: Clarke and Soni Uhler.
Year Founded/History of Bookstore: 1981.
Number of Volumes: 80,000.
Types/Classifications: Hardbound (50,000), paperback (30,000), magazines, used, out-of-print.
General Subject Areas: General.
Mail/Telephone Orders; Credit Cards: Both; no credit cards.
Business Hours: Summer: Tuesday through Saturday 1:00 PM - 6:00 PM. Winter: by appointment only.
Parking Facilities: Ample parking.
Special Features: Search service
Catalogue: Infrequently.
Collections/Individual Items Purchased: Collections only.

348
Owen Davies, Bookseller
200 West Harrison Street
Oak Park, Illinois 60304   (312) 848-1186

Owen Davies is the oldest bookstore in the United States specializing in the history of transportation. The store carries old and new books on trains, ships, and airplanes from around the world. Boxes of railroad timetables, travel folders, steamship schedules, photographs, railroad annual reports, and dining car menus fill shelves along the walls.

How to Get There: The bookstore is located at the corner of Harrison Street and Lombard Avenue in Oak Park, 1 block north of the Eisenhower Expressway and 3 blocks west of Austin Boulevard.
Owner/Biography: Thomas R. Bullard.
Year Founded/History of Bookstore: 1929. The shop was founded by the late Owen Davies in 1929 and located in Chicago from that date until 1980; owned by the founder's widow from 1968 to 1980. The shop was moved to Oak Park in 1980.
Number of Volumes: 5,000.
Types/Classifications: Hardbound, paperback, related ephemera, new, out-of-print.
General Subject Areas: Transportation History.
Mail/Telephone Orders; Credit Cards: Both. No credit cards.
Business Hours: Tuesday through Saturday 9:00 AM - 5:00 PM.
Parking Facilities: Street parking on Harrison Street and Lombard Avenue.
Special Features: Search service.
Catalogue: Published quarterly.
Collections/Individual Items Purchased: Both.

349
Powell's Book Warehouse
1020 South Wabash
8th Floor
Chicago, Illinois 60605 (312) 341-0748

Powell's Book Warehouse has a stock of used, rare, and out-of-print books. It emphasizes French, German, Italian, and British History, plus South Asia, Australia, Africa, Literary Criticism, Science, and University Press remainders.
How to Get There: Located at the south edge of the Loop in downtown Chicago.
Owner/Biography: Michael Powell.
Year Founded/History of Bookstore: 1973.
Types/Classifications: Hardbound, paperback, prints, maps, out-of-print.
General Subject Areas: General.
Specific Specialties: Literary Criticism, Sciences, Foreign Language, British History, Australia, South Asia, Africa.
Other Specialties: University Press remainders.
Mail/Telephone Orders; Credit Cards: No mail or phone orders. Visa and Mastercard accepted.
Business Hours: Tuesday through Saturday 10:30 AM - 5:00 PM or by appointment.
Parking Facilities: Street parking, public parking lots.
Collections/Individual Items Purchased: Both.
Booksellers' Memberships: Midwest Bookhunters.
Miscellaneous: See also POWELL'S BOOKSTORE, Chicago, Illinois.

350
Powell's Bookstore
1501 East 57th Street
Chicago, Illinois 60637 (312) 955-7780

Powell's is a large general used bookstore located in the Hyde Park/University of Chicago neighborhood. The store is particularly strong in academic and university press books but also has intensive art and fiction collections. The store occupies 4,000 square feet of space.
How to Get There: The store is located 2 1/2 blocks west of the 57th Street Exit from Lake Shore Drive.
Owner/Biography: Michael Powell, owner; Bradley Jones, manager.
Year Founded/History of Bookstore: 1973.
Number of Volumes: 200,000.
Types/Classifications: Hardbound, paperback, prints, maps.
General Subject Areas: African History, American History, American Indians, Americana, Ancient History, Anthropology, Archaeology, Architecture, Art, Black Studies, Books About Books, British History,

Canadian History, Chinese History, Cookbooks, Drama, East Asian History, Economics, European History, Fiction, Film, Foreign Language, Geology, History and Philosophy of Science, Indian History, Japanese History, Judaica, Latin American History, Law, Linguistics, Literary Criticism, Marxism, Mathematics, Medieval History, Mideastern History, Music, Mysteries, Philosophy, Photography, Poetry, Political Science, Psychology, Russian History, Science, Science Fiction, Sociology, Sports, Theology, Transportation, Westerns, Women's Studies.

Mail/Telephone Orders; Credit Cards: No mail or phone orders. Visa and Mastercard accepted.
Business Hours: Seven days a week 9:00 AM - 11:00 PM; closed Christmas Day.
Parking Facilities: Ample street parking.
Special Features: Books purchased at the store will be mailed if requested.
Collections/Individual Items Purchased: Both.
Booksellers' Memberships: Midwest Bookhunters.
Miscellaneous: Powell's also has a warehouse at 1020 South Wabash, 8th Floor, which is open to the public 10:30 AM - 5:00 PM, Tuesday through Saturday.

351
Prairie Archives
641 West Monroe
Springfield, Illinois 62704   (217) 522-9742

This is a general line of used, out-of-print, and rare books. Also handled are paper collectibles such as postcards, posters, and prints.

Owner/Biography: John R. Paul.
Year Founded/History of Bookstore: 1971.
Number of Volumes: 20,000.
Types/Classifications: Hardbound, paperbacks, ephemera, first editions, fine bindings, out-of-print, association copies, press books, signed copies, presentation copies, limited editions, color plate books.
General Subject Areas: General.
Specific Specialties: Abraham Lincoln, Illinois History, Civil War (U.S.)
Author Specialties: Vachel Lindsay, Edgar Lee Masters.
Mail/Telephone Orders; Credit Cards: Both. Visa and Mastercard accepted.
Business Hours: Monday through Saturday 11:00 AM - 5:00 PM.
Parking Facilities: Street parking.
Special Features: Search service.
Collections/Individual Items Purchased: Both.

352
Preservation Book Shop
1911 Central Street
Evanston, Illinois 60201   (312) 864-4449

This is a general subject used bookstore with a selection of history, literature, philosophy, religion, art, and science fiction. It also has rare, unusual, and hard to find books. Customers are encouraged to have a cup of coffee and discuss books with the owners.

How to Get There: The store is in northwest Evanston at the corner of Central Street and Green Bay Road.
Owner/Biography: Dave and Theresa Wilhelm.
Year Founded/History of Bookstore: 1984.
Number of Volumes: 8,000.
Types/Classifications: Hardbound, paperback.
General Subject Areas: Anthropology, Archaeology, Art, Business, Children's Books, Cooking, Drama, Health, History, Language, Law, Music, Mysteries, Philosophy, Photography, Poetry, Religion, Science, Science Fiction.
Mail/Telephone Orders; Credit Cards: No mail or phone orders.
Business Hours: Monday through Saturday 11:00 AM - 7:00 PM.

Parking Facilities: Street parking.
Special Features: Search service.
Collections/Individual Items Purchased: Both.

353
Renaissance Books in Ravinia
591A Roger Williams Avenue
Highland Park, Illinois 60035   (312) 432-0432

This bookstore has two rooms of books. Each section is categorized by author and marked as to type of book. It occupies 400 square feet of space. The shop has an antiquarian atmosphere with seating for reading and casual browsing. It is carpeted and has wood paneled walls.

How to Get There: The store is located 2 blocks east of Green Bay Road; Roger Williams Avenue is the main street of the business district in Ravinia, a suburb of Highland Park.
Owner/Biography: Juanita Shearer.
Year Founded/History of Bookstore: 1972.
Number of Volumes: 5,000.
Types/Classifications: Hardbound only, out-of-print, rare.
General Subject Areas: Americana, Art, Aviation, Baseball, Birds, Books About Antiques, British History, Business, Cookbooks, Fishing, Gardening, Golf, Heritage Press, History, Hobbies, Horses, Humor, Hunting, Juvenile, Literature, Military, Mysteries, Natural History, Philosophy, Political Science, Religion, Science Fiction and Fantasy, Travel.
Mail/Telephone Orders; Credit Cards: Both. Cash with order; 10 day return policy; libraries billed. No credit cards.
Business Hours: Daily 10:00 AM - 5:00 PM; Sunday 12:00 Noon - 5:00 PM; closed Friday.
Parking Facilities: Street parking, public parking lot.
Special Features: Search service; appraisals.
Catalogue: Lists published (all books on lists by category).
Collections/Individual Items Purchased: Both.

354
Richard S. Barnes & Company
821 Foster Street
Evanston, Illinois 60201   (312) 869-2272

The bookstore is located in the old bindery building of Northwestern University Press. It is a large store with categorized book stacks, designated work areas, and an area for finer and rare books. It occupies 3,000 square feet of space.

How to Get There: The store is located in the first suburb north of Chicago. Travelling north on Sheridan Road in Evanston, one passes the Northwestern University Campus; turn west (left) onto Foster Street. The store is three blocks west of Sheridan Road and two blocks east of Ridge Avenue.
Owner/Biography: Richard S. Barnes and Patricia N. Barnes. Mr. Barnes has been in the book business for nearly 40 years in the Chicago area.
Year Founded/History of Bookstore: 1942.
Number of Volumes: Over 25,000.
Types/Classifications: Hardbound, some paperbacks in collector's fields, some ephemera, European import-ed art cards, first editions, fine bindings, press books, out-of-print, signed copies, limited editions, sets.
General Subject Areas: Americana, Biography, Books About Books, Detective Fiction, History, Literature, Science Fiction and Fantasy.
Other Specialties: Scholarly Works.
Mail/Telephone Orders; Credit Cards: Both. Postage is paid if cash with order. No credit cards.
Business Hours: Monday through Saturday 11:00 AM - 6:00 PM.
Parking Facilities: Driveway and street parking.
Special Features: Quotes to libraries and individuals.

Collections/Individual Items Purchased: Both.
Booksellers' Memberships: Antiquarian Booksellers Association of America, Midwest Bookhunters.

355
Rogers Park Bookstore
1422 West Morse
Chicago, Illinois 60626 (312) 262-3765

This is a general used bookstore with stock in all subject areas. It occupies 1,250 square feet of space.
Owner/Biography: Jeffrey Ennis.
Year Founded/History of Bookstore: 1974.
Number of Volumes: 30,000.
Types/Classifications: Hardbound, out-of-print, first editions.
General Subject Areas: General.
Other Specialties: Scholarly remainders.
Mail/Telephone Orders; Credit Cards: Both. No credit cards.
Business Hours: Seven days per week 12:00 Noon - 8:00 PM.
Collections/Individual Items Purchased: Both.

356
Second City Books, Inc.
2922 North Clark Street
Chicago, Illinois 60657 (312) 477-1999

This bookstore carries a general stock of used, out-of-print, and rare books with emphasis upon quality and condition. It has one of the larger stocks of photography books in the country as well as a large section of professional level mental health books. Fiction and literary criticism are well represented and the rare books number in the hundreds. The shop occupies 1,000 square feet of space.
How to Get There: The shop is located in the "New Town" section of Chicago between Diversey and Belmont Avenues.
Owner/Biography: Paul Rohe, Irving Leiden, Barbara Leiden. Paul is an experienced bookstore operator with a background in English and publishing. Irving and Barbara are major collectors of photographica and also work in the mental health field.
Year Founded/History of Bookstore: 1982.
Number of Volumes: 20,000.
Types/Classifications: Mostly hardbound, extensive number of individual photographs, large section of autographed books, many volumes in galley or proof, extensive art and architecture collection, first editions, fine bindings, limited editions, out-of-print, leather bound books, books with fine graphics.
General Subject Areas: American History, Art and Architecture, Biography, Classic Literature, Cookbooks, Fiction and Literary Criticism, Foreign History, Juveniles, Linguistics, Mental Health, Music, Mysteries, Philosophy, Photography, Religion, Science Fiction, Theater and Film.
Specific Specialties: Chicago, Nineteenth Century Photography, Psychoanalysis.
Author Specialties: Henry Miller, James Joyce.
Other Specialties: Scholarly Works.
Mail/Telephone Orders; Credit Cards: Both. Cash with order and postage will be included in the price.
Business Hours: Seven days per week 12:00 Noon - 9:00 PM.
Parking Facilities: Street parking, public garage within 2 blocks.
Collections/Individual Items Purchased: Both.

357
Seven Oaks Press
405 South Seventh Street
Saint Charles, Illinois 60174 (312) 584-0187

A general bookstore.
Owner/Biography: Tom Bowie.
Year Founded/History of Bookstore: 1960.
Number of Volumes: 5,000.
Types/Classifications: General.
General Subject Areas: General.
Mail/Telephone Orders; Credit Cards: Both.
Business Hours: Friday 12:00 Noon - 9:00 PM; Saturday 9:00 AM - 6:00 PM; other times by appointment.
Catalogue: Twice yearly.
Collections/Individual Items Purchased: Both.

358
Storey Book Antiques and Books
1325 East State - Highway 64
Sycamore, Illinois 60178   (815) 895-5910

This bookstore carries a general line of used books. The store occupies five rooms in two buildings. The site was a former gas station.
How to Get There: The bookstore is located 60 miles west of Chicago and 10 miles northeast of Northern Illinois University in DeKalb.
Owner/Biography: Jean A. Larkin.
Year Founded/History of Bookstore: 1972.
Number of Volumes: 9,000.
Types/Classifications: Hardbound, some paperback, ephemera, out-of-print, signed copies.
General Subject Areas: American Indians, Architecture, Art, Biography, Christmas, Civil War (U.S.), Cookbooks, Crafts, Gerontology, Humor, Illinois, Juvenile, Mysteries, Poetry, Psychology, Sports, World War I, World War II.
Specific Specialties: Money, Sex, Politics, Religion.
Author Specialties: Gene Fowler, Alexander King, Richard Halliburton.
Mail/Telephone Orders; Credit Cards: Both. No credit cards.
Business Hours: Wednesday through Sunday 11:00 AM - 5:00 PM.
Parking Facilities: Ample parking.
Special Features: Search service.
Collections/Individual Items Purchased: Both.
Booksellers' Memberships: Midwest Bookhunters.

359
Swiss Village Book Store
907 Main Street
Highland, Illinois 62249   (618) 654-2521

The Swiss Village Book Store is in a lovely old bank. Most of the better antiquarian books are in the Board Room. There are also many quilts and handmade articles and a large selection of books for children as well as new and old books. Another Swiss Village Book Store is located at Laclede's Landing in St. Louis, Missouri.
How to Get There: Highland, Illinois is located 30 miles east of St. Louis on Route 40, just off Interestate 70.
Owner/Biography: Elaine Stratton. Ms. Stratton is a teacher, librarian, writer, and oral historian.
Year Founded/History of Bookstore: 1978.
Number of Volumes: 4,000.
Types/Classifications: Hardbound, autographs, ephemera, first editions, out-of-print, signed copies, limited editions.
General Subject Areas: Children's Books, Cookbooks, History, Mississippi River, Victorian Books, Women Authors, Women's Biography, Women's Studies.
Specific Specialties: Abraham Lincoln.

Author Specialties: Mark Twain.
Mail/Telephone Orders; Credit Cards: Both. American Express, Visa, and Mastercard accepted.
Business Hours: Seven days a week.
Parking Facilities: Ample parking.
Catalogue: Published every 2 or 3 months.
Collections/Individual Items Purchased: Individual items; collections sometimes.
Miscellaneous: Many customers have claimed that the Swiss Village Book Store is the most interesting they have ever visited.

360
Thomas J. Joyce and Company
14th Floor
431 South Dearborn
Chicago, Illinois 60603   (312) 922-0980

This is a general antiquarian bookstore with a wide selection of subject matter. The 14th-floor shop contains 1,200 square feet of space.
How to Get There: Located in Chicago's South Loop, just north of Printer's Row, the company operates from the Manhattan Building, a landmark structure designed by William LeBaron Jenney.
Owner/Biography: Thomas J. Joyce.
Year Founded/History of Bookstore: The Company was founded in 1974 in Chicago. It moved to a walk-up office in Geneva, Illinois in May 1975 under the name The Scholar Gypsy, Ltd. In 1981 the name was changed to its present one and the business expanded into a first floor store front in the same building. In mid-1983 the shop was moved to its present address in Chicago's South Loop area.
Number of Volumes: 4,000.
Types/Classifications: Hardbound, paperback, prints, maps, pamphlets, ephemera, framed work, rare books, first editions, fine bindings, association copies, press books, autographs, fine printing.
General Subject Areas: Abraham Lincoln, Americana, Architecture, Books About Books, Chicago, Children's Books, Exploration, Fur Trade, Illinois, Ireland, Irish People, Law, Medicine, Midwest, Overland Narratives, Science, Science Fiction and Fantasy, Sherlockiana, Theology, Travel, Voyages, Western Americana, World's Fairs.
Specific Specialties: World's Columbian Exposition, Chicago's Century of Progress Exposition, Chicago Ante-Fire Imprints, Midwest Private Presses.
Author Specialties: Vincent Starrett, Thomas Merton, Arthur Conan Doyle, George MacDonald, Ulysses S. Grant.
Mail/Telephone Orders; Credit Cards: Both; no credit cards.
Business Hours: This is a full-time professional firm; however, it operates by appointment only. In addition, appointments may be made during and after normal business hours.
Parking Facilities: Street and public parking lot.
Special Features: Search service, collection development, appraisals.
Catalogue: Four times a year.
Collections/Individual Items Purchased: Both.
Booksellers' Memberships: Antiquarian Booksellers Association of America, Midwest Bookhunters.

361
Thomas L. Brisch - Bookseller
304 South Main Street
Galena, Illinois 61036   (815) 777-0814

This is a general bookstore with some specializations.
Owner/Biography: Thomas L. Brisch.
Year Founded/History of Bookstore: The bookstore was formerly known as Valley Book Shop.
Number of Volumes: 20,000.
General Subject Areas: Architecture, Catholic Americana, Illinois, Iowa, Mississippi River, Railroads, Southern Americana, Western Americana.

Mail/Telephone Orders; Credit Cards: Both. No credit cards. Mailing address: same as above except add P.O. Box 37.

Business Hours: Daily 9:00 AM - 4:00 PM; closed Sunday.

Collections/Individual Items Purchased: Both.

362
Titles, Inc.
1931 Sheridan Road
Highland Park, Illinois 60035

(312) 432-3690

This is a small personal shop with the look of a private library, providing a comfortable antiquarian ambiance. It contains 500 square feet of space.

How to Get There: The bookstore is in the downtown business area of Highland Park, which is a suburb 25 miles north of Chicago. It is readily accessible by auto or railroad.

Owner/Biography: Florence Shay.

Year Founded/History of Bookstore: 1973.

Number of Volumes: 6,000.

Types/Classifications: Hardbound, autographs, maps, prints, ephemera, first editions, fine bindings, out-of-print, association copies, press books, signed copies, presentation copies, limited editions, color plate books, sets in leather bindings.

General Subject Areas: Americana, Architecture, Art, Books About Books, Civil War (U.S.), Detective, Juveniles, Medical, Natural History, Photography, Poetry, Science Fiction and Fantasy, Travel.

Specific Specialties: Chicago, 19th Century First Edition Literature, 20th Century First Edition Literature.

Mail/Telephone Orders; Credit Cards: Both. No credit cards.

Business Hours: Daily except Sunday 10:30 AM - 5:00 PM.

Parking Facilities: Street and public lot around the corner.

Special Features: Search service.

Collections/Individual Items Purchased: Both.

Booksellers' Memberships: Antiquarian Booksellers Association of America, Midwest Book Hunters.

363
Unicorn Bookstore
4104 South Archer Avenue
Chicago, Illinois 60632

(312) 523-3685

The bookstore specializes in astrology, hypnosis, Extrasensory Perception (ESP), witchcraft, and the occult.

How to Get There: The bookstore is located 1/2 block west of California Avenue on Archer, one of the oldest streets in Chicago. Archer was once an Indian trail, and runs on an angle from the rest of the streets.

Owner/Biography: Elinor Jaksto, owner, is a professional astrologer and gifted psychic. She has been an antiquarian book person for over 20 years and also deals in rare and unusual telling cards and Tarot decks. She has been written about in Brad Steiger's book "Psychic City, Chicago."

Year Founded/History of Bookstore: 1964.

Number of Volumes: 50,000.

Types/Classifications: Hardbound, paperback, magazines, first editions, out-of-print, rare.

General Subject Areas: Astrology, Extrasensory Perception (ESP), Hypnosis, Occult, Witchcraft.

Mail/Telephone Orders; Credit Cards: Mail orders.

Business Hours: By appointment only.

Parking Facilities: Street parking.

Special Features: Search service, publishing.

Collections/Individual Items Purchased: Collections.

364
Valerie Kraft, Fine Books
309 North Elmhurst Road
Prospect Heights, Illinois 60070   (312) 253-1419

The bookstore, sometimes known as "Valerie's Gallery," is located on a large tree-shaded lot, with rare books and prints in the residence. There is a separate bookhouse in Prospect Heights, in the northwest suburbs of Chicago, 1/2 hour north of O'Hare Airport. The shops contain 3,500 square feet of space.

How to Get There: Elmhurst Road is State Highway 83, running through the state to the Wisconsin border.

Owner/Biography: Valerie Kraft, owner, has been a book lover since childhood in northern Michigan. She studied journalism at Northwestern University, wrote and sold articles and fiction to national magazines, taught adult writing workshops. She then "succumbed" to her first love: books. For 14 years now she has been specializing in buying and selling artist-illustrated books, children's books, and illustrated sporting books.

Year Founded/History of Bookstore: Founded in 1970, the bookstore in still on its original site, with gradual expansion into all corners of the house, then into the "Little Bookhouse on the Prairie," a shelf-lined, paneled, carpeted, metal second house in Prospect Heights.

Number of Volumes: 7,500.

Types/Classifications: Hardbound, a few paperbacks of distinction, ephemera, many prints, first editions, fine bindings, press books, signed copies, limited editions, many color plate books.

General Subject Areas: Art, Children's Books, Decorative Arts, Mystery, Natural History, Sporting, Travel.

Specific Specialties: Derrydale Press.

Author Specialties: Ian Fleming, Erle Stanley Gardner.

Mail/Telephone Orders; Credit Cards: Both. No credit cards.

Business Hours: Daily 9:00 AM - 9:00 PM.

Parking Facilities: Street and driveway.

Special Features: Personal attention to all individual requests.

Catalogue: Catalogue published.

Collections/Individual Items Purchased: Both.

Booksellers' Memberships: Founding member 10 years ago of the Midwest Bookhunters.

365
W. Graham Arader III
110 East Delaware Place
Suite 1504
Chicago, Illinois 60611

See: W. GRAHAM ARADER III, King of Prussia, Pennsylvania.

366
Yesteryear Books
420 Lincoln Avenue
Lincoln, Illinois 62656   (217) 732-6474

The bookstore features a cross section of good, collectible books neatly arranged. The store welcomes beginning collectors as well as advanced collectors and fellow dealers. It contains 500 square feet of space.

How to Get There: The bookstore is only five minutes off I-55, in a lovely residential area. This is the only city christened by Abraham Lincoln before he became famous.

Owner/Biography: Bob and Pat Weimer.

Year Founded/History of Bookstore: The owners explain that the bookstore, founded in 1972, is mainly a "Mom and Pop Operation, featuring a well rounded, clean stock of books."

Number of Volumes: 12,000.

Types/Classifications: Hardbound, ephemera, postcards, first editions, fine bindings, press books, out-of-print, signed copies, presentation copies, color plate books.

General Subject Areas: Adventure, Americana, Biography, Civil War (U.S.), Juvenile, Lincolniana, Litera-

ture, Travel.
    Mail/Telephone Orders; Credit Cards: Both. No credit cards.
    Business Hours: By appointment only.
    Parking Facilities: Street.
    Special Features: Quiet, undisturbed browsing. Late hours no problem.
    Collections/Individual Items Purchased: Both.

INDIANA

367
Books Unlimited
922 East Washington
Indianapolis, Indiana 46202   (317) 634-0949

Books Unlimited is a family bookshop offering a complete line of hardbound, paperback books, mostly non-fiction. It also features comics. The shop occupies 850 square feet of space.
How to Get There: The bookstore is within easy walking distance of all downtown hotels.
Owner/Biography: James Ware.
Year Founded/History of Bookstore: 1978. The shop has been in the same location since its founding.
Number of Volumes: 8,000.
Types/Classifications: Hardbound, paperback, maps, comics, out-of-print, first editions.
General Subject Areas: General.
Specific Specialties: Indiana History and Authors.
Author Specialties: James Whitcomb Riley, Gene Stratton Porter.
Mail/Telephone Orders; Credit Cards: Both. Visa and Mastercard accepted.
Business Hours: Monday through Saturday 9:30 AM - 6:00 PM.
Parking Facilities: Business parking lot.
Special Features: Search service.
Collections/Individual Items Purchased: Both
Miscellaneous: Complete line of new and collector comic books is offered.

368
Bookstack
112 West Lexington
Elkhart, Indiana 46516   (219) 293-3815

The Bookstack is a bright, spacious shop in an 1890's vintage metal-fronted building. The shop caters to all ages with a general stock of fine used books complemented with paperbacks, comics, scarce books, and collector's items. The store maintains what is perhaps the best selection of Western Americana, natural history (from hunting and fishing through gardening and flower arranging), and Notre Dame football to be found in the State of Indiana.
How to Get There: The bookstore is located 3 miles south of the Indiana Toll Road (Elkhart exit) in downtown Elkhart.
Owner/Biography: Charles and Judy Brothers, George and Mary Foster.
Year Founded/History of Bookstore: 1975.
Number of Volumes: 25,000.
Types/Classifications: Hardbound, paperback, comics, first editions, out-of-print.
General Subject Areas: American History, Animals, Art, Auto Repair, Birds, Cookbooks, Crafts, European History, Fishing, Flower Arranging, Gardening, Horticulture, Hunting, Indiana History, Literature, Music, Nature, Philosophy, Psychology, Railroads, Religion, Science, Western Americana.
Mail/Telephone Orders; Credit Cards: Both. Prepayment necessary. No credit cards.
Business Hours: Monday through Saturday 10:30 AM - 5:30 PM or by appointment.
Parking Facilities: Steet parking, public parking lot 1 block away.
Special Features: Search service.
Catalogue: Published 2 to 3 times per year.
Collections/Individual Items Purchased: Both.

369
Chanticleer Books
1120 Michigan Avenue
Fort Wayne, Indiana 46804   (219) 424-0746

Most of the stock of Chanticleer Books is located in an old carriage house and some books are in the owner's private residence. Visits can be by chance or appointment.
How to Get There: Go south on Broadway to the end of 2000 block, turn west on Michigan Avenue for 1/2 block.
Owner/Biography: Mary and Ralph W. Clark.
Year Founded/History of Bookstore: 1975.
Number of Volumes: 1,000.
Types/Classifications: Hardbound, paperback, magazines, first editions, out-of-print.
General Subject Areas: Americana, Indiana Authors, Indiana History.
Specific Specialties: Indiana State Historical Society Publications, Indiana County Histories.
Mail/Telephone Orders; Credit Cards: Both. Cash with order; any book, except city directories, may be returned within 10 days for a full refund. No credit cards.
Business Hours: By chance or by appointment.
Parking Facilities: Private parking lot for 4 cars.
Collections/Individual Items Purchased: Both.

370
Corner Cupboard Cookbooks
58 North Main Street
Suite B
Zionsville, Indiana 46077   (317) 872-4319

Corner Cupboard Cookbooks began as a mail order only business in 1976 and opened a small retail store in October 1982. The store specializes in carefully selected new, out-of-print, hard-to-get, scarce cookbooks with heavy emphasis on the spiral bound church and community cookbooks. The store has customers all over the world.
Owner/Biography: Helen L. Jump. The business developed from a personal hobby of collecting cookbooks during travels.
Year Founded/History of Bookstore: 1976.
Types/Classifications: Hardbound, spiral bound, paperback, magazines, newsletters.
General Subject Areas: Cookbooks.
Specific Specialties: Church and Community Cookbooks.
Mail/Telephone Orders; Credit Cards: Both. Visa and Mastercard accepted.
Business Hours: Tuesday through Friday 11:00 AM - 4:00 PM; other hours by appointment.
Parking Facilities: Public parking lot, street parking.
Special Features: Publishing sideline ("Cookbook Collector Favorite Recipes" and international newsletter).
Catalogue: Published monthly; write for latest lists and/or catalogue.
Miscellaneous: Ms. Jump and her store were described in detail in an article which appeared in the "Chicago Sun Times," Thursday, December 1, 1983.

371
Erasmus Books
1027 East Wayne
South Bend, Indiana 46617   (219) 232-8444

Erasmus Books has a general stock of used and out-of-print titles which fills the first floor and basement of a prairie-style house. It occupies 1,800 square feet of space.
How to Get There: South Bend is 80 miles east of Chicago; take Notre Dame Exit off Indiana Tollway; the shop is across the river from downtown South Bend.

Owner/Biography: Philip Schatz and William Storey.
Year Founded/History of Bookstore: 1978. The shop was purchased by the present owners in 1980.
Number of Volumes: 30,000.
Types/Classifications: Hardbound, paperback, first editions, fine bindings, out-of-print, association copies, press books, signed copies, presentation copies, limited editions, color plate books.
General Subject Areas: General.
Mail/Telephone Orders; Credit Cards: Both. No credit cards.
Business Hours: Tuesday through Sunday 12:00 Noon - 6:00 PM.
Parking Facilities: Street parking.
Special Features: Search service.
Collections/Individual Items Purchased: Both.

372
Forest Park Book Shop
1412 Delaware Avenue
Fort Wayne, Indiana 46805   (219) 424-1058

Since 1970 the shop has been located in a former grocery store building in a quiet residential area. It is large enough for browsing, but "too small for very much junque." The shop carries mostly hardbound books in very good to fine condition.
How to Get There: The bookstore is located 2 blocks north of Lakeside Park Rose Gardens, about 1 mile northeast of downtown.
Owner/Biography: Lois Morris, et al.
Year Founded/History of Bookstore: 1970.
Number of Volumes: 10,000.
Types/Classifications: Hardbound, first editions, out-of-print.
General Subject Areas: Americana, Art, Biography, Detective Fiction, General, History.
Specific Specialties: Indiana, Fort Wayne.
Mail/Telephone Orders; Credit Cards: Both. Cash with order and a self-addressed stamped envelope. Visa and Mastercard accepted.
Business Hours: Tuesday through Saturday 1:30 PM - 5:30 PM.
Parking Facilities: Street parking.
Special Features: Search service; selected author and subject checklists; genealogy supplies including "easy-read" census forms; National Geographic maps; fee appraisals for insurance purposes and attorneys.
Collections/Individual Items Purchased: Both.

373
Kathleen Rais - Books
612 N. Dunn
Bloomington, Indiana 47401   (812) 336-7687

This is a small operation, open by appointment only, specializing in fine books on the dog and Albert Payson Terhune and the Terhune family. Catalogues are issued on these and general subjects.
How to Get There: Bloomington, the home of Indiana University and the Lilly Library, is located about 50 miles south of Indianapolis. The bookstore is situated near downtown, within walking distance of the campus.
Owner/Biography: Originally from Huntington, Long Island, Ms. Rais began collecting Terhune's works at age six. After graduating from Indiana University she apprenticed to Applegate Books East, in Philadelphia. She returned to Indiana University and completed the MLS degree. Ms. Rais is working on a bibliography of Albert Payson Terhune for publication.
Year Founded/History of Bookstore: 1978. Stock is small but select, with a growing emphasis on fine catalogues in many areas, but especially on fine books about dogs and Terhune. The first office is now a parking lot, and Ms. Rais presently works out of her home.
Types/Classifications: Hardbound, paperback, prints, rare, antiquarian.

General Subject Areas: Coursing, Dogs, Foxhunting.

Specific Specialties: Albert Payson Terhune, Marion Harland, Alice Terhune, Edward Payson Terhune, Christine Terhune Herrick, Virginia Terhune Van deWater, State of Indiana, Indiana University.

Mail/Telephone Orders; Credit Cards: Both. Mail orders: cash with order unless otherwise arranged; overseas customers billed; no credit cards.

Business Hours: By appointment only.

Parking Facilities: Street.

Special Features: Search service, checklists of the Terhune family.

Catalogue: Four times a year.

Collections/Individual Items Purchased: Both.

374
Mason's Rare & Used Books

264 South Wabash Street

Wabash, Indiana 46992

(219) 563-6421

The bookstore is one of Indiana's largest antiquarian dealers, containing 110,000 volumes in 54,000 square feet of space.

How to Get There: The shop is situated on Indiana Route 13 in downtown Wabash, and is 1 1/2 hours north of Indianapolis via US 31 & 24; 2 1/2 hours southeast of Chicago via US 31 & 24; 45 minutes west of Ft. Wayne via US 24.

Owner/Biography: Jon D. Mason.

Year Founded/History of Bookstore: 1974.

Number of Volumes: 110,000.

Types/Classifications: Hardbound, paperback, magazines.

General Subject Areas: General.

Specific Specialties: Religion, Theology, Military History, Natural History, Old Northwest, Indiana Authors, Industrial Arts, Technology, American Indians.

Author Specialties: Gene Stratton Porter, Kin Hubbard.

Mail/Telephone Orders; Credit Cards: Both; no credit cards.

Business Hours: Monday through Saturday 9:30 AM - 5:00 PM.

Parking Facilities: Street and parking lots.

Special Features: Search service.

Catalogue: Six times a year.

Collections/Individual Items Purchased: Both.

375
Odds & Eads

1127 Prospect

Indianapolis, Indiana 46203

(317) 635-2592

This is a general bookstore, housed in a building erected in 1930 and designed to be a dry goods store, with a broad stairway to the downstairs rooms. The stairway is now filled with books. The shop contains 8,000 square feet of space.

How to Get There: The shop is in the center of Indianapolis.

Owner/Biography: Hereford and Winona Eads.

Year Founded/History of Bookstore: 1979.

Number of Volumes: 350,000.

Types/Classifications: Hardbound, paperback, general classifications.

General Subject Areas: General, Mysteries.

Mail/Telephone Orders; Credit Cards: Both; no credit cards.

Business Hours: Monday through Saturday 10:00 AM - 6:00 PM.

Parking Facilities: Street.

Special Features: Search service.

376
Rick Grunder - Books
915 Maxwell Terrace
Bloomington, Indiana 47401　　　　　　　　　　　　　　　　　　　　(812) 336-6808

Rick Grunder carries a small select rare stock on private premises. Visits can be arranged by appointment.
How to Get There: Travel east on First Street to the end then east on Maxwell two blocks to Maxwell Terrace Apartments.
Owner/Biography: Rick Grunder. Mr. Grunder was former Chairman of the Bibliographic Department of Brigham Young University Library.
Year Founded/History of Bookstore: 1981.
Number of Volumes: 1,000.
Types/Classifications: Rare, antiquarian in all categories.
General Subject Areas: Aldine and Estienne Presses, American Religious Movements (19th Century), Americana, French Sixteenth Century, Mormonism, Victorian Literature.
Specific Specialties: Mormons Before 1850, signed or association Victorian Literary First Editions.
Author Specialties: Ethan Smith, Sara Josepha Hale, James Seixas, Joshua Seixas.
Other Specialties: Accepts referrals for anything even remotely connected to Mormonism prior to 1850, including all newspaper mentions, ephemera, letters, and manuscripts.
Mail/Telephone Orders; Credit Cards: Both. New customers may be asked to remit before shipment is made on first order; shipping charges are additional. No credit cards.
Business Hours: Anytime by appointment.
Parking Facilities: Ample parking available.
Special Features: Large number of items sold for private parties and institutions on consignment.
Catalogue: Published monthly; lists include a broad subject selection of antiquarian items priced from $5 to several thousand dollars.
Collections/Individual Items Purchased: Both.
Booksellers' Memberships: Antiquarian Booksellers Association of America.

377
Used Book Place
P.O. Box 206
2027 Hart Street
Dyer, Indiana 46311　　　　　　　　　　　　　　　　　　　　　　　(219) 322-4247

The bookstore features out-of-print books in most general categories, and contains 850 square feet of space.
How to Get There: Dyer, Indiana is 1/2 mile from the Illinois state line; the store is 1/2 block north of U.S. 30, at the traffic light.
Owner/Biography: Albert McCasey.
Year Founded/History of Bookstore: 1976.
Number of Volumes: 20,000.
Types/Classifications: Hardbound, paperback, out-of-print.
General Subject Areas: General.
Specific Specialties: Libertarian Philosophy, Self-Sufficiency, Austrian Economics.
Author Specialties: Ayn Rand.
Mail/Telephone Orders; Credit Cards: Mail orders only. No credit cards.
Business Hours: Monday, Tuesday, Wednesday, Friday, Saturday 9:15 AM - 5:00 PM.
Parking Facilities: Business parking lot.
Special Features: Search service.
Collections/Individual Items Purchased: Mostly individual items; collections on a limited basis.

IOWA

378
Different Drummer Used Books
333 5th Street
West Des Moines, Iowa 50265   (515) 279-2969

Different Drummer is a small shop which offers personal service. All books are hand-picked for their value as literature. The stock is limited but each book is a "beauty." The shop occupies 600 square feet of space.

How to Get There: 5th Street runs north and south off Grand Avenue; take the 63rd Street exit off the I-235 Freeway, south to Walnut Street and 5th.

Owner/Biography: Barbara L. Croft and Norman R. Hane. The owners are academics and interested in reading and writing.

Year Founded/History of Bookstore: 1978.

Number of Volumes: 3,500.

Types/Classifications: Hardbound, paperback, prints, phonograph albums, out-of-print, some American first editions.

General Subject Areas: Civil War (U.S.), Classic and Contemporary Fiction, General, History, Iowa History, Philosophy, Poetry, World War II.

Mail/Telephone Orders; Credit Cards: Both. Check with order; store pays postage. Visa and Mastercard accepted.

Business Hours: Saturdays only 11:00 AM - 4:30 PM.

Parking Facilities: Street parking.

Special Features: Small publishing venture; free-lance writing.

Collections/Individual Items Purchased: Individual items only.

379
Murphy-Brookfield Books
219 North Gilbert
Iowa City, Iowa 52240   (319) 338-3077

The bookstore is located in the historic Wentz House. Built in 1847, it is the only extant two-story house of native sandstone remaining in Iowa City. Originally a boarding house, it now provides shelter and a background of history for the scholarly works sold here. The shop contains 1,500 square feet of space.

Owner/Biography: Jane Murphy and Mark Brookfield.

Year Founded/History of Bookstore: 1980.

Number of Volumes: 15,000.

Types/Classifications: Hardbound, paperback, literary magazines, in-print, out-of-print books in mostly scholarly fields.

General Subject Areas: Art, History, Literature, Philosophy, Religion, Science, Social Sciences.

Specific Specialties: Irish Literature.

Other Specialties: University Press Titles.

Mail/Telephone Orders; Credit Cards: Both; no credit cards.

Business Hours: Tuesday through Saturday 11:00 AM - 6:00 PM; Sunday 1:00 PM - 5:00 PM.

Parking Facilities: Parking lot in the rear, street parking in front.

Special Features: Search service for out-of-print scholarly books.

Collections/Individual Items Purchased: Both.

380
Source Book Store
232 West 3rd Street
Davenport, Iowa 52801   (319) 324-8941

This is a very large bookstore with a general stock of nearly every subject, mostly out-of-print. Some books date back to the 17th Century. The store has two full floors with 5,200 square feet of space. The bookstore is well known in the Mid-West area.

How to Get There: Davenport is situated on the eastern border of Iowa, on the Mississippi River. The bookstore is located in downtown Davenport on one of its main streets. Interstate Highways I-80 and I-74 intersect here.

Owner/Biography: Robert and Virginia Pekios. The Pekios family has been in the book business for 45 years. George Pekios started the store and has since retired, selling it to his son Robert. Grandson Daniel Pekios is now learning the business and is planning to take over in a few years from his father Robert.

Year Founded/History of Bookstore: 1940.

Number of Volumes: 200,000.

Types/Classifications: Hardbound, paperback, magazines, broadsides, autographs, ephemera, comics, collectibles, first editions, fine bindings, out-of-print, association copies, press books, signed copies, presentation copies, limited editions, color plate books.

General Subject Areas: General.

Mail/Telephone Orders; Credit Cards: Both. No credit cards.

Business Hours: Monday through Saturday 9:30 AM - 5:30 PM.

Parking Facilities: Street.

Special Features: Search service.

Collections/Individual Items Purchased: Both.

381
Stone House Books
307 North Jackson Street
Charles City, Iowa 50616   (515) 228-1764

The bookstore is located in the owners' old limestone house, thus the name.

How to Get There: When entering the town of Charles City from either east or west, turn north on main street and go to Central Park. The bookstore is on the next street, on the west side of the park.

Owner/Biography: Maurice and Catherine Schrup.

Year Founded/History of Bookstore: Founded in 1970 in the owners' home, the shop has remained there, but moved to larger quarters as space demanded.

Number of Volumes: 2,000.

Types/Classifications: Hardbound, a few paperback and magazines.

General Subject Areas: General.

Specific Specialties: Iowa.

Author Specialties: Iowa Authors.

Mail/Telephone Orders; Credit Cards: Both. No credit cards.

Business Hours: Monday through Saturday 2:00 PM - 5:00 PM; other times by appointment.

Parking Facilities: Street.

Special Features: Search service.

Collections/Individual Items Purchased: Both.

KANSAS

382
Green Dragon Books
2730 Boulevard Plaza
Wichita, Kansas 67217   (316) 681-0746

The Green Dragon is a medium sized general store dealing in used, antiquarian, and rare books. The stock is arranged by category with a good selection of books in all sections.
Owner/Biography: Charles and Larue Basom. Both owners have attended the Antiquarian Booksellers School at the University of Denver.
Year Founded/History of Bookstore: 1974.
Number of Volumes: 20,000 hardbound; 50,000 paperback.
Types/Classifications: Hardbound, paperback, first editions, limited editions, signed books, ephemera.
General Subject Areas: General.
Specific Specialties: Southwest Americana, Kansas History, Civil War (U.S.), Aviation, Theater.
Mail/Telephone Orders; Credit Cards: No credit cards.
Business Hours: Tuesday through Saturday 10:00 AM - 6:00 PM; closed Sunday and Monday.
Parking Facilities: Small mall with plenty of parking.
Collections/Individual Items Purchased: Both.

383
J. Hood, Booksellers
1401 Massachusetts
Lawrence, Kansas 66044   (913) 841-4644

The bookstore offers out-of-print scholarly books in all fields with a strong collection in psychology and literary criticism. The shop contains 2,000 square feet of space.
Owner/Biography: John and Chick Hood.
Year Founded/History of Bookstore: 1972.
Number of Volumes: 75,000.
Types/Classifications: Hardbound, paperback, out-of-print.
General Subject Areas: Scholarly books.
Specific Specialties: Psychology, Literary Criticism, Philosophy.
Mail/Telephone Orders; Credit Cards: Mail orders accepted, and must have cash with order; no credit cards.
Business Hours: Closed Monday; Tuesday through Saturday 11:00 AM - 6:00 PM; Sunday 1:00 AM - 6:00 PM.
Parking Facilities: Street.
Collections/Individual Items Purchased: Both.

KENTUCKY

384
Glover's Books
862 South Broadway
Lexington, Kentucky 40504   (606) 253-0614

Glover's Books offers one of the finest selections of used and rare books in the Bluegrass Country. Old and rare volumes in all fields are particularly well represented with a wide variety of works worthy of the most discriminating collector. Book lovers interested in Kentucky history or horse books can choose from Kentucky's rarest works. In addition to books, Glover's has antiquarian maps and prints dating back centuries and offers quality museum mounting and picture framing.

How to Get There: Lexington is 80 miles east of Louisville and 80 miles south of Cincinnati. After Interstates 75 and 64 merge, exit off Route 68 (North Broadway) and travel through downtown, continue on South Broadway one mile past Main Street and watch for Glover's on the left side in an old 2-story Victorian house.

Owner/Biography: John T. Glover.
Year Founded/History of Bookstore: 1978.
Number of Volumes: 20,000.
Types/Classifications: Hardbound, maps and prints, broadsides, autographs, ephemera, out-of-print, first editions, signed copies, presentation copies, atlases, color plate books.
General Subject Areas: Americana, Biography, Biological Sciences, Fiction, History.
Specific Specialties: Kentuckiana, Midwest History, Southern Americana, Civil War (U.S.), Horses.
Author Specialties: Kentucky Authors.
Other Specialties: Cartography - maps, town views, atlases.
Mail/Telephone Orders; Credit Cards: Both. Cash with order; include $1 postage. No credit cards.
Business Hours: Monday through Friday 11:00 AM - 5:30 PM; Saturday 12:00 Noon - 4:00 PM.
Parking Facilities: Business parking lot behind building.
Special Features: Search service; publishing; picture framing.
Catalogue: Published when merited.
Collections/Individual Items Purchased: Both.
Booksellers' Memberships: Antiquarian Booksellers Association of America.

385
Old Louisville Books
426 West Oak Street
Louisville, Kentucky 40203   (502) 637-6411

This is a general bookstore featuring books, collectible paperbacks, and magazines.

How to Get There: The shop is located just off Interstate 65; take Exit 135 (St. Catherine West) 5 blocks to Garvin, left 1 block to Oak, left on West Oak. From downtown Louisville, take Route 6 south, left on Oak.
Owner/Biography: Don Grayson.
Year Founded/History of Bookstore: Founded in 1976, the bookstore remains in its original location under the original owner. The shop's 1984 plans call for expansion in square footage and volumes stocked.
Number of Volumes: 13,000.
Types/Classifications: Hardbound, collectible paperbacks, collectible magazines, first editions, out-of-print, presentation copies, signed copies, limited editions, sets, antiquarian, imprints.
General Subject Areas: Americana, Art, Biography, Civil War (U.S.), Fiction, Natural History, Poetry, Religion, Sporting, World History, World War I, World War II, 19th Century Literature, 20th Century Literature.
Specific Specialties: Kentucky History, Kentucky Literature, Early Regional Travel Accounts and Narratives, African History, European History, Western Americana.

Author Specialties: Kentucky Authors, Jesse Stuart, Wendell Berry, Elizabeth Madox Roberts, J. Winston Coleman, Jr., Thomas D. Clark, Ernest Hemingway, Erskine Caldwell.

Mail/Telephone Orders; Credit Cards: Both. Cash with order. No credit cards. Personal check acceptable.

Business Hours: Monday through Saturday 10:30 AM - 4:30 PM; also by appointment. In the evening phone (502) 451-1130 until 10 PM.

Parking Facilities: Street.

Special Features: Search service; want lists solicited; collection building, especially regional authors such as Jesse Stuart, E.S.Cobb, E.M. Roberts, Wendell Berry, J.W. Coleman, Jr., James Still.

Catalogue: Anticipated two to four times a year.

Collections/Individual Items Purchased: Both.

Miscellaneous: The stock includes gift books which are often quite old and in lovely condition.

386
T & S Books

1545 Scott Boulevard

Covington, Kentucky 41011 (606) 261-6435

The bookstore is located in what was originally a grocery store. It consists of a large front room and a smaller back room which was once the walk-in refrigerator. The two rooms total 2,200 square feet of space.

How to Get There: Covington is located immediately across the Ohio River from Cincinnati. The shop, at the corner of Scott Boulevard and 16th Street, is within five to ten minutes' driving time from downtown Cincinnati.

Owner/Biography: Dan Nagle.

Year Founded/History of Bookstore: 1978.

Number of Volumes: 20,000.

Types/Classifications: Hardbound, paperback, some ephemera, first editions, out-of-print, signed copies, limited editions.

General Subject Areas: Africa, Alaska, American Indians, Americana, Archaeology, Arctic, Art, Aviation, Baseball, Biography, Children's Books, Cookbooks, Fiction, Fishing, Flowers, Gardening, Golf, History, Humor, Hunting, Kentucky History, Kentucky Literature, Literature, Medical, Military History, Poetry, Reference, Religion, Science Fiction and Fantasy, Sea, Ships, Travel, True Crime, Western Americana, Western Art, Western Fiction, World History.

Author Specialties: Jesse Stuart, Kentucky Authors, Kenneth Roberts, Alan Eckert.

Mail/Telephone Orders; Credit Cards: Both. Cash with order except for libraries and other institutions which will be billed by invoice. Visa, Mastercard.

Business Hours: Wednesday, Thursday 10:00 AM - 6:00 PM; Friday 10:00 AM - 8:00 PM; Saturday, Sunday 10:00 AM - 5:00 PM.

Parking Facilities: Street.

Special Features: Search service.

Catalogue: Published at various times.

Collections/Individual Items Purchased: Both.

LOUISIANA

387
Bayou Books, Inc.
1005 Monroe Street
Gretna, Louisiana 70053   (504) 368-1171

Bayou Books is housed in a turn-of-the-century two-story dwelling which has a quaintness that enhances its collection of books. The front room displays current Louisiana books as well as leather bound books, first editions, rare, and autographed editions. The second room is filled with other Louisiana books arranged in alphabetical order by author and includes an extensive selection of local interest cookbooks. Other rooms display general used books, categorized and alphabetized within each category.

How to Get There: From New Orleans drive across the Greater New Orleans Mississippi River Bridge to the Westbank. Take the General DeGaulle West exit (last exit past the bridge), proceed through 3 traffic lights plus one block to stop sign. Bayou Books is on the corner.

Owner/Biography: Milburn and Nancy Calhoun.

Year Founded/History of Bookstore: 1961.

Number of Volumes: 20,000.

Types/Classifications: Hardbound, paperback, some magazines, Alva museum replicas, ephemera, leather bound, first editions, signed copies.

General Subject Areas: Americana, Archaeology, Architecture, Art, Biography, British History, Classics, Cookbooks, Early Texts, Economics, Education, Essays, Fiction, Hobbies, Humor, Juveniles, Language, Literature, Louisiana, Medical, Military, Music, Philosophy, Photography, Poetry, Psychology, Reference, Religion, Science, Sociology, South (U.S.), Travel, U.S. History, World History.

Specific Specialties: New Orleans, Louisiana State University Press, Pelican Publishing Company, Center for Louisiana Studies.

Author Specialties: Stanley C. Arthur, George W. Cable, Lafcadio Hearn, Harnett Kane, Frances Parkinson Keyes, Grace King, Lyle Saxon, Robert Tallant, Edward Tinker.

Mail/Telephone Orders; Credit Cards: Both. Visa and Mastercard accepted.

Business Hours: Monday through Saturday 10:00 AM to 5:00 PM.

Parking Facilities: Street parking.

Special Features: Search service.

Catalogue: Published occasionally.

Collections/Individual Items Purchased: Both.

388
Beckham's Bookshop
228 Decatur Street
New Orleans, Louisiana 70116   (504) 522-9875

Beckham's Bookshop is contained in an early (1836) commercial building with stock displayed on two floors in general categories. The shop occupies 3,000 square feet of space.

How to Get There: The shop is just two blocks into the French Quarter from Canal Street.

Owner/Biography: Alton L. Cook and Carey Beckham.

Number of Volumes: 40,000.

Types/Classifications: Hardbound, paperback, ephemera, old prints, out-of-print, first editions.

General Subject Areas: General.

Mail/Telephone Orders; Credit Cards: Both. No credit cards.

Business Hours: Daily 10:00 AM - 6:00 PM.

Parking Facilities: Public parking lots.

Collections/Individual Items Purchased: Both.

389
City Book and Coin Store
521 Crockett Street
Shreveport, Louisiana 71101 (318) 425-5142

The City Book and Coin Store occupies 1,000 square feet of space and offers both hardbound and paperback books in Americana and Science Fiction and Fantasy. It also carries new books in Parapsychology. The coin department has been a minor item for over 15 years.

Owner/Biography: Vida and Bernie Payton. The Paytons purchased the store 20 years ago and have been in the present location for 15 years.

Year Founded/History of Bookstore: 1963. The store originally opened in 1960 and had three different owners before the Paytons took over.

Types/Classifications: Hardbound, paperback, magazines, out-of-print.

General Subject Areas: Americana, Arkansas History, Civil War (U.S.), Louisiana History, Texas History.

Mail/Telephone Orders; Credit Cards: Mail orders accepted. No credit cards.

Business Hours: Monday through Saturday 9:30 AM - 5:00 PM.

Parking Facilities: Public parking lot, street parking.

Special Features: Search service.

Collections/Individual Items Purchased: Both.

390
J. Raymond Samuel, Ltd.
2727 Prytania Street
New Orleans, Louisiana 70130 (504) 891-9061

Located in a 100-year-old building which began as a roller skating rink built for the 1884 World's Fair in New Orleans, the bookstore has become one of the "must visit" stops in the old Garden District. This is the second most famous historic area in the city after the French Quarter. The shop contains 850 square feet of space.

How to Get There: The bookstore is located at Prytania Street and Washington Avenue, one block from the famous Commander's Palace Restaurant. It is in "The Rink," one block from the St. Charles Avenue streetcar line. It is easily reached from all hotels.

Owner/Biography: J. Raymond Samuel, owner, is a retired corporation executive, published author, and President of the Louisiana Historical Society. He has been active in historical and preservation circles for years, and has been a collector of Louisiana material for over 40 years. He is a member of the Order of the British Empire, having served as Honorary Consul of Great Britain for 10 years before retirement. Mr. Samuel is a lecturer, writer, and appraiser.

Year Founded/History of Bookstore: The shop was opened in 1981 at its present site, and with the same owner.

Number of Volumes: 500.

Types/Classifications: Hardbound, documents, autographs, prints, maps.

General Subject Areas: Battle of New Orleans, Deep South (U.S.), Louisiana, Mississippi River, Steamboats.

Mail/Telephone Orders; Credit Cards: Both; no credit cards.

Business Hours: Monday through Saturday 10:00 AM - 5:30 PM, or by special appointment.

Parking Facilities: Covered parking in the same building.

Special Features: Center of interest for those collecting Louisiana and Deep South material such as books, maps, documents.

Collections/Individual Items Purchased: Both.

391
Librairie Bookshop
829 Royal Street
New Orleans, Louisiana 70116 (504) 525-4837

The bookstore features general second-hand books arranged by topic, with a selection of older books chiefly of the 19th Century, and some earlier, housed in a quaint building containing 750 square feet of space.

How to Get There: The shop is near the center of the Vieux Carre, in the 800 block of the principal business street of the French Quarter.

Owner/Biography: Carey Beckham.

Year Founded/History of Bookstore: The bookstore has remained in the same building since its founding in 1967 and is one of the oldest antiquarian bookstores in the city of New Orleans. It has spawned additional bookshops: "Old Books" at 811 Royal, and "Beckham's Bookshop," 228 Decatur, now one of the city's largest antiquarian bookshops.

Number of Volumes: 20,000.

Types/Classifications: Hardbound, paperback, old prints, ephemera.

General Subject Areas: Americana, Antiques, Architecture, Art, Cooking, Dance, Folklore, Foreign Language Books, History, Literary Criticism, Medicine, Military, Music, Mystery, New Orleans, Occult, Philosophy, Poetry, Psychology, Religion, South (U.S.), Technical, Theater, Travel, True Crime.

Mail/Telephone Orders; Credit Cards: Both; no credit cards; there is no search service.

Business Hours: Daily 10:00 AM - 10:00 PM.

Parking Facilities: There is no parking lot; parking is unpredictable.

Collections/Individual Items Purchased: Both.

392
Maple Street's Second-Hand and Rare Book Shop
7529 Maple Street
New Orleans, Louisiana 70118 (504) 861-2105

The bookstore is an offshoot of the Maple Street Book Shop; it is located next door to the original shop and shares a converted New Orleans "Shotgun" house with the Maple Street Children's Book Shop. Although the shop is just a year old, it is growing rapidly.

Owner/Biography: Rhoda K. Faust.

Year Founded/History of Bookstore: 1982.

Number of Volumes: 12,000.

Types/Classifications: Hardbound, paperback, autographs, magazines, first editions, fine bindings, out-of-print, signed copies, color plate books.

General Subject Areas: Anthropology, Art, Biography, Children's Books, Criticism, Essays, Fiction, History, Mystery, Philosophy, Poetry, Psychology, Reference, Science Fiction and Fantasy, Sociology.

Mail/Telephone Orders; Credit Cards: Both. Visa and Mastercard accepted.

Business Hours: Monday through Saturday 10:00 AM - 6:00 PM.

Parking Facilities: Street.

Special Features: Search service.

393
Taylor Clark Inc.
2623 Government
Baton Rouge, Louisiana 70806 (504) 383-4929

The bookstore has a limited stock, mostly of color plate books and Louisiana material.

Year Founded/History of Bookstore: 1956.

Number of Volumes: 50.

Types/Classifications: Leather bound mostly; color plate books.

General Subject Areas: Americana.

Specific Specialties: Louisiana Material.
Mail/Telephone Orders; Credit Cards: Both. American Express, Mastercard.
Business Hours: By appointment only.
Special Features: Art Gallery.
Catalogue: Published infrequently.
Collections/Individual Items Purchased: Both.
Booksellers' Memberships: Antiquarian Booksellers Association of America.

MAINE

394
Bill Lippincott Paper/Books
547 Hammond Street
Bangor, Maine 04401   (207) 942-4398

This shop appears to be an old house from the exterior and one enters into a large, well-lit area that is full of bookshelves. The walls are covered floor to ceiling with fiction on one side and literature, poetry, and drama on the other side, all alphabetically arranged. Maine books face the front door; free standing shelves arranged by subject cover the room. A row of magazines rests alongside a counter. A second room contains one of the best selections of vintage paperbacks in the country, arranged by publisher, numerically. Important authors are alphabetically arranged in another section. The shop occupies over 736 square feet of space.

How to Get There: Take exit 46 off Interstate 95; head downtown; shop is 1/2 mile on the left.

Owner/Biography: Bill Lippincott. Mr. Lippincott has collected books since he began haunting used bookshops as a child. He started dealing as a means of paying for his collecting habit; then as a substitute for that habit. In 1976 he began to concentrate on early paperbacks and has watched the field grow from a few hundred collectors to several thousand.

Year Founded/History of Bookstore: 1975. Mr. Lippincott began his business as mail order only. He opened a shop in Bingham, Maine four years ago when he ran out of space in his home. He moved to Bangor to a much larger shop in the fall of 1983.

Number of Volumes: 20,000.

Types/Classifications: Hardbound, paperback, magazines, comic books, out-of-print, first editions.

General Subject Areas: Big Little Books, General, Hunting and Fishing, Maine, Mystery and Detective Fiction, Vintage Paperbacks.

Specific Specialties: Boys' Books.

Author Specialties: David Goodis, Arthur Macdougall, Jim Thompson, Richard Stark, Cornell Woolrich.

Mail/Telephone Orders; Credit Cards: Both. Personal checks accepted. No credit cards.

Business Hours: Tuesday through Saturday 10:00 AM - 5:30 PM. Closed Sunday and Monday.

Parking Facilities: Ample street parking, parking lot next door.

Special Features: Informal search service, appraisals. Mr. Lippincott has published a bibliography of Arthur Macdougall and an underground comic book.

Catalogue: Published 3 times per year. Current catalogue is $1. Also available are lists of boys' books, mysteries, pulps which can be obtained by sending a long self-addressed stamped envelope.

Collections/Individual Items Purchased: Both.

Booksellers' Memberships: Maine Antiquarian Booksellers Association.

395
Book Cellar
36 Main Street
Freeport, Maine 04032   (207) 865-3157

Approximately 40,000 books are shelved in the basement of a brick cape house built by shipbuilders in 1800. The shop occupies 800 square feet of space and is located two blocks from the L.L. Bean store.

How to Get There: The Book Celler is located on U.S. Route 1, 20 miles from Portland, Maine on Casco Bay.

Owner/Biography: Dean Chamberlin. Mr. Chamberlin is a retired foreign service officer and a former college teacher.

Year Founded/History of Bookstore: 1970.

Number of Volumes: 40,000.

Types/Classifications: Hardbound, paperback.
General Subject Areas: Biography, General, Juveniles, Maine.
Mail/Telephone Orders; Credit Cards: Both. No credit cards.
Business Hours: Mornings only, year around.
Parking Facilities: Driveway and street parking.
Special Features: Search service.
Collections/Individual Items Purchased: Both.
Booksellers' Memberships: Maine Antiquarian Booksellers.

396
Bookbarn
286 Main Street
Route 109
Springvale, Maine 04083   (207) 324-8255

The Bookbarn is, in typical New England fashion, attached to a ten-room Victorian house built in 1850. The large entrance opens into a front room behind which are two additional rooms. The second floor is one large room. Each floor measures 32 x 44 feet for a total of 2,800 square feet. The barn is spacious and allows for easy browsing. The books are well organized and are in very good or better condition with a few ex-library books.

How to Get There: Take Exit 2 off the Maine Turnpike and go north (a right) on Route 109 for approximately 12 miles, through Sanford to Springvale on Main Street (which is Route 109) to a large white Victorian house and The Bookbarn.

Owner/Biography: Allen Scott. After teaching at the College of Wooster, Millikin University, and the University of Arizona, Allen Scott came to Springvale to teach at in the English Department at Nasson College. A native Virginian (Bridgewater College and the University of Virginia), he opened The Bookbarn as a summer preoccupation in 1972. In 1983 with the closing of Nasson College, antiquarian and out-of-print books became his singular profession.

Year Founded/History of Bookstore: 1972.
Number of Volumes: 25,000.
Types/Classifications: Hardbound, some paperback, some magazines and scholarly journals, broadsides, autographs, prints, newspapers, sheet music (when older material is available); principally out-of-print books with some first editions, a few leather bound sets, signed copies, color plate books, some scarce and unusual items.

General Subject Areas: Americana, Architecture, Art, Art History, Children's Books, Cinema, Civil War (U.S.), Cookbooks, Drama, European History, Feminist Books (By and About Women), Fiction, Fishing, Foreign Language, Hunting, Literary Criticism, Maritime, Medicine, Music, Natural History, Photography, Poetry, Reference, Social Science, Technical, Theology, Travel, Western Americana.

Specific Specialties: Of particular interest are a signed F. Scott Fitzgerald, a Kenneth Roberts letter, a William Morris' Kelmscott Press book, a collection of 24 Robert Browning first editions, and an Albert Einstein letter.

Other Specialties: In each of the subject areas, effort is made to stock scholarly works, and emphasis is given to collecting out-of-print and hard-to-find standard scholarly books.

Mail/Telephone Orders; Credit Cards: Both. Personal checks accepted.
Business Hours: Seven days a week June through September 10:00 AM - 5:00 PM; evenings by appointment; October through May by appointment welcomed day or evening.
Parking Facilities: Parking in driveway, street, and on the front lawn.
Special Features: Special orders; search service; bilbiographies; subject area lists.
Catalogue: Published on an erratic schedule.
Collections/Individual Items Purchased: Both.
Booksellers' Memberships: Maine Antiquarian Booksellers Association.
Miscellaneous: Beginning in May 1984, Bed and Breakfast will be offered at $35 double and $20 single. Reservations are requested and recommended. The Bookbarn is centrally located and within commuting distance of at least ten bookshops.

397
Bridgton Book House
Depot Street
Bridgton, Maine 04009   (207) 647-2546

The Bridgton Book House is located in a century-old blacksmith shop which has been weather beaten to a soft restful gray color. Inside are books of all categories in both hardbound and paperback, most of which are alphabetized by author (biographies by subject). The shop occupies 900 square feet of space.

How to Get There: The bookstore is located on Route 302 which runs through Bridgton. A black and white sign in Olde English script points across a parking lot to the store on the next street.

Owner/Biography: Mrs. Sawyer E. Medbury. Mrs. Medbury is a graduate of Pembroke College of Brown University with a BA in English and Psychology. The bookstore has been run as summer business since 1970.

Year Founded/History of Bookstore: 1970. The business represents "retirement" for the Medburys. The store is open from the end of June until the Saturday of Labor Day Weekend.

Number of Volumes: 8,000.

Types/Classifications: Hardbound, paperback, first editions.

General Subject Areas: Biography, Children's Books, Classics, Dictionaries, Foreign Language, General Fiction, Gothic Novels, Historical Novels, History, How-To, Mysteries, New England Authors, Religion, Romance, Science Fiction.

Mail/Telephone Orders; Credit Cards: Both (during summer only). No credit cards.

Business Hours: Summers only Monday, Tuesday, Thursday, Friday 10:00 AM - 4:30 PM; Saturday 10:00 AM to 1:00 PM; closed Wednesday and Sunday.

Parking Facilities: Public parking lot, street parking.

Collections/Individual Items Purchased: Both.

398
Bunkhouse Books
Route 5A
Gardiner, Maine 04345   (207) 582-2808

Bunkhouse Books is a small book shop with only out-of-print books on Maine subjects. The shop specializes in Maine town histories, county histories, atlases of Maine, and town registers of Maine. It also has fishing books of Maine. The shop occupies 1,000 square feet of space.

How to Get There: The shop is located on Route 126, 5 miles west of Gardiner; also, 1/2 mile west of the Gardiner exit of the Maine Turnpike, and Interstate 95 (Gardiner exit). Watch for sign - Maine Books.

Owner/Biography: Isaac Davis, Jr. Mr. Davis has taught U.S. history for 23 years at Gardiner High School.

Year Founded/History of Bookstore: 1976. The bookstore was founded as a part-time supplement to teaching.

Number of Volumes: 14,000.

Types/Classifications: Hardbound, out-of-print, some first editions.

General Subject Areas: Maine, Maine Authors.

Author Specialties: Kenneth Roberts, Robert Tristam Coffin, Edmund W. Smith.

Other Specialties: Maine Gems and Geology, Maine and the Civil War (U.S.).

Mail/Telephone Orders; Credit Cards: Both. Check with order and include postage. No credit cards.

Business Hours: Monday through Friday 12:00 Noon - 9:00 PM.

Parking Facilities: Business parking lot.

Special Features: Free search service.

Catalogue: Published once or twice per year.

Collections/Individual Items Purchased: Both, but Maine items only.

Booksellers' Memberships: Maine Antiquarian Booksellers Association.

399
C. Seams - Books
P.O. Box 66
Randall Street
Anson, Maine 04911

(207) 696-3138

C. Seams - Books is located in a private residence. Books are found in a room at the rear of house and are mostly catalogued on shelves. Most categories are covered with strong coverage:History, Literature, Biography, Social Science, Mysteries, and Modern First Editions. The stock has been selected with emphasis on condition and desirability.

How to Get There: Take Interstate 95 to Waterville, route 8 to Norridgewock, 201A to Anson, right turn at sign before railroad tracks.

Owner/Biography: Colby J. Seams. Mr. Seams was a new book buyer for a large retail chain for 5 years and operated a used bookshop (Ex Libris) in Bangor for 5 years. He "retired" to his home town to work at home. He is a voracious reader with wide and varied interests.

Year Founded/History of Bookstore: 1980.

Number of Volumes: 15,000.

Types/Classifications: Hardbound, paperbound, some magazines, broadsides, some autographs and ephemera, first editions, out-of-print, signed copies, presentation copies, limited editions, color plate books.

General Subject Areas: History, Literature, Maine, Mysteries, Social Science.

Specific Specialties: Modern First Editions.

Mail/Telephone Orders; Credit Cards: Both. No credit cards.

Business Hours: When at home.

Parking Facilities: Parking in yard.

Special Features: Lists.

Catalogue: Catalogue published.

Booksellers' Memberships: Maine Antiquarian Booksellers Association.

400
Charles Robinson Rare Books
Box 299
Pond Road
Manchester, Maine 04351

(207) 622-1885

Rare and fine books are available in many fields including illustrated books, fine bindings, science and medicine, and western Americana. The readers' annex (open June to September) offers over 5,000 books in fine condition.

How to Get There: Call for an appointment and easy directions. The shop is located 8 miles from the Augusta exit of the Maine Turnpike.

Owner/Biography: Charles Robinson.

Year Founded/History of Bookstore: 1974.

Number of Volumes: 7,000.

Types/Classifications: Rare and fine hardbound.

General Subject Areas: General.

Mail/Telephone Orders; Credit Cards: Both. Cash with order. No credit cards.

Business Hours: By appointment only.

Parking Facilities: Private parking.

Special Features: Appraisals; annual rare book auction each Fall.

Catalogue: Published once per year.

Collections/Individual Items Purchased: Both.

Booksellers' Memberships: Maine Antiquarian Booksellers Association.

401
Ciderpress Bookstore
Cleve Tripp Road, RFD 1
Poland Spring, Maine 04274

The Ciderpress Bookstore is located in the cellar of the owner's house at the edge of Range Pond in Poland Spring. The well-ordered collection of between 5,000 and 10,000 books occupies 650 square feet of space.
How to Get There: From Route 26 in Poland Spring take the Range Hill Road .7 of a mile from the Shaker Village to the Cleve Tripp Road. Poland Spring is 24 miles from Portland and 12 miles from Lewiston and Auburn.
Owner/Biography: Virginia Chute.
Year Founded/History of Bookstore: 1974.
Number of Volumes: Between 5,000 and 10,000.
Types/Classifications: Hardbound, paperback, out-of-print.
General Subject Areas: Biography, Black Americans, Books By and About Women, Children's Books, Cookbooks, History, Literary Criticism, Literature, Natural History, Natural Science, Philosophy, Poetry, Religion, Science Fiction and Fantasy.
Mail/Telephone Orders; Credit Cards: Both. No credit cards.
Business Hours: By chance or appointment.
Collections/Individual Items Purchased: Both.
Booksellers' Memberships: Maine Antiquarian Booksellers Association.

402
Cross Hill Books
866 Washington Street
P.O. Box 798
Bath, Maine 04530   (207) 443-5652

Cross Hill Books is located in a private residence. Visitors are welcome by chance or appointment. The stock occupies approximately 500 square feet of space in a "sea captain's house."
How to Get There: Approximately 1/4 mile north of Route 1.
Owner/Biography: William W. Hill. Mr. Hill was Rare Books Librarian at Colby College in Waterville, Maine from 1969-1976. He has been a full-time antiquarian bookseller since 1977.
Year Founded/History of Bookstore: 1977.
Number of Volumes: 5,000.
Types/Classifications: Hardbound, paperback, prints, rare, antiquarian.
General Subject Areas: Antarctic, Arctic, Boatbuilding, Maritime History, Nautical, Naval History, Pirates, Sailing Ships, Shipbuilding, Whaling, Yacht Voyages, Yachting.
Specific Specialties: Maine Maritime History, Maine Ships and Shipbuilding (especially Bath, Maine).
Author Specialties: G.L. Eskew, Basil Lubbock, E.K. Chatterton, Alan Viliers, Samuel Eliot Morison, Howard Chapelle.
Other Specialties: Thomas Bird Mosher Press Books (Portland, Maine 1891-1923).
Mail/Telephone Orders; Credit Cards: Both. Cash with order (postage is paid). No credit cards.
Business Hours: By appointment or chance.
Parking Facilities: Street parking.
Special Features: Nautical search service; rare book appraisals in all areas.
Catalogue: Published 2 or 3 times per year.
Collections/Individual Items Purchased: Both.
Booksellers' Memberships: Maine Antiquarian Booksellers Association.
Miscellaneous: Mr. Hill states that he has the largest stock of nautical books in the state of Maine.

403

D. Isaacson, Books & Prints

11 Ash Street

Lewiston, Maine 04240   (207) 784-3937

D. Isaacson has a general stock of selected used, out-of-print, and antiquarian books with an emphasis on Maine, the arts, and travel. The ground floor location is always cool in summer.

How to Get There: Lewiston is 17 miles from L.L. Bean (Freeport) and 35 miles from Portland. The shop is in downtown Lewiston next to the municipal parking garage and 2 blocks from Bates Fabrics.

Owner/Biography: Deborah Isaacson.

Year Founded/History of Bookstore: 1977.

Number of Volumes: 5,000.

Types/Classifications: Hardbound, paperback, ephemera, prints, first editions, out-of-print.

General Subject Areas: Americana, Art, Biography, British History, Children's Literature, Civil War, Dance, Fashion Prints, Film, French, Harper's Weekly Prints, Himalayas, Literary Criticism, Literature, Maine, Mysteries, Philosophy, Religion, Scholarly Books, Social Science, Theatre, Travel, World Wars I and II.

Mail/Telephone Orders; Credit Cards: Both. No credit cards.

Business Hours: Monday, Tuesday, Thursday, Friday, Saturday 11:00 AM - 5:00 PM; closed Sunday and Wednesday; closed weekends during July and August.

Parking Facilities: Public parking garage, street parking.

Special Features: Search service; attention to want lists.

Collections/Individual Items Purchased: Both.

404

East Coast Books

Depot Street at Route 109

P.O. Box 849

Wells, Maine 04090   (207) 646-3584

East Coast Books is located in an 1840's red dwelling which is brim full of books, prints, historical documents, and autographs. It occupies 1,800 square feet of space.

How to Get There: Take Exit 2 (Wells) of Maine Turnpike, turn left.

Owner/Biography: Merv and Kaye Slotnick.

Year Founded/History of Bookstore: 1976.

Number of Volumes: 10,000.

Types/Classifications: Hardbound, paperback, out-of-print, rare, ephemera, autographs, prints, drawings, paintings, historical documents, signed copies, first editions.

General Subject Areas: Art, Books with Etchings, Children's Literature, History, Humor, Literature, Maine, Marine, Medical, Natural History Reference, Presidents (U.S.), Religion, Science, Sports, Travel, War.

Author Specialties: Kenneth Roberts, Booth Tarkington.

Mail/Telephone Orders; Credit Cards: Both. Personal check with order, postage charged to all orders. Visa and Mastercard accepted.

Business Hours: April through November: Daily 10:00 AM - 6:00 PM; December through March: 11:00 AM -5:00 PM Daily.

Parking Facilities: Ample parking available.

Special Features: Mail and phone auctions during the Fall and Winter with illustrated catalogue; on-site auctions of books, art, autographs with mail and phone bids accepted in June, July, and August; no buyers premium; reasonable commission schedule.

Catalogue: Auction catalogue published at least 5 times per year.

Collections/Individual Items Purchased: Both.

Booksellers' Memberships: Maine Antiquarian Booksellers Association.

405
F. M. O'Brien - Antiquarian Bookseller
34 & 36 High Street
Portland, Maine 04101 (207) 774-0931

The bookstore specializes in autographs, historical documents and papers, pamphlets, prints and paintings of American interest plus American, English, and foreign literature. Mr. O'Brien also offers expert appraisals.
How to Get There: The bookshop is near the waterfront in the central part of town.
Owner/Biography: Francis M. O'Brien.
Year Founded/History of Bookstore: The bookstore began in Portsmouth, New Hampshire in 1934, was in Portland, Maine from 1935 to 1937, then briefly in Pasadena, California in 1938; in Northampton, Massachusetts during 1938 and 1939, then moved back to stay in Portland, Maine in 1939.
Number of Volumes: 100,000, divided between the city house and a farm 40 miles upcountry.
Types/Classifications: Hardbound, broadsides, autographs, ephemera, first editions, fine bindings, out-of-print, association copies, press books, signed copies, presentation copies, limited editions, color plate books, general old, rare, and second-hand.
General Subject Areas: American Literature, English Literature, Foreign Literature, Historical Documents and Papers, Prints and Paintings of American Interest.
Specific Specialties: State of Maine, Early American Education, Irish History and Literature.
Mail/Telephone Orders; Credit Cards: Mail orders; no credit cards.
Business Hours: Monday through Saturday 10:00 AM - 5:00 PM.
Parking Facilities: Business parking lot.
Collections/Individual Items Purchased: Both.
Booksellers' Memberships: Antiquarian Booksellers Association of America; Maine Antiquarian Booksellers Association.

406
Falls Book Barn
P. O. Box 58, Main Street
Farmington Falls, Maine 04940 (207) 778-3429

The bookstore is located on the first floor of a large barn attached to a Civil War period house. Of the two rooms, one shows the original construction, the other displays old pine paneling with French doors looking out on the bank of the Sandy River.
How to Get There: The shop is located off Route No. 2, between Skowhegan and Farmington; off Route No. 27, between Belgrade and Farmington; five miles east of Farmington, in the village bypassed by new Route No. 2. Watch for state highway signs to direct the turn-offs.
Owner/Biography: Ethel P. Emerson, owner, is a science graduate of Colby College in Waterville, Maine. A retired State of Maine teacher, she is the wife of the village postmaster.
Year Founded/History of Bookstore: The bookstore started as a barn sale in 1973, and has been progressively changing to a bookstore. It now occupies an area of 1,500 square feet.
Number of Volumes: 5,000.
Types/Classifications: General line of hardbound and paperback books; magazines, newspapers, ephemera, pictures, book-related items such as bookends, lamps, bookmarks, etc.; out-of-print.
General Subject Areas: Archaeology, Biography, Classics, Cooking, Criminology, History, Juvenile, Medicine, Nature, Religion, State of Maine.
Mail/Telephone Orders; Credit Cards: No mail or telephone orders; no credit cards.
Business Hours: Summer: Daily 10:00 AM - 6:00 PM; Winter: (unheated) 10:00 AM - 4:00 PM.
Parking Facilities: Blacktop driveway area.
Special Features: Selling off the shelf to readers and dealers.
Collections/Individual Items Purchased: Individual items.

407
Frederica de Beurs - Books
RFD 1
Box 2880
Dexter, Maine 04930

(207) 924-7474

The bookstore is part of an 18th Century farmhouse. The setting is rural and a worthwhile detour for those travelling to the Northwoods and the Moosehead Lake region. The librarian-owner has collected a general stock of interesting books with special emphasis on Maine, books by Maine authors, art books, and works in the field of science and technology.

How to Get There: The location of the store is in Garland, Maine on Upper Garland Road, an unpaved road which starts off Route 94, just 2 miles west of the center of Garland.
Owner/Biography: Frederica de Beurs.
Year Founded/History of Bookstore: 1980.
Number of Volumes: 6,000.
Types/Classifications: Hardbound, some paperback, first editions, signed copies, out-of-print, illustrated books.
General Subject Areas: Americana, Art, Biography, Literature, Maine, Science and Technology.
Specific Specialties: Electronics, Steam.
Mail/Telephone Orders; Credit Cards: Both. Cash with order. No credit cards.
Business Hours: By appointment and by chance.
Parking Facilities: Off-street parking.
Special Features: Search service.
Booksellers' Memberships: Maine Antiquarian Booksellers Association.
Miscellaneous: Nice lawn for picnics.

408
Grey Matter Service
South China, Maine 04358

(207) 445-2245

Grey Matter Service deals in general hardbound stock in all subjects emphasizing children's books and all authors.

How to Get There: From Augusta, go east on Route 202-3-9 about 11 miles.
Owner/Biography: Mabel Charles.
Year Founded/History of Bookstore: 1970.
Number of Volumes: Over 20,000.
Types/Classifications: Hardbound, magazines, ephemera, first editions, out-of-print.
General Subject Areas: General.
Specific Specialties: Children's Books.
Mail/Telephone Orders; Credit Cards: Both. No credit cards.
Business Hours: By appointment or chance.
Parking Facilities: Business parking lot.
Special Features: Search service.
Collections/Individual Items Purchased: Both.
Booksellers' Memberships: Maine Antiquarian Booksellers Association.

409
Harland H. Eastman - Books & Prints
66 Main Street
P.O. Box 276
Springvale, Maine 04083

(207) 324-2797

The shop occupies the second floor of a large old barn which has been handsomely lined with bookshelves and furnished with antiques, old china, glassware, and braided rugs to give it the atmosphere of a large home library. Only the books and prints are for sale; the furnishings are family heirlooms which have been handed down from generation to generation in the owner's family, whose home has been on the property for over 165 years.

How to Get There: Main Street in Springvale is Route 109 from Wells west to New Hampshire; look for a large white house with black shutters on more than 2 acres of land surrounded by a white board fence.

Owner/Biography: Harland H. Eastman. Mr. Eastman is a retired American diplomat who served in Europe, Asia, the Middle East, and Washington in his 26 year career. His last post was as the American Consul General in Tangier, Morocco.

Year Founded/History of Bookstore: 1949.

Number of Volumes: 8,000.

Types/Classifications: Hardbound, antiquarian prints, some ephemera, first editions, fine bindings, out-of-print.

General Subject Areas: Juveniles, Maine Fiction and Non-Fiction, Maine Town Histories, Nineteenth Century Religion.

Specific Specialties: Boys' Series Books.

Author Specialties: G.A. Henty, Jacob Abbott, Elijah Kellogg, Kate Douglas Wiggin, Gene Stratton Porter.

Mail/Telephone Orders; Credit Cards: Both. No minimum order. No credit cards.

Business Hours: Anytime. If coming from a distance, it is advised that one call ahead.

Parking Facilities: Ample parking on street and in driveway.

Collections/Individual Items Purchased: Both.

Booksellers' Memberships: Maine Antiquarian Booksellers Association (President).

410
Leon Tebbetts Bookstore
164 Water Street
Hallowell, Maine 04347   (202) 623-4670

The bookstore is located in the center of old Hallowell on the bank of the Kennebec River. Hallowell is an antique center, with many antique shops; the area is listed in the National Register of Historic Sites, and is in the process of being restored. The shop occupies the first floor of a brick structure dating back to the early 1830's.

Owner/Biography: Leon Tebbetts, owner, is a former newspaperman. He has owned his own publishing firm in Portland, Maine for 20 years.

Year Founded/History of Bookstore: Mr. Tebbetts established the bookstore in 1957.

Number of Volumes: 30,000.

Types/Classifications: Hardbound, paperback, most all other classifications.

General Subject Areas: General.

Mail/Telephone Orders; Credit Cards: Mail orders accepted; no credit cards.

Business Hours: Summer: Monday through Saturday 10:00 AM - 5:00 PM; Winter: Saturday 10:00 AM - 5:00 PM.

Parking Facilities: Street.

Collections/Individual Items Purchased: Both.

Booksellers' Memberships: Maine Antiquarian Booksellers Association.

411
Lobster Lane Book Shop
Spruce Head, Maine 04859   (207) 594-7520

The bookstore is located in a small fishing village on the water, in an unfinished building with a beautiful view. For customer convenience the nearly 40,000 volumes are catalogued as follows: fiction, by author; non-fiction, by topic.

How to Get There: If driving from Rockland, the nearest big city, one should take Route 73 for eight miles to Spruce Head, where a sign points the way to the shop.

Owner/Biography: Mrs. Vivian York.

Year Founded/History of Bookstore: Mr. and Mrs. York established the bookstore in 1963 in one unfinished room; since then it has has three additions. Mr York died in 1974 and Mrs. York has continued to operate the shop since then.

Number of Volumes: 40,000.
Types/Classifications: A general stock of used and out-of-print hardbound, paperback, and magazines.
General Subject Areas: Agriculture, Biography, Domestic Science, Earth Science, Fiction, Foreign Travel, Juveniles, Maine, Medical, Nature, Occult, Philosophy, Religion, Social Science, Transportation.
Author Specialties: State of Maine Authors.
Mail/Telephone Orders; Credit Cards: No credit cards.
Business Hours: Summer: Daily 12:30 PM - 5:00 PM.
Parking Facilities: Business parking lot.
Collections/Individual Items Purchased: Both.

412
MacDonald's Military
Eustis, Maine 04936

(207) 297-2751

This dealer specializes in the U.S. Civil War and other military subjects. The business is mail order only.
Year Founded/History of Bookstore: 1974.
Number of Volumes: 5,000.
General Subject Areas: Military, U.S. Civil War.
Mail/Telephone Orders; Credit Cards: Both. No credit cards.
Business Hours: Telephone until 10:00 PM Eastern Time.
Catalogue: Published every 6 weeks.
Collections/Individual Items Purchased: Both.
Booksellers' Memberships: Maine Antiquarian Booksellers Association.

413
Old Book Shop
61 York Street (Route 1)
Kennebunk, Maine 04043

(207) 985-3748

The bookstore consists of 3 rooms of old, rare, and scarce books located in an old service station built around 1923. The building was turned into a bookstore in 1960.
How to Get There: Route 1 is the main road through the village of Kennebunk, and is approximately 3 miles from Exit 3 of the Maine Turnpike.
Owner/Biography: Tom and Viola Drysdale, owners, started the bookshop in 1960 in the service station, which had been in Viola's family since 1923.
Year Founded/History of Bookstore: 1960.
Number of Volumes: 65,000.
Types/Classifications: Hardbound, autographs, first editions, out-of-print, press books, limited editions, signed copies, color plate books.
General Subject Areas: Boy Scouts, Cookbooks, Maine, New England, Old Fiction.
Author Specialties: Kenneth Roberts.
Mail/Telephone Orders; Credit Cards: Both. No credit cards.
Business Hours: Summer: daily 10:00 AM - 6:00 PM; Winter: by chance.
Collections/Individual Items Purchased: Both.
Booksellers' Memberships: Maine Booksellers Association.

414
Old Books
136 Maine Street
Brunswick, Maine 04011

(207) 725-4524

This is a general bookstore featuring used books with an emphasis on literature and belles lettres.
How to Get There: From Coastal Highway 1 use the Brunswick Down Town exit to Pleasant Street. At the second traffic light (a dead end) turn left. The shop is on the left-hand side in the first block. It is situated

above Macbeans, a new-book shop, and contains 800 square feet of space.
Owner/Biography: Clare C. Howell.
Year Founded/History of Bookstore: 1977.
Number of Volumes: 15,000.
Types/Classifications: Hardbound, paperback, out-of-print.
General Subject Areas: General.
Mail/Telephone Orders; Credit Cards: Both. No credit cards.
Business Hours: Monday through Wednesday, Friday, Saturday 10:00 AM - 5:00 PM; Thursday 11:00 AM - 4:00 PM.
Parking Facilities: Street.
Special Features: Search service.
Collections/Individual Items Purchased: Both.
Booksellers' Memberships: Maine Antiquarian Booksellers Association.

415
Oliver's Books
16 A Hanover Street
Skowhegan, Maine 04976   (207) 474-9850

Oliver's Books occupies an old garage attached to a private residence. It houses a general stock of paperbacks and hardcovers with emphasis on science fiction and fantasy, mysteries, detective fiction, and modern literature.
How to Get There: Take the Skowhegan exit from I-95 to Skowhegan; travel through the town around the rotary and watch for signs saying Madison, Jackman, Quebec; go up Madison Avenue 1 mile from downtown. The street sign says "anover" (H is missing); turn left here and go 1 1/2 blocks to a yellow house with brown trim.
Owner/Biography: Lynn Oliver.
Year Founded/History of Bookstore: 1982.
Number of Volumes: 6,000.
Types/Classifications: Hardbound, paperback, comics, magazines, first editions, out-of-print.
General Subject Areas: Detective Fiction, Modern Literature, Mysteries, Science Fiction and Fantasy.
Specific Specialties: Maine.
Mail/Telephone Orders; Credit Cards: Both. Cash with order including postage; returnable first class insured. No credit cards.
Business Hours: Evenings Monday through Friday 4:00 PM - 8:00 PM; Sunday 12:00 Noon - 5:00 PM.
Parking Facilities: Driveway and lawn if necessary.
Collections/Individual Items Purchased: Both.
Booksellers' Memberships: Maine Antiquarian Booksellers Association.

416
Pro Libris
10 Third Street
Bangor, Maine 04401   (207) 942-3019

Pro Libris is primarily a used paperback shop with a select stock of hardcovers, magazines, and accessory items. All sections are very strictly arranged; most are alphabetized by author or categorized by subject where appropriate. The store is comfortable, spacious, and well-lighted. Casual browsing is encouraged.
How to Get There: Take Union Street (Route 222) Exit from I-95, go east 1.1 miles; Pro Libris is in the large building at the southeast corner of Union and Third. From the east, the shop is 4 blocks east of the intersection of the Bar Harbor Road (Route 1A) and Main Street.
Owner/Biography: Eric A. Furry. Mr. Furry, a native of Ohio, previously worked for B. Dalton Booksellers in Ohio, Oklahoma, and Maine.
Year Founded/History of Bookstore: 1980.
Number of Volumes: 20,000.

Types/Classifications: Paperback, limited selection of hardbound, magazines, LP phonograph records, comics; small stock of new books from regional small presses.

General Subject Areas: Art, Business, Cooking, Diet and Health, Drama, Family and Child Care, Gardening, General Fiction, History, Horror, Humor, Literature, Music, Mystery and Suspense, Nature, Occult, Philosophy, Poetry, Political Science, Psychology, Reference, Religion, Romance, Science, Science Fiction and Fantasy, Sociology and Anthropology, Sports, Study Aids, Television and Movies, Travel, True Crime, War Fiction, Westerns, Young Folks.

Other Specialties: French language editions, collectible paperbacks.

Mail/Telephone Orders; Credit Cards: Both. Payment in advance for price as quoted. No credit cards.

Business Hours: Monday through Thursday 10:00 AM - 6:00 PM; Friday 10:00 AM - 7:00 PM; Saturday 10:00 AM - 5:00 PM; Sunday: often.

Parking Facilities: Street or supermarket lot across the street.

Special Features: Search service; publishing sideline; semi-public "salon"; occasional poetry readings and art showings.

Collections/Individual Items Purchased: Both.

Miscellaneous: Pro Libris trades paperbacks at a rate of 1 for 2 of equal value plus a 10 cent per copy fee; dealer and institutional discounts on quantity purchases; gift certificates available.

417
Robert E. Dysinger - Books
5 Stanwood Street
Brunswick, Maine 04011   (207) 729-1229

This is a small select collection of Americana, especially of the Northeast and West. It includes literary firsts and a general line of older materials (very few 20th Century items).

How to Get There: The shop is 100 feet off U.S. 1 as one enters Brunswick which is 26 miles east of Portland.

Owner/Biography: Robert E. Dysinger. Mr. Dysinger is a former university librarian.

Year Founded/History of Bookstore: 1981.

Number of Volumes: 2,000.

Types/Classifications: Hardbound, first editions, out-of-print, signed copies, mostly 19th Century items.

General Subject Areas: Americana.

Specific Specialties: Maine.

Mail/Telephone Orders; Credit Cards: Both. No credit cards.

Business Hours: Daily 7:00 AM - 10:00 PM or by chance.

Parking Facilities: Ample parking.

Special Features: Search service.

Catalogue: Published occasionally.

Collections/Individual Items Purchased: Both.

Booksellers' Memberships: Maine Antiquarian Booksellers Association.

Miscellaneous: Very casual atomsphere; wine offered.

418
Sail Loft
Main Street
Newcastle, Maine 04553   (207) 563-3209

The Sail Loft is in a small 1840 building by a reverse falls of the Damariscotta River. The stock is general with a specialty of Maine histories, town reports, commemorative booklets, postcards, children's books, and old music. The shop occupies 1,350 square feet of space.

How to Get There: The shop is located by the bridge and behind the Post Office.

Owner/Biography: Mr. and Mrs. Wallace J. Williams.

Year Founded/History of Bookstore: 1932. The store was originally at the end of the pier for 8 years. After World War II it was relocated to a building that had been a horse barn for American Express. The owners added two wings and a deck porch.

Types/Classifications: Hardbound, magazines, ephemera, limited editions, color plate books, fine bindings, illustrated books, out-of-print, reading copies.

General Subject Areas: Americana, Atlantic Coast, British History, Children's Books, Cookbooks, Maine, Natural History, Nautical.

Specific Specialties: Maine Histories and Town Reports.

Mail/Telephone Orders; Credit Cards: Both. Check with order. Visa and Mastercard accepted.

Business Hours: Daily during July, August, and September until 6:00 PM and by appointment.

Parking Facilities: Street parking, church yard near shop.

Special Features: Search service; appraisals.

Collections/Individual Items Purchased: Individual items; collections sometimes.

Booksellers' Memberships: Maine Antiquarian Booksellers Association; New England Appraisers Association.

Miscellaneous: The owners enjoy "book talk" and coffee anytime; they are in Lexington, Kentucky during the winter and can be reached at (606) 269-6348.

419
Snug Harbor Books
P.O. Box 8 - Route 1
Wells, Maine 04090   (207) 646-4124

The bookstore carries many general subjects and specializes in Western Americana, fine bindings, and autographs. It contains 1,200 square feet of space.

How to Get There: From the Maine Turnpike take Exit 2, turn left 1.5 miles to Wells Corners, Route 1. Turn right, drive about 1 mile. The shop is on Route 1, ocean side of the street, 500 yards south of Macdonald's.

Owner/Biography: Gary and Karen Austin. Gary's background is in teaching and collecting. He has a degree in history with a minor in English. Karen's degree is in marketing management. She is a former retail buyer and administrator.

Year Founded/History of Bookstore: In 1981 the present owners took over a business that was basically a shop of uncatalogued paperbacks. They have completely changed the stock and doubled the space. The shop caters heavily to tourists in the summer, but is a year-round business. Winter activity is show and catalogue oriented.

Number of Volumes: 15,000.

Types/Classifications: Hardbound, paperback, autographs, documents, prints, paintings, first editions, fine bindings, out-of-print, signed copies, sets.

General Subject Areas: Americana, Art, Civil War (U.S.), Detective Fiction, History, Literature.

Specific Specialties: General George A. Custer, West (U.S.), American Historical Autographs, American Literary Autographs, American Indians, General Robert E. Lee, Confederacy (U.S. Civil War).

Author Specialties: Ernest Hemingway.

Mail/Telephone Orders; Credit Cards: Both. Visa, Mastercard.

Business Hours: Summer (May 30 through September 30): Daily 9:00 AM - 9:00 PM.

Parking Facilities: Business parking lot adjacent to building.

Special Features: Search service.

Catalogue: Published infrequently.

Collections/Individual Items Purchased: Both.

Booksellers' Memberships: Maine Antiquarian Booksellers Association.

Miscellaneous: The bookstore strives for a friendly atmosphere. It is in a beach resort area, with four other book dealers within a five-minute radius.

420
Varney's Volumes
Quaker Ridge Road
Box 1175, RFD 2
Casco, Maine 04015   (207) 655-4605

Adjacent to the owner's home, the bookstore was newly constructed in early 1984, and contains 440 square feet of space. A beep of the car horn will bring the owner.

How to Get There: Located in the famous Sebago Lake area, 25 miles northwest of Portland, Maine, the bookstore is four-tenths of a mile from the state highway, on Route 302, the route to the White Mountains. The town is the boyhood home of Nathaniel Hawthorne.

Owner/Biography: A. Lois Varney, owner, and also a teacher, began the business as a hobby for summertime amusement. She plans to continue the bookstore as a supplement to retirement income.

Year Founded/History of Bookstore: Founded in 1978, the bookstore has been located in what was a small country post office. Aging foundations required the construction of the new location next door to the owner's residence.

Number of Volumes: 6,000.

Types/Classifications: Hardbound, paperback, ephemera, postcards, out-of-print, miscellaneous classifications.

General Subject Areas: Biography, Boys and Girls Series Books, Children's Literature, Detective, History, Maine, Mysteries, Nature, Sporting.

Mail/Telephone Orders; Credit Cards: Both; cash with order. No credit cards.

Business Hours: July and August: 10:00 AM - 5:00 PM; other times by appointment.

Parking Facilities: Driveway will accommodate five or six cars.

Special Features: Search service; coffee.

Catalogue: Two times per year.

Collections/Individual Items Purchased: Individual items.

Booksellers' Memberships: Maine Antiquarian Booksellers Association.

Miscellaneous: Year-round booth at the Green Mountain Antique and Craft Center, on Route 16, in Ossipee, New Hampshire.

421
Victorian House
East Main Street
Stockton Springs, Maine 04981   (207) 567-3351

The bookstore is contained in four large rooms in a big Victorian House, which, in itself, has proved to be an attraction. The books are arranged by subject, and in many cases, alphabetically by author within the subject. There are lawns and fields for children and pets to enjoy, and a small riding school held from the nearby barn, all giving added interest especially to children. The four rooms of the bookstore contain a total of 3,200 square feet of space.

How to Get There: Stockton Springs is situated at the mouth of the Penobscot River on Penobscot Bay. It lies between Bucksport and Searsport, homes of former Maine sea captains. East Main Street and Victorian House are parallel to Route 1 by a few hundred yards. The bookstore is easily visible from Route 1.

Owner/Biography: Andrew B.W. MacEwen.

Year Founded/History of Bookstore: The bookstore was founded in 1960 on a small side street in Bangor, Maine, and moved later to Main Street. In 1968, due to urban renewal and the removal of the entire block housing the store, it was moved to Stockton Springs, to the home of the owner, Aimee B. MacEwen. In 1980 her son Andrew bought the store and has carried on the business since.

Number of Volumes: 30,000.

Types/Classifications: Hardbound, paperback, some magazines, fine bindings, first editions, out-of-print, signed copies.

General Subject Areas: Biography, Children's Books, Science Fiction and Fantasy.

Specific Specialties: Americana, Maine, Mystery, Detective.

Mail/Telephone Orders; Credit Cards: Both. No credit cards.

Business Hours: April through October: Daily 10:00 AM - 4:30 PM; mail order, year 'round.

Parking Facilities: Very large parking area attached to the store.

Special Features: Search service.

Collections/Individual Items Purchased: Both.

Booksellers' Memberships: Maine Booksellers Association.

422
Village Bookshop, Inc.
Route 130 (Box 169)
New Harbor, Maine 04554 (207) 677-2429

This is a general bookstore with 800 square feet of space.
How to Get There: Take Route 130 south from Damariscotta, Maine, to New Harbor village; the bookstore is opposite the Methodist Church.
Owner/Biography: Jon and Peggy Richardson.
Year Founded/History of Bookstore: Founded in 1981, the bookstore opened in the summer of 1982. It has experienced increasing year 'round mail order business.
Number of Volumes: 6,000.
Types/Classifications: Hardbound books only. First editions, out-of-print.
General Subject Areas: American Literature, Americana, Civil War (U.S.), Cookbooks, English History, English Literature, Maine, Medicine, Medieval History, Religion.
Author Specialties: Virginia Woolf, Bloomsbury Group, Sarah Orne Jewett, Kenneth Roberts.
Mail/Telephone Orders; Credit Cards: Both. Cash with order per quotes only; personal check acceptable. An additional telephone number is (207) 677-3720.
Business Hours: Open June 20 to Labor Day only. Monday through Friday 10:00 AM - 4:00 PM; Saturday by appointment.
Parking Facilities: Business parking lot.
Catalogue: Two times per year.
Collections/Individual Items Purchased: Both.
Booksellers' Memberships: Maine Antiquarian Booksellers Association.

423
Wells Bookstore & Gallery
Route No. 1
Wells, Maine 04090 (207) 646-7022

The bookstore was the first out-of-print shop established in Wells. It is housed in an old barn attached to the main house which was built in 1840. The bookstore/barn contains 1,600 square feet of space on two floors.
How to Get There: The shop is located on U.S. Route 1, one-half mile north of Wells Corner.
Owner/Biography: A. Davis Paulhus, owner, has been in the book business for 15 years part time and 6 years full time.
Year Founded/History of Bookstore: 1970.
Number of Volumes: 35,000.
Types/Classifications: The bookstore handles mostly hardbound with a scattering of anything old, and most classifications, but specializes in finely bound sets.
General Subject Areas: General, Louisiana, Texas.
Author Specialties: Kenneth Roberts, Thomas Wolf, William Faulkner, Mark Twain, L. Frank Baum, Will James, Tom Lea, Joel Chandler Harris.
Other Specialties: Children's Books, especially those illustrated by Arthur Rackham, Maxfield Parrish, J.W. Smith, Edmund Dulac.
Mail/Telephone Orders; Credit Cards: Both. No credit cards.
Business Hours: Daily 10:00 AM - 6:00 PM.
Parking Facilities: Private driveway.
Catalogue: Catalogue issued.
Collections/Individual Items Purchased: Both.

MARYLAND

424

B & B Smith, Booksellers

710 Park Avenue
Mt. Airy, Maryland 21771   (301) 549-1227

Archaeology, classical literature, and ancient history are the only subject categories stocked by this firm. It is one of the few American importers of European books in Classical Studies, stocking these as well as the titles of most American presses. Also for sale are several thousand second-hand titles. All trade is strictly mail order with catalogs issued three to five times per year. The shop occupies 600 square feet of space.

How to Get There: Mail order only.
Owner/Biography: Barbra L. Smith and William P. Smith.
Year Founded/History of Bookstore: 1980. B & B Smith, Booksellers began in 1980 as a part-time business selling second-hand titles in the Classics by mail. It now stocks the titles of several dozen publishers on Classical subjects, importing books from as far away as Australia and Argentina to meet the needs of its customers, primarily scholars and libraries.
Number of Volumes: 5,000.
General Subject Areas: Ancient History, Archaeology, Classical Studies, Epigraphy, Greek and Latin Literature, Numismatics (Ancient).
Other Specialties: Foreign language titles on all subject specialities listed.
Mail/Telephone Orders; Credit Cards: Both. Prepayment required on initial orders for more than $100. No credit cards.
Business Hours: Monday through Saturday 10:00 AM - 8:00 PM.
Special Features: Search service.
Catalogue: Published 3 to 5 times per year; catalogue lists both used and new books on ancient studies in many languages.
Collections/Individual Items Purchased: Both.
Booksellers' Memberships: Antiquarian Booksellers Association of America.

425

Drusilla's Books

202 West Seminary Avenue
Lutherville, Maryland 21093   (301) 321-6687

Drusilla's Books has a specialist collection of out-of-print, used, and rare children's and illustrated books and related items, ranging from the 19th Century to the present. The business is primarily mail order, with an occasional book or antique show exhibit. Visits are by appointment only.

How to Get There: Call for an appointment and directions.
Owner/Biography: Drusilla Park Jones.
Year Founded/History of Bookstore: 1977.
Number of Volumes: 3,000.
Types/Classifications: Hardbound, out-of-print, magazines and ephemera relating to children's books and childhood with some illustrated stock, first editions, fine bindings, association copies, signed copies, presentation copies, limited editions, color plate books.
General Subject Areas: Children's Fantasy, Children's Literature, Children's Literature Reference.
Other Specialties: Children's books in foreign languages, especially French and German.
Mail/Telephone Orders; Credit Cards: Both. No credit cards.
Business Hours: By appointment only.
Catalogue: Published 2 to 3 times per year.

Collections/Individual Items Purchased: Both.

426
Firstborn Books
1007 East Benning Road
Galesville, Maryland 20765   (301) 867-7050

The shop is located in a converted Turkey House beside the owner's home. Firstborn Books has always purveyed Western Americana, modern first editions, and local histories to institutions and private collectors. The bookstore has a branch known as Main Street Books in Annapolis.

How to Get There: From Annapolis, go south on Route 2 to Maryland Route 214 (left), to Maryland Route 468 (right) for 6 miles to blinking traffic light, left at light onto Galesville Road; go left at Woodfield Road for 1 block then right onto East Benning; second house on right.

Owner/Biography: James W. and Cecelia P. Clark. Mr. Clark is a poet, journalist, and author of regional (Maryland) mysteries. His work has appeared in many literary magazines and he is contributing editor to "Chesapeake Country Life" magazine. He has been engaged in the used, rare, and out-of-print book trade for nearly a decade and is a specialist in Westrn Americana. Cecelia P. Clark is a food writer and bilbiophile. She studied Rare Books at Columbia University and is currently compiling a Bibliography of Maryland in Fiction.

Year Founded/History of Bookstore: 1976.

Number of Volumes: 15,000 (includes stock at Annapolis location - Main Street Books).

Types/Classifications: Hardbound, broadsides, fine printing, maps, limited editions.

General Subject Areas: Cooking, Food, Local History, Marylandia, Music, Natural History, Western Americana.

Specific Specialties: Country and Western Music, Regional Cooking, Western Travel, Lakeside Classics, Loeb Classical Library, Maryland Fiction.

Author Specialties: Gertrude Atherton, Willa Cather, Zane Grey, Robinson Jeffers, Alfred Henry Lewis, Eugene Manlove Rhodes, Jack Schaefer, Mari Sandoz, Stewart Edward White, Owen Wister.

Mail/Telephone Orders; Credit Cards: Both. Cash with order including postage. Visa and Mastercard accepted.

Business Hours: By appointment only.

Parking Facilities: Ample parking on premises.

Special Features: Search service; appraisals.

Collections/Individual Items Purchased: Both.

427
John Gach Books
5620 Waterloo Road
Columbia, Maryland 21045   (301) 465-2518

The bookstore has one of the largest and most selective inventories of out-of-print and rare books on psychology, psychiatry, psychoanalysis, and philosophy in the world.

How to Get There: Call for directions.

Owner/Biography: John and Frank Gach.

Year Founded/History of Bookstore: Opened in 1968, the bookstore was known as The Gach Bookshop; the antiquarian branch was started in 1972 as The John Gach Bookservice. In 1979 the shop was moved to its present location.

Number of Volumes: 20,000.

Types/Classifications: Hardbound, autographs, out-of-print, rare.

General Subject Areas: Philosophy, Psychiatry, Psychoanalysis, Psychology.

Specific Specialties: Very strong in antiquarian German books in its specialties.

Author Specialties: Sigmund Freud.

Mail/Telephone Orders; Credit Cards: Both; Visa, Mastercard.

Business Hours: By appointment only.

Parking Facilities: Private parking.
Special Features: Search service within the shop's specialties.
Catalogue: Four or five times a year.
Collections/Individual Items Purchased: Both.
Booksellers' Memberships: Antiquarian Booksellers Association of America, International League of Antiquarian Booksellers.

428
Kelmscott Bookshop
32 West 25th Street
Baltimore, Maryland 21218   (301) 235-6810

The Kelmscott Bookshop carries old and rare books in all fields.
How to Get There: Call for directions.
Types/Classifications: First editions, illustrated books, fine bindings and sets, out-of-print, rare.
General Subject Areas: General.
Mail/Telephone Orders; Credit Cards: Mail orders.
Business Hours: Call for information.

429
Marilyn Braiterman
20 Whitfield Road
Baltimore, Maryland 21210   (301) 235-4848

Marilyn Braiterman is an antiquarian bookseller operating by mail order and appointment only.
How to Get There: Call for an appointment and directions.
Owner/Biography: Marilyn Braiterman.
Year Founded/History of Bookstore: 1977.
Number of Volumes: 2,000.
Types/Classifications: First editions, fine bindings, out-of-print, association copies, press books, signed copies, presentation copies, limited editions, color plate books, illustrated books.
General Subject Areas: Architecture, Art, Books About Books, Children's Books, Design, Fine Printing, Judaica, Natural History, Travel.
Mail/Telephone Orders; Credit Cards: Both. No credit cards.
Business Hours: By appointment only.
Catalogue: Published occasionally.
Collections/Individual Items Purchased: Both.
Booksellers' Memberships: Antiquarian Booksellers Association of America.

430
Old Hickory Book Shop, Ltd.
20225 New Hampshire Avenue
Brinklow, Maryland 20862   (301) 924-2225

The bookstore contains a large stock of old, rare, and out-of-print books about medicine, dentistry, and the life sciences. It is open by appointment only.
How to Get There: The shop is three miles north of Ashton, Maryland, in a large private home in the Maryland countryside, half-way between Baltimore and Washington.
Owner/Biography: Johanna and Ralph Grimes.
Year Founded/History of Bookstore: 1940.
Number of Volumes: 50,000.
Types/Classifications: Hardbound, old, rare, out-of-print.
General Subject Areas: Dentistry, Life Sciences, Medicine, Science.

Mail/Telephone Orders; Credit Cards: Both. No credit cards.
Business Hours: By appointment only.
Parking Facilities: Ample private parking.
Special Features: Two or three times a year.
Collections/Individual Items Purchased: Both.

431
Old Printed Word
10630 Connecticut Avenue
Kensington, Maryland 20895   (301) 949-7350

The Old Printed Word has one of the largest selections of rare and scholarly items under one roof in the Washington area. It has a line of general stock including prints, maps, documents, pamphlets, autographs, and photography.

How to Get There: The bookstore is easily accessible by the Washington Metro.

Types/Classifications: First editions, out-of-print, autographs, signed books, limited editions, documents, leather bound books.

General Subject Areas: Americana (Regional), Biography, Books About Books, Geology, Minorities and Slavery, Nautical, Presidents (U.S.), Women Authors, Women's Biography.

Mail/Telephone Orders; Credit Cards: Mail orders.

Business Hours: Monday through Saturday 10:00 AM - 7:00 PM; Sunday 11:00 AM - 5:00 PM.

Parking Facilities: Street parking, commercial parking lots and garages.

Special Features: Appraisals; search service.

Catalogue: Catalogues published.

Collections/Individual Items Purchased: Both.

432
Quill & Brush
7649 Old Georgetown Road
Bethesda, Maryland 20814   (301) 951-0919

The Quill & Brush is a bright and open bookshop, carefully arranged for comfortable browsing. The extensive collection of modern first editions is supplemented with a well-chosen stock of 19th Century fiction, travel, and exploration first editions. A handsome bust of Dante overlooks shelves of books and the walls are hung with the work of noted area artists.

How to Get There: Located in Bethesda Square, the bookstore is at the corner of Old Georgetown Road and Woodmont Avenue, 2 blocks west of Wisconsin Avenue. There is also an Old Georgetown Road exit off the Washington Beltway.

Owner/Biography: Patricia and Allen Ahearn.

Year Founded/History of Bookstore: 1972.

Number of Volumes: 10,000.

Types/Classifications: Hardbound, some paperback, first author appearances in magazines, broadsides, ephemera, autographs, first editions, out-of-print, association copies, signed copies, presentation copies, limited editions, press books, bibliographies, proof copies, pricing guides.

General Subject Areas: Exploration, Fiction, Travel.

Specific Specialties: Modern First Editions (British and American), 19th Century First Editions, 19th Century Travel and Exploration.

Author Specialties: James Agee, W.H. Auden, Samuel Beckett, Thomas Berger, Ray Bradbury, John Dickson Carr, Willa Cather, Raymond Chandler, Agatha Christie, John Gardner, Robert Graves, Graham Greene, Dashiell Hammett, Ernest Hemingway, Langston Hughes, Shirley Jackson, Robinson Jeffers, James Joyce, Jack Kerouac, Stephen King, Wyndham Lewis, Jack London, H.P. Lovecraft, Malcolm Lowry, Larry McMurtry, John McPhee, Herman Melville, H.L. Mencken, Marianne Moore, Anais Nin, Tim O'Brien, Flannery O'Connor, Hart Crane, Countee Cullen, "H.D." (Hilda Doolittle), Arthur Conan Doyle, W.E.B. DuBois, Lawrence Durrell, William Faulkner, F. Scott Fitzgerald, Ian Fleming, George Orwell, Edgar Allan Poe, Ezra Pound, Thomas Pynchon, Theodore Roethke, Thorne Smith, Gertrude Stein, John Steinbeck, Rex

Stout, Henry David Thoreau, Mark Twain, Anne Tyler, John Updike, Eudora Welty, Nathanael West, Evelyn Waugh, William Carlos Williams, Edmund Wilson, P.G. Wodehouse, Thomas Wolfe, Virginia Woolf, William Butler Yeats, Kurt Vonnegut.

Mail/Telephone Orders; Credit Cards: Both. Personal check with first order or credit references. American Express, Visa, Mastercard accepted.

Business Hours: Monday through Saturday 10:00 AM - 6:00 PM, with seasonal changes.

Parking Facilities: Street parking, public parking garage.

Special Features: Search service; collection development; appraisals; art shows by local artists; poetry readings.

Catalogue: Monthly.

Collections/Individual Items Purchased: Both.

Miscellaneous: Allen Ahearn is the author of "The Book of First Books." Now in its 3rd edition, the book lists the first books of over 2,000 authors, with values, along with general guidelines for collecting and identifying first editions.

433
Rug Book Shop
2603 Talbot Road
Baltimore, Maryland 21216

(301) 367-8194

The Rug Book Shop has one of the largest collections of in-print and out-of-print books on Oriental rugs and Navajo blankets in the United States. The titles include everything in the U.S. and Great Britain as well as selections from France, Germany, Italy, Turkey, Yugoslavia, and the Far East. The shop also has more ephemeral items such as exhibition catalogues, auction catalogues, rug dealers' brochures, and periodicals with articles about rugs. Visitors are welcome by appointment.

How to Get There: The book shop is located in western Baltimore overlooking scenic Leakin Park in the section of the city bounded by Garrison Boulevard, Forest Park Avenue, and Windsor Mill Road. People unfamiliar with Baltimore should call for directions.

Owner/Biography: Paul Kreiss.

Year Founded/History of Bookstore: 1976.

Number of Volumes: 500.

Types/Classifications: Hardbound, paperback, magazines, auction catalogues, museum catalogues, exhibition catalogues, notecards, postcards, calendars, maps, first editions, out-of-print.

General Subject Areas: Balkan Costume, Kilims, Navajo Blankets, Oriental Rugs, Tapestries, Textiles.

Specific Specialties: Rugs: Persian, Caucasian, Turkish, Turkmen, Chinese, Spanish, Flat-Weaves, Iranian, Afghan, Indian.

Mail/Telephone Orders; Credit Cards: Both. Prepayment preferred; postpaid except for orders from outside North America; foreign customers should ask for a pro forma invoice and then pay in U.S. funds. No credit cards.

Business Hours: By appointment; best time to call is evenings and weekends.

Parking Facilities: Street parking.

Special Features: Search service.

Catalogue: Published about every 9 months.

Collections/Individual Items Purchased: Both.

434
Second Story Books
3322 Greenmount Avenue
Baltimore, Maryland 21218

(301) 467-4344

See SECOND STORY BOOKS, 3236 P Street NW, Washington, DC.

435
Second Story Books
7730 Old Georgetown Road
Bethesda, Maryland 20014   (301) 656-0170

See SECOND STORY BOOKS, 3236 P Street NW, Washington, DC.

436
Stewarts Book Store
6504 Old Branch Avenue
Camp Springs, Maryland 20748   (301) 449-6766

This is a general bookstore with an emphasis on history in all areas including military and biographies. The majority of the stock is very clean with dust jackets where possible. Dealers are welcome. The shop contains 1,200 square feet of space.

How to Get There: Camp Springs, Maryland is a suburb of Washington, D.C., and can easily be reached off the beltway (Route 95) around the city. Take Exit 7-S south on Route 5 from the beltway to the second light; turn right one block, then left for three blocks. The shop is on the left.

Owner/Biography: Frances M. Stewart.
Year Founded/History of Bookstore: 1975.
Number of Volumes: 25,000.
Types/Classifications: General stock, primarily hardbound, some paperback.
General Subject Areas: Biography, History, Military.
Mail/Telephone Orders; Credit Cards: Both; Visa, Mastercard.
Business Hours: Tuesday through Saturday 11:00 AM - 5:00 PM; Friday nights until 8:00 PM.
Parking Facilities: Business parking lot.
Special Features: Search service.
Collections/Individual Items Purchased: Both.

437
Takoma Books
6847 Eastern Avenue
Takoma Park, Maryland 20912   (301) 270-8194

This is a new bookstore, opened in 1983. It is situated on the first floor of an old house; the owners live above their shop which contains 800 square feet of space.

How to Get There: The bookstore is at the intersection of Eastern and Laurel Avenues, three blocks from the Takoma Park Metro station.

Owner/Biography: Donald F. and Angelika Burke.
Year Founded/History of Bookstore: 1983.
Number of Volumes: 15,000.
Types/Classifications: Hardbound two-thirds, paperback one-third; mostly out-of-print.
General Subject Areas: General.
Mail/Telephone Orders; Credit Cards: Mail orders.
Business Hours: Saturday 11:00 AM - 5:00 PM; other days call ahead.
Parking Facilities: Street.
Collections/Individual Items Purchased: Both.

438
Unicorn Bookshop
P.O. Box 154 - Route 50
Trappe, Maryland 21673   (301) 476-3838

The bookstore is located in a one-story, brick, pseudo-colonial, former bank building, with an attractive and well-lit location. It carries the full range of secondhand and rare books. The shop contains 1,200 square feet of space.

How to Get There: The bookstore is located on the east side of Route 50 approximately 7 miles south of Easton, Maryland, and just south of the Trappe Frozen Foods fiberglass igloo.

Owner/Biography: James Dawson.

Year Founded/History of Bookstore: Originally formed in 1975 as a partnership located on Dover Street in Easton, Maryland, the shop was moved in 1978 to Washinton Street in Easton. It became single ownership in 1980, then moved to its present location in September 1983.

Number of Volumes: 12,000.

Types/Classifications: Hardbound, some paperback, first editions, fine bindings, out-of-print, association copies, press books, signed copies, presentation copies, limited editions, color plate books.

General Subject Areas: Americana, Art, Children's Books, Fiction, Gardening, Maryland History, World War I, World War II.

Specific Specialties: Maryland Eastern Shore History.

Author Specialties: H.L. Mencken, John Barth, Henry David Thoreau.

Mail/Telephone Orders; Credit Cards: Both. Cash with order. No credit cards.

Business Hours: Daily except Wednesday and Sunday 9:30 AM - 5:00 PM; other times by appointment.

Parking Facilities: Business parking lot.

Special Features: Search Service. Publishing sideline of books of local interest in paperback and hardbound; limited and autographed editions. Published two books by author Gilbert Byron: (1) "Sunbathing With the Professor," 1982, eastern shore poetry; (2) "Cove Dweller," 1983, semi-autobiographical, and nature.

Catalogue: Published occasionally.

Collections/Individual Items Purchased: Both.

MASSACHUSETTS

439
Andover Antiquarian Books
41 Chandler Circle
Andover, Massachusetts 01810 (617) 475-1645

This book business is open by appointment only. It features a select stock of out-of-print and rare books in all fields but with an emphasis on illustrated, children's Christmas, and New England material. Also available are some maps, prints, photographs, and ephemera of local and regional interest. Items are housed in 375 square feet of space. The shop is small with a friendly atmosphere. Serious readers, collectors, and dealers are always welcome.

How to Get There: Directions will be given when calling for an appointment.

Owner/Biography: V. David Rodger.

Year Founded/History of Bookstore: 1977.

Number of Volumes: 4,000 items.

Types/Classifications: Hardbound, maps, prints, photographs, ephemera, first editions, fine bindings, out-of-print, association copies, press books, signed copies, presentation copies, limited editions, color plate books.

General Subject Areas: Americana, Antiques, Art, Biography, Black History, Books About Books, Children's Literature, Christmas, Civil War, Cooking, Crafts, Decorative Arts, Gardening, Literature, Nature, New England, Poetry, Printing Arts, Religion, Science/Technical, Travel, Women's Studies.

Mail/Telephone Orders; Credit Cards: Both. Mail orders accepted in response to catalogues. Cash with order. No credit cards.

Business Hours: By appointment only.

Parking Facilities: Street parking.

Special Features: Appraisals; regional book shows.

Catalogue: Published quarterly.

Collections/Individual Items Purchased: Both.

Booksellers' Memberships: Massachusetts and Rhode Island Antiquarian Booksellers Association, The Ephemera Society of America.

440
Annie's Book Swap
39 South Street
Westborough, Massachusetts 01581 (617) 366-5840

See ANNIE'S BOOK SWAP INC., Westborough, MA.

441
Annie's Book Swap
60 Great Road
Acton, Massachusetts 01720 (617) 263-3158

See ANNIE'S BOOK SWAP INC., Westborough, MA.

442
Annie's Book Swap
158 East Central Street
Natick, Massachusetts 01760 (617) 653-6402

See ANNIE'S BOOK SWAP INC., Westborough, MA.

443
Annie's Book Swap
237 Main Street
West Yarmouth, Massachusetts 02673 (617) 775-5056

See ANNIE'S BOOK SWAP INC., Westborough, MA.

444
Annie's Book Swap
125 Main Street
Groton, Massachusetts 01450 (617) 448-6040

See ANNIE'S BOOK SWAP INC., Westborough, MA.

445
Annie's Book Swap
Route 7 and Commonwealth
Great Barrington, Massachusetts 01230 (413) 528-3794

See ANNIE'S BOOK SWAP INC., Westborough, MA.

446
Annie's Book Swap
26 Alpine Lane
Chelmsford, Massachusetts 01824 (617) 256-9056

See ANNIE'S BOOK SWAP INC., Westborough, MA.

447
Annie's Book Swap
Marshall's Mall
Leominster, Massachusetts 01453 (617) 534-7997

See ANNIE'S BOOK SWAP INC., Westborough, MA.

448
Annie's Book Swap
70 Atlantic Avenue
Marblehead, Massachusetts 01945 (617) 631-3805

See ANNIE'S BOOK SWAP INC., Westborough, MA.

449
Annie's Book Swap
Second and Main Streets
North Andover, Massachusetts 01845   (617) 683-7684

See ANNIE'S BOOK SWAP INC., Westborough, MA.

450
Annie's Book Swap
Lowell Square
Orleans, Massachusetts 02653   (617) 896-6046

See ANNIE'S BOOK SWAP INC., Westborough, MA.

451
Annie's Book Swap
403 Parker Street
Gardner, Massachusetts 01440   (617) 632-1448

See ANNIE'S BOOK SWAP INC., Westborough, MA.

452
Annie's Book Swap
344 West Boylston Street
West Boylston, Massachusetts 01583   (617) 853-3297

See ANNIE'S BOOK SWAP INC., Westborough, MA.

453
Annie's Book Swap
4 Man Mar Drive
Plainville, Massachusetts 02762   (617) 695-2396

See ANNIE'S BOOK SWAP INC., Westborough, MA.

454
Annie's Book Swap
85 River Street
Waltham, Massachusetts 02154   (617) 899-4384

See ANNIE'S BOOK SWAP INC., Westborough, MA.

455
Annie's Book Swap
27 Broadway
Wakefield, Massachusetts 01880
                                                          (617) 246-3730

See ANNIE'S BOOK SWAP INC., Westborough, MA.

456
Annie's Book Swap
188 Main Street
Haverhill, Massachusetts 01830
                                                          (617) 373-5193

See ANNIE'S BOOK SWAP INC., Westborough, MA.

457
Annie's Book Swap
230 Main Street
Williamstown, Massachusetts 01267
                                                          (413) 458-4639

See ANNIE'S BOOK SWAP INC., Westborough, MA.

458
Annie's Book Swap Inc.
15 Lackey Street
Westborough, Massachusetts 01581
                                                          (617) 366-9547

If one has not yet been in an Annie's, the very first thing to do is to totally erase from one's mind any preconceived image of what constitutes a used book store. These stores are truly unlike any others. Their windows are sparkling clean glass fronts edged with old New England gingham or calico prints, showing off a warmly-lit, neat, fully-stocked and inviting bookstore. Nearly all of their books are paperbacks and are shelved by category and then alphabetically by author. There are over 40 categories of books with an emphasis on novels and bestsellers, historical novels, and the occult. Every book sells for approximately half price and customers are offered credit for books they bring in to swap.

How to Get There: Annie's Book Swap, Inc. has over 50 franchise operations. The corporate office is located at the above address with office hours from 9:00 AM to 5:00 PM, Monday through Friday.

Owner/Biography: Anne and David Adams.

Year Founded/History of Bookstore: 1974. The original site was in Westboro, Massachusetts, a single store operated by Anne Adams. She opened two additional stores and began franchising in 1981. Stores vary in size from 750 square feet to 1,200 square feet.

Number of Volumes: Minimum of 6,000 in each store just to open.

Types/Classifications: Paperbacks.

General Subject Areas: Anthropology, Art, Biography, Children's Literature, Detective, Ecology, Education, Foreign Languages, General Reference, Health and Nutrition, History, Hobbies, Humor and Satire, Large Print, Literature, Movies, Music, Mysteries, Natural History, Occult, Parenting, Philosophy, Political Science, Religion, Romantic Novels, Science, Science Fiction and Fantasy, Sociology, Sports, Television, Theater.

Specific Specialties: Adventure and Espionage, Assorted Harlequins, Family Sagas, Contemporary Romances, Gothic Novels, Historical Novels, Literary Anthologies and Criticism, Bestsellers, Political Profiles, Romantic Anthologies, Silhouette Romances, Women's Issues, Young Romance, True Crime, War Stories.

Mail/Telephone Orders; Credit Cards: Neither. No credit cards.

Business Hours: Sunday 12:00 Noon - 5:00 PM; Monday, Tuesday, Thursday, Saturday 10:00 AM - 6:00 PM; Wednesday and Friday 10:00 AM - 8:00 PM.

Parking Facilities: Business parking lot, public parking lot, and street.

459
Ars Libri, Ltd.
286 Summer Street
Boston, Massachusetts 02210 (617) 357-5212

Ars Libri, Ltd. specializes in rare and scholarly books in the fine arts and in illustrated books from the Fifteenth through the Twentieth Centuries. Its stock of art reference material includes monographs, catalogues, periodicals, and documents relevant to all periods and all fields of art history.
Owner/Biography: Elmar W. Seibel.
Types/Classifications: Rare, out-of-print, first editions, illustrated books, catalogues, periodicals, documents.
General Subject Areas: Art History, Art Reference, Fine Arts, German and French Illustrated Books, Photography.
Mail/Telephone Orders; Credit Cards: Mail orders.
Business Hours: Call for information.
Parking Facilities: Available.
Catalogue: Catalogues published.
Collections/Individual Items Purchased: Both.
Booksellers' Memberships: Antiquarian Booksellers Association of America.

460
Artistic Endeavors
24 Emerson Place
Boston, Massachusetts 02114 (617) 227-1967

Artistic Endeavors is operated by by a general antiquarian bookdealer specializing in the musical and fine arts. It is located in a private home and visits can be arranged by appointment only.
How to Get There: The business is located across from Massachusetts General Hospital.
Owner/Biography: B. R. Gantshar. Mr. Gantshar majored in music, sang with the Tanglewood Festival Chorus, and is currently on several operatic boards.
Year Founded/History of Bookstore: 1975.
Number of Volumes: 1,000 books plus autographs and art.
Types/Classifications: Hardbound, autographs, ephemera, prints, fine art, first editions, association copies, press books, signed copies, presentation copies, limited editions.
General Subject Areas: Biography, Children's Books, Early Pamphlet Material, Monographs and General Art Reference, Music.
Specific Specialties: Opera.
Mail/Telephone Orders; Credit Cards: Both. Stamped return envelope along with check if ordering.
Business Hours: Varied.
Parking Facilities: Public parking lot.
Catalogue: Published 1 to 2 times per year; $3 each.
Collections/Individual Items Purchased: Both.
Booksellers' Memberships: Antiquarian Booksellers Asssociation of America, International League of Antiquarian Booksellers, Massachusetts and Rhode Island Antiquarian Booksellers Association.

461
Atavist Books
274 North Pleasant Street
Amherst, Massachusetts 01002 (413) 253-5393

The bookstore specializes in scholarly and eclectic categories.
How to Get There: Located in the rear of the Amity Real Estate building, the bookstore is near Amherst Center. If driving, take the Northampton exit off Route I-91, proceed east on Route 9 to Amherst.
Number of Volumes: 7,000.

Types/Classifications: Primarily hardbound, with many paperbound monographs and pamphlets.
General Subject Areas: Eclectic Materials, Scholarly Works.
Specific Specialties: The bookstore specializes in scholarly and eclectic categories, with strengths in Classical/Medieval Studies, Philosophy, Languages and Linguistics, World Literature, Anthropology, Comparative Religions, Occultist Belief Systems, Modern World History, Political and Social (Labor) Movements (quite a bit of Radical Literature on hand), Social Theory, General Esoterica.
Mail/Telephone Orders; Credit Cards: Both. Mail orders require coherence and specificity. No credit cards.
Business Hours: Monday through Saturday 10:30 AM - 5:30 PM.
Parking Facilities: Ample.
Collections/Individual Items Purchased: Both.

462

Avenue Victor Hugo Bookshop
339 Newbury Street
Boston, Massachusetts 02115   (617) 266-7746

Somewhat out of place on Boston's fashionable Newbury Street, the shop is an old fashioned general bookstore with specialties in all genres of fiction. A large selection of back issue magazines supplements an eclectic collection, from science fiction and mystery to turn-of-the-century romance writers. It contains 1,500 square feet of space.
How to Get There: The bookstore is located in midtown Boston, two blocks from the Prudential Building, and a half a block from the Auditorium stop on the Green Line Trolley; it is between Hereford Street and Massachusetts Avenue.
Owner/Biography: Vincent McCaffrey and Thomas Owen.
Year Founded/History of Bookstore: The bookstore was begun as a publisher and bookseller in Vermont in 1972. The Boston store opened in 1975, dealing primarily in new books until 1980 when it was reorganized to deal in used and rare books and magazines. For the two years 1973-74 used books were sold from a bright yellow cart across the street from the Boston Public Library.
Number of Volumes: 75,000 books, 100,00 magazines.
Types/Classifications: Hardbound, paperback, sheet music, catalogues, new and old magazines, comics, maps, first editions, fine bindings, out-of-print, association copies, press books, signed copies, presentation copies, limited editions, color plate books, sets, reasonably priced reading copies.
General Subject Areas: General.
Specific Specialties: Beyond the specialties in fiction genres, the shop features good collections of Western Americana, Books About Books, Literary Biographies, The Kennedys, Libertarian Literature, Children's Books, and a growing collection of Foreign Language Books.
Author Specialties: Willa Cather, Ernest Hemingway, D.H. Lawrence, Ayn Rand, Frederick Manfred, Rafael Sabatini, P.G. Wodehouse, Victor Hugo, H.P. Lovecraft, C.S. Forester, H.L. Mencken, Arthur Conan Doyle, Mark Twain, Harlan Ellison, Anthony Trollope, Alexander Dumas, Robert Heinlein, Robert Louis Stevenson.
Mail/Telephone Orders; Credit Cards: Both; payment with order except for libraries. Visa and Mastercard accepted.
Business Hours: Monday through Friday 9:00 AM - 9:00 PM; Saturday 10:00 AM - 8:00 PM; Sunday 12:00 Noon - 8:00 PM.
Parking Facilities: Street.
Special Features: Search service, publishing sideline, preparation of bibliographies.
Catalogue: Semi-monthly.
Collections/Individual Items Purchased: Both.

463

Barrow Bookstore
79 Main Street
Concord, Massachusetts 01742   (617) 369-6084

Since its establishment in 1971, the bookstore has been known for its exceptionally clean, well chosen, hand picked stock. While specializing in Concord history and the Concord authors (Thoreau, Emerson, Hawthorne, the Alcotts), the shop also has an excellent collection of old children's books, and good general stock.

How to Get There: When driving or walking through Concord Center, look for the hand barrow displaying paperbacks. The bookstore is just off Main Street, behind Kussin's Children's Shop, off their parking lot.

Owner/Biography: Claiborne W. Dawes, owner, is an avid reader and collector, with a background in publishing and selling of new books.

Year Founded/History of Bookstore: Founded in 1971, the bookstore was first located in the Concord railroad depot. It was moved to its present location in 1978, where the previous active growth has continued. The business was run as a partnership with Elizabeth Woodward until 1979; it is now a sole proprietorship.

Number of Volumes: 3,000.

Types/Classifications: Hardbound, some paperbacks, some magazines; first editions, out-of-print, used, and rare.

General Subject Areas: American History, American Literature, Art, Children's Books, Cookbooks, Crafts, English Literature, Gardening, Hobbies, Natural History, Philosophy, Poetry, Religion, Sports, World History.

Specific Specialties: Concord History from the period of the Revolution, the Concord Authors: Thoreau, Emerson, Hawthorne, the Alcott Family, Transcendentalism.

Author Specialties: Henry David Thoreau, Ralph Waldo Emerson, Nathaniel Hawthorne, Bronson Alcott, Louisa May Alcott, Margaret Fuller.

Mail/Telephone Orders; Credit Cards: Mail orders: cash with order only; telephone orders accepted. No credit cards.

Business Hours: Monday through Saturday 9:30 AM - 5:00 PM; in addition, during December, open until 9:00 PM on Thursday, and 1:00 PM - 5:00 PM on Sunday.

Parking Facilities: Private parking lot belonging to Kussin's Children's Shop.

Special Features: Active search service; appraisals and evaluations.

Collections/Individual Items Purchased: Both.

Booksellers' Memberships: Massachusetts and Rhode Island Antiquarian Booksellers Association.

464
Bigelow Bookshop
90 Green Street
Northampton, Massachusetts 01060   (413) 584-3912

This is a general trade store for new books, but it specializes in New England titles with a concentration on the Pioneer Valley of Massachusetts. The bookstore also stocks out-of-print books in its area of specialization. It contains 3,000 square feet of space.

How to Get There: The bookstore is adjacent to Smith College in the center of Northampton, just off Route I-91.

Owner/Biography: Paul and Marilyn Bigelow.

Year Founded/History of Bookstore: The bookstore was started in 1950, and grew over the years. At one time it was the textbook store for Smith College.

Number of Volumes: 15,000.

Types/Classifications: Hardbound, paperback, magazines, broadsides, autographs, ephemera, prints.

General Subject Areas: General.

Specific Specialties: Pioneer Valley of Massachusetts from Springfield to Greenfield; any item on Smith College and/or Northampton, Massachusetts.

Mail/Telephone Orders; Credit Cards: Both. Visa, Mastercard, and American Express accepted.

Business Hours: Monday through Saturday 9:00 AM - 5:30 PM; Sunday 12:00 Noon - 4:00 PM.

Parking Facilities: Street.

Collections/Individual Items Purchased: Both.

465
Blands Book Bin
58 Day Street
Box 5
Norwood, Massachusetts 02062 (617) 769-1008

Blands Book Bin covers general interests with emphasis on Americana, New England, juveniles, cookery, and literature.

Owner/Biography: Eleanor M. Bland.
Types/Classifications: First editions, out-of-print, rare, color plate books.
General Subject Areas: Americana, Cookery, Juveniles, Literature.
Specific Specialties: New England.
Mail/Telephone Orders; Credit Cards: Mail orders.
Business Hours: April - October: Monday through Saturday 11:00 AM - 5:00 PM; November - April: Monday through Saturday 10:00 AM - 4:00 PM.
Parking Facilities: Ample parking.

466
Blue Rider Books
1640 Massachusetts Avenue
Cambridge, Massachusetts 02138 (617) 576-3634

The bookstore, in association with H. L. Mendelsohn, Fine European Books, offers pleasant, relaxed browsing for collectors of scholarly art and architecture books. For horse lovers, the store also carries one of New England's largest stocks of out-of-print non-fiction and fiction horse books, together with selected new and imported titles. Just a few blocks from the hurly-burly of Harvard Square, the shop is hidden from the street at the rear of a garden. It contains 600 square feet of space. Customers often ask about the source of the name "Blue Rider Books." It comes from "Der Blaue Reiter," a school of Pre-World War I German artists, some of whom painted brightly colored horses and thus it reflects the bookstore's two specialties of art and horse books.

How to Get There: The bookstore is located opposite the Cambridge Holiday Inn, a five minute walk north of the Harvard Square subway station, and on a major bus route.
Owner/Biography: Robin Bledsoe.
Year Founded/History of Bookstore: 1973.
Number of Volumes: 3,000.
Types/Classifications: Chiefly hardbound. Some horse prints, reproductions, postcards, and ephemera. Out-of-print, scarce, including foreign language.
General Subject Areas: Archaeology, Architecture, Horse Books (except Wagering and Handicapping), Photography, Scholarly Art History.
Specific Specialties: Art: Art Reference, Artist Monographs, Women Artists, Exhibition Catalogues, Ancient, Middle-Eastern, Oriental, European, American. Horses: all Sports (Racing, Trotting, Hunting, Polo, Eventing, Rodeo, etc.), Riding (Jumping, Dressage, Sidesaddle, Western, etc.), Driving and Carriages, Harness and Equipment Catalogues, Veterinary Care, Shoeing, Breeding and Bloodlines, Behavior, Breeds (Arabian, American Saddlebred, Morgan, Quarter Horse, etc.), the Horse in Art, Reference Books (Bibliographies, Stud Books, Statistical Yearbooks, etc.), Children's Fiction, Collector's Editions.
Author Specialties: Paul Brown, Alois Podhajsky, Children's Authors.
Mail/Telephone Orders; Credit Cards: Mail orders to 65 Mt. Auburn Street, Cambridge, MA 02138; telephone orders accepted. Visa and Mastercard accepted. An additional telephone number is (617) 354-4894.
Business Hours: Wednesday 2:00 PM - 5:00 PM, Thursday 2:00 PM - 8:00 PM, Friday 2:00 PM - 5:00 PM, Saturday 1:00 PM - 6:00 PM. Other times by appointment. Summer hours may be shorter. It is always best to check ahead if one is coming from a distance.
Parking Facilities: Street.
Special Features: Appraisals, search service, in-print books ordered.
Catalogue: Four to eight times a year.
Collections/Individual Items Purchased: Both.

225

Booksellers' Memberships: Massachusetts and Rhode Island Antiquarian Booksellers Association.

467
Book Collector
375 Elliot Street
Newton, Massachusetts 02164   (617) 964-3599

This bookstore is a general used and out-of-print shop. The volumes are well categorized and arranged alphabetically by author. Browsers are welcome. The bookstore is located in what was once an old silk mill and occupies 1,200 square feet of space.

How to Get There: The bookstore can be reached from Rte. 9 (a main east-west road). Elliot Street runs south west from Rte. 9 at a point about one mile east of Rte. 128 (Circumferal Highway). About one mile down Elliot Street, at the corner of Chestnut Street is the Old Mill Building, shaped like a "U." Drive into the center of the "U," and the shop is on the right side.

Owner/Biography: Theodore Berman.

Year Founded/History of Bookstore: Founded in 1972, the bookstore has had three locations: one in Wellesley, Massachusetts, one in Newton, Massachusetts, and the present one, also in Newton, where it has been for five years.

Number of Volumes: 30,000.

Types/Classifications: Hardbound (90 percent), paperback (10 percent), autographed, leatherbound, first editions, fine bindings, out-of-print, association copies, press books, signed copies, presentation copies, limited editions, color plate books.

General Subject Areas: General.

Mail/Telephone Orders; Credit Cards: Both. No credit cards.

Business Hours: Monday through Saturday 10:00 AM - 5:00 PM.

Parking Facilities: Parking lot.

Special Features: Search service, appraisals.

Collections/Individual Items Purchased: Both.

Booksellers' Memberships: Massachusetts and Rhode Island Antiquarian Booksellers Association.

468
Book Den East
New York Avenue
P. O. Box 721
Oak Bluffs, Massachusetts 02557   (617) 693-3946

Situated on the island of Martha's Vineyard, the bookstore is housed on two floors of an atmospheric turn-of-the-century carriage barn behind the owners' Victorian home. It offers a carefully selected stock on all subjects. The emphasis is on out-of-print and hard-to-find titles, but one will also find nearly new copies of recent books, nice editions of classic titles, first editions, fine, illustrated, and rare books. The owners' aim is to provide useful or desirable books for all types of readers and collectors, so they do not specialize. However, by virtue of location, they try to have strong collections related to Martha's Vineyard, whaling, and other marine subjects. The owners favor books on the arts, literature, and travel, as well as juveniles; but those in search of nearly every other subject, from antiques to cooking, psychology to anthropology, mythology to natural science, sports to religion, history to carpentry, will find a respectable selection.

How to Get There: The bookstore is located on the island of Martha's Vineyard, off the Massachusetts coast; it is situated one half mile from the Oak Bluffs ferry terminal on the road to Vineyard Haven. A sign hangs by the road; drive in to the barn at the rear of the house.

Owner/Biography: Dick and Susan Phelps, after careers in government and education, and experience in other small businesses, entered into the used and rare book business in 1947 by purchasing the Book Den in Santa Barbara, California. For a time they operated both Book Dens, but have since sold the Santa Barbara store.

Year Founded/History of Bookstore: Founded in 1977, the bookstore opened with a stock of 2,500 books which gradually and selectively has been expanded. It contains 2,000 square feet of space. Although the proprietors of the Book Den East buy selectively from collections when offered, they have built their stock largely by handpicking books from other stocks (of dealers, estate libraries, sales, etc.) during their extensive and continuous travels. They attempt to keep a stock of titles for which there is always demand and they do not subscribe to the maxim "for every book there is a buyer."

Number of Volumes: 18,000.

Types/Classifications: Principally hardcover, but also paperbacks, some magazines, ephemera, postcards, and prints.

General Subject Areas: General.

Mail/Telephone Orders; Credit Cards: Both. No credit cards.

Business Hours: Mid-May to mid-October: Monday through Saturday 10:00 AM - 6:00 PM; Sunday afternoon. During the rest of the year, call ahead.

Parking Facilities: On premises.

Catalogue: Intermittently during the Winter.

Collections/Individual Items Purchased: Both.

Booksellers' Memberships: Massachusetts and Rhode Island Antiquarian Booksellers Association.

469
Book Store

222 North Main Street
West Bridgewater, Massachusetts 02379   (617) 588-4774

The Book Store contains rare, used, and out-of-print stock in general categories. It occupies 2,500 square feet of space.

Owner/Biography: David E. Johnson.

Year Founded/History of Bookstore: 1971.

Number of Volumes: 50,000.

Types/Classifications: Hardbound, paperback, rare, out-of-print.

General Subject Areas: General.

Mail/Telephone Orders; Credit Cards: Both. Cash with order. No credit cards.

Business Hours: Wednesday, Thursday, Friday 7:00 PM - 9:00 PM; Saturday and Sunday 12:00 Noon - 6:00 PM.

Parking Facilities: Parking lot.

Special Features: Search service.

Catalogue: Published once per year.

Collections/Individual Items Purchased: Both.

470
Books

Route 23 and Tyrrel Road
South Egremont, Massachusetts 01258   (413) 528-2327

"Books" has a large general stock of used, rare, out-of-print books. It also carries a line of remainders. The specialty is 19th Century women's fashion (especially American and English) and hand colored plate books. The shop occupies 864 square feet of space.

How to Get There: The shop is located at the intersection of Route 23 and Tyrrel Road. It is 1 mile east of the New York/Massachusetts state line or 2.2 miles west of the village of South Egremont.

Owner/Biography: Bruce Gventer and Susan Gventer.

Year Founded/History of Bookstore: 1980. After three expansions, "Books" is now in a new and larger shop.

Number of Volumes: 10,000.

Types/Classifications: Hardbound, paperback, old magazines, ephemera, first editions, fine bindings, signed copies, out-of-print, limited editions, hand colored plate books, remainders.

General Subject Areas: Americana, Biography, Fiction, History, Literature, Travel.

Specific Specialties: 19th Century Women's Fashion (especially American and English), Limited Editions Club, Heritage Press.

Mail/Telephone Orders; Credit Cards: Both. Visa and Mastercard accepted.

227

Business Hours: Wednesday through Saturday 10:30 AM - 5:00 PM; closed Monday and Tuesday; longer hours during summer; other times by appointment.
Parking Facilities: Parking on grounds.
Catalogue: Women's Fashion catalogue published.
Collections/Individual Items Purchased: Both.
Booksellers' Memberships: Massachusetts and Rhode Island Antiquarian Booksellers Association.

471
Books With A Past
17 Walden Street
Concord, Massachusetts 01742　　　　　　　　　　　　　(617) 371-0180

Books With A Past is a general used bookstore with 7,000 to 8,000 volumes — some rare, some out-of-print, some reading copies of old favorites. The store is in the center of historic Concord where lived the nineteenth century writers that the store features: Thoreau, Emerson, Hawthorne, and the Alcotts. One can sit and rock and browse overlooking what was once called the "little Athens of America." The shop occupies 750 square feet of space.
Owner/Biography: Bonnie Bracker, Susan Tucker, Ann Wanzer. All of the owners are book lovers with experience in old bookstores and rare book libraries.
Year Founded/History of Bookstore: 1981.
Number of Volumes: 7,000 to 8,000.
Types/Classifications: Hardbound, paperback, a few literary magazines, out-of-print.
General Subject Areas: Biography, General, Literature, Music, Natural History, New Englandiana, Poetry, Western History.
Specific Specialties: Concord (Massachusetts) History and Authors.
Author Specialties: Henry David Thoreau, Ralph Waldo Emerson, Bronson Alcott, Louisa May Alcott, Nathaniel Hawthorne, Elizabeth P. Peabody, Margaret Fuller Ossoli, F. B. Sanborn, William Brewster, C. Cranch, Jones Very, Margaret Sidney.
Mail/Telephone Orders; Credit Cards: Both. No credit cards.
Business Hours: Monday through Saturday 10:00 AM - 5:00 PM.
Parking Facilities: Business parking lot, street parking.
Special Features: Free search service, growing interest in sheet music.
Collections/Individual Items Purchased: Both.
Booksellers' Memberships: Massachusetts and Rhode Island Antiquarian Booksellers Association.

472
Boston Book Annex
906 Beacon Street
Boston, Massachusetts 02215　　　　　　　　　　　　　(617) 266-1090

The Boston Book Annex is a used and rare book store with a special emphasis on literature. The collection of rare books includes over 10,000 first editions of American and British titles of the 19th and 20th Centuries. The store occupies 2,000 square feet of space.
Owner/Biography: Helen Kelly, Francine L. Ness.
Year Founded/History of Bookstore: 1979.
Number of Volumes: 30,000.
Types/Classifications: Hardbound, paperback, magazines, broadsides, autographs, ephemera, first editions.
General Subject Areas: Detective Fiction, Fantasy, First Editions (19th and 20th Century), Literature.
Mail/Telephone Orders; Credit Cards: Both. Visa and Mastercard accepted.
Business Hours: Monday through Saturday 10:00 AM - 10:00 PM; Sunday 12:00 Noon - 10:00 PM.
Parking Facilities: Street parking.
Special Features: Search service.
Catalogue: Published 5 times per year.
Collections/Individual Items Purchased: Both.

Booksellers' Memberships: Massachusetts and Rhode Island Antiquarian Booksellers Association.
Miscellaneous: The Boston Book Annex has both a used and a rare section. The rare books are housed on the second floor.

473
Brattle Book Shop
25 West Street
Boston, Massachusetts 02111   (617) 542-0210

The Brattle Book Shop is a well-known Boston "institution," famous for its longevity and the dedication given to the business by the Gloss family.
How to Get There: The book shop is located in downtown Boston on West Street between Washington and Tremont Streets; 1 block from the Jordan Marsh department store and the Boston Common; 2 blocks from the Park Street subway station.
Owner/Biography: George J. Gloss and Kenneth Gloss. George J. Gloss has been called the "dean of the Boston book trade" and is widely known by authors, educators, librarians, and a loving public who seek him out for his knowledge of books and the antiquarian book trade. He has been profiled in "The Christian Science Monitor," January 28, 1970, the "Wall Street Journal," September 13, 1976, and "The Boston Globe," May 7, 1980. His son Ken is a partner in the business.
Year Founded/History of Bookstore: 1825. Prior to a disastrous fire in 1980 which destroyed the entire stock of 400,000 volumes plus manuscripts, letters, photos, and other materials, the Brattle Book Shop was known as the "oldest continous antiquarian bookstore in America." It had its beginning in 1825 and was operated by the Burnhams and Colesworthys over the years and was acquired by Mr. Gloss in 1945. After the fire, the Brattle Book Shop rose like the phoenix from the ashes and began rebuilding. The shop retains the title "successor to America's oldest continuous antiquarian bookshop." The new location occupies 6,000 square feet of space.
Number of Volumes: 150,000.
Types/Classifications: Hardbound, paperback, magazines, broadsides, autographs, ephemera, first editions, fine bindings, out-of-print, association copies, press books, signed copies, presentation copies, limited editions, color plate books.
General Subject Areas: General.
Mail/Telephone Orders; Credit Cards: Both. American Express, Visa, Mastercard accepted.
Business Hours: Monday through Saturday 9:00 AM - 5:00 PM.
Parking Facilities: Public parking lot next door.
Collections/Individual Items Purchased: Both.
Booksellers' Memberships: Antiquarian Booksellers Association of America, Massachusetts and Rhode Island Antiquarian Booksellers Association.

474
Bromer Booksellers
607 Boylston Street, 2nd Floor
Boston, Massachusetts 02116   (617) 247-2818

Bromer Booksellers is a specialist rare book shop and gallery with a selection of fine items in the areas of literature and the art of the book. It has a comfortable atmosphere in which to browse and chat about fine books. The shop occupies 1,500 square feet of space.
How to Get There: Located in Copley Square on the corner of Dartmouth Street and Boylston Street; the shop is on the second floor.
Owner/Biography: Anne and David Bromer. Anne is a former librarian with an M.S. degree and David is a former research scientist with a Ph.D. Both left their former professions to become booksellers because of their love for beautiful books.
Year Founded/History of Bookstore: 1966. Bromer Booksellers originally operated out of the Bromer's house in Watertown. In the summer of 1980 the business was moved to a shop on Copley Square across from the Public Library.
Number of Volumes: 4,000.

Types/Classifications: Hardbound, prints, autographs, first editions, private press books, illustrated books, miniature books, early printed books, fine bindings.

General Subject Areas: Juveniles.

Specific Specialties: Designer Bindings, Moveable Children's Books.

Author Specialties: Edward Gorey, Aldous Huxley.

Mail/Telephone Orders; Credit Cards: Both. Payment with order or acceptable references for persons unknown to the owners. No credit cards.

Business Hours: Monday through Friday 9:30 - 5:30 PM; Saturday by appointment.

Parking Facilities: Small parking lots in vicinity, street parking.

Catalogue: Published 3 or 4 times per year.

Collections/Individual Items Purchased: Both.

Booksellers' Memberships: Anitquarian Booksellers Association of America, Massachusetts and Rhode Island Antiquarian Booksellers Association (Founding Member).

Miscellaneous: Exhibitions of the book arts are mounted in the store's gallery.

475
Brookline Village Bookshop
23 Harvard Street
Brookline, Massachusetts 02146 (617) 734-3519

Brookline Village Bookshop is situated in an older neighborhood business district which has evolved into a center for antique specialty shops. The shop is attractively laid out maintaining an open ambiance while displaying an impressive number of titles. It occupies 1,000 square feet of space.

How to Get There: Brookline is 3 miles from downtown Boston. The store is near Route 9 and also the Brookline Village subway stop on the Riverside Green Line.

Owner/Biography: James Lawton. Mr. Lawton has a Master's degree in English and Library Science and is an experienced bookman of 22 years. He has worked in the Rare Book libraries of the Unviersity of Michigan, Syracuse Unviersity, and the Boston Public Library before initiating his own business.

Year Founded/History of Bookstore: 1980.

Number of Volumes: 20,000.

Types/Classifications: Hardbound, broadsides, autographs, ephemera, fine bindings, out-of-print, rare, press books, limited editions, signed copies, presentation copies, early American imprints, quality remainders.

General Subject Areas: Afro Americana, Americana, Antiques, Art, Children's Literature, Cookbooks, English History, Fiction, Folklore, History, Irish History, Literature, Nautical, Philosophy, Photography, Poetry, Religion, Women, Yachting.

Specific Specialties: New England History.

Author Specialties: Samuel Eliot Morison, Edward Rowe Snow.

Other Specialties: Scholarly Works.

Mail/Telephone Orders; Credit Cards: Both. Visa and Mastercard accepted.

Parking Facilities: Public parking lot, street parking.

Catalogue: Published 4 to 6 times per year.

Collections/Individual Items Purchased: Both.

Booksellers' Memberships: Massachusetts and Rhode Island Antiquarian Booksellers Association.

476
Bryant's
467 Commercial Street
Provincetown, Massachusetts 02657 (617) 487-0134

The bookstore is located at the edge of Provincetown harbor and is housed in two old buildings which are joined together. One was the headquarters of the E. & E.K. Cook & Co., ship chandlers and whaling and fishing vessel agents and the other was the shop of David C. Stull (1844-1926), the "ambergris king" and dealer in marine curios. The shop occupies 3,000 square feet of space.

How to Get There: Follow signs on U.S. Route 6 to Shore Road at the east end of Provincetown.

Owner/Biography: Marie-Louise Bryant, George Bryant. George Bryant is a native of Provincetown, a graduate of Wesleyan University and the Massachusetts Institute of Technology. He is a fisheries historian.
Year Founded/History of Bookstore: The building is a general store as it has been since 1837.
Number of Volumes: 5,000.
Types/Classifications: Hardbound, paperback, magazines, broadsides, autographs, ephemera, out-of-print.
General Subject Areas: Americana.
Specific Specialties: The Fisheries as an industry (commercial), Whaling and the Fin Fisheries, books about Provincetown and Cape Cod, federal serials about the Fisheries and Lifesaving.
Mail/Telephone Orders; Credit Cards: Both. No credit cards.
Business Hours: Monday through Saturday 9:00 AM - 6:00 PM.
Parking Facilities: Business parking lot.
Collections/Individual Items Purchased: Both.

477
Bryn Mawr Book Sale
373 Huron Avenue
Cambridge, Massachusetts 02138   (617) 661-1770

The Bryn Mawr Book Sale is a non-profit organization which sells donated books to raise scholarship funds for Bryn Mawr College. The stock is old, rare, and out-of-print in all categories.
Number of Volumes: Thousands.
Types/Classifications: Hardbound, paperback, rare, out-of-print, first editions, reading copies.
General Subject Areas: Americana, Art, Asia and Africa, Biography, Children's Books, History, Languages, Literature, Music, Philosophy, Psychology, Religion, Science and Technology, Travel.
Mail/Telephone Orders; Credit Cards: No mail or phone orders; no credit cards.
Business Hours: Monday through Saturday 10:00 AM - 4:00 PM.
Parking Facilities: Ample parking available.
Collections/Individual Items Purchased: Neither. Donations accepted.
Miscellaneous: Staffed by alumnae volunteers.

478
Cape Cod Book Center
Route 28
Mashpee, Massachusetts 02649   (617) 477-9903

The Cape Cod Book Center has a motto "We make it fun to browse." It features both new and used books in general subjects and offers coffee to all customers. There is a large selection of price guides and antiques guides. The shop occupies 1,500 square feet of space.
Owner/Biography: Carole W. Aronson.
Year Founded/History of Bookstore: 1975.
Number of Volumes: Over 20,000.
Types/Classifications: Hardbound, paperback, magazines, first editions, out-of-print.
General Subject Areas: General.
Author Specialties: Nevil Shute, Joseph C. Lincoln, Phoebe Atwood Taylor, Samuel Eliot Morison, Edward Rowe Snow.
Mail/Telephone Orders; Credit Cards: Both. Visa and Mastercard accepted.
Business Hours: Seven days a week 10:00 AM - 6:00 PM.
Parking Facilities: Parking in front of shop.
Special Features: Search service; puzzles; some antiques; coffee always available.
Collections/Individual Items Purchased: Both.
Booksellers' Memberships: American Booksellers Association.

479
Carriage-Barn Book Shop
Cold Spring Road - Routes 2 and 7
Williamstown, Massachusetts 01267 (413) 458-5534

This book shop occupies a huge century-old red carriage barn and carries a general stock of antiquarian books, specializing in Americana, Art, Social Sciences, Children's, and beautiful old books. The shop also has antiques and prints.

How to Get There: Williamstown is located in the beautiful Berkshire Hills, 35 miles east of Albany, New York and 12 miles south of Bennington, Vermont. The shop is two miles south of the village.

Owner/Biography: Martha Mercer.

Year Founded/History of Bookstore: 1975.

Number of Volumes: 20,000.

Types/Classifications: Hardbound, first editions, fine bindings, out-of-print.

General Subject Areas: Americana, Art, Children's Color Plate Books, Social Science.

Other Specialties: Scholarly Works (all topics).

Mail/Telephone Orders; Credit Cards: Telephone orders only; an additional telephone number is (413) 458-3608. No credit cards.

Business Hours: May through November, seven days a week 10:00 AM -5:00 PM; other times by appointment.

Parking Facilities: Spacious on-grounds parking.

Collections/Individual Items Purchased: Both.

Booksellers' Memberships: Massachusetts and Rhode Island Antiquarian Booksellers Association.

480
Common Reader Bookshop
Old Main Street
New Salem, Massachusetts 01355 (617) 544-3002

In the center of a quaint New England town, the Common Reader Bookshop is housed in an 1840 schoolhouse during the summer only. In the off season, women's studies materials are available by chance or appointment. An additional telephone number is (617) 544-7039.

How to Get There: Located on route 202 between Amherst and Orange, the shop is 1/4 mile off Route 202 in the center of New Salem.

Owner/Biography: Dorothy A. Johnson and Doris E. Abramson.

Year Founded/History of Bookstore: 1977. The shop began in a barn in the back of the owner's home and recently changed to its location in the schoolhouse. For the summer, general stock is available, but all year round women's studies materials are available.

Number of Volumes: 5000.

Types/Classifications: Hardbound, ephemera, fine bindings, signed copies.

General Subject Areas: General, Women Authors, Women's Biography, Women's Rights and Suffrage.

Mail/Telephone Orders; Credit Cards: Both. No credit cards.

Business Hours: Summer: May 15 through October 15, Monday through Saturday 10:00 AM - 5:00 PM; Sunday 12:00 Noon - 5:00 PM.

Parking Facilities: Street parking.

Booksellers' Memberships: Massachusetts and Rhode Island Antiquarian Booksellers Association.

481
Dower House
North Main Street
Petersham, Massachusetts 01366 (617) 724-3283

Dower House is a "Carpenter Gothic House" located on the edge of a small New England town. Petersham is noted for its Greek Revival architecture.

How to Get There: Petersham is located 6 miles from Route 2 on Route 32. Dower House is across Main

Street from the Craft Center.

Owner/Biography: Ann G. Swindells.

Year Founded/History of Bookstore: 1980.

Number of Volumes: 2,000.

Types/Classifications: Hardbound, first editions, fine bindings, out-of-print, signed copies, presentation copies.

General Subject Areas: Early Children's Literature, General, Illustrated Children's Books, Mysteries.

Specific Specialties: Children's Illustrated Fairy Stories, Children's Series.

Author Specialties: Thornton Burgess, Tasha Tudor, Cecily Barker, Jessie W. Smith, Cecil Aldin, Dugald Walker Stewart, N.C. Wyeth, Anne Anderson, Bessie Pease.

Mail/Telephone Orders; Credit Cards: Both. Check with order, add $1.50 postage first book, $.50 for each additional book; insurance and UPS extra. No credit cards.

Business Hours: By appointment only.

Parking Facilities: Street parking.

Special Features: Search service.

Catalogue: Published 2 times per year.

Collections/Individual Items Purchased: Both.

482
Edward Morrill & Son, Inc.

25 Kingston Street

Boston, Massachusetts 02111   (617) 482-3090

Edward Morrill & Son, Inc. occupies a 4-story building. The shop deals in old and rare books, pamphlets, broadsides, prints, and autographs. The main floor of the building is the retail store with the remainder of the 9,706 square feet devoted to storage.

How to Get There: The bookstore is located in downtown Boston.

Owner/Biography: Samuel R. Morrill, President.

Year Founded/History of Bookstore: 1939. A branch shop was operated in Cambridge from 1947 to 1955, but now it is exclusively in Boston.

Number of Volumes: 50,000.

Types/Classifications: First editions, out-of-print, association copies, signed copies, presentation copies.

General Subject Areas: Americana, Arts and Crafts, Business and Industry, Foreign Travel, Science.

Mail/Telephone Orders; Credit Cards: Both. Cash with order or credit references. No credit cards.

Business Hours: Monday through Friday 8:00 AM - 4:00 PM.

Parking Facilities: Public parking across the street.

Catalogue: Published 10 times per year.

Collections/Individual Items Purchased: Both.

Booksellers' Memberships: Antiquarian Booksellers Association of America, Antiquarian Booksellers Association (International).

483
English Bookshop

22 Rocky Neck Avenue

Gloucester, Massachusetts 01930   (617) 283-8981

Gloucester is a working town with fishing and fishery products as the main industries. The English Bookshop is happily situated overlooking a busy and beautiful inner cove off the harbor; all on the ground floor with an upper loft. It has a wide collection of sea-going titles, books on religion, poetry, children's and illustrated books, and especially women's writing before 1920.

Owner/Biography: A family trust owns the shop. Peggy Sibley is the manager and in sole charge. She is an Englishwoman by birth, now an American citizen and the widow of a fishing skipper who fished out of Gloucester for 45 years.

Year Founded/History of Bookstore: 1968.

Number of Volumes: 5,000.
Types/Classifications: Hardbound, ephemera, first editions, fine bindings, out-of-print, press books, color plate books, illustrated books.
General Subject Areas: British History, Children's Books, Religious Books for Young People, Religious Tracts, Sunday School Prizes (Before 1920), Women Authors (Before 1920).
Specific Specialties: Illustrators: Hammett Billings, Charles Bennett, W.H. Robinson, Alice Barber Stephens, Stella Langdale, Florence Harrison.
Author Specialties: May Wilkins Freeman, Rudyard Kipling.
Mail/Telephone Orders; Credit Cards: Both. Cash with order, except libraries. No credit cards.
Business Hours: Tuesday through Sunday 1:30 PM - 7:00 PM; closed Monday.
Parking Facilities: Street parking, public parking lot opposite store.
Special Features: Search service for out-of-print titles and rarities; new books ordered.
Collections/Individual Items Purchased: Both.
Miscellaneous: The bookshop carries a stock of new traditional books for children, fairy tales and classics, chosen for their illustrations and standard of production, mostly imported from England.

484
George Robert Minkoff, Inc.
RFD 3, Box 147
Great Barrington, Massachusetts 01230 (413) 528-4575

George Robert Minkoff deals in antiquarian books, manuscript material, original art, and autographs. Visits may be arranged by appointment.
How to Get There: Call for an appointment and directions.
Owner/Biography: George Robert Minkoff.
Year Founded/History of Bookstore: 1970.
Types/Classifications: Hardbound, modern first editions, out-of-print, manuscripts, original art, autographs, fine press books, European illustrated books, association copies, presentation copies, original drawings.
General Subject Areas: English and American Literature, Photography.
Mail/Telephone Orders; Credit Cards: Both. Visa and Mastercard accepted.
Business Hours: By appointment.
Catalogue: Published 10 times per year.
Collections/Individual Items Purchased: Both.
Booksellers' Memberships: Antiquarian Booksellers Association of America, International League of Antiquarian Booksellers.

485
Globe Bookshop
38 Pleasant
Northampton, Massachusetts 01060 (413) 584-0374

The Globe Bookshop carries both new and used books, foreign periodicals, and literary and art journals. The Globe is an excellent resource for scholarly and literary secondhand books. It is located in the center of Northampton in an historic building dating to 1907.
How to Get There: Northampton is 15 miles north of Springfield and 5 miles west of Amherst.
Owner/Biography: John D. and Patricia F. Riley.
Year Founded/History of Bookstore: 1981.
Number of Volumes: 30,000.
Types/Classifications: Hardbound, paperback, periodicals, rare, illustrated books, first editions.
General Subject Areas: Art, Belles Lettres, Classical Scholarship, Poetry.
Other Specialties: Foreign languages: French, Italian, Spanish, German.
Mail/Telephone Orders; Credit Cards: Mail orders only.
Business Hours: Monday through Saturday 9:00 AM - 9:00 PM; Sunday 10:00 AM - 5:00 PM.
Parking Facilities: Available.

Special Features: Search service; appraisals.
Collections/Individual Items Purchased: Both.
Miscellaneous: The Globe Bookshop is always interested in purchasing scholarly material.

486
Goodspeed's Book Shop, Inc.
7 Beacon Street
Boston, Massachusetts 02108

(617) 523-5970

A general bookstore.
Owner/Biography: George T. Goodspeed, President.
Year Founded/History of Bookstore: 1898.
Types/Classifications: First editions, old and rare books, prints, autographs, manuscripts.
General Subject Areas: Americana, Genealogy, Local History.
Mail/Telephone Orders; Credit Cards: Both; personal check with order; include delivery charge; no credit cards.
Business Hours: Monday through Friday 9:00 AM - 5:00 PM; and from September to June: Saturday 10:00 AM - 3:00 PM.
Catalogue: Catalogue published.
Collections/Individual Items Purchased: Both.
Booksellers' Memberships: Antiquarian Booksellers Association of America, International League of Antiquarian Booksellers.

487
Grolier Book Shop
6 Plympton Street
Cambridge, Massachusetts 02138

(617) 547-4648

This shop is a small one room shop with over 9,000 poetry and related titles. It also serves as the information center for the poetry community. Also stocked are recordings, periodicals, and a section of limited, signed editions (all poetry) and some broadsides.
How to Get There: From the Red Line subway stop in Harvard Square, walk along Massachusetts Avenue keeping the Harvard Yard to your left; proceed on down the avenue 5 to 7 blocks where Plympton Street enters Massachusetts; the Grolier is two doors down on the left.
Owner/Biography: Louisa Solano. Ms. Solano wandered into the bookstore at age 15 and essentially never left (although she spent 7 years during the day at Goodspeed's).
Year Founded/History of Bookstore: 1927. The Grolier Book Shop stands as the oldest continuous poetry book shop in the United States. The founders, Gordon Cairnie and Adrian Gambet, initially stocked private press books, some poetry, a sampling of avant-garde literature, and a grab-bag of secondhand volumes. With Conrad Aiken's taking up residence at 8 Plympton Street in 1929, Cairnie, then the sole proprietor, shifted his focus more and more to poetry. The store, with its comfortable couch, armchairs, tables of disorderly piled books and pamphlets, and the constant presence of Aiken and his friends, grew into a poetry book shop and a meeting place for poets. The archive of Cairnie's correspondence in Houghton Library at Harvard University gives testimonial to the breadth of this contact: A.E. Houseman, Ezra Pound, Marianne Moore, Anais Nin, Richard Eberhart, Donald Hall, to name only a few. In the world of poetry, the Grolier is considered a monument. Famous for its function of bringing poets together, as an information center, and as a major retail outlet for poetry in this country, the Grolier represents the vitality of the art it serves.
Number of Volumes: 9,000.
Types/Classifications: Hardbound, paperbound, periodicals, broadsides, cassettes, some first editions, out-of-print small press, some contemporary press and signed editions.
General Subject Areas: Poetry.
Mail/Telephone Orders; Credit Cards: Both. Cash with order. Visa and Mastercard accepted.
Business Hours: Tuesday through Friday 10:00 AM - 6:00 PM; Saturday 10:00 AM - 5:30 PM.
Parking Facilities: "Awful."

Catalogue: Published 2 times annually.

488
H. L. Mendelsohn, Fine European Books
1640 Massachusetts Avenue
Cambridge, Massachusetts 02138   (617) 484-7362

H. L. Mendelsohn, in association with Blue Rider Books, offers pleasant, relaxed browsing for collectors of scholarly art and architecture books. The bookstore has one of the Boston area's largest and finest collections of books on architecture. The shop contains 600 square feet of space.

How to Get There: Located opposite the Cambridge Holiday Inn, the shop is a five minute walk north of the Harvard Square subway station and is on a major bus route. Note that the shop is hidden from the street at the rear of a garden.

Owner/Biography: Harvey L. Mendelsohn.

Year Founded/History of Bookstore: 1981.

Number of Volumes: 1,500.

Types/Classifications: Hardbound, out-of-print, scarce, foreign language.

General Subject Areas: City Planning, Dance, Design, Gardens, History of Architecture, Landscape, Theater, Travel.

Specific Specialties: European Architecture and Design, especially Scandanavia, Holland, Germany, France, Italy.

Other Specialties: Foreign languages.

Mail/Telephone Orders; Credit Cards: Both. Mail orders: all mail should be sent to Post Office Box 317, Belmont, MA 02178. No credit cards. An additional telephone number is (617) 576-3634.

Business Hours: Wednesday 2:00 PM - 5:00 PM; Thursday 2:00 PM - 8:00 PM; Friday 2:00 PM - 5:00 PM; Saturday 1:00 PM - 6:00 PM. Summer hours may be shorter. It is always best to phone ahead.

Parking Facilities: Street.

Special Features: Search service.

Catalogue: Three times a year.

Collections/Individual Items Purchased: Collections and individual items.

Booksellers' Memberships: Massachusetts and Rhode Island Antiquarian Booksellers Association.

489
Hall's Nostalgia
389 Chatham Street
Lynn, Massachusetts 01902   (617) 595-7757

See HALL'S NOSTALGIA, Arlington, Massachusetts.

490
Hall's Nostalgia
25 Mystic Street
Arlington, Massachusetts 02174   (617) 646-7757

Hall's Nostalgia specializes in sports memorabilia and there are thousands of hardcover and softcover books and magazines. These are all out of date issues and in excellent condition. The enterprise is a family partnership. There is a branch store in Lynn, Massachusetts.

How to Get There: The Arlington store is in the center of town. The Lynn store is just off Route 107/129.

Owner/Biography: Walter, David, and Joel Hall. Walter is a professional accountant with over 25 years' experience and has been a collector for over 45 years; David is a certified appraiser and a hobbyist for 18 years; Joel is also a certified appraiser and has been a hobbyist for over 15 years.

Year Founded/History of Bookstore: 1976. The Mystic Street store has been expanded 3 times; the Chatham Street store in Lynn was opened in 1980.

Number of Volumes: Several thousand.

Types/Classifications: Hardbound, paperback, magazines, out-of-print.
General Subject Areas: Movies, Sports.
Mail/Telephone Orders; Credit Cards: Both. No credit cards.
Business Hours: Arlington: Monday through Saturday 11:00 AM - 6:00 PM; Lynn: Monday through Friday 10:00 AM - 5:00 PM.
Parking Facilities: Public parking at Arlington; street parking at Lynn.
Collections/Individual Items Purchased: Both.

491
Howard S. Mott, Inc.
South Main Street
P.O. Box 309
Sheffield, Massachusetts 01257

(413) 229-2019

Howard S. Mott, Inc. has a large, hand-picked and comprehensive stock of broadsides, autographs, maps, globes, first editions, and rare books. It occupies a 1780 mansion of 17 rooms, many of which are not open to the public. Visits must be arranged by appointment.
How to Get There: The shop is located on Route 7, an interstate highway from Canada to New York.
Owner/Biography: Donald N. Mott, Phyllis N. Mott, Howard S. Mott.
Year Founded/History of Bookstore: 1936.
Types/Classifications: Broadsides, autographs, maps, globes, first editions, rare; all from the 16th to 20th Centuries.
General Subject Areas: American Fiction, British Fiction (16th to 20th Centuries).
Specific Specialties: American Fiction of the "Wright" Period; West Indies.
Mail/Telephone Orders; Credit Cards: Both. No credit cards.
Business Hours: By appointment only.
Parking Facilities: Ample parking for at least 50 cars.
Catalogue: Catalogue published.
Collections/Individual Items Purchased: Both.
Booksellers' Memberships: Antiquarian Booksellers Association of America, Antiquarian Booksellers Association (International), Manuscript Society.

492
Howland and Company
P.O. Box 88
Jamaica Plain, Massachusetts 02130

(617) 522-5281

Howland and Company specializes in rare and out-of-print books and graphics relating to Yachting and Boating, Ships and the Sea. Visits should be arranged by appointment only.
Owner/Biography: Llewellyn Howland III.
Year Founded/History of Bookstore: 1978.
Number of Volumes: 3,500.
Types/Classifications: Rare, out-of-print, graphics.
General Subject Areas: Boating, Sea, Ships, Yachting.
Mail/Telephone Orders; Credit Cards: Both. No credit cards.
Business Hours: By appointment only.
Catalogue: Published 3 times per year.
Collections/Individual Items Purchased: Both.

493
Imagine That Bookstore
58 Dalton Avenue
Pittsfield, Massachusetts 01201 (413) 445-5934

The bookstore is a multi-faceted shop, selling used, rare, current, new, reprint, collector, antique, and remainder books. Also sold are tapes, comic books, magazines, pulps, big-little books, sportcards, postcards, and old-time radio shows. The fiction section is arranged by author; the non-fiction, by subject. Most non-collectible items are at discount prices, especially the paperbacks. There is a branch store in North Adams, Massachusetts which also has an extensive hardback fiction section. The Pittsfield store contains 2,000 square feet of space; the one in North Adams, 4,000.

How to Get There: The Pittsfield store is on the main artery to downtown, Routes 8 and 9.

Owner/Biography: Donna S. Connors, owner, was born in North Adams, Massachusetts. She has been assisted in the bookstores by her husband, two daughters, family, and friends. Ms. Connors is also the president of a food co-op.

Year Founded/History of Bookstore: The bookstore began as a paperback book exchange in 1975. Robert and Donna Connors purchased it in 1976, increasing both inventory and selection in most reading and listening areas. Sales have increased every year, and a second store was started in North Adams, Massachusetts in 1982. The North Adams store is managed by the owner's sister, Betty Wells.

Number of Volumes: Including magazines, paperback, hardback: 30,000 in the Pittsfield store, 20,000 in the North Adams store.

Types/Classifications: Hardbound, paperback, sets, magazines, comic books, pulps, postcards, records, sportcards, old-time radio tapes.

General Subject Areas: American Biographies, Americana, Anthropology, Antique Collecting, Architecture, Art, Business, Children's Books, Cinema, Collecting, Cookbooks, Crafts, Dance, Drama, Economics, Essays, Family, Foreign Language Reference, Games, Hobbies, How-To Books, Kennedy Family, Literature, Marriage, Music, Mysteries, Opera, Philosophy, Photography, Poetry, Psychology, Radio, Religion, Romance, Science Fiction and Fantasy, Sociology, Sports, Television, Transportation, Travel, U.S. Government, U.S. History, Westerns, World War I, World War II.

Specific Specialties: Rare Pre-1960 Paperbacks.

Author Specialties: Joseph Lincoln.

Mail/Telephone Orders; Credit Cards: Both. The store prefers bulk mailing of paperbacks rather than specific author or title. Visa, Mastercard.

Business Hours: Monday, Tuesday, Wednesday, Friday, Saturday 10:00 AM - 5:00 PM; Thursday 10:00 AM - 9:00 PM; Sunday 12:00 Noon - 5:00 PM.

Parking Facilities: Both business locations have business parking lots in the rear and street parking in front.

Special Features: Stock can be interchanged between branch stores, for the convenience of customers.

Catalogue: Old-time radio catalogue only.

Miscellaneous: In addition to home purchases, both stores offer a trade-in system allowing store credit to purchase other used items. Consignment is offered for certain items, allowing a higher value to customer.

494
Imagine That Bookstore
59 Main Street
North Adams, Massachusetts 01247 (413) 663-5195

See IMAGINE THAT BOOKSTORE, Pittsfield, Massachusetts.

495
Isaiah Thomas Books & Prints, Inc.
980 Main Street
Worcester, Massachusetts 01603 (617) 754-0750

The bookstore is in a large Victorian house full of rare books, original prints, and reproductions. The books are arranged by subject, then alphabetically by author.

How to Get There: The shop is near Clark University in Worcester.
Owner/Biography: James A. Visbeck.
Year Founded/History of Bookstore: 1970.
Number of Volumes: 50,000.
Types/Classifications: Hardbound, rare books, original prints, art reproductions, paperback, autographs, ephemera, first editions, fine bindings, out-of-print, association copies, press books, signed copies, presentation copies, limited editions, color plate books.
General Subject Areas: General.
Mail/Telephone Orders; Credit Cards: Both. Visa, Mastercard.
Business Hours: Tuesday, Thursday, Friday, Sunday 12:00 Noon - 5:00 PM; Wednesday 12:00 Noon - 8:00 PM; Saturday 9:00 AM - 5:00 PM. Other times by appointment.
Parking Facilities: Street.
Special Features: Search service, appraisals.
Catalogue: Intermittently.
Collections/Individual Items Purchased: Both.
Booksellers' Memberships: American Booksellers Association of America, Massachusetts and Rhode Island Antiquarian Booksellers.
Miscellaneous: Lecturer on collecting books.

496
J & J Lubrano
Main Street
South Lee, Massachusetts 01260   (413) 243-2218

How to Get There: If driving from points along the Massachusetts Turnpike, one should take the Lee exit, following Route 102 towards Stockbridge. The shop is 3 1/2 miles from the Turnpike on the left-hand side of the road, a yellow colonial with black shutters. Coming from the opposite direction, it is approximately 1 1/2 miles outside of Stockbridge, and would be on the right.
Owner/Biography: John and Jude Lubrano.
Year Founded/History of Bookstore: 1977.
Number of Volumes: 2,000.
Types/Classifications: Antiquarian books, prints, autographs, manuscripts, ephemera in the performing arts.
General Subject Areas: Circus, Conjuring, Dance, Music, Performing Arts, Puppetry, Theater.
Specific Specialties: First and Early Editions of Printed Music by Major Composers, 18th Century Music in America, Dance Prints of the Romantic Era.
Mail/Telephone Orders; Credit Cards: Both; telephone orders accepted if from established customers; no credit cards.
Business Hours: By appointment only.
Parking Facilities: Off-street parking.
Special Features: Bid on commission at auctions.
Catalogue: Three times a year.
Collections/Individual Items Purchased: Both.
Booksellers' Memberships: Antiquarian Booksellers Association of America, Massachusetts and Rhode Island Antiquarian Booksellers Association.

497
Jean S. McKenna - Books
131 Dodge Street (Rt. 1-A)
Beverly, Massachusetts 01915   (617) 927-3067

According to the owner of the bookstore, if one is looking for a neat, pristine shop, this is not the place to go. Books are arranged in categories for the most part, but do tend to spill over. There is a section with books priced $1 and under, and friendly conversation is offered. The shop has 500 square feet of space.
How to Get There: The shop is located in North Beverly, Massachusetts; when driving, one should take

Exit 20 North off Route 128. The shop is about 1/2 mile on the right, and is set back from the street.

Owner/Biography: Jean S. McKenna.

Year Founded/History of Bookstore: The business was opened in 1973 as a mail order function from the owner's home. In 1976 the shop was opened and has been in the same location since.

Number of Volumes: 6,000.

Types/Classifications: Hardbound, paperback, prints, magazines, ephemera, autographed material, paper related material, first editions, fine bindings, out-of-print, signed copies.

General Subject Areas: General.

Specific Specialties: Children's Books, Illustrated Books, Local Massachusetts History, Fiction.

Author Specialties: Horatio Alger, Frank Baum, Thornton W. Burgess, Maude Humphrey, Robert B. Parker.

Mail/Telephone Orders; Credit Cards: Both; no credit cards.

Business Hours: Tuesday through Friday 12:00 Noon - 5:00 PM; Saturday 12:00 Noon - 4:30 PM.

Parking Facilities: Front and side street parking.

Special Features: Search service, lists sent, instant coffee.

Collections/Individual Items Purchased: Both.

Booksellers' Memberships: Massachusetts and Rhode Island Antiquarian Booksellers.

498
Johnson's Bookstore
1379 Main Street
Springfield, Massachusetts 01103   (413) 732-6222

One of the largest and oldest second hand bookstores in New England, the shop is located in scenic Western Massachusetts. It features used books and remainders, and contains 2,200 square feet of space. It does not stock rare books.

How to Get There: The bookstore is located in downtown Springfield. If driving, take Exit 5 from Interstate 91.

Owner/Biography: Charles Johnson.

Year Founded/History of Bookstore: Founded in 1893, this is a family owned bookstore with seven departments: new books, card shop, gift shop, toy shop, office supplies, art shop, and second hand bookshop. It is currently being run by the third and fourth generation owners.

Number of Volumes: 50,000.

Types/Classifications: Hardbound, paperback, magazines, ephemera, remainders, reprints.

General Subject Areas: General.

Specific Specialties: Springfield, Massachusetts History; Western Massachusetts History.

Mail/Telephone Orders; Credit Cards: Mail orders accepted for single titles only; telephone orders. Visa, Mastercard, Johnson's Charge.

Business Hours: Monday through Saturday 9:00 AM - 5:30 PM; Thursday 9:00 AM - 9:00 PM.

Parking Facilities: Validated public parking, street.

Special Features: Single title search service; personal service.

Collections/Individual Items Purchased: Both.

Booksellers' Memberships: Massachusetts and Rhode Island Antiquarian Booksellers Association.

499
Lord Randall Book & Print Shop
22 Main Street (Rt. 3A)
Marshfield, Massachusetts 02050   (617) 837-1400

The bookstore contains a selected general stock of 10,000 volumes. It is housed in a 100-year old heated barn.

How to Get There: The shop is located 25 miles south of Boston. If driving on Route 3, one should take the Marshfield exit, Route 139 to the first traffic light, right onto Route 3A; the shop is the first building on the right.

Owner/Biography: Gail Wills.

Year Founded/History of Bookstore: 1972.
Number of Volumes: 10,000.
Types/Classifications: Hardbound.
General Subject Areas: Americana, Art, Children's Books, Literature, Nautical.
Mail/Telephone Orders; Credit Cards: Both; cash with order; no credit cards.
Business Hours: Monday through Saturday 11:00 AM - 5:00 PM; closed Sunday.
Parking Facilities: Business parking lot.
Special Features: Search service.
Collections/Individual Items Purchased: Both.
Booksellers' Memberships: Massachusetts and Rhode Island Antiquarian Booksellers Association.

500
M & S Rare Books, Inc.
45 Colpitts Road
Weston, Massachusetts 02193   (617) 891-5650

The bookstore is located next to the post office in the heart of downtown Weston, a pleasant residential community just a dozen miles from Boston and near to major highways including Route 128. Best known for its 19th Century American reform materials, the shop also offers 18th and 19th Century books in all fields plus 16th to 19th Century European material in many fields including 19th Century Russian literature. It contains 1,200 square feet of space.

How to Get There: If driving from Boston, take the Massachusetts Turnpike to Route 128, north two miles to Route 20, west two miles to Colpitts Road; on the right is a sign for the U.S. Post Office. The trip is about 20 to 30 minutes from Boston.

Owner/Biography: Daniel G. Siegel, President.
Year Founded/History of Bookstore: The bookstore was founded along with M & S Press in 1969 by Daniel G. Siegel.
Number of Volumes: 6,000.
Types/Classifications: Hardbound, pamphlets, broadsides, prints, photographs, first editions, association copies, color plate books, research collections, high spots.
General Subject Areas: American History, Economics, Literature, Medicine, Political Science, Reform, Russian 19th Century Literature, Science.
Specific Specialties: American Utopias, Communities, Anti-Slavery, Spiritualism, Chicago Imprints, Western Narratives, Color Plate Books, Early Broadsides.
Mail/Telephone Orders; Credit Cards: Both; pre-payment required by new customers; no credit cards.
Business Hours: Monday through Friday 9:00 AM - 5:00 PM; however, it is suggested that the visitor call first.
Parking Facilities: Business parking lot.
Special Features: M & S Press, Inc., publishers of books important in American intellectual history (new editions with new introductory material of rare 19th Century American material).
Catalogue: Two to three times a year.
Collections/Individual Items Purchased: Both.
Booksellers' Memberships: Antiquarian Booksellers Association of America, Massachusetts and Rhode Island Antiquarian Booksellers Association.

501
Murray Books
477 Main Street
Wilbraham, Massachusetts 01095   (413) 596-3801

Murray Books is a wholesale-only supplier to the used book trade from a large stock of books and emphemera which occupies 2,000 square feet of space in a barn and a house. The Murrays request that appointments be made for visits.

How to Get There: The location is 8 miles due east of Springfield, Massachusetts.

Owner/Biography: Samuel and Paul Murray.
Year Founded/History of Bookstore: 1950.
Number of Volumes: Over 20,000.
Types/Classifications: General stock of collectible books and paper ephemera; color plate books, antiquarian desiderata.
General Subject Areas: Americana, Juvenilia.
Mail/Telephone Orders; Credit Cards: Both. No credit cards. An additional telephone number is (413) 596-9372.
Business Hours: By appointment only.
Special Features: Wholesale only.
Collections/Individual Items Purchased: Both.
Booksellers' Memberships: Antiquarian Booksellers Association of America, International League of Antiquarian Booksellers.

502
Old Book Store

32 Masonic Street
Northampton, Massachusetts 01060   (413) 586-0576

The bookstore contains a general stock, and is located in the basement of a 100 year old former bicycle factory. The shop contains 1,000 square feet of space. Situated in the "Five College Area," home of Smith, Amherst, Mount Holyoke, and Hampshire Colleges, and the University of Massachusetts, the bookstore supplies reading material to many college-age customers.
How to Get There: The shop is located just off Main Street in downtown Northampton, Massachusetts. Nearby is Smith College.
Owner/Biography: H. Walz.
Year Founded/History of Bookstore: Founded in 1958, the bookstore is in its third location. It is still a family owned business.
Number of Volumes: 25,000.
Types/Classifications: Hardbound, paperback, general stock.
General Subject Areas: General.
Mail/Telephone Orders; Credit Cards: Mail orders only; no telephone orders accepted. The shop will respond to written requests with a quote. No credit cards.
Business Hours: Monday through Saturday 10:00 AM - 5:00 PM.
Parking Facilities: Public parking lot across the street.
Collections/Individual Items Purchased: Collections.
Booksellers' Memberships: Pioneer Valley Book Dealers Association.

503
Omega Books

213 Main Street
Northampton, Massachusetts 01060   (413) 586-2271

Omega Books is a specialty house offering comics, movie items, American illustration, and science fiction and fantasy. Visits can be arranged by appointment.
How to Get There: Located in the center of downtown, the bookstore faces City Hall.
Owner/Biography: Norman Witty.
Year Founded/History of Bookstore: 1972.
Number of Volumes: 35,000 comics; 5,000 movie items.
Types/Classifications: Posters, comics, magazines, paperbacks, ephemera.
General Subject Areas: Animation, Children's Literature, Comics and Comic Art, Movies, Science Fiction and Fantasy.
Specific Specialties: Silent Film Material (books, posters, ephemera); Classic Comic Strip Art; Film Noir.
Other Specialties: French and Italian Comic Books, Foreign Movie Posters.

Mail/Telephone Orders; Credit Cards: Both. No credit cards.
Business Hours: Daily by appointment.
Special Features: Imports European comics.
Collections/Individual Items Purchased: Both.

504
Pangloss Bookshop
65 Mount Auburn Street
Cambridge, Massachusetts 02138   (617) 354-4003

This bookshop carries scholarly books in the humanities and social sciences. It occupies 2,000 square feet of space.
How to Get There: The shop is located 3 blocks from the Harvard Square subway station facing Lowell House.
Owner/Biography: Herbert R. Hillman, Jr.
Year Founded/History of Bookstore: 1950. From 1950-57 the shop was on MacDougall Street in New York City's Greenwich Village. In 1957 it was moved to Cambridge.
Number of Volumes: 50,000.
Types/Classifications: Primarily hardbound books focusing on the out-of-print and rare book needs of scholars; small stock of off-beat literary, political, and film magazines.
General Subject Areas: Cinema, History of Science, Humanities, Philosophy, Religion, Social Sciences, Theater.
Other Specialties: Western European languages only.
Mail/Telephone Orders; Credit Cards: Both. No credit cards.
Business Hours: Daily 10:00 AM - 7:00 PM; Thursday and Friday until 10:00 PM.
Parking Facilities: Street parking, public parking lots nearby.
Special Features: Search service; small reading area with fireplace; separate rare book room with fireplace.
Collections/Individual Items Purchased: Both.
Booksellers' Memberships: Antiquarian Booksellers Association of America, International League of Antiquarian Booksellers.

505
Parnassus Book Service
Route 6A
P.O. Box 33
Yarmouthport, Massachusetts 02675   (617) 362-6420

Parnassus Book Service has a general antiquarian stock of hardbound and paperback out-of-print books including magazines, broadsides, autographs, and ephemera.
How to Get There: Take Exit 7 of the Mid-Cape Highway (Route 6) and travel north until you reach Route 6A, turn right and the bookstore is located on the left 1 1/2 miles ahead.
Owner/Biography: Ben and Ruth Muse.
Year Founded/History of Bookstore: 1951. The Parnassus Book Service was originally located in Hicksville, New York as a mail order firm. It moved to Hyannis in 1957 and then to its present location in 1959.
Number of Volumes: 150,000.
Types/Classifications: Hardbound, paperback, magazines, broadsides, autographs, ephemera, first editions, fine bindings, out-of-print, association copies, press books, signed copies, presentation copies, limited editions, color plate books.
General Subject Areas: Americana, Antiques, Archaeology, Biography, Cape Codiana, Children's Literature, Civil War (U.S.), Cookbooks, Crafts, Drama, Economics, European History, Fine Arts, Greek Literature, Literature, Maritime and Naval History, Medicine, Music, Nature, Occult, Ornithology, Poetry, Railroadiana, Religion, Roman Literature, Russia, Women.
Mail/Telephone Orders; Credit Cards: Both. Credit references required for new customers wanting to charge, or cash with order. No credit cards.
Business Hours: Daily 9:00 AM - 5:00 PM.

Parking Facilities: Business parking lot.
Catalogue: Published 4 to 6 times per year.
Collections/Individual Items Purchased: Both.
Booksellers' Memberships: Antiquarian Booksellers Association of America, Massachusetts and Rhode Island Antiquarian Booksellers Association.

506
Paul C. Richards, Autographs
High Acres
Templeton, Massachusetts 01468   (800) 637-7711

Paul C. Richards has a quaint office with the walls covered with framed autographs of famous writers, Presidents, composers, artists, and statesmen. His filing cabinets contain original letters, documents, and manuscripts. The walls are lined with book shelves which are adorned with signed books from a host of diversified well-known persons. Most people find a visit is a unique experience. Visits are by appointment only.

How to Get There: The village of Templeton is located in the north central part of Massachusetts just off Route 2. When making an appointment, precise directions will be given.

Owner/Biography: Paul C. Richards and Gladys W. Richards. Mr. Richards has been an avid collector of autographs and signed books since 1953 and a full-time dealer since 1961. The firm has issued over 180 illustrated catalogues. He is recognized as an expert in the field of autographs and is often called upon to authenticate and appraise.

Year Founded/History of Bookstore: 1961. The office has been located in Brookline, Bridgewater, and has been in Templeton since 1976.

Number of Volumes: 10,000 letters and documents; 1,500 books.

Types/Classifications: Specializing in original letters, documents, and manuscripts signed by famous people; also signed photographs and books; some broadsides (mostly from the American Revolution); obsolete stocks and bonds; financial Americana; American lottery tickets; some political ephemera.

General Subject Areas: Autographs.

Specific Specialties: Presidents (U.S.), American and European Literature including fiction and poetry; Biographies of famous individuals; in autograph material all categories from the 12th Century to the present. Very large stock of signed Presidential Books; also signed books by Robert Frost.

Other Specialties: Engraved portraits of famous people suitable for framing or displaying with autographs.

Mail/Telephone Orders; Credit Cards: Both. Cash with first order. No credit cards.

Business Hours: Monday through Friday 8:00 AM - 9:00 PM; weekends by chance.

Parking Facilities: Private parking lot.

Special Features: The company specializes in finding that different gift for someone special; in this regard it has been of service to the State Department, politicians on all levels, and many professional people; it tries to tailor the gift to the individual.

Catalogue: Monthly catalogues (sample sent free on request) available by subscription at $10 per year (refundable with $50 purchase).

Collections/Individual Items Purchased: Both.

Booksellers' Memberships: Antiquarian Booksellers Association of America, Massachusetts and Rhode Island Antiquarian Booksellers Association, Manuscript Society, Universal Autograph Collectors's Club, Ephemera Society of America.

507
Pepper & Stern - Rare Books, Inc.
P.O. Box 160
Sharon, Massachusetts 02067   (617) 784-7618

Pepper & Stern does most of its business by catalogues but visitors are always welcome by appointment. It maintains a very large stock emphasizing material that is rare or unique.

How to Get There: Directions will be given when phoning for an appointment.

Owner/Biography: James Pepper, Deborah Sanford, Peter L. Stern.

Number of Volumes: 20,000.

Types/Classifications: First editions, association copies, signed copies, presentation copies, limited editions, autograph letters, original manuscripts.

General Subject Areas: American and English Literature, Detective Fiction, Mysteries, Rare Cinema Material, Science Fiction.

Author Specialties: Aldous Huxley, Ring Lardner, John Le Carre, Ross MacDonald, H.L. Mencken, George Orwell, Ellery Queen, Agatha Christie, Bram Stoker, Rex Stout, James Thurber, S.J. Perelman, John Updike, Larry McMurtry, S.S. Van Dine, Nathanael West, Paul Bowles, Robert Van Gulik, H.G. Wells, Eric Ambler, Len Deighton, Zane Grey, Thomas Wolfe, Ray Bradbury, Jack London, Ernest Hemingway, F. Scott Fitzgerald, Dashiell Hammett, Raymond Chandler, John Dickson Carr, Arthur Conan Doyle, Cornell Woolrich, P.G. Wodehouse, Edgar Rice Burroughs, Mark Twain, John Steinbeck, William Faulkner, W. Somerset Maugham, Kurt Vonnegut, Ross MacDonald, Earl Derr Biggers, Sax Rohmer, C.S. Forester, Dick Francis, R. Austin Freeman, Graham Greene, Stephen King, Willa Cather, D.H. Lawrence.

Mail/Telephone Orders; Credit Cards: Both. Visa and Mastercard accepted.

Business Hours: Anytime by prior appointment Monday through Friday 10:00 AM - 5:00 PM.

Catalogue: Published 8 times per year.

Collections/Individual Items Purchased: Both.

Booksellers' Memberships: Antiquarian Booksellers Association of America.

Miscellaneous: Pepper & Stern - Rare Books, Inc. also has an office in Santa Barbara, California.

508
Peter L. Masi - Books
17 Central Street
Montague, Massachusetts 01351 (413) 367-2628

This is a small bookstore housed in a renovated 19th Century general store. It specializes in antiquarian, scholarly, and good used books. The emphasis is on non-fiction architecture, arts, technology, sciences, industry and business, Americana. The store carries some juveniles and ephemera.

How to Get There: From Exit 24 of Interstate 91, turn right at top of ramp and first right onto Route 16 south; go 1 mile into Sunderland, turn left at light onto route 47 north and go 5 miles into Montague. The bookstore is on the north side of the town green.

Owner/Biography: Peter and Deborah Masi.

Year Founded/History of Bookstore: 1979.

Number of Volumes: 10,000.

Types/Classifications: Hardbound, pamphlets, broadsides, out-of-print, antiquarian, ephemera.

General Subject Areas: Agriculture, Americana, Architecture, Business and Industry, Engineering and Technology, Film, Fine and Decorative Arts, Horticulture, Juveniles, Music, Photography, Religion, Science and Medicine, Trade Catalogues.

Mail/Telephone Orders; Credit Cards: Both. No credit cards.

Business Hours: By appointment only.

Parking Facilities: Street parking.

Catalogue: Published 3 to 4 times per year.

Collections/Individual Items Purchased: Both.

Booksellers' Memberships: Antiquarian Booksellers Association of America, Massachusetts and Rhode Island Antiquarian Booksellers Association.

509
Printers' Devil
One Claremont Court
Arlington, Massachusetts 02174 (617) 646-6762

The Printers' Devil is the only shop in New England specializing in the History of Medicine, a specialty since 1976. The showroom is stocked with a wide range of scholarly and rare books, prints relating to medicine, antique medical instruments, and other antique medical artifacts. Visits are by appointment only.

How to Get There: Arlington is a quiet residential suburb of Boston located between Cambridge and

Lexington. The shop is easily accessible by public transportation and by car from Route 2 or Massachusetts Avenue. A telephone call will provide simple directions.

Owner/Biography: Barry A. Wiedenkeller.
Year Founded/History of Bookstore: 1976.
Number of Volumes: Over 2,500.
Types/Classifications: Scholarly and rare hardbound, broadsides, ephemera, prints, antiques.
General Subject Areas: History of Medicine, Medical Antiques, Medical Monographs.
Mail/Telephone Orders; Credit Cards: Both. Visa and Mastercard accepted.
Business Hours: By appointment only.
Parking Facilities: Street parking.
Special Features: Occasional reprints published in the field of Medical History.
Catalogue: Published 4 to 5 times per year.
Collections/Individual Items Purchased: Both.
Booksellers' Memberships: Antiquarian Booksellers Association of America, International League of Antiquarian Booksellers, Massachusetts and Rhode Island Antiquarian Booksellers Association, New England Appraisers Association, Scientific Instrument Society.
Miscellaneous: Collection development.

510
Priscilla Juvelis, Inc.
89 Beacon Street
Boston, Massachusetts 02108   (617) 367-8452

Priscilla Juvelis, Inc. offers rare books in literature, livres d'artiste, fine bindings, autographs, and manuscripts. Visits are by appointment only.
Types/Classifications: Rare, fine bindings, autographs, manuscripts, hardbound, livres d'artiste.
Business Hours: By appointment only.
Catalogue: Catalogue published.

511
Pro Libris - Gertrude B. Toll
10 Littell Road
Brookline, Massachusetts 02146   (617) 739-0523

Pro Libris is not a bookstore; it is a search service which specializes in tracking down rare, hard to find, and out-of-print books and magazines. Everything is done by mail order as no stock is maintained.
Owner/Biography: Gertrude B. Toll. Ms. Toll has learned from previous experience in the retail book business just where to find the unusual.
Year Founded/History of Bookstore: 1983.
General Subject Areas: India, Mysteries, Women's Books.
Mail/Telephone Orders; Credit Cards: Mail order only. No credit cards.
Business Hours: Monday through Friday 9:00 AM - 5:00 PM.
Special Features: Search service. In addition to the cost of the book, there is a $5 non-refundable search fee per title or category to cover the cost of advertising that title in trade journals for up to three months; customer is kept posted regularly on the status of the order.

512
Rebecca B. Desmarais, Rare Books
1 Nixon Road
Framingham, Massachusetts 01701   (617) 877-4564

This is an antiquarian bookstore open by appointment only and dealing in first edition literature (19th and 20th Centuries), press books, books about books, and Americana.
How to Get There: The bookstore is about 2 miles off Route 9, between Routes 128 and 495.

Owner/Biography: Rebecca and Gil Desmarais. Rebecca has been selling books for about 8 years and has served as President of the Massachusetts and Rhode Island Antiquarian Booksellers Association and is presently on the Board of Governors for the Antiquarian Booksellers Association of America.
Year Founded/History of Bookstore: 1978.
Number of Volumes: 10,000.
Types/Classifications: Hardbound, broadsides, autograph material, first editions, press books.
General Subject Areas: American Literature (19th Century), Americana, Books About Books, Modern First Editions.
Specific Specialties: Armed Services Editions.
Mail/Telephone Orders; Credit Cards: Both. Cash with order for new customers or 2 ABAA references. No credit cards.
Business Hours: By appointment only.
Catalogue: Published 6 times per year.
Collections/Individual Items Purchased: Both.
Booksellers' Memberships: Antiquarian Booksellers Association of America, Massachusetts and Rhode Island Antiquarian Booksellers Association, Manuscript Society, Bibliographic Society of America.

513
Rendells Inc.
154 Wells Avenue
Newton, Massachusetts 02159   (617) 965-4670

The Rendells Inc. is located in a modern office park on the Charles River west of Boston. It maintains "the largest inventory in the world of autograph letters, manuscripts, and documents from ancient through medieval to modern times, in all western languages, and from virtually all areas of human endeavor." The shop also maintains an inventory of printed books concerning the American West, as well as other American subjects, fine bindings, and signed, inscribed, and annotated books by noted persons in virtually all fields.
How to Get There: The Rendells Inc. is just off Route 128 near the junction of Route 9.
Owner/Biography: Kenneth Rendell and Diana Rendell. Mr. Rendell is the co-editor of "Autographs and Manuscripts: A Collector's Manual" which was selected by the American Library Association as one of the outstanding reference books of 1979. He was also a consultant for "Newsweek" in disclosing that the "Hitler Diaries" were forged.
Year Founded/History of Bookstore: 1961.
Types/Classifications: Autographs, Americana.
General Subject Areas: Western Americana.
Mail/Telephone Orders; Credit Cards: Both. No credit cards.
Business Hours: Daily 9:00 AM - 5:00 PM.
Parking Facilities: Business parking lot.
Catalogue: Published 15 times per year.
Collections/Individual Items Purchased: Both.
Booksellers' Memberships: Antiquarian Booksellers Association of America, International League of Antiquarian Booksellers, Antiquarian Booksellers Association (International).

514
Robert and Barbara Paulson - Books
Allen Coit Road
Huntington, Massachusetts 01050   (413) 667-3208

This bookstore is situated in a two-story barn in a country setting. Fiction is found downstairs and non-fiction upstairs.
How to Get There: The store is located 10 miles southwest of Northampton, just off Route 66; easy to follow signs are found from Route 66.
Owner/Biography: Robert A. Paulson.
Number of Volumes: 20,000.

Types/Classifications: Hardbound, out-of-print, first editions, postcards, trade cards.
General Subject Areas: General.
Author Specialties: Rockwell Kent.
Other Specialties: Business and Industrial History.
Mail/Telephone Orders; Credit Cards: Both. No credit cards.
Business Hours: Seven days per week 10:00 AM - 5:00 PM; by appointment in January, February, March.
Collections/Individual Items Purchased: Both.
Booksellers' Memberships: Antiquarian Booksellers Association of America, Massachusetts and Rhode Island Antiquarian Booksellers Association.

515
Robert F. Lucas
Main Street
P.O. Box 63
Blandford, Massachusetts 01008   (413) 848-2061

Located in an 1840 parsonage, this shop occupies the front half of the house. It contains a small general stock with an emphasis on Americana. Open by appointment, the owners welcome collectors, librarians, and booksellers.
How to Get There: The shop is a 20 minute drive from Exit 3 of the Massachusetts Pike; take Route 10 to Route 20 to Route 23; the shop is in the center of the village of Blandford, 3 houses east of the only general store.
Owner/Biography: Robert and Patricia Lucas.
Year Founded/History of Bookstore: 1976.
Number of Volumes: 3,000.
Types/Classifications: Hardbound, ephemera, out-of-print, rare, first editions, signed copies, illustrated books, manuscript historical items.
General Subject Areas: Americana, Antiques, Art, Biography, Books About Books, Children's Books, Literature, Literature (19th Century), Maritime, Photographica, Travel, Women's Books.
Specific Specialties: Whaling, Hawaii, Pacific Islands, New England, Transcendentalism, Western Americana, Shakers, Textiles, Diaries and Journals, Letters, Civil War (U.S.), Western Massachusetts.
Author Specialties: Henry David Thoreau, Ralph Waldo Emerson.
Mail/Telephone Orders; Credit Cards: Both. No credit cards.
Business Hours: By appointment only.
Parking Facilities: Driveway.
Special Features: Predominantly mail order.
Catalogue: Published about 6 times per year.
Collections/Individual Items Purchased: Both.
Booksellers' Memberships: Antiquarian Booksellers Association of America, Massachusetts and Rhode Island Antiquarian Booksellers Association, Ephemera Society.

516
Robert L. Merriam, Rare and Used Old Books
Newhall Road
Conway, Massachusetts 01341   (413) 369-4052

This is a bookstore in the country with a stock of rare, used, and old books. The specialties are Americana, books on books, bibliography, antiques, and decorative arts. Miniature books are also published.
How to Get There: Take route 91 North and Exit 24 to Routes 5 and 10, travel about a mile to Route 116 to Conway; in Conway take Shelburne Falls Road to fork (about 2 miles), take left 1/4 mile to Newhall Road.
Owner/Biography: Robert L. Merriam.
Year Founded/History of Bookstore: 1955.
Number of Volumes: 10,000.
Types/Classifications: Hardbound, first editions, out-of-print.

General Subject Areas: Americana, Antiques, Bibliography, Books About Books, Decorative Arts, Miniature Books.
Mail/Telephone Orders; Credit Cards: Both. No credit cards.
Business Hours: Sunday 1:00 PM - 5:00 PM or by chance or appointment. The best time to call for an appointment is after 7:00 PM.
Catalogue: Published every two months.
Collections/Individual Items Purchased: Both.
Booksellers' Memberships: Massachusetts and Rhode Island Antiquarian Booksellers Association.

517
Running Fence Books
148 North Street
Pittsfield, Massachusetts 01201

(413) 442-6876

Running Fence Books has a general stock of used and rare books classified by subject. Specialties are books on Berkshire County (Massachusetts) and books by nature writer Hal Borland. The shop occupies 1,200 square feet of space.
Year Founded/History of Bookstore: 1975. The business was founded as Second Floor Books and in 1984 the name and location were changed as above.
Number of Volumes: 25,000.
Types/Classifications: Hardbound, paperback, new magazines, first editions, out-of-print.
General Subject Areas: General.
Specific Specialties: Berkshire County (Massachusetts).
Author Specialties: Hal Borland.
Mail/Telephone Orders; Credit Cards: Both. Visa and Mastercard accepted.
Business Hours: Monday through Saturday 10:00 AM - 5:00 PM; Thursday until 9:00 PM.
Parking Facilities: Public parking, street parking.
Special Features: Appraisals; search service.
Collections/Individual Items Purchased: Both.
Booksellers' Memberships: New England Antiquarian Booksellers Association.

518
Samuel L. Lowe, Jr. Antiques Inc.
80 Charles Street
Boston, Massachusetts 02114

(617) 742-0845

Samuel L. Lowe Jr. Antiques Inc. is a nationally known concern catering to the needs of the serious marine collector. The stock includes marine original art and prints, scrimshaw, ship models, nautical instruments, China trade items, and out-of-print books and manuscripts.
How to Get There: Charles Street runs along the west side of historic Beacon Hill in Boston. It is easily accessible from Storrow Drive which follows the bank of the Charles River. From Storrow Drive, watch for signs for Government Center and the Charles Street shopping area. If Boston is unfamiliar, call for precise directions from wherever you are.
Owner/Biography: Samuel L. Lowe, Jr.
Year Founded/History of Bookstore: 1964.
Number of Volumes: 1,000.
Types/Classifications: Hardbound, rare paperback, out-of-print.
General Subject Areas: Marine Subjects.
Specific Specialties: Clipper Ships and the Clipper Era, Whales, Whaleships, Whaling, Famous Yachts, Famous Shipbuilders of the Days of Sail, Merchant Sail and Their Captains, Pirates and Piracy, Steamboats and Steamboat Days, China Trade, Scrimshaw/Knots/Sailor Arts, Ocean Liners including the Titanic, Ship Models, Figureheads/Marine Carvings, Books of Ship Photographs and Prints; Listings/Registers/Enrollments of Ships (Yachts - early only), Salem Research Society Publications, Original Logs, Manuscripts, Ships Papers.
Mail/Telephone Orders; Credit Cards: Cash with order. No credit cards.

Business Hours: Monday through Friday 10:30 AM - 5:00 PM; Saturday 10:30 AM - 4:00 PM; no Saturday hours during the summer.
Parking Facilities: Street parking, nearby parking lots.
Collections/Individual Items Purchased: Both.

519
Saxifrage Books
14 Derby Square
Salem, Massachusetts 01970 (617) 745-7170

Saxifrage Books carries general antiquarian stock including natural history, antique reference, photography, art, children's illustrated literature, Americana, and nautical. The shop occupies 7,000 square feet of space.
How to Get There: The store is located in the center of the historic city of Salem, across from the Old Town Hall. Salem is located about 15 miles north of Boston and can be reached most easily by taking Route 1 out of Boston, north to Route 128 and using Exit 114.
Owner/Biography: Gina Shulimson, Deborah Wender, Gerry Williams.
Year Founded/History of Bookstore: 1976. The store originally opened at 13 Central Street. It combined with Robert Murphy, Bookseller in 1983 and moved to its present location.
Number of Volumes: 20,000.
Types/Classifications: Hardbound, first editions, limited editions, color plate books, fine bindings, binding services.
General Subject Areas: Americana, Antique Reference, Art, Children's Books, Literature, Natural History, Nautical, Photography.
Specific Specialties: Salem and Local History, Modern First Editions, Cookbooks.
Mail/Telephone Orders; Credit Cards: Both. Visa and Mastercard accepted.
Business Hours: Tuesday through Saturday 12:00 Noon - 6:00 PM.
Parking Facilities: Public parking lot, street parking.
Special Features: Bookbinding services; some publishing of poetry.
Catalogue: Published once per year.
Collections/Individual Items Purchased: Both.
Booksellers' Memberships: Massachusetts and Rhode Island Antiquarian Booksellers Association.

520
Second Life Books
Quarry Road - P.O. Box 242
Lanesborough, Massachusetts 01237 (413) 447-8010

The bookstore is located in the owners' home on the side of Mt. Greylock. It contains 800 square feet of space and features first editions of literature of the 17th through the 20th Centuries.
How to Get There: The bookstore is easily accessible off Route 7 in Berkshire County, Massachusetts, just north of Pittsfield. One and a half miles north of the Lanesborough Supermarket and post office is the turnoff for Mt. Greylock Summit. Proceed 1/2 mile, take the right fork, then another 1/2 mile and another right fork onto a dirt road. The house is a blue Cape Cod with a white pickett fence, on the left side of the street.
Owner/Biography: Russell and Martha Freedman.
Year Founded/History of Bookstore: Founded in 1972 in Williamstown, Massachusetts, the shop was moved in 1974 to Adams, Massachusetts, then to its present location in 1983.
Number of Volumes: 15,000.
Types/Classifications: Hardbound books, literary magazines, broadsides, autographs, ephemera, some paperbacks, first editions, out-of-print, association copies, presentation copies, press books (especially Pennyroyal and Gehenna).
General Subject Areas: Agriculture, American Revolution, American Utopias, Anti-Slavery Movement, Beat Generation, Bohemian Movements, Feminism, Horticulture, Pacifist Movements, Reform Movements, Revolts, Rural Crafts, Seventeenth through Twentieth Century Literature, Women's Suffrage Movement.
Author Specialties: George Bernard Shaw, Mark Twain, William Morris, Jack Kerouac, William Burroughs, Gregory Corso, Lew Welch, Gary Snyder, Wendell Berry, Sarah Orne Jewett, Willa Cather, Henry

to Antiquarian Bookstores

James, Ernest Hemingway, James Joyce, Virginia Woolf, Susan B. Anthony, Margaret Fuller, Henry David Thoreau, Robert Owen, Margaret Sanger, Allen Ginsberg.

Mail/Telephone Orders; Credit Cards: Both; no credit cards.
Business Hours: By appointment only; telephone calls accepted 9:00 AM - 11:00 PM, Eastern Time.
Parking Facilities: Driveway.
Special Features: Search service.
Catalogue: Four times a year.
Collections/Individual Items Purchased: Both.
Booksellers' Memberships: Antiquarian Booksellers Association of America, Massachusetts and Rhode Island Antiquarian Booksellers Association, International League of Antiquarian Booksellers.

521
Starr Book Co. Inc.
186 South Street
Boston, Massachusetts 02111

(617) 542-2525

The bookstore is located in a basement with counters and nine-foot-high stacks. It is well lighted with a linoleum cover on a cement floor. The store also has three warehouses of books. The shop contains 2,000 square feet of space, and the three warehouses a total of 3,000 square feet.

Owner/Biography: Ernest and Norman Starr (father and son). Both owners are specialists in English and American literature and American fiction.
Year Founded/History of Bookstore: 1930.
Number of Volumes: 300,000.
Types/Classifications: Hardbound, paperback, ephemera, fine bindings, first editions, limited editions, out-of-print, sets.
General Subject Areas: American Literature, Americana, Cookbooks, Detective Fiction, Drama, English Fiction, English Literature, Judaica, Music, Mysteries, Photography, Science Fiction and Fantasy, Technical.
Specific Specialties: President John F. Kennedy, Kennedy Family, Southwest Americana, American Short Stories.
Author Specialties: Bret Harte, John F. Kennedy, Upton Sinclair, Ralph Waldo Emerson, Albion Tourgee, George Santayana.
Other Specialties: Scholarly Works, Foreign Language Titles, English Translations from Foreign Languages.
Mail/Telephone Orders; Credit Cards: Both. Visa, Mastercard.
Business Hours: Monday through Friday 9:00 AM - 5:00 PM; Saturday 9:00 AM - 4:00 PM.
Parking Facilities: Parking lot next door to the shop; metered street parking.
Catalogue: Lists published occasionally.
Collections/Individual Items Purchased: Collections only.
Booksellers' Memberships: Antiquarian Booksellers Association of America, Massachusetts and Rhode Island Antiquarian Booksellers Association.

522
Sterling Bookstore
Route 12, North
Sterling, Massachusetts 01564

(617) 422-6897

The Sterling Bookstore is unique in that it was built in a rural location in 1954 specifically to be a bookstore and has never been anything else. Located in a field with an apple-tree setting on 1.5 acres of land in an easy-to-find location, it is a traveler's landmark in central New England. There is adequate customer elbow room inside with a total of 2,000 square feet of space.

How to Get There: Sterling is located halfway between Worcester and Fitchburg in central Massachusetts. The bookstore is one mile north of Sterling Center on Route 12 near the Route I-90 interchange. Both sides of the building and the top front read "Books."

Owner/Biography: Hopfmann Enterprises, Inc.

Year Founded/History of Bookstore: The bookstore was built as a bookstore in 1954 by Paul Roland and sold by his estate to the present owner in 1970.

Number of Volumes: 50,000.

Types/Classifications: New and used hardbound and paperback, ephemera, collector's comic books, antique books, author-autographed books, first editions, fine bindings, out-of-print, association copies, press books, signed copies, presentation copies, limited editions, color plate books.

General Subject Areas: Biography, Boys' Classics, Chess, Classics, Conservatism, Cooking, Flying, Gardening, Girls' Classics, History, Libertarianism, Local Histories, Mysteries, Occult, Practical Arts, Reference, Religions, Romances, Science, Science Fiction and Fantasy, Sports, Travel, Westerns.

Specific Specialties: National Geographic Magazines, Collector's Comic Books, Early 1900's Fiction.

Author Specialties: Richard Halliburton, Rupert Hughes, G.A. Henty, Percy Fitzhugh, Richard Harding, Raphael Sabatini, Nesta Webster, Thomas Costain, Laura Lee Hope, Sinclair Lewis, John P. Marquand, Theodore Roosevelt, Ralph Connor, Peter Kyne, Upton Sinclair.

Other Specialties: Pre-1800 Books.

Mail/Telephone Orders; Credit Cards: Mail orders only; inquire first; cash with order. No credit cards.

Business Hours: Wednesday and Friday 6:00 PM - 9:00 PM; Saturday 10:00 AM - 9:00 PM; Sunday 11:00 AM - 7:00 PM.

Parking Facilities: Business parking lot.

Catalogue: Annual catalogue of author-autographed books only.

Collections/Individual Items Purchased: Both.

523

Taste of Honey Bookstore
1749 North Main Street
Fall River, Massachusetts 02720   (617) 679-8844

This is a general bookstore, carrying many subject areas.

How to Get There: The shop is located 50 miles southeast of Boston. Take Route 24 to the North Main Street Exit.

Owner/Biography: James McKenna.

Year Founded/History of Bookstore: 1972.

Number of Volumes: 25,000.

Types/Classifications: Hardbound, paperback, magazines, ephemera, first editions, fine bindings, color plate books.

General Subject Areas: Americana, Children's Books, Fiction, General, Hollywood Stars, New England, Poetry, Religion, Sports.

Specific Specialties: Fall River (Massachusetts), Fall River Line (Old Steamship Line), Lizzie Borden, Whaling, New Bedford (Massachusetts), Cape Cod.

Author Specialties: Victoria Lincoln, Edmond Pearson, Roger Williams McAdams, Edwin Porter, Barbara Hunt, Arthur Phillips, Edward Radin.

Mail/Telephone Orders; Credit Cards: Both. No credit cards.

Business Hours: Tuesday through Saturday 9:00 AM - 5:00 PM.

Parking Facilities: Street.

Special Features: Search service.

Catalogue: Published annually.

Collections/Individual Items Purchased: Both.

524

Ten Pound Island Book Co.
108 Main Street
Gloucester, Massachusetts 01930   (617) 283-7312

The bookstore was named for an island in the Gloucester Harbor. It carries a general stock of old, scarce, and out-of-print books in most all subject areas. The shop provides pleasant surroundings for browsing, and is conveniently located in the downtown area. It contains 750 square feet of space.

How to Get There: Take Route 128 to Main Street in Gloucester.
Owner/Biography: Gregory Gibson.
Year Founded/History of Bookstore: 1976.
Number of Volumes: 10,000.
Types/Classifications: Old and rare hardbound books, modern first editions, out-of-print, fine bindings.
General Subject Areas: Anthropology, Architecture, Art, Children's Books, Cookbooks, Drama, English Language Illustrated, Fiction, Foreign Languages, Gardening, General Americana, Hobbies, Local History, Maritime, Military, Music, Natural History, Philosophy, Photography, Poetry, Regional Americana, Religion, Sports, Technical, Travel, World History.
Specific Specialties: North Atlantic Commercial Fisheries, Wooden Boat and Ship Building, Whaling, 19th Century Yachting, Maritime History.
Author Specialties: Black Mountain Poets, Post-Modernist Poets.
Other Specialties: Essex County (Massachusetts) History and Ephemera.
Mail/Telephone Orders; Credit Cards: Both. Visa, Mastercard.
Business Hours: Monday through Friday 12:00 Noon - 5:00 PM; Saturday 10:00 AM - 5:00 PM. Closed Sunday.
Parking Facilities: Street and municipal lots.
Catalogue: Maritime lists published bi-monthly.
Collections/Individual Items Purchased: Both.
Booksellers' Memberships: Massachusetts and Rhode Island Antiquarian Booksellers Association.

525
Titcomb's Bookshop
432 Route 6A
East Sandwich, Massachusetts 02537   (617) 888-2331

Housed in a charming antique Cape Cod house on the scenic highway of the North Shore of Cape Cod, this is a small shop of carefully selected books in many subject areas. The shop contains 800 square feet of space.
How to Get There: East Sandwich is located on Cape Cod eight miles from Cape Cod Canal on the Old King's Highway, Route 6A. The shop is four miles east of the traffic light in Sandwich, on the right side of the road, and clearly identified by a life-size statue of a colonial man.
Owner/Biography: Ralph and Nancy Titcomb.
Year Founded/History of Bookstore: Established at this location in 1969, the bookstore is a long wing attached to a 200-year old Cape Cod house. It is a family operated shop.
Number of Volumes: 8,000.
Types/Classifications: Hardbound, out-of-print, rare, unusual, first editions, limited editions.
General Subject Areas: Americana, Art, Biography, Cape Cod, Children's Books, Crafts, Fishing, Glass, Marine, Natural History, Poetry, Sports.
Specific Specialties: Cape Cod History, Whaling, American Glass.
Author Specialties: New England Authors, Thornton W. Burgess, Joseph C. Lincoln.
Mail/Telephone Orders; Credit Cards: Both. Visa, Mastercard.
Business Hours: Monday through Saturday 10:00 AM - 5:00 PM; Sunday 1:00 AM - 5:00 PM.
Parking Facilities: Parking area.
Collections/Individual Items Purchased: Both.
Booksellers' Memberships: Massachusetts and Rhode Island Antiquarian Booksellers Association.

526
Valley Book Shop
5 East Pleasant Street
Amherst, Massachusetts 01002   (413) 549-6052

The bookstore is one of the largest such shops in western Massachusetts, with a stock of nearly 40,000 hardbound and paperbacks in all subjects. The stock consists of old, recent, out-of-print, first editions, as well as unused hardbound and paperback, current and recent, at 40 to 80 percent off publisher's list price. There are two floors of books for a total of 1,700 square feet of space, organized by subject, shelved alphabetically by author.

How to Get There: From Route 91 North take the Amherst Exit onto Route 9, then east on 9 for 6 miles to the traffic lights at Amherst College. Turn left, proceed through two lights. The bookstore is on the right, next to the Hampshire National Bank.

Owner/Biography: Larry Pruner.

Year Founded/History of Bookstore: 1975.

Number of Volumes: 40,000.

Types/Classifications: Hardbound, paperback, out-of-print, first editions, limited editions, press books.

General Subject Areas: Anthropology, Antiques, Architecture, Art, Biography, Business, Children's Books, Cinema, Cooking, Crafts, Drama, Economics, Education, Energy, Exploration, Fiction, Fishing, Food, Greek Classics, Health, History, Hobbies, How-To Books, Humor, Literary Criticism, Local (Massachusetts) History, Medicine, Men, Military, Music, Mystery, Mythology, Natural History, Occult, Outdoors, Philosophy, Photography, Poetry, Political Science, Psychology, Reference, Religion, Roman Classics, Science, Science Fiction and Fantasy, Social Science, Sports, Theater, Women, World War II.

Specific Specialties: Quality Fiction From 1950 to Present, Baseball, Field Guides, Bibliographies.

Mail/Telephone Orders; Credit Cards: Both. No credit cards.

Business Hours: Monday through Friday 10:00 AM - 5:30 PM; Saturday 10:00 AM - 5:00 PM; Sunday 12:00 Noon - 4:00 PM.

Parking Facilities: Business parking lot.

Catalogue: Infrequently.

Collections/Individual Items Purchased: Both.

Booksellers' Memberships: Massachusetts and Rhode Island Booksellers Association, New England Booksellers Association.

527
Western Hemisphere, Inc.
144 West Street
P.O. Box 178
Stoughton, Massachusetts 02072   (617) 344-8200

The bookstore is located in an 1850 farm house, with its stock in the basement and barn, for a total of 3,000 square feet of space. Most of its business is done by mail. Directions for reaching the shop will be given to those calling for an appointment.

Year Founded/History of Bookstore: 1967.

Number of Volumes: 7,500.

Types/Classifications: Hardbound books, government documents.

General Subject Areas: Americana, Business, Economics, Literature, Political Science, Social Science, U.S. Government Publications.

Specific Specialties: Publications of the U.S. Census, Business History, Economic History. Scholarly Books and Journals in Business, Economics, Political Science.

Mail/Telephone Orders; Credit Cards: Mail orders accepted. Institutions billed; individuals not known to the shop require cash with order until credit is established. Books are returnable for any reason within 7 days of receipt. No credit cards.

Business Hours: Weekdays 9:00 AM - 5:00 PM.

Collections/Individual Items Purchased: Both.

Booksellers' Memberships: Antiquarian Booksellers Association of America.

528
Yankee Book Exchange
5 North Street
Plymouth, Massachusetts 02360   (617) 747-2691

This is a quaint bookshop located on one of America's oldest streets. A stone's throw from the Plymouth Rock and beautiful Plymouth Harbor, the shop greets the passer-by with 2 large bay windows where one can spend several leisurely minutes window shopping or digging through the 25 cent books in the wheelbarrow parked outside. Inside, the shopper is greeted by a wide selection of books in many subjects, with special focus on the fascinating history of the Pilgrims. Also featured are first editions and private press books. The walls above the bookshelves are covered with prints, photographs, and original art. The shop contains 400 square feet of space, with an additional 400 square feet in the basement.

How to Get There: Approximately 45 minutes from Boston, the shop can be reached by taking the South East Expressway to Route 3 towards Cape Cod, exiting at Route 44 (Exit 6 East), and a right at the light to the center of Plymouth. The shop is near the corner of North and Main Streets.

Owner/Biography: Charles and Linda Purro.

Year Founded/History of Bookstore: Founded in 1981, the shop was originally at 46 Court Street in Plymouth. The present location was occupied in November 1982; since then the business has more than doubled.

Number of Volumes: 10,000.

Types/Classifications: Hardbound, paperback, magazines, broadsides, autographs, ephemera, prints, photographs, original art, first editions, fine bindings, out-of-print, association copies, press books, signed copies, presentation copies, limited editions, color plate books, leather bound sets, incunabula, miniature books, manuscripts, illustrated books, much more.

General Subject Areas: Americana, Antiques, Bibles (Before 1800), Books About Books, Caxton Press, Children's Books, Clocks, Colonial History (U.S.), Derrydale Press, Massachusetts History, Newspapers (19th Century), Ships' Logs, Sundials, Watches, Whaling.

Specific Specialties: Pilgrim History, Puritan History, Early Exploration of the Northeast U.S. Coast (Norse Exploration), Genealogy of Mayflower Descendants.

Author Specialties: Ernest Hemingway, F. Scott Fitzgerald, John Steinbeck, e.e. cummings, Robert Frost, Irwin Shaw, Thornton W. Burgess, Gene Stratton Porter, Joseph Lincoln, W.T. Davis, William Bradford, Edward Winslow, Alexander Young.

Mail/Telephone Orders; Credit Cards: Both. Libraries and institutions are billed, all others must furnish cash with order. American Express.

Business Hours: Monday through Saturday 10:00 AM - 5:00 PM; Sunday by appointment.

Parking Facilities: Street, public parking lot.

Special Features: Search service, appraisals.

Collections/Individual Items Purchased: Both.

Booksellers' Memberships: Massachusetts and Rhode Island Antiquarian Booksellers Association.

MICHIGAN

529
Arnolds of Michigan (Arnolds Books)
511 South Union Street
Traverse City, Michigan 49684   (616) 946-9212

Owner/Biography: John and Elizabeth Griffin.
Year Founded/History of Bookstore: Founded in 1932, the bookstore has moved only once since opening; the new management and owners took over in 1971.
Number of Volumes: 10,000.
Types/Classifications: Hardbound, paperback, ephemera, fine maps, fine literary sets.
General Subject Areas: American History, American Literature, British History, British Literature, Children's Illustrated Books, Fine Fishing Material, Fine Literary Sets, Maps of the Great Lakes Area, Michigan, Michigan History, WPA Guides.
Mail/Telephone Orders; Credit Cards: Telephone orders. Mastercard accepted.
Business Hours: Monday through Friday 10:30 AM - 5:00 PM; Saturday 10:30 AM - 3:30 PM.
Special Features: Search service.
Collections/Individual Items Purchased: Both.
Booksellers' Memberships: Antiquarian Booksellers Association of America including Midwest Chapter, International League of Antiquarian Booksellers.

530
Baker Book House
2768 East Paris
Grand Rapids, Michigan 49506   (616) 957-3110

The Baker Book House specializes in used and out-of-print theological works. The shop occupies 6200 square feet of space.
How to Get There: One mile east of Woodland Mall, two doors north of 28th Street on East Paris (near Kent County Airport).
Owner/Biography: Herman Baker. Mr. Baker began his business 44 years ago as a used book dealer. Since that time he has developed a large publishing program in which reprints of theological works are emphasized. He remains a leader in the used and out-of-print book business.
Year Founded/History of Bookstore: 1939. The bookstore was originally located at 1019 Wealthy Street and relocated to larger facilities at 2768 East Paris.
Number of Volumes: 20,000.
Types/Classifications: Hardbound, out-of-print.
General Subject Areas: Theology.
Mail/Telephone Orders; Credit Cards: Both. Visa and Mastercard accepted.
Business Hours: Monday through Saturday 8:30 AM to 5:30 PM.
Parking Facilities: Adequate parking near door.
Collections/Individual Items Purchased: Both.

531
Bicentennial Bookshop
820 South Westnedge Avenue
Kalamazoo, Michigan 49008   (616) 345-5987

Bicentennial Bookshop deals in general used books with an emphasis on American history.
How to Get There: Take I-94 to Westnedge exit, 4 miles north.
Owner/Biography: Vaughn and Arlene Baber.
General Subject Areas: American History, General.
Mail/Telephone Orders; Credit Cards: Both.
Business Hours: Monday through Friday 10:00 AM - 5:30 PM; Saturday 10:00 AM - 4:00 PM.

532
Bohling Book Company
P.O. Box 215
Lawton, Michigan 49065

(616) 624-6002

The Bohling Book Company welcomes collectors by appointment. It has more than 800 shelf feet of fine stock, particularly in the field of Americana.
How to Get There: Call for directions when making an appointment.
Owner/Biography: Curt and Lynn Bohling.
Types/Classifications: First editions, out-of-print, 19th Century and earlier material.
General Subject Areas: Agriculture, Alabama, Allied Nineteenth Century Technology, Americana, Denominational Religion, Discovery, Exploration, Great Lakes, Immigrant Groups, Indians, Literature, Michigan, Missions and Missionaries, Mississippi River, Natural History, Old Northwest, Pioneering, Railroads, Settling, Texas, Travel.
Mail/Telephone Orders; Credit Cards: Mail orders.
Business Hours: By appointment.
Parking Facilities: Ample parking.
Catalogue: Catalogues published.
Collections/Individual Items Purchased: Both.

533
Cellar Book Shop
18090 Wyoming
Detroit, Michigan 48221

(313) 861-1776

The Cellar Book Shop is a 100 percent mail order bookshop dealing in certain geographical areas only. The shop handles books both in and out-of-print and in many languages. The main interest is to provide material of intrinsic value and it invites inquiries and catalogue requests.
Owner/Biography: Morton J. and Petra F. Netzorg.
Year Founded/History of Bookstore: 1946.
Number of Volumes: 10,000 plus.
Types/Classifications: Hardbound, paperback, magazines, broadsides, autographs, ephemera.
General Subject Areas: Australia, New Zealand, Pacific Islands, Southeast Asia.
Specific Specialties: Philippines, Hawaii, Guam, the new Republic of Kiribati, Tahiti, Samoa, Fiji, Solomons, New Guinea, and all of the many islands in both the Western and Southern Pacific.
Mail/Telephone Orders; Credit Cards: Both. No credit cards.
Business Hours: Business operates by mail order only.
Catalogue: Catalogue published.
Collections/Individual Items Purchased: Both.
Booksellers' Memberships: Antiquarian Booksellers Association of America, International League of Antiquarian Booksellers.

534
David's Books
622 East Liberty
Ann Arbor, Michigan 48104

(313) 665-8017

This shop has a very wide general stock of used books, hardbound and paperback bestsellers, scarce and rare items. Search and special orders are also available. A branch of the Gutenberg Bindery located in the shop is "the world's smallest bindery." The shop occupies 1,600 square feet of space.

How to Get There: The bookstore is on the corner of State and Liberty, upstairs; enter on Liberty.
Owner/Biography: Edward S. Koster.
Year Founded/History of Bookstore: 1977.
Number of Volumes: 40,000.
Types/Classifications: Hardbound, paperback, magazines (Playboy, Life, National Geographic, many art and scientific).
General Subject Areas: General.
Mail/Telephone Orders; Credit Cards: Mail orders. No credit cards.
Business Hours: Seven days per week 10:00 AM - 10:00 PM.
Parking Facilities: Street parking, nearby public parking lots and structures.
Special Features: Searches, bookbinding.
Collections/Individual Items Purchased: Both.
Booksellers' Memberships: Ann Arbor Antiquarian Booksellers Association.

535
Dawn Treader Book Shop
525 East Liberty
Ann Arbor, Michigan 48104   (313) 995-1008

The Dawn Treader Book Shop is contained in five rooms under the classic Michigan Theatre. Seemingly mazelike, everything is easy to find once the sense of order is absorbed. Reading copies and first editions are both extensively represented in literature, the arts, and scholarly subjects generally. The shop occupies 1,500 square feet of space.

How to Get There: Located together with Bill's Bindery downstairs opposite Maynard Street.
Owner/Biography: William Gillmore.
Year Founded/History of Bookstore: 1979.
Number of Volumes: 40,000.
Types/Classifications: Hardbound, paperback, autographed material, first editions, out-of-print, press books, signed copies, early printing, reading copies.
General Subject Areas: Art and Art Criticism, Detective Fiction, Exploration, Folklore, Literary Criticism, Modern First Editions, Mysteries, Mythology, Natural History, Philosophy, Poetry, Science Fiction.
Specific Specialties: Analytic Philosophy, 20th Century Poetry.
Mail/Telephone Orders; Credit Cards: Both. Visa and Mastercard accepted.
Business Hours: Monday through Saturday 10:00 AM - 6:00 PM.
Catalogue: Published seldomly.
Collections/Individual Items Purchased: Both.

536
Don's Book Store
663 Bridge N.W.
Grand Rapids, Michigan 49504   (616) 454-7300

Don's Book Store is a general antiquarian bookstore and is the "second oldest in Michigan." The store features a Michigan history room.

Owner/Biography: Donald D. Teets.
Year Founded/History of Bookstore: 1953.
Number of Volumes: 20,000.
Types/Classifications: Hardbound, first editions, fine bindings, out-of-print, association copies, press books, signed copies, presentation copies, limited editions, color plate books.
General Subject Areas: General.
Specific Specialties: Michigan History, Lakeside Classics, Civil War (U.S.).

Author Specialties: Michigan Authors.
Mail/Telephone Orders; Credit Cards: Both. No credit cards.
Business Hours: Wednesday through Saturday 10:00 AM - 5:00 PM.
Parking Facilities: Street parking, parking lot in rear of store.
Special Features: Search service; publishing under name of Black Letter Press since 1969.
Collections/Individual Items Purchased: Both.

537
George Tramp - Books
709 Second Street
Jackson, Michigan 49203

(517) 784-1057

George Tramp - Books is located in a century-old home on a quiet side street. The house is Michigan Pom-Pom yellow with white trim and wooden red rosettes near the roof like the Victorian wedding present it was. It looms on a small hill at the end of the block on which the "Under the Oaks" Republican Party was founded to oppose slavery in 1854. The marker may be seen through the window.

Owner/Biography: George Dewey Tramp. Mr. Tramp taught at Jackson High School for 30 years and since retirement has been operating his book business full-time.
Year Founded/History of Bookstore: 1975.
Number of Volumes: 10,000.
Types/Classifications: Hardbound, out-of-print.
General Subject Areas: Abraham Lincoln, American Revolution, Antarctic, Anthropology, Arctic, Asia and the Pacific, Biography, Black History, Canada, Children's Books, Civil War (U.S.), Classical, England, German, Hunting and Fishing, Irish, Latin America, Literature, Michigan, Natural History, Poetry, Pre Civil War Imprints, Religion, Science Fiction, Ships and the Sea, West, World Wars I and II.
Author Specialties: Zane Grey, J.O. Curwood.
Other Specialties: German language titles.
Mail/Telephone Orders; Credit Cards: Both. Cash with order except libraries. No credit cards.
Business Hours: Monday through Saturday 9:00 AM - 5:00 PM.
Parking Facilities: Street parking.
Special Features: Search service; appraisals.
Catalogue: Published quarterly.
Collections/Individual Items Purchased: Both.
Booksellers' Memberships: Michigan Book Dealers Association.

538
Hartfield Fine and Rare Books
117 Dixboro Road
Ann Arbor, Michigan 48105

(313) 662-6035

Hartfield Fine and Rare Books is located in a large private home in a rural setting on the Huron River east of Ann Arbor. A spacious library and other rooms are lined with books and arranged according to period, author, and subject.

How to Get There: The shop is located a few hundred yards from U.S. Highway 23; from the Geddes Road Exit, go east to Dixboro Road and south 200 feet to the private drive on the right.
Owner/Biography: Ruth and Robert Iglehart. The Igleharts are retired university professors of English literature and art history and were collectors for many years before launching Hartfield Books.
Year Founded/History of Bookstore: 1971.
Number of Volumes: 8,000.
Types/Classifications: Hardbound, broadsides, ephemera, pamphlets, first editions, fine bindings, out-of-print, association copies, press books, presentation copies, limited editions, color plate books, fore-edge paintings.
General Subject Areas: Book Collecting, Books About Books, English Literature, Printing, Scholarly Works.
Specific Specialties: Johnson, Boswell, Goldsmith and Their Circle; Pope, Swift, and Their Contemporaries;

Scott, Byron, and Their Contemporaries; Dickens, Trollope, Thackeray; Women Writers of the 17th, 18th, and 19th Centuries.

Other Specialties: English Literature of the 17th, 18th, and 19th Centuries (emphasis on the 18th Century).
Mail/Telephone Orders; Credit Cards: Both. No credit cards.
Business Hours: By appointment only.
Parking Facilities: Private parking area.
Catalogue: Published 4 times per year.
Collections/Individual Items Purchased: Both.
Booksellers' Memberships: Antiquarian Booksellers Association of America.

539
J. E. Sheldon Fine Books
645 West Green
Hastings, Michigan 49058
(616) 948-2131

The bookstore specializes in Civil War books while carrying a general out-of-print stock. The present location on historic Green Street in Hastings doubles as a bookshop and residence. There is ample room for both (1,200 square feet of space in the shop) in the brick facade structure built originally as a Christian Science Church. Collectors and dealers are welcome by appointment. Want lists in all subject areas are solicited, and descriptive quotes are mailed every day.

Owner/Biography: Julie E. Sheldon.
Year Founded/History of Bookstore: The bookstore was founded in 1974 and moved to Hastings, Michigan in 1980, leaving a bookshop location in Charlotte, Michigan, where the business operated under the name Sheldon & Van Sickle Fine Books. The ownership of the business hasn't changed.
Number of Volumes: 6,500.
Types/Classifications: Hardbound, pamphlets, older magazines, general out-of-print.
General Subject Areas: Americana, Biographies, Books About Books, Children's Books, Children's Illustrated Books, Military History, Nature, Occult, Popular Authors, Scholarly Non-Fiction.
Specific Specialties: Civil War (U.S.), Michigan History.
Author Specialties: Arthur Conan Doyle, Johnny Gruelle.
Other Specialties: Foreign Language Dictionaries.
Mail/Telephone Orders; Credit Cards: Both; no credit cards.
Business Hours: By appointment only.
Parking Facilities: Parking on Young Street.
Special Features: Appraisals of book collections.
Catalogue: Published occasionally.
Collections/Individual Items Purchased: Both.
Miscellaneous: Also for sale in the bookshop are hand crafted folding bookcases.

540
Kregel's Bookstore
525 Eastern Avenue, S.E.
Grand Rapids, Michigan 49503
(616) 459-9444

This bookstore specializes in used books on theology, mainly Protestant.
Owner/Biography: Robert L. Kregel.
Year Founded/History of Bookstore: 1919.
Number of Volumes: 100,000.
Types/Classifications: Mostly hardbound.
General Subject Areas: Theology.
Mail/Telephone Orders; Credit Cards: Both. Visa and Mastercard accepted.
Business Hours: Monday through Friday 8:30 AM - 5:30 PM; Saturday 8:30 AM - 5:00 PM; closed Saturday during June, July, and August.
Parking Facilities: Business parking lot, street parking.

Catalogue: Published 3 times per year.
Collections/Individual Items Purchased: Both.

541
Leaves Of Grass (Rare Books)
2433 Whitmore Lake Road
Ann Arbor, Michigan 48103

(313) 995-2300

Located at the northern edge of Ann Arbor, Michigan, the bookstore is housed in a rambling century-old farmhouse and adjacent red barn. The stock emphasizes 17th to 20th Century American and English literature, Americana, and books about books.

How to Get There: If driving, take Route 23 to Route 14 West and exit at the Whitmore Lake Road exit, just north of the Huron River. Turn right at the stop sign. The bookstore is the first building on the left.

Owner/Biography: Tom Nicely, owner, is a graduate of Williams College and the University of Michigan, where he received his Ph.D. in American Culture. He is the author of "Adam & His Work: A Bibliography of Sources By and About Paul Goodman (1911-1972)," as well as articles for "AB Bookman's Weekly," and "New Letters."

Year Founded/History of Bookstore: 1973.
Number of Volumes: 10,000.
General Subject Areas: American Literature, Americana, Books About Books, English Literature.
Mail/Telephone Orders; Credit Cards: Both; no credit cards.
Business Hours: By appointment only.
Special Features: Appraisals are a specialty.
Catalogue: Three times a year; free on request.
Collections/Individual Items Purchased: Both.
Booksellers' Memberships: Ann Arbor Antiquarian Book Seller's Association.

542
Marion the Antiquarian Librarian
3668 South Shimmons Circle
Auburn Hills, Michigan 48057

(313) 373-8414

This business is primarily a book search service. The stock is of a general nature. Mail orders are accepted and visits are by appointment only.

Owner/Biography: Marion E. Brodie.
Types/Classifications: First editions, out-of-print.
General Subject Areas: General.
Business Hours: By appointment only.
Special Features: Search service.

543
Mayflower Bookshop
2645 12 Mile Road
Berkley, Michigan 48072

(313) 547-8227

The shop is one of the most complete metaphysical bookstores in the world with its selection of new, used, and rare books in all price ranges. The store features an old world setting with old oak cabinets, stained glass, and soft music, creating a serene, studious environment. It contains 3,500 square feet of space, including storage.

How to Get There: The bookstore is located on Twelve Mile Road, 3 buildings west of Coolidge, on the south side of the street.

Owner/Biography: Robert Thibodeau, Proprietor; John Barnwell, Manager. Thibodeau is the author of four books; Barnwell has witten one book and is the Vice President of Trismegistus Press.

Year Founded/History of Bookstore: Founded in 1971, the bookstore was recently moved from Ferndale,

Michigan to the present address.
  Number of Volumes: 80,000.
  Types/Classifications: Hardbound, paperback, magazines, broadsides, autographs, ephemera, crystals, incense, records and tapes, Tarot cards, flower essences, gem elixirs, first editions, out-of-print, limited editions.
  General Subject Areas: Ancient Civilizations, Astrology, Children's Books, Hermetics, Kabbalah, Magic, Masonic, Metaphysics, Mysticism, Natural Healing, Occult, Oriental Medicine, Philosophy, Psychic Development, Religions, Rosicrucian, Self Help, Sufism, Theosophy, Yoga.
  Specific Specialties: Tarot Books, Druids, Alchemy, Holy Grail, Pythagoras, Plato, Egypt, Babylon, Knights Templar, Fairy Tales, Legends, Myths, Numerology, Palmistry, Phrenology, Astrology, Christology, Philology, Cryptology, I-Ching, Paganism, Christianity, Islam, Judaism, Zoroastrianism, Buddhism, Taoism, Confucianism, Hinduism, Zen, Gnosticism, Acupuncture, much more.
  Author Specialties: Rudolf Steiner, H.P. Blavatsky, A. Crowley, Gerald Massey, Frank Higgins, Godfrey Higgins, Albert Pike, Jacob Boehme, Thomas Taylor, Wallis Budge, Thomas Inman, Abner Doubleday, Albert Churchward, W.B. Yeats, Carl Jung, Wilhelm Reich, Walter Russell, and more.
  Mail/Telephone Orders; Credit Cards: Both; Visa, Mastercard.
  Business Hours: Tuesday, Wednesday, Thursday, Saturday 10:00 AM - 7:00 PM; closed Sunday and Monday.
  Special Features: Publishing under the names Hermes Press and Trismegistus Press.
  Catalogue: Periodic Book lists.
  Collections/Individual Items Purchased: Both.
  Miscellaneous: The owners also offer astrology and card readings, lectures, classes, public appearances, appraisals, consignments (on approval, art, etc.).

544
Old Curiosity and Book Shop
1202 Packard
Ann Arbor, Michigan 48104   (313) 663-4614

  Housed in a former campus area residence, the bookstore is a combination antique, piano, and used book shop; it contains 1,800 square feet of space.
  Owner/Biography: Eric and Gael Eklund.
  Year Founded/History of Bookstore: 1979.
  Number of Volumes: 15,000.
  Types/Classifications: Hardbound, paperback, magazines, ephemera, first editions, rare, out-of-print.
  General Subject Areas: American Indians, Biography, Cookbooks, Education, Exploration, Heritage Press Books, History, How-To Books, Humor, Literary Criticism, Michigan History, Music, Psychology, Science Fiction and Fantasy, Sports, Travel.
  Mail/Telephone Orders; Credit Cards: Both. No credit cards.
  Business Hours: Monday through Saturday 10:00 AM - 6:00 PM; Sunday 1:00 PM - 5:00 PM.
  Parking Facilities: Street.
  Special Features: Search Service.
  Collections/Individual Items Purchased: Both.

545
Phillip J. Pirages Rare Books
315 North Prospect
Kalamazoo, Michigan 49007   (616) 345-7220

  Phillip J. Pirages Rare Books deals in hardbound and manuscript material emphasizing early printing, 17th and 18th Century books, literary first editions of all periods, early and illuminated manuscripts, and the finest of private press materials. The collection is located on private premises, a large house serving both as a residence and business. Visits can be arranged by appointment.
  How to Get There: From I-94, take US 131 north to M-43 (West Main) Exit; go east on West Main for about 3 miles and Prospect is the first left just below crest of a long hill.
  Owner/Biography: Phillip J. Pirages. Dr. Pirages earned his Ph.D. at the University of Michigan in English

Literature with an emphasis in dramatic literature and the 18th Century.
Year Founded/History of Bookstore: 1977.
Number of Volumes: 2,000.
Types/Classifications: Hardbound, manuscript material, first editions, fine bindings, association copies, press books, signed copies, presentation copies, limited editions, color plate books.
General Subject Areas: Early Printing, English and American Literature and History, Incunabula, Medieval Subjects, Natural History, Science and Medicine, Travel and Exploration.
Specific Specialties: Incunabula in original bindings and with embellishment by hand; literary high spots, 18th Century Fiction, 17th Century Drama, Books of Hours and other devotional illuminated manuscript material, either complete or fragmentary; fine illustrated materials (before 1800 or before 1850 if hand-colored).
Author Specialties: Mark Twain, Samuel Johnson, Joseph Conrad, William Faulkner, Charles Dickens.
Mail/Telephone Orders; Credit Cards: Both. No credit cards.
Business Hours: By appointment only.
Parking Facilities: Street parking.
Catalogue: Published once every 8 months.
Collections/Individual Items Purchased: Both.
Miscellaneous: Dr. Pirages is interested in dealing with the finest quality material possible in terms of condition, beauty, and importance.

546
Pisces & Capricorn Books
514 Linden Avenue
Albion, Michigan 49224   (517) 629-3267

Pisces & Capricorn Books is primarily a mail order business but visits can be arranged by appointment. It deals in field sports and Notable British Trials Series only and is very critical about condition.
How to Get There: Access to Albion is from I-94 Exit 124 from the east or Exit 121 from the west.
Owner/Biography: Joseph V. Wilcox.
Year Founded/History of Bookstore: 1975.
Number of Volumes: 2,000.
Types/Classifications: Hardbound, some catalogues and ephemera relating to field sports.
General Subject Areas: Field Sports, Notable British Trials Series.
Specific Specialties: Angling, Upland Bird Hunting, Waterfowl Shooting, Canoes and Canoeing, Fly Fishing, Hunting, Archery.
Author Specialties: William Roughead, Edmund Pearson, John T. Foote, Corey Ford, Van Campen Heilner, Edward R. Hewitt, George M.L. LaBranche, Arnold Gingrich, Robert Traver (John Donaldson Voelker), Oscar Wilde.
Other Specialties: Lizzie Borden, Jack the Ripper.
Mail/Telephone Orders; Credit Cards: Both. No check with order, customer will be billed; telephone orders strongly encouraged; U.S. funds only. No credit cards.
Business Hours: By appointment.
Parking Facilities: Street parking.
Special Features: Search service, annual lists.
Catalogue: Published annually ($4).
Collections/Individual Items Purchased: Both.
Booksellers' Memberships: Antiquarian Book Society of Ann Arbor (Michigan).
Miscellaneous: Customers assisted in research on authors and titles; appraisals; candid advice on acquisition of books and literary properties.

547
Thrifty Reader
9 West Burdick
Oxford, Michigan 48051   (313) 628-6817

This is a general bookstore with subjects in most areas. Books are shelved in alphabetical order according to author. The shop contains 400 square feet of space.

How to Get There: The bookstore is on the main cross-street in Oxford, behind the museum.

Owner/Biography: Suzanne D. Komarzec.

Year Founded/History of Bookstore: 1978.

Number of Volumes: 35,000.

Types/Classifications: Hardbound, paperback, magazines, out-of-print, first editions.

General Subject Areas: General.

Specific Specialties: Biography, Children's Books, Science Fiction and Fantasy, History, U.S. History, Hobbies, Harlequins, Romances, Fiction, Natural History, Science, Occult, Westerns, Adventure, Spy, Humor, Religion, Social Science, Physical Science, Self-Help, Technical, Mathematics, Computers.

Mail/Telephone Orders; Credit Cards: Both. Self addressed stamped envelope, cash with order. No credit cards.

Business Hours: Daily except Tuesday and Sunday 9:00 AM - 5:00 PM.

Parking Facilities: Street and public parking lot.

Special Features: Two types of search service with trade prices: active at $1 per volume; inactive at no charge.

Collections/Individual Items Purchased: Individual items.

548
West Side Book Shop
113 West Liberty
Ann Arbor, Michigan 48103   (312) 995-1891

The bookstore is located on Ann Arbor's "Old West Side," situated in an attractive example of late nineteenth century mercantile architecture which was originally used as a bookstore in the 1880's. The shop contains 1,100 square feet of space plus an additional 800 square feet in storage.

How to Get There: Ann Arbor is immediately off Route I-84, 40 miles west of Detroit. The shop is in downtown Ann Arbor one-half block west of Main Street.

Owner/Biography: Jay Platt, owner, came to Ann Arbor in 1963 to attend the University of Michigan, graduating with a degree in Naval Architecture. However, bibliophilism took control in 1970, and Jay has worked in various local bookshops since. He opened his own shop in 1975. His wife, poet Marilyn Churchill, and he have two sons.

Year Founded/History of Bookstore: The bookstore opened in 1975 as a partnership, with an original stock of 3,000 books. In 1978 Jay Platt bought out his partner and to date has increased the stock to 20,000 volumes.

Number of Volumes: 20,000.

Types/Classifications: Mostly used out-of-print and rare hardbound books; some paperbacks, mainly of a scholarly nature. First editions, fine bindings, association copies, press books, signed copies, presentation copies, limited editions, color plate books, ephemera, view books, paintings, posters.

General Subject Areas: Great Lakes History, Michigan History, Polar Exploration, Sea, Ships.

Specific Specialties: Arctic Exploration Pre-1925, Alaska, Antarctic, Faulkland Islands, South Georgia Island, Clipper Ships, Early Voyages and Travels, Small Boat Voyages, Michigan Counties Histories, Northern Michigan, Early Michigan Imprints, Logging, Great Lakes Car Ferries, Cruise Ships, Steamboats, Log Books, Michigan Counties Atlases.

Author Specialties: Jack London, James Oliver Curwood.

Other Specialties: Great Lakes Steamship Ephemera, Nautical Ephemera.

Mail/Telephone Orders; Credit Cards: Both; Visa, Mastercard.

Business Hours: Monday through Saturday 11:00 AM - 6:00 PM.

Parking Facilities: Street and public lot behind the shop.

Catalogue: Three to four times a year, mainly on Polar items.

Collections/Individual Items Purchased: Both.

Booksellers' Memberships: Antiquarian Booksellers Association of America, International League of Antiquarian Booksellers, Ann Arbor Antiquarian Booksellers Association.

549
Wine and Food Library
1207 West Madison
Ann Arbor, Michigan 48103

(313) 663-4894

The bookstore is an antiquarian bookshop devoted to all matters gastronomic. It stocks selected new, out-of-print, scarce, and rare items on cookery, wine, and gastronomy. Books in every language and from all years of printed history are available. The shop prides itself on the depth and imagination of its stock, and would welcome inquiries for one book or for help in buiding a library.

How to Get There: The shop is open by appointment only. Call for directions.

Owner/Biography: Jan Longone, owner, is the founder of the bookstore and of the Culinary Historians of Michigan. Ms. Longone is on the Board of Advisors for the American Institute of Food and Wine, and is a writer and lecturer on food history and food literature.

Year Founded/History of Bookstore: 1972.

Number of Volumes: 10,000.

Types/Classifications: All types of material relating to Gastronomy.

General Subject Areas: Cooking, Food History, Gastronomy, Wine.

Mail/Telephone Orders; Credit Cards: Both. No credit cards.

Business Hours: By appointment only.

Special Features: Search service, evaluations, library and collection building.

Catalogue: One catalogue plus several lists per year. Charge for catalogue $2.00.

Collections/Individual Items Purchased: Both.

Booksellers' Memberships: Ann Arbor Antiquarian Booksellers Association.

MINNESOTA

550
Arch Books
5916 Drew Avenue, South
Minneapolis, Minnesota 55410   (612) 927-0298

Arch Books is a closed shop, conducting business by mail only. The shop utilizes a fully computerized, cross-referenced inventory of general stock and specializes in the full spectrum of Children's Books.

Owner/Biography: Ruth P. Hendrickson. Ms. Hendrickson is a former English teacher with a heavy library science background. She decided to pursue her own book business four years ago.

Year Founded/History of Bookstore: 1980.

Number of Volumes: 24,000.

Types/Classifications: Hardbound, children's magazines and ephemera, first editions, out-of-print, signed copies, illustrated books, color plate books.

General Subject Areas: Books About Children's Authors and Illustrators, Books About Children's Books, Children's Books - 19th and 20th Century, Christmas Books, Cookery, Decorative Arts, Gardening.

Specific Specialties: Children's Picturebooks, Children's Modern Fantasy, Children's Fairy Tales; Children's Fables, Children's Myths, Children's Poetry, Children's Modern and Historical Fiction, Children's Biography, Children's Informational Books, Children's Cookbooks, Children's Minority Literature, Children's Series Books, Children's Classics, Children's Animal Stories, Children's Reference Works; Children's Bible Stories, Children's Anthologies, Children's Shape Books, Coloring Books, Pop-Ups, ABC Books, Toy Books.

Author Specialties: Books by award-winning and honor-book authors and illustrators as well as more obsure children's authors and illustrators.

Other Specialties: Bader's "American Picturebooks" citations, books about research on children's literature, books on criticism of children's literature.

Mail/Telephone Orders; Credit Cards: Both. Check with order; terms available for libraries and institutions. No credit cards.

Business Hours: Monday through Friday 10:00 AM - 10:00 PM.

Special Features: Prompt review and notification of want lists; computerized children's titles want file, children's titles search service.

Catalogue: Published semi-annually.

Collections/Individual Items Purchased: Both.

Miscellaneous: Individualized quotes or specialized lists prepared on wants from totally catalogued and computerized stock; gift wrap and card enclosure; ten-day return policy.

551
Book Post
22234 Woodland Avenue
Duluth, Minnesota 55803   (218) 724-7643

The store recently moved from a downtown Duluth location to a private residence.

Owner/Biography: Mrs. Barbara Landfield. Mrs. Landfield is a former journalist and encyclopedia editor and is currently editor of a quarterly regional magazine.

Year Founded/History of Bookstore: 1971. The Book Post opened in an architecturally charming former post office in a residential area selling only new books. It was profiled in Brady and Lawless' "Favorite Bookstores" (1978). In 1980 the bookstore moved 7 blocks to a shopping strip and in 1981 ventured into the used and antiquarian field. In 1983, the Book Post moved to the heart of the revitalized downtown and in 1984 to a private residence.

Number of Volumes: 10,000.

Types/Classifications: Hardbound, paperback, ephemera, first editions.
General Subject Areas: Adventure, Humanities, Literature, Local and Regional History, Natural Science.
Specific Specialties: Lake Superior, Minnesota.
Author Specialties: Margaret Culkin Banning, Sinclair Lewis, Claude Washburn.
Mail/Telephone Orders; Credit Cards: Both. Visa and Mastercard accepted.
Business Hours: Monday through Saturday 9:30 AM - 5:00 PM and by appointment.
Parking Facilities: Available.
Special Features: Search service.
Collections/Individual Items Purchased: Individual items only.

552
Booksellers et al
167 North Snelling Avenue
St. Paul, Minnesota 55104   (612) 647-1471

Located conveniently in the heart of St. Paul, but very close to Minneapolis, Booksellers et al shelters three used bookdealers under one roof. Each bookseller has brought his/her specialties to the business besides offerings of general out-of-print books.
How to Get There: Located 4 blocks from Highway 94, exit at Snelling. The shop is one door away from the corner of Selby and Snelling.
Owner/Biography: McKee, McKee, Viner, and Anderson. Harper McKee, Bookseller, has been in the trade for 15 years now specializing in religion/theology and cookery. Ann McKee, along with Virg Viner, has sold books pertaining to the cinema (also theater and true crime) under the name of Tinseltown Titles. Steve Anderson of Ross & Haines Old Books Co. has been involved in the book business for 16 years.
Year Founded/History of Bookstore: 1983.
Number of Volumes: 40,000.
Types/Classifications: Hardbound, paperback, ephemera, out-of-print, first editions.
General Subject Areas: Biography, Books on Women, British History, Cooking, Film Biographies, History, Indians, Military History, Religion, Theater, Theology, True Crime, West (U.S.).
Mail/Telephone Orders; Credit Cards: Both. No credit cards.
Business Hours: Monday through Friday 11:00 AM - 7:00 PM; Saturday 10:00 AM - 5:00 PM; Sunday 12:00 Noon - 5:00 PM.
Parking Facilities: Street parking.
Catalogue: Ross & Haines Old Books Co. has a catalogue of its books in American History with a heavy emphasis on American Indian history.
Collections/Individual Items Purchased: Both.

553
Dinkytown Bookstore
1316 SE 4th Street
Minneapolis, Minnesota 55414   (612) 378-1286

This bookstore has a general out-of-print stock and specializes in modern fiction and literature of all types. The owners attend some of the major book fairs around the country. The store occupies 1,800 square feet of space.
How to Get There: Dinkytown is the prime student area just off campus from the University of Minnesota. The store is on the 2nd floor of the Dinkytown Mall, a few miles from downtown Minneapolis.
Owner/Biography: Larry and Mary Dingman.
Year Founded/History of Bookstore: 1971. The bookstore began as a five-owner cooperative but has been owned by Larry and Mary Dingman for the past six years.
Number of Volumes: 30,000 plus 30,000 more in storage.
Types/Classifications: Hardbound, paperback, broadsides, autographs, ephemera, out-of-print.
General Subject Areas: Crafts, Modern Fiction, Mysteries, Nature, Poetry, Sports.
Specific Specialties: Knitting, Crochet, Needlepoint.

Mail/Telephone Orders; Credit Cards: Both. No credit cards.
Business Hours: Monday through Saturday 10:30 AM - 5:30 PM; closed Sunday.
Parking Facilities: Street and hourly parking within 1 block of shop.
Catalogue: Published 5 to 6 times per year.
Collections/Individual Items Purchased: Both.
Booksellers' Memberships: Antiquarian Booksellers Association of America.

554
Fort Snelling Antiquarian
1294 Bohland Place
St. Paul, Minnesota 55116   (612) 690-5702

Fort Snelling Antiquarian Bookstore occupies the greater portion of a private home located five minutes from Fort Snelling. The home has been restored to its original 1830 condition. The colonial dwelling is furnished with midwest works of art from the late 19th Century.
How to Get There: Call for specific directions.
Owner/Biography: Roland M. and Jeanne A. Griep. Mr. Griep is a life member of the Minnesota Historical Society.
Year Founded/History of Bookstore: 1979.
Number of Volumes: 5,000.
Types/Classifications: Hardbound, broadsides, autographs, ephemera, first editions, out-of-print, signed copies, color plate books, atlases, fine bindings.
General Subject Areas: Atlases and Maps Relating to the Upper Midwest, Diaries, Explorations, Histories, Midwest Americana, Minnesota Authors and Artists, Travel.
Specific Specialties: Minnesota.
Author Specialties: Sinclair Lewis.
Mail/Telephone Orders; Credit Cards: Both. Cash with order. No credit cards.
Business Hours: By appointment only.
Parking Facilities: Street parking.
Special Features: Minnesota Art.
Catalogue: Published once per year.
Collections/Individual Items Purchased: Both.
Booksellers' Memberships: James F. Bell Library Association.

555
James & Mary Laurie, Booksellers
251 South Snelling
St. Paul, Minnesota 55105   (612) 699-1114

How to Get There: The bookstore is located 2 miles south of Highway I-94 on Snelling Avenue.
Owner/Biography: James and Mary Laurie.
Year Founded/History of Bookstore: The bookstore was founded in 1971 in Stillwater, Minnesota, and moved to St. Paul in 1978 where it has remained in the same location. It contains 1,000 square feet of space.
Number of Volumes: 20,000.
Types/Classifications: Hardbound, limited editions, signed copies, fine printing, private press books.
General Subject Areas: American Literature, Bibliography, Bookbinding, Books About Books, English Literature, Minnesota, Printing, Reference Books, Typography.
Other Specialties: English Literary Criticism, American Literary Criticism, Bookplates.
Mail/Telephone Orders; Credit Cards: Both; Visa, Mastercard.
Business Hours: Monday through Wednesday 11:00 AM - 7:00 PM; Saturday 9:00 AM - 5:00 PM; Sunday 12:00 Noon - 5:00 PM.
Parking Facilities: Unmetered street parking.
Special Features: Search service, appraisals.
Catalogue: Four times a year.

Collections/Individual Items Purchased: Both.
Booksellers' Memberships: Antiquarian Booksellers Association of America.

556
Leland N. Lien, Bookseller
413 South 4th Street
Minneapolis, Minnesota 55415 (612) 332-7081

In this bookstore the book shelves surround the outer walls from floor to ceiling (12') in the rear half of the store, and floor to ceiling (8') in the front half. There are also two free-standing shelves running from front to rear of the shop. Altogether, there is 3,000 square feet of space.

How to Get There: The bookstore is located in downtown Minneapolis at 4th Street South and 4th Avenue South.

Owner/Biography: Leland N. and Rae T. Lien.

Year Founded/History of Bookstore: The business was founded in 1952 and has had three owners. The Liens purchased it in 1971.

Number of Volumes: 75,000.

Types/Classifications: Hardbound, prints, out-of-print, first editions (modern and antiquarian), fine bindings, signed copies.

General Subject Areas: American History, American Literature, Architecture, Art, Biography, Children's Books, Cinema, Detective Fiction, Drama, European History, European Literature, Journalism, Military, Music, Philosophy, Travel.

Specific Specialties: Minnesota History, American Indians, Indian Wars, Civil War (U.S.), American Presidential Biographies.

Author Specialties: F. Scott Fitzgerald, Ernest Hemingway, Jack Kerouac.

Mail/Telephone Orders; Credit Cards: Both; Visa, Mastercard.

Business Hours: Monday through Saturday 10:00 AM - 5:00 PM.

Parking Facilities: Street, public parking ramps and lots.

Special Features: The bookstore does collection building for institutional and private collectors; offers a search service for out-of-print titles; orders new books for clients.

Catalogue: Catalogue and occasional lists.

Collections/Individual Items Purchased: Both.

Booksellers' Memberships: National and Midwest Chapters of the Antiquarian Booksellers Association of America, International League of Antiquarian Booksellers, American Booksellers Association.

557
Mary Twyce Antiques & Books
601 East 5th Street
Winona, Minnesota 55987 (507) 454-4412

The bookstore features approximately 10,000 carefully selected books including fiction and non-fiction arranged by categories; they are alphabetized when appropriate. The bookstore contains 3,500 square feet of space.

How to Get There: The shop is located 4 blocks west of Mankato Avenue, and 1 block north of Broadway.

Owner/Biography: Mary, John, and David Pendleton.

Year Founded/History of Bookstore: Founded in 1969, the shop was moved to its present location in 1977; it is now housed in a three-level 100 year old former pharmacy building.

Number of Volumes: 10,000.

Types/Classifications: Hardbound, magazines, old postcards, sheet music, miscellaneous paper, out-of-print.

General Subject Areas: Air, Americana, Architecture, Art, Biography, Blacks, Children's Books, Cinema, Cookbooks, Drama, Fiction, Games, Humor, Literature, Medical, Military, Minnesota, Music, Nature, Photography, Science, Sea, Sports, Technical, Travel, Westerns, Wisconsin.

Author Specialties: Hamlin Garland.

Mail/Telephone Orders; Credit Cards: Both; self addressed stamped envelope; no credit cards.
Business Hours: Monday through Saturday 10:00 AM - 5:00 PM; shorter Winter hours.
Parking Facilities: Street; no problem.
Special Features: Search service.
Collections/Individual Items Purchased: Both.

558
Midway Bookstore, Inc.
1579 University Avenue
St. Paul, Minnesota 55104 (612) 644-7605

The bookstore has a general stock of thousands of out-of-print hardbound, paperback, and rare editions. The owners boast of having the "complete" used bookstore, as they also stock new and collector comics, science fiction pulps, and thousands of vintage magazines in the lower level. The shop also specializes in illustrated books, science fiction, and books about books. It contains approximately 3,000 square feet of space.

How to Get There: Coming from downtown St. Paul drive 4 miles west on I-94. Exit on Snelling Avenue; go north two blocks. Coming from downtown Minneapolis drive 5 miles east on I-94. Exit on Snelling Avenue; go north two blocks. The bookstore is at the corner of University and Snelling Avenues.

Owner/Biography: Tom and Kathy Stransky.

Year Founded/History of Bookstore: The bookstore was founded in 1965; the present owners bought it in 1980.

Number of Volumes: Several thousand.

Types/Classifications: Hardbound, paperback, magazines, comics, first editions, out-of-print, color plate books.

General Subject Areas: Art, Books About Books, Illustrated Books, New and Collector Comics, Photography, Science Fiction and Fantasy.

Specific Specialties: Illustrators: Arthur Rackham, Dulac, Nielsen Clarke, Robinson, Wyeth. Science fiction: Weird Tales, Arkham House (both in-print and out-of-print titles); Comics: Golden Age Comics, early Marvel and DC comics.

Mail/Telephone Orders; Credit Cards: Both; money orders (include postage) with order. No credit cards.

Business Hours: Monday through Friday 9:00 AM - 9:30 PM; Saturday 9:30 AM - 7:00 PM; Sunday 12:00 Noon - 6:00 PM.

Parking Facilities: Street.

Collections/Individual Items Purchased: Both.

Booksellers' Memberships: James Ford Bell Library Associates; Ampersand Club.

559
North Woods Books
5400 London Road
Duluth, Minnesota 55804 (218) 525-7218

The owners believe that their shop is "another example of book collecting going beyond the limits of sanity." Thousands of books are housed in the owners' residence and are available by appointment only. Storage problems and the weather make a visit in the summer time most desirable. Especially strong are the sporting and Americana sections.

Owner/Biography: Kay and Mark Kilen.

Year Founded/History of Bookstore: 1980.

Number of Volumes: 10,000.

Types/Classifications: Hardbound.

General Subject Areas: Americana, Children's Books (Illustrated), Fishing, Hunting, Lake Superior, Logging, Lumberjacks, Paul Bunyan, Sporting.

Author Specialties: Robert Travers, Sinclair Lewis, Sig Olson.

Mail/Telephone Orders; Credit Cards: Both. No credit cards.

Business Hours: By appointment only, chiefly evenings.

Parking Facilities: Street.
Catalogue: In preparation.
Collections/Individual Items Purchased: Both.

560
Northern Lights Book Shop
103 West Thriol Street
Winona, Minnesota 55987   (507) 454-5838

The Northern Lights Book Shop specializes in hardbound books on Minnesota, the Upper Mississippi River before 1900, maps, atlases, and county and regional histories.
Types/Classifications: Hardbound, first editions, out-of-print, maps, atlases.
General Subject Areas: Minnesota, Regional and County Histories, Upper Mississippi River.
Mail/Telephone Orders; Credit Cards: Mail orders.
Business Hours: By appointment.

561
Once Read
629 South Front
Mankato, Minnesota 56001   (507) 388-8144

Once Read carries mostly paperback stock with a hardcover section devoted to Minnesota history.
How to Get There: The shop is located 2 blocks south of the downtown mall.
Owner/Biography: Mark Hustad.
Year Founded/History of Bookstore: 1977.
Types/Classifications: Paperback, some hardcover.
General Subject Areas: General.
Specific Specialties: Minnesota History.
Author Specialties: Maude Heart Lovelace.
Mail/Telephone Orders; Credit Cards: Check with order. No credit cards.
Business Hours: Monday through Saturday 10:00 AM - 5:00 PM; Monday Evening 6:00 PM - 9:00 PM.
Parking Facilities: Street parking.
Collections/Individual Items Purchased: Individual items only.

562
Rulon-Miller Books
716 North First Street
Minneapolis, Minnesota 55401   (612) 339-5779

Rulon-Miller offers rare and fine books from diverse periods and in diverse fields.
Owner/Biography: Robert Rulon-Miller, Jr.
Year Founded/History of Bookstore: 1969. The company was founded under the name of The Current Company and was originally located in Bristol, Rhode Island. Mr. Rulon-Miller, Jr. purchased the business from his father in the fall of 1983 and the name was changed to Rulon-Miller Books. Barbara Walzer now operates a branch office in Providence, Rhode Island while the main offices are in Minneapolis.
Number of Volumes: 5,000.
Types/Classifications: Rare and fine books, first editions, fine bindings, association copies, press books, signed and presentation copies, limited editions, prints.
General Subject Areas: Americana, Letters, Literature, Manuscripts, Science, Yachting and Sporting.
Specific Specialties: America's Cup Races, Mountaineering, Polar Material, Rhode Island and Minnesota Material, American Literature (19th Century), Early American Science and Technology.
Author Specialties: Herman Melville, Henry David Thoreau, J.D. Salinger, John Fowles, Ian Fleming, Mark Twain, James Fenimore Cooper, Philip Freneau, John Gardner, Alan Brody.
Mail/Telephone Orders; Credit Cards: Both. Visa and Mastercard accepted.

Business Hours: Monday Through Friday 9:00 AM - 4:30 PM.
Parking Facilities: Parking lot.
Catalogue: Published 6 times per year.
Collections/Individual Items Purchased: Both.
Booksellers' Memberships: Antiquarian Booksellers Association of America, International League of Antiquarian Booksellers, Manuscript Society.

563
S & S Books
80 North Wilder
St. Paul, Minnesota 55104   (612) 645-5962

S & S Books is housed in the basement of a residence near the College of St. Thomas. The shelves hold an extensive collection of out-of-print antiquarian science fiction and fantasy, horror, mystery, and detective fiction. Back issues of magazines of the same genre are boxed nearby. Additional items on religion (mostly Catholica), occult, fiction, non-fiction, and computer books are finding their way into the collection. The business is primarily mail order.

Owner/Biography: Jack Sticha and Pat Sticha.
Year Founded/History of Bookstore: 1971.
Number of Volumes: 10,000.
Types/Classifications: Hardbound, paperback, magazines, first editions, antiquarian, signed copies, limited editions.
General Subject Areas: Computers, Detective Fiction, Horror, Mysteries, Occult, Religion, Science Fiction and Fantasy.
Mail/Telephone Orders; Credit Cards: Mail order only. No credit cards.
Special Features: Search service.
Collections/Individual Items Purchased: Both.

MISSISSIPPI

564
Nouveau Rare Books
5005 Meadow Oaks Park Drive
Jackson, Mississippi 39211   (601) 956-9950

The bookstore handles 20th Century first editions. An extensive collection of signed and limited editions in literature, poetry, and drama can be found easily on alphabetically arranged shelves. The general literature specialty is augmented by subspecialties in Southern and women authors. The bookstore contains 400 square feet of space.

How to Get There: The shop is located in the northeast sector of the city of Jackson, Mississippi. It can be reached by turning off Interstate 55 at the Northside Drive Exit. More detailed instructions will be provided by contacting the bookstore by phone or mail.

Owner/Biography: Stephen L. Silberman.

Year Founded/History of Bookstore: 1980.

Number of Volumes: 2,000.

Types/Classifications: Hardbound, paperback originals, broadsides, autographed editions, limited editions, ephemera, magazines (literary and out-of-print), first editions, out-of-print, association copies, press books, presentation copies, signed copies.

General Subject Areas: Modern Literature, Science Fiction and Fantasy, Southern Literature, Women.

Specific Specialties: Black Literature, Fugitives, Eudora Welty, Mississippi Authors, Poetry, English Translations of Foreign Authors.

Author Specialties: Eudora Welty, William Faulkner, James Dickey, Willian Stryon, Katherine Anne Porter, Carson McCullers, Robert Penn Warren, Mississippi Authors.

Other Specialties: Herman Hesse, William Golding, J.R.R. Tolkien, American Expatriates.

Mail/Telephone Orders; Credit Cards: Both. Mail order prepayment if unknown to owner. Visa, Mastercard.

Business Hours: By appointment only.

Parking Facilities: Street.

Special Features: Search service, publishing sideline under logo of Nouveau Press.

Catalogue: Three to five times a year.

Collections/Individual Items Purchased: Both.

565
Old Bookshop
208 North McCrary Road
Columbus, Mississippi 39701   (601) 328-6239

The bookstore strives to keep a neat, well-arranged, and good general stock shop. There are many categories, all alphabetically arranged by author. The store is open part time, and features a search service, special order of new books, and is also open by appointment. It contains 800 square feet of space.

How to Get There: If driving on Highway 82 into Columbus, turn north on McCrary Road. The shop is in the immediate vicinity.

Owner/Biography: Gene and Lynn Gumfory.

Year Founded/History of Bookstore: 1982.

Number of Volumes: 12,000.

Types/Classifications: Hardbound, paperback, magazines, used, out-of-print; some new books.

General Subject Areas: American History, Animals, Biography, Business, Children's Literature, Civil War, Comics, Cookbooks, Gardening, Hobbies, How-To Books, Law, Management, Medicine, Music, Mysteries, Novels, Old South History, Photography, Political, Psychology, Radio Broadcasting, Religion, Science Fiction and Fantasy, Self Motivation, Space, Sports, Travel, Westerns, World History, World War I, World War II.

Specific Specialties: Mississippi.

Mail/Telephone Orders; Credit Cards: Both. Cash with order. Visa, Mastercard.

Business Hours: Thursday through Saturday 11:00 AM - 6:00 PM, or by appointment.

Parking Facilities: Business parking.

Special Features: Search service, special ordering of new books.

Catalogue: Catalogue published.

Collections/Individual Items Purchased: Both.

Booksellers' Memberships: American Booksellers Association; Friends of the Library, Lowndes County.

MISSOURI

566
Adams Books & Hobbies
214 North 8th Street
Columbia, Missouri 65201

(314) 449-6416

The bookstore features a large stock of used books, men's magazines, stamps, coins, and collector supplies. It contains 1,600 square feet of space, plus five warehouses.

Owner/Biography: I. C. Adams, Jr.
Year Founded/History of Bookstore: 1946; same location, same owner for 37 years.
Number of Volumes: 80,000.
Types/Classifications: Hardbound, paperback, magazines, out-of-print.
General Subject Areas: Early Pocket Books, Men's Magazines, Missouri, National Geographic Magazines, Western Americana.
Mail/Telephone Orders; Credit Cards: Both; no credit cards.
Business Hours: Tuesday through Sunday 12:00 Noon - 5:00 PM; closed Monday.
Parking Facilities: Street, public parking.
Special Features: Search service.
Collections/Individual Items Purchased: Both.

567
Becky Thatcher Bookshop
211 Hill Street
Hannibal, Missouri 63401

(314) 221-0822

The Becky Thatcher Bookshop is located in the 1840's home of Laura Hawkins who was the prototype of Becky Thatcher in Mark Twain's classic "The Adventures of Tom Sawyer." Laura's house, which is listed in the National Register of Historic Places, faces Hill Street and just across that street is the home of Sam Clemens who became the celebrated author, Mark Twain. It is fitting that the bookshop inside Laura's house contains what is probably the single largest collection of books by and about Mark Twain of any place in the United States. Not only is it famous for its collection of Mark Twain books, new and used, but it also carries a large selection of general children's books and unusual children's books which are generally thought to be hard to find. The bookshop also contains collections of regional cookbooks, Americana, nostalgia, and many volumes on crafts and handwork. Up the narrow stairway, one can view a parlor and bedroom which have been restored as they might have been when little Laura Hawkins lived here.

Owner/Biography: Charles P. Anton III and Leroy S. Richardson.
Year Founded/History of Bookstore: 1949. The Becky Thatcher Bookstore was founded by John A. Winkler to provide books for and about Mark Twain to the many visitors to the Mark Twain Boyhood Home and the Mark Twain Museum. It has been in the same location since its inception. Mr. Winkler sold the bookstore to the present owners in 1974. The bookstore occupies 995 square feet of space.
Number of Volumes: 5,993.
Types/Classifications: Hardbound, paperback, prints, maps, first editions, out-of-print, signed copies.
General Subject Areas: Americana, Biography, Children's Literature.
Specific Specialties: Mark Twain.
Mail/Telephone Orders; Credit Cards: Both. Mail orders accepted on book price plus postage basis, normally prepaid before shipping. No credit cards.
Business Hours: Seven days per week 8:00 AM - 5:00 PM.
Parking Facilities: Public and street parking.
Collections/Individual Items Purchased: Individual items only.

568
Cramer Book Store
Box 7235
Kansas City, Missouri 64113

Formerly a retail antiquarian bookstore, the business is now mail order only. The books are shelved in a warehouse and sold largely by quotes and correspondence. The establishment occupies 5,000 square feet of space.

Owner/Biography: Terence W. Cassidy. Mr. Cassidy has over 25 years' experience in the antiquarian book trade and work as a librarian in acquisitions and cataloguing specialties.

Year Founded/History of Bookstore: 1884. The bookstore was established July 22, 1884 at 1321 Grand Avenue in Kansas City, Missouri where it remained, with a brief exception, until April 1973. There, the business was a true "store" and filled a four-story loft building. If legends are to be believed, it held as many as 500,000 volumes during its heydays into the 1920's. A gradual sell-off of stock, coupled with "lack of ability to secure good general material for restocking" reduced the size to about 50,000 volumes at the time the retail store was closed in 1973.

Number of Volumes: 6,000.

Types/Classifications: Non-fiction material in all forms, out-of-print, antiquarian, old postcards.

General Subject Areas: Airships, Dirigibles, Kansas City, Street Railways, Zeppelins.

Specific Specialties: Horse, cable, steam, or electric powered street railways; early material of Kansas City, especially views and street guides.

Author Specialties: Charles B. Fairchild, George Francis Train.

Other Specialties: Street Railway Gazette, Electric Railway Gazette, Interurban Railway Journal, Street Railway Review, Electric Railway Review, Street Railway Journal (1884-1900).

Mail/Telephone Orders; Credit Cards: Mail orders only. No credit cards.

Collections/Individual Items Purchased: Both.

569
D. Halloran - Books
7629 Wydown Boulevard
St. Louis, Missouri 63105   (314) 863-1690

D. Halloran - Books deals in out-of-print, scarce, and rare books with sporting books a specialty, generally hunting, big game, and fishing.

How to Get There: The store can be reached easily from Highway 40. Take Hanley Road exit north to Wydown Boulevard, 1/2 block east of Hanley on north side of street.

Owner/Biography: Donne S. Halloran.

Year Founded/History of Bookstore: 1977. The store is an outgrowth of book scouting for a New York rare book dealer.

Number of Volumes: Varies greatly.

Types/Classifications: Hardbound, autographs, some pamphlets, first editions, fine bindings, out-of-print, association copies, press books, signed copies, presentation copies, limited editions, color plate books, leatherbound sets.

General Subject Areas: Americana, Children's Literature, Missouriana, Private Press Books, St. Louis.

Specific Specialties: Derrydale Press.

Mail/Telephone Orders; Credit Cards: Both. Cash with order. No credit cards.

Business Hours: Seven days per week 8:00 AM - 8:00 PM.

Parking Facilities: Public parking lot, street parking.

Special Features: Appraisals of libraries, prints, maps, etc. for banks, estates, and private parties for insurance purposes.

Collections/Individual Items Purchased: Both.

Miscellaneous: Sold only to the trade by appointment; must be recognized dealer, but D. Halloran will buy from anyone at anytime; will sell to anyone if sales tax is not involved; will travel for collections.

570
David R. Spivey
1708 West 45th Avenue
Kansas City, Missouri 66103   (816) 531-6088

This shop is situated with a group of small specialty stores, i.e. antiques, etc. It occupies 400 square feet of space.

How to Get There: The bookstore is located seven blocks west of the Country Club Plaza in the State Line Antiques Center.

Owner/Biography: David R. Spivey. Mr. Spivey is a dealer in maps, prints, and books.

Year Founded/History of Bookstore: 1978.

Number of Volumes: 2,500.

Types/Classifications: Hardbound, first editions, fine bindings, out-of-print, association copies, press books, signed copies, presentation copies, limited editions, color plate books.

General Subject Areas: Books About Books, Cookbooks, Western Americana.

Specific Specialties: Maps of America; Bird prints by George Catlin, Karl Bodmer, George C. Bingham.

Mail/Telephone Orders; Credit Cards: Both.

Business Hours: Monday through Saturday 10:00 AM - 5:00 PM.

Collections/Individual Items Purchased: Both.

Booksellers' Memberships: American Historical Print Collectors Society.

571
Glenn Books, Inc.
1227 Baltimore
Kansas City, Missouri 64105   (816) 842-9777

The owner describes her bookstore as " a typical old English Bookstore!" This common exclamation means in translation: "Enchanting, full of nooks and crannies, absolutely stuffed with books of every kind, with heavy emphasis on fine, old and rare, but including thousands of well-selected secondhand books. Subject areas are just about anything except computers, law, and textbooks - although there are some even in those subjects."

How to Get There: Located in downtown Kansas City, the bookstore is across the street from the Radisson-Muehlebach Hotel.

Owner/Biography: Ardis L. Glenn.

Year Founded/History of Bookstore: 1933.

Number of Volumes: 15,000.

Types/Classifications: Hardbound, prints, illuminated manuscripts, objets d'art, first editions, fine bindings, out-of-print, association copies, private press books, signed copies, presentation copies, limited editions, color plate books, rare, fine printing.

General Subject Areas: Americana, Ancient History, Anthropology, Archaeology, Art, Autobiography, Biography, Books About Books, Calligraphy, Children's Books, Civil War, Classics, Crafts, History, Literature, Music, Natural History, Philosophy, Photography, Printing, Psychology, Reference, Religion, Science, Travel, United States History, Western Americana.

Specific Specialties: Western Americana.

Mail/Telephone Orders; Credit Cards: Both. Cash with first order except for institutions, established customers, or references from ABAA colleague(s). Visa and Mastercard accepted.

Business Hours: Tuesday through Friday 11:00 AM - 5:30 PM; Saturday 11:00 AM - 4:00 PM; also by appointment; closed Monday.

Parking Facilities: Street parking; business parking lot.

Catalogue: Published 4 to 5 times per year.

Collections/Individual Items Purchased: Both.

Booksellers' Memberships: Antiquarian Booksellers Association of America, American Booksellers Association, Bibliographical Society of America, Manuscript Society of America.

Miscellaneous: The staff of this bookstore delights in infecting neophyte collectors with their enthusiasm for book collecting; no question is considered stupid or out of line; be preprared for a delightful experience.

572
R. Dunaway, Bookseller
6138 Delmar Boulevard
St. Louis, Missouri 63112

(314) 725-1581

This is a shop with general stock and an emphasis on literature and history. It occupies 660 square feet of space.

Owner/Biography: Reginald P. Dunaway.
Year Founded/History of Bookstore: 1965.
Number of Volumes: 50,000.
Types/Classifications: Hardbound, paperback, magazines, broadsides, autographs, ephemera, first editions, fine bindings, out-of-print, association copies, press books, signed copies, presentation copies, limited editions, color plate books.
General Subject Areas: General.
Mail/Telephone Orders; Credit Cards: Both. Check must accompany order. No credit cards.
Business Hours: Monday through Saturday 10:00 AM - 5:00 PM.
Parking Facilities: Street parking.
Catalogue: Published 10 times per year.
Collections/Individual Items Purchased: Both.
Booksellers' Memberships: Antiquarian Booksellers Association of America.

573
Readmore Books
3607 Meramec
St. Louis, Missouri 63116

(314) 352-3769

Readmore Books has a little bit of just about everything including both paperbacks and hardbound. The selection ranges from novels to technical and from current to first editions. All stock is well categorized. The shop occupies 750 square feet of space.

How to Get There: The shop is situated in south St. Louis, just west of South Grand Avenue.
Owner/Biography: Ed Fix. Mr. Fix is a former teacher and bookseller for two major publishing companies.
Year Founded/History of Bookstore: 1978.
Number of Volumes: 10,000.
Types/Classifications: Hardbound, paperback, first editions, out-of-print, signed copies.
General Subject Areas: General.
Mail/Telephone Orders; Credit Cards: Both. No credit cards.
Business Hours: Monday through Saturday 9:00 AM - 4:00 PM.
Parking Facilities: Street parking.
Special Features: Search service.
Collections/Individual Items Purchased: Individual items only.

574
Shirley's Old Book Shop
1948-G South Glenstone
Springfield, Missouri 65804

(417) 882-3734

The bookstore is small but packed with used books; no magazines except for a few foreign language copies kept primarily for college students. The fiction (except for children's literature) is alphabetized by author on the shelves; everything else is categorized by subject.

How to Get There: The bookstore is located in the Glenstone Plaza Shopping Center which lies on the east side of Glenstone Avenue (business highway 65) and which extends south from the corner of Sunshine. The shopping center is in the shape of an upsidedown U, and although the bookstore carries a Glenstone address, it does not face the avenue; instead, it is located on the south arm of the Plaza, close to the east end.
Owner/Biography: Sherlu R. Walpole.

Year Founded/History of Bookstore: Founded in January 1980 by Shirley Garrett who sold the bookstore to Ms. Walpole in August 1981, the bookstore is still in the original location.

Types/Classifications: Hardbound and paperback almost exclusively. Out-of-print hardbound primarily; however, through search service, special requests are filled for all types of books, including first editions.

General Subject Areas: General.

Specific Specialties: Since the change of ownership three years ago, every effort has been made to broaden the base of stock so that if a specific title is not available, another volume written along the same lines can be suggested, whatever the topic.

Other Specialties: A small but growing section of foreign language titles.

Mail/Telephone Orders; Credit Cards: Both; payment in advance; all items returnable; no credit cards.

Business Hours: Monday and Friday 10:00 AM - 6:00 PM; Tuesday through Thursday 10:00 AM - 5:00 PM; Saturday 10:00 AM - 3:30 PM.

Parking Facilities: Free parking in front of the door.

Special Features: Search service is the speciality.

Collections/Individual Items Purchased: Both.

575

Swiss Village Book Store
711 North First Street
Laclede's Landing
St. Louis, Missouri 63102

(314) 231-2782

This bookstore is a stone's throw north of the Jefferson Memorial Arch. The store, located in a restored old tobacco warehouse, features many antiques as well as new and antiquarian books. Another Swiss Village Book Store is located in Highland, Illinois.

Owner/Biography: Elaine Stratton. Ms. Stratton is a teacher, librarian, writer, and oral historian.

Year Founded/History of Bookstore: 1978.

Number of Volumes: 4,000.

Types/Classifications: Hardbound, autographs, ephemera, first editions, out-of-print, signed copies, limited editions.

General Subject Areas: Children's Books, Cookbooks, History, Mississippi River History, Victorian Books, Women Authors, Women's Biography, Women's Studies.

Specific Specialties: Abraham Lincoln.

Author Specialties: Mark Twain.

Mail/Telephone Orders; Credit Cards: Both. American Express, Visa, Mastercard accepted.

Business Hours: Seven days a week.

Parking Facilities: Ample parking.

Catalogue: Published every 2 or 3 months.

Collections/Individual Items Purchased: Individual items; collections sometimes.

Miscellaneous: Many customers claim that the Swiss Village Bookstore is the most interesting they have ever visited.

576

Westport Bookstore
14 Westport Road
Kansas City, Missouri 64111

(816) 931-9822

This is a general used bookstore, with good, well organized stock. It contains 2,500 square feet of space.

How to Get There: The bookstore is located in midtown Kansas City, between Crown Center and The Plaza.

Owner/Biography: Jane Gilbreath.

Year Founded/History of Bookstore: 1965.

Number of Volumes: 20,000.

Types/Classifications: General used stock.

General Subject Areas: General.

Business Hours: Monday through Saturday 10:00 AM - 6:00 PM.
Parking Facilities: On the street and in lot on the side of the building.
Collections/Individual Items Purchased: Both.

577
William J. Cassidy
109 East 65th Street
Kansas City, Missouri 64113　　　　　　　　　　　　　　　　(816) 361-4271

The bookstore is located in a warehouse with 2,000 square feet of space. It is clean, well-lighted, and comfortable. Visits are by appointment only.

How to Get There: Telephone for directions.
Owner/Biography: William J. Cassidy.
Year Founded/History of Bookstore: 1953.
Number of Volumes: 15,000.
Types/Classifications: Hardbound, paperback, ephemera.
General Subject Areas: Dance, Economics.
Mail/Telephone Orders; Credit Cards: Both. Required for mail orders: author, title, publisher, date. No credit cards.
Business Hours: By appointment only.
Parking Facilities: Business parking lot.
Special Features: Search service.
Catalogue: Published annually.
Collections/Individual Items Purchased: Both.
Booksellers' Memberships: Antiquarian Booksellers Association of America, International League of Antiquarian Booksellers.

MONTANA

578
Bird's Nest Books
136 East Broadway
P.O. Box 8809
Missoula, Montana 59807

(406) 721-1125

Bird's Nest Books features a large stock of general and out-of-print books.
Owner/Biography: Betty R. Anderson.
Number of Volumes: 20,000.
Types/Classifications: Hardbound, paperbound, out-of-print.
General Subject Areas: General, Western Americana.
Specific Specialties: Montana.
Author Specialties: A.B. Guthrie, Jr., Dorothy M. Johnson, B.M. Bower, Mildred Walker, James W. Schultz, Frank B. Linderman, George B. Grinnell.
Mail/Telephone Orders; Credit Cards: Both. Visa and Mastercard accepted.
Parking Facilities: Stree parking, public parking lot in back of building.
Special Features: Search service.
Catalogue: Published 1 or 2 times per year.
Collections/Individual Items Purchased: Both.

579
Book Exchange
Holiday Village Shopping Center
Missoula, Montana 59801

(406) 728-6342

The Book Exchange is organized along the lines of a new bookstore with distinct subject categories neatly organized to make browsing easy and pleasurable. The stock occupies 1,200 square feet of space.
How to Get There: Turn off Highway 90 onto Highway 93-S. Holiday Village Shopping Center is in the middle of newer Missoula.
Owner/Biography: Rebecca Haddad, Nabil Haddad, Fouad Haddad, Fadwa Haddad. Rebecca Haddad is a former university and public librarian and Nabil Haddad is a former university professor.
Year Founded/History of Bookstore: 1979. The bookstore was established at its current location.
Number of Volumes: 20,000.
Types/Classifications: Hardbound, paperback, back issues of selected magazines, new and collectible comics, sheet music, out-of-print.
General Subject Areas: Americana, Children's Books, Classics, General, Historical Fiction, Mysteries, Romances, Science Fiction and Fantasy, Westerns.
Specific Specialties: Montana, Northwest Americana.
Author Specialties: Dorothy Johnson, A. B. Guthrie, Jr.
Mail/Telephone Orders; Credit Cards: No telephone orders. Send self addressed stamped envelope with mail orders. No credit cards.
Business Hours: Monday through Saturday 9:00 AM - 9:00 PM; Sunday 10:00 AM - 7:00 PM.
Parking Facilities: Business parking lot.
Collections/Individual Items Purchased: Both.

580
Jane Graham
528 Dell Place
Bozeman, Montana 59715 (406) 587-5001

Jane Graham specializes in books relating to Montana and the West including cattle items. The business is operated by mail order and appointment only.

How to Get There: Call in advance for an appointment and directions will be given.

Owner/Biography: Jane Graham. Ms. Graham was a retail bookseller from 1950 to 1960, a librarian from 1960 to 1972, a used book dealer from 1972 to 1978, and since 1978 has been a specialist antiquarian bookseller.

Year Founded/History of Bookstore: Founded in 1974 as Sage Book Store.

Number of Volumes: 300.

Types/Classifications: Hardbound, first editions, fine bindings, out-of-print, association copies, signed copies, presentation copies, limited editions, color plate books.

General Subject Areas: Cattle, Montana and the West.

Specific Specialties: Pacific Northwest.

Author Specialties: A.B. Guthrie, Jr.

Mail/Telephone Orders; Credit Cards: Both. No credit cards.

Business Hours: By appointment only.

Parking Facilities: Street.

Special Features: Search service is a specialty. Coffee, tea, and sherry served.

Catalogue: Published irregularly.

Collections/Individual Items Purchased: Both.

581
Sidneys Used Books
319 East Broadway
Missoula, Montana 59802 (406) 543-5343

The bookstore is housed in an old apartment building built in 1911. The books are in two of the former bedrooms and the former parlor. The store is named for Sidney, the owner's black cat-in-residence who came with the store. The shop's specialty is the liberal arts and material of local interest. It contains 1,500 square feet of space.

How to Get There: The shop is located in the third block east of Missoula's central downtown intersection. From Route I-90 take any of the three Missoula Exits to Broadway.

Owner/Biography: Carol Stem, owner, is originally from Florida, and is a graduate of the University of Florida. She was a newspaper and magazine writer, and continues to freelance. Ms. Stem moved to Montana in 1976.

Year Founded/History of Bookstore: The business was founded in 1978 in Helena, Montana as a small paperback exchange. The present owner bought it in 1979 and moved it to the current location in 1982.

Number of Volumes: 10,000.

Types/Classifications: Hardbound, paperback, ephemera, comic books, baseball cards, non-sports cards, post cards, some first editions, signed copies (by Montana authors).

General Subject Areas: Adventure, Biography, Classics, Collected Works, Contemporary Literature, Cooking, Detective Fiction, Drama, Environment, Erotica, Essays, Gardening, History, Humor, Juvenile, Literary Women, Montana History, Nature, Nostalgia, Philosophy, Poetry, Psychology, Religion, Science, Science Fiction and Fantasy, Sociology, Sporting, Technical, True Crime, Western Americana.

Specific Specialties: Out-of-print Masonic History and Reference.

Author Specialties: A.B. Guthrie, Jr., Dorothy M. Johnson, Montana Authors.

Other Specialties: Foreign Language Books.

Mail/Telephone Orders; Credit Cards: Both; payment in advance. No credit cards.

Business Hours: Monday through Saturday 10:00 AM - 5:00 PM.

Parking Facilities: Street.

Special Features: Search service.

Collections/Individual Items Purchased: Individual items only.

582
Thomas Minckler Historic Books & Art
Suite 221
111 North 30th Street
Billings, Montana 59101   (406) 245-2969

   The bookstore describes itself as having one of the best inventories of books about the U.S. West. The shop contains 600 square feet of space.
   Year Founded/History of Bookstore: 1975.
   Number of Volumes: 3,000.
   Types/Classifications: Hardbound, autographs, maps, ephemera, first editions, out-of-print, signed copies, limited editions, newspapers.
   General Subject Areas: Western Americana.
   Specific Specialties: Lewis and Clark, Fur Trade, Cattle Trade, American Indians, Military, Yellowstone National Park, Art.
   Author Specialties: Will James, F. B. Linderman, G. B. Grinnell.
   Mail/Telephone Orders; Credit Cards: Both. No credit cards.
   Business Hours: Daily 10:00 AM - 4:00 PM.
   Parking Facilities: Street and parking garage.
   Special Features: Preparation of bibliography on Montana.
   Catalogue: Catalogue published.
   Collections/Individual Items Purchased: Both.

NEBRASKA

583
Long's Book Store
905 O Street
Lincoln, Nebraska 68508   (402) 474-4697

This is a large bookstore, with 4,000 square feet of space and 150,000 volumes covering all fields.
Owner/Biography: Ernest G. Long.
Year Founded/History of Bookstore: The shop was founded in 1914 as "Long's College Book Store."
Number of Volumes: 150,000.
Types/Classifications: Hardbound, paperback, all general classifications.
General Subject Areas: General.
Mail/Telephone Orders; Credit Cards: Both; self addressed envelope; Visa, Mastercard.
Business Hours: Weekdays 9:00 AM - 5:00 PM.
Parking Facilities: Street.
Collections/Individual Items Purchased: Both.

584
Mostly Books
1025 South 10th Street
Omaha, Nebraska 68108   (402) 345-0999

The bookstore features rare, scholarly, and out-of-print items only. It includes no paperbacks. The building housing the shop is being renovated, and when it is completed there will be 4,000 square feet of space.
Owner/Biography: Roger O'Connor.
Year Founded/History of Bookstore: The present building was purchased three years ago; the main floor and the basement are now completely renovated, and work is progressing on the upstairs.
Number of Volumes: 40,000.
Types/Classifications: Rare, scholarly, out-of-print hardback only; no paperback; first editions, fine bindings, association copies, press books, signed copies, presentation copies, limited editions, color plate books.
General Subject Areas: Americana, Biography, Children's Books, History, Science Fiction and Fantasy.
Specific Specialties: American West, Nebraska, Midwestern History, History.
Author Specialties: Loren Eiseley, John G. Neilhardt, Willa Cather, Mari Sandoz, Wright Morris.
Mail/Telephone Orders; Credit Cards: Both; no credit cards, but personal checks welcome.
Business Hours: Monday through Saturday 11:00 AM - 5:00 PM, and by appointment.
Parking Facilities: Business parking lot, public parking lot, street parking.
Catalogue: Quarterly.
Collections/Individual Items Purchased: Both.

NEVADA

585
Book Stop III
3732 East Flamingo
Las Vegas, Nevada 89121

(702) 456-4858

This bookstore carries general used and out-of-print stock covering most categories. The establishment occupies 1,000 square feet of space.

How to Get There: Located in the Flamingo Sandhill Shopping Center.
Owner/Biography: Gini Segedi.
Year Founded/History of Bookstore: 1973.
Types/Classifications: Hardbound, paperback.
General Subject Areas: General.
Mail/Telephone Orders; Credit Cards: Mail orders only. Visa and Mastercard accepted.
Business Hours: Daily 11:00 AM - 7:00 PM.
Parking Facilities: Business parking lot.
Special Features: Search service; appraisals.
Collections/Individual Items Purchased: Both.

586
Gambler's Book Shop
630 South 11th Street
Las Vegas, Nevada 89101

(702) 382-7555

The Gambler's Book Shop is housed in a 5,000 square foot building and carries a stock of new and out-of-print hardbound and paperback books related to gambling. The store has 15 subcategories of gambling, each with its own shelf area, plus 2,000 used books relating to gambling and organized crime. There are more than 125 in-print titles in the areas of horse race handicapping and casino wagering, more than 60 picture books with a gambling theme, and 50 titles for the sports bettor, with separate shelving for those interested in baseball, football, or basketball. There are sections for the person interested in the sociology, psychology, biographical, or historical aspects of gambling and a section for the antique slot or coin-operated antique collector. Other sections cover books on general card games, poker, backgammon, bridge, magic, dog racing, and probabilities.

How to Get There: Most taxi drivers in Las Vegas know where the Gambler's Book Club is located, but "South 11th Street and Garces, just off Charleston Boulevard" is as specific as you can get in directions, but add "right behind the Minit-Lube" for good measure. There is a large sign on the roof of the book shop displaying the biggest pair of red dice in town. If one is coming from the downtown area, go down Fremont Street and make a right on South 11th Street and continue until reaching Garces.

Owner/Biography: John and Edna Luckman. John is a former dealer and floorman at several Las Vegas Strip casinos, including the Tropicana and Caesars Palace, who turned a hobby into a business and is now considered one of the most authoritative individuals in the bookselling-publishing business on the subject of gambling. Mrs. Luckman has a background in accounting and is considered as knowledgeable as her husband on all in-print and out-of-print books on the subject of gambling. Both hail from Skokie, Illinois and arrived in Las Vegas in the 1950's via Santa Monica, California.

Year Founded/History of Bookstore: 1964. Originally located at 8th and Charleston, the business began a small walk-in operation where customers could see where they had been ordering by mail. It also offered people a chance to get together and discuss, argue, and exchange ideas about various systems and methods of gambling. Thus the alternate name by which the business is also known was formulated: The Gambler's Book Club.

Types/Classifications: Hardbound, paperbound, some magazines and newsletters, first editions, out-of-print.

General Subject Areas: Gambling, Magic, Organized Crime.

Specific Specialties: How-To Books (how to win, how to develop a method of beating particular games, history of various games of chance and how the rules and format evolved over the years, how people have tried to beat the games or how they failed).

Mail/Telephone Orders; Credit Cards: Both. Telephone orders on new books only. On used books, customer must visit store to pick out what is available; holdings change by the day. Visa and Mastercard accepted.

Business Hours: Monday through Saturday 9:00 AM - 5:00 PM.

Parking Facilities: Street parking; off-street parking for 25 cars.

Catalogue: Published annually (by January 15).

Collections/Individual Items Purchased: Both.

Booksellers' Memberships: American Booksellers Association.

Miscellaneous: The Gambler's Book Shop mails out 20,000 to 30,000 free catalogues a year in the U.S. and overseas (first class in U.S.; overseas airmail). There is a toll-free number for catalogue requests: (800) 634-6243; call from 9:00 AM - 5:00 PM Pacific time Monday through Saturday.

587
Gundy's Book World
1442 East Charleston Boulevard
Las Vegas, Nevada 89104   (702) 385-6043

Gundy's Book World carries a general stock of used and antiquarian books plus some magazines. Specialties include organized crime, sports, gambling, religions, and fiction. The store occupies 1,000 square feet of space.

How to Get There: The bookstore is located two miles from the Las Vegas Strip. It is in downtown Las Vegas, on the east side of town.

Owner/Biography: Sol Levco and Elaine Levco. A former printer and a needlepointer combined to make one happy used bookstore.

Year Founded/History of Bookstore: 1977.

Number of Volumes: 10,000.

Types/Classifications: Hardbound, paperback, magazines, broadsides, autographs, ephemera, first editions, out-of-print, signed copies.

General Subject Areas: General.

Mail/Telephone Orders; Credit Cards: Both. C.O.D. Telephone orders will be held until payment received. Visa and Mastercard accepted.

Business Hours: Monday through Friday 10:00 AM - 5:30 PM; Saturday 10:00 AM - 3:00 PM; closed Sunday.

Parking Facilities: Business parking lot.

Collections/Individual Items Purchased: Both.

NEW HAMPSHIRE

588
Annie's Book Swap
493 Amherst Street
Nashua, New Hampshire 03060   (603) 882-9178

    See ANNIE'S BOOK SWAP INC., Westborough, MA.

589
Annie's Book Swap
122 West Broadway
Londonderry, New Hampshire 03053   (603) 434-5363

    See ANNIE'S BOOK SWAP INC., Westborough, MA.

590
Annie's Book Swap
264 Mammouth Road
Manchester, New Hampshire 03103   (603) 622-5526

    See ANNIE'S BOOK SWAP INC., Westborough, MA.

591
Annie's Book Swap
821 Layfayette Road
Hampton, New Hampshire 03842   (603) 926-8696

    See ANNIE'S BOOK SWAP INC., Westborough, MA.

592
Antiquarian Old Book Store
1070 Lafayette Road (U.S. Route 1)
Portsmouth, New Hampshire 03801   (603) 436-7250

The bookstore specializes in wholesale, large bulk lots and collections transactions. However, it also has a very large volume of neatly organized hardbound books on its shelves and a large volume of paperbacks at 50 cents each, for the retail trade. Also, not on display, are 1/4 million periodicals available in wholesale lots only. The bookstore contains 2,200 square feet of space, fully heated, air conditioned, carpeted, lighted, and arranged for easy access.

How to Get There: The bookstore is located next to New England's landmark restaurant, Yoken's Whale Restaurant, 50 miles north of Boston and 50 miles south of Portland, Maine.

Year Founded/History of Bookstore: Founded in 1973, the bookstore has always been under the same ownership. In 1981 it moved to its present location, one mile from the old one and in new, custom built quarters.

Number of Volumes: Hardbound 60,000; paperback 50,000.

Types/Classifications: Hardbound, paperback, magazines, first editions, fine bindings, out-of-print, signed copies.
General Subject Areas: Biography, Erotica, Literature.
Mail/Telephone Orders; Credit Cards: Both. Mail orders must be for over $100 per transaction. Visa and Mastercard accepted.
Business Hours: Monday through Saturday 10:00 AM - 6:00 PM.
Parking Facilities: Business parking lot.
Collections/Individual Items Purchased: Collections only.

593
Barn Loft Bookshop
96 Woodland Avenue
Laconia, New Hampshire 03246   (603) 524-4839

The Barn Loft Bookshop is in an upstairs loft portion of a barn and is fairly well hidden by trees from the street and from the world. The barn is surrounded by trees and a vegetable garden. One of the main attractions of the Barn Loft Bookshop is an overhanging porch facing the south which serves as a marvelous reading or sunbathing spot for all who can take a few extra minutes from a busy day. The shop occupies 480 square feet.
How to Get There: From Laconica High School on Union Avenue go north towards Lakeport, take first right (Lyman Street), next right (Butler Street), and left onto Woodland Avenue.
Owner/Biography: Lee Burt.
Year Founded/History of Bookstore: 1979.
Number of Volumes: 8,000.
Types/Classifications: Hardbound, some magazines and ephemera. Main interest is Children's Books - picture, color plate, and first editions up to and including modern authors and illustrators.
General Subject Areas: General.
Specific Specialties: Children's Literature, New England, New Hampshire, White Mountains.
Mail/Telephone Orders; Credit Cards: Both. No credit cards.
Business Hours: By appointment or chance.
Parking Facilities: Parking in yard.
Collections/Individual Items Purchased: Both.
Booksellers' Memberships: New Hampshire Antiquarian Booksellers Association.

594
Celtic Cross Books
Route 12
Westmoreland, New Hampshire 03467   (603) 399-4342

See HURLEY BOOKS, Westmoreland, New Hampshire.

595
Evelyn Clement (Dealer in Old Books)
45 Central Street
Franklin, New Hampshire 03235   (603) 934-5496

The bookstore is located in a private residence, with overflow stock housed in an adjacent barn. The collection is segregated by subject: in the house, the first room at the top of the stairs includes all technical and related subjects; in the second room, New England and especially the White Mountains, are featured. Upstairs in the nearby barn is housed the general stock such as mystery, science fiction, metaphysics, biography, and more.
How to Get There: Traveling west through the small city of Franklin, on Central Street, the bookstore is the fourth house after the high school, on the same side. There is a sign worded "Books" under the bay window.

Owner/Biography: Evelyn Clement.
Types/Classifications: Hardbound.
General Subject Areas: General, New Hampshire, White Mountains.
Specific Specialties: Early Technical which includes Gas and Steam Engines, Metallurgy, Logging, Automotive, Railroads, Hydro-Electric Power, Music Boxes, Marine and Nautical, Electricity.
Mail/Telephone Orders; Credit Cards: Both.
Business Hours: There are no established business hours; it is suggested that the visitor call first.
Collections/Individual Items Purchased: Both.
Booksellers' Memberships: New Hampshire Antiquarian Booksellers Association.

596
Homestead Bookshop
Route 101
P.O. Box 90
Marlborough, New Hampshire 03455   (603) 876-4213

The Homestead Bookshop is an artistically restored old woolen mill building. Inside are wide aisles with well organized general stock. There is an especially large collection of old fiction and juvenile books.
How to Get There: Located on New Hampshire Route 101, the shop is just east of the village of Marlborough; take Exit 3 (Route 9) east of I-91.
Owner/Biography: Harry, Connie, and Robert Kenney.
Year Founded/History of Bookstore: 1970.
Number of Volumes: 60,000.
Types/Classifications: Hardbound, paperback, magazines, ephemera, first editions, fine bindings, sheet music, illustrated books.
General Subject Areas: Americana, Biography, Children's Literature, History, Marine, Religion.
Mail/Telephone Orders; Credit Cards: Both. Send stamped self-addressed envelope with order. No credit cards.
Business Hours: Monday through Friday 9:00 AM - 5:00 PM; Saturday 9:00 AM - 4:30 PM.
Parking Facilities: Business parking lot.
Special Features: Informal search service.
Collections/Individual Items Purchased: Both.
Booksellers' Memberships: New Hampshire Antiquarian Booksellers Association.

597
Hurley Books/Celtic Cross Books
Route 12
Westmoreland, New Hampshire 03467   (603) 399-4342

Hurley Books specializes in scholarly works in agricultural history, Catholic theology, non-Catholic theology, and books about books. It prints its own catlogues and an occasional miniature book. The shop occupies 1,800 square feet of space.
How to Get There: The shop is located on Route 12 about 200 yards north of Route 63.
Owner/Biography: Henry and Janet Hurley.
Year Founded/History of Bookstore: 1966.
Number of Volumes: 25,000.
Types/Classifications: Hardbound, broadsides, ephemera, out-of-print, press books, miniature books.
General Subject Areas: Agricultural History, Books About Books, Early American Imprints, Protestant Church History, Twentieth Century Catholic Theology.
Specific Specialties: Liturgical History, Christian Mystics, Reformation History, Early Agriculture, Agricultural Magazines and Catalogues.
Other Specialties: Stone and Kimball Publications.
Mail/Telephone Orders; Credit Cards: Both. Payment in advance for new customers. No credit cards.
Business Hours: By chance or appointment.

Parking Facilities: Business parking lot.
Catalogue: Published 6 times per year.
Collections/Individual Items Purchased: Both.
Booksellers' Memberships: Antiquarian Booksellers Association of America, New Hampshire Antiquarian Booksellers Association.

598
John F. Hendsey Bookseller
Route 125
Epping, New Hampshire 03042   (603) 679-2428

Mr. Hendsey deals in antiquarian books in all fields. Visits may be arranged by appointment only.
How to Get There: Directions will be given when calling for an appointment.
Owner/Biography: John F. Hendsey.
Year Founded/History of Bookstore: 1960.
Number of Volumes: 5,000.
Types/Classifications: Hardbound, manuscripts, autographs, maps, first editions.
General Subject Areas: Americana.
Mail/Telephone Orders; Credit Cards: Both. No credit cards.
Business Hours: By appointment only.
Catalogue: Published 2 times per year.
Collections/Individual Items Purchased: Both.
Booksellers' Memberships: Antiquarian Booksellers Association of America, New Hampshire Antiquarian Booksellers Association.

599
Mary Robertson, Books
U.S. Route 3
Meredith, New Hampshire 03253   (603) 279-8750

One approaches the bookstore through the wide doors of a big 200 year old barn with hand hewn timbers and well worn 4 inch thick floorboards. A greeting by darting barnswallows is possible; they nest far overhead. Glass doors in the rear of the barn also open into this unique bookshop where can be found a mixture of old, used, out-of-print, and rare books, along with a selection of new books. Children have a room of their own with shelves of previously owned and loved books as well as new copies of old favorites of all generations. There is about 800 square feet of space in the shop, plus the loft and barn floor.
How to Get There: The bookstore can be found one mile south of Meredith, just past the Parade Road intersection, on the right; four miles north of Weirs Beach, on the left; from I-93 one should take the New Hampton exit from Route 104 and turn right at the Route 3 intersection, then one quarter mile, on the right.
Owner/Biography: Mary Robertson.
Year Founded/History of Bookstore: The bookstore was founded in 1954 as a mail order business; Ms. Robertson then opened a small home-based shop in her village home in 1963. In 1980 the shop was moved to its present location.
Types/Classifications: Hardbound, paperback, magazines, ephemera, prints, maps, sheet music, postcards, needlework designs and transfers.
General Subject Areas: Americana, Animals, Antiques, Art, Biography, Cooking, Crafts, Farming, Gardening, History, Music, Nature, Outdoors, Poetry, Railroads, Religion, Ships, Sports, Theater, Trains, Travel, War.
Specific Specialties: Needlework, Needlepoint, Crewel, Quilts, Crochet, Tatting, Jewelry, Weaving, Stencilling, Woodworking, Stained Glass, Collecting, Dolls, China, Furniture, Metals, Clocks, Price Guides, New Hampshire.
Mail/Telephone Orders; Credit Cards: Both; no credit cards.
Business Hours: Summer: Daily 10:00 AM - 5:00 PM; Spring and Fall: Most Days 12:00 Noon - 4:00 PM, or by appointment.
Parking Facilities: On-site parking.

Collections/Individual Items Purchased: Both.
Booksellers' Memberships: New Hampshire Antiquarian Booksellers Association.

600
Old Almanack Shop
5 South State Street
Concord, New Hampshire 03301 (603) 225-5411

The bookstore is situated in the basement of an old 19th Century brick building. The stock ranges from the 18th to the 20th Century in all subject areas. A large collection of 19th Century prints may be found including original Currier & Ives. There are also maps and ephemera.

How to Get There: The shop is located in downtown Concord, New Hampshire, one block from Main Street, at the corner of Pleasant and South State Streets. It can easily be reached in 60-75 minutes from Boston via I-95, 45 minutes from the coast via Rt. 4, and 60 minutes from Vermont via I-89.

Owner/Biography: Craig B. Holmes.

Year Founded/History of Bookstore: Founded in 1975, the shop has operated at the present location for the past six years. It has recently expanded to add shelf space for 2,000 additional volumes.

Number of Volumes: 10,000.

Types/Classifications: Hardbound, paperback, magazines, broadsides, autographs, ephemera, prints, first editions, fine bindings, out-of-print, association copies, press books, signed copies, presentation copies, limited editions, color plate books.

General Subject Areas: Americana, Biography, British History, Children's Books, Gardening, Greek, Latin, Law, Medicine, Music, Natural History, New England History, Poetry, Religion, Science, Science Fiction and Fantasy, Theater.

Specific Specialties: British Biography, New England Social History, Victorian Bindings.

Author Specialties: Charles Dickens, Henry David Thoreau, Nathaniel Hawthorne, A. Conan Doyle, Robert Frost.

Mail/Telephone Orders; Credit Cards: Both; cash with order; Visa, Mastercard.

Business Hours: Monday through Saturday 10:00 AM - 5:00 PM.

Parking Facilities: Street.

Catalogue: The first catalogue is being published in 1984.

Collections/Individual Items Purchased: Both.

Booksellers' Memberships: New Hampshire Antiquarian Booksellers Association.

601
Stinson House Books
Quincy Road
Rumney Village, New Hampshire 03266 (603) 786-9300

The bookstore consists of nearly 20,000 books shelved in a large barn plus another stock of 2,000 books housed in two rooms in the residence adjacent to the barn. The total area contains 1,600 square feet of space.

How to Get There: The shop is located off I-93 and Route 75, about seven miles west of Plymouth, New Hampshire.

Owner/Biography: George and Ann Kent. Both attended Oberlin College; George is a retired USAF Lt. Colonel.

Year Founded/History of Bookstore: 1962.

Number of Volumes: 20,000.

Types/Classifications: Hardbound, broadsides, ephemera, out-of-print.

General Subject Areas: Americana, New England, New Hampshire.

Specific Specialties: White Mountains (New Hampshire).

Mail/Telephone Orders; Credit Cards: Both. No credit cards.

Business Hours: Generally open year 'round 9:00 AM - 5:00 PM, but if travelling any distance, it is best to call ahead.

Parking Facilities: Residential driveway.

Catalogue: Once per year.
Collections/Individual Items Purchased: Both.
Booksellers' Memberships: Antiquarian Booksellers Association of America; New Hampshire Antiquarian Booksellers Association.
Miscellaneous: The owners serve cold drinks in the Summer, hot coffee during the other seasons.

602
Typographeum Bookshop
Bennington Road
Francestown, New Hampshire 03043

The shop features modern first editions with a special emphasis on English and European literature, books about books, private press publications, and books about music. By appointment only.
How to Get There: Francestown is in southern New Hampshire about twelve miles from Peterborough. The shop is one mile north of the village of Francestown, on Route 47.
Owner/Biography: R.T. Risk.
Year Founded/History of Bookstore: 1976.
Number of Volumes: 2,000.
Types/Classifications: All hardbound with some fine leather bindings, first editions, press books, out-of-print, signed copies, presentation copies, limited editions.
General Subject Areas: Books About Books, Books About Music, English Literature, European Literature.
Specific Specialties: Twentieth Century Literature, British Fiction, European Fiction, Biography, Poetry.
Mail/Telephone Orders; Credit Cards: Mail orders only; no credit cards.
Business Hours: By appointment only. There is no telephone; write for an appointment.
Special Features: The owner of the bookstore operates a private press on the premises.
Catalogue: Four times per year.
Collections/Individual Items Purchased: Both.

603
Village Book Store, Inc.
102 Main Street
Littleton, New Hampshire 03561   (603) 444-5263

Located in the center of downtown Littleton, New Hampshire, the bookstore stocks 35,000 volumes of new books, and has a small but very active New Hampshire and White Mountains antiquarian section. The store contains 4,000 square feet of space.
Owner/Biography: Ned Densmore.
Year Founded/History of Bookstore: 1971.
Number of Volumes: 35,000.
Types/Classifications: Hardbound, out-of-print.
General Subject Areas: New Hampshire, White Mountains (New Hampshire).
Mail/Telephone Orders; Credit Cards: Both. Visa, Mastercard.
Business Hours: Daily during normal business hours; evenings Wednesday through Saturday.
Parking Facilities: Street.
Collections/Individual Items Purchased: Individual items only.

NEW JERSEY

604
Acres Of Books
35 East State Street
Trenton, New Jersey 08608   (609) 392-0459

Situated in a four story building on the Trenton Commons, the bookstore has 300 square feet of space on each floor, for a total of 1,200. The stock is general but with an emphasis on Americana.

How to Get There: The bookstore is in the block between the northbound and southbound streets of Alternate Route I (north to Princeton, south to Philadelphia). It is an eight minute walk from the railroad station.

Owner/Biography: Dr. John A. Muscalus, owner, is a prolific writer of non-fiction who served as special features editor for a monthly periodical. He is a graduate of the University of Pennsylvania.

Year Founded/History of Bookstore: Founded in the late 1890's in Buffalo, New York, the bookstore was named Keel's Bookstore. Under Dr. Muscalus' ownership the name changed to Genesee & Michigan Bookstore, and then was moved to Trenton after several years, taking its present name.

Number of Volumes: 200,000.

Types/Classifications: Hardbound, ephemera, prints, bound early magazines, first editions, out-of-print.

General Subject Areas: Banking, Biography, Bound Periodicals, Children's Literature, Dictionaries, Fiction (Early), Foreign Languages, History, Juvenile Fiction, Literary Annuals (Early), National Geographics, Paper Money, Poetry, Prints, Psychology, Railroads, Sheet Music (1800's to 1950), Street & Smith Paperbacks, Travel.

Specific Specialties: Buffalo, New York, Niagara Frontier, Bank Notes prior to 1866, Works on Paper Money of the World.

Business Hours: There are no designated business hours; it is suggested that the visitor call first.

Parking Facilities: Street and public parking lot.

Special Features: Search service.

Catalogue: Specialized lists issued.

Collections/Individual Items Purchased: Both.

Miscellaneous: Appointments are available.

605
Book Store at Depot Square
8 Depot Square
Englewood, New Jersey 07631   (201) 568-6563

This store is a general antiquarian bookstore with fine, out-of-print, and scarce books in most categories including medicine, cookery, children's literature, Russian history, World War II, and illustrated books. Prices range from $1 to $1,000. There is also an annex containing about 20,000 books. The store carries whatever good books in any category they can purchase from local estates. The shop occupies 1,100 square feet of space.

How to Get There: The bookstore is located 3.5 miles from the George Washington Bridge. From the bridge take Route 4, exit at Grand Avenue in Englewood, left at Palisade Avenue, right into the municipal parking lot before the railroad tracks to the rear of the store.

Owner/Biography: Rita Alexander.

Year Founded/History of Bookstore: 1978. The business was established in Teaneck, New Jersey in 1978 and moved in 1979 to the ground floor of a turn-of-the-century house. There has been no change in ownership.

Number of Volumes: 15,000 plus a barn annex with 20,000 volumes.

Types/Classifications: Hardbound, out-of-print, first editions, illustrated books, leather bound books.

General Subject Areas: Art, Biography, Children's Books, Cookery, Fiction, History, Humor, Medicine, Nature, New Jersey History, Orientalia, Poetry, Space Exploration, Sports, Transportation, Travel, World

War I, World War II.
  Specific Specialties: Alice in Wonderland, Federal Writers Project, Bergen County (New Jersey) History.
  Mail/Telephone Orders; Credit Cards: Both. No credit cards.
  Business Hours: Tuesday through Saturday 10:30 AM - 5:30 PM and by appointment.
  Parking Facilities: Free parking in rear.
  Special Features: Personal search service.
  Collections/Individual Items Purchased: Both.

606
Chatham Bookseller
8 Green Village Road
Madison, New Jersey 07940   (201) 822-1361

  This is a general used bookstore, stocking over 10,000 books in about 75 subject categories. While it has a number of rare books, most of the hardbound books are priced from $3 to $5. It also handles second hand paperbacks in the areas of literary fiction, science fiction and fantasy, and mysteries. The shop has a definite commitment to quality.
  How to Get There: The bookstore is in downtown Madison, New Jersey, not in the town of Chatham, as the name implies. From New York City, the shop can be reached by rail, which lets one off about a block from the shop, or by Lakeland Bus from the N.Y.C. Port Authority Bus Terminal. It is just off Route 24 and can easily be reached by auto.
  Owner/Biography: Frank Deodene, owner, is an ex-librarian, inveterate reader, and has sold books in this store for 15 years.
  Year Founded/History of Bookstore: The business was founded in 1968; the bookstore, in 1970. Originally, the shop was very small, as most of the business was mail order for university libraries. It is now much larger in terms of stock and space (1,200 square feet in the store, and twice that in storage), and does 80 percent of its business directly with the public. It has always been owned by Mr. Deodene at this location.
  Number of Volumes: 10,000 in the store; an additional 20,000 in storage.
  Types/Classifications: Hardbound, paperback, magazines, ephemera, phonograph records, used books.
  General Subject Areas: General.
  Mail/Telephone Orders; Credit Cards: Both; postage paid by the customer; Visa, Mastercard.
  Business Hours: Monday through Saturday 9:00 AM - 5:30 PM.
  Parking Facilities: Street and public parking.
  Special Features: Only good quality used books, and a pleasant atmosphere.
  Collections/Individual Items Purchased: Both.
  Booksellers' Memberships: Antiquarian Booksellers Association of America.

607
Cranbury Book Worm
54 North Main Street
Cranbury, New Jersey 08512   (609) 655-1063

  This book shop is housed in an 1840's Greek Revival style home. Inside the atmosphere is relaxed and friendly with classical music always in the background. Each room is a warren of books and bookcases. The flow of new material into the shop is often visually apparent. The shop occupies 5,000 square feet of space.
  How to Get There: Cranbury is easily reached from Routes 1 and 130 on Exit 8A of the New Jersey Turnpike.
  Owner/Biography: Ralph C. Schremp.
  Year Founded/History of Bookstore: 1974.
  Number of Volumes: 80,000.
  Types/Classifications: Hardbound, paperback, magazines, ephemera, first editions, fine bindings, out-of-print, association copies, press books, signed copies, presentation copies, limited editions, color plate books.
  General Subject Areas: Americana, Art, Biography, Business, Chemistry, Children's Literature, Foreign Language, Humor, Literary Criticism, Mathematics, Music, Natural Science, New Jersey History, Performing Arts, Physics, Plays, Poetry, Religion, Science Fiction and Fantasy, Social Sciences, Sports, Technical, World

History.
Mail/Telephone Orders; Credit Cards: Both. No credit cards.
Business Hours: Monday through Friday 9:00 AM - 8:00 PM; Saturday 9:00 AM - 5:00 PM; Sunday 12:00 Noon - 5:00 PM.
Parking Facilities: Business parking lot.
Collections/Individual Items Purchased: Both.
Booksellers' Memberships: New Jersey Booksellers Association.
Miscellaneous: The shop also carries phonograph records, art, and antiques.

608
Egg Harbor Books
612 White Horse Pike (Route 30)
Egg Harbor, New Jersey 08215 (609) 965-1708

Egg Harbor Books is a general antiquarian bookstore filled to overflowing with a collection of books in all areas.
Owner/Biography: Norman Arrington and William Spangler.
Year Founded/History of Bookstore: 1967. The shop was formerly located in the Atlantic City area, but with the "advent of casinos, was forced to repair to the hinterlands."
Number of Volumes: 50,000.
Types/Classifications: Hardbound, paperback, ephemera.
General Subject Areas: General.
Mail/Telephone Orders; Credit Cards: Both. No credit cards.
Business Hours: Monday through Saturday 11:00 AM - 6:00 PM.
Parking Facilities: Available.
Collections/Individual Items Purchased: Both.
Booksellers' Memberships: Antiquarian Booksellers Association of New Jersey.

609
Elisabeth Woodburn
Booknoll Farm
Hopewell, New Jersey 08525 (609) 466-0888

Elisabeth Woodburn is a dealer in old and new books in the fields of horticulture, landscape gardening, herbs, and early farming. She sells primarily by catalogue but visits may be arranged by appointment.
How to Get There: Call for directions and appointment.
Owner/Biography: Elisabeth Woodburn.
Year Founded/History of Bookstore: 1946.
Number of Volumes: 13,000.
Types/Classifications: Hardbound, ephemera, periodicals, rare, out-of-print, used, new.
General Subject Areas: Agriculture before 1900, Bees, Bibliography, Biography, Cacti and Succulents, Cattle, Ferns, Flora, Flower Arrangement, Grasses and Weeds, Herbs, Horticultural History, Horticulture, Landscape and Garden Design, Language of Flowers, Lilies, Mushrooms, Oriental Gardens, Rock Gardens, Roses, Sheep, Travel, U.S. Seed and Nursery Catalogues, Vegetables, Violets, Wildflowers.
Other Specialties: Preparation of collections on a topic, e.g. Andrew Jackson Downing, U.S. Botany, United States Landscape, American Horticultural History.
Mail/Telephone Orders; Credit Cards: Both. Send request, do not pre-pay; order will be sent with invoice. No credit cards.
Business Hours: Monday through Friday 9:00 AM - 5:00 PM; other hours by appointment.
Parking Facilities: Private parking.
Special Features: Search service.
Catalogue: Published approximately 4 times per year on selected topics.
Collections/Individual Items Purchased: Both.
Booksellers' Memberships: Antiquarian Booksellers Association of America (President, 1982-84), including Mid-Atlantic Chapter.

610
Escargot Books
503 Route 71
Brielle, New Jersey 08730   (201) 528-5955

Escargot Books has a general stock of out-of-print used books plus sheet music, comics, and baseball cards. The shop occupies 1,500 square feet of space.
How to Get There: Call for specific directions.
Year Founded/History of Bookstore: 1979.
Number of Volumes: 10,000.
Types/Classifications: Hardbound, paperback, magazines, sheet music, comics, baseball cards, first editions, fine bindings, out-of-print, association copies, press copies, signed copies, presentation copies, limited editions, color plate books.
General Subject Areas: General.
Mail/Telephone Orders; Credit Cards: Both. American Express, Visa, Mastercard accepted.
Business Hours: Monday through Saturday 10:00 AM - 5:00 PM.
Parking Facilities: Business parking lot.
Collections/Individual Items Purchased: Both.
Booksellers' Memberships: New Jersey Antiquarian Booksellers Association.

611
Frank Michelli Books
45 Halsey Street
Newark, New Jersey 07102   (201) 623-4289

This shop handles mostly out-of-print titles of general and collectible books. It occupies 800 square feet of space.
How to Get There: The bookstore is located in the downtown business section of Newark across the street from Hahnes Department Store.
Owner/Biography: Paul Grippo and Frank Michelli.
Year Founded/History of Bookstore: 1952.
Number of Volumes: 15,000.
Types/Classifications: Hardbound, first editions, out-of-print, limited editions.
General Subject Areas: Americana, Art, Biography, Children's Literature, Cookbooks, History, Mysteries, Travel.
Author Specialties: T.E. Lawrence, J. Frank Dobie, G.A. Henty.
Mail/Telephone Orders; Credit Cards: Both. Cash with order. No credit cards.
Business Hours: By appointment only.
Parking Facilities: Street parking, public parking lot.
Special Features: Search service.

612
Harold R. Nestler
13 Pennington Avenue
Waldwick, New Jersey 07463   (201) 444-7413

Harold R. Nestler deals in antiquarian Americana material. The stock is in a private residence with books on shelves, manuscripts in folders, and pamphlets in drawers. An appointment is absolutely necessary.
How to Get There: Phone ahead for directions.
Owner/Biography: Harold R. Nestler. Mr. Nestler is the compiler of "Bibliography of New York State Communities" published in 1968 with a supplement issued in 1975.
Year Founded/History of Bookstore: 1972.
Number of Volumes: 3,500.
Types/Classifications: Hardbound, pamphlets, manuscripts, autographs, maps, broadsides, rare, out-of-print.

General Subject Areas: Americana.
Specific Specialties: New York State, New Jersey, New England, Pennsylvania, South (U.S.), Revolutionary War (U.S.), Shakers, Early American History, Genealogy.
Mail/Telephone Orders; Credit Cards: Both. Payment with order for new customers. No credit cards.
Business Hours: By appointment only.
Parking Facilities: Street parking.
Catalogue: Published approximately 8 times per year.
Collections/Individual Items Purchased: Both.
Booksellers' Memberships: Antiquarian Booksellllers Association of America.

613
Heinoldt Books
1325 West Central Avenue
Egg Harbor, New Jersey 08215   (609) 965-2284

A famous art critic once desribed his home as a library with living quarters; Heinoldt Books is truly a bookstore with living quarters. Only the bathrooms and kitchen have escaped the invasion of book shelves or cases. The American Scene is the theme of the collection which is broken down into local history by area and subjects such as Indians, American Revolution, etc. All aspects are covered including social, historic, and economic. The red brick ranch house is in the small town of Egg Harbor, 17 miles inland from Atlantic City.
How to Get There: From the north via Garden State Parkway, Exit 44, Pomona. From the west and south, Atlantic Expressway, Exit Egg Harbor City. The house is a few blocks south of Highway 30 and 2 blocks east of Route 50 on the corner of West Central and Buffalo Avenues.
Owner/Biography: Theodore H. Heinoldt and Margaret T. Heinoldt. Ted Heinoldt was with the "New York Sun" for 22 years, then with the "New York World Telegram," remaining with them when merged with the "New York Journal" and "Herald Tribune." When the combination newspaper closed in 1968, he decided to make his avocation a vocation.
Year Founded/History of Bookstore: 1956. Margaret Heinoldt shared her husband's interest in books and started a mail order business which thrived. When Ted joined her in 1968 this was expanded and has grown steadily since.
Number of Volumes: 6,000.
Types/Classifications: Hardbound, pamphlets, first editions, fine bindings, out-of-print.
General Subject Areas: American Revolution, Americana, Civil War and Slavery, Cowboys and the Range, Early Travels, Explorations, Indians, Local History, Mexican War, Transportation, War of 1812, Western Expansion.
Specific Specialties: New Jersey, Pennsylvania, New York, Railroads, Ocean Liners, Western Art, Fur Trade, Gunfighters and Law Men.
Author Specialties: J. Frank Dobie.
Mail/Telephone Orders; Credit Cards: Both. No credit cards.
Business Hours: Around the clock.
Parking Facilities: Driveway and street.
Special Features: Personal service.
Catalogue: Published 3 times per year.
Collections/Individual Items Purchased: Both.
Booksellers' Memberships: Antiquarian Booksellers Association of America, International League of Antiquarian Booksellers.
Miscellaneous: Ted Heinoldt is a hand bookbinder and personally rebinds books.

614
James Cummins Bookseller
Fairmount Road
Pottersville, New Jersey 07929   (201) 439-3803

See JAMES CUMMINS BOOKSELLER, New York, N.Y.

615
Keith Library
The Antique Center, Building 1
217 West Front Street
Red Bank, New Jersey 07701   (201) 741-5331

This is the oldest bookshop in Monmouth County, occupying three 400 square foot stalls of the Antique Center of Red Bank since 1968. The Keith Library is the only book, map, and print collection among a mass of antique dealers. It is the sales outlet of the private library of the Keith family in Britain and America going back several centuries, but its general stock reflects a wide variety of interests. New Jerseyana is a specialty.

How to Get There: Take the Garden State Exit 109 (Red Bank), travel east 1 mile to Shrewsbury Avenue, then north to West Front Street which parallels the Navesink River and is 200 yards from the Molly Pitcher Hotel.

Owner/Biography: Quentin and Sylvia Keith. Mr. Keith is a retired professor of English and Army colonel, writer, editor and publisher, and an expert in Anglo-American affairs. He was educated at Eton and Cambridge.

Year Founded/History of Bookstore: 1953. The first shop was located in the south wing of the Old Mill in Tinton Falls. It was moved to Ballantine's in Red Bank in 1955 and then to its present site in 1967.

Number of Volumes: 8,000.

Types/Classifications: Hardbound, periodicals, autographs, broadsides, letters, prints, maps, newspapers, out-of-print, first editions, fine bindings, press books, association copies, limited editions.

General Subject Areas: Americana, Children's Literature, English Biography, English Literature, Exploration, French Classics, French Literature, German Literature, Greek and Latin Classics, Military, Sea and Sailing, Travel.

Specific Specialties: New Jerseyana, Monmouth and Ocean Counties (New Jersey), Battle of Monmouth, "Worthies of Monmouth": Philip Freneau, George Keith, Harry B. Smith, Lily Langtry, Lewis Morris, Henry Morford.

Author Specialties: D.H. Lawrence, E.M. Forster, Robert Louis Stevenson, John Lloyd Stephens, Edmund Wilson, Henry Morford, Harry Bache Smith, Charles Kingsley, Aphra Behn, Sir Walter Raleigh, John Maynard Keynes, A.N.L. Munby, John Carter, William Burton Todd, Ann Royall.

Other Specialties: Special collection of printed material on "El Dorado" (The Guianas: French, British, Dutch) including original diaries, notebooks, manuscripts; contemporary accounts of the births, marriages, enthronements, and deaths of British monarchs from Victoria to the present.

Mail/Telephone Orders; Credit Cards: Both. Cash with order. Visa and Mastercard accepted.

Business Hours: Monday through Saturday 10:00 AM - 5:00 PM; Sunday 12:00 Noon - 5:00 PM.

Parking Facilities: Business parking lot, street parking.

Special Features: Book appraisals; editing; ghost writing; lecturing; publishing small and limited editions of history, poetry, biography.

Catalogue: Published infrequently.

Collections/Individual Items Purchased: Both.

Miscellaneous: This shop is a prototype antiquarian book shop of the large "antique center" variety found in London, New York, and the larger cities of America and Europe. It is probably one of the first in a suburban area on either side of the Atlantic.

616
Margaret Inman - Books
207 Gorham Avenue
North Cape May, New Jersey 08204   (609) 886-2596

While currently not open to visitors, Margaret Inman - Books has a stock of several thousand used and out-of-print books in many subjects including some foreign language books. It is anticipated that these books will be classified and catalogued in 1984 at which time the issuance of catalogues will begin. Meanwhile, mail inquiries are welcomed and processed.

How to Get There: No current facility open for visitors.

Owner/Biography: Margaret and Joseph Inman.

Year Founded/History of Bookstore: 1975. Margaret Inman - Books was created as a branch of the Book House of Plainfield, New Jersey and Cape May, New Jersey with responsibility for handling requests for out-of-print book searches.

Number of Volumes: 5,000.

Types/Classifications: Hardbound, paperback, magazines, professional journals, some ephemera, first editions, fine bindings, signed copies, color plate and illustrated books, limited editions.

General Subject Areas: General.

Author Specialties: John Steinbeck.

Other Specialties: Foreign language titles.

Mail/Telephone Orders; Credit Cards: Mail orders only. Cash with order; send self-addressed stamped envelope. No credit cards.

Business Hours: Irregular.

Special Features: Search service.

Catalogue: To be published.

Collections/Individual Items Purchased: Both.

617
Old Book Shop

75 Spring Street
Morristown, New Jersey 07960   (201) 538-1210

This is a general bookstore, dealing in out-of-print books with a wide variety of subject matter as well as all types of old books.

How to Get There: Morristown is 30 miles due west of New York City, and is easily reached by car via Routes 287 or 24. Train service (Erie Lackawana) and bus service (N.J. Transit) are regular.

Owner/Biography: Virginia Faulkner, R. Chris Wolff.

Year Founded/History of Bookstore: Founded in 1945 by Harry Turitz, the bookstore was purchased in 1974 by the present owners. Currently the shop is in the same location it has been for the last 35 years. The building was built in the 1920's on the site of Dickerson's Tavern where, in the winter of 1779, Benedict Arnold was tried for treason.

Number of Volumes: 30,000.

Types/Classifications: Hardbound, magazines, paperback, ephemera, postcards, out-of-print.

General Subject Areas: Adventure, Americana, General, Scholarly Nonfiction, Travel.

Specific Specialties: New Jersey History.

Other Specialties: Old Postcards.

Mail/Telephone Orders; Credit Cards: Both. No credit cards.

Business Hours: Monday through Saturday 10:00 AM - 5:30 PM.

Catalogue: Catalogue published.

Collections/Individual Items Purchased: Both.

Booksellers' Memberships: New Jersey Booksellers Association.

618
Oz and Ends Book Shoppe

14 Dorset Drive
Kenilworth, New Jersey 07033   (201) 276-8368

This is a mail order business only that specializes in Oziana and related material including: Oz books, Oz music, Oz toys, original Oz art, Oz ephemera; also other books and materials by Oz authors and illustrators, e.g. anything by or about L. Frank Baum, W.W. Denslow, John R. Neill, Ruth P. Thompson, Jack Snow, Rachel Cosgrove, and Eloise McGraw. The owner requests that telephone calls be made between 6:00 PM and 10:00 PM only.

Owner/Biography: Judy A. Bieber. Ms. Bieber is very active in the International Wizard of Oz Club.

Year Founded/History of Bookstore: 1978.

Number of Volumes: 750.

Types/Classifications: Any and all material related to Oz.
General Subject Areas: Oziana.
Specific Specialties: All Oz editions are stocked; books can range from fine inscribed first editions in dust jackets to ex-libris reading copies; Oz reference material and scholarly criticism.
Other Specialties: Foreign Oz books.
Mail/Telephone Orders; Credit Cards: Both. Payment with order; all material returnable for full refund for any reason. No credit cards.
Business Hours: Evenings and Weekends.
Special Features: Search service.
Catalogue: Published 1 to 5 times per year ($1 each).
Collections/Individual Items Purchased: Both.
Booksellers' Memberships: New Jersey Antiquarian Book Dealers Association.

619
P. M. Bookshop
321 Park Avenue
Plainfield, New Jersey 07060   (201) 754-3900

The P.M. Bookshop carries antiquarian, used, and remaindered books with over 100,000 volumes in stock.
Owner/Biography: Sidney Pinn.
Year Founded/History of Bookstore: 1940.
Number of Volumes: 100,000.
Types/Classifications: Hardbound, paperback, magazines, out-of-print, first editions.
General Subject Areas: General.
Mail/Telephone Orders; Credit Cards: No credit cards.
Business Hours: Monday through Saturday 10:00 AM - 5:00 PM.
Parking Facilities: Public parking lot, street parking.
Collections/Individual Items Purchased: Both.

620
Pickwick Book Shop
201 Cedar Street
Tuckerton, New Jersey 08087   (609) 296-3343

The shop is located in a carriage house behind a 100 year old Victorian home on a back country street. It occupies 500 square feet of space.
How to Get There: Call for precise directions.
Owner/Biography: Bill and Elaine McClure.
Number of Volumes: 7,000.
Types/Classifications: Hardbound, magazines.
General Subject Areas: Biography, Children's Books, Fiction, History.
Mail/Telephone Orders; Credit Cards: Both. No credit cards.
Business Hours: By appointment only.
Parking Facilities: Business parking lot.
Collections/Individual Items Purchased: Individual items only.

621
Princeton Antiques Bookshop
2915-17-31 Atlantic Avenue
Atlantic City, New Jersey 08401   (609) 344-1943

This bookshop is an international search service for out-of-print books, with over 175,000 different titles in stock, all indexed by author, title, and subject. Visits can be arranged by appointment.
Owner/Biography: Robert Eugene Ruffolo II. Mr. Ruffolo is a member of the American Society of Apprais-

ers.

Year Founded/History of Bookstore: 1974.
Number of Volumes: 175,000.
Types/Classifications: Hardbound, out-of-print.
General Subject Areas: Antiques, Architecture, Art, Film, Illustrated Books, Science and Technology.
Specific Specialties: Marilyn Monroe.
Author Specialties: Gladys Taber, P.G. Wodehouse, Martha Finley, Beverly Nichols, Patricia Wentworth, L.M. Montgomery.
Mail/Telephone Orders; Credit Cards: Both. No credit cards.
Business Hours: By appointment only; Monday through Friday 8:00 AM - 4:00 PM; Saturday 9:00 AM - 1:00 PM.
Parking Facilities: Street parking.
Special Features: Search service.
Collections/Individual Items Purchased: Both.

622
Time Again Books, Records, Collectibles
P.O. Box 385
420 South Main Street
Pennington, New Jersey 08534   (609) 737-0361

The bookstore offers retail and wholesale books in general subjects, by appointment only.
How to Get There: Pennington, New Jersey is a few miles north of Interstate 95 on Route 31; it is twenty minutes north of Trenton, fifteen miles from Princeton, one hour each from New York or Philadelphia.
Owner/Biography: Dr. Charles C. McCracken, owner, has been a bookseller for eight years. He has a Doctorate in the library and information fields, a background in the arts, human services, as an educational consultant, and in research.
Year Founded/History of Bookstore: 1980.
Number of Volumes: 2,000 in the showroom, 50,000 in the warehouse.
Types/Classifications: Hardbound, paperback.
General Subject Areas: General.
Mail/Telephone Orders; Credit Cards: Both. No credit cards.
Business Hours: By appointment only.
Parking Facilities: Private parking.
Special Features: The bookstore has a large stock with rapid turnover; it works with individual dealers, collectors, students, researchers, and the general public.
Collections/Individual Items Purchased: Both.
Booksellers' Memberships: Antiquarian Booksellers Association of New Jersey.

623
Wangner's Book Shop
9 Midland Avenue
Montclair, New Jersey 07042   (201) 744-4211

The bookstore has a large stock of books located on shelves by category, alphabetically arranged, and index carded. The stock listings will be on computer by the end of 1984. The shop contains 1,200 square feet of space.
Owner/Biography: Victor and Lorraine Wangner.
Year Founded/History of Bookstore: Founded in 1977, the bookstore is on its original site.
Number of Volumes: 25,000.
Types/Classifications: Hardbound, magazines, autographs, ephemera, first editions, fine bindings, out-of-print, association copies, press books, signed copies, presentation copies, limited editions, color plate books.
General Subject Areas: Americana, Biography, British History, Children's Books, Science Fiction and Fantasy.
Specific Specialties: British Statesmen, Aesop, Victorian Period, Pacific Northwest.

Mail/Telephone Orders; Credit Cards: Both. Cash with order, personal checks and money orders. No credit cards.

Business Hours: Saturday 10:00 AM - 5:00 PM; other times by appointment.

Parking Facilities: Street, public parking.

Special Features: Search service, free appraisal service.

Collections/Individual Items Purchased: Both.

624
White's Galleries
607 Lake Avenue
Asbury Park, New Jersey 07712   (201) 531-4535

The bookstore was founded over 17 years ago and is probably the largest antiquarian bookstore on the Jersey Shore. It has a very large stock of out-of-print titles in both hardbound and paperback, in nearly all fields.

How to Get There: The shop is situated in the beautiful resort city of Asbury Park on the New Jersey Shore. It is in the heart of the business section, a few blocks from the beach and boardwalk. The shop is on the southern-most street of the town, separating Asbury Park from the quaint Victorian town of Ocean Grove.

Owner/Biography: Evelyn White.

Year Founded/History of Bookstore: The bookstore was founded in 1967. Due to the death recently of Alex Sandri White, the store is operated by Mrs. White who has an extensive knowledge of the book business.

Number of Volumes: 200,000.

Types/Classifications: Hardbound, paperback, prints, first editions, out-of-print.

General Subject Areas: Americana, Art, Biography, Children's Books, Cinema, Fiction, General, Literary Biography, Military, Music, Occult, Psychology, Religion, Theater.

Other Specialties: Some foreign language books: French, Spanish, German.

Mail/Telephone Orders; Credit Cards: Mail orders only; cash with order. No credit cards. Mailing address: P.O. Box 46 (rest of address same as above). An additional telephone number: (201) 774-9300.

Business Hours: Monday through Saturday 10:00 AM - 5:00 PM.

Parking Facilities: Street.

Special Features: Large discounts given on quantity and bulk purchases. Dealers are welcomed.

Collections/Individual Items Purchased: Individual items only.

625
Wilsey Rare Books
80 Watchung Avenue
Upper Montclair, New Jersey 07043   (201) 744-8366

The bookstore is located in a second-floor apartment. The stock is small but very choice in its specialties. Visits are by appointment only. The shop contains 400 square feet of space.

How to Get There: The shop is about 15 miles from central Manhattan, New York City, a twenty-five minute drive along New Jersey Route 3 from the Lincoln Tunnel. It is also easily accessible by frequent bus service fron the New York City Port Authority bus terminal. Call for more detailed directions.

Owner/Biography: Edward Ripley-Duggan and Carol Maltby.

Year Founded/History of Bookstore: 1975.

Number of Volumes: 500.

Types/Classifications: Hardbound, individual fine bindings (not shelf sets), color plate books, private press books.

Specific Specialties: Notable Illustrated Books from 1600 to the Present; Bibliography, Books on the Arts of the Book: Papermaking, Bookbinding, Calligraphy, Typography; Early Color Printing.

Mail/Telephone Orders; Credit Cards: Both. Payment in U.S. dollars for foreign orders; cash with order for parties not known to the bookstore. No credit cards.

Business Hours: By appointment only.

Parking Facilities: Street.

Catalogue: Two times a year.

Collections/Individual Items Purchased: Both.

Booksellers' Memberships: Antiquarian Booksellers Association of America, International League of Antiquarian Booksellers.

NEW MEXICO

626
Adobe Booksellers
2416 Pennsylvania Street N.E.
Albuquerque, New Mexico 87110 (505) 299-1670

> *Owner/Biography:* Hy S. Adler
> *Year Founded/History of Bookstore:* 1970.
> *Number of Volumes:* 5,000.
> *Types/Classifications:* Hardbound, out-of-print, first editions, association copies, press books.
> *General Subject Areas:* Americana, Southwest (U.S.).
> *Specific Specialties:* New Mexico, Arizona, Texas, Colorado, University of New Mexico Press.
> *Mail/Telephone Orders; Credit Cards:* Both. No credit cards.
> *Business Hours:* Monday through Saturday 9:00 AM - 5:00 PM.
> *Collections/Individual Items Purchased:* Both.

627
Ancient City Books
109 East Palace Avenue
Santa Fe, New Mexico 87501 (505) 455-7539

The bookstore has specialized in Soutwest Americana for 22 years, and carries a hand picked selection of rarities the year 'round in a shop of 250 square feet. The mailing address is P.O. Box 1986, Santa Fe, New Mexico 87501.

> *How to Get There:* The shop is located in Santa Fe's historic Old City, in the courtyard.
> *Owner/Biography:* Nicole Romanov.
> *Year Founded/History of Bookstore:* 1961.
> *Number of Volumes:* 2,500.
> *Types/Classifications:* Hardbound, paperback, current, out-of-print.
> *General Subject Areas:* American Indian, Southwest Americana.
> *Specific Specialties:* New Mexico.
> *Mail/Telephone Orders; Credit Cards:* Both; no credit cards.
> *Business Hours:* Monday through Saturday 10:00 AM - 5:00 PM.
> *Parking Facilities:* Street.
> *Special Features:* Search service, publishing sideline.
> *Catalogue:* Six times a year.
> *Collections/Individual Items Purchased:* Both.
> *Booksellers' Memberships:* Antiquarian Booksellers Association of America.

628
Chaparral Books of Santa Fe
Sena Plaza
Santa Fe, New Mexico 87501 (505) 988-1076

Chapparal Books of Santa Fe is located in a Spanish hacienda that was built in the 1820's and is just one block east of the historic Palace of Governors, the oldest public building in the United States. The shop occupies 400 square feet of space. The owners also have stock in their private residence.

> *Owner/Biography:* Riley and Betty Parker.

Year Founded/History of Bookstore: 1980. The business was begun mostly for mail order, but in 1983 a retail location was opened. The owners still do an extensive catalogue and mail order business in the home. The mail address is 300 Lomita, Santa Fe 87501.
Number of Volumes: 4,000.
Types/Classifications: Hardbound, broadsides, ephemera, out-of-print, rare.
General Subject Areas: History, Literature, Western Americana.
Specific Specialties: History and Literature of New Mexico, Texas, Arizona.
Author Specialties: Willa Cather, D.H. Lawrence, Paul Horgan, Mary Austin, J. Frank Dobie.
Mail/Telephone Orders; Credit Cards: Both. American Express, Visa, Mastercard accepted.
Business Hours: Monday through Saturday 10:00 AM - 5:30 PM.
Parking Facilities: Business parking lot behind building.
Catalogue: Published 3 to 4 times annually.
Collections/Individual Items Purchased: Both.

629
El Paisano Books
1000 Park Avenue S.W.
Albuquerque, New Mexico 87102   (505) 242-9121

El Paisano Books specializes in the Southwest and carries a general stock.
Owner/Biography: Katherine Stamm.
Year Founded/History of Bookstore: 1965.
Types/Classifications: Hardbound (except for some new Southwest trade paperback).
General Subject Areas: General.
Specific Specialties: Southwest.
Mail/Telephone Orders; Credit Cards: Both. Visa and Mastercard accepted.
Business Hours: Monday through Saturday 11:00 AM - 5:00 PM.
Parking Facilities: Street parking, driveway.
Collections/Individual Items Purchased: Both.
Booksellers' Memberships: American Booksellers Association.

630
Jane Zwisohn Books
524 Solano Drive, N.E.
Albuquerque, New Mexico 87108   (505) 255-4080

Jane Zwisohn deals in fine antiquarian books from her private residence.
How to Get There: Directions will be given when calling for an appointment.
Owner/Biography: Jane Zwisohn.
Year Founded/History of Bookstore: 1981.
Number of Volumes: 1,200.
Types/Classifications: Old and rare, some pamphlets, first editions.
General Subject Areas: Latin Americana, Travel (Literary), Western Americana.
Mail/Telephone Orders; Credit Cards: Both. Cash with order for first-time customers. No credit cards.
Business Hours: Call for appointment anytime; best time to call is 8:00 AM - Noon.
Parking Facilities: Street or driveway.
Catalogue: Published 2 times per year.
Collections/Individual Items Purchased: Both.

631
La Galeria De Los Artesanos Bookstore
220 North Plaza
Las Vegas, New Mexico 87701   (505) 425-8331

This specialist bookstore is housed in a restored law office with a warm, friendly atmosphere, including working fireplaces. It deals in Western Americana books and ephemera.

How to Get There: Located on the north side of the Old Town Plaza, the shop is housed in a red brick building with a large sign on top and two lower signs.

Owner/Biography: Joseph W. and Diana G. Stein. Joe came to Las Vegas first, arriving after World War II, and by the end of the forties, opening a bookstore and art gallery, establishing poetry readings, and having twice-monthly offerings of paintings, sculpture, and silverwork. Diana, an adventurous New York girl with a yen for the West, came to Las Vegas via Mexico City where she was an executive secretary for a World Health Organization International Conference.

Year Founded/History of Bookstore: Established in 1950 as an art gallery with paintings, crafts, objets d'art, books, and interior furnishings. The shop gradually grew a large inventory of books, and over the years developed an all Western Americana stock, still with art. In 1975 the Steins restored a small, old building formerly used as a law office, on the Old Town Plaza, and transferred the bookstore to their restoration. Later that same year they received an award from the State of New Mexico for their efforts.

Number of Volumes: 20,000.

Types/Classifications: Hardbound, paperback, used, rare, ephemera, first editions, fine bindings, out-of-print, association copies, press books, signed copies, presentation copies, limited editions, color plate books.

General Subject Areas: American Indians, Cattle Trade, Early Conquest of Western America, Folklore, History of the West, Juveniles, Medicine, Military, Music, Outlaws, Western Americana, Western Fiction, Westward Expansion and Overland Trails, Women of the West.

Specific Specialties: Southwest Juveniles, Women of the West.

Author Specialties: Paul Horgan, William Eastlake, Will James, Oliver LaFarge, R.E. Twitchell, Evits Haley, Frank Dobie, Tom Lea, Paul Wellman.

Other Specialties: Books About Books.

Mail/Telephone Orders; Credit Cards: Both; cash with order; no credit cards.

Business Hours: Monday through Saturday 10:00 AM - 5:00 PM.

Parking Facilities: All around the Plaza.

Special Features: Search service, special ordering of prints; coffee, tea; apartment behind shop for out of town visitors on occasion, and for lunch for customers. The Steins feel that they are off the beaten path, so they want to make their people feel comfortable. The shop also has many albums of historic photographs and memorabilia for research, available to historians.

Collections/Individual Items Purchased: Both.

Miscellaneous: The owners appraise libraries and estates, and act as an historical information center.

632
Margolis & Moss
129 West San Francisco Street
Santa Fe, New Mexico 87501   (505) 982-1028

The bookstore has a constantly changing stock of collector's editions from nearly all fields, especially Western Americana, Americana, photography, illustrated books, and culinary arts. It also offers a large stock of decorative prints from the late 15th Century through the early 20th Century, selected 19th Century photographs, a large collection of ephemera, and a choice selection of American regional printmakers. It contains 450 square feet of space.

How to Get There: The shop is located 2 blocks west of the Plaza, upstairs.

Owner/Biography: David Margolis, Jean Moss.

Year Founded/History of Bookstore: 1979.

Number of Volumes: 5,000.

Types/Classifications: General antiquarian stock books, photographs, ephemera, prints, first editions, fine bindings, out-of-print, association copies, press books, signed copies, presentation copies, limited editions, color plate books, 19th Century photography, early 20th Century regional printmakers, decorative prints from the 15th Century through the early 20th Century.

General Subject Areas: Americana, Children's Books, Cookbooks, Illustrated Books, Photography, Western Americana.

Mail/Telephone Orders; Credit Cards: Both; mailing address is P.O. Box 2042, Santa Fe, NM 87501. Visa and Mastercard accepted.

Business Hours: Monday through Saturday 11:00 AM - 5:00 PM.

Parking Facilities: Street, public parking lot.
Catalogue: Quarterly.
Collections/Individual Items Purchased: Both.

633
Nicholas Potter - Bookseller
203 East Palace
Santa Fe, New Mexico 87501

(505) 983-5434

This is probably Santa Fe's oldest established used bookstore, offering a general stock of hardbound books, a large selection of used classical and jazz recordings, and a gallery of contemporary and vintage photographs. It contains 650 square feet of space.

Owner/Biography: Nicholas Potter, owner, is a graduate of Princeton University (B.A. History). He started working in his father's bookstore in 1969 during school vacations, and took over after his father's death in January, 1975.

Year Founded/History of Bookstore: Jack Potter, veteran Chicago bookman, started in the book business after World War II. He opened the Broadway Bookstore in Chicago in 1952. In 1969 he moved to Santa Fe and opened the shop at its present location. After his death in 1975 his son Nicholas took over the business and has expanded it steadily since then.

Number of Volumes: 7,500.

Types/Classifications: Hardbound books, classical and jazz LP recordings, photographs, illustrated books, sets, and all general classifications.

General Subject Areas: Americana, Anthropology, Archaeology, Architecture, Art, Biography, Books About Books, Children's Books, Drama, Economics, Food and Wine, History of Science, Language, Literary Criticism, Literature, Metaphysics, Music, Mythology, Natural History, Philosophy, Photography, Poetry, Psychology, Travel, Western Americana, World History.

Specific Specialties: Southwestern American History, Southwestern American Literature, Modern First Editions of Literature and Poetry.

Author Specialties: Willa Cather, D.H. Lawrence, James Joyce, Paul Horgan, Frank Waters.

Mail/Telephone Orders; Credit Cards: Both; the owner generally answers requests if the book is in stock; otherwise, the request is filed until a copy can be located; not all requests can be filled, especially general requests; no credit cards.

Business Hours: Monday through Saturday 10:00 AM - 5:00 PM.

Parking Facilities: Street parking when available.

Special Features: Appraisals, good music, photography gallery.

Collections/Individual Items Purchased: Both.

Booksellers' Memberships: Antiquarian Booksellers Association of America, New Mexico Book League.

Miscellaneous: Extra effort is expended for the customer.

NEW YORK

634
A Gatherin'
Route 150
West Sand Lake, New York 12196 (518) 674-2979

This enterprise operates out of the home of the owners, a much modified turn-of-the-century village cottage. Clients are welcome to browse the stock which covers 1,000 square feet of space.

How to Get There: A Gatherin' is open by appointment only. More precise directions will be given upon inquiry.

Owner/Biography: Robert Dalton Harris and Diane DeBlois. Rob, an ex-physicist, came to rare books via stamp collecting and a love of historic "evidence." Diane, an ex-educator, came to A Gatherin' via a love for Rob and an interest in people's collecting passions.

Year Founded/History of Bookstore: 1972.

Number of Volumes: Several hundred thousand paper items.

Types/Classifications: Rare volumes on postal history, trade catalogs, music sheets, pamphlets, documents, manuscripts, ephemera.

General Subject Areas: Advertising Ephemera - 19th Century, Drug Trade (19th Century), Music (U.S. - 19th Century), Postal History (U.S. and Worldwide), Trade and Commerce (U.S. - 19th Century).

Mail/Telephone Orders; Credit Cards: Both. Mail order address: P.O. Box 175, Wynantskill, NY 12198. No credit cards.

Business Hours: By appointment only.

Parking Facilities: Private parking lot.

Special Features: A Gatherin' publishes a journal entitled "P.S., A Quarterly Journal of Postal History."

Catalogue: Published 2 to 4 times per year.

Collections/Individual Items Purchased: Both.

Booksellers' Memberships: Antiquarian Booksellers Association of America.

635
A Photographer's Place
133 Mercer Street
New York, New York 10012 (212) 431-9358

A comfortable bookplace specializing in photographic books of all sorts: technical, aesthetic, out-of-print, and historical. The walls are covered with old photographs; photographic antiques line the tops of the bookshelves. The staff is generally knowledgeable about photography and the partners who run the shop are both ex-photographers steeped in technical and historical photographic lore.

How to Get There: Located in New York City, the shop's nearest subway stop is the Prince Street stop on the RR (local) train of the BMT line. It is one block west of the subway station. The shop contains 1,300 square feet of space.

Owner/Biography: Harvey Zucker and Gene Bourne. Mr. Zucker is a former president of the Photographic Historical Society of New York, an ex-technical editor of Photo World magazine, and instructor in photographic technique and photographic history at several colleges in the New York area. Mr. Bourne is a former professional photographer, having shared a commercial studio in New York. He graduated from Alfred University with a major in photography. He is a former photographic therapist, having worked on theories involving the use of photography in therapy with mentally disturbed patients at a New York State mental hospital.

Year Founded/History of Bookstore: Originally started as a mail order operation in 1979 out of the home of Harvey Zucker, the business was later moved to New York's famous Soho Disrtict and enlarged to include the shop and a photographic gallery, first located on Greene Street; Bourne joined the business at this time.

The shop moved to its present site in 1981.

Number of Volumes: 5,000.

Types/Classifications: All types of books and material related to photography; in-print, out-of-print, collectors' interest, used books, bargain and super value bargain books, remainders, hurt, overstocked.

General Subject Areas: Aesthetic Photography, Historical Photography, Technical Photography.

Mail/Telephone Orders; Credit Cards: Mail orders are accepted, but customers are encouraged to send for the store's mail order catalogue, use the special mail order forms provided, and read the terms for ordering. Telephone inquiries invited. Visa and Mastercard accepted.

Business Hours: Monday through Saturday 11:00 AM - 6:00 PM; Sunday 12:00 Noon - 5:00 PM.

Parking Facilities: Street or local public lots.

Special Features: One of the best selections of out-of-print photographic books available anywhere. The owners actively seek out and buy photographic books by the single volume or entire library. They maintain want lists for their customers on the specific titles being sought.

Catalogue: Four or five times a year.

Collections/Individual Items Purchased: Both.

Miscellaneous: To a very limited degree, the bookstore deals in photographic antiques: tintypes, daguerreotypes, cameras, prints, etc. It also rents out photographic antiques as props, and has a relatively large and professional selection.

636
Academy Book Store
10 West 18th Street
New York, New York 10011
                                                                    (212) 242-4848

The bookstore is one of New York City's largest for used, rare, and out-of-print books. It specializes in scholarly works in all subjects, with strong holdings in psychology, philosophy, music, fiction, and art. It selects the stock carefully and acquires new collections often. It also has one of New York City's finest and most extensive collections of classical recordings. The shop contains 3,500 square feet of space.

How to Get There: The bookstore is located a few doors west of Fifth Avenue.

Owner/Biography: Alan Weiner.

Year Founded/History of Bookstore: 1973.

Number of Volumes: 100,000 books; 35,000 recordings.

Types/Classifications: Hardbound, paperback; used, out-of-print, rare, first editions, illustrated, signed copies; classical and show records.

General Subject Areas: Ancient History, Anthropology, Archaeology, Art, Children's Books, Classical Literature, Eastern Studies, Fiction, History, Literature, Music, Mystery, New York, Occult, Performing Arts, Philosophy, Photography, Poetry, Political Science, Psychology, Reference Books, Religion, Scholarly, Science Fiction and Fantasy, Travel.

Mail/Telephone Orders; Credit Cards: Both. No credit cards.

Business Hours: Monday through Friday 10:30 AM - 7:00 PM; Saturday 10:30 AM - 6:00 PM; Sunday 11:00 AM - 5:00 PM.

Collections/Individual Items Purchased: Both.

637
Adirondack Yesteryears Inc.
Drawer 209, Lower Lake
Saranac Lake, New York 12983
                                                                    (518) 891-3206

The bookstore occupies two rooms (2,500 square feet) of what was formerly a country club clubhouse. It specializes in out-of-print Adirondack books, paintings, and prints. The bulk of the stock consists of books which the owner has written and published independently.

How to Get There: It is suggested that the customer telephone first for directions.

Owner/Biography: Maitland DeSormo.

Year Founded/History of Bookstore: Founded in 1967, the first shop was located at 10 Dorsey Street, Saranac Lake. In 1974 the business was moved to the owner's home on Lower Lake.

Number of Volumes: 10,000.
Types/Classifications: Hardbound, out-of-print.
General Subject Areas: Adirondacks, Paintings, Prints.
Author Specialties: Verplanck Colvin, Alfred L. Donaldson, Samuel Hammond, Henry Abbott, Alfred Street, Maitland DeSormo.
Mail/Telephone Orders; Credit Cards: Both; no credit cards.
Business Hours: By appointment only.
Parking Facilities: Business parking lot.
Collections/Individual Items Purchased: Collections.

638
Albert J. Phiebig Inc.
5 Rutherford Avenue
White Plains, New York 10605   (914) 948-0138

This is primarily a mail order business dealing in foreign books and periodicals, both current and out-of-print. It is located in an office building in midtown White Plains and occupies approximately 2,000 square feet of space.
How to Get There: The bookstore is located 1 block from Mamaroneck Avenue; visits are welcomed but mail order is preferred.
Owner/Biography: Albert J. Phiebig, President. Mr. Phiebig is listed in "Who's Who in the East."
Year Founded/History of Bookstore: 1947. Mr. Phiebig moved his business to the present location in 1980.
Types/Classifications: Foreign books and periodicals, current and out-of-print.
General Subject Areas: General.
Specific Specialties: Irregular Foreign Serials, International Congresses.
Other Specialties: Scholarly Works.
Mail/Telephone Orders; Credit Cards: Both. No credit cards. Mail address: P.O. Box 352 and as above.
Business Hours: Monday through Friday 9:00 AM - 4:45 PM.
Parking Facilities: Business parking lot.
Special Features: Search service.
Collections/Individual Items Purchased: Neither.
Booksellers' Memberships: Antiquarian Booksellers Association of America, American Booksellers Association.

639
Aleph-Bet Books
670 Waters Edge
Valley Cottage, New York 10989   (914) 268-7410

The bookstore specializes in rare and collectible children's and illustrated books. Want-lists are welcome and quotes will be given on individual titles. The owner also participates in several book shows per year in various parts of the country.
How to Get There: The dealer is located 50 minutes from midtown Manahattan near the Tappan-Zee Bridge in Rockland County, New York.
Owner/Biography: Helen Younger. Ms. Younger is a former librarian who has always loved being around books.
Year Founded/History of Bookstore: 1978. Aleph-Bet Books has always operated by appointment only.
Number of Volumes: 4,000.
Types/Classifications: Rare, antiquarian and collectible children's and illustrated books.
General Subject Areas: Children's Books, Fantasy.
Mail/Telephone Orders; Credit Cards: Both. Payment with order; fully refundable within 10 days of receipt provided books are insured and received in the same condition as sent. No credit cards.
Business Hours: Daily 9:00 AM - 9:00 PM. Appointment required.
Catalogue: Published 4 times per year.

Collections/Individual Items Purchased: Both.
Booksellers' Memberships: Antiquarian Booksellers Association of America.

640
Andrew Wittenborn
152 Mountain Road
Pleasantville, New York 10570 (914) 941-2744

This dealer specializes in books about automobiles only and operates by direct mail order only.
General Subject Areas: Automobiles.
Specific Specialties: Graham Paige, Franklin, Chrysler Products, Repair Books.
Mail/Telephone Orders; Credit Cards: Mail orders only. No credit cards.

641
Antheil Booksellers
2177 Isabelle Court
North Bellmore, New York 11710 (516) 826-2094

These booksellers specialize in World War I and World War II books with emphasis on naval, maritime, military, and aviation subjects. They carry an extensive line of imported items (Britain, Japan, Australia, France, Austria, Germany) in their fields of specialization. They do not have an open shop but visits may be arranged by appointment only.
How to Get There: Directions will be given when making an appointment.
Owner/Biography: Nate and Sheila Rind.
Year Founded/History of Bookstore: 1958.
Number of Volumes: 10,000.
Types/Classifications: Hardbound.
General Subject Areas: Aviation, Maritime History, Military History, Naval History, World Wars I and II.
Mail/Telephone Orders; Credit Cards: Both. Payment with order, postage extra. No credit cards.
Business Hours: By appointment. Phone orders accepted Monday through Saturday 9:00 AM - 6:00 PM.
Special Features: Search service available to all at no obligation to buy and no fee required.
Catalogue: Published 4 times yearly. Subscription fee for catalogue: $3 yearly which entitles subscriber to receive 4 issues.
Collections/Individual Items Purchased: Both.

642
Appelfeld Gallery
1372 York Avenue
New York, New York 10021 (212) 988-7835

An unusual, old fashioned bookshop featuring fine bindings, illustrated books, color plate books, sets, paintings, first editions, and rare books.
How to Get There: The bookstore is located at 73rd Street and York Avenue in Manhattan, New York City.
Owner/Biography: Louis Appelfeld, owner, has been in the book business for over 40 years.
Number of Volumes: 7,000.
Types/Classifications: Old and rare books, fine leather bindings, illustrated books, first editions, press books, color plate books, standard sets, exhibition bindings.
General Subject Areas: American History, Americana, Art, Books About Books, Children's Books, Decoration, European History, Fine Illustrations (French and English), Literature, Travel, Typography.
Mail/Telephone Orders; Credit Cards: Both; personal check with order on the first purchase; no credit cards.
Business Hours: Monday through Friday 10:00 AM - 6:00 PM; Saturday 11:00 AM - 4:30 PM.

311

Parking Facilities: Very limited street parking.
Special Features: Unusually fine collection of rare books of high quality; few used or out-of-print books.
Catalogue: Four times a year.
Collections/Individual Items Purchased: Both.
Booksellers' Memberships: Antiquarian Booksellers Association of America.

643
Argosy Book Store, Inc.
116 East 59th Street
New York, New York 10022 (212) 753-4455

The Argosy Book Store is considered one of the largest and best stocked bookstores in New York City. It carries a large stock of 19th and 20 Century first editions and rare books in many subject areas. It also specializes in medical books published before 1900, Americana, autographs, and old maps. Bins and shelves for browsing by passers-by are outside the entrance and contain prints, maps, and reading copies.

How to Get There: The bookstore is located just off Lexington Avenue on the south side of 59th street toward Park Avenue; a few steps across and beyond Lexington from Bloomingdale's.
Owner/Biography: Louis Cohen.
Types/Classifications: Rare, out-of-print, first editions, limited editions, press books, illustrated books, autographs, maps.
General Subject Areas: Early Medicine, Literature (19th Century), Literature (20th Century), Modern First Editions.
Mail/Telephone Orders; Credit Cards: Mail orders.
Business Hours: Daily.
Parking Facilities: Commercial parking lots and garages.
Catalogue: Catalogues published.
Collections/Individual Items Purchased: Inquire as to current special wants of the store.
Booksellers' Memberships: Antiquarian Booksellers Association of America.

644
Arthur H. Minters, Inc.
84 University Place
New York, New York 10003 (212) 989-0593

The bookstore features books and magazines related to the fine and decorative arts and architecture, as well as various art movements and photography. The shop contains 2,200 square feet of space. Visits are by appointment only.

How to Get There: The business is located in New York City's Greenwich Village, between 11th and 12th Streets, on the third floor.
Owner/Biography: Arthur H. Minters.
Year Founded/History of Bookstore: 1957.
Number of Volumes: 9,800.
Types/Classifications: Hardbound, magazines, broadsides, ephemera, out-of-print, press books, signed copies, presentation copies, limited editions.
General Subject Areas: Architecture, Art Movements, Decorative Arts, Fine Arts, Music (Sheet), Photography.
Specific Specialties: Dada, Surrealism, Expressionism, Constructivism, Bauhaus, Futurism, Abstract Art, 19th Century European Art and Architecture, 20th Century European Art and Architecture.
Mail/Telephone Orders; Credit Cards: Both; payment with order reqired. Visa and Mastercard accepted.
Business Hours: Monday through Friday 10:00 AM - 6:00 PM by appointment only.
Parking Facilities: Street and public lot.
Special Features: Search service.
Catalogue: Six times a year.
Collections/Individual Items Purchased: Both.

645
As You Like It
2185 Bullis Road
Elma, New York 14059

(716) 652-0060

This is a small bookstore (250 square feet of space) crammed full of almost every type of reading material.

How to Get There: The bookstore is located fifteen miles southeast of Buffalo, three miles from the transit road between Lancaster and East Aurora.

Owner/Biography: Jim and Cathy Kraynik; Jim Kraynik's primary occupation is optician; Cathy Kraynik is a free lance artist.

Year Founded/History of Bookstore: The bookstore was started in 1976 in what was previously the Elma public library, founded before World War II.

Number of Volumes: 5,000.

Types/Classifications: Hardbound, paperback, magazines, broadsides, autographs, ephemera, comics, pulps, house portraits by Cathy Kraynik, first editions, out-of-print.

General Subject Areas: American Heritage, Animals, Art Books, Aviation, Biography, Children's Books, Cinema, Classics, Comedy, Cooking, Detective, Gardening, Historical Romance, History, Horror, Mysteries, National Geographics, Naval, Occult, Poetry, Religion, Science Fiction and Fantasy, Shakespeare, Spy, Teen-age Books, War, Western Americana, Western New York State History, Women.

Specific Specialties: Tom Swift, Early Science Fiction, Presidential History.

Author Specialties: Gene Stratton Porter, H.G. Wells, Jules Verne.

Mail/Telephone Orders; Credit Cards: Both; cash with order. No credit cards.

Business Hours: Daily 11:00 AM - 5:30 PM.

Parking Facilities: Business parking lot.

Special Features: Search service; house portraits.

Collections/Individual Items Purchased: Both.

646
Asian Rare Books Inc.
234 Fifth Avenue
Suite 3-F
New York, New York 10001

(212) 259-3732

This is a bookstore specializing in scholarly old and antiquarian books about Asia; it contains 2,300 square feet of space.

Owner/Biography: Stephen Feldman.

Year Founded/History of Bookstore: 1974.

Number of Volumes: 7,500.

Types/Classifications: Hardbound scholarly old books and serials.

General Subject Areas: Arabia, Asia, China, Japan, Middle East, Persia.

Specific Specialties: European Travel, Descriptions of Asia and the Middle East, Art Books, History, the Humanities.

Author Specialties: M.A. Stein, S. Hedin, R. van Gulik.

Mail/Telephone Orders; Credit Cards: Mail orders; stock lists will be sent with a payment of $1.50; no credit cards.

Business Hours: Monday through Saturday 9:00 AM - 5:30 PM.

Special Features: Search service, collection building.

Catalogue: Catalogue is published.

Collections/Individual Items Purchased: Both.

647
Austin Book Shop
82-64 Austin Street
Kew Gardens, New York 11415 (212) 441-1199

The Austin Book Shop has two parts: (1) a bargain outlet shop which is open on Friday and Saturday where books are sold which do not fit into the shop's various catalogues (science, technology, social science, world history, current books, and paperbacks), and which sell at very low prices, and (2) a mail order department which issues catalogues of old, rare, and out-of-print books.

How to Get There: The bookstore is located in central Queens, equidistant between New York City's LaGuardia and Kennedy Airports. It can be reached via Independent Subway line (E or F Train) at the Kew Gardens/Union Turnpike station. If in doubt, call for friendly instructions.

Owner/Biography: Bernard Titowsky, owner, was born in 1925 and became a bookman officially in 1952. He trained to be a history teacher at Queens College (BA 1947) and at the University of Wisconsin (MA 1948). He wrote his Masters thesis on Historiography. Mr. Titowsky returned to school in 1962 to receive a graduate degree in Library Science at the Graduate School of Queens College (CUNY). His thesis, entitled "American History - A Guide to Student Reading for Teachers and Librarians," was published by McKinley Publishing Co. in 1964 and was selected by the American Library Association as one of the outstanding reference books of the year.

Year Founded/History of Bookstore: The Shop was founded in 1952 at the present address as a retail used bookshop. By 1962 Mr. Titowsky had closed the retail store to devote himself to issuing catalogues of old, rare, and out-of-print books, in expanded quarters (4400 square feet) at 82-60 A Austin Street. The retail shop (320 square feet) reopened at 82-64 Austin Street in 1974.

Number of Volumes: 75,000.

Types/Classifications: Hardbound, paperback, pamphlets, autographed books, old, rare, out-of-print.

General Subject Areas: American History, American Literature, English Literature, Ethnic Studies, Immigration Studies, Women's Studies, World Literature in Translation.

Author Specialties: John Steinbeck, Upton Sinclair, William Dean Howells, S. J. Perelman, New Yorker Magazine Writers.

Other Specialties: Books in foreign languages concerning the immigration experience in America.

Mail/Telephone Orders; Credit Cards: Mail orders accepted; a check with the order will result in full postage and handling being provided; telephone orders accepted. No credit cards, but credit is granted to established customers. Mail address: Box 36, Kew Gardens, New York 11415.

Business Hours: The retail shop is open Friday and Saturday only, 12:00 Noon - 6:00 PM. Mail orders fulfilled Monday through Saturday 9:00 AM - 5:00 PM.

Parking Facilities: Parking lot, metered street parking.

Catalogue: Four to six times a year.

Collections/Individual Items Purchased: Both.

Miscellaneous: Mr. Titowsky believes his catalogue on immigration and ethnic studies to be the only one of its kind issued in the United States.

648
B & J Books
91-16 63rd Drive
Rego Park, New York 11374 (212) 896-1272

B & J Books is a general bookstore with hardbound and paperback stock and with a specialty in military history. The shop occupies 1200 square feet of space.

How to Get There: Independent subway; E or F train from Jamaica or Manhattan to 63rd Drive, Rego Park.

Owner/Biography: Barry Skolnick.

Year Founded/History of Bookstore: 1977.

Number of Volumes: 30,000.

Types/Classifications: Hardbound, paperback.

General Subject Areas: General.

Specific Specialties: Military History.

Mail/Telephone Orders; Credit Cards: Both. No credit cards.

Business Hours: Monday through Saturday 11:00 AM - 6:00 PM; Sunday 12:00 Noon - 5:00 PM.
Parking Facilities: Street parking.
Catalogue: Published 2 times per year.
Collections/Individual Items Purchased: Both.

649
Ballet Shop
1887 Broadway
New York, New York 10023

(212) 581-7990

This bookstore specializes in ballet, opera, and theater books, both new and used. The shop occupies 500 square feet of space.
How to Get There: The shop can be reached by subway and bus.
Owner/Biography: Norman Crider.
Year Founded/History of Bookstore: 1974.
Number of Volumes: 2,000.
Types/Classifications: Hardbound, paperback, magazines, broadsides, autographs, ephemera, prints, first editions, fine bindings, out-of-print, signed copies, limited editions, color plate books.
General Subject Areas: Ballet, Opera, Theater.
Specific Specialties: Diaghilev Period (19th Century Ballet).
Mail/Telephone Orders; Credit Cards: Both. Prepaid if order is over $100. American Express, Visa, Mastercard accepted.
Business Hours: Monday through Saturday 11:00 AM - 8:00 PM.
Parking Facilities: Street parking.
Collections/Individual Items Purchased: Both.

650
Barn East Books
29 Montgomery Street
Tivoli, New York 12583

(914) 757-4294

Barn East Books is housed in a barn behind the residence of Richard Wiles. Books are categorized and fiction titles are alphabetized. Regional United States literature is a specialty. The shop occupies 1,000 square feet of space.
How to Get There: The bookstore is located in the village of Tivoli, 1/2 mile off New York State Highway 9G.
Owner/Biography: Richard C. Wiles. Dr. Wiles is Profesor of Economics at nearby Bard College where he is also Director of Hudson Valley Study Program.
Year Founded/History of Bookstore: 1978.
Number of Volumes: 15,000.
Types/Classifications: Hardbound, out-of-print.
General Subject Areas: Biography, Children's Literature, Regional Americana, Travel.
Mail/Telephone Orders; Credit Cards: Both. No credit cards.
Business Hours: Weekends and by appointment.
Parking Facilities: Parking space at house for 4 cars.
Collections/Individual Items Purchased: Both.

651
Ben Franklin Bookshop
318 North Broadway
Upper Nyack, New York 10960

(914) 358-0440

Ben Franklin Bookshop is a quaint shop in an old Victorian building. A general stock of used, old, and rare books occupies 900 square feet of space.

Owner/Biography: Steven and Donna Schwartz.
Year Founded/History of Bookstore: 1979.
Number of Volumes: 12,000.
Types/Classifications: Hardbound, paperback, first editions, out-of-print.
General Subject Areas: General.
Specific Specialties: New York State, Hudson River.
Mail/Telephone Orders; Credit Cards: Both. Postage additional. Visa and Mastercard accepted.
Business Hours: Closed Wednesday. Monday, Tuesday, Thursday, Friday 9:00 AM - 6:00 PM; Saturday and Sunday 12:00 Noon - 6:00 PM.
Parking Facilities: Street parking.
Special Features: Bookbinding, appraisals, printing.
Collections/Individual Items Purchased: Both.
Miscellaneous: Paperbacks are all 1/2 cover price.

652
Bernice Weiss - Rare Books
36 Tuckahoe Avenue
Eastchester, New York 10707
(914) 793-6200

Bernice Weiss - Rare Books offers a fine and varied selection in the fields of literature, poetry, and the arts. The constantly changing stock is sold to institutions and private collectors worldwide. Appraisals are available and the store is particularly interested in purchasing fine literary material.
Owner/Biography: Mrs. Bernice P. Weiss.
Year Founded/History of Bookstore: 1963. This is a mail order and telephone business established twenty years ago solely by the present owner.
Number of Volumes: Over 6,000.
Types/Classifications: Hardbound, broadsides, autographs, illustrated material, ephemera, miniature books, first editions, fine bindings, out-of-print, association copies, press books, signed copies, presentation copies, limited editions, color plate books, fine printing, manuscripts.
General Subject Areas: Children's Literature, Literature, Poetry, Private Press Books.
Author Specialties: Elizabeth Bogan, Roy Campbell, Willa Cather, Samuel Beckett, Djuna Barnes, Basil Bunting, Truman Capote, Charles Dickens, William Faulkner, Eugene Field, Allen Ginsberg, Edward Gorey, Graham Greene, Lafcadio Hearn, James Joyce, Galway Kinnell, Jerzy Kosinski, D.H. Lawrence, Henry Miller, Anais Nin, Liam O'Flaherty, Walker Percy, Katherine Anne Porter, William Saroyan, Isaac B. Singer, Maurice Sendak, John Steinbeck, Wallace Stevens, Arthur Szyk, James Tate, Peter Taylor, William Thackeray, Paul Theroux, Henry Thoreau, Anne Tyler, Robert Penn Warren, Eudora Welty, Tennessee Williams, Edmund Wilson.
Other Specialties: First foreign editions of major writers.
Mail/Telephone Orders; Credit Cards: Both. No credit cards.
Business Hours: Monday through Friday 9:00 AM - 6:00 PM. Business is conducted by mail order or phone only. Quotations for specific titles are sent to serious collectors.
Catalogue: Published 3 to 4 times per year.
Collections/Individual Items Purchased: Both.
Booksellers' Memberships: Antiquarian Booksellers Association of America including Middle Atlantic Chapter.

653
Berry Hill Book Shop
Route 12-B, Box 118
Deansboro, New York 13328
(315) 821-6188

A converted two-story (soon to be three-story) barn, Berry Hill Book Shop stocks a general selection of used, rare, and out-of-print books in all subjects. The shop also offers a free search service.
How to Get There: The bookstore is 15 miles south of Utica in the center of New York State on Route 12-B between Deansboro and Oriskany Falls.

Owner/Biography: D.L. Swarthout.
Year Founded/History of Bookstore: 1966.
Number of Volumes: 75,000.
Types/Classifications: Hardbound, out-of-print, some prints, paper items, autographs which are mostly entertainment related.
General Subject Areas: Art, Literary Criticism, Literature, New York State, Show Business, Travel, World History.
Mail/Telephone Orders; Credit Cards: Both. No credit cards.
Business Hours: Monday through Saturday 10:00 Am to 6:00 PM. Closed Sunday.
Parking Facilities: Small parking area - driveway and across the street.
Special Features: Search Service.
Catalogue: Special lists on various subjects (e.g. Civil War, Art) are published.
Collections/Individual Items Purchased: Both.
Booksellers' Memberships: Central New York Antiquarian Booksellers Association.

654
Bevan Davies, Books
431 West Broadway
New York, New York 10012

(212) 925-9132

Bevan Davies, Books is a mail order business which is open to the public by appointment. Mr. Davies specializes in books on American art and 20th Century photography. Most of the books are out-of-print, but a number of in-print titles which are felt to be of scholarly interest are also carried. The shop occupies 2,000 square feet of space.

How to Get There: The shop is located in Manhattan's historic SoHo (SOuth of HOuston) which is convenient to all public transportation.
Owner/Biography: Bevan Davies.
Year Founded/History of Bookstore: 1980.
Number of Volumes: 5,000.
Types/Classifications: Out-of-print, magazines, ephemera on 20th Century art and photography, limited editions, some press books, some signed books.
General Subject Areas: Art, Photography.
Mail/Telephone Orders; Credit Cards: Both. No credit cards.
Business Hours: By appointment Monday through Saturday 9:00 AM - 5:00 PM.
Parking Facilities: Street parking, parking lots.
Catalogue: Published 4 to 8 times per year.
Collections/Individual Items Purchased: Both.
Booksellers' Memberships: Antiquarian Booksellers Association of America.

655
Bibliomania
129 Jay Street
Schenectady, New York 12305

(518) 393-8069

The bookstore is a pleasant and unpretentious general bookshop well suited for browsing. The stock is carefully chosen and arranged neatly in categories. In addition to the continually growing stock of used and out-of-print titles, the bookstore carries many interesting remainders in literature, art, and the social sciences. It also carries some new books in areas such as book collecting and New York State history. The atmosphere is relaxed, with soft music (usually jazz) in the background. Able assistance and friendly conversation are available when needed or desired.

How to Get There: The bookstore is located one block from State Street (Rte. 5), Schenectady's main street. Jay Street is one way into State Street, meeting directly in front of Proctor's Theatre in the heart of downtown. A map with the location of the bookstore and directions is available; send a self addressed stamped envelope.
Owner/Biography: William M. Healy.

Year Founded/History of Bookstore: The bookstore opened in September 1981 at its present location. Four catalogues have been published; they will be issued more frequently as good books become available.

Number of Volumes: 9,000.

Types/Classifications: Hardbound used and out-of-print books only. Some ephemera sold in catalogues. Within the bookstore's subject areas there are many first editions, signed copies, limited editions, and general out-of-print books.

General Subject Areas: Americana, Anthropology, Archaeology, Art, Biography, Books and Book Collecting, Civil War, Cooking, Fishing, Furniture and Antiques, General Fiction, Hunting, Literary First Editions, Music, Mystery Fiction, Natural History, New York State History, Photography, Travel and Exploration, World War II.

Specific Specialties: Adirondacks, Canoeing, North American Small Boat and Foot Travels, Fly Fishing, Modern First Editions, Literary Biography, Mountaineering.

Author Specialties: The bookstore has several author interests such as Edward Abbey, Colin Fletcher, Ernest Hemingway, John McPhee, Jack London, Robert B. Parker, and John Steinbeck, but their books rarely stay in the shop long enough to be considered a specialty.

Mail/Telephone Orders; Credit Cards: Mail orders: payment by check or money order required with the order. Telephone orders accepted. No credit cards.

Business Hours: Monday through Saturday 10:00 AM - 5:00 PM; Thursday to 9:00 PM.

Parking Facilities: Street parking on Jay Street; free public lots on adjacent parallel streets.

Catalogue: One or two times per year.

Collections/Individual Items Purchased: Both.

656
Black Sun Books
667 Madison Avenue
Suite 305
New York, New York 10021   (212) 688-6622

Black Sun Books occupies two rooms containing rare and important books and artwork.

How to Get There: The bookstore is located at the above address which is at 61st Street in Manhattan. It can be reached by subway and surface transportation.

Owner/Biography: Linda and Harvey Tucker.

Year Founded/History of Bookstore: 1969.

Types/Classifications: First editions, illustrated books with original graphics, fine bindings, fine press books, original filmscripts, authors' letters and manuscript material, autographs, inscribed books.

General Subject Areas: American and English Literature (First Editions), Art Books, Photography Books.

Author Specialties: All major 19th and 20th Century authors.

Mail/Telephone Orders; Credit Cards: Both. Personal checks, money orders, Visa, Mastercard accepted.

Business Hours: Monday through Friday 9:00 AM - 5:00 PM and by appointment.

Parking Facilities: No parking facilities except in public and private parking lots.

Special Features: Collections built for clients; want lists kept on file for all clients; appraisals.

Catalogue: Published once a year plus monthly lists.

Collections/Individual Items Purchased: Both.

Booksellers' Memberships: Antiquarian Booksellers Association of America.

657
Bob Fein Books
150 Fifth Avenue
Room 623
New York, New York 10011   (212) 807-0489

This is a unique bookstore which specializes in out-of-print books on Indians of North and South America including Eskimos. There is a large collection of pre-Columbian art and culture. Original artifacts are also sold and some current books on Indian cultures are also stocked. Also available is a large supply of Bureau of American Ethnology Bulletins and Annual Reports. The shop occupies 400 square feet of space.

318

How to Get There: Located in midtown Manhattan, the bookstore can be reached via subway and surface transportation.

Owner/Biography: Bob Fein.

Year Founded/History of Bookstore: 1980.

Number of Volumes: 4,000.

Types/Classifications: Hardbound, paperback, ephemera, out-of-print, signed copies, limited editions.

General Subject Areas: Anthropology, Archaeology, North American Indians, South American Indians.

Specific Specialties: Maya, Inca, Eskimo, Pacific Northwest Coast, American Indians.

Mail/Telephone Orders; Credit Cards: Both. Payment in U.S. dollars payable on a U.S. bank. No credit cards.

Business Hours: Monday through Saturday 11:00 AM - 5:00 PM.

Parking Facilities: Metered parking on street, parking lots.

Special Features: Search service.

Catalogue: Published 8 times per year.

658
Book Chest
19 Oxford Place
Rockville Centre, New York 11570

(516) 766-6105

The Book Chest specializes in natural history, voyages and travels, and fine illustrated books. It operates as a mail order business but customers may visit by appointment only.

How to Get There: Rockville Centre is located in Nassau County on Long Island and can be reached via various parkways from New York City.

Owner/Biography: Estelle Chessid.

Year Founded/History of Bookstore: 1972.

Number of Volumes: 1,200.

Types/Classifications: Hardbound, out-of-print, rare, scarce, color plate books, finely illustrated.

General Subject Areas: Natural History, Voyages and Travels.

Mail/Telephone Orders; Credit Cards: Both. No credit cards.

Business Hours: By appointment only.

Catalogue: Published 1 to 2 times per year.

Collections/Individual Items Purchased: Both.

Booksellers' Memberships: Antiquarian Booksellers Association of America including Middle Atlantic Chapter.

659
Book End
521 Jewett Avenue
Staten Island, New York 10302

(212) 273-0303

The Book End was Staten Island's only used and out-of-print bookstore from 1977 to 1983. There are over 10,000 hardbound and paperback books in many categories with no particular specialization. All books are categorized. The shop occupies 2,400 square feet of space.

How to Get There: From the Staten Island Expressway connecting the Verrazano and Goethals Bridges, use Barclay Avenue exit north to Victory Boulevard, then east to Jewett Avenue (1-1/2 miles from Expressway on the North Shore).

Owner/Biography: Harlow and Loretta McMillen. Both are teachers with over 10 years in bookselling.

Year Founded/History of Bookstore: 1977. The shop has been on its current site since inception with no changes in ownership.

Number of Volumes: 10,000.

Types/Classifications: Hardbound, paperback, ephemera, greeting cards, first editions, illustrated books, leather bindings.

General Subject Areas: Adventure, Aircraft, Americana, Anthologies, Antiques, Art, Automobiles, Biography, Celebrities, Children's Books, Classics, Cookbooks, Crafts, Economics, Erotica, Essays, Fiction, Fishing,

History, How-To-Books, Humor, Hunting, Judaica, Medicine, Nature, New York City, Philosophy, Photography, Politics, Psychology, Railroads, Reference, Religion, Science, Sports, Technical, Travel.

Specific Specialties: American Humor, Staten Island.

Mail/Telephone Orders; Credit Cards: Both. Cash with mail order; quotations made to want lists. Telephone orders with written confirmation. No credit cards.

Business Hours: Wednesday through Friday 12:00 Noon - 5:00 PM; Saturday 10:00 AM - 5:00 PM.

Parking Facilities: Small parking lot, street parking.

Special Features: Free search service.

Catalogue: Periodic lists of general books.

Collections/Individual Items Purchased: Both.

660
Book Exchange
90 West Market Street
Corning, New York 14830   (607) 936-8536

The Book Exchange is a small general stock bookstore located on the main street in the historic district of Corning, New York. The bookstore occupies 800 square feet of space.

Owner/Biography: Elizabeth and James Iraggi.

Year Founded/History of Bookstore: 1978. The current shop is the third location since the founding of the business. It began with a stock of paperback books but has grown to out-of-print and rare books in various subject areas.

Number of Volumes: 7,000.

Types/Classifications: Hardbound, broadsides, ephemera, out-of-print, color plate books.

General Subject Areas: Americana, Arctic, Decorative Arts, Glass Reference Material, Natural History, New York State, Scholarly Works.

Specific Specialties: The Book Exchange maintains what is probably the largest collection of out-of-print glass reference material in the United States, if not the world. The stock covers stained glass from antiquity as well as all aspects of glass. There is also a large collection on ceramics, pottery, and porcelain.

Mail/Telephone Orders; Credit Cards: Both. No credit cards.

Business Hours: Monday through Saturday 10:30 AM - 5:30 PM.

Parking Facilities: Street parking, public parking lot.

Special Features: Cappuccino and expresso offered.

Catalogue: Published 4 times per year.

Collections/Individual Items Purchased: Both.

661
Book Look
51 Maple Avenue
Warwick, New York 10990   (914) 986-1981

The Book Look is an out-of-print book finder that operates by mail order only. The manager states that 94 percent of the books requested are successfully located. Most books are located within 30 to 90 days.

Owner/Biography: Jerry D. Dodd.

Year Founded/History of Bookstore: 1966.

Types/Classifications: Out-of-print.

General Subject Areas: General.

Mail/Telephone Orders; Credit Cards: Mail order only. Visa and Mastercard accepted.

662
Book Revue
313 New York Avenue
Huntington, New York 11743   (516) 271-1442

320

The Book Revue is a large general bookstore that consists of approximately equal thirds of new, remaindered, and out-of-print books. A substantial section of modern first editions and other valuable books has been recently established. The shop occupies 4,800 square feet of space.

How to Get There: The bookstore is located 30 yards north of Route 25A in Huntington Village.
Owner/Biography: Richard Klein, Robert Klein.
Year Founded/History of Bookstore: 1977.
Number of Volumes: 75,000.
Types/Classifications: Hardbound, paperback, first editions, limited editions, signed copies, presentation copies.
General Subject Areas: General.
Specific Specialties: Signed first editions.
Mail/Telephone Orders; Credit Cards: Visa and Mastercard accepted.
Business Hours: Monday through Friday 10:00 AM - 9:00 PM; Saturday 10:00 AM - 6:00 PM; Sunday 12:00 Noon - 5:00 PM.
Parking Facilities: Public parking lot, street parking, small private lot.
Miscellaneous: A large clearance room is located in the rear of the store which has many out-of-print bargains.

663
Book Stop
384 East Meadow Avenue
East Meadow, New York 11554

(516) 794-9129

The Book Stop features one of Long Island's largest selections of old and new paperbacks, categorized and alphabetized. The shop specializes in out-of-print paperbacks and occupies 1,000 square feet of space.
How to Get There: The bookstore is located close to the North and South Shores of Long Island in Nassau County; call for directions. The shop is about 45 minutes from Manhattan or Brooklyn.
Owner/Biography: Beverly and Milton Rafalof.
Year Founded/History of Bookstore: 1974. The shop has been in the same location with the same ownership since its inception.
Number of Volumes: Over 100,000.
Types/Classifications: Paperback, magazines, comic books, out-of-print.
General Subject Areas: Biography, Cookbooks, Health, Mysteries, Philosophy, Psychology, Romances, Science Fiction and Fantasy, Westerns.
Specific Specialties: Back issues of adult magazines.
Mail/Telephone Orders; Credit Cards: Both. Send self addressed stamped envelope with inquiry. No credit cards.
Business Hours: Monday through Saturday 11:00 AM - 6:00 PM.
Parking Facilities: Business parking lot, street parking.
Special Features: Search service; subscription service on Romances with a 10 percent discount.
Collections/Individual Items Purchased: Both.
Miscellaneous: Friendly service.

664
Book-Nook
366 Route 9W
Upper Nyack, New York 10960

(914) 358-1114

The Book-Nook is located in Rockland County within an area devoted to antiques, crafts, and other bookstores. Accessibility is excellent as the shop is on a major highway reached via the New York State Thruway. The cedar shingled building is easily discernible as it stands alone amidst a picturesque area. The shop occupies 750 square feet of space.
How to Get There: The Tappan Zee Bridge will lead to Route 59 and immediately to Route 9W North. The shop is located 3/4 mile past the huge Nyack Hospital.
Owner/Biography: Mildred Marowitz. Mrs. Marowitz is a devotee of the written word. She also has taught

piano and theory for 30 years as well as having performed professionally.
   Year Founded/History of Bookstore: 1973. The shop was originally located in Montvale, New Jersey and has been at the present location for one year.
   Number of Volumes: 10,000.
   Types/Classifications: Hardbound, magazines (Life, Colliers, Holiday, Fortune, Esquire, Harpers, Vogue, National Geographic), first editions, out-of-print, signed copies, presentation copies, color plate books, illustrated books.
   General Subject Areas: Americana, Art and Architecture, Astronomy, Automobiles, Aviation, Biography, Black History, Botany, Cartoon Books, Chess, Children's Books, Civil War (U.S.), Cookbooks, Crime, Drama, Foreign Countries, Foreign Language, Hollywood, Humor, Law, Literature, Medical, Modern Library, Music, Mysteries, Natural History, Nautical, Philosophy, Photoplays, Poetry, Presidents (U.S.), Psychology, Radio, Religion, Science Fiction, Sewing, Spiritualism, Sports, Theater, Westerns, World Wars I and II, Zoology.
   Specific Specialties: Winston Churchill, British Royalty, Napoleon, Children's Series.
   Author Specialties: Pearl Buck, Taylor Caldwell, Marie Corelli, William Faulkner, Edna Ferber, Paul Gallico, Nathaniel Hawthorne, Ernest Hemingway, Alexander King, Joseph C. Lincoln, Hendrik Van Loon, W. Somerset Maugham, John Steinbeck, T.S. Stribling, Mark Twain, Philip Wylie.
   Other Specialties: Foreign novels in German, Norwegian, Greek, Russian, Italian, Swedish.
   Mail/Telephone Orders; Credit Cards: Both. All prices include postage and insurance (domestic shipping only). No personal checks; bank/business check or postal money order; check to be forwarded prior to shipment of order. No credit cards.
   Business Hours: Daily 12:00 Noon - 5:30 PM; closed Tuesday.
   Parking Facilities: Business parking lot.
   Special Features: Free search service.
   Collections/Individual Items Purchased: Individual items only.
   Miscellaneous: 95 percent of inventory is in the realm of bookdom; the other 5 percent is of a decorative nature such as glass and porcelain; also available are postcards and sheet music.

665
Bookery
Dewitt Mall
Ithaca, New York 14850   (607) 273-5055

   The Bookery has two locations in the Dewitt Mall which is a former school building converted to specialty shops, offices, and apartments. The original Bookery is an antiquarian shop featuring quality out-of-print and rare books. The new Bookery II offers a wide selection of new French, German, and Spanish books along with a travel section in English which carries guides, atlases, globes, and an in-depth collection of maps from around the world. Both shops occupy 2,500 square feet of space.
   How to Get There: The Dewitt Mall is located in downtown Ithaca at the corner of Buffalo and Cayuga Streets. The antiquarian section of The Bookery is on the ground floor of the bulding. The Bookery II travel and foreign language section has its own entrance on Buffalo Street.
   Owner/Biography: Jack Goldman.
   Year Founded/History of Bookstore: 1975. From 1975 to 1983 The Bookery operated as a general antiquarian shop. Within the past year, it has opened a second shop in the same building featuring new travel and foreign language books.
   Number of Volumes: 10,000.
   Types/Classifications: Hardbound, paperback, atlases, maps, first editions, out-of-print, sets, color plate books.
   General Subject Areas: Anthropology, Archaeology, Cornell University, Dance, Economics, History of Science, Labor History, Linguistics, Literary Theory, Music, Natural Science, New York State, Philology, Philosophy, Photography, Psychology, Theater.
   Other Specialties: Scholarly Books; French, German, and Spanish Books, Structuralism, Semeiotics, Marxism.
   Mail/Telephone Orders; Credit Cards: Both. Visa and Mastercard accepted.
   Business Hours: Monday through Saturday 10:00 AM - 5:30 PM.
   Parking Facilities: Steet parking.

Special Features: Search service; appraisals.
Catalogue: Catalogue published.
Collections/Individual Items Purchased: Both.

666
BookMarx, Inc.
28 Lincoln Avenue
Roslyn Heights, New York 11577

(516) 621-0095

A large picture window and a 12-foot high ceiling give BookMarx in Roslyn Heights its open, airy, and well-lit appearance. There are approximately 30 hand-made bookcases located throughout the store with some coming out towards the center and others flat against the wall. The chairs, carpeting, classical music, and fresh coffee brewing makes the store a comfortable place to browse. The store occupies 800 square feet of space.

How to Get There: Take the Northern State Parkway Exit 29 (Roslyn Road North), to the third traffic light, make a left turn onto Lincoln. By train, take the Long Island Railroad to Roslyn and walk 1 block east of the train station.

Owner/Biography: Evan Marx. Mr. Marx is a journalism graduate of Northeastern University in Boston (1975). He got into the book business in 1979 when his father bought a large collection of books while Evan was managing a local bookstore. Space was rented at the store to display the new collection which gradually grew large enough to become a full-time occupation. Mr. Marx has a large collection of early baseball books and memorabilia.

Year Founded/History of Bookstore: 1979. Originally the BookMarx was conducted in a 9 x 12 rented room in a local bookstore which was operated as a part-time business for 2 years, then full-time for 1 year. It was then operated out of a private residence for 1 year as a mail order business until the store was rented in April 1983.

Number of Volumes: 20,000.

Types/Classifications: Hardbound, paperback, magazines, broadsides, autographs, ephemera, prints, sheet music, photographs, illustrated books, press books.

General Subject Areas: Americana, Antiques, Art, Books About Books, Children's Books, Literature, Military, Mysteries, Science Fiction, Sports, Transportation, Travel.

Specific Specialties: Long Island, Big Game Hunting, Derrydale Press, Baseball Memorabilia (Pre-1930).

Author Specialties: Jack Kerouac, Jack London, Arthur Conan Doyle, P.G. Wodehouse, Lewis Carroll.

Mail/Telephone Orders; Credit Cards: Both. Cash with order, 10 day return privilege. Visa and Mastercard accepted.

Business Hours: Monday through Friday 11:00 AM - 7:00 PM; Saturday 11:00 AM - 5:00 PM.

Parking Facilities: Street parking.

Special Features: Search service, book repair.

Collections/Individual Items Purchased: Both.

Booksellers' Memberships: Long Island Antiquarian Bookdealers Association.

667
Books 'N Things
64 East 7th Street
New York, New York 10003

(212) 533-2320

This bookstore gives one the feeling of being in a small town. It is on the street level of an old brownstone townhouse on a side street in the East Village of Manhattan. It has an iron gate enclosing the front of two windows set at angles. The shop occupies 600 square feet of space.

How to Get There: The bookstore can be reached by nearby subway and surface transportation.

Owner/Biography: Gertrude Briggs. Mrs. Briggs' late husband was a poet and book scout before they opened their first bookstore in 1941 just off 4th Avenue on 10th Street. Before that year was over, they moved to the corner of 4th Avenue and 10th street where they remained for over 20 years. Mrs. Briggs continued the business in a new location after the death of her husband in 1969 and remained there until the most recent move. A reference to their shop appeared in "Publishers Weekly," October 27, 1969, Page 52.

Year Founded/History of Bookstore: 1941.

323

Number of Volumes: 10,000.
Types/Classifications: Hardbound, paperback, ephemera, rare postcards, trade cards, sheet music, valentines.
General Subject Areas: Children's Illustrated Books, Dance, Drama, Film, Modern Art, Modern Fiction, Photography, Poetry, Women Authors.
Mail/Telephone Orders; Credit Cards: Both.
Business Hours: Monday through Saturday 12:00 Noon - 6:00 PM.
Parking Facilities: Street parking, commercial parking lots.
Special Features: The bookstore offers good books to read, enjoy, and put on one's shelf.
Collections/Individual Items Purchased: Both.

668
Books of Wonder
464 Hudson Street
New York, New York 10014   (212) 989-3270

Books of Wonder specializes in children's and illustrated books, particularly those which entice and expand the imagination. Classic illustrated editions, juvenile fantasy, and historical children's literature are all to be found here. One of the shop's major specialties is the Oz books and other works of L. Frank Baum. Two to three hundred books in this area are maintained at all times. The shop occupies 700 square feet of space.
How to Get There: Located at the corner of Barrow Street in Greenwich Village, the bookstore is easily reached by nearby subway or surface transportation.
Owner/Biography: Peter Glassman and James Carey.
Year Founded/History of Bookstore: 1980. Originally at 444 Hudson Street for two years, the bookstore recently moved to the current location which is 4 times the size and located on a corner.
Number of Volumes: 5,000.
Types/Classifications: Hardbound, ephemera, first editions, out-of-print, signed books, limited editions, presentation copies, association copies.
General Subject Areas: Children's Books, Illustrated Books.
Specific Specialties: Oz and the works of L. Frank Baum; Juvenile Fantasy, Children's Classics (Mid-19th Century through 20th Century).
Author Specialties: L. Frank Baum, John R. Neill, Jack Snow, W.W. Denslow, N.C. Wyeth, Maurice Sendak, Willy Pogany, Robert Lawson, Jessie Wilcox Smith, Howard Pyle, Maxfield Parrish.
Mail/Telephone Orders; Credit Cards: Both. Payment with order in U.S. dollars drawn on a U.S. bank. American Express, Visa, Mastercard accepted.
Business Hours: Monday through Thursday 11:00 AM - 7:00 PM; Friday and Saturday 12:00 Noon - 9:00 PM; Sunday 12:00 Noon - 6:00 PM.
Parking Facilities: Street parking; commercial parking lots.
Catalogue: Published 3 to 4 times per year.
Collections/Individual Items Purchased: Both.

669
Bookswappers
1400 Wantagh Avenue
Wantagh, New York 11793   (516) 785-9029

The Bookswappers is a used paperback bookstore specializing in mysteries, science fiction and fantasy, romances, and general fiction. There is also a large selection of children's books.
How to Get There: Wantagh is on the South Shore of Long Island and can be reached via the Southern State Parkway east from Manhattan; take the Wantagh exit south.
Owner/Biography: Bengta Woo.
Year Founded/History of Bookstore: 1975. The Bookswappers is still at the original site. The store was purchased in 1980 by Bengta Woo.
Number of Volumes: 20,000 paperback, 5,000 hardbound.

Types/Classifications: Paperback, some hardbound, out-of-print, first editions.

General Subject Areas: Adventure, American History, Anthropology, Biography, Black History, Children's Literature, Children's Series, Cinema, Classics, Contemporary Romances, Cookbooks, Drama, Essays, Gothics, Historical Romances, Mysteries, Occult, Philosophy, Poetry, Psychology, Religion, Science Fiction and Fantasy, Sociology, Sports, War Novels, Westerns, World History.

Specific Specialties: Harlequins, Dell Candlelight-Ecstasy, Nancy Drew, Hardy Boys, Women Authors.

Author Specialties: Robert A. Heinlein, C.S. Lewis, Agatha Christie, Rex Stout, Ellery Queen, John Creasey, Elsie Lee, Elizabeth Peters, Ellis Peters, Barbara Michaels, Patricia Wentworth.

Mail/Telephone Orders; Credit Cards: Both. Contact the bookstore for mailing specifications. No credit cards.

Business Hours: Monday through Saturday 9:00 AM - 5:00 PM.

Parking Facilities: Business parking lot.

Special Features: Search service; want lists accepted.

Catalogue: Catalogue of Mystery and Detective first editions and out-of-print hardbound and paperback books is issued once a month.

Collections/Individual Items Purchased: Individual items only.

Booksellers' Memberships: Long Island Antiquarian Booksellers Association.

Miscellaneous: Mystery and Detective Fiction hardbound books are not kept at the store but can be viewed by appointment at the owner's home.

670
Bookworm
18 West Market
P.O. Box 263
Corning, New York 14830

(607) 962-6778

The Bookworm features antiquarian and used books arranged by category. The store has a beautiful oak front and occupies 1,400 square feet of space. It is listed in the Historical Register.

How to Get There: The bookstore is off Highway 17 in the heart of restored downtown Corning, home of the Corning Glass Museum.

Owner/Biography: Billie and Howard Weetall.

Year Founded/History of Bookstore: 1974. The Bookworm began in Horseheads, New York and moved to Corning in 1977.

Number of Volumes: 20,000.

Types/Classifications: Hardbound, autographs, maps, prints, ephemera, first editions, fine bindings, out-of-print, association copies, press books, signed copies, presentation copies, limited editions, color plate books.

General Subject Areas: General.

Specific Specialties: Guns, Children's Literature, American Indians, Horticulture, Americana, Medical, Art, Architecture, Religion, Travel, West (U.S.), Cookbooks, Early School Books.

Author Specialties: Mark Twain.

Mail/Telephone Orders; Credit Cards: Both. Cash with order. Visa and Mastercard accepted.

Business Hours: Monday through Saturday 9:00 AM - 5:00 PM.

Parking Facilities: Street parking.

Special Features: Search service.

Collections/Individual Items Purchased: Both.

Miscellaneous: Very little fiction, no paperbacks.

671
Boro Book Store
146 Lawrence Street
Brooklyn, New York 11201

(212) 522-5278

The Boro Book Store is a general used bookstore which carries over 100 subjects in fiction and non-fiction.

How to Get There: The bookstore can be reached by any subway line to the downtown Brooklyn area.

Owner/Biography: R. Colton.
Year Founded/History of Bookstore: 1952. The store was originally on Montague Street in Brooklyn Heights and was founded by Samuel and Silvia Colton. It was moved to its present location in May 1978.
Number of Volumes: 75,000.
Types/Classifications: Hardbound, paperback, some magazines, out-of-print; all non-text subjects.
General Subject Areas: Biography, General, Judaica, Music, Politics, Religion, Science, Technical.
Mail/Telephone Orders; Credit Cards: Both. Cash with order. No credit cards.
Business Hours: Monday through Saturday 11:30 AM - 6:00 PM. Closed Sunday and major holidays.
Parking Facilities: Street parking, commercial parking lots.
Special Features: Search service; the bookstore has published some books on Brooklyn and the Brooklyn Bridge.
Catalogue: George A. Bernstein operates a catalogue business from this store, specializing in Sciences and Judaica plus other subjects.
Collections/Individual Items Purchased: Both.

672
Brazen Head Bookshop
215 East 84th Street
New York, New York 10028   (212) 861-4704

The Brazen Head Bookshop is a small bookshop located on East 84th Street between 2nd and 3rd Avenues. It features general out-of-print and first editions. All books are neatly organized.
How to Get There: The shop can be reached via nearby subway and surface transportation.
Owner/Biography: Michael Seidenberg.
Year Founded/History of Bookstore: 1979. The shop was originally located in Brooklyn and moved to Manhattan in 1981.
Number of Volumes: 10,000.
Types/Classifications: Hardbound, paperback, first editions, out-of-print, signed copies.
General Subject Areas: Art, Belles Lettres, Biography, Fiction, History, Humor, Mysteries, Performing Arts, Philosophy, Poetry, Science Fiction, Travel.
Author Specialties: John Cowper Powys, Robert Graves.
Mail/Telephone Orders; Credit Cards: Both. Cash with order. No credit cards.
Business Hours: Monday through Friday 4:00 PM - 8:00 PM; Saturday 1:00 PM - 8:00 PM; call for Sunday hours; appointments can be made before 4:00 PM.
Parking Facilities: Street parking, commercial parking lots.
Collections/Individual Items Purchased: Both.

673
Brighton-Nostrand Book Shop
276 Brighton Beach Avenue
Brooklyn, New York 11235   (212) 891-2849

This book shop has shelves filled alphabetically with new and used paperbacks, used magazines, and shool supplies blended together with new and rare comics. The shop also has a new and used children's section. It occupies approximately 980 square feet of space.
How to Get There: To reach the bookstore, take Brooklyn's Belt Parkway to Ocean Parkway, south to Brighton Beach Avenue (under the elevated subway line).
Owner/Biography: Bernice Bogash.
Year Founded/History of Bookstore: 1955. A first store on Nostrand Avenue in Brooklyn was destroyed by fire and in 1969 a move was made to the present location.
Number of Volumes: Approximately 500,000 items.
Types/Classifications: Hardbound, paperback, magazines, comics, school supplies.
General Subject Areas: Americana, Biography, Boating, Children's Books, Classics, Comics, Cookbooks, Games, Gothic Novels, Health, Humor, Judaica, Maps, Mysteries, Mythology, Nature, Occult, Philosophy, Puzzle Books, Science Fiction and Fantasy, Spy Novels, Westerns.

Mail/Telephone Orders; Credit Cards: Both. Payment in full in advance (will hold items two weeks until check clears; if money order, next day shipment). No credit cards.
Business Hours: Monday through Saturday 10:00 AM to 5:30 PM.
Parking Facilities: Public parking lot, street parking.
Catalogue: Catalogue published.
Collections/Individual Items Purchased: Both (for paperbacks, collections only).
Miscellaneous: The bookstore is family owned and offers personal attention to each customer.

674
Broude Brothers Limited
170 Varick Street
New York, New York 10013

(212) 242-7001

Broude Brothers Limited are antiquarian book dealers specializing in early books on music, art and the theater, and fine facsimile reprints. Visitors are welcome by appointment only.
How to Get There: Located in lower Manhattan, the shop is reachable by subway and surface transportaton.
Owner/Biography: Ronald Broude.
Year Founded/History of Bookstore: 1935.
Types/Classifications: Hardbound, rare, out-of-print, fine facsimile reprints.
General Subject Areas: Art, Dance, Music, Theater.
Mail/Telephone Orders; Credit Cards: Both. No credit cards.
Business Hours: By appointment only.
Parking Facilities: Street parking, commercial parking lots.
Catalogue: Catalogue published.
Booksellers' Memberships: Antiquarian Booksellers Association of America including Middle Atlantic Chapter.

675
Bryn Mawr Book Shop
170 Grand Street
White Plains, New York 10514

(914) 946-5356

This book shop is a non-profit organization stocked by donations. It occupies 800 square feet of space and has out-of-print books in all categories.
Owner/Biography: Bryn Mawr Club of Westchester.
Year Founded/History of Bookstore: 1977.
Number of Volumes: 12,000.
Types/Classifications: Hardbound, paperback, out-of-print, some first editions.
General Subject Areas: Afro American, Art, Biography, Business, Children's Literature, Classics, Cookbooks, Gardening, History, Philosophy, Political Science, Psychology, Reference, Religion, Science, Short Stories, Travel, Women's Studies.
Mail/Telephone Orders; Credit Cards: Both. No credit cards.
Business Hours: Monday through Saturday 10:00 AM - 4:00 PM.
Parking Facilities: Street parking, nearby public parking lot.
Collections/Individual Items Purchased: None; stocked by donations only.

676
Bryn Mawr Book Shop
1 Spring Street
Albany, New York 12210

(518) 865-8126

The Bryn Mawr Book Shop was the first of nine book shops to open as a fund raising project for Bryn Mawr College scholarships. The shop is run by alumnae of Bryn Mawr and the funds go to the Upstate New York Scholarship Fund. The shop occupies 3,000 square feet of space.

How to Get There: The bookstore is located 2 blocks west of the Capitol Building.

Owner/Biography: Co-managers: Mrs. Barbara McNamee Dudley and Mrs. Virginia Bennett.

Year Founded/History of Bookstore: 1968. After 10 years in an old fire house, the shop settled in the present location, a building that was originally designed for and used as the city library.

Number of Volumes: 30,000.

Types/Classifications: Hardbound, paperback, autographs, ephemera, records, sheet music, prints, frames, first editions, fine bindings, signed copies, illustrated books, out-of-print.

General Subject Areas: Americana, Ancient History, Art, Automotive, Aviation, Biography, Children's Books, Economics, Essays, Gardening, Hobbies, International Affairs, Journalism, Law, Literary Biography, Medicine, Modern History, Music, Natural Science, Philosophy, Poetry, Political Science, Presidential Biography, Psychology, Railroads, Religion, Science Fiction, Sociology, Textbooks, Travel, War, Women.

Mail/Telephone Orders; Credit Cards: Both. No credit cards.

Business Hours: Tuesday through Saturday 10:30 AM - 4:00 PM.

Parking Facilities: Street parking.

Special Features: Search service; appraisals.

Collections/Individual Items Purchased: Both.

677
Bryn Mawr Book Shop
135 East Avenue
Rochester, New York 14604   (716) 454-2910

This bookstore is a non-profit organization which sells donated books to raise scholarship funds for Bryn Mawr College. The stock is old, rare, and out-of-print in all categories.

Number of Volumes: Thousands.

Types/Classifications: Hardbound, paperback, rare, out-of-print, first editions, reading copies.

General Subject Areas: Americana, Art, Asia and Africa, Biography, Children's Books, History, Languages, Literature, Music, Philosophy, Psychology, Religion, Science and Technology, Travel.

Mail/Telephone Orders; Credit Cards: No mail or phone orders; no credit cards.

Business Hours: Monday through Saturday 10:00 AM - 4:00 PM.

Parking Facilities: Street parking, public parking lot.

Collections/Individual Items Purchased: Neither. Donations accepted.

Miscellaneous: Staffed by alumnae volunteers.

678
Bryn Mawr Book Shop
502 East 79th Street
New York, New York 10021   (212) 744-7682

The Bryn Mawr Book Shop of New York City is a non-profit organization which sells donated books to raise scholarship funds for Bryn Mawr College. The stock is old, rare, and out-of-print in all categories.

Number of Volumes: Thousands.

Types/Classifications: Hardbound, paperback, rare, out-of-print, first editions, reading copies.

General Subject Areas: Americana, Art, Asia and Africa, Biography, Children's Books, History, Languages, Literature, Music, Philosophy, Psychology, Religion, Science and Technology, Travel.

Mail/Telephone Orders; Credit Cards: No mail or phone orders; no credit cards.

Business Hours: Monday through Saturday 10:00 AM - 4:00 PM.

Parking Facilities: Commercial parking lots and garages.

Collections/Individual Items Purchased: Neither. Donations accepted.

Miscellaneous: Staffed by alumnae volunteers.

679
C.J. Scheiner, Books
275 Linden Boulevard
Brooklyn, New York 11226   (212) 469-1089

C.J. Scheiner, Books is possibly the only specialty bookseller in the United States dealing exclusively in Erotica, Curiosa, and Sexology. They deal in fine, rare, and related material, almost exclusively by mail order.

Owner/Biography: C.J. Scheiner. Mr. Scheiner is one of America's foremost authorities on printed Erotica and is a recognized expert throughout the world. He has been actively researching the genre of Erotica for over twenty years. His annotated catalogues are kept in the reference sections of such institutions as the Institute for Sex Research and the British Library. Mr. Scheiner has written several articles on the subject and has been interviewed by major publications in the United States and Europe. His own research archives contain in excess of 40,000 volumes on the subject of Erotica.

Year Founded/History of Bookstore: 1977.

Number of Volumes: 4,000.

Types/Classifications: Hardbound, paperback, magazines, film, newspapers, comics, art, ephemera; fine, rare, reference and collectible items including first editions and illustrated editions.

General Subject Areas: Curiosa, Erotica, Sexology.

Other Specialties: Foreign language material is stocked.

Mail/Telephone Orders; Credit Cards: Both. Check with order. No credit cards.

Business Hours: Variable. 24 hour answering service.

Special Features: Extensive search service; literature quotes and illustrations provided for commercial re-use.

Catalogue: Published twice per year; latest catalogue available for $2.

Collections/Individual Items Purchased: Both.

Miscellaneous: Personalized service; collections built for serious collectors.

680
Cabin in the Pines Bookshop
Route 2
Potsdam, New York 13676   (315) 265-9036

This bookshop is a log cabin that the owner had built next to his 1822 brick farmhouse. It is constructed of hemlock logs cut from his land. He carries a general stock and the majority of books are hardbound and arranged alphabetically by author in 350 square feet of space.

How to Get There: The shop is located 1/2 mile west of West Potsdam on the Buck's Bridge Road. Potsdam is 60 miles north of Watertown and 90 miles south of Ottawa. From Potsdam take the road to Madrid for 3 miles; at the top of a hill there is a sign for West Potsdam.

Owner/Biography: Charles Penrose. Mr. Penrose was a librarian at the Clarkson College Library for 30 years and is now retired. Before that time he was at the Bethany College Library in West Virginia. He is a graduate of the College of William and Mary and the University of Michigan. He served in the U.S. Army for 4 1/2 years including service in India and Iran.

Year Founded/History of Bookstore: 1978.

Number of Volumes: 4,000.

Types/Classifications: Hardbound, some paperback, out-of-print, some association copies and limited editions.

General Subject Areas: Adirondackana, Art, Biography, History, Novels, Poetry.

Author Specialties: Irving Bachellor.

Mail/Telephone Orders; Credit Cards: Both. Cash with order. No credit cards.

Business Hours: Monday through Saturday 9:00 AM - 5:00 PM.

Parking Facilities: Parking just outside the cabin among the pine trees.

Special Features: Search service, no charge unless book is located, $7 commission added to price of book; $5 commission added if the patron picks up the book.

Collections/Individual Items Purchased: Individual items; collections are rarely purchased.

Booksellers' Memberships: Upstate New York Antiquarian Booksellers Association.

681
Caravan-Maritime Books
87-06 168th Place
Jamaica, New York 11432

Caravan-Maritime Books does not have an open shop but deals by mail order only. It carries rare and out-of-print books relating to the sea, the ship, and the sailor.

Owner/Biography: Anne Klein.
Year Founded/History of Bookstore: 1946.
Number of Volumes: Over 4,000.
Types/Classifications: Hardbound, ephemera, first editions, fine bindings, out-of-print, association copies, press books, signed copies, presentation copies, limited editions, color plate books.
General Subject Areas: Sailors, Sea, Ships.
Specific Specialties: World wide maritime specialty.
Other Specialties: Any and all foreign languages on maritime subjects.
Mail/Telephone Orders; Credit Cards: Mail order only. Cash with order. No credit cards.
Special Features: Search service.
Catalogue: Published 3 to 4 times per year.
Collections/Individual Items Purchased: Both; maritime subjects only, especially rare and hard-to-find.
Booksellers' Memberships: Antiquarian Booksellers Association of America.

682
Carlson - Booksellers
7883-7885 Main Street
Box 194
Springwater, New York 14560   (716) 669-2450

Open to the public most weekends the year round, the bookstore has its books shelved in an 1840 building that operated originally as the post office and bank. The owners state that the stock is western New York's largest of rare and out-of-print books. There are more than 250,000 books with 80,000 shelved. The owners are specialists in Americana with wide-ranging collections on Alaska, Arctic Americana, the American West, American Indians, Revolutionary and Civil War, Western Hemispheric Discovery, Atlases, and Histories of the American States. The stock occupies over 8,000 square feet of space.

How to Get There: Nestled in the scenic center of western New York's Finger Lakes, the village of Springwater is in the heart of the area's antiques and crafts country, 35 miles south of Rochester, midway between the New York Thruway (U.S. 90) and the new Southern Tier Expressway (NY 17).
Owner/Biography: Reid and Nancy Carlson. They are successors to the Midland Rare Book Company of Mansfield, Ohio who were the principal builders of the Thomas W. Streeter Collection.
Year Founded/History of Bookstore: 1953.
Number of Volumes: Over 250,000.
Types/Classifications: Hardbound, fine bindings, some fine prints and early paintings, autographs, excellent collection of pamphlets and ephemera on or related to the Western Hemisphere before 1875, first editions, out-of-print, association copies, signed copies, presentation copies, limited editions, color plate books, European and American view books.
General Subject Areas: American Indians, American Revolutionary War, Black History, Discovery of the American West, Lincoln-Douglas Debates, World War II.
Specific Specialties: Pre-Colonial Wars through Vietnam; Western Discovery and Migration; illustrated and early Children's Books; History of Russian and Soviet Union; Abraham Lincoln; small stock of Science Fiction and Fantasy; Magic/Occult; Medicine and Health; Sex; Cooking.
Mail/Telephone Orders; Credit Cards: Both. Check with order; shipped satisfaction guaranteed on items returned as sent (postpaid and insured) within 7 days of receipt. No credit cards.
Business Hours: Although usually working daily, appointment is advised. Open to the public most weekends.
Parking Facilities: Street, business parking lot suitable for trucks and motorhomes.
Special Features: Wholesale supplier to most professional bookdealers in northeastern and midwestern United States and eastern Canada.

Catalogue: Published twice per year.
Collections/Individual Items Purchased: Both.

683
Carnegie Book Shop
30 East 60th Street
New York, New York 10022

(212) 755-4861

The Carnegie Book Shop is an antiquarian bookstore dealing in rare books, autographed material, autographs, and manuscripts. A specialty is Americana.

How to Get There: The shop is located in midtown Manhattan and can be reached by nearby subway and surface transportation.

Owner/Biography: David Kirschenbaum.

Year Founded/History of Bookstore: 1910. The shop was formerly located at 140 East 59th Street.

Types/Classifications: Hardbound, broadsides, autographs, ephemera, first editions, fine bindings, out-of-print, association copies, press copies, signed copies, presentation copies, limited editions, color plate books.

General Subject Areas: Americana.

Mail/Telephone Orders; Credit Cards: No telephone orders.

Business Hours: Monday through Saturday 9:00 AM - 4:00 PM.

Collections/Individual Items Purchased: Both.

684
Collectors Antiques, Inc.
286 A Main Street
Port Washington, New York 11050

(516) 883-2098

The Collectors Antiques offers rare antique books, fine bindings, history, children's books, antique reference, medical, cookery, and fine illustrated books. It also stocks books on Judaica, early Bibles, and miscellaneous ephemera.

How to Get There: The shop is located in a former bank building near Shore Road.

Owner/Biography: Jean Feigenbaum, President. Ms. Feigenbaum has over 25 years' experience dealing and living with antiques and books.

Year Founded/History of Bookstore: 1964.

Number of Volumes: 2,000.

Types/Classifications: Hardbound, rare, out-of-print, fine bindings, color plate books.

General Subject Areas: Bibles, Children's Books, Cookery, Judaica, Medical, Reference.

Mail/Telephone Orders; Credit Cards: Neither; no credit cards.

Business Hours: Monday through Saturday 9:00 AM - 5:00 PM.

Parking Facilities: Public parking lot, street parking.

Collections/Individual Items Purchased: Both.

Booksellers' Memberships: Long Island Antiquarian Book Dealers Association.

Miscellaneous: Also includes an antique shop.

685
Copper Fox Farm Books
Box 763 (Route 44, Mabbettsville)
Millbrook, New York 12545

(914) 677-3013

Copper Fox Farm Books has a general antiquarian collection. The stock occupies 1,050 square feet of space.

How to Get There: Call for specific directions.

Owner/Biography: George B. Davis.

Year Founded/History of Bookstore: 1968.

Number of Volumes: 40,000.

Types/Classifications: Hardbound, paperback, out-of-print, signed copies.

General Subject Areas: American and English Literature, Antiques, Children's Books, Collectibles, Cookbooks, Gardening, Horses and Hounds, Military History, Natural History, Needlework, New York History, Old Farming, U.S. History.

Mail/Telephone Orders; Credit Cards: Both. No credit cards.

Business Hours: Saturday and Sunday 9:00 AM - 5:00 PM.

Parking Facilities: Adequate parking.

Special Features: Free search service.

Catalogue: Catalogue published (no specific date).

Collections/Individual Items Purchased: Both.

686
Corner-Stone Bookshop
110 Margaret Street
Plattsburgh, New York 12901   (518) 561-0520

This bookshop carries over 75,000 out-of-print and used books neatly organized and arranged on the ground floor and basement. All categories are available as well as thousands of old comics and phonograph records.

How to Get There: The shop is located in downtown Plattsburgh next to Lake Champlain. Take the Plattsburgh exit on Adirondack Northway 87, then Route 3 east to downtown; shop is at corner of Court and Margaret. Route 9N and 9S pass right by the door.

Owner/Biography: Nancy Duniho.

Year Founded/History of Bookstore: 1975.

Number of Volumes: 75,000.

Types/Classifications: Hardbound, paperback, out-of-print, comics, phonograph records.

General Subject Areas: Adventure, American History, Anthropology, Biography, Business, Canadian Books, Children's Books, Cookbooks, European History, Hunting and Fishing, Lake Champlain and Adirondack History, Literature, Medical, Parapsychology, Poetry, Psychology, Science, Science Fiction, Theology, World War II.

Specific Specialties: National Geographic Magazines.

Mail/Telephone Orders; Credit Cards: Both. Orders accepted only from the store's published lists. Visa and Mastercard accepted.

Business Hours: Monday through Saturday 9:00 AM - 9:00 PM.

Parking Facilities: Public parking lot, street parking.

Catalogue: Catlogue published "once in a while."

Collections/Individual Items Purchased: Collections only.

Miscellaneous: The owner does not want solicitation or sales calls from publishers of new books.

687
David Tunick Inc.
12 East 81st Street
New York, New York 10028   (212) 570-0090

David Tunick Inc. is a gallery dealing primarily in old master and modern prints and old master drawings. Books containing fine original prints are a small but important part of the gallery's inventory. The gallery is housed in a 100-year old townhouse with a beautiful wood-paneled viewing room. Clients include major museums both in the United States and abroad.

How to Get There: Located on the east side of Manhattan, the shop is easily accessible by nearby subway and surface transportation.

Owner/Biography: David P. Tunick.

Year Founded/History of Bookstore: 1966.

Types/Classifications: Hardbound books containing fine orginial graphic art.

General Subject Areas: Old Master Prints and Drawings.

Mail/Telephone Orders; Credit Cards: Both. Customers must have had previous business with the firm or have proper references; return of works not purchased within 1 week, registered and fully insured. No credit cards.

Business Hours: Monday through Friday 10:00 AM - 5:00 PM.
Parking Facilities: Street parking, parking lot at Metropolitan Museum nearby.
Catalogue: Published irregularly.
Collections/Individual Items Purchased: Both.
Booksellers' Memberships: Antiquarian Booksellers Association of America; International League of Antiquarian Booksellers.

688
De Simone Company, Booksellers
54 Charles Street
New York, New York 10014 (212) 242-1252

De Simone Company, Booksellers are specialists in antiquarian bibliography, Americana, and 18th Century books. Visits may be arranged by appointment.
How to Get There: Charles Street is 6 blocks south of 14th Street off 7th Avenue South in the heart of Greenwich Village in Manhattan.
Owner/Biography: Daniel De Simone.
Year Founded/History of Bookstore: 1978.
Number of Volumes: 1,000.
Types/Classifications: 18th Century books in original leather and paper bindings.
General Subject Areas: Americana, Antiquarian Bibliography, Eighteenth Century Books.
Specific Specialties: History of Printing, Bookbinding, Papermaking; Library, Auction, and Booksellers Catalogues; 18th and 19th Century Books relating to America; French and Italian 18th Century Books (in original bindings).
Mail/Telephone Orders; Credit Cards: Both. References required. No credit cards.
Business Hours: By appointment only.
Parking Facilities: Street parking, commercial parking lots.
Catalogue: Published 3 to 4 time per year.
Collections/Individual Items Purchased: Both.
Booksellers' Memberships: Antiquarian Booksellers Association of America, International League of Antiquarian Booksellers.

689
Denning House
Orrs Mills Road
Salisbury Mills, New York 12577 (914) 496-6771

Denning House deals in general out-of-print and unusual books and paper items. Business is by appointment and via catalogues.
How to Get There: Call for directions.
Owner/Biography: P.R. McTague.
Year Founded/History of Bookstore: 1963.
Types/Classifications: Hardbound, out-of-print, paper items.
General Subject Areas: General.
Mail/Telephone Orders; Credit Cards: Both. No credit cards.
Business Hours: By appointment only.
Catalogue: Catalogue published every month.
Collections/Individual Items Purchased: Both.

690
Depot Attic
377 Ashford Avenue
Dobbs Ferry, New York 10522   (914) 693-5858

The Depot Attic is a haven for railroad historians and enthusiasts. Occupying a large old fashioned basement with high ceilings, the store resembles a cluttered museum of railroad books, ephemera, chinaware, and hardware. Visitors step back in history as they enter. Modern fixtures are almost nonexistent.

How to Get There: Dobbs Ferry is one half hour north of Manhattan via New York State Thruway or Saw Mill River Parkway.

Owner/Biography: Fred Arone and John Martin. Mr. Arone is the son of a railroad telegrapher and was raised in various railroad depots where his father worked. He also became a railroader. John Martin is an advanced collector of rare railroad books, ephemera, and chinaware.

Year Founded/History of Bookstore: 1954. The store is in its original site.

Number of Volumes: 75,000 plus thousands of booklets, brochures, etc.

Types/Classifications: Hardbound, paperback, magazines, broadsides, ephemera, first editions, out-of-print, signed copies, presentation copies, limited editions, color plate books.

General Subject Areas: Railroad items of all types.

Specific Specialties: Canadian Railroads, U.S. Railroads.

Other Specialties: Some ship, express, and early airline ephemera.

Mail/Telephone Orders; Credit Cards: Both. No credit cards.

Business Hours: Saturday and Sunday only 12:00 Noon - 5:00 PM. Mail order any day; by phone after 6:00 PM. An additional telephone number is (914) 693-1832.

Parking Facilities: Street parking.

Special Features: Search service; collection appraisals; special service to decorators seeking railroad motif; advisors to authors, film makers, etc.

Catalogue: Published 8 times yearly; send $2 for next 4 issues.

Collections/Individual Items Purchased: Both.

Booksellers' Memberships: National Railway Historical Society, Railway and Locomotive Historical Society.

Miscellaneous: Coffee pot is always on and the owners like to discuss their field with all visitors and customers; The Depot Attic is "the largest specialized railroad artifact and antiquarian business in America."

691
Discount Book Warehouse
3735 Nostrand Avenue
Brooklyn, New York 11235   (212) 646-5225

One of the largest bookstores in Brooklyn, Discount Book Warehouse is open seven days weekly. It has a comprehensive selection of new, used, and out-of-print paperbacks. The stock occupies 1,700 square feet of space.

How to Get There: From the Belt Parkway, take exit 9A (Knapp Street). The store is 10 blocks away.

Owner/Biography: Michael Simms.

Year Founded/History of Bookstore: 1975.

Number of Volumes: 100,000.

Types/Classifications: Paperbacks, magazines, comics, self-help tapes, old radio tapes, complete line of "Dungeons and Dragons."

General Subject Areas: Automotive, Children's Books, Computer Books, Literature, Mysteries, Reference, Romance, Science Fiction, Show Business, Westerns.

Mail/Telephone Orders; Credit Cards: Mail orders only; send self addressed stamped envelope with request for easy and quick response. Visa and Mastercard accepted.

Business Hours: Seven days a week 10:00 AM - 7:30 PM.

Parking Facilities: Street parking.

Special Features: Old paperback search; romance series subscriptions, comic and magazine subscriptions; photocopies.

Collections/Individual Items Purchased: Both.

692
Donan Books
235 East 53rd Street
New York, New York 10022

(212) 421-6210

Donan Books is an east side Manhattan bookstore dealing in hardbound used books in all general classifications. It occupies 1,000 square feet of space.
How to Get There: The store is easily accessible by nearby subway and surface transportation.
Owner/Biography: Donald Dryfoos.
Year Founded/History of Bookstore: 1969.
Number of Volumes: 20,000.
Types/Classifications: Hardbound.
General Subject Areas: General.
Mail/Telephone Orders; Credit Cards: Both. No credit cards.
Business Hours: Monday through Friday 9:00 AM - 4:00 PM.
Parking Facilities: Street parking is hard to come by in Manhattan; commercial parking lots in neighborhood.
Special Features: Free search service.
Collections/Individual Items Purchased: Both.

693
Edward J. Monarski, Antiquarian Books
1050 Wadsworth Street
Syracuse, New York 13208

(315) 455-1716

The collection is located in the basement of the Monarski home. The stock occupies 1,200 square feet of space.
How to Get There: The bookstore is located on the north side of Syracuse; exit Route 81 North at Court Street Exit, go to Wadsworth Street, turn left (5 minutes from Route 81).
Owner/Biography: Edward J. Monarski.
Year Founded/History of Bookstore: 1967.
Number of Volumes: 14,000.
Types/Classifications: Hardbound, magazines, broadsides, autographs, ephemera, signed copies, limited editions, color plate books.
General Subject Areas: General.
Specific Specialties: New York State History, World War II Military Research Material and World War II Germany.
Author Specialties: L. Frank Baum.
Mail/Telephone Orders; Credit Cards: Both. No credit cards.
Business Hours: By appointment or chance.
Special Features: Free search service.
Catalogue: Published 4 times per year.
Collections/Individual Items Purchased: Both.

694
Elgen Books
336 DeMott Avenue
Rockville Centre, New York 11570

(516) 536-6276

Elgen Books specializes in medicine, science, technology, and mathematics including biography in these areas.
Owner/Biography: Esther and Leonard Geller.
Year Founded/History of Bookstore: 1977.
Number of Volumes: 5,000.

335

Types/Classifications: Hardbound, out-of-print, first editions.
General Subject Areas: Biography, Mathematics, Medicine, Science, Technology.
Mail/Telephone Orders; Credit Cards: Both. No credit cards.
Special Features: Appraisals.
Catalogue: Published 1 or 2 times annually.

695
Elysian Fields, Booksellers
80-50 Baxter Avenue
Suite 339
Elmhurst, New York 11373   (212) 424-2789

Elysian Fields is a mail order only business and deals in out-of-print gay literature, gay journals, magazines, periodicals, paperbacks, and ephemera.
Owner/Biography: Ed Drucker.
Year Founded/History of Bookstore: 1973.
Number of Volumes: 10,000.
Types/Classifications: Hardbound, paperback, magazines, ephemera, rare, out-of-print.
General Subject Areas: Erotica, Gay Literature, Transexualism, Transgenderism, Transvestism.
Specific Specialties: Ronald Firbank.
Mail/Telephone Orders; Credit Cards: Both. Visa and Mastercard accepted.
Business Hours: Mail order only. 24 hour telephone answering machine.
Special Features: Search service.
Catalogue: Published 2 to 3 times yearly plus lists.
Collections/Individual Items Purchased: Both.

696
Emil Offenbacher, Old and Rare Books
84-50 Austin Street
P.O. Box 96
Kew Gardens, New York 11415   (212) 849-5834

This business is conducted from the owner's home. He specializes in old and rare books, particularly in the fields of early medicine, science, and technology.
Owner/Biography: Emil Offenbacher.
Year Founded/History of Bookstore: 1945.
Number of Volumes: 1,000.
Types/Classifications: Old and rare only.
General Subject Areas: Early Medicine, Science, Technology.
Mail/Telephone Orders; Credit Cards: Both. Prepayment required from unknown buyers. No credit cards.
Business Hours: Variable.
Catalogue: Published once per year.
Collections/Individual Items Purchased: Both.
Booksellers' Memberships: Antiquarian Booksellers Association of America.

697
Ex Libris - A Division of T. J. Art Inc.
160-A East 70th Street
New York, New York 10021   (212) 249-2618

Situated on the ground floor of a New York City townhouse, the 800-square foot offices are designed in the De Stijl manner, with strong accents of blue, red, and green, amid prevailing white modern furniture and burgundian wood furniture. The shop contains one of the largest existant stocks documenting the art and architecture of the 20th Century, consisting of rare original editions, periodicals, posters, photographs (1920's and 1930's predominating), graphic design, graphic ephemera, and autographs.

Owner/Biography: Arthur A. and Elaine Lustig Cohen. Arthur A. Cohen, novelist, theologian, essayist, and art historian, is the author and editor of more than sixteen works. Founder of Meridian Books and former editor-in-chief of Holt, Rinehart, Winston, Mr. Cohen has been managing editor of "Documents of 20th Century Art" and co-editor with his wife Elaine Lustig Cohen of the new series, "The Avant-Garde In Print." Mrs. Cohen, former graphic designer, is a painter widely exhibited in the United States, and represented in many American corporate and museum collections.

Year Founded/History of Bookstore: Originally operated from an apartment on East 69th Street in 1974 in Manhattan, Ex Libris was moved to its present location during the fall of 1978.

Number of Volumes: 4,000.

Types/Classifications: Hardbacks, periodicals, posters, photographs, graphic design, graphic ephemera, autographs. Most all classifications, including first editions, fine bindings, out-of-print.

General Subject Areas: Art Movements of the 20th Century, Avant-Garde Architecture.

Specific Specialties: Only rare and recherché materials relating to the major Avant-Garde Architectural and Art Movements of the 20th Century. No reprints or facsimiles; "the original or nothing."

Other Specialties: Bauhaus, Dada, Futurism, Russian Avant-Garde Illustrated Books (1910- 1935), Surrealism, Cubism, Vorticism, Fluxus, Architecture, Rare Avant-Garde posters, Graphic Design, De Stijl, German Expressionism, Design and Topography, Vienna Secession.

Mail/Telephone Orders; Credit Cards: Mail orders: cash with order for new clients; material returnable with full refund within two weeks. Telephone orders. No credit cards.

Business Hours: Monday through Friday 10:00 AM - 5:00 PM; closed weekends.

Parking Facilities: Generally available in the area, with business parking and street parking.

Catalogue: Four times a year.

Collections/Individual Items Purchased: Both.

Booksellers' Memberships: Antiquarian Booksellers Association of America; Deutscher Verband (associate member).

Miscellaneous: Continual exhibition of rare works of Avant-Garde photography, posters, Dada ephemera, as well as rare works by Marcel Duchamp.

698

F. A. Bernett Inc.

2001 Palmer Avenue
Larchmont, New York 10538
(914) 834-3026

The bookstore carries out-of-print and rare books on the fine arts, architecture, archaeology, and history of the theater.

How to Get There: The bookstore is situated thirty-five minutes by train from Grand Central Station in New York City. If travelling by car, Palmer Avenue is just off Interstate 95.

Owner/Biography: The Bernetts.

Year Founded/History of Bookstore: 1944.

Number of Volumes: 4,000.

Types/Classifications: Out-of-print, rare.

General Subject Areas: Archaeology, Architecture, Fine Arts, Theater History.

Mail/Telephone Orders; Credit Cards: Both; no credit cards accepted.

Business Hours: Monday through Friday 9:00 AM - 5:00 PM.

Parking Facilities: Street parking.

Catalogue: Six times a year.

Collections/Individual Items Purchased: Both.

Booksellers' Memberships: Antiquarian Booksellers Association of America.

699
Fantasy Archives
71 8th Avenue
New York, New York 10014 (212) 929-5391

Fantasy Archives is an antiquarian science fiction and fantasy rare bookseller dealing in first editions, original manuscripts, and original fantasy art. The shop occupies 1,000 square feet of space.

How to Get There: Located between 13th and 14th Streets, Fantasy Archives is on the third floor. Ring bell for 3R.

Owner/Biography: Eric Kramer.

Year Founded/History of Bookstore: 1977.

Types/Classifications: Hardbound, paperback, broadsides, autographs, ephemera, original fantasy art and manuscripts, uncorrected proofs, first editions, signed copies, presentation copies, limited editions.

General Subject Areas: Science Fiction and Fantasy.

Specific Specialties: Original pulps such as Weird Tales, Astounding, Wonder Stories.

Author Specialties: Ray Bradbury, Stephen King, Edgar Rice Burroughs, C.A. Smith, R.E. Howard, A.C. Clarke, Talbot Mundy, H. Rider Haggard, R.A. Heinlein, H.P. Lovecraft.

Mail/Telephone Orders; Credit Cards: Both. Cash with order; UPS address preferred. No credit cards.

Business Hours: Daily by appointment 11:00 AM - 7:00 PM .

Parking Facilities: Street parking; commercial parking lot.

Special Features: Search service.

Catalogue: Published at varying intervals.

Collections/Individual Items Purchased: Both.

700
G. J. Askins - Bookseller
2 West Street
Box 386
New Lebanon, New York 12125 (518) 794-8833

This is a traditional small general used bookstore with single proprietorship. It has stock in many subjects in a wide range of price and quality. Books are organized by subject. The store occupies 700 square feet of space.

How to Get There: Located just off Highway 20/22 in New Lebanon, New York in the Berkshires, the store is close to Tanglewood and the Hancock Shaker Village.

Owner/Biography: Grover J. Askins.

Year Founded/History of Bookstore: 1982.

Number of Volumes: 10,000.

Types/Classifications: Hardbound, paperback, prints, out-of-print.

General Subject Areas: Agriculture, Americana, Animals, Anthropology, Antiques, Art, Art History, Automobile, Business, Chemistry, Chess, Children's Books, Classics, Cookbooks, Crafts, Dance, Drama, Economics, Education, Engineering, European History, Foreign Languages, Games, Geology, How-To Books, Humor, Law, Literary Criticism, Medicine, Music, Natural History, Philosophy, Physics, Poetry, Psychology, Reference, Religion, Self-Help, Sociology, Sports, Theater, Women's Literature, World History.

Specific Specialties: Midwest Americana.

Author Specialties: P.G. Wodehouse, William Shakespeare.

Other Specialties: Rivers of America Series, Shaker Books and Papers.

Mail/Telephone Orders; Credit Cards: Both. No credit cards.

Business Hours: Friday through Monday 10:00 AM - 6:00 PM.

Parking Facilities: Business parking lot.

Collections/Individual Items Purchased: Both.

Booksellers' Memberships: Upsate New York Antiquarian Booksellers Association.

701
Good Times Bookshop
150 East Main Street
Port Jefferson, New York 11777 (516) 928-2664

Housed in a two-story brick building built in 1848, the Good Times Bookshop is a browser's store with over 30,000 titles arranged by sections and alphabetized by author. Both floors are open to the public. Included in the selection offered are rare, scholarly, and out-of-print books in most fields, hardbound, and some paperbacks.

How to Get There: Located on the North Shore of Long Island, the shop is about 1 1/2 hours east of New York City. By auto, it is north of the Long Island Expressway Exit 67; by train, the Long Island Railroad to Port Jefferson Station; from Connecticut, take the Bridgeport/Port Jefferson Ferry, a delightful cruise of about one hour across the sound (operates from April to January).

Owner/Biography: Michael and Mary Mart.
Year Founded/History of Bookstore: 1972.
Number of Volumes: 30,000.
Types/Classifications: Hardbound, paperbacks, rare, scholarly, out-of-print, limited editions, first editions, fine bindings, illustrated books, signed copies.
General Subject Areas: Art, Children's Books, Drama, Exploration, History, Literature, Military, Philosophy, Photography, Psychology, Theology.
Mail/Telephone Orders; Credit Cards: Both. Cash with order; institutions billed. Visa and Mastercard accepted in store only.
Business Hours: Tuesday through Saturday 11:00 AM - 6:00 PM.
Parking Facilities: Street parking; public lot behind shop.
Collections/Individual Items Purchased: Both.
Booksellers' Memberships: Long Island Antiquarian Book Dealers Association.

702
Gotham Book Mart & Gallery, Inc.
41 West 47th Street
New York, New York 10036 (212) 719-4448

The Gotham is somewhat specialized in literature, theater, film, and the arts. Both in-print and out-of-print books are carried in these fields, including rare books, manuscripts, literary correspondence, and archives. The shop occupies 10,000 square feet of space.

How to Get There: The shop is located in midtown Manhattan between Fifth and Sixth Avenues.
Owner/Biography: Andreas Brown.
Year Founded/History of Bookstore: 1920. The Gotham Book Mart was founded by Frances Steloff. From the beginning, it has been a gathering place for writers, film makers, theater people, artists, editors, and publishers - from the early days of H.L. Mencken, Eugene O'Neill, Theodore Dreiser, Ezra Pound, T.S. Eliot, Christopher Morley until today's Norman Mailer, John Updike, Arthur Miller, Woody Allen, Katharine Hepburn, Warren Beatty, and many others.
Number of Volumes: 500,000.
Types/Classifications: Hardbound; includes about 300 current literary magazines; the Gallery exhibits literary broadsides, photographs, literary posters, literary portraits, book illustrations, etc.
General Subject Areas: American Film Industry, American Playwrights After 1920, American Writers After 1910.
Author Specialties: James Joyce, Henry Miller, the work of Edward Gorey.
Mail/Telephone Orders; Credit Cards: Both. Visa and Mastercard accepted.
Business Hours: Monday through Friday 9:30 AM - 6:30 PM; Saturday 9:30 AM - 6:00 PM; closed Sunday.
Parking Facilities: Commercial parking lots.
Special Features: Search service for out-of-print books in the Gotham's field of specialization; a separate department specializes in literary archives for writers, editors, publishers, literary agents (probably the largest dealer in this country specializing in this service).
Catalogue: Published occasionally (film, small press, rare books).
Collections/Individual Items Purchased: Both.

Booksellers' Memberships: Antiquarian Booksellers Association of America, American Booksellers Association.

703
Gryphon Bookshop
216 West 89th Street
New York, New York 10024   (212) 362-0706

The Gryphon is a general used bookshop with carefully selected stock. It occupies 800 square feet of space.
How to Get There: The bookstore is located between Broadway and Amsterdam Avenue on Manhattan's upper West Side.
Owner/Biography: Henry Holman and Marc Lewis.
Year Founded/History of Bookstore: 1974.
Number of Volumes: 10,000.
Types/Classifications: Hardbound, paperback, autographs, art prints, first editions, out-of-print, fine illustrated books, signed copies, limited editions, color plate books.
General Subject Areas: Art, Ballet, Black Literature, Humor, Literature, Music, New York City, Reference, Theater.
Specific Specialties: Oziana.
Author Specialties: L. Frank Baum, George MacDonald, Robert Benchley.
Other Specialties: Foreign language titles.
Mail/Telephone Orders; Credit Cards: Both. Visa and Mastercard accepted.
Business Hours: Seven days per week 11:00 AM - 11:00 PM.
Parking Facilities: Street parking.
Special Features: Search service.
Collections/Individual Items Purchased: Both.
Booksellers' Memberships: American Booksellers Association.
Miscellaneous: Custom book restoration.

704
Gutenberg's
431 South Avenue
Rochester, New York 14620   (716) 454-4245

Gutenberg's is a warm cozy store designed to fit the owner's image of an old fashioned English bookstore. It has easy chairs (including a red rocker), footstools, and coffee or wine is served. There is often a group of book dealers, book lovers, and neighborhood folks just "hanging out."
How to Get There: Just off Route 490, the bookstore is south of the downtown area and across the Expressway from the Margaret Woodbury Strong Museum.
Owner/Biography: Fran Glover and Kurt Feverherm. Fran is a psychotherapist in private practice and Kurt is an artist and educator.
Year Founded/History of Bookstore: 1980. Gutenberg's is one of the first of the new businesses of the South Wedge neighborhood which is an old Rochester area being restored.
Number of Volumes: 20,000.
Types/Classifications: Hardbound, photographica, postcards, magazines, prints, ephemera, first editions, out-of-print.
General Subject Areas: Anthropology, Archaeology, Art, Automobiles, Biography, Black Americana, Books About Books, Children's Books, Classics, Erotica, Etiquette, Foreign Language, Gardening, History, Humor, Linguistics, Medicine, Music, Mysteries, Philosophy, Photography, Poetry, Psychology, Railroads, Reference, Religion, Sailing, Science Fiction, Ships, Sociology, Sports, Theater, Travel, Westerns, Women's Studies.
Mail/Telephone Orders; Credit Cards: Mail orders. Visa and Mastercard accepted.
Business Hours: Thursday 4:00 PM - 7:00 PM; Friday and Saturday 12:00 Noon - 6:00 PM; Sunday 12:00 Noon - 4:00 PM.
Parking Facilities: Street parking.

Collections/Individual Items Purchased: Both.

705
Hacker Art Books Inc.
54 West 57th Street
New York, New York 10019

(212) 757-1450

Hacker Art Books proudly states that it is the largest art book store in the world with over 1,000,000 books in stock. The establishment occupies over 10,000 square feet of space. It is devoted exclusively to art books and includes Art History, the Fine and Applied Arts, and Architecture.

How to Get There: Located in midtown Manhattan just off Fifth Avenue, the bookstore is easily accessible from nearby subway and surface transportation.

Owner/Biography: Seymour Hacker.
Year Founded/History of Bookstore: 1946.
Number of Volumes: Over 1,000,000.
Types/Classifications: Art books only.
General Subject Areas: Africa, Antiques, Applied Arts, Archaeology, Architecture, Art, Art History, Fine Arts.
Mail/Telephone Orders; Credit Cards: Mail order only; no telephone orders. No credit cards.
Business Hours: Monday through Saturday 9:00 AM - 6:00 PM.
Parking Facilities: Commercial parking lots and garages.
Catalogue: Published 4 times annually.
Collections/Individual Items Purchased: Both.

706
Harmer Johnson Books Ltd.
667 Madison Avenue
New York, New York 10021

(212) 752-1189

Harmer Johnson Books Ltd. is probably the only bookstore in New York City specializing in ancient and tribal art and archaeology. The shop occupies 500 square feet of space.

How to Get There: The shop's midtown Manhattan location can be reached by nearby subway, bus, and other surface transportation.

Owner/Biography: Harmer Johnson and Peter Sharrer.
Year Founded/History of Bookstore: 1975.
Number of Volumes: 5,000.
Types/Classifications: Hardbound, paperback, out-of-print, in-print.
General Subject Areas: Ancient Art, Archaeology, Tribal Art.
Specific Specialties: Ancient Near East, Egypt, Greece, Rome, Africa, South Pacific, Indonesia, Pre-Columbian, North American Indian, Eskimo.
Mail/Telephone Orders; Credit Cards: Both. Payment with order for new clients. No credit cards.
Business Hours: Monday through Friday 11:00 AM - 5:00 PM.
Parking Facilities: Street parking, commercial parking lots.
Catalogue: Published approximately 5 times per year.
Collections/Individual Items Purchased: Both.

707
Harvin Bookshop
209 Martine Avenue
White Plains, New York 10601

(914) 948-2416

The Harvin Bookshop carries used and out-of-print books on all subjects. The shop occupies 1,000 square feet of space.

Owner/Biography: Andrew C. Lee.

Year Founded/History of Bookstore: 1975.
Number of Volumes: 25,000.
Types/Classifications: Hardbound, paperback, out-of-print.
General Subject Areas: General.
Specific Specialties: Asia.
Mail/Telephone Orders; Credit Cards: Mail orders only. Visa and Mastercard accepted.
Business Hours: Tuesday through Saturday 11:30 AM - 5:00 PM.
Parking Facilities: Public parking lot, street parking.
Collections/Individual Items Purchased: Both.

708
Hennesseys
4th and Woodlawn
Saratoga, New York 12866   (518) 584-4921

The Hennesseys offers used books in the stable portion of an old brick carriage house in a residential section of Saratoga.
How to Get There: The shop is off North Broadway, the main street in Saratoga.
Owner/Biography: Helen B. Hennessey.
Year Founded/History of Bookstore: 1961.
Number of Volumes: 10,000.
Types/Classifications: Hardbound, prints, first editions, fine bindings, out-of-print, press books, signed copies, presentation copies, limited editions, color plate books.
General Subject Areas: General.
Specific Specialties: Sporting.
Mail/Telephone Orders; Credit Cards: Both. No credit cards.
Business Hours: Seven days per week 10:00 AM - 5:00 PM; it is suggested that one phone for an appointment.
Parking Facilities: Street parking.
Catalogue: Published occasionally.
Collections/Individual Items Purchased: Both.
Booksellers' Memberships: Antiquarian Booksellers Association of America including Middle Atlantic Chapter.

709
Hope Farm Press and Bookshop
Strong Road
Cornwallville, New York 12418   (518) 239-4745

This is a rural bookshop serving the community with the main objective of easing the difficulty of securing books. The shop has three rooms in an annex to the owner's residence. The shop specializes in material on the Catskill Region and the Hudson Valley.
How to Get There: The shop is located 20 miles west of Catskill between Routes 23 and 45.
Owner/Biography: Charles E. Dornbusch. Mr. Dornbusch is a retired bibliographer and staffer at the New York Public Library. His published contributions include the three volume "Military Bibliography of the Civil War."
Year Founded/History of Bookstore: 1962.
Number of Volumes: 2,000.
Types/Classifications: All kinds of material on the Catskill Region and the Hudson Valley.
General Subject Areas: Albany County, Archaeology, Architecture, Art, Columbia County, Cookbooks, Covered Bridges, Delaware and Hudson Canal, Delaware County, Folklore, Genealogy, Greene County, Herbs, Historical Background, Hudson River, Indians, Local History, Maps, Out-of-Doors, Palatines, Railroads, Schoharie County, Self-Sufficiency, Shawangunk Mountains, Ulster County.
Author Specialties: John Burroughs, Brooks Atkinson.

Other Specialties: Civil War (U.S.)
Mail/Telephone Orders; Credit Cards: Both. Clients invoiced.
Business Hours: Daily 10:00 AM - 5:00 PM except non-holiday Mondays.
Parking Facilities: Parking area.
Special Features: Search service for out-of-print books.
Catalogue: Published twice a year.
Collections/Individual Items Purchased: Individual items only.

710
Howard Frisch Books
Old Post Road
Livingston, New York 12541   (518) 851-7493

Howard Frisch Books has a general stock of hardbound, out-of-print books.
How to Get There: Livingston is a small village 100 miles north of New York City and 40 miles south of Albany. It is easily accessible by the Taconic Parkway. The bookstore is located in the center of the village.
Owner/Biography: Howard Frisch and Fred Harris.
Year Founded/History of Bookstore: 1954. The store was originally situated in New York City's Greenwich Village area and moved to Livingston in 1970.
Number of Volumes: 30,000.
Types/Classifications: Hardbound, out-of-print, first editions, fine bindings, association copies, press books, signed copies, presentation copies, limited editions, color plate books.
General Subject Areas: General.
Mail/Telephone Orders; Credit Cards: Both. No credit cards.
Business Hours: Closed during the winter; call for hours other seasons.
Parking Facilities: Unlimited parking facilities.
Special Features: Search service.
Catalogue: Published 4 times per year.
Collections/Individual Items Purchased: Both.
Booksellers' Memberships: Antiquarian Booksellers Association of America.

711
Irving Zucker Art Books
256 Fifth Avenue
New York, New York 10001   (212) 679-6332

The shop is on the sixth floor and features rare art books, some color plate books, and some modern French illustrated books. It contains 2,500 square feet of space.
How to Get There: Public transportation or taxi.
Owner/Biography: Irving Zucker.
Year Founded/History of Bookstore: 1940.
Number of Volumes: 1,000.
Types/Classifications: Rare, fine bindings, signed copies, limited editions, color plate books.
General Subject Areas: Art.
Mail/Telephone Orders; Credit Cards: No credit cards.
Business Hours: Monday through Friday 10:00 AM - 5:00 PM.
Parking Facilities: Public parking lot.
Catalogue: Occasionally.
Collections/Individual Items Purchased: Both.
Booksellers' Memberships: Antiquarian Booksellers Association of America.

712
Isaac Mendoza Book Co.
15 Ann Street
New York, New York 10038   (212) 227-8777

This bookstore, carrying a large stock, features science fiction and fantasy as well as detective fiction.
Owner/Biography: Walter Caron.
Year Founded/History of Bookstore: Founded in 1894, the bookstore is still in the same location.
Number of Volumes: 200,000.
Types/Classifications: Hardbound, paperback, magazines, modern first editions.
General Subject Areas: Detective Fiction, Science Fiction and Fantasy.
Collections/Individual Items Purchased: Both.
Booksellers' Memberships: Antiquarian Booksellers Association of America.

713
J. N. Herlin, Inc.
68 Thompson Street
New York, New York 10012   (212) 431-8732

This is a bookstore devoted exclusively to the 20th Century Visual Arts. It contains 350 square feet of space.
Owner/Biography: Jean-Noel Herlin.
Year Founded/History of Bookstore: 1972.
Number of Volumes: 10,000.
Types/Classifications: Hardbound, paperback, exhibition catalogues, magazines, posters, ephemera, out-of-print.
General Subject Areas: Twentieth Century Art and Film.
Specific Specialties: Avant-Garde, Experimental Art.
Mail/Telephone Orders; Credit Cards: Both; Visa.
Business Hours: Monday through Friday 11:00 AM - 6:30 PM; Saturday 2:00 PM - 6:30 PM.
Catalogue: Twice a year.
Collections/Individual Items Purchased: Both.

714
Jackson Heights Discount Books
77-15 37th Avenue
Jackson Heights, New York 11372   (212) 426-0202

The bookstore features a huge collection of books specializing in mystery, science fiction and fantasy, romance, and westerns. The shop also carries new hardback and paperback bestsellers at discount. In addition, it offers a full line of collector comics, old and new. The store contains 1,300 square feet of space.
How to Get There: The bookstore is located in a residential community in the Borough of Queens, New York City; the Independent and Flushing Line subways both stop at the Roosevelt Avenue-Jackson Heights stop.
Owner/Biography: Ava and Elliott Grubman.
Year Founded/History of Bookstore: 1976.
Number of Volumes: 250,000.
Types/Classifications: New and used hardbound, paperback, National Geographics, collector comics, student aids and assigned readings.
General Subject Areas: American Indians, Americana, Antiques, Architecture, Art, Barron's Educational Books, Biography, Black Studies, Business, Cinema, Civil Service Exam Books, Collector Comics, Cookbooks, Crafts, Dance, Economics, Feminism, Foreign Language Books, Gardening, General Fiction, Harlequins, Health, History, Home Repair, Humor, Literature, Monarch and Cliff Notes, Music, Mystery, Mythology, National Geographics, Nature, Occult, Philosophy, Photography, Poetry, Political Science, Psychology, Reference Books, Religion, Romance, Science, Science Fiction and Fantasy, Secretarial Studies, Sewing, Shakespeare, Sociology, Spanish Language Books, Sports, Television, Theater, Travel, War, Westerns.

Specific Specialties: Out-of-print Books and Comics.
Other Specialties: Very large selection of used classics from Jane Austin to Emil Zola; Russian Classics.
Mail/Telephone Orders; Credit Cards: Mail orders only; full payment and shipping costs in advance; Visa, Mastercard.
Business Hours: Monday through Saturday 9:00 AM - 9:00 PM; Sunday 11:30 AM - 6:30 PM.
Parking Facilities: Metered street parking.
Collections/Individual Items Purchased: Both.
Miscellaneous: The shop will special-order new books at 20 percent off the cover price.

715
Jamaica Book Center
146-16 Jamaica Avenue
Jamaica, New York 11435   (212) 526-5899

This very large bookstore carries all categories of new and used books. There are 1/2 million books on two floors, with 7,500 square feet of space.
How to Get There: The bookstore can be reached by a variety of ways: New York City Bus System, Independent Subway (to Jamaica Railroad Station stop), 5 minutes by car from New York City's La Guardia or Kennedy Airports.
Owner/Biography: Joseph Landau, owner, has been in the book business for 15 years; he was formerly with Brentano's Fifth Avenue Store.
Year Founded/History of Bookstore: Founded in 1925, the bookstore has had only three owners over the years. Still in the same original location, it is probably the longest continuously operating bookstore in the Borough of Queens.
Number of Volumes: 500,000.
Types/Classifications: Hardbound, paperback, magazines, broadsides, autographs, ephemera, first editions, fine bindings, out-of-print, signed copies, presentation copies, limited editions.
General Subject Areas: Antiques, Best Sellers, Bibles, Black Studies, Boating, Chemistry, Cinema, Civil War (U.S.), Crafts, Drama, English Studies, Feminism, Home Repair, Humor, Mathematics, Occult, Physics, Politics, Religion, Science Fiction and Fantasy.
Specific Specialties: Oceanography, Seamanship, History, Technical, New York, Art, Literature, Engineering, Railroads, Military History, Psychology, Philosophy, Judaica.
Mail/Telephone Orders; Credit Cards: Both; personal check with order; $1 postage for each book; Visa, Mastercard.
Business Hours: Monday through Saturday 9:00 AM - 6:00 PM.
Parking Facilities: Free parking.
Collections/Individual Items Purchased: Both.
Miscellaneous: The shop owns a second store: Washington Street Bookstore, 119 Washington Street, South Norwalk, Connecticut 06854.

716
James Cummins Bookseller
Suite 1005
667 Madison Avenue
New York, New York 10021   (212) 371-4151

In addition to this bookstore in the heart of Manhattan, New York City, the owners have a shop in New Jersey, at: Fairmount Road, Pottersville, New Jersey 07929; phone (201) 439-3803.
How to Get There: Pottersville, New Jersey is 50 miles southwest of New York City; the driver should take Route 80W to 287 south, to 206 north, then 5 miles to Pottersville Road.
Owner/Biography: James and Carol Cummins.
Year Founded/History of Bookstore: 1978.
Number of Volumes: 50,000.
Types/Classifications: Hardbound, broadsides, autographs, first editions, fine bindings, association copies, press books, signed copies, presentation copies, limited editions, color plate books, fine sets.

General Subject Areas: Angling, Exploration, Fishing, Fox Hunting, Hunting, Sporting, Travel.
Mail/Telephone Orders; Credit Cards: Both; no credit cards.
Business Hours: New York store: Monday through Friday 9:30 AM - 5:30 PM; at the New Jersey Store: by appointment only.
Catalogue: Four to six times a year.
Collections/Individual Items Purchased: Both.
Booksellers' Memberships: Antiquarian Booksellers Association of America.

717
James Lowe Autographs, Ltd.
Suite 907
30 East 60th Street
New York, New York 10022 (212) 889-8204

One of the foremost shops in New York City dealing in autographs, manuscripts, signed books, and 19th Century photographs, it is located near Madison Avenue and 61st Street, an area which is fast becoming the book and autograph center of Madison Avenue. The shop offers a wide range of browsing pleasures.
Owner/Biography: James Lowe, owner, is well known throughout the world as a leading autograph and manuscript authority. He is editor of The Professional Rare Bookseller, the journal of the Antiquarian Booksellers Association of America, and an officer of the Association. He is a trustee of the Manuscript Society and a frequent lecturer and contributor to book trade and manuscript-related journals.
Year Founded/History of Bookstore: 1970.
Types/Classifications: Autographs, manuscripts, and documents in all fields of endeavor; 19th Century photographs and manuscript material of noted photographers; signed and limited editions.
General Subject Areas: Autographs, Manuscripts, Photographs.
Mail/Telephone Orders; Credit Cards: Both; no credit cards.
Business Hours: Monday through Friday 11:00 AM - 6:00 PM.
Special Features: Appraisals, auction representation.
Catalogue: Four or five times a year.
Collections/Individual Items Purchased: Both.
Booksellers' Memberships: Antiquarian Booksellers Association of America, International League of Antiquarian Booksellers.

718
Jenison's Books & Antiques
23 Gouverneur Street
Canton, New York 13617 (315) 386-3022

This is a general used bookstore, also carrying prints, paintings, and furniture.
How to Get There: The bookstore is located on Route 11 in the village of Canton, New York.
Owner/Biography: T. C. Jenison.
Year Founded/History of Bookstore: 1975.
Number of Volumes: 7,000.
Types/Classifications: Hardbound, prints, paintings, ephemera, catalogues, out-of-print, etchings, trade catalogues.
General Subject Areas: General.
Specific Specialties: Adirondacks, New York State.
Mail/Telephone Orders; Credit Cards: Both; no credit cards.
Business Hours: Thursday through Saturday 12:00 Noon - 5:00 PM, all year.
Parking Facilities: Off street.
Special Features: Search service.
Catalogue: Published on demand.
Collections/Individual Items Purchased: Both.

719
John Cashman Books
327 Sea Cliff Avenue
Sea Cliff, New York 11579   (516) 676-6088

This is an old style bookstore which was named the best old bookstore in Nassau County (New York) by the newspaper Newsday. The shop features easily accessible shelves, bookcases, and bric-a-brac. It also features continuous Baroque music. It is a one-man store, and contains 1,000 square feet of space.

How to Get There: Sea Cliff, a 100 year old Victorian village nestled in the hills of Long Island's fabled North Shore, is easily reached via the Long Island Expressway. It is about a 30 minute drive from New York City.

Owner/Biography: John Cashman, owner, is an ex-newspaperman who "walked away from the deadlines and headlines" three years ago after more than 25 years as a writer and editor. He wanted to see if being around his books full time would be a rewarding experience; it is.

Year Founded/History of Bookstore: The bookstore was founded in the late 1940's by Mark Thompson who ran it for 35 years. John Cashman took it over in 1981, remodeled it, and brought in new stock, especially antiquarian books.

Number of Volumes: 30,000.

Types/Classifications: Hardbound books only; some ephemera; old, used, rare, color plate books, illustrated, old bindings, first editions, signed books.

General Subject Areas: Alcohol, American Indians, Americana, Beats, Biography, Cinema, Cocaine, Communes, Counter-Culture, Culture, Dance, Drugs, Eighteenth Century Literature, Heroin, Hippies, History, Language and Writing, Magazines, Marijuana, Media, Minorities, Music, Newspapers, Nineteenth Century Literature, Occult, Performing Arts, Photography, Publishing, Radio News, Reference, Science Fiction and Fantasy, Sex Studies, Television, Television News, Temperance, Theater, Tobacco, True Crime, Women's Movement.

Author Specialties: F. Scott Fitzgerald, Ernest Hemingway, John Steinbeck, Jack Kerouac, William Faulkner, James Joyce, John Masefield, Frank Harris, James T. Farrell.

Other Specialties: Media (Journalism), Temperance (Prohibition).

Mail/Telephone Orders; Credit Cards: Both; personal check with order; no credit cards.

Business Hours: Tuesday through Sunday 1:00 PM - 6:00 PM; closed Monday.

Parking Facilities: Plenty of street parking.

Collections/Individual Items Purchased: Both.

Booksellers' Memberships: Long Island Antiquarian Book Dealers Association.

Miscellaneous: Large selection of 18th and 19th Century wood and steel engravings and color lithographs; 17th, 18th, and 19th Century maps.

720
John H. Stubbs Rare Books & Prints
3rd Floor
28 East 18th Street
New York, New York 10003   (212) 982-8368

This is a rare-book store and art gallery located in a loft space overlooking lower Broadway in Manhattan, New York City. It features an antiquarian bookstore atmosphere with architectural fragments, antiques, and similar artifacts. The gallery always has a display of prints and drawings from its stock on the subjects of architecture, decorative arts, and archaeology.

Owner/Biography: John H. Stubbs.

Year Founded/History of Bookstore: Founded in 1980, the expanding specialty bookstore/gallery recently relocated to a larger space of 1,400 square feet.

Number of Volumes: 1,500.

Types/Classifications: Hardbound, pamphlets, ephemera, trade catalogues, prints, original drawings, color plate books, fine bindings, out-of-print, folio-size books, prints.

General Subject Areas: Architecture, Classical Archaeology, Decorative Arts, Egypt, Egyptology, Landscape Architecture.

Specific Specialties: Archaeological Excavation Reports, Lithographs by David Roberts, History of Archaeology, History of Architecture, Travel Accounts, especially Egypt.

Other Specialties: Scholarly Books, Foreign Languages (European).

Mail/Telephone Orders; Credit Cards: Both; payment on ordering from new customers, deferred payments accepted from institutions.

Business Hours: Monday through Saturday 9:00 AM - 5:00 PM by appointment only.

Parking Facilities: Street.

Special Features: Book Gallery, Art Gallery.

Catalogue: Twice a year.

Collections/Individual Items Purchased: Both.

721
Johnson & O'Donnell Rare Books

1015 State Tower Building
Syracuse, New York 13202   (315) 476-5312

Open by appointment only, the shop features first editions of 19th and 20th Century literature.

How to Get There: The bookstore is located on the corner of South Warren and East Genesee Streets in Syracuse, New York.

Owner/Biography: Bruce Johnson, Ed O'Donnell.

Types/Classifications: Hardbound, first editions, fine bindings, signed copies, presentation copies.

General Subject Areas: Nineteenth Century Literature, Twentieth Century Literature.

Mail/Telephone Orders; Credit Cards: Both. Visa, Mastercard.

Business Hours: By appointment only.

Catalogue: Two or three times per year.

Collections/Individual Items Purchased: Both.

Booksellers' Memberships: Antiquarian Booksellers Association of America.

722
Justin G. Schiller, Ltd.

36 East 61st Street
New York, New York 10021   (212) 832-8231

Although specializing in historical children's literature, this bookseller handles both the rarefied museum-quality first editions and a browsing stock for more moderately-priced collectible children's books (these latter under the subsidiary name of "Battledore Books," operated from the same premises). There is also original artwork for children's books at the gallery upstairs.

How to Get There: Justin G. Schiller, Ltd. occupies the first two floors of an old New York mansion building (not an obvious storefront), located on the south side of East 61st Street between Park and Madison Avenues. The name of the establishment is on the doorbell.

Owner/Biography: Justin G. Schiller and Raymond M. Wapner.

Year Founded/History of Bookstore: 1959 (incorporated 1969).

Number of Volumes: 3,500.

Types/Classifications: Rare, first editions, chapbooks, manuscript material and related original drawings, all focused on the evolution of historical children's literature from the beginnings to the present, including foreign languages.

General Subject Areas: Children's Literature.

Specific Specialties: Bibliographies (children's book-related), Fables.

Author Specialties: John Newbery, Maurice Sendak, L. Frank Baum, George MacDonald, Randolph Caldecott, Kate Greenaway, Walter Crane.

Other Specialties: First editions of major children's literature in their original language as well as important translations, such as Hans Christian Andersen in Danish, Grimm Brothers in German, and so forth.

Mail/Telephone Orders; Credit Cards: Both. Trade references required from new clients or pre-payment on orders from catalogues. Visa and Mastercard accepted.

Business Hours: Justin G. Schiller, Ltd. is open by appointment only; Battledore Books is open Tuesday through Friday 10:00 AM - 6:00 PM and Saturday 11:00 AM - 4:00 PM.

Parking Facilities: Commercial parking available directly across the street.
Catalogue: Catalogue published.
Collections/Individual Items Purchased: Both.
Booksellers' Memberships: Antiquarian Booksellers Association of America, International League of Antiquarian Booksellers, Antiquarian Booksellers Association (International).

723
Keshcarrigan Bookshop
90 West Broadway
New York, New York 10007   (212) 962-4237

This bookshop specializes in Irish and American history, literature, both out-of-print and in-print. The selection is strong on Irish language material. The shop occupies 500 square feet of space.
How to Get There: The shop is five blocks north of the World Trade Center.
Owner/Biography: Angela Carter.
Year Founded/History of Bookstore: 1979.
Types/Classifications: Hardbound, paperback, out-of-print.
General Subject Areas: Biography, Fiction, History, Literature.
Specific Specialties: Irish History and Literature, American History and Literature.
Mail/Telephone Orders; Credit Cards: Mail orders. Visa and Mastercard accepted.
Business Hours: Monday through Saturday 11:00 AM - 5:00 PM.
Parking Facilities: Commercial parking lots.
Special Features: Search service.
Catalogue: Catalogue published.
Collections/Individual Items Purchased: Both.

724
L. Gobrecht - Books
Rt. 94
Kinderhook, New York 12106   (518) 758-7341

The bookstore is located in the Kinderhook Antique Center and includes a general line of both used and antiquarian books. The shop contains 300 square feet of space.
How to Get There: The store is located one mile north of the Martin Van Buren home, Lindenwald, a national historic site.
Owner/Biography: L. E. Gobrecht.
Year Founded/History of Bookstore: 1970.
Number of Volumes: 3,000.
Types/Classifications: Hardbound, magazines; first editions.
General Subject Areas: American History, Biography, European History, Literature.
Other Specialties: Scholarly works in American History.
Mail/Telephone Orders; Credit Cards: Both; cash with order, returnable in 10 days; Visa, Mastercard. An additional telephone number is (518) 758-7939.
Business Hours: Sunday through Saturday 10:00 AM - 5:00 PM. Weekends only, January through April. First editions by appointment only.
Parking Facilities: Business parking lot.
Collections/Individual Items Purchased: Both.

725
L. H. McGill - Rare Books
41 Third Streeet
New City, New York 10956   (914) 634-0729

L. H. McGill - Rare Books is conducted by mail order and by appointment only. There is a general stock with emphasis on non-fiction and scholarly publishing.

How to Get There: Located 21 miles northwest of George Washington Bridge in Rockland County. The bookstore is near the junction of Route 304 and Third Street.

Owner/Biography: L. H. McGill was formerly an acquisitions librarian and has been active in educational and scholarly publishing for eighteen years.

Year Founded/History of Bookstore: 1979.

Number of Volumes: 5,000.

Types/Classifications: Hardbound, first editions, fine bindings, out-of-print, association copies, press books, signed copies, presentation copies, limited editions, color plate books.

General Subject Areas: General, Non-fiction, Scholarly Works.

Mail/Telephone Orders; Credit Cards: Cash with mail order. No telephone orders. No credit cards.

Business Hours: Visits by appointment only.

Parking Facilities: Minimal parking.

Collections/Individual Items Purchased: Both.

726
Landmark Book Company
119 West 57th Street
New York, New York 10019   (212) 765-5252

This company is primarily a wholesale supplier of remainders of fine art books, scholarly books in all fields, nonfiction (history, literature, philosophy), and other discontinued titles and specials. The business caters to new bookstores, antiquarian book dealers, and libraries worldwide. The company maintains an office and showroom in midtown Manhattan.

Owner/Biography: Norman Blaustein and Nina Neimark. Mr. Blaustein was part owner of Harlem Book Company, Tudor Publishing Company, and William Penn Publishing Company and their successors from 1927 to 1976 when he established this specialty firm.

Year Founded/History of Bookstore: 1976. Harlem Book Company was the first large scale distributor of remainders at wholesale; Tudor Publishing Company was the first publisher of reprints at off prices.

Number of Volumes: 3,000 titles.

Types/Classifications: Remainders.

General Subject Areas: General.

Mail/Telephone Orders; Credit Cards: Both. No credit cards.

Business Hours: Monday through Friday, 9:00 AM - 5:00 PM.

Parking Facilities: Various nearby parking lots.

Catalogue: Published 10 times annually.

Collections/Individual Items Purchased: Both.

727
Lathrop C. Harper, Inc.
300 Madison Avenue
New York, New York 10017   (212) 490-3412

Lathrop C. Harper, Inc. specializes in early printed books, illuminated manuscripts, incunabula, and medieval and renaissance material. The shop occupies 1,000 square feet of space. An appointment is necessary.

How to Get There: The location is easily reached by various forms of public transportation.

Owner/Biography: Felix Oyens.

Year Founded/History of Bookstore: 1881.

Number of Volumes: 1,500.

Types/Classifications: Hardbound, manuscripts, early printed books, illustrated books.

General Subject Areas: Incunabula, Medieval and Renaissance Books.

Mail/Telephone Orders; Credit Cards: Both. No credit cards.

Business Hours: By appointment only.

Parking Facilities: Public parking lots nearby.
Catalogue: Published once each year.
Collections/Individual Items Purchased: Both.
Booksellers' Memberships: Antiquarian Booksellers Association of America.

728
Leona Rostenberg & Madeleine B. Stern
40 East 88th Street
New York, New York 10128   (212) 831-6628

The bookstore specializes in significant books (mostly foreign) printed between 1500 and 1800. It highlights texts on political theory, history, and literature. The owners are particularly interested in ephemeral material (pamphlets) of the 16th and 17th Centuries, as well as in the major Renaissance printer-publishers Aldus Manutius, Etienne Dolet, and the Estiennes. The shop also stocks an occasional unusual Americanum.

Owner/Biography: Leona Rostenberg and Madeleine B. Stern, owners, are both known for their numerous publications as well as for their bookselling careers. Ms. Rostenberg has written several books and numerous articles on 17th Century English publishing history; she is past president of the Antiquarian Booksellers Association of America, and present delegate to the International League of Antiquarian Booksellers. Ms. Stern is the author of numerous books and articles on 19th Century American publishing history, feminism, and biography. She is the author of the forthcoming "History of the American Antiquarian Booktrade to 1945." Both partners lecture extensively in their fields. They are co-authors of "Old & Rare: Thirty Years In the Book Business," and of "Between Boards: New Thoughts On Old Books."

Year Founded/History of Bookstore: Leona Rostenberg founded the firm in September 1944 at 152 East 179th Street, Bronx, NY. She was joined in partnership by Madeleine B. Stern in April 1945. The partners have continued the business with only one change of location, in 1969, to the present address.

Number of Volumes: 2,000.

Types/Classifications: Antiquarian, old, rare, hardbound, pamphlets, ephemera.

General Subject Areas: History, Literature from the 15th through the 19th Century, Political Theory.

Specific Specialties: Sixteenth Century Pamphlets, Seventeenth Century Pamphlets, Renaissance Printer-Publishers, Aldus Manutius, Etienne Dolet, the Estiennes, Americana, Foreign Language Books dated 1500 to 1800.

Mail/Telephone Orders; Credit Cards: Both.

Business Hours: Weekdays 9:00 AM - 5:00 PM.

Catalogue: Three times a year.

Collections/Individual Items Purchased: Both.

Booksellers' Memberships: Antiquarian Booksellers Association of America, including the Middle Atlantic Chapter.

729
Liberty Rock Book Shoppe
55 Orange Turnpike
Sloatsburg, New York 10974   (914) 476-9115

The bookstore maintains a general collection of old and out-of-print material covering most every subject. It is housed in a quaint building which was once a 1930's gas station, capped by two tall white chimneys. Each subject area is carefully kept in alphabetical order for easy reference, with separate sections for older and rarer material. Deceiving from the outside, the store's barnwood interior with its large stock in a small but cozy store elicits surprise from customers. The store contains 750 square feet of space.

How to Get There: The shop is situated on Route 17 in the center of the village of Sloatsburg, New York. It is 4 miles north of the New Jersey border, four miles south of Tuxedo Park, New York, and 32 miles north of New York City via the New York Thruway, Exit 15.

Owner/Biography: James Bartlett Mahoney, Mrs. Frank J. Mahoney, Thomas J. Liotta. James Mahoney, former librarian, is the editor and publisher of an historical journal. He is experienced in the major antiquarian book trade. Virginia Mahoney, the operating manager, has 40 years of experience in the retail trade, and is a library trustee.

Year Founded/History of Bookstore: The bookstore began in 1976 with one estate purchase in conjunction with an antique business (soon abandoned); it was enlarged with the purchase of stock of another bookstore in 1979, and was moved to a larger building on a major road. Business improved by twelve times in the first year. Always outgrowing its quarters, the shop now has a separate location for storage and additional stock.

Number of Volumes: 15,000.

Types/Classifications: Hardbound, paperback, magazines, ephemera, prints, first editions, fine bindings, out-of-print, signed copies, limited editions.

General Subject Areas: American Catholic Church History, Americana, Antiques, Biography, Boy Scout Literature, Children's Books, Collecting, Ecclesiastical Architecture, Ecclesiastical Literature, French History, French Literature, Medicine.

Specific Specialties: New York State History, New Jersey History, Ramapo Mountains (N.Y.), Tuxedo Park (N.Y.), Rockland County (N.Y.).

Author Specialties: Albert Payson Terhune, Amelia Barr, Dan Beard, E. P. Roe, Orange County (N.Y.) Authors.

Mail/Telephone Orders; Credit Cards: Both; no credit cards.

Business Hours: Tuesday through Friday 10:00 AM - 5:00 PM; Saturday 10:00 AM - 6:00 PM; Sunday 12:00 Noon - 4:00 PM; closed Monday except when a holiday.

Parking Facilities: Business parking lot.

Special Features: Search service.

Catalogue: One or two times a year.

Collections/Individual Items Purchased: Both.

730
Librarium
RD 190 Black Bridge Road
East Chatham, New York 12060   (518) 392-5209

The bookstore is a four room shop in a wing of an 1820's farmhouse with a country setting. The large general stock of old, used, out-of-print, and rare books is neatly arranged by subject. In addition, there is a barn just a pleasant short walk from the shop that contains a large collection of inexpensive books arranged by subject, with fiction shelved alphabetically by author.

How to Get There: When driving, take Route 90 (Berkshire Extension); from the east, Route 22 north to Route 295 west, 5 miles to Black Bridge Road; from the west or south, Taconic Parkway to Route 295 east 4 miles, left on Black Bridge Road.

Owner/Biography: Richard and Ella Socky, Sharon S. Lips.

Year Founded/History of Bookstore: 1979.

Number of Volumes: 25,000.

Types/Classifications: Hardbound, paperback, used, out-of-print, rare.

General Subject Areas: General.

Mail/Telephone Orders; Credit Cards: Both; no credit cards.

Business Hours: April - December: Friday through Monday 10:00 AM - 6:00 PM; January - March: Saturday and Sunday 10:00 AM - 5:00 PM; and by appointment.

Parking Facilities: Driveway and street.

Special Features: Search service.

Collections/Individual Items Purchased: Both.

731
Littwin & Feiden
735 East Boston Post Road
Mamaroneck, New York 10543   (914) 698-6504

This is not an open shop; it operates by appointment only, but is willing to meet people at most times.

How to Get There: The business is located in Westchester County, a 40-minute drive north of New York City, or a like ride on the New Haven RR.

Owner/Biography: Suzanne Littwin and Elaine S. Feiden.

Year Founded/History of Bookstore: Founded in 1976, the shop has changed from an open shop with both rare and scholarly out-of-print books to an office-like atmosphere open by appointment only. It no longer carries out-of-print books.
Number of Volumes: 8,000.
Types/Classifications: Hardbound, maps, prints, first editions, illustrated, art, color plate books, signed copies, presentation copies.
General Subject Areas: Americana, Art, Literature.
Mail/Telephone Orders; Credit Cards: Both; personal check with order unless for a customer with whom the shop has done business, or a library; no credit cards.
Business Hours: By appointment only, including weekends and evenings if convenient.
Parking Facilities: Street, and parking lot.
Catalogue: Once a year.
Collections/Individual Items Purchased: Both.
Booksellers' Memberships: Antiquarian Booksellers Association of America.

732
Lucien Goldschmidt, Inc.
1117 Madison Avenue
New York, New York 10028 (212) 879-0070

This is a bookstore dealing in rare books on architecture and the fine arts, many European.
How to Get There: The bookstore is located at Madison Avenue and 84th Street in Manhattan, New York City.
Owner/Biography: Lucien C. Goldschmidt.
Year Founded/History of Bookstore: 1953.
Types/Classifications: Rare books, illustrated books, fine bindings.
General Subject Areas: Architecture, Continental European Illustrated Books 1500-1950, Fine Arts, French Literature in First Edition.
Mail/Telephone Orders; Credit Cards: Both; no credit cards.
Business Hours: Monday through Friday 10:00 AM - 6:00 PM; Saturday 10:00 AM - 5:00 PM.
Catalogue: Twice a year.
Collections/Individual Items Purchased: Both.
Booksellers' Memberships: Antiquarian Booksellers Association of America.

733
Lyrical Ballad Bookstore
7 Phila Street
Saratoga Springs, New York 12866 (518) 584-8779

This is one of the most unusual bookstores in upstate New York, in that it has its rare books displayed in an old bank vault. The stock is very strong in illustrated books, leatherbound classics, and American thoroughbred horseracing, but it also includes a wide variety of antiquarian books.
How to Get There: Saratoga Springs is a one-half hour drive north of Albany, New York on Rt. 87, the Northway; it is half way between New York City and Montreal, Canada. The bookstore is just off Broadway, east of the Adelphi Hotel. It is the second shop on the left, on Phila Street.
Owner/Biography: John J. and Carolyn DeMarco.
Year Founded/History of Bookstore: Founded in 1971 by the DeMarcos, the bookstore is still in its original location, but has expanded from 200 square feet of space to 1,200.
Number of Volumes: 25,000.
Types/Classifications: Hardbound, magazines, postcards, ephemera, prints, first editions, fine bindings, out-of-print, rare, illustrated books.
General Subject Areas: Adirondack Mountains, Ballet, Children's Books, Folklore, Horse Racing, New York State, Saratoga Springs (N.Y.).
Specific Specialties: American Thoroughbred Horse Racing, Polo, Coaching, Fairy Tales.

Author Specialties: Herman Melville, William Blake, Samuel Taylor Coleridge.
Mail/Telephone Orders; Credit Cards: Both; Visa, Mastercard.
Business Hours: September - June: Tuesday through Saturday 10:00 AM - 5:30 PM; July - August: Monday through Saturday 9:30 AM - 6:00 PM.
Parking Facilities: Street, plus public parking lot nearby.
Special Features: Search Service.
Collections/Individual Items Purchased: Both.
Booksellers' Memberships: Antiquarian Booksellers Association of America, International League of Antiquarian Booksellers.
Miscellaneous: Saratoga Springs in August is the national center of thoroughbred horse racing; in July it is the summer home of the New York City Ballet.

734
Magazine Center
1133 Broadway
New York, New York 10010   (212) 929-5255

This bookstore specializes in back-issue magazines, especially for the years 1900 to 1960. The magazines are in what might be termed the general field. The bookstore contains 1,000 square feet of space.
How to Get There: The shop is located in the heart of Manhattan, New York City, and can be reached easily from all points by bus, subway, or walking.
Owner/Biography: H. B. Koyun.
Year Founded/History of Bookstore: 1970.
Number of Volumes: 150,000 magazines.
Types/Classifications: Out-of-print magazines, paper ephemera, some first editions and presentation copies by leading authors such as P.G. Wodehouse and "beat" generation authors; photography books by 19th Century and 20th Century photographers.
Specific Specialties: General out-of-print magazines such as: Vogue, Ladies Home Journal, Cosmopolitan, Redbook, Hearst's International, Green Book, Play Pictorial, Collier's, Saturday Evening Post, McCall's, Theatre, and Harper's Bazaar.
Mail/Telephone Orders; Credit Cards: Both.
Special Features: Search service for magazines published in the years 1900 to 1960.

735
Mahoney & Weekly Booksellers
513 Virginia Street
Buffalo, New York 14202   (716) 856-6024

Mahoney & Weekly offers antiquarian fine books, paintings, prints, and autographs.
Owner/Biography: Thomas D. Mahoney and Jon W. Weekly.
Types/Classifications: Rare, out-of-print, first editions, paintings, prints, autographs.
General Subject Areas: General.
Mail/Telephone Orders; Credit Cards: Mail orders.
Business Hours: Wednesday through Saturday 11:00 AM - 5:00 PM.
Parking Facilities: Available.

736
Many Feathers Books
Route 212 and Sickler Road
Lake Hill, New York 12448   (914) 679-6830

This bookstore stocks fine literature in many fields. The owner states that his bookstore contains "a little something for everyone."
How to Get There: Five miles west of Woodstock.

Owner/Biography: Anthony Sackett.
Types/Classifications: Most categories.
General Subject Areas: Children's Illustrated Books, Cooking, Gardening, Mystery, Natural History, Poetry, Religion, Travel, True Crime.
Author Specialties: W.B. Yeats, George Eliot, W.H. Auden, Dylan Thomas, Robert Lowell, Graham Greene, Dr. Samuel Johnson.
Business Hours: By appointment only.

737
McDonald's Book Ends
125 Water Street
Catskill, New York 12414
                                                                        (518) 943-3520

McDonald's Book Ends deals in antiquarian books, prints, and maps, particularly on the Catskill Mountains.
How to Get There: Catskill is located on the Hudson River 30 miles south of Albany; it can be reached via the New York State Thruway.
Types/Classifications: Hardbound, first editions, out-of-print, maps, prints.
General Subject Areas: Catskill Mountains, Greene County, Hudson River, New York State, Railroads.
Other Specialties: American and European Maps, Atlases, Prints.
Mail/Telephone Orders; Credit Cards: Mail orders.
Business Hours: Monday through Saturday 10:00 AM - 9:00 PM.
Parking Facilities: Available.
Special Features: Want lists maintained.
Collections/Individual Items Purchased: Both.

738
Military Bookman Ltd.
29 East 93rd Street
New York, New York 10128
                                                                        (212) 348-1280

The bookstore offers a selection of about 10,000 out-of-print titles on military, naval, and aviation history. It is located on the ground floor (old servants' quarters) of a brownstone townhouse, and contains 650 square feet of space.
How to Get There: The shop is situated in a beautiful largely residential area of landmark old brownstones in Manhattan, and can be reached by the Madison Avenue bus to 93rd Street or the IRT subway express stop at 86th Street.
Owner/Biography: Harris and Margaretta Colt.
Year Founded/History of Bookstore: This bookstore is the successor to an older store on this specialty in Boston; its inventory was acquired by the present owners in 1976 and relocated to an address on 92nd Street, Manhattan; it was moved to its present location in 1978.
Number of Volumes: 10,000.
Types/Classifications: Out-of-print, signed copies, presentation copies, limited editions, color plate books.
General Subject Areas: Aviation History, Military History, Naval History.
Specific Specialties: American Wars, Napoleonic Wars, Civil War (U.S.), Warfare of 17th, 18th, and 19th Centuries, World War I, World War II, Ancient Warfare, Medieval Warfare, Military Strategy and Tactics, British Army, Ordnance, Fortifications, Engineering, Tanks, French Foreign Legion.
Other Specialties: Foreign languages within specialty.
Mail/Telephone Orders; Credit Cards: Both; the bookstore will respond on the phone to specific inquiries; it will reserve and ship the ordered material upon receipt of a personal check or money order; no credit cards.
Business Hours: Tuesday through Saturday 10:30 AM - 5:30 PM.
Parking Facilities: Street (limited), several nearby pay garages.
Special Features: The stock is organized for browsing by subject matter.
Catalogue: Three times a year; each issue covers different material and shows a selection of original World War I and World War II posters and good uniform prints. Write or call for information about catalog

subscriptions.
Collections/Individual Items Purchased: Both.
Miscellaneous: The stock includes classic historians, personal memoirs, technical writings, and unit histories.

739
Mysterious Bookshop
129 West 56th Street
New York, New York 10019   (212) 765-0900

The bookstore occupies two floors of a converted brownstone townhouse in the heart of Manhattan, New York City. The two floors are connected by a spiral staircase, in the best mysterious manner, and plush carpeting, soft classical music, and mahogany bookshelves enhance the comfortable ambience. The shop boasts of one of the finest collections of out-of-print hardcover mystery books in the country. Aimed to satisfy both readers and collectors, the selection ranges from inexpensive reading copies to superb first editions. A special feature is an extensive stock of autographed books. The bookstore contains 2,000 square feet of space.
How to Get There: The shop is located in midtown Manhattan.
Owner/Biography: Otto Penzler, owner and collector of mystery fiction for 20 years, started The Mysterious Press in 1976, and the bookstore in 1979. He also won a special Edgar Allan Poe Award for co-editing the Encyclopedia of Mystery & Detection.
Year Founded/History of Bookstore: 1979.
Number of Volumes: 5,000 hardbound.
Types/Classifications: New and old hardbound, new paperbacks, a few old mystery magazines, first editions, fine bindings, out-of-print, association copies, signed copies, presentation copies, limited editions.
General Subject Areas: Crime, Detective Fiction, Espionage, Mystery, Suspense.
Specific Specialties: Sherlock Holmes Books and Ephemera.
Mail/Telephone Orders; Credit Cards: Both; mail orders: $10 minimum for cash, $20 minimum for credit cards; Visa, Mastercard, Diners, American Express. Postage charges are $2 for the first book on an order, 50 cents thereafter; double these rates for foreign mail.
Business Hours: Monday through Friday 11:00 AM - 7:00 PM.
Parking Facilities: No free parking, but there are many pay parking lots in the area.
Special Features: Search service, want lists, autograph parties, many signed books.
Catalogue: Twice a year; also a newsletter on new books.
Collections/Individual Items Purchased: Both.

740
Nelson's Book Stores
26 Central Avenue
Albany, New York 12210   (518) 465-0256

The bookstore occupies two buildings on Central Avenue in the business section of Albany, New York. It carries a general stock of used books. There is also a section of remaindered books, and a very liberal dealer's discount.
Owner/Biography: John L. Nelson, Sr.
Year Founded/History of Bookstore: The bookstore was established in 1969 in two buildings with a connecting hallway in the historic Townsend Square Park area. There is a branch of the bookstore in a family-owned sporting goods store at 331 Central Avenue in Albany. The bookstores have a combined area of 2,200 square feet of space.
Number of Volumes: 70,000.
Types/Classifications: Hardbound, paperbacks, magazines, ephemera, first editions, out-of-print, color plate books, used prints, and paintings.
General Subject Areas: Albany (N.Y.) History, Americana, Birds, Fishing, French Foreign Legion, Guns, Hunting, Lighthouses, Literature, Military, Nature, Political Science, Science Fiction and Fantasy, Weapons, World History.
Mail/Telephone Orders; Credit Cards: Both; Visa, Mastercard, American Express.

Business Hours: Monday through Saturday 11:00 AM - 5:30 PM; closed Sunday. Evening telephone: (518) 459-1291.

Parking Facilities: Public parking, 1.5 hours free.

Special Features: Free search service; publishes a monthly newsletter called The Book Scout, for no charge; holds a semi-annual gigantic dealer's book sale.

Catalogue: Semi-annually.

Collections/Individual Items Purchased: Both.

741

New York Bound Bookshop
43 West 54th Street
New York, New York 10019
                                         (212) 245-8503

This shop is probably the only bookstore to specialize in New York City. Most of the material is old, rare, and out-of-print. The store publishes and reprints unusual or important related material. The stock includes a range of material, from 18th Century documents and 19th Century atlases of New York, to current worthwhile books and prints. The emphasis is on the 19th Century and important out-of-print books, ranging in price from $5 to $5,000. In addition to the walk-in business, the shop has an extensive mail order business, and issues catalogues on old and rare New York City material.

How to Get There: The shop is located in the heart of midtown Manhattan, New York City, in a little brownstone townhouse, on the fourth floor (there is an elevator). It contains 450 square feet of space.

Owner/Biography: Barbara L. Cohen.

Year Founded/History of Bookstore: Founded in 1974, the business grew from appointments at home, to a stall in the South Street Seaport Museum, to its present midtown location. The store was founded by Barbara Cohen who remains the sole proprietor. The original concept of carrying everything relating to New York City past and present has continued and has expanded with the publishing efforts.

Number of Volumes: 3,000.

Types/Classifications: Old and rare hardbound, ephemera, pamphlets, documents, prints, limited editions, out-of-print.

General Subject Areas: New York City, New York State.

Specific Specialties: All areas relating to New York: Wall Street, Literature, History, Diaries, Social History, Crime, Biography, Theater, Immigrants; Special Topics: Brooklyn Bridge Centennial, Statue of Liberty Centennial, Transportation, Architecture, Real Estate.

Author Specialties: Joseph Mitchell, A.J. Liebling.

Other Specialties: Pictorial New York City Maps.

Mail/Telephone Orders; Credit Cards: Both; payment on order for new customers; Visa, Mastercard.

Business Hours: Tuesday through Friday 10:00 AM - 5:30 PM; Saturday 12:00 Noon - 5:00 PM; closed Saturday June through August.

Parking Facilities: Adjacent parking garage.

Special Features: Search service, appraisals, publishing, occasional special events such as lectures and special exhibits.

Catalogue: Three times a year. Special catalogues issued for special events such as the Brooklyn Bridge Centennial and the Statue of Liberty Centennial.

Collections/Individual Items Purchased: Both.

Booksellers' Memberships: Antiquarian Booksellers Association of America.

742

Nineteenth Century Bookshop
Corner of U.S. 20 and N.Y. 8
Bridgewater, New York 13313
                                         (315) 855-7530

The bookstore is housed in a 19th Century brick building, the simple architectural style of which is Federal; it was at one time an inn. The large front room is filled with books, while the former bar room features old tools, small antiques, and some prints.

Owner/Biography: Mrs. Halbert Hiteman and son, James Hiteman.

Year Founded/History of Bookstore: The bookstore was founded by Halbert Hiteman in 1972, and was enjoyed as a retirement project until his death in December 1982. Originally known as the Corner Store, the shop started across the street from its present location, in a vacant grocery store. The old brick building which now houses the shop was purchased and restored in the late 1970's.

Number of Volumes: 6,000.

Types/Classifications: Hardbound, magazines, ephemera, out-of-print, old, first editions, limited editions, color plate books, fine bindings.

General Subject Areas: Agriculture, American History, American Literature, Americana, Architecture, Art, Biography, Drama, General Fiction, General Non-Fiction, Geology, History, How-To Books, Juveniles, Music, Nature, Oneida County (N.Y.) History, Philosophy, Religion, Travel, World History, World Literature.

Mail/Telephone Orders; Credit Cards: No credit cards.

Business Hours: Summer: Monday, Thursday through Sunday 1:00 PM - 6:00 PM; closed Tuesday and Wednesday. Winter: Friday through Sunday 1:00 PM - 6:00 PM.

Parking Facilities: Parking lot.

Collections/Individual Items Purchased: Both.

Booksellers' Memberships: Upstate New York Antiquarian Booksellers, Tri-County Antiques.

743
North Shore Books Ltd.
8 Green Street
Huntington, New York 11743   (516) 271-5558

North Shore Books Ltd. carries a stock of American, English, and European literature as well as books on all subjects.

How to Get There: Located on the north shore of Long Island, the bookstore is approximately 40 miles from Manhattan; take the Long Island Expressway and then north on Route 110.

Types/Classifications: First editions, signed copies, presentation copies, out-of-print, illustrated books, association copies, manuscripts.

General Subject Areas: Detective Fiction, Long Island, Modern First Editions, Scholarly Books, Science Fiction and Fantasy, Seven Arts.

Other Specialties: German, French, Italian Books.

Mail/Telephone Orders; Credit Cards: Mail orders.

Business Hours: Seven days per week 10:30 AM - 6:00 PM.

Parking Facilities: Ample parking.

Special Features: Search service; want lists maintained.

Collections/Individual Items Purchased: Both.

744
OAN Oceanie-Afrique Noir, Ltd.
Box 85
Ancram, New York 12502   (518) 325-5400

The bookstore is located in a large (22,000 square feet), new, modern building designed to house one of the world's largest stocks of "Primitive/Tribal" art publications. Out-of-print, used, and in-print titles are completely computerized for immediate access. Open stock for each title is divided into geographical regions and again divided into subjects (textiles, metal, pottery, jewelry), or re-divided into countries within regions (Nigeria, New Guinea). The regions covered are Africa, Oceania, Indonesia, and the Americas.

How to Get There: The shop is located at the New York/Massachusetts/Connecticut border, in the town of Hillsdale, New York, on Route 22 just 600 yards south of Route 23.

Owner/Biography: Kevin and Lynda Cunningham.

Number of Volumes: 100,000.

Types/Classifications: Hardbound, paperback, magazines, periodicals, exhibition catalogues, auction catalogues, reprints, first editions, fine bindings, scarce, rare, out-of-print, in-print, color plate books.

General Subject Areas: Africa, Americas, Anthropology, Early Voyages and Travel, Ethnology, Pre-

Columbian Americas, Primitive and Tribal Art Publications, South Seas, Southeast Asia, Tribal Cultures, Tribal Peoples.

Specific Specialties: Jewelry, Pottery, Metal, Music, Textiles, Costumes, Body Decoration, Weapons, Art and Artifacts of Tribal Peoples; Cartography and Color Plates of Voyages and Early Travel to the South Seas, Africa, and Northwest Coast of the Americas; all countries of North, West, Central, and South Africa; all countries of Melanesia, Polynesia, Micronesia, and Australia; all Southeast Asia countries including Indonesia, Malaysia, and India; World-Wide Titles in all Languages.

Author Specialties: Capt. James Cook, Sidney Parkinson, L. DuPerrey, Salomon Muller, C. Lumholtz, A.C. Haddon, H.L. Roth, T.S. Raffles, B. Spencer, F.J. Gillen, S. Chauvet, O. Finsch, DeClerq, Schmeltz, A. Kramer, R. Parkinson, R.S. Rattray, Olbrechts, Von Sydow, Pitt-Rivers, Kaudern.

Other Specialties: Museum and University Monographs, Catalogues, and Publications from France, Germany, Belgium, Russia, Netherlands, Denmark, Italy, most other foreign languages.

Mail/Telephone Orders; Credit Cards: Both; Visa, Mastercard.

Business Hours: Tuesday through Thursday 10:00 AM - 5:00 PM.

Parking Facilities: Business parking lot.

Special Features: The store will back-order and search for all unavailable out-of-print material, will order new titles as published, will compile suggested lists for libraries and university courses.

Catalogue: Catalogues semi-annually; lists four times a year.

Collections/Individual Items Purchased: Both.

745
Oceanside Books Unlimited

2856 St. John Road

Oceanside, New York 11572   (516) 764-3378

The bookstore is mainly a mail-order business, but is open by appointment. It issues formal catalogues regularly and specializes in mystery, detective, and bibliography. The shop caters mainly to collectors, featuring first editions, signed copies, uncorrected books, good reprints.

How to Get There: Call for an appointment and directions.

Owner/Biography: Adrienne and Raymond Williams, owners, have been in the book business for 11 years. Prior to that, Adrienne worked for a maritime rare book dealer.

Year Founded/History of Bookstore: Founded in 1973, the bookstore is still in the original location. It grew from a general stock to a specialty bookstore in 3 years; from there it went from average-priced material to good collectible items in mystery and bibliography.

Number of Volumes: 8,000.

Types/Classifications: Hardbound, only first edition paperbacks, autographs, ephemera, first editions, out-of-print, association copies, signed copies, presentation copies, limited editions.

General Subject Areas: Bibliography, Detective, Mystery.

Specific Specialties: Golden Age of Mystery: 1920-1945.

Author Specialties: All Mystery and Detective Authors.

Mail/Telephone Orders; Credit Cards: Both; Visa, Mastercard; the mail order catalogue subscription is $2 for one year, and customers remain on the mailing list indefinitely.

Business Hours: Daily 9:30 AM - 5:30 PM.

Special Features: Search service, preparation of bibliographies, personalized service, service to chain bookstores.

Catalogue: Six times a year; $2 annual subscription.

Collections/Individual Items Purchased: Both.

Booksellers' Memberships: Long Island Antiquarian Bookdealers Association.

Miscellaneous: The owners travel to search for collections, and work with clients to purchase their needs, on an agreed-upon payment schedule. They also service out-of-print material to libraries in the U.S.

746
Old Book Room
111 Grand Street
Croton-on-Hudson, New York 10520 (914) 271-6802

This relatively small store of used and out-of-print books is situated in the old, now revitalized, shopping area of Croton, and it shares space with an art gallery. The bookstore has three rooms, for a total of 250 square feet of space. The first room begins at the far end of the art gallery and contains the rare books, art, first editions, and New York and Hudson River history. Next is a small room for children's books, and last, a larger room with stock covering all categories.

How to Get There: Croton-on-Hudson is 45 miles north of New York City; if driving the New York Thruway, exit at Tarrytown, go north on Rt. 9 to Taconic/Rt. 129 exit, proceed on Rt. 129 to the first stoplight; then left 1 block to Grand Street, left again 1/2 block.

Owner/Biography: Mrs. Jane Northshield, owner, founded the bookstore in 1979 when she and Cornelia Cotton opened connecting shops. The other shop, an art gallery, has frequent shows, and carries old maps, prints, and ephemera. Both women have other jobs: Jane is Village Historian, Cornelia is a free-lance photographer. Jane was a serious book collector before opening her shop; she now has customers in Europe and in most states in this country.

Year Founded/History of Bookstore: The bookstore was started in 1979 by its present owner in a building north of Croton and was one of four stores. When the building was sold all moved to the old Upper Village area of Croton and started a "Merchants' Association" to encourage other small specialty shops. Their success led to a revitalization project, an annual Village Fair, fashion shows, and other group projects.

Number of Volumes: 3,000.

Types/Classifications: Hardbound, paperback, old magazines, posters, rock music recordings, color plate books, out-of-print, signed copies, first editions, old leather bound, pamphlets, booklets, new books by local authors.

General Subject Areas: Adventure, Airplanes, Americana, Antiques, Art, Astronomy, Automobiles, Biography, Birds, Black History, Black Literature, Books About Books, Business, Cats, Children's Books, Christmas, Cinema, Classic Fiction, Cooking, Crafts, Dance, Diaries, Dictionaries (including Foreign), Dogs, Drama, Ethnology, Etymology, Fishing, Folklore, Geology, History, Horticulture, Hudson River, Humor, Hunting, Jewish History, Labor, Literary Criticism, Medicine, Memoirs, Music, Mythology, Nature, Orient, Philosophy, Photography, Poetry, Psychology, Radical Movements, Radio, Reference, Religion, Sailing, Ships, Sports, Television, Theater, Travel, Westchester County (New York), Wild Foods, Witchcraft, Women's Books.

Specific Specialties: Caricature, Woodcuts, German Expressionists, American Artists, New York State, New York City, American Labor, WPA Artists, WPA Writers, Cookbooks, American Socialist, Communist, Anarchist.

Other Specialties: Small but growing collection of Latin and Greek books and unusual foreign dictionaries, Japanese and Chinese Art and Literature.

Mail/Telephone Orders; Credit Cards: Both; cash with order, libraries billed; postage paid usually except large shipments and foreign; will hold phone orders for 2 weeks; no credit cards.

Business Hours: October - January: Wednesday through Saturday 10:00 AM - 5:00 PM; in December: Sunday 2:00 PM - 5:00 PM; February - November: Thursday through Saturday 10:00 AM - 5:00 PM.

Parking Facilities: Street.

Special Features: Search service, lists sent on request; a connecting walled garden for openings, book parties, sales, and reading; free coffee and tea.

Catalogue: No catalogue, but upon acquiring specialty libraries, lists sent to appropriate dealers and customers.

Collections/Individual Items Purchased: Both.

Miscellaneous: Special art shows with related books on sale; open extra times by appointment, appraisals on a small scale.

747
Old Book Room
115 Buffalo Street
Gowanda, New York 14070 (716) 532-3714

The bookstore is located in a large room in the loft of a barn. Climbing the stairs one will enter a barnwood paneled area, heated by a pot bellied stove. The walls are covered with shelves of books; no matter where one looks or walks or sits he is surrounded by books. The shop contains 1,200 square feet of space.

How to Get There: From the New York State Thruway at the Hamburg Exit (No. 57), drive south on Route 62 for about 40 miles. Buffalo Street in Gowanda is Route 62. There is no exterior sign on the bookstore, just the number 115.

Owner/Biography: Lee and Ernest Kionke. Ernest is a retired schoolteacher; he and his wife enjoy gardening, woodcarving, traveling, and raising a horse.

Year Founded/History of Bookstore: Founded around 1959, the bookstore is in its original location, and, as the owners report, is growing older and more crowded as the years pass.

Number of Volumes: 10,000.

Types/Classifications: Hardbound, magazines, ephemera, first editions, out-of-print, signed copies, color plate books, boxed sets.

General Subject Areas: Airplanes, Americana, Animals, Arts, Children's Books, Cooking, Crime, Fiction, Gardening, Health, Histories of Towns, Hobbies, How-To Books, Music, Sheet Music, Sports, Trains.

Other Specialties: Ships and the Sea; the owner makes ship models as a hobby and occasionally for sale.

Mail/Telephone Orders; Credit Cards: Both; no credit cards.

Business Hours: By appointment only.

Parking Facilities: Large driveway and yard for off-street parking.

Special Features: Search service, appraisals, customer want lists.

Collections/Individual Items Purchased: Both.

748
Old Editions Book Shop
3124-26 Main Street
Buffalo, New York 14214 (716) 885-6473

The bookstore is located in a large, old brick building, and contains 2,500 square feet of space. The shop is divided into three sections: paperbacks, hardcovers, rare books.

How to Get There: The shop is located on Main Street in Buffalo less than a mile from the University of Buffalo's Main Street campus. If driving, take the N.Y. State Thruway Exit No. 50 to Main Street; proceed 3 to 4 miles west to the bookstore.

Owner/Biography: Ronald Cozzi, owner, is a former New York State, City, and County chess champion, and is presently the collector of a large antiquarian chess library which branched off into the antiquarian book business.

Year Founded/History of Bookstore: Founded in 1976, the bookstore was originally called The Buffalo Book Studio because of its upstairs location. The name was changed in 1978 to its present one, and the shop moved to a new location in February 1984.

Number of Volumes: 40,000.

Types/Classifications: Most all types and classifications.

General Subject Areas: General.

Mail/Telephone Orders; Credit Cards: Both; Visa, Mastercard.

Business Hours: Monday through Friday 9:00 AM - 9:00 PM; Saturday 9:00 AM - 6:00 PM; Sunday 12:00 Noon - 6:00 PM.

Parking Facilities: Street.

Special Features: Open shop, direct sales, mail order service.

Catalogue: Once a year.

Collections/Individual Items Purchased: Both.

Miscellaneous: The shop also stocks old prints and engravings.

361

749
Once Upon A Time Books
146 Front Street
2nd Floor
Hempstead, New York 11550 (516) 486-9427

   This is a general book store consisting of stacks on military history, aviation history, art, books about books, children's and illustrated books, Americana, Western Americana, cinema, and theater. The stock is hardbound exclusively.
   How to Get There: The bookstore is located directly behind the Abraham & Strauss department store; take the Southern State Parkway to Exit 19 (Peninusla Boulevard-Hempstead), then left at President Street; at 3rd traffic light make a right turn onto Front Street.
   Owner/Biography: Harvey Stanson and James Dore.
   Year Founded/History of Bookstore: 1980.
   Number of Volumes: 20,000.
   Types/Classifications: Hardbound only, first editions, fine bindings, out-of-print, association copies, press books, signed copies, presentation copies, limited editions, color plate books.
   General Subject Areas: General.
   Specific Specialties: Arts, Military History.
   Other Specialties: Modern first editions.
   Mail/Telephone Orders; Credit Cards: Both. Cash with order. Visa and Mastercard accepted.
   Parking Facilities: Parking lot.
   Special Features: Search service; appraisals.
   Collections/Individual Items Purchased: Both.
   Booksellers' Memberships: Long Island Antiquarian Booksellers Association.

750
Owl Pen
Riddle Road
Greenwich, New York 12834 (518) 692-7039

   The Owl Pen is a general used bookstore situated on a back road off a back road in the hills of Washington County, New York. The large stock includes books in all areas, shelved according to subject. Owl Pen's stock is housed in converted barns belonging to what was once a working farm consisting of 30 acres of woods and fields with a view of Vermont's Green Mountains. Visitors are welcome to walk and picnic on the grounds.
   How to Get There: For the adventurous: Follow Route 29 east out of Saratoga Springs, take Route 40 north in Greenwich, proceed 1.5 miles and take the first right (Spraguetown Road), continue 3.4 miles to first Owl Pen sign (small red shingle) on a telephone pole, follow red signs from that point. For the less brave: Call and the owners will send you a map.
   Owner/Biography: Hank Howard and Edie Brown.
   Year Founded/History of Bookstore: 1960. The Owl Pen began with 2,500 volumes housed in a one-time hog house. Its present stock is stored in 4 barns, 2 of which are open to customers. Owl Pen was the brain child of Barbara Probst and on her retirement was sold to the present owners.
   Number of Volumes: 60,000.
   Types/Classifications: Hardbound, paperback, prints, some magazines, some ephemera, out-of print, first editions, fine bindings, illustrated books.
   General Subject Areas: American History, Antiques, Arctic, Art, Biography, Classics, Cooking, Crafts, Crime, Drama, Economics, Fiction, Fishing, Foreign Languages, Humor, Hunting, Juveniles, Literary Criticism, Music, Mysteries, Natural History, Nautical, Occult, Philosophy and Religion, Photography, Poetry, Psychology, Science, Science Fiction, Social Sciences, Sports, Technical, Travel, Victoriana, Westerns, World History.
   Specific Specialties: New York State History, Adirondack Mountains, Revolutionary War (U.S.).
   Other Specialties: Biological and Aquatic Sciences.
   Mail/Telephone Orders; Credit Cards: Both. Check with order. No credit cards.
   Business Hours: May 1 - November 1: Wednesday through Sunday 12:00 Noon - 6:00 PM or by appointment; Winter: by appointment or chance.

Parking Facilities: Business parking lot.
Special Features: Search service.
Catalogue: Published once per year (on Biological and Aquatic Sciences).
Collections/Individual Items Purchased: Both.
Miscellaneous: Should collectors plan a trip to the area, be advised that there are 10 or more bookstores within a half hour of The Owl Pen.

751
Pageant Book and Print Shop
109 East 9th Street
New York, New York 10003

(212) 674-5296

This is a family run second-hand bookstore with books in all subjects on two levels. The prints are on the first floor along with open bins for easy viewing. The shop occupies 4,500 square feet of space.

How to Get There: Located between 3rd and 4th Avenues, the bookstore is one block from the Astor Place Station on the Lexington Avenue subway line.

Owner/Biography: Sidney B. Solomon, Shirley Solomon. Mr. Solomon has been an antiquarian bookdealer for over 35 years in the "Book Row" district. His daughter, Shirley, is following in her father's footsteps.

Year Founded/History of Bookstore: 1945. This is the 3rd location of the shop which was once on "Book Row" with the former name Pageant Book Co. The current name is more descriptive of the stock.

Number of Volumes: 300,000.

Types/Classifications: Hardbound, paperback, magazines, broadsides, autographs, ephemera, first editions, fine bindings, out-of-print, press books, signed copies, presentation copies, limited editions, color plate books.

General Subject Areas: American Literature, Americana, Antiques, Architecture, Art, Black Studies, British History, British Literature, Catholica, Cookery, Crime, Economics, European Literature, Fiction, Film, Foreign Languages, Gardening, Judaica, Language, Law, Medical, Music, Mysteries, Mythology, Natural History, Occult, Photography, Plays, Poetry, Reference, Religion, Science Fiction and Fantasy, Social Sciences, Sports, Technical, Theater, Transportation, Travel, Women, World History.

Specific Specialties: Art Deco, Art Nouveau, American First Editions, John F. Kennedy, Royalty.

Other Specialties: Translated books.

Mail/Telephone Orders; Credit Cards: Both. Check with order. American Express, Visa, Mastercard accepted.

Business Hours: Monday through Saturday 10:00 AM - 6:30 PM.

Parking Facilities: Commercial parking lots, street parking.

Special Features: Search service (in store).

Catalogue: Published occasionally.

Collections/Individual Items Purchased: Both.

Booksellers' Memberships: Antiquarian Booksellers Association of America including Local and Middle Atlantic Chapters.

Miscellaneous: The store has over 1/2 million antique prints; it specializes in incunabula leaves, old rare maps, original art, etchings, New York, American views, European views, world views, fashion, political cartoons, botany, Audubons, Victoriana, ephemera.

752
Paragon Book Gallery, Ltd.
"The Oriental Book Store of America"
14 East 38th Street
New York, New York 10016

(212) 532-4920

The Paragon carries current and out-of-print titles on the Near East, Far East, South and Southeast Asia, mostly in translation in English.

How to Get There: The bookstore, located in Manhattan, is between Fifth and Madison Avenue, on the fifth floor.

Owner/Biography: Joseph Abraham.

363

Year Founded/History of Bookstore: 1936.
Types/Classifications: Out-of-print, current titles.
General Subject Areas: Far East, Near East, South Asia, Southeast Asia.
Mail/Telephone Orders; Credit Cards: Both. Prepayment required. No credit cards.
Business Hours: Monday through Friday 9:30 AM - 5:45 PM; Saturday (except July and August) 10:00 AM - 4:00 PM; closed Sunday.
Parking Facilities: Commercial parking lots are advised.
Catalogue: Published 2 times per year.
Collections/Individual Items Purchased: Individual items only with asking price by seller.

753
Paulette Greene Rare Books
140 Princeton Road
Rockville Centre, New York 11570   (516) 766-8602

Paulette Green Rare Books is a select stock of antiquarian books which are catalogued and sold through the mail. Occasionally book collectors are able to shop but by appointment only.
How to Get There: Call for directions when making an appointment.
Owner/Biography: Paulette Greene.
Year Founded/History of Bookstore: 1963.
Number of Volumes: 5,000.
Types/Classifications: Hardbound, first editions, out-of-print, press books, signed copies, author letters.
General Subject Areas: American and English Literature, Detective Fiction, Mysteries, Science Fiction and Fantasy.
Specific Specialties: Sherlock Holmes.
Author Specialties: Arthur Conan Doyle, Edna St. Vincent Millay, John F. Kennedy.
Mail/Telephone Orders; Credit Cards: Both. Letter or phone orders to confirm book order; directions for payment made at that time. No credit cards.
Business Hours: Daily 9:00 AM - 5:00 PM by appointment.
Special Features: Special publications relating to Sherlock Holmes.
Catalogue: Published annually ($3).
Collections/Individual Items Purchased: Both.
Booksellers' Memberships: Antiquarian Booksellers Association of America including Middle Atlantic Chapter, Long Island Antiquarian Book Dealers Association.

754
Peter Thomas Fisher Bookseller
41 Union Square West
New York, New York 10003   (212) 255-6789

Mr. Fisher carries new and used American and German books.
Owner/Biography: Peter Thomas Fisher. Mr. Fisher is a former Sales and Promotion Manager of the New York Graphic Society and a former manager of the Harcourt Brace Store in New York City.
Year Founded/History of Bookstore: 1939.
Number of Volumes: 12,000.
Types/Classifications: Hardbound, paperback, out-of-print, signed copies, presentation copies.
General Subject Areas: General.
Author Specialties: Stefan Zweig.
Other Specialties: German books.
Mail/Telephone Orders; Credit Cards: No telephone orders. No credit cards.
Business Hours: By appointment.
Special Features: Search service.
Catalogue: Catalogue published.

755
Peter Tumarkin Fine Books, Inc.
310 East 70th Street
New York, New York 10021 (212) 348-8187

This is a primarily a mail order business in a private residence. It specializes in first editions of German literature, rare books from the Continent (mainly German from the 16th to 19th Centuries), antiquarian German titles, and illustrated children's books until 1930. Visits may be arranged by appointment.
Owner/Biography: Peter Tumarkin.
Year Founded/History of Bookstore: 1973. The business was founded originally in Cambridge, Massachusetts.
Number of Volumes: 2,000.
Types/Classifications: See above.
General Subject Areas: German Literature.
Specific Specialties: German Baroque Titles.
Mail/Telephone Orders; Credit Cards: Both. No credit cards.
Business Hours: By appointment; generally between 10:00 AM - 5:00 PM.
Catalogue: Published 4 times per year.
Collections/Individual Items Purchased: Both.
Booksellers' Memberships: Antiquarian Booksellers Association of America, International League of Antiquarian Booksellers, Verband Deutscher Antiquare.

756
Phoenix Book Shop
22 Jones Street
New York, New York 10014 (212) 675-2795

The Phoenix Book Shop emphasizes first editions of 20th century literature.
How to Get There: The shop is located in New York City's Greenwich Village, easily reached by nearby subway and surface transportation.
Owner/Biography: Robert A. Wilson. Mr. Wilson is the author of "Modern Book Collecting" published in 1980 by Alfred A. Knopf. He is also the compiler of bibliographies of Gregory Corso, Denise Levertov, and Gertrude Stein.
Year Founded/History of Bookstore: 1931. The store has had two locations and five owners, the present owner since 1962.
Number of Volumes: 14,000.
Types/Classifications: Hardbound first editions of 20th Century literature, manuscripts, letters.
General Subject Areas: Drama, Modern First Editions, Poetry.
Author Specialties: Gertrude Stein, Ezra Pound, Wystan Hugh Auden.
Mail/Telephone Orders; Credit Cards: Both. No credit cards.
Business Hours: Daily 12:00 Noon - 7:00 PM.
Parking Facilities: Street parking, commercial parking garages.
Special Features: Preparation of bibliographies.
Catalogue: Published bi-monthly.
Collections/Individual Items Purchased: Both.

757
Pomander Bookshop
252 West 95th Street
New York, New York 10025 (212) 866-1777

The Pomander Bookshop, named for the adjacent New York City landmark Pomander Walk, is a small, select, out-of-print and antiquarian shop with a bit of an English "air" about it. Visiting author Jonathan Miller claimed that this sort of book shop no longer exists in London. Primarily a client-oriented, word-of-mouth establishment, the shop has been mentioned favorably in the "New Yorker" magazine and the "New

York Times" and welcomes new faces. Neatly stocked subjects include art, history, fiction, poetry, belles lettres, philosophy, performing arts, and travel. Art and travel are especially strong. Book requests are pursued vigorously and book condition is stressed. The owners strive to present a good turn-over of handsome editions of interesting titles in attractive condition. This neighborhood "spot" has gathered a lively crowd of in and out of town regulars whose informed interests have animated every book on the Pomander's shelves. Dogs are welcome.

How to Get There: The shop is just west of Broadway on Manhattan's Upper West Side next to the historic Thalia Theatre (seen in Woody Allen's "Annie Hall"). The closest subway stop is the IRT 1, 2, or 3 train at 96th Street. If driving, exit the West Side Highway at 95th Street.

Owner/Biography: Carlos R. Goez and William L. Hamilton.

Year Founded/History of Bookstore: 1976.

Number of Volumes: 8,000.

Types/Classifications: Hardbound, original paperback titles and editions, out-of-print, first editions, some illustrated books, some signed and association copies.

General Subject Areas: Architecture, Art, Belles Lettres, Fiction, History, Literary Criticism, Performing Arts, Poetry, Religion, Travel.

Specific Specialties: 20th Century Decorative Arts, art monographs and exhibition catalogues, scholarly titles, neglected modern fiction.

Mail/Telephone Orders; Credit Cards: Both. Send self-addressed stamped envelope for reply. No credit cards.

Business Hours: Daily 12:00 Noon - 8:00 PM.

Collections/Individual Items Purchased: Both.

758
Question Mark

P.O. Box 9107
Albany, New York 12209   (518) 434-8465

The Question Mark occupies a two-room office at Number 1 Columbia Place in Albany, New York. It deals mostly in Americana and unusual items of interest. Visits can be arranged by appointment.

How to Get There: The shop is located 1 block from City Hall in downtown Albany.

Owner/Biography: Michael R. Linehan.

Year Founded/History of Bookstore: 1979.

Number of Volumes: 1,000.

Types/Classifications: Rare, out-of-print, autographs, photographs, broadsides, historically significant artifacts.

General Subject Areas: Americana, General.

Mail/Telephone Orders; Credit Cards: Both. Cash with order. No credit cards.

Business Hours: By appointment only.

Parking Facilities: Arrangements for parking will be made.

Special Features: Appraisals.

Collections/Individual Items Purchased: Both.

759
Radio City Book Store

324 West 47th Street
New York, New York 10036   (212) 245-5754

The Radio City Book Store specializes in books on professional cooking and books for hotels.

How to Get There: The store is located in midtown Manhattan, easily reached by nearby subway and surface transportation.

Owner/Biography: Seymour Gaynor.

General Subject Areas: Cooking.

760
Reference Book Center, Inc.
175 Fifth Avenue
New York, New York 10010
(212) 677-2160

The Reference Book Center has a large stock of used encyclopedias and dictionaries plus all kinds of reference books.
How to Get There: The Center is in Room 701 of the historic Flatiron Building located at the junction of 23rd Street, Broadway, and Fifth Avenue.
Owner/Biography: Saul and Margery Shine.
Year Founded/History of Bookstore: 1961.
Number of Volumes: 6,000.
Types/Classifications: Hardbound only.
General Subject Areas: Dictionaries, Encyclopedias, Reference.
Other Specialties: Some foreign language dictionaries and encyclopedias.
Mail/Telephone Orders; Credit Cards: Both. Check with order. No credit cards.
Business Hours: Monday through Friday 10:00 AM - 4:30 PM.
Parking Facilities: Commercial parking lots.
Catalogue: Published 2 times per year.
Collections/Individual Items Purchased: Both.

761
Renate Halpern Galleries, Inc.
325 East 79th Street
New York, New York 10021
(212) 988-9316

Books are sold from the owners' apartment by appointment only to serious collectors and dealers. They specialize in books and catalogues on oriental rugs and textiles.
How to Get There: Directions will be given by phone when an appointment is requested.
Owner/Biography: Renate Halpern and Arthur Halpern.
Year Founded/History of Bookstore: 1974.
Number of Volumes: 500.
Types/Classifications: Hardbound and soft cover books and catalogues, out-of-print, in-print, first editions.
General Subject Areas: Oriental Rugs and Textiles.
Mail/Telephone Orders; Credit Cards: Both. Minimum order $25, postage extra. No credit cards.
Business Hours: By appointment.
Parking Facilities: Metered street parking and commercial parking garages.
Special Features: The Halperns buy, sell, and restore oriental rugs and textiles.
Collections/Individual Items Purchased: Both.

762
Richard B. Arkway, Inc.
538 Madison Avenue
New York, New York 10022
(212) 751-8135

This antiquarian bookstore carries fine rare books, maps, and globes.
How to Get There: The store is easily reached by nearby subway and surface transportation.
Owner/Biography: Richard B. Arkway.
Year Founded/History of Bookstore: 1972.
Types/Classifications: Fine, rare, first editions, out-of-print, maps, globes, prints.
General Subject Areas: Americana, Architecture, Botanical Prints, Early Travels, Medicine, Science, Social History, Voyages.
Mail/Telephone Orders; Credit Cards: Both. No credit cards.
Business Hours: Monday through Saturday 10:00 AM - 5:00 PM.

Parking Facilities: Commercial parking garages.
Catalogue: Published 4 times annually.
Collections/Individual Items Purchased: Both.
Booksellers' Memberships: Antiquarian Booksellers Association of America.

763
Richard C. Ramer, Old & Rare Books
225 East 70th Street
New York, New York 10021   (212) 737-0222

The bookstore is open by appointment only and features old and rare Spanish and Portuguese books, 16th through 19th Centuries, and Latin Americana. Brazil is a major speciality. Also featured are books concerned with the Spanish and Portuguese presence in Africa and Asia, e.g., Morocco, Angola, Cabo Verde, Guinea, Mozambique, India, China, Japan, the Philippines. Included is bibliography relating to the above. The bookstore contains approximately 1,000 square feet of space.

Owner/Biography: Richard C. Ramer, owner, has an M.A. in Latin American history from Indiana University. Mr. Ramer has been in business since 1969.
Year Founded/History of Bookstore: 1969.
Number of Volumes: 6,000.
Types/Classifications: Old and rare books.
General Subject Areas: Portuguese Literature, Spanish Literature.
Specific Specialties: Old and Rare Spanish and Portuguese, 16th through 19th Centuries; Latin America; Spanish and Portuguese Presence in Africa and Asia; Brazil.
Mail/Telephone Orders; Credit Cards: Both. No credit cards.
Business Hours: By appointment only.
Parking Facilities: Street parking (extremely difficult); public parking garages.
Special Features: Search service for Portuguese titles.
Catalogue: Infrequently.
Collections/Individual Items Purchased: Both.
Booksellers' Memberships: Antiquarian Booksellers Association of America including the Middle Atlantic Chapter.

764
Richard Stoddard - Performing Arts Books
90 East 10th Street
New York, New York 10003   (212) 982-9440

This bookstore offers both popular and scholarly books and ephemera related to all of the performing arts as well as autographs, photographs, posters, and original scenic and costume designs. It has the largest stock of Broadway Playbills in the city (and perhaps in the country); all are catalogued by title.

How to Get There: The shop is located between 3rd and 4th Avenues in the old 4th Avenue bookstore district of Manhattan, just two blocks north of Joseph Papp's Public Theatre.
Owner/Biography: Richard Stoddard. Mr. Stoddard holds a Ph.D. in the History of Theatre from Yale University. He is a former university professor.
Year Founded/History of Bookstore: 1975.
Number of Volumes: 8,000.
Types/Classifications: Hardbound, paperback, ephemera, autographs, posters, photographs, original science and costume designs, back-issue periodicals, rare, out-of-print.
General Subject Areas: Circus, Conjuring/Magic, Costume Design, Dance, Film, Popular Entertainments, Scenic Design, Show Business, Theater.
Author Specialties: Edward Gordon Craig, Jo Mielziner, Adolph Appia, Leon Bakst.
Mail/Telephone Orders; Credit Cards: Both. Check with order. No credit cards.
Business Hours: Wednesday through Saturday 11:00 AM - 6:00 PM; Sunday 1:00 PM - 6:00 PM; closed Monday and Tuesday.
Parking Facilities: Commercial parking lots nearby; street parking catch-as-catch-can.

Special Features: Search service, appraisals.
Catalogue: Published 5 times per year.
Collections/Individual Items Purchased: Both.

765
Rivendell Bookshop, Ltd.
149 First Avenue
New York, New York 10003   (212) 533-2501

This is a small specialized bookstore devoted to Celtic studies.
How to Get There: The store is located in lower Manahattan, easily reached by First Avenue bus, 2nd Avenue bus, and subway. The Lexington Avenue subway stop at Astor Station and the Broadway Local stop at 8th Street are within a short walking distance.
Owner/Biography: Eileen Campbell Gordon.
Year Founded/History of Bookstore: 1978.
Number of Volumes: 5,000.
General Subject Areas: Arthurian Legend, Celtic Studies, Norse Legend.
Specific Specialties: Celtic: History, Language, Art, Folkore, Music; Arthurian and Norse Legend: The Inklings, Faerie.
Mail/Telephone Orders; Credit Cards: No telephone orders. No credit cards.
Business Hours: Monday through Saturday 12:00 Noon - 8:00 PM.
Parking Facilities: Street parking, commercial parking lots and garages.
Catalogue: Catalogue published.
Collections/Individual Items Purchased: Both.

766
Riverow Bookshop
204 Front Street
Owego, New York 13827   (607) 687-4094

Riverow Bookshop carries new, used, and rare books. It occupies 750 square feet of space.
How to Get There: The shop is in downtown Owego along the river; Owego is 25 miles west of Binghamton and 30 miles south of Ithaca.
Owner/Biography: John D. Spencer.
Year Founded/History of Bookstore: 1976.
Number of Volumes: 15,000.
Types/Classifications: Hardbound only in used and rare book section; ephemera, trade catalogues, autographs, broadsides, maps, trade cards, stereocards, travel guides, first editions, fine bindings, out-of-print.
General Subject Areas: Americana, Antique Reference, Architectural Drawings, Architecture, Art, Biography, Cookbooks, Literature, Reference, Technology, World History.
Mail/Telephone Orders; Credit Cards: Both. Visa and Mastercard accepted.
Business Hours: Monday through Saturday 9:30 AM - 5:30 PM; Thursday until 8:00 PM.
Parking Facilities: Street parking.
Catalogue: Published 2 times per year.
Collections/Individual Items Purchased: Both.
Booksellers' Memberships: Antiquarian Booksellers Association of America, Ephemera Society.

767
Rodgers Book Barn
Rodman Road
Hillsdale, New York 12529   (518) 325-3610

Rodgers Book Barn maintains a stock of over 35,000 hardbound books and paperbacks.

How to Get There: The bookstore is located off NY Route 22 via Whipperwill Road.
Number of Volumes: 35,000.
Types/Classifications: Hardbound, paperback, out-of-print, first editions, reading copies.
General Subject Areas: General.
Mail/Telephone Orders; Credit Cards: Mail orders.
Business Hours: April 1 - December 31: Monday, Thursday, Friday 2:00 PM - 6:00 PM; Saturday and Sunday 10:00 AM - 6:00 PM. Winter hours vary; it is best to call first.
Parking Facilities: Ample parking.
Collections/Individual Items Purchased: Both.

768
Roy W. Clare - Antiquarian and Uncommon Books
47 Woodshire South
P.O. Box 136
Getzville, New York 14068   (716) 688-8723

Roy W. Clare is an antiquarian bookman specializing in incunabula, early science and medicine, 16th and 17th Century books in English in all subjects, early witchcraft, and early illustrated books. Visits can be arranged by appointment.
How to Get There: The bookstore is located in suburban Buffalo. Call for directions when making an appointment.
Owner/Biography: Roy W. Clare.
Types/Classifications: Incunabula, rare, out-of-print, illustrated books.
General Subject Areas: General (16th and 17th Century), Science and Medicine, Witchcraft.
Mail/Telephone Orders; Credit Cards: Mail orders.
Business Hours: By appointment only.
Parking Facilities: Ample parking.
Catalogue: Catalogue published.
Collections/Individual Items Purchased: Both. Quotations appreciated.
Booksellers' Memberships: Antiquarian Booksellers Association of America.

769
Russica Book and Art Shop, Inc.
799 Broadway
New York, New York 10003   (212) 473-7486

This shop specializes in rare and out of print Russian, Ukrainian, and Slavic books and manuscripts. It has a small stock of books in Baltic languages (Latvian, Lithuanian, Estonian) and old prints and drawings in the same area. The shop occupies 3,000 square feet of space.
Owner/Biography: Valery Kuharets. Mr. Kuharets was born in Orenburg (USSR) and was graduated from the Leningrad School of Library Science. He emigrated to the United States in 1974.
Year Founded/History of Bookstore: 1975.
Number of Volumes: 50,000.
Types/Classifications: Hardbound, paperback, magazines, broadsides, autographs, ephemera, first editions, fine bindings, out-of-print, association copies, press books, signed copies, presentation copies, limited editions, color plate books.
General Subject Areas: Russian Books, Slavic Materials, Ukranian Books.
Specific Specialties: First editions of Russian classics in Russian; books on the history of science in Russia and the USSR; limited editions of art books.
Author Specialties: Vladimir Nabokov first editions.
Other Specialties: Rare photographs by Russian and East European photographers.
Mail/Telephone Orders; Credit Cards: Both. Cash with order. No credit cards.
Business Hours: Monday through Friday 9:00 AM - 6:00 PM; Saturday 11:00 AM - 4:00 PM.
Parking Facilities: Street parking, commercial parking lots and garages.

Special Features: Search service; publishing sideline; preparation of bibliographies.
Catalogue: Published 3 to 5 times per year.
Collections/Individual Items Purchased: Both.

770
Ruth Berman - Book Gallery
15 Overlook Road
White Plains, New York 10605   (914) 949-5406

The Book Gallery specializes in Art, Architecture, and Photography. Visits are welcome by appointment only.
Owner/Biography: Ruth Berman.
Year Founded/History of Bookstore: 1960.
Number of Volumes: 5,000.
Types/Classifications: Hardbound, first editions, out-of-print.
General Subject Areas: Architecture, Art, Photography.
Business Hours: By appointment only.
Catalogue: Published infrequently.
Collections/Individual Items Purchased: Both.

771
Science Fiction Shop
56 Eighth Avenue
New York, New York 10014   (212) 741-0270

This is a street-level shop in the West Village area of Manhattan. Bookshelves are hung between curving baffles which gives the mock appearance of a spaceship interior. The shop deals exclusively in science fiction and fantasy. It occupies 350 square feet of space.
How to Get There: Located in the Greenwich Village section of Manhattan, the shop is easily reached by nearby subway and surface transportation.
Owner/Biography: Pellucidar Corporation. One corporate officer is a long-time book reviewer for Isaac Asimov's "Magazine of Science Fiction" and film reviewer for the "Magazine of Fantasy & Science Fiction." He and other corporate officers along with employees authored "The Reader's Guide to Science Fiction" and "The Reader's Guide to Fantasy," both published by Avon Books.
Year Founded/History of Bookstore: 1973.
Number of Volumes: 5,000.
Types/Classifications: Hardbound, paperback, magazines, limited editions, signed editions, British hardbound and paperback.
General Subject Areas: Science Fiction and Fantasy.
Mail/Telephone Orders; Credit Cards: Both. Payment in advance unless charged. Visa and Mastercard accepted. See catalogue for specific mail order requirements.
Business Hours: Monday through Friday 11:00 AM - 8:00 PM; Saturday 11:00 AM - 6:00 PM; Sunday 12:00 Noon - 6:00 PM.
Parking Facilities: Street parking, commercial parking lots and garages.
Catalogue: Published 4 times per year.
Collections/Individual Items Purchased: Both.
Miscellaneous: The staff has an excellent knowledge of the genre.

772
Soldier Shop Inc.
1222 Madison Avenue
New York, New York 10128   (212) 535-6788

The Collector's Guide

The bookstore specializes in all facets of military history and military collecting. It contains 800 square feet of space.

Year Founded/History of Bookstore: Founded in 1965, the bookstore remained at its original location, 1013 Madison Avenue, New York City, for 18 years. In 1983 it moved to its present address.

Number of Volumes: 3,000.

Types/Classifications: Hardbound, paperbacks, in-print, out-of-print.

General Subject Areas: Military, Military History, Military Uniforms, Military Weapons, Model Soldiers.

Specific Specialties: All facets of Military History and Military Collecting.

Mail/Telephone Orders; Credit Cards: Mail orders only; orders must be through the store's catalogue. No credit cards.

Business Hours: Monday through Saturday 10:00 AM - 5:00 PM.

Parking Facilities: Metered parking.

Catalogue: Two times a year.

Collections/Individual Items Purchased: Collections only.

773
Strand Bookstore
828 Broadway
New York, New York 10003 (212) 473-1452

The Strand Bookstore is a well-known spot for booklovers. It has over two million books on three floors, on all subjects, arranged in subject areas and alphabetically by author. This vast stock includes reviewers' copies of the latest publications, quality remainders of scholarly interest, and antiquarian books which are especially strong in the arts and humanities. There is also a rare book room. The management of the Strand proudly declares that its bookstore is reportedly "the best-stocked antiquarian and used bookshop of quality books in the English-speaking world."

How to Get There: Located on Broadway, the shop is two blocks south of Union Square (Fourteenth Street) in Manhattan, New York City.

Owner/Biography: Fred Bass.

Year Founded/History of Bookstore: 1927. The store was originally located in Greenwich Village and was moved to Fourth Avenue in the late 1930's. In the late 1950's it was moved to its present location. The store was founded by Benjamin Bass (1901-1978) and has been continued as a sole proprietorship by his son.

Number of Volumes: 2,000,000.

Types/Classifications: Hardbound, paperback, magazines, broadsides, autographs, ephemera, first editions, fine bindings, association copies, press books, signed copies, presentation copies, limited editions, color plate books.

General Subject Areas: Americana, Antiques, Architecture, Art, Aviation, Bibliography, Biological Sciences, Black Studies, Children's Books, Crime, Dance, Drama, Fiction, Gardening, History, Journalism, Judaica, Latin America, Linguistics, Literature, Mathematics, Music, Mysteries, Occult, Philosophy, Photography, Physical Sciences, Poetry, Reference, Religion, Science Fiction, Social Sciences, Travel, War.

Other Specialties: Reviewers' copies of latest publications.

Mail/Telephone Orders; Credit Cards: Both. American Express, Visa, and Mastercard accepted.

Business Hours: Monday through Saturday 9:30 AM - 6:30 PM; Sunday 11:00 AM - 5:00 PM.

Parking Facilities: Street parking on Saturday; private parking lots nearby.

Special Features: Appraisals of libraries and fine individual items.

Catalogue: Published monthly.

Collections/Individual Items Purchased: Both.

Booksellers' Memberships: Antiquarian Booksellers Association of America.

774
Swann Galleries, Inc.
104 East 25th Street
New York, New York 10010 (212) 254-4710

Swann Galleries is possibly the most active rare book auctioneer in the United States. It conducts weekly auctions of rare and antiquarian books, maps, atlases, photographica, autographs, and manuscripts.

Owner/Biography: George S. Lowry, President.

Year Founded/History of Bookstore: 1941.

General Subject Areas: General.

Catalogue: Published 40 times per year.

775
Sydney R. Smith Sporting Books
Canaan, New York 12029   (518) 794-8998

Sydney R. Smith Sporting Books specializes in equestrian books in all subjects, e.g. foxhunting, polo, racing, breeding, vet, training, showing, dressage. It also offers books on dogs, shooting, and fishing. Both out-of-print and new books are available.

How to Get There: Directions will be furnished when making an appointment.

Owner/Biography: Camilla P. Smith.

Year Founded/History of Bookstore: 1940. The business was started by Sydney R. Smith, a retired Cavalry Officer and Master of Foxhounds. It was continued by his daughter.

Number of Volumes: Probably the largest number of equestrian books in the United States.

Types/Classifications: Hardbound, paperback, magazines, out-of-print, first editions, fine bindings, association copies, press copies, signed copies, presentation copies, limited editions, color plate books.

General Subject Areas: Dogs, Equestrian Books, Fishing, Shooting.

Other Specialties: Derrydale Press.

Mail/Telephone Orders; Credit Cards: Both. Prepaid orders only, plus postage. No credit cards. Items can be shipped C.O.D.

Business Hours: Daily by appointment only.

Special Features: Search service; appraisals.

Collections/Individual Items Purchased: Both.

Booksellers' Memberships: Antiquarian Booksellers Association of America including Mid-Atlantic Chapter.

776
Theatrebooks, Inc.
Room 312
1576 Broadway
New York, New York 10036   (212) 757-2834

The bookstore specializes in all aspect of the theater, and carries new, used, and out-of-print books on that subject. It contains 850 square feet of space.

How to Get There: The shop is located between 47th and 48th Streets, on the third floor.

Owner/Biography: Jane and Robert Emerson.

Year Founded/History of Bookstore: 1979.

Number of Volumes: 50,000.

Types/Classifications: Hardbound, paperback, magazines, autographs, first editions, signed copies, out-of-print.

General Subject Areas: Theater.

Specific Specialties: Musicals, Musical Scores, Plays, Acting, Directing (Theater), Biography, Playwriting, Shakespeare, Stage Design.

Author Specialties: William Shakespeare.

Mail/Telephone Orders; Credit Cards: Both. Visa, Mastercard.

Business Hours: Monday through Friday 10:30 AM - 6:00 PM; Saturday 12:00 Noon - 5:00 PM.

Parking Facilities: Public parking lot.

Special Features: Search service.

Catalogue: Three times a year.

777 NEW YORK The Collector's Guide

Collections/Individual Items Purchased: Both.
Booksellers' Memberships: Antiquarian Booksellers Association of America.

777
Timothy Trace
144 Red Mill Road
Peekskill, New York 10566 (914) 528-4074

The bookstore is on private premises in the country and specializes in books for the collector of antiques, including pottery, porcelain, glass, brass, silver, furniture, needlework, textiles. The shop is open by appointment only.
How to Get There: Directions will be furnished when calling for an appointment.
Owner/Biography: Timothy Trace.
Year Founded/History of Bookstore: 1950.
Number of Volumes: 6,000.
Types/Classifications: Hardbound, ephemera, rare, out-of-print.
General Subject Areas: Antiques, Architecture, Decorative Arts, Early Science, Early Trades, Furniture Pattern Books, Needlework Pattern Books.
Specific Specialties: Collecting of: Pottery, Porcelain, Glass, Brass, Silver, Textiles.
Mail/Telephone Orders; Credit Cards: Both. Personal check with order. No credit cards.
Business Hours: By appointment only.
Parking Facilities: Private parking.
Collections/Individual Items Purchased: Both.
Booksellers' Memberships: Antiquarian Booksellers Association of America.

778
Trebizond Rare Books
667 Madison Avenue
New York, New York 10021 (212) 371-1980

The bookstore features first or significant early editions of American, English, and Continental works in literature and travel. It contains 720 square feet of space.
How to Get There: Located in central Manhattan, New York City, the bookstore is on the east side of Madison Avenue between 60th and 61st Streets.
Owner/Biography: Williston R. and Rosalind C. Benedict.
Year Founded/History of Bookstore: Founded in 1975, the bookstore's original location was at 14 East 60th Street; later that year it was moved to its present location. The business was founded by its present owners.
Number of Volumes: 1,500.
Types/Classifications: Principally hardbound books, but also volumes in original wrappers; autographs, first editions, significant early editions, signed copies, association copies, color plate books.
General Subject Areas: American Literature, Continental Literature, English Literature, Travel.
Mail/Telephone Orders; Credit Cards: Both. No credit cards.
Business Hours: Monday through Friday 10:00 AM - 5:00 PM; Saturday by appointment.
Catalogue: Three times per year.
Collections/Individual Items Purchased: Both.
Booksellers' Memberships: Antiquarian Booksellers Association of America (Middle Atlantic Chapter).

779
Tryon County Bookshop
RD 1, Box 207
Route 29
Johnstown, New York 12095 (518) 762-1060

The bookstore is a fifty foot mobile home located on a quarter acre in the foothills of the Adirondack Mountains. The stock consists of a general line of used, rare, and out-of-print books, paper material, stereo views, postcards, antiques, minerals, and wood carvings.

How to Get There: The bookstore is located four miles east of Johnstown, New York on Route 29, and twenty-four miles west of Saratoga.

Owner/Biography: Roger S. Montgomery, owner, started buying and selling books and antiques part time in 1953, and then full time in 1957. He also does silversmithing, wood carving, collecting minerals, and raising animals.

Year Founded/History of Bookstore: Founded in 1953, the bookstore was located in Fonda, New York for 21 years. At one time the shop had two stores on Main Street in Fonda. In 1979 the stock was moved into the mobile home which is located behind the Montgomery residence, and contains 500 square feet of space.

Number of Volumes: 4,000.

Types/Classifications: Hardbound, magazines, photographs, paper material, postcards, stereo views, catalogues, out-of-print.

General Subject Areas: Americana, Biography, Children's Books, Civil War, Fiction, Natural History, New York State History, Poetry, Travel.

Mail/Telephone Orders; Credit Cards: Both; no credit cards.

Business Hours: Daily 8:00 AM - 8:00 PM except during book fairs, shows, buying trips, etc.; it is advisable to call ahead.

Parking Facilities: Free parking nearby.

Special Features: Search service.

Collections/Individual Items Purchased: Both.

780
University Place Book Shop
821 Broadway
New York, New York 10003
(212) 254-5998

The bookstore features used and out-of-print books mainly on Black Studies and radical movements. It contains 3,000 square feet of space.

How to Get There: Located in Manhattan, New York City, the shop can be reached by the East Side subway to Union Square, then walk south two blocks; the shop is at Broadway and 12th Street.

Owner/Biography: Walter Goldwater, owner, started the shop in 1932 on University Place. Prior to that, after college, he had been in the radical movement and in publishing. Mr. Goldwater has been the President of the Marshall Chess Club for the past 15 years.

Year Founded/History of Bookstore: The bookstore was opened in 1932 as a tiny shop on University Place and has been moved several times since. It has been in its present location since 1972.

Number of Volumes: 80,000.

Types/Classifications: Hardbound, pamphlets, old, rare, early printed books, first editions.

General Subject Areas: Africa, American Negro, Anarchism, Black Studies, Checkers, Chess, Communism, Socialism, West Indies.

781
Urban Center Books
457 Madison Avenue
New York, New York 10022
(212) 935-3595

The bookstore specializes in architecture, design, urban planning, and historic preservation. It is operated by the Municipal Art Society of New York with the support of the J.M. Kaplan Fund. The store deals mainly in new books in its specialty, but has a small collection of out-of-print books mainly in 20th Century architecture of America and Europe. The shop contains 500 square feet of space.

How to Get There: Between 50th and 51st Streets on Madison Avenue in midtown Manhattan, New York City, the shop is located in the north wing of the historic Villard House. Directly behind St. Patrick's Cathedral enter the courtyard of the Helmsley Palace Hotel and turn left.

Owner/Biography: The Municipal Art Society of New York, owner, is a civic organization founded in 1892 and is concerned with the physical environment of the city in planning and preservation.

Year Founded/History of Bookstore: The bookstore was founded in 1980 and serves a growing clientele of design practitioners, students, and the public. It sponsors Spring and Fall lecture series by authors of books on the built environment.

Number of Volumes: 4,000.

Types/Classifications: Hardbound, paperback, magazines, exhibition catalogues, journals, some prints, first editions, out-of-print.

General Subject Areas: Architecture, Design, Historic Preservation, Landscape Architecture, New York City, Urban Planning.

Specific Specialties: Le Corbusier, Frank Lloyd Wright.

Mail/Telephone Orders; Credit Cards: Both. Payment with order including postage and handling fee of $2.50 for the first book, $.50 for each additional book. Visa, Mastercard, American Express.

Business Hours: Monday through Saturday 10:00 AM - 6:00 PM.

Parking Facilities: Business parking lot.

Special Features: Search service.

Catalogue: Published in the Fall and in the Spring.

Collections/Individual Items Purchased: Individual items only.

782
Ursus Books Ltd.

1011 Madison Avenue
New York, New York 10021   (212) 772-8787

How to Get There: The bookstore is near the corner of Madison Avenue and 78th Street in Manhattan.

Owner/Biography: T. Peter Kraus.

Number of Volumes: 100,000.

Types/Classifications: Out-of-print art reference books, early color printing, fine illustrated books, fine decorative prints.

General Subject Areas: Art, Color Prints, Illustrated Books.

Mail/Telephone Orders; Credit Cards: Both. American Express, Visa, and Mastercard accepted.

Business Hours: Monday through Friday 10:00 AM - 6:00 PM; Saturday 11:00 AM - 5:00 PM.

Catalogue: Six times a year.

Collections/Individual Items Purchased: Both.

Booksellers' Memberships: Antiquarian Booksellers Association of America.

783
Victor Tamerlis

911 Stuart Avenue
Mamaroneck, New York 10543   (914) 698-8950

The bookstore features art, illustrated books, early printing, and prints. It is open by appointment only.

Owner/Biography: Victor Tamerlis.

Year Founded/History of Bookstore: 1959.

Number of Volumes: 15,000.

Types/Classifications: Hardbound, illustrated books, prints.

General Subject Areas: Art, Early Printing, Illustrated Books, Scholarly Works.

Business Hours: By appointment only.

Collections/Individual Items Purchased: Both.

Booksellers' Memberships: Antiquarian Booksellers Association of America.

784
Victoria Book Shop
Suite 809
303 Fifth Avenue
New York, New York 10016   (212) 683-7849

The bookstore is situated in one of New York's earliest skyscrapers, following the flatiron building by only three years. The owner describes the entrance: "The door to our office is the original one of circa 1907, with chicken wire glass. Somewhere a Dashiell Hammet character has a duplicate key." The store features very early children's, illustrated, and miniature books, some from the 16th Century. It contains 750 square feet of space.
How to Get There: The shop is located on the corner of 31st Street and Fifth Avenue, within walking distance of many of the city's great department stores.
Owner/Biography: Milton Reissman.
Year Founded/History of Bookstore: 1965.
Number of Volumes: 4,500.
Types/Classifications: Hardbound; first editions only, except for early rarities; illustrated books, color plate books, signed copies, limited editions, fine bindings, original book illustrations, miniature books, ephemera, manuscripts, games, moveable plate books.
General Subject Areas: Children's Books.
Specific Specialties: Children's Books from the 16th to the 20th Century, from all countries, in a dozen or more languages, mainly English, French, German, Latin, Russian; Juvenile Classics.
Mail/Telephone Orders; Credit Cards: Both. Pre-payment with order unless established customer. No credit cards.
Business Hours: Monday through Friday 10:00 AM - 4:00 PM; other times by appointment.
Parking Facilities: Business parking lot.
Catalogue: Three times a year.
Collections/Individual Items Purchased: Both.
Booksellers' Memberships: Antiquarian Booksellers Association of America (National and Middle Atlantic Chapters).

785
Village Booksmith
223 Main Street
Hudson Falls, New York 12839   (518) 747-3261

The bookstore has a large general stock of used and out-of-print books with special holdings in the areas of behavioral sciences, Americana, regional history, and the performing arts including magic and conjuring. The shop is air conditioned for summer comfort and contains 1,600 square feet of space.
How to Get There: Hudson Falls, New York is 15 miles north of Saratoga Springs, 10 miles south of Lake George, and 2 miles east of Glens Falls. The bookstore is located just north of the park, on U.S. Route 4, in the heart of historic Hudson Falls, directly across from the Town Hall.
Owner/Biography: Clifford E. Bruce.
Year Founded/History of Bookstore: The owner originally operated a mail order business from his home. The present building was purchased in 1976.
Number of Volumes: 30,000.
Types/Classifications: Hardbound, paperback, some paper items.
General Subject Areas: Art, Biography, Children's Books, Fiction, Games, History, Literature, Mathematics, Music, Mystery, Nature, Occult, Philosophy, Poetry, Religion, Science, Science Fiction and Fantasy, Sports, Westerns.
Specific Specialties: Americana, Behavioral Science, Regional New York State History, Magic, Conjuring.
Mail/Telephone Orders; Credit Cards: Both. Visa, Mastercard.
Business Hours: Weekdays (closed Tuesday) 1:00 PM - 5:00 PM.
Parking Facilities: Street and public parking lot.
Special Features: Search service.

Collections/Individual Items Purchased: Both.
Miscellaneous: Dealers are welcome.

786
W. Graham Arader III
23 East 74th Street
Suite 5A
New York, New York 10021 (212) 628-3668

See: W. GRAHAM ARADER III, King of Prussia, Pennsylvania.

787
W. Somers, Bookseller
841 Union Street
Schenectady, New York 12308 (518) 393-5266

The owner describes his bookstore this way: "We belong to the neat, clean, spacious, well-lighted school of bookstore decor because that is how we like to spend our days. We also belong to the price-'em-low, sell-a-lot-to-dealers school." The shop contains 2,000 square feet of space.
How to Get There: The store is located one block from Union College.
Owner/Biography: Wayne Somers.
Year Founded/History of Bookstore: The business was founded in 1971 in Delanson, New York as a catalogue business specializing in scholarly books under the name Hammer Mountain Book Halls. The catalogue business continues under this name from the above address, but with the scope narrowed to European history, European literature, and economics. The store was opened in 1981 and carries a general stock.
Number of Volumes: 10,000.
Types/Classifications: Hardbound, out-of-print, used, rare.
General Subject Areas: Economics, European History, French Literature, German Literature.
Mail/Telephone Orders; Credit Cards: Both.
Business Hours: Monday through Friday 1:00 PM - 5:00 PM; Saturday 10:00 AM - 5:00 PM.
Parking Facilities: Street.
Catalogue: Two times per year.
Collections/Individual Items Purchased: Both.
Booksellers' Memberships: Antiquarian Booksellers Association of America.

788
Weiser's Bookstore
740 Broadway
New York, New York 10003 (212) 777-6363

The bookstore specializes in oriental philosophy and all aspects of the occult. Some psychology and related subjects are included. Egyptology and theosophy are available. The store sells new and used books, but specializes in rare and out-of-print material. Customers can write, call, or come in to browse in the rare book section. The bookstore contains 3,000 square feet of space.
How to Get There: The shop is on lower Broadway in New York City south of 8th Street, near New York University.
Owner/Biography: Donald Weiser. The bookstore was started in 1926 by Samuel Weiser for whom the business is named. He gradually began to specialize in hard-to-obtain occult books at the request of his customers. Donald is Samuel's son, and took over the business when his dad retired. Both father and son bought books in the occult field extensively, gradually developing one of the largest collections of this kind anywhere.
Year Founded/History of Bookstore: Founded in 1926, the bookstore started on 4th Avenue (Book Row) and has since moved to several locations on 4th Avenue, did a stint at 13th Street and Broadway, and has

finally settled on lower Broadway near New York University.

Number of Volumes: 200,000.

Types/Classifications: Hardbound books, manuscripts, out-of-print, limited editions, signed copies, fine bindings, color plate books.

General Subject Areas: Alchemy, Astrology, Egyptology, Occult, Orientalia, Philosophy, Psychology, Tarot, Theology, Witchcraft.

Mail/Telephone Orders; Credit Cards: Both. Mastercard.

Business Hours: Monday through Saturday 9:00 AM - 6:00 PM.

Parking Facilities: Metered street parking, garage across the street.

Special Features: Wants lists department; anyone can write for information about specific titles.

Collections/Individual Items Purchased: Both.

Booksellers' Memberships: Antiquarian Booksellers Association of America.

Miscellaneous: New and used books are also sold in the store. Weiser's is probably the biggest occult bookstore in the United States and also has a world-wide reputation in this field.

789
Weyhe Art Books, Inc.
794 Lexington Avenue
New York, New York 10021   (212) 838-5466

The bookstore features art books in the following categories: fine arts, applied arts, architecture, decoration, drawings, graphics, textiles. The bookstore is on the street floor of the building. The Weyhe Gallery, specializing in American prints, is on the second floor. An additional telephone number is (212) 838-5478.

How to Get There: The shop is located on Lexington Avenue in Manhattan, New York City, between 61st and 62nd Streets.

Owner/Biography: Gertrude Weyhe Dennis.

Year Founded/History of Bookstore: The bookstore was founded by Erhard Weyhe in 1919, and has been at its present location for over 60 years.

Types/Classifications: Hardbound books, prints.

General Subject Areas: Applied Arts, Architecture, Art, Decoration, Drawings, Fine Arts, Graphics, Textiles.

Mail/Telephone Orders; Credit Cards: Both; no credit cards.

Business Hours: Monday through Friday 9:30 AM - 5:30 PM; Saturday 9:30 AM - 5:00 PM.

Collections/Individual Items Purchased: Both.

Booksellers' Memberships: Antiquarian Booksellers Association of America.

790
Wildwood Books and Prints
Route 28
P.O. Box 560
Old Forge, New York 13420   (315) 369-3397

Since its founding five years ago the bookstore has expanded from one to six rooms in a renovated 65 year old building on the main street of the Adirondack resort village of Old Forge. The proprietors, both former museum professionals, chose to broaden the appeal of their store by offering sporting antiques such as old wooden canoes and fishing tackle side by side with their specialty books on the out-of-doors and their large stock of Adirondackiana. In addition, a growing selection of general stock now occupies an adjoining store. The total area consists of 1,800 square feet of space.

How to Get There: The shop is located in the Adirondack Mountains of New York State, fifty miles north of Utica. The store is in the center of the village of Old Forge.

Owner/Biography: Ted and Sarah Comstock.

Year Founded/History of Bookstore: 1979.

Number of Volumes: 5,000.

Types/Classifications: Hardbound, broadsides, ephemera, prints, paintings, photographs, maps.

General Subject Areas: Adirondacks, Canoeing, Natural History, Sporting.
Specific Specialties: Adirondack History, Lake George (N.Y.) History, Lake Champlain (N.Y.) History, Outdoors.
Author Specialties: Adirondack Authors.
Mail/Telephone Orders; Credit Cards: Both. Personal check with order. Visa, Mastercard.
Business Hours: Monday through Saturday 9:30 AM - 5:00 PM. In the Winter, by appointment.
Parking Facilities: Street, business parking lot.
Special Features: A large selection of in-print regional books on the Adirondacks complements the out-of-print stock.
Collections/Individual Items Purchased: Both.
Booksellers' Memberships: The bookstore is listed in two regional directories: Upstate New York Antiquarian Booksellers Directory, Central New York Antiquarian Booksellers Directory.

791
With Pipe and Book
91 Main Street
Lake Placid, New York 12946 (518) 523-9096

The owners take pride in declaring that their store is "a unique shop offering two of life's finest pleasures: good books and high quality pipes, cigars, and tobacco." The store offers a complete selection of the finest imported pipes and cigars as well as its own custom blended tobaccos. The shop carries a large selection of good, readable used books at low prices as well as antiquarian books in many subject areas. It specializes in Adirondack books and has over 1,000 titles in stock. In addition there are old Adirondack prints and maps. The store contains 2,000 square feet of space.
How to Get There: Lake Placid is just a beautiful 30 minute drive from Interstate 87 (The Adirondack Northway). It can also be reached from the south and west on well maintained scenic roads.
Owner/Biography: Breck and Julie Turner.
Year Founded/History of Bookstore: 1977.
Number of Volumes: 8,000.
Types/Classifications: Hardbound, ephemera, prints, maps, first editions, out-of-print, used, antiquarian, new (Adirondack) books.
General Subject Areas: Americana, Biography, Education, Fiction, Military, Natural History, Poetry, Politics, Sports, Travel.
Specific Specialties: Adirondacks, Lake George, Lake Champlain.
Other Specialties: Old Adirondack Prints and Maps.
Mail/Telephone Orders; Credit Cards: Both. Visa, American Express, Mastercard.
Business Hours: Monday through Saturday 10:00 AM - 6:00 PM. In Summer, also on Sunday 10:00 AM - 4:00 PM.
Parking Facilities: Public parking lot across the street.
Catalogue: Adirondack book catalogue published twice a year.
Collections/Individual Items Purchased: Both.

792
Witkin Gallery, Inc.
41 East 57th Street, Suite 802
New York, New York 10022 (212) 355-1461

Tucked in a corner of the Witkin Gallery is one of the best stocked in-print and out-of-print photography bookshops in New York City. It contains everything from today's deluxe coffee table books to slender 19th Century manuals. Many hard-to-find show catalogues and small book publishers who are not carried by major New York City bookstores can be found here. Many of the books are signed by the photographers. The gallery contains 2,500 square feet of space, the bookshop 800.
How to Get There: The shop is on the corner of Madison Avenue and 57th Street in the heart of Manhattan, New York City. Take the elevator to the 8th floor.
Owner/Biography: Lee D. Witkin, owner, is the author of "The Photographic Collector Guide," New York

Graphic Society, and "A Ten Year Salute." He is also Adjunct Professor of Photography, New York University, School of the Arts, as well as a lecturer and appraiser.

Year Founded/History of Bookstore: 1969.

Number of Volumes: 2,000.

Types/Classifications: Hardbound, softbound, paperback, magazines, catalogues, photographic illustrated books, postcards, posters, first editions, fine bindings, out-of-print, association copies, press books, signed copies, presentation copies, limited editions, color plate books.

General Subject Areas: Photography.

Mail/Telephone Orders; Credit Cards: Both. Prepayment required if not a previous customer. No credit cards.

Business Hours: Tuesday through Friday 11:00 AM - 6:00 PM; Saturday 12:00 Noon - 5:00 PM.

Catalogue: Once a year.

Collections/Individual Items Purchased: Both.

Booksellers' Memberships: Antiquarian Booksellers Association of America.

793
Yankee Peddler Bookshop
94 Mill Street
Pultneyville, New York 14538   (315) 589-2063

The bookstore is located in a century-old building on Lake Ontario in Pultneyville, New York. It houses about 12,000 volumes of general Americana. In the front is a small gallery of paintings, prints, photographs, and ephemera. There is a branch shop named Yankee Peddler Bookshop Volume 2 in downtown Rochester, New York. It is situated in a renovated old factory complex surrounded by antique and craft shops. The address there is Peddlers Village, 274 North Goodman Street, Rochester, N.Y. 14607; the telephone is (716) 271-5080. The main shop contains 675 square feet of space, the Rochester branch, 900.

How to Get There: The main shop is located 30 miles east of Rochester on Lake Ontario. It is 30 minutes north of Exit 43 of the New York State Thruway. The branch shop may be reached by exiting the Expressway (Route 490) at North Goodman Street in Rochester.

Owner/Biography: John and Janet Westerberg, owners; Douglas Westerberg, associate.

Year Founded/History of Bookstore: Founded in 1970, the shop is still in the same location, but all the cataloguing, research, and shop preparation takes place at the residence, 4299 Lake Road.

Number of Volumes: 40,000.

Types/Classifications: Hardbound books, prints, paintings, photographs, autographs, broadsides, postcards, trade cards, stereo cards, sculpture, ephemera, a few remainders, first editions, illustrated books, signed editions, limited editions, press books, color plate books, fine bindings, views of American cities, American and Canadian maps.

General Subject Areas: Abraham Lincoln, Aeronautics, American Indians, American Revolution, Americana, Anti-Slavery Movement, Arctic, Art (American), Canada, Children's Books, Cinema, Civil War (U.S.), Classsical Music, Confederacy (U.S. Civil War), Dance, Discovery, Erie Canal, Exploration, Great Lakes, Harpers Weekly Magazines, Illustrators Before 1930, Itinerants, Juveniles, Ku Klux Klan, Ladies Home Journals before 1930, Mormonism, Natural History, New York City, New York State, Peddlers, Railroads, Rochester (N.Y.), Roycroft Press, Saudi Arabia, Shakers, Theater, Thousand Islands (N.Y.), Travels, Underground Railroad, Voyages, Western Americana, Women's Movement, Women's Rights Movement, World War II.

Specific Specialties: James Boswell, George Henty, Charles Finney, Theodore Weld, Henry David Thoreau, American Transcendentalists, George Proctor, Maxfield Parrish, Winslow Homer, Elbert Hubbard, N.C. Wyeth, Minor White, Frederick Douglass, Susan B. Anthony, Elizabeth Cady Stanton, George Eastman, Glenn Curtis, Eastman Kodak Before 1920, L. Frank Baum, Maude Humphrey, Ansel Adams, Alfred Steiglitz, Edward Steichen, Margaret Fuller.

Author Specialties: Samuel Clemens, James Fenimore Cooper, Emily Dickinson, Paul Laurence Dunbar, Walter D. Edmonds, Ralph Waldo Emerson, William Faulkner, C.S. Forester, Robert Frost, Joel Chandler Harris, Lafcadio Hearn, Ernest Hemingway, John Muir, Frederick Remington, Edna St. Vincent Millay, Thomas Hardy, D.H. Lawrence, Thomas Wolfe, F. Scott Fizgerald, Anthony Trollope, Mark Twain.

Other Specialties: Classical Mediterranean Archaeology, James Boswell's and Samuel Johnson's Literary Circle, Gloucester, Massachusetts History.

Mail/Telephone Orders; Credit Cards: Both. Cash with order; or, ship and bill for those known to the store.

Visa, Mastercard. Mailing address: 4299 Lake Road (rest same as above.)
Business Hours: Pultneyville: Thursday through Sunday 1:00 PM - 5:00 PM. Rochester: Thursday and Friday 11:00 AM - 5:00 PM; Saturday and Sunday 10:00 AM - 5:00 PM.
Parking Facilities: Pultneyville, street; Rochester, parking lot.
Special Features: Search service, Publishers of New York State Americana, Book Collecting Course Instructor, Hand Coloring, Book Binding, Print Cleaning, Appraising.
Catalogue: Published annually.
Collections/Individual Items Purchased: Both.
Booksellers' Memberships: Antiquarian Booksellers Association of America.

794
Yankee Peddler Bookshop Vol 2
Peddlers Village
274 North Goodman Street
Rochester, New York 14607   (716) 271-5080

See: YANKEE PEDDLER BOOKSHOP, Pultneyville, New York.

795
Zita Books
760 West End Avenue
New York, New York 10025   (212) 866-4715

The bookstore consists of private premises in an apartment house, with approximately 500 square feet, including multiple-purpose rooms with shelving along the walls.
How to Get There: Open by appointment only, the business is located near the 7th Avenue IRT subway stop at 96th St.
Owner/Biography: G. Laderman.
Year Founded/History of Bookstore: Founded in 1965, the bookstore has had the same ownership and location since founding. Books were originally sold only by mail order through the catalogue, but now visits may be arranged by appointment.
Number of Volumes: 10,000.
Types/Classifications: Hardbound books, pamphlets, sheet music, ephemera, manuscripts, prints, drawings, photographs, albums, game boards (both oriental and western); no modern first editions, usually rare and antiquarian rather than out-of-print; some out-of-print among books about Japan; inscribed, fine bindings, limited editions within areas of specialization and biographies; ephemera includes above subjects plus trade cards, cloth labels, paper toys.
General Subject Areas: Comic Illustrated Early American Fiction, Early and Historical Juveniles (especially American), Early Songsters, Exotic Printing (especially Mission Press and Japanese), Graphic Humor (Comic Illustration), History of Art and Music (16th Century to Present), Japanese Prints and Sugoroku, Japanese Woodcut Illustrated Books (including Crepe Paper Books), Joke Books, Judaica and Hebraica, Nineteenth Century and Earlier Sheet Music, Oriental Photography, Poetry, Political Caricature, Regional American publications from 1795 to 1945, Social Caricature, South American Illustrations.
Specific Specialties: Albums of American Caricatures printed locally from 1829 to 1945; Mexican 19th Century Illustrations; American Juveniles pre-1821; American and European Paper Toys, 19th Century and earlier, both printed and hand made, i.e. Harlequinades, Movables, Games, Paper Dolls, Toy Paper Furniture, Paper Soldiers; Japanese Woodcut Illustrated Books of the Nanga, Bunjingwa, and Classical Schools; Tobaye; Rare Japonica and Malasiana; K. Ogawa and Tamamura, Photographers; American Mission Presses; Early Japanese Printing in European Languages; D.C. Johnston, F.O.C. Darley, A. Hoppin, F. Beard, T. Nast, W. Homer, J.W. Barber, Rev. W. Cook, all Early American Illustrators; Early American Poetry, Fiction, and Literary Essays, especially minor and locally printed through 1875; Anti-Masonic Books and Pamphlets; Sectarian Americana, especially Communitarian Movements such as Hopedale, Oneida, Shakers, Mormons, Brook Farm, Icarians, Rappites; Early German printing in the U.S., especially Henkel Press in Virginia and Peters in Pennsylvania.
Author Specialties: George G. Small, Rev. Wm. Cook; illustrator specialities, rather than authors.

Other Specialties: American comic illustrators; social and political caricaturists; American art; social and sexual life of Japanese (scholarly only); Shunga books; 19th Century American popular culture including the underworld, gambling, racetrack, bordello. Languages include Japanese, Malay, French, German, Yiddish, Hebrew, Italian, Portuguese, Spanish, in the store's areas of interest.

Mail/Telephone Orders; Credit Cards: Mail orders: primarily from the catalogue to new customers, who must pre-pay. Want lists in the store's specialties accepted. Telephone orders: from the store's catalogue. No credit cards.

Business Hours: By appointment only.

Parking Facilities: Parking garage or street parking.

Catalogue: Eight or more times yearly.

Collections/Individual Items Purchased: Both.

Booksellers' Memberships: Ephemera Society.

NORTH CAROLINA

796
Andrew Cahan, Bookseller
P.O. Box 882
Chapel Hill, North Carolina 27514 (919) 967-3069

Mr. Cahan's book business is operated from a private residence. His stock is general antiquarian with particular attention paid to the South. Other areas of depth include modern literature, the arts, Americana, and the Civil War. Most of the business is generated from catalogues issued on a regular basis.

How to Get There: The stock is housed in downtown Chapel Hill. When calling for an appointment, Mr. Cahan will give you easy directions.

Owner/Biography: Andrew Cahan.

Year Founded/History of Bookstore: 1976. The business was formerly conducted in New York City.

Number of Volumes: 2,500.

Types/Classifications: Broadsides, maps, autographs, prints, photographs, hardbound, first editions, special editions, association copies, out-of-print.

General Subject Areas: American South, American West, Americana, Black History, Dance, Literary First Editions, Modern Art, Photography, U.S. Civil War.

Mail/Telephone Orders; Credit Cards: Both. Items requested must be listed in the catalogues. No credit cards.

Business Hours: By appointment only.

Parking Facilities: Street parking.

Special Features: Cordial hospitality.

Catalogue: Published six times per year.

Collections/Individual Items Purchased: Collections only.

797
Book House
Brightleaf Square
Main Street and Gregson
Durham, North Carolina 27707 (919) 688-5311

The Book House is situated in Brightleaf Square, a group of renovated tobacco warehouses on the National Register of Historic Sites. The bookstore specializes in antiquarian books of general Americana with emphasis on North Carolina and the South. The store occupies 600 square feet of space.

How to Get There: From I-85, use the Gregson Street exit.

Owner/Biography: Lin and Tucker Respess.

Year Founded/History of Bookstore: 1979.

Number of Volumes: 5,000.

Types/Classifications: Hardbound, first editions.

General Subject Areas: Americana, English and American First Editions, Fine Sporting Books, North Carolina, South (U.S.).

Mail/Telephone Orders; Credit Cards: Both. Visa and Mastercard accepted.

Business Hours: Monday through Saturday 12:00 PM - 6:00 PM.

Parking Facilities: Business parking lot.

Catalogue: Published 8 times per year.

Collections/Individual Items Purchased: Both.

798
Book Mart
7 Biltmore Plaza
Asheville, North Carolina 28803   (704) 274-2241

The Book Mart deals in general antiquarian and out-of-print books but also carries a small stock of new books on regional topics. It also has a side line of fine greeting cards. The shop occupies 700 square feet of space.

How to Get There: The bookstore is located near exits from Interstates 40 and 26, 2 blocks from the entrance to the Biltmore Estate, home of the late George Vanderbilt.

Owner/Biography: Nancy Brown. The Book Mart was established by Helen Martha Wilson and Nancy Brown. Miss Wilson died in 1971 and the business was carried on by Nancy Brown.

Year Founded/History of Bookstore: 1947. The Book Mart opened April 1, 1947 in downtown Asheville at 21 Wall Street. It moved to larger quarters and present location in August 1949.

Number of Volumes: 20,000.

Types/Classifications: Hardbound, paperback, magazines (National Geographic only), first editions, out-of-print, signed copies.

General Subject Areas: Americana, Biography, Children's Literature.

Specific Specialties: Southern Appalachian Mountains, North Carolina and South Carolina History, Americana.

Author Specialties: Thomas Wolfe.

Mail/Telephone Orders; Credit Cards: Both. Payment in advance. No credit cards.

Business Hours: Tuesday through Sunday 10:00 AM - 5:00 PM; closed Monday.

Parking Facilities: Street parking.

Special Features: Search service.

Collections/Individual Items Purchased: Both.

799
Carolina Bookshop
1601 East Independence Boulevard
Charlotte, North Carolina 28205   (704) 375-7305

The Carolina Bookshop is located in a former brick residence with an enclosed porch. Five rooms and the porch house a large general stock with one room devoted exclusively to North Carolina material. The stock occupies 2,000 square feet of space.

How to Get There: The shop is located at the corner of Independence Boulevard and St. Julien Street, one block east of the Plaza.

Owner/Biography: Gordon Briscoe, Jr.

Year Founded/History of Bookstore: 1975.

Number of Volumes: 10,000.

Types/Classifications: Hardbound, out-of-print.

General Subject Areas: Americana, Biography.

Specific Specialties: Civil War (U.S.), North Caroliniana, South Caroliniana, Southern States.

Author Specialties: Thomas Dixon, Thomas Wolfe.

Mail/Telephone Orders; Credit Cards: Both. Cash with order; libraries or institutions billed; postage and insurance extra. Visa and Mastercard accepted.

Business Hours: Saturday 11:00 AM - 6:00 PM; Tuesday through Friday by prior appointment only.

Parking Facilities: Business parking lot.

Special Features: Search service.

Catalogue: Published 2 to 3 times annually; catalogues issued on The Carolinas and the Civil War.

Collections/Individual Items Purchased: Both.

800
Grandpa's House
Route 1, Box 208
Highway 27 West
Troy, North Carolina 27371 (919) 572-3484

The main building, which is also an antique shop, has sections of Americana emphasizing North Carolina material and a good selection of Military and Sporting books. The old house next door has nostalgic novels, textbooks, juveniles, magazines, and reading copies of modern novels.

How to Get There: Troy is in the center of North Carolina about one hour from Charlotte, Greensboro, Winston-Salem, and Fayetteville. The bookstore is located 3 1/2 miles southwest of Troy on Highway 24-27 W; at first cross road, turn south, 200 yards on left.

Owner/Biography: Mary R. Parks.

Year Founded/History of Bookstore: 1963. When the owners built a new shop next to their home, they moved Grandpa's House (Grandfather Strickland's 100 year old house which was purchased by his granddaughter and was an antique shop just outside of Troy's town limits) from its original site to where it now houses rooms of books.

Number of Volumes: Varies, always several thousand.

Types/Classifications: Hardbound, some paperback, old postcards, ephemera, out-of-print.

General Subject Areas: General.

Specific Specialties: North Carolina.

Mail/Telephone Orders; Credit Cards: Both. Cash with order including postage and insurance unless otherwise indicated. No credit cards.

Business Hours: Week Days 9:00 AM - 5:00 PM by chance or appointment.

Parking Facilities: Ample parking on shop grounds.

Special Features: Search service; collection building.

Collections/Individual Items Purchased: Both.

801
Keith & Martin Book Shop
310 West Franklin Street
Chapel Hill, North Carolina 27514 (919) 942-5178

The bookstore offers general stock in all fields except technical, and contains approximately 1,600 square feet of space.

How to Get There: The entrance to the bookstore is on the east side of the building.

Owner/Biography: Bill Loeser.

Year Founded/History of Bookstore: The bookstore opened in New Bern, North Carolina, in October 1979, and moved to Chapel Hill in May 1981. In April 1983, 600 square feet of new space was added.

Number of Volumes: 30,000.

Types/Classifications: Hardcover, collectible paperbacks, first editions, reading copies.

General Subject Areas: General.

Specific Specialties: North Carolina, Southern (U.S.) Fiction and Non-fiction, Detective Fiction.

Other Specialties: Scholarly books in the Humanities.

Mail/Telephone Orders; Credit Cards: Both; prepayment required from individuals unknown to the bookstore; no credit cards.

Business Hours: Monday through Saturday 11:00 AM - 6:00 PM or by appointment.

Parking Facilities: Public parking lot 1 block away.

Special Features: Free search service; books-wanted file maintained.

Catalogue: Six times a year.

Collections/Individual Items Purchased: Both.

802
Little Hundred Gallery
6028 Bentway Drive
Charlotte, North Carolina 28226

(704) 542-3184

This is a mail order only business dealing exclusively in antique maps, prints, documents, and Americana.
Owner/Biography: Paul Whitfield.
Year Founded/History of Bookstore: 1975.
Types/Classifications: Maps; prints; vellum, parchment, and paper documents; autographs, ephemera.
General Subject Areas: Americana.
Mail/Telephone Orders; Credit Cards: Both. Visa and Mastercard accepted.
Catalogue: Catalogue published.
Collections/Individual Items Purchased: Both.

OHIO

803
Barbara Agranoff, Books
4025 Paddock Road No. 501
Cincinnati, Ohio 45229   (513) 281-5095

Barbara Agranoff, Books does business by mail order, by appointment, and by chance from a private residence. They have a select stock of a books, ephemera, and old postcards. The shop occupies 300 square feet of space.

How to Get There: Paddock Road is Route 4 and is 2 minutes south of the Norwood Lateral connecting I-71 and I-75; 15 minutes from downtown Cincinnati.

Owner/Biography: Barbara Agranoff.

Year Founded/History of Bookstore: 1973. The business has always been at the above location.

Number of Volumes: 3,000.

Types/Classifications: Hardbound, ephemera (documents, postcards, photographs, stereopticons, trade cards, maps), first editions, fine bindings, out-of-print, association copies, press books, signed copies, presentation copies, limited editions, color plate books, illustrated books.

General Subject Areas: Americana, Architecture, Art, Atlases, Children's Books, Civil War (U.S.), Cookery, Literature, Natural History, Photography, Trades.

Author Specialties: Gene Stratton Porter, Daniel Drake, Jesse Stuart.

Mail/Telephone Orders; Credit Cards: Both. No credit cards.

Business Hours: By appointment or chance.

Parking Facilities: Parking in rear.

Special Features: Search service.

Catalogue: Subject lists available upon request.

Collections/Individual Items Purchased: Both.

804
Book Stop
2705 Far Hills Avenue
Dayton, Ohio 45419   (513) 298-3156

The Book Stop is a medium sized store featuring fine used books and paperbacks with an emphasis on literature, history, and nature. Their search service is a popular feature. The shop occupies 1,000 square feet of space.

How to Get There: Far Hills Avenue is an extension of South Main Street and the store is located 3 miles south of central Dayton in the Oakwood shopping district.

Owner/Biography: Marilyn H. Bohlander.

Year Founded/History of Bookstore: 1978.

Number of Volumes: 20,000.

Types/Classifications: Hardbound, paperback, first editions, fine bindings, out-of-print, signed copies.

General Subject Areas: Americana, Biography, Gardening, History, Hobbies, Juvenile, Literature, Military, Nature, Philosophy, Regional History, Religion, Sports.

Mail/Telephone Orders; Credit Cards: Both. Visa and Mastercard accepted.

Business Hours: Monday through Friday 11:00 AM - 6:00 PM; Saturday 10:00 AM - 5:00 PM.

Parking Facilities: Business parking lot.

Special Features: Search service.

Collections/Individual Items Purchased: Both.

805
Bookhaven of Springfield
1549 Commerce
Springfield, Ohio 45504

(513) 322-9021

This is a general used bookstore which recently changed ownership. There is a wide selection of non-fiction and fiction hardbound books of general interest. Non-fiction is arranged by category and fiction alphabetically. Also available is an abundance of paperbacks for pleasure reading arranged according to type. The store occupies 3,000 square feet of space.

How to Get There: Take I-70 to Route 68 on the west side of Springfield, north on Route 68 for 1-1/2 miles, east on Route 40 for 1-1/2 miles, left on Bechtle, cross railroad tracks, then left at 1st traffic light. The store is behind the AAA.

Owner/Biography: Marc Beckwith and Karen Wickliff.
Number of Volumes: 15,000.
Types/Classifications: Hardbound, paperback, magazines, comics, records, out-of-print.
General Subject Areas: Americana, Art, Arts and Crafts, Biography, Children's Books, Drama, Fiction, Local History, Military, Music, Poetry, Reference, Religion, Science, Science Fiction and Fantasy, Technical.
Mail/Telephone Orders; Credit Cards: No mail or phone orders. No credit cards.
Business Hours: Monday through Thursday, Saturday 12:00 Noon- 6:00 PM; Friday 12:00 Noon - 8:00 PM.
Parking Facilities: Business parking lot.
Collections/Individual Items Purchased: Both.

806
Bookseller, Inc.
521 West Exchange Street
Akron, Ohio 44302

(216) 762-3101

The Bookseller, Inc. carries antiquarian stock in many subject areas. The shop welcomes dealers, book scouts, librarians, and collectors.

How to Get There: The shop is located on I-76 and I-77, close to the Ohio Turnpike (I-71). Call for precise directions.

Types/Classifications: First editions, out-of-print, limited editions.
General Subject Areas: Aviation, Bookbinding, Entertainment, History of Rubber Industry, Movies, Ohioana, Theater, U.S. Army in Vietnam, U.S. Military History.
Mail/Telephone Orders; Credit Cards: Mail orders.
Business Hours: Monday through Saturday 10:00 AM - 6:00 PM.
Parking Facilities: Ample parking.
Catalogue: Published regularly.
Collections/Individual Items Purchased: Both.

807
Dragon's Lair, Inc.
110 West Fifth Street
Dayton, Ohio 45402

(513) 222-1479

The Dragon's Lair has over 12,000 square feet of floor space distributed over 6 floors. The store stocks more than 250,000 different items including books, maps, comic books, and paperbacks.

How to Get There: The store is 1 1/2 blocks west of the Convention Center in downtown Dayton.
Owner/Biography: Richard E. Clear and Joanne Clear.
Year Founded/History of Bookstore: 1973.
Number of Volumes: 100,000 books, 100,000 maps, 50,000 comic books, 25,000 paperbacks.
Types/Classifications: Hardbound, paperback, magazines, broadsides, autographs, ephemera.
General Subject Areas: General.
Specific Specialties: Pre-1940's magazines, Science Fiction and Fantasy, Comic Books.

Mail/Telephone Orders; Credit Cards: Mail orders. Visa and Mastercard accepted.
Business Hours: Monday through Saturday 10:00 AM - 6:45 PM.
Parking Facilities: Street parking and public lots available.
Collections/Individual Items Purchased: Both.

808
Duttenhofer's Book Treasures
214 West McMillan Street
Cincinnati, Ohio 45219   (513) 381-1340

Duttenhofer's is a large traditionally operated store which is well organized in all categories. It occupies 5,000 square feet of space.

How to Get There: Midway between I-75 and I-71, the bookstore is located near the University of Cincinnati.

Owner/Biography: Stanley A. Duttenhofer.
Year Founded/History of Bookstore: 1975. The original site was located 1 block east.
Number of Volumes: 41,000.
Types/Classifications: Hardbound, paperback, magazines, newspapers, maps, globes, atlases, first editions, fine bindings, out-of-print, association copies, press books, signed copies, presentation copies, limited editions, color plate books.
General Subject Areas: Biography, Bookbinding, Books About Books, Botany, Earth Science, History.
Specific Specialties: U.S. Public Works Administration, Rivers of America, Overland Narratives.
Author Specialties: Gene Stratton Porter, D.H. Lawrence, Julian Huxley, Charles Darwin.
Other Specialties: Book conservancy and binding; scholarly works.
Mail/Telephone Orders; Credit Cards: Both. Visa and Mastercard accepted.
Business Hours: Seven days per week 8:30 AM - 10:00 PM.
Parking Facilities: Public lot and street parking.
Special Features: Search service.
Collections/Individual Items Purchased: Both.

809
Heritage Book Store
4145 North High Street
Columbus, Ohio 43214   (614) 262-0615

"Just a little ole used bookstore" nestled in an old building with four small stores, a violin repair and sales on one side and a Far East grocery store on the other. The shop occupies 450 square feet of space.

How to Get There: Situated on the south corner of Westwood and North High Street, the bookstore is 3 miles north of the Ohio State University campus, 2 blocks south of Cooke Road.

Owner/Biography: Larry Cosner.
Year Founded/History of Bookstore: 1980.
Number of Volumes: Over 5,000.
Types/Classifications: Hardbound, posters, ephemera, military collectibles, out-of-print, press books, signed copies.
General Subject Areas: Americana, Fishing, Hunting, Military History, Ohioana, Sports, Weapons.
Specific Specialties: Civil War (U.S.), World War II.
Mail/Telephone Orders; Credit Cards: Both. Cash with order. No credit cards.
Business Hours: Tuesday through Friday 6:00 AM - 9:00 PM; Saturday 12:00 Noon - 5:00 PM.
Parking Facilities: Parking lot in rear of building.
Special Features: Civil War Round Table held at 7:30 PM on 2nd Friday of each month; all are welcome.
Catalogue: Lists published 2 to 3 times per year.
Collections/Individual Items Purchased: Both.

810
Irving M. Roth, Antiques & Old Books
89 Whittlesey Avenue
Norwalk, Ohio 44857

(419) 668-2893

This bookstore is open by appointment only. In addition to old books it features old postcards, tradecards, and old advertising.

Owner/Biography: Irving M. Roth.
Year Founded/History of Bookstore: 1946.
Number of Volumes: 20,000.
Types/Classifications: Hardbound, magazines, ephemera, old postcards, tradecards, advertising.
General Subject Areas: Americana, Antiques, Civil War (U.S.), Expositions, Freemasonry, Numismatics, Ohio.
Mail/Telephone Orders; Credit Cards: Both. No credit cards.
Business Hours: By appointment only.
Parking Facilities: Business parking lot.
Collections/Individual Items Purchased: Both.

811
John T. Zubal, Inc.
2969 West 25th Street
Cleveland, Ohio 44113

(216) 241-7640

The bookstore has two buildings where stock is organized by subjects (literary criticism, Latin America, Art, others), and by categories (rare books, periodicals, governmental, others). The stacks are open to visitors but the periodicals area is closed to the public. The total area is 58,000 square feet.

How to Get There: The location is one mile north of I-71 and the West 25th Street Exit; 15 minutes from Cleveland's Public Square; 20 minutes from the airport.
Owner/Biography: John T. Zubal, President; Marilyn C. Zubal, Vice President.
Year Founded/History of Bookstore: The business was established in 1965 as the Charterhouse of Parma, in Parma, Ohio. Shops and warehouses were maintained simultaneously in 5 separate locations from 1965 to 1973 when all stock was gathered at the present address. Ohio law required the name to be changed when the business became a corporation in 1976.
Number of Volumes: 200,000.
Types/Classifications: The vast majority is hardbound; some paperback, magazines, autographed works, ephemera. The shop's main focus is on scholarly books for research libraries. Other areas include literary first editions, illustrated books.
General Subject Areas: Anthropology, Economics, History, Literary Criticism, Philosophy, Political Economy, Psychology, Sociology, Theology.
Other Specialties: Backstock of Catholic University of America Press's dissertations on the social sciences and humanities.
Mail/Telephone Orders; Credit Cards: Both. Cash with order; no credit cards.
Business Hours: Monday through Friday 8:00 AM - 4:00 PM. Saturday and Evenings by appointment.
Parking Facilities: The store has its own parking lot.
Special Features: Since 1980 the bookstore has published 18 scholarly reprints (such as Ramon Adams' Six Guns, and Rampaging Herd), and two original works.
Catalogue: Nine times per year.
Collections/Individual Items Purchased: Both.
Miscellaneous: The bookstore is one of the chief suppliers of backdate scholarly periodicals to libraries and individuals.

812
Karen Wickliff Books
2579 North High Street
Columbus, Ohio 43202

(614) 263-2903

This store is located within walking distance of Ohio State University. The store tries to stock a wide variety of books that would be of interest to students, researchers, and collectors. New stock is added weekly. The shop occupies 1,400 square feet of space.

How to Get There: The shop is 12 blocks north of Ohio State University at Hudson.

Owner/Biography: Karen Wickliff.

Year Founded/History of Bookstore: 1973.

Number of Volumes: 25,000.

Types/Classifications: Hardbound, paperback, used magazines, postcards, sheet music, ephemera, out-of-print.

General Subject Areas: Americana, Ancient and Medieval History, Arts and Crafts, Biography, Fine Arts, Foreign Language, Government, Juvenile, Literature, Local History, Medicine and Psychology, Military, Music, Natural Science, Occult, Philosophy, Poetry, Reference, Sporting, Technical, Theater and Drama, Theology, Travel.

Other Specialties: Scholarly works in all areas.

Mail/Telephone Orders; Credit Cards: No mail orders; telephone orders accepted. No credit cards.

Business Hours: Monday through Saturday 11:30 AM - 5:30 PM.

Parking Facilities: Street parking.

Collections/Individual Items Purchased: Both.

813
Odyssey Shop
1743 South Union Avenue
Alliance, Ohio 44601

(216) 821-9958

The bookstore offers a general antiquarian stock with major emphasis on mystery, science fiction and fantasy, and modern first editions. It also stocks large quantities of vintage paperbacks, pulp magazines, and digests. Catalogues are issued regularly and mail orders are a specialty. The shop contains 300 square feet of space.

How to Get There: If driving from Canton, Ohio, take Route 62 east 12 miles to Mt. Union College exit, turn right, go 5 miles to Route 183 (Union Avenue), turn left; shop is 2 blocks further, next to the Mt. Union theater.

Owner/Biography: Scott D. Edwards.

Year Founded/History of Bookstore: 1978.

Number of Volumes: 20,000.

Types/Classifications: Hardbound, paperback, magazines, first editions, signed copies, small press books, illustrated books.

General Subject Areas: Americana, Children's Books, Classics, General Fiction, History, Mystery, Natural History, Poetry, Poetry First Editions, Science Fiction and Fantasy.

Specific Specialties: First Edition Science Fiction and Fantasy, First Edition Mysteries, Science Fiction Magazines including Astounding, F & SF, Galaxy, Amazing; Mystery Magazines including Ellery Queen, Alfred Hitchcock.

Mail/Telephone Orders; Credit Cards: Both; no credit cards; billing available for established accounts.

Business Hours: Monday through Friday 10:00 AM - 5:00 PM; Saturday 10:00 AM - 3:00 PM.

Parking Facilities: Large business parking lot.

Catalogue: Twelve times a year.

Collections/Individual Items Purchased: Both.

Booksellers' Memberships: Northern Ohio Bibliographic Society.

814
Ohio Bookhunter
323 Park Avenue West
Mansfield, Ohio 44906

(419) 526-1249

The bookstore stocks rare and scarce books; customers are received on an appointment only basis. An additional telephone number is (419) 756-0655.

Owner/Biography: John Stark.
Year Founded/History of Bookstore: 1952.
Number of Volumes: 5,000.
Types/Classifications: Rare and scarce books, autographs, collections.
General Subject Areas: General.
Business Hours: By appointment only.
Parking Facilities: Parking lot at the rear of the shop.
Catalogue: Four times a year.
Collections/Individual Items Purchased: Both.
Booksellers' Memberships: Antiquarian Booksellers Association of America, International League of Antiquarian Booksellers.

815
Old Erie Street Bookstore
2128 East Ninth Street
Cleveland, Ohio 44115

(216) 575-0743

The shop is a general, out-of-print, rare bookstore located in a commercial block in the heart of downtown Cleveland. It inventories 15,000 books in all fields, and contains 1,000 square feet of space.

How to Get There: From all major Interstate highways take the East Ninth Street exit to downtown Cleveland.

Owner/Biography: Mark Stueve.
Year Founded/History of Bookstore: 1980.
Number of Volumes: 15,000.
Types/Classifications: Fine hardbound, limited editions, signed copies, press books, sets, fine bindings, first editions, out-of-print, association copies, presentation copies, color plate books.
General Subject Areas: Americana, Art, Aviation, Biography, Books About Books, Children's Books, Cinema, Civil War (U.S.), Classics, Cooking, Drama, Illustrated Atlases, Journalism, Literature, Local (Ohio) History, Medicine, Military History, Music, Natural History, Nautical, Photography, Plays, Poetry, Railroads, Religions, Science, Sporting, Sports, Technical, Transportation, Travel, True Crime, Urban Studies.
Author Specialties: Nelson Algren, Charles Bukowski, Sherwood Anderson, John Gardner.
Mail/Telephone Orders; Credit Cards: Both. No credit cards.
Business Hours: Monday through Saturday 10:30 AM - 6:00 PM.
Parking Facilities: Private parking lot next door.
Catalogue: Published quarterly.
Collections/Individual Items Purchased: Both.

816
Owl Creek Books
309 West Vine Street
Mt. Vernon, Ohio 43050

(614) 397-9337

Owl Creek Books carries a general stock of used, out-of-print, and rare books. It occupies 1,200 square feet of space.

Owner/Biography: B.K. Clinker.
Year Founded/History of Bookstore: 1968.
Number of Volumes: 9,000.

Types/Classifications: Hardbound, first editions, out-of-print, fine bindings, association copies, press books, signed copies, presentation copies, limited editions, color plate books.
General Subject Areas: General.
Mail/Telephone Orders; Credit Cards: Both. No credit cards.
Business Hours: Monday 6:00 PM - 10:00 PM or by appointment.
Parking Facilities: Street parking.
Special Features: Search service.
Collections/Individual Items Purchased: Both.

817
Paul H. North, Jr.
81 Bullitt Park Place
Columbus, Ohio 43209 (614) 252-1826

Paul H. North, Jr. carries antiquarian and rare books in the fields of literature and Americana. The collection is housed on private premises and visits can be arranged by appointment.
How to Get There: Mr. North is located around the corner from 2500 East Broad Street.
Owner/Biography: Paul H. North, Jr. Mr. North is a bookseller, art dealer, and clergyman.
Year Founded/History of Bookstore: 1948.
Number of Volumes: 10,000.
Types/Classifications: Antiquarian, rare.
General Subject Areas: Americana, Literature.
Mail/Telephone Orders; Credit Cards: Both. No credit cards.
Business Hours: By appointment.
Catalogue: Catalogue published.
Collections/Individual Items Purchased: Both.

818
Robert G. Hayman Antiquarian Books
575 West Street
Carey, Ohio 43316 (419) 396-6933

Primarily a mail order business, this shop is located in a private residence. Visitors are welcome but an appointment is suggested. The stock includes first editions and out-of-print Americana.
How to Get There: Call for directions.
Owner/Biography: Robert G. and Arnelva Hayman.
Year Founded/History of Bookstore: 1962.
Number of Volumes: 5,000.
Types/Classifications: Hardbound, pamphlets, broadsides, ephemera, first editions, out-of-print.
General Subject Areas: Americana.
Specific Specialties: Historical and literature in the regions of the Great Lakes, Midwest; Western Americana.
Mail/Telephone Orders; Credit Cards: Both. No credit cards.
Business Hours: By appointment only.
Catalogue: Published 5 times per year.
Collections/Individual Items Purchased: Both.
Booksellers' Memberships: Antiquarian Booksellers Association of America including Midwest Chapter, Northern Ohio Bibliophilic Society.

819
Significant Books
3053 Madison Road
Cincinnati, Ohio 45209 (513) 321-7567

The bookstore specializes in used and rare books with an emphasis on non-fiction and some collectible literature and illustrated books. The shop contains 2,300 square feet of space.

How to Get There: Cincinnati is served by Routes 175, 174, and 171. Madison Road is a short distance south of I-71, at Exit 6.

Owner/Biography: Bill and Carolyn Downing.

Year Founded/History of Bookstore: 1977.

Number of Volumes: 10,000.

Types/Classifications: The books are 90 percent hardbound and include rare, used, collectible illustrated books; there are also prints, maps, stamps, ephemera, antiques.

General Subject Areas: Art, History, Literature, Medicine, Nature, Non-Fiction, Philosophy, Sciences, Technology, Travel.

Specific Specialties: The stock is strong in books of historical interest such as classic works and reference works; also some How-To Books.

Other Specialties: Scholarly and Important Works.

Mail/Telephone Orders; Credit Cards: Both. Cash with order from individual buyers; institutions should submit purchase orders. Visa, Mastercard.

Business Hours: Monday and Friday 11:00 AM - 6:00 PM; Tuesday, Wednesday, Thursday 11:00 AM - 9:00 PM; weekends by appointment.

Parking Facilities: Free parking in lot behind the store.

Special Features: Search service; special order of new books.

Catalogue: Quarterly.

Collections/Individual Items Purchased: Both.

Miscellaneous: The business features supplying books and some other items of historical and antiquarian interest as well as associated reference material.

820
Susan Heller Books
P.O. Box 22723
Beachwood, Ohio 44122

(216) 283-2665

Susan Heller runs this book business from her home and it is rapidly encroaching on the living area with 20,000 books in stock, all alphabetically arranged on shelves for easy inspection. Several fireplaces and perpetual coffee bring warmth to winter visitors. Summer guests may enjoy long, cool drinks and a flower/rock garden. A changing supply of books can be enjoyed all year long.

How to Get There: Beachwood, an eastern suburb of Cleveland, can be rached via the Chagnin Road Exit of I-271; travel west on Chagnin to Green Road, turn right on Green Road and at the first traffic light turn left onto Halburton; Susan Heller Books is the seventh home on the right, backing up to a golf course.

Owner/Biography: Susan Heller.

Year Founded/History of Bookstore: 1976. To accommodate growing stock, a cathedral ceiling was built with shelves on all walls. A spiral staircase leads to still more books.

Number of Volumes: 20,000.

Types/Classifications: Rare, fine, and out-of-print, some autographs, photographica, first editions, fine bindings, sets, some press books, association and signed copies, color plate books.

General Subject Areas: Americana, Architecture, Art, Books About Books, Fine Arts, Juveniles, Literature, Medicine, Mysteries, Natural History, Nautical, Science, Science Fiction and Fantasy, Sporting, Travel and Exploration.

Other Specialties: Scholarly works.

Mail/Telephone Orders; Credit Cards: Both. No credit cards.

Business Hours: By appointment only.

Parking Facilities: Driveway parking.

Special Features: Computerized search service; computer software for bookdealers and search services.

Catalogue: Published irregularly.

Collections/Individual Items Purchased: Both.

Booksellers' Memberships: Antiquarian Booksellers Association of America, International League of Booksellers, Northern Ohio Bibliophilic Association.

OREGON

821
Authors of the West
191 Dogwood Drive
Dundee, Oregon 97115   (503) 538-8132

The bookstore is in the daylight basement of a hillside home overlooking the Willamette River and Valley, in this fertile nut, berry, and vinyard district. Although coffee is served to visitors, the business is primarily mail order; if planning to visit the store, it is wise to call ahead. The shop contains 2,000 square feet of space, and features fine books by Westerners on the West.

How to Get There: By car, 20 miles southwest of Portland on Highway 99W, Dundee is three miles beyond Newberg. Turn up the hill on 5th Street by the school, and turn right onto Dogwood.

Owner/Biography: Lee and Grayce Nash. Grayce, a native of Alberta, Canada, is a former college psychology teacher; Lee now teaches history at a nearby college.

Year Founded/History of Bookstore: The business began in Flagstaff, Arizona in 1973, and moved to its present location in 1975. It has published seventeen catalogues and numerous special lists.

Number of Volumes: 5,000.

Types/Classifications: Hardbound, collector's paperbacks.

General Subject Areas: Exploration, Fiction, Nature, Poetry, Travel, West (U.S.).

Specific Specialties: Pacific Northwest, Southwest (U.S.), Rocky Mountains, Alaska, Texas, Great Plains (U.S.), Midwest (U.S.).

Author Specialties: Edward Abbey, Mary Austin, Willa Cather, Walter V.T. Clark, Harvey Fergusson, Vardis Fisher, A.B. Guthrie, Zane Grey, Louis L'Amour, Hamlin Garland, Jack London, Frederick Manfred, E.M. Rhodes, Frank Walters, C.S. Lewis, Western (U.S.) Authors.

Mail/Telephone Orders; Credit Cards: Both; personal check with order until becoming an established customer. No credit cards.

Business Hours: All hours, but call for appointment.

Parking Facilities: Street.

Special Features: Search service.

Catalogue: Two times a year.

Collections/Individual Items Purchased: Both.

822
Book Bin
121 West First
Albany, Oregon 97321   (503) 926-6869

The Book Bin has a comprehensive assortment of books in most fields. Used hardbound and paperback books are offered at reasonable prices. The shop occupies 2,000 square feet of space.

Owner/Biography: Bob and Phyllis McMaster, Bob and Maria Baird.

Year Founded/History of Bookstore: 1973. The Book Bin began at the current Albany location with Phyllis McMaster in charge. Bob McMaster left his job as a high school English teacher in 1977 as the store expanded. Bob and Maria Baird joined the partnership in 1983 with the opening of a 2,300 square foot branch store in Corvallis.

Number of Volumes: 50,000 (additional 30,000 volumes in Corvallis).

Types/Classifications: Hardbound, paperback, magazines (National Geographics and some others).

General Subject Areas: General.

Mail/Telephone Orders; Credit Cards: Both. Check with order including adequate amount for postage. Visa and Mastercard accepted.

Business Hours: Monday through Thursday 10:00 AM - 6:00 PM; Friday 10:00 AM - 8:00 PM; Saturday

10:00 AM - 5:00 PM.
Parking Facilities: Adequate parking in front of store and around the corner.
Special Features: Search service; titles available from either store.
Collections/Individual Items Purchased: Both.

823
Book Bin
351 NW Jackson
Corvallis, Oregon 97330

(503) 752-0040

See BOOK BIN, Albany, Oregon.

824
Camerons Books & Magazines
2833 South East 33rd Place
Portland, Oregon 97204

(503) 228-2391

The bookstore deals in old, rare, and out-of-print hardbacks; it is Portland's oldest bookstore dealing in out-of-print books. Also included are vintage magazines. The shop refers to itself as a true "bargain bookstore," where new arrivals still in boxes and stacks are subject to browsing. The bookstore contains 2,500 square feet of space.
How to Get There: This is the only used bookstore remaining in Portland's downtown core area.
Owner/Biography: Fred and Ann Goetz. Fred is a former outdoor columnist who bought the shop from R.E. Cameron (who still works a few hours in the store each day) in 1973. Ann is a real estate sales person who works the mail order department of the bookstore in her spare time.
Year Founded/History of Bookstore: The bookstore was founded in 1940 by Grace and R.E. Cameron and purchased by Fred and Ann Goetz in 1973. Grace is retired from the store while Bob works for the new owner 2 hours a day.
Number of Volumes: 50,000.
Types/Classifications: Hardbound, paperback, magazines, first editions, out-of-print, association copies.
General Subject Areas: Biography, Crafts, Fiction, Technical.
Specific Specialties: Sporting, Angling, Hunting, Children's Books, Military, Art, Sports, Baseball, Golf, Antique Lore, Photography.
Mail/Telephone Orders; Credit Cards: Both; cash with order; Visa, Mastercard.
Business Hours: Daily 10:00 AM - 6:00 PM.
Parking Facilities: Street.
Special Features: Search service; the shop is strong on vintage magazines, and features a unique filing system and shelving. Thousands of these charming, old magazines, which are rarely found elsewhere, are available for browsing.
Catalogue: Quarterly.
Collections/Individual Items Purchased: Both.
Booksellers' Memberships: Antiquarian Booksellers Association of America.

825
Holland's Books
3522 S.E. Hawthorne
Portland, Oregon 97214

(503) 232-3596

Holland's Books is in a neighborhood shopping area. The store is small but selectively stocked with mostly non-fiction, mostly hardbound, mostly with a specific, often scholarly focus. The store occupies 1,000 square feet.
How to Get There: From downtown Portland, cross the Hawthorne Bridge and travel east 35 blocks.
Owner/Biography: Stephen Holland.

Year Founded/History of Bookstore: 1980.

Number of Volumes: 10,000.

Types/Classifications: Hardbound, some paperback, first editions, fine bindings, out-of-print, association copies, press books, signed copies, presentation copies, limited editions, color plate books.

General Subject Areas: Americana, Arts, Feminism, History, Literary Criticism, Literature, Marxism, Philosophy, Psychology, Radicalism, Science, Social Theory.

Mail/Telephone Orders; Credit Cards: Neither. Visa and Mastercard accepted.

Business Hours: Monday through Saturday 12:00 Noon - 6:30 PM.

Parking Facilities: Business parking lot, street parking.

Collections/Individual Items Purchased: Both.

826
Longfellow's Bookstore
6229-31 S. E. Milwaukee Avenue
Portland, Oregon 97202 (503) 239-5222

The bookstore is located in a high-ceilinged 1912 building. The basement is devoted to periodicals which include Life magazines from 1936, National Geographics from 1914 to the present, and vintage American Mercury and Esquire collections. The 1,500 lineal feet of pine bookcases on the main floor house the general stock books (with emphasis on standard works), the sheet music collection, and the resident stuffed owl. The shop contains a total of 1,960 square feet of space.

How to Get There: Just five minutes from downtown Portland by car, the bookstore is located in southeast Portland near the Willamette River, between the Ross Island and Sellwood Bridges. It is ten blocks north of Sellwood's Antique Row, Portland's largest collection of antique shops.

Owner/Biography: Edwin Jon Hagen, owner, describes himself as an unfulfilled bookseller, with more-or-less successful careers as a saw filer, remodeling contractor, student sociologist, youth services specialist, and professional athlete. A once zealous paratrooper, he claims that he is now a committed peacenik.

Year Founded/History of Bookstore: The shop opened in 1981, doubled its square footage two years later, and added a search service in 1983.

Number of Volumes: 30,000.

Types/Classifications: Hardbound, paperback, magazines, maps, ephemera, Sunday funnies, vintage sheet music, L.P. records, first editions, out-of-print.

General Subject Areas: American Cooking, American Literature, Biography, Cookbooks, Disarmament, Drama, Humanities, Life Magazines from 1936, Military, Music, Mystery, National Geographic Maps, National Geographic Publications, National Geographics 1916 to Date, Poetry, Religion, Science Fiction and Fantasy, Sheet Music 1900-1960, Social Science, Sports.

Author Specialties: H.L. Mencken, Pearl Buck, Stewart Holbrook.

Other Specialties: Political Science, Political Materials, Black Studies.

Mail/Telephone Orders; Credit Cards: Both; cash with order; personal checks accepted; Visa, Mastercard.

Business Hours: Tuesday through Saturday 10:00 AM - 6:00 PM, and by appointment.

Parking Facilities: Street and business parking lot.

Special Features: Search service.

Collections/Individual Items Purchased: Both.

Miscellaneous: In the very near vicinity of the shop are a delicatessen, pizzeria, and pastry shop. Coffee with the customers is a regular occurrence for the owner. Dealers are welcome, and are given a dealer discount.

827
Manuscript
223 High Street NE
Salem, Oregon 97301 (503) 370-8855

This quaint used bookstore is owned and operated by a self-designated bibliomanic, and features neatness and organization. The owner specializes in a desire to find the books the customers want.

How to Get There: The bookstore is located between Court Street and Chemeketa Street NE.

Owner/Biography: Barbara J. Haskell.
Year Founded/History of Bookstore: Founded in 1979, the shop is still under the original ownership.
Number of Volumes: 10,000.
Types/Classifications: Hardbound, ephemera, first editions, fine bindings, out-of-print, signed copies, limited editions, color plate books, rare.
General Subject Areas: Art, Children's Literature, Cookbooks, History, Literature, Religion, Science, Western Americana.
Specific Specialties: Pacific Northwest, 19th Century English Literature, Modern Literature, Regional Fiction of the Early 20th Century, Color Plate Children's Books, Arctic Adventure and Exploration, Fairy Tales, Mythology.
Author Specialties: Thomas Hardy, Hugh Thomson (illustrator), Mary E. Wilkins Freeman, Ernest Hemingway, William Faulkner, John Steinbeck, W.B. Yeats, Gene Stratton Porter, Jessie Wilcox, Joseph C. Lincoln, Sara Ware Bassett, Willa Cather, Louisa May Alcott, L.M. Montgomery, Margaret Deland, G.L. Hill, Robert Graves.
Mail/Telephone Orders; Credit Cards: Both. Visa and Mastercard accepted.
Business Hours: Monday through Friday 10:00 AM - 5:00 PM; Saturday 11:00 AM - 4:00 PM.
Parking Facilities: Street.
Special Features: Search service, appraisals.
Catalogue: Two times a year.
Collections/Individual Items Purchased: Both.

828
McLaughlin's Books
78196 Highway 99 South
Cottage Grove, Oregon 97424 (503) 942-0745

The bookstore features books about hunting, fishing, Alaska, and the Arctic, with 1,000 square feet of space.
How to Get There: The shop is located 1/2 mile south of the Cottage Grove city limits; if driving from the north or south take the first exit on I-5.
Owner/Biography: Robert F. McLaughlin, owner, has been in the out-of-print business for over 35 years.
Year Founded/History of Bookstore: Mr. McLaughlin started his first bookstore in 1946 in Oregon, and has opened others in California and Arizona.
Number of Volumes: 5,000.
Types/Classifications: Hardbound, paperback, ephemera, first editions, fine bindings, signed copies, out-of-print, limited editions, pulps.
General Subject Areas: Alaska, Americana, Arctic, Arctic Canada, Big Game, Big Game Hunting, Eskimos, Fishing, Guns, Outdoors, Science Fiction and Fantasy, Trappers, Trapping, Traps, Western Canada.
Specific Specialties: Pacific Northwest, Boone & Crockett Club Publications.
Author Specialties: Charles Sheldon, Elmer Keith, Jack O'Conner.
Mail/Telephone Orders; Credit Cards: Both; no credit cards; mail address: P.O. Box 753, rest same as above.
Business Hours: By appointment only.
Parking Facilities: Parking lot.
Special Features: Search service.
Catalogue: Ten times a year.
Collections/Individual Items Purchased: Both.

829
Midvale Books
155 SW Midvale Road
Portland, Oregon 97219 (503) 636-7952

Midvale Books is a mail order only business and specializes in books on bikes and bicycling.
Owner/Biography: Ron and Cheryl Clevenger.
Year Founded/History of Bookstore: 1980.

Number of Volumes: 400.
Types/Classifications: Hardbound, paperback, in-print, out-of-print, used.
General Subject Areas: Bikes and Bicycling.
Mail/Telephone Orders; Credit Cards: Mail orders: $1.00 for catalogue; no credit cards.
Business Hours: Mail order only.
Catalogue: Catalogue published.
Collections/Individual Items Purchased: Both.

830
Old Oregon Book Store
525 S.W. 12th Avenue
Portland, Oregon 97205 (503) 227-2742

The Old Oregon Book Store carries a general stock in all fields with emphasis on American history, economics, political science, literature, and Russian history. The store occupies 3,400 square feet of space.
How to Get There: The bookstore is located between Alder Street and Washington Street on 12th Avenue.
Owner/Biography: Preston and Phyllis McMann.
Year Founded/History of Bookstore: 1949.
Number of Volumes: 100,000.
Types/Classifications: Hardbound, ephemera, out-of-print, first editions.
General Subject Areas: American History, Economics, Literature, Political Science, Russian History.
Specific Specialties: Pacific Northwest History.
Mail/Telephone Orders; Credit Cards: Both. No credit cards.
Business Hours: Monday through Saturday 11:00 AM - 5:00 PM.
Parking Facilities: Street parking.
Catalogue: Catalogue Published.
Collections/Individual Items Purchased: Both.
Booksellers' Memberships: Antiquarian Booksellers Association of America.

831
Paper Moon Bookstore
3530 S.E. Hawthorne Boulevard
Portland, Oregon 97214 (503) 236-5195

This is a used bookstore with general stock and emphasis on literature, poetry, the fine arts, photography, and illustrated children's books. It also has paper ephemera, photographs, and prints. The store occupies 1,200 square feet of space.
How to Get There: The store is located on the south side of the Hawthorne Bridge.
Owner/Biography: Andrea K. Drinard.
Year Founded/History of Bookstore: 1978.
Number of Volumes: 40,000.
Types/Classifications: Hardbound, paperback, old magazines, ephemera, old photographs, out-of-print, reading copies.
General Subject Areas: Children's Books, Fine Arts, Literature, Photography, Poetry.
Specific Specialties: Early 20th Century Book Illustrators, 20th Century Photographers, Modern Writers.
Mail/Telephone Orders; Credit Cards: Both. Mail orders should include postage and handling charges.
Business Hours: Monday through Saturday 12:00 Noon - 5:00 PM.
Parking Facilities: Parking lot behind store.
Special Features: Search service.
Collections/Individual Items Purchased: Both.

PENNSYLVANIA

832

Americanist

1525 Shenkel Road

Pottstown, Pennsylvania 19464 (215) 323-5289

The bookstore is a full service antiquarian shop housed in a converted Pennsylvania Dutch barn, offering books in major categories of scholarly and collecting interest in all price ranges. It contains over 5,000 square feet of space.

How to Get There: The bookstore is out in the country, in northern Chester County, Pennsylvania. It is just south of State Route 724, about 15 miles north of the Downingtown exit of the Pennsylvania Turnpike. It is best to call for directions.

Owner/Biography: Norman and Michal Kane, owners, have been in the antiquarian book business for over 30 years.

Year Founded/History of Bookstore: 1954.

Number of Volumes: 20,000.

Types/Classifications: Used and rare books in all fields, maps, manuscripts, ephemera, prints.

General Subject Areas: General.

Mail/Telephone Orders; Credit Cards: Both; cash with order. Visa and Mastercard accepted.

Business Hours: Usual business hours, seven days a week, but it is well to call if planning to visit on Sunday.

Parking Facilities: Plenty of free space.

Catalogue: Ten times a year.

Collections/Individual Items Purchased: Both.

Booksellers' Memberships: Antiquarian Booksellers Association of America.

Miscellaneous: Under the name Kane Antiquarian Auction, the Kanes conduct auction sales of books, prints, graphics, and ephemera.

833

Bernard Conwell Carlitz, Books-Manuscripts-Prints

1901 Chestnut Street

Philadelphia, Pennsylvania 19103 (215) 563-6608

This bookshop occupies 2,100 square feet of space on the second floor of the above address.

Owner/Biography: Bernard C. Carlitz. Mr. Carlitz was formerly a chemical engineer and is a Disabled Veteran of World War II. He began his book business after his discharge.

Year Founded/History of Bookstore: 1946.

Number of Volumes: 10,000.

Types/Classifications: Hardbound, broadsides, autographs, ephemera, first editions, fine bindings, out-of-print, association copies, press books, signed copies, presentation copies, limited editions, color plate books.

General Subject Areas: General.

Mail/Telephone Orders; Credit Cards: Both. No credit cards.

Business Hours: Monday through Friday 12:00 Noon - 5:30 PM.

Parking Facilities: Street parking.

Collections/Individual Items Purchased: Both.

Booksellers' Memberships: Philobiblon.

834
Bikes and Books
5952 Germantown Avenue
Philadelphia, Pennsylvania 19144   (215) 843-6071

This bookstore has a voluminous stock neatly shelved which includes basically non-fiction and functional books - dictionaries, Bibles, and atlases. The store also carries many How-To-Do-It books, standard American and European literature, and health books. A nearby storage area has fiction, scholarly books on Americana, literature, psychology, history, anthropology, etc. The majority of books in the shop (15,000) are paperbound and those in storage (30,000) are mainly hardbound. Seventy five percent of the stock is out-of-print. The shop is a large rectangular area occupying approximately 4,000 square feet of space. There are glass doors and a large window area on two streets. To the right as one enters is a bicycle repair shop. In the far left corner is a separate room full of bicycles, used and rebuilt, for sale or being repaired. The remainder of the shop is shelved with books.

Owner/Biography: Arthur (Art) Carduner. Mr. Carduner has been in the book business since 1949. He operated Vanity Fair in New York City from 1949 to 1958 and Vanity Fair in New Hope, Pennsylvania from 1958 to 1966. Mr. Carduner has been in the bike business since 1975.

Year Founded/History of Bookstore: The business has been in its present format since 1975.

Number of Volumes: 50,000.

Types/Classifications: Hardbound, paperback, some old magazines, out-of-print.

General Subject Areas: Americana, Anthropology, Art, Black History, Books By and About Women, European History, Fiction, How-To Books, Juvenile, Literature, Music, Philosophy, Poetry, Psychology, Science Fiction and Fantasy.

Mail/Telephone Orders; Credit Cards: Both. Remittance with order, except libraries and institutions. No credit cards.

Business Hours: Monday through Saturday 9:00 AM - 6:00 PM.

Parking Facilities: Street parking.

Special Features: Search service.

Catalogue: Published 4 times per year.

Collections/Individual Items Purchased: Both.

835
Book Haven
154 North Prince Street
Lancaster, Pennsylvania 17603   (717) 393-0920

The Book Haven is a full service bookstore offering 30,000 better books on two floors arranged in over 30 categories for ease of browsing. Though a general bookstore, it is particularly strong in children's and illustrated books, Americana, military history, first edition fiction, and Pennsylvania. The store occupies 1,000 square feet of space.

How to Get There: Lancaster is located 60 miles due west of Philadelphia in the heart of the Pennsylvania Dutch (and Amish) country. The store is located downtown, just 3 blocks from the square. Prince Street is also Route 222 south through Lancaster.

Owner/Biography: Kinsey Baker.

Year Founded/History of Bookstore: 1978. The Book Haven is located on its original site. The store has expanded from 2 rooms and 5,000 books to 5 rooms and 30,000 books.

Number of Volumes: 30,000.

Types/Classifications: Hardbound, paperback, magazines, ephemera, autographs, prints, paintings.

General Subject Areas: General.

Mail/Telephone Orders; Credit Cards: Both. No credit cards.

Business Hours: Monday through Friday 10:00 AM - 5:00 PM; Friday Evening 6.00 PM - 9:00 PM; Saturday 11:00 AM - 4:00 PM.

Parking Facilities: Metered street parking, parking garage 1 block away.

Special Features: Search service; personal quoting; appraisals.

Collections/Individual Items Purchased: Both.

836
Book Mark
2049 West Rittenhouse Square
Philadelphia, Pennsylvania 19103   (215) 735-5546

Largely a general used and out-of-print bookstore, the shop includes unusual books in a variety of subjects.
How to Get There: The bookstore is located between 20th and 21st Streets, and Locust and Spruce Streets, in the center of the city of Philadelphia.
Owner/Biography: Valerie J. Polin and Robert C. Langmuir, Jr.
Year Founded/History of Bookstore: Founded in 1978 in what was originally a carriage house/stable, the bookstore has been in this same location since it opened.
Number of Volumes: 7,000 to 10,000.
Types/Classifications: Hardbound, prints, ephemera, out-of-print, fine bindings.
General Subject Areas: Antiques, Architecture, Children's Books, Fiction, Gardening, History, Natural History, Poetry, Travel.
Specific Specialties: Architecture of all periods.
Mail/Telephone Orders; Credit Cards: Both.
Business Hours: Monday through Saturday 10:00 AM - 5:00 PM; later in the evening by appointment.
Parking Facilities: Street; parking lot 1/4 block from shop (charges a fee).
Special Features: Personal service; browsing encouraged with no solicitation to purchase; quiet, friendly atmosphere; specific want lists welcome.
Catalogue: Two to three times a year; only architecture or gardening titles are included in the catalogue.
Collections/Individual Items Purchased: Both.

837
Book Trader
501 South Street
Philadelphia, Pennsylvania 19147   (215) 925-0219

The Book Trader is a "browser's paradise" where there are thousands of used hardbound and paperback books in all categories. The shop occupies 4,500 square feet of space.
Owner/Biography: Peter C. Hiler.
Year Founded/History of Bookstore: 1976.
Number of Volumes: 75,000.
Types/Classifications: Hardbound, paperback, rare, out-of-print, photographic posters, out-of-print phonograph records (lp's).
General Subject Areas: General.
Mail/Telephone Orders; Credit Cards: Both. Visa and Mastercard accepted.
Business Hours: Daily 10:00 AM - Midnight (365 days per year).
Catalogue: Published annually.
Collections/Individual Items Purchased: Both.

838
Booksource, Ltd.
7 South Chester Road
P.O. Box 43
Swarthmore, Pennsylvania 19081   (215) 328-5083

Located in the business village of Swarthmore, the bookstore is adjacent to the campus of Swarthmore College. The shop has a general stock of quality books both for the enjoyment and scholarly pursuits of customers. It occupies 1,000 square feet of space.
Owner/Biography: Constance and Patrick Flanigan.
Year Founded/History of Bookstore: 1979.
Number of Volumes: 10,000.

Types/Classifications: Hardbound, first editions, out-of-print.
General Subject Areas: Americana, General.
Mail/Telephone Orders; Credit Cards: Both. No credit cards.
Business Hours: Monday through Thursday 10:00 AM - 6:00 PM; Friday 10:00 AM - 8:00 PM; Saturday 10:00 AM - 4:00 PM.
Parking Facilities: Ample parking available.
Special Features: Search service.
Catalogue: Published periodically.
Collections/Individual Items Purchased: Both.

839
Bruce McKittrick Rare Books
2240 Fairmount Avenue
Philadelphia, Pennsylvania 19130 (215) 235-3209

Bruce McKittrick Rare Books is a rare book dealer emphasizing the Renaissance, incunabula, antiquarian bibliography, pedagogy, science, medicine, humanism, and neo-Latinity. The business is conducted from the owner's private residence and visits are by appointment only.
How to Get There: Located five minutes from Philadelphia's Center City by car; take 22nd Street north to Fairmount Avenue, turn left one block, second house from the corner of 23rd Street on south side of Fairmount Avenue; frequent and convenient bus service or 20 minute walk from Center City.
Owner/Biography: Bruce McKittrick.
Year Founded/History of Bookstore: 1979.
Number of Volumes: 500.
Types/Classifications: Printed books of the Reniassance, 17th and 18th Century Europe, manuscripts of the same period.
General Subject Areas: Renaissance.
Other Specialties: Continental printed books and manuscripts from the 15th Century to the end of the 18th Century.
Mail/Telephone Orders; Credit Cards: Both. Prepayment or satisfactory trade references.
Business Hours: Monday through Saturday by appointment only.
Parking Facilities: Public parking across the street.
Catalogue: Published 3 times yearly.
Collections/Individual Items Purchased: Both.
Booksellers' Memberships: Antiquarian Booksellers Association of America.

840
Bryn Mawr-Vassar Book Store, Inc.
4612 Winthrop Street
Pittsburgh, Pennsylvania 15213 (412) 687-3433

The Bryn Mawr-Vassar Book Store is a non-profit organization which sells donated books to raise scholarship funds for Bryn Mawr College and Vassar College. The stock is old, rare, and out-of-print in all categories.
Number of Volumes: Thousands.
Types/Classifications: Hardbound, paperback, rare, out-of-print, first editions, reading copies.
General Subject Areas: Americana, Art, Asia and Africa, Biography, Children's Books, History, Languages, Literature, Music, Philosophy, Psychology, Religion, Science and Technology, Travel.
Mail/Telephone Orders; Credit Cards: No mail or phone orders; no credit cards.
Business Hours: Monday through Saturday 10:00 AM - 4:00 PM.
Parking Facilities: Ample parking available.
Collections/Individual Items Purchased: Neither. Donations accepted.
Miscellaneous: Staffed by alumnae volunteers.

841
Cantrell's Books
15 South Pearl Street
North East, Pennsylvania 16428

(814) 725-3681

Cantrell's Books is a small, specialized, mostly mail order operation. It was started as a "retirement buisness" after the Cantrells sold the new and antiquarian store which had held their attention for thirty-two years (sold to their daughter).

Owner/Biography: Glenn and Sabra Cantrell.
Year Founded/History of Bookstore: 1979.
Number of Volumes: 1,000.
Types/Classifications: Hardbound, paperback, pamphlets, some magazines, broadsides, autographs, stock certificates.
General Subject Areas: American Inland Waterways.
Specific Specialties: American Rivers, American Canals, American Lakes, Canoes, Steamboats, Rafting, Folklore, Logbooks.
Author Specialties: Captain Frederick Way, Jr.
Mail/Telephone Orders; Credit Cards: Both. Cash with order. No credit cards.
Business Hours: Irregular. Call for appointment.
Parking Facilities: Street parking.
Special Features: Search service.
Collections/Individual Items Purchased: Both.
Booksellers' Memberships: Antiquarian Booksellers Association of America including Middle Atlantic Chapter.

842
Carmen D. Valentino, Rare Books & Manuscripts
2956 Richmond Street
Philadelphia, Pennsylvania 19134

(215) 739-6056

The store is located near major highways and streets only 10 minutes from Center City Philadelphia. Appointments are absolutely necessary and one may call between 9:00 AM and 4:00 PM seven days a week for such. A wide variety of antiquarian material is carried and wants are solicited by mail and phone. The shop and storage area occupy 3,000 square feet of space.

How to Get There: Richmond Street is parallel to I-95 and the Delaware River. The shop is located between the I-95 exits of Aramingo and Allegheny (both are very close to Center City Philadelphia).
Owner/Biography: Carmen D. Valentino.
Year Founded/History of Bookstore: 1973. The shop has always been in its present location.
Number of Volumes: Literally thousands of items.
Types/Classifications: Hardbound, pamphlets, newspapers, broadsides, autographs, documents, manuscripts, pictorial art, much ephemera, anything in paper, periodicals, out-of-print, fine bindings, signed copies, color plate books, association copies.
General Subject Areas: Americana, Business History, Exploration, Law, Medicine, Numismatics, Pennsylvania, Philadelphia, Photography, Printing, Religion, Science, Textiles, Trade Catalogues, Travel, World History.
Specific Specialties: Romania, Transylvania.
Other Specialties: Manuscript collections in all categories.
Mail/Telephone Orders; Credit Cards: Neither. No credit cards.
Business Hours: Strictly by appointment.
Parking Facilities: Public parking lot, street parking.
Special Features: Wants cheerfully solicited from collectors, dealers, and institutions.
Collections/Individual Items Purchased: Both.
Miscellaneous: Quotes sent and expected to be answered.

843
Cesi Kellinger, Bookseller
735 Philadelphia Avenue
Chambersburg, Pennsylvania 17201   (717) 263-4474

Cesi Kellinger, Bookseller is located in a refurbished coach house and has a stock of hardbound first editions. Visits can be arranged by appointment.

How to Get There: From Interstate 81, take exit 6.
Owner/Biography: Cesi Kellinger.
Year Founded/History of Bookstore: 1973.
Number of Volumes: 10,000.
Types/Classifications: Hardbound, first editions.
General Subject Areas: Americana, Art.
Mail/Telephone Orders; Credit Cards: Both. No credit cards.
Business Hours: By appointment.
Parking Facilities: Street parking.
Catalogue: Published 2 times per year.
Collections/Individual Items Purchased: Both.
Booksellers' Memberships: Chambersburg Area Booksellers.

844
Dale W. Starry, Sr. - Bookseller
115 North Washington Street
Shippensburg, Pennsylvania 17257   (717) 532-2690

A general stock is housed in a bookbarn in a wide variety of subjects. Open only by appointment.

How to Get There: Call for directions.
Owner/Biography: Dale W. Starry, Sr.
Year Founded/History of Bookstore: 1965.
Number of Volumes: 20,000
Types/Classifications: Hardbound, paperback, magazines, first editions, out-of-print, signed copies, illustrated books.
General Subject Areas: Americana, Biography, Children's Series, Horticulture, Medical, Military, Music, Natural History, Pennsylvania History, Plays, Poetry, Religious, Travel, Western Novels.
Author Specialties: Edgar Rice Burroughs, Albert Payson Terhune, Clarence Budington Kelland, Max Brand, Henry W. Shoemaker, Ellery Queen, Earl Derr Biggers, E. Phillips Oppenheim, Robert Chambers.
Mail/Telephone Orders; Credit Cards: Both. No credit cards.
Business Hours: By appointment only.
Parking Facilities: Street parking.
Collections/Individual Items Purchased: Both.
Booksellers' Memberships: Chambersburg Area Booksellers.

845
Family Album
RD 1, Box 42
Glen Rock, Pennsylvania 17327   (717) 235-2134

The Family Album shares with librarians, collectors, and fellow antiquarian booksellers throughout the world an ongoing commitment to our cultural heritage. It is engaged in active collection development programs that embrace many diverse disciplines and nourish a clientele of eclectic tastes. The Family Album is located in a farmhouse that is over 100 years old and occupies 1,600 square feet of space.

How to Get There: Phone for appointment and specific directions.
Owner/Biography: Ronald Lieberman.
Year Founded/History of Bookstore: 1969.

Number of Volumes: 40,000.

Types/Classifications: Fine books and manuscripts, out-of-print, hardbound, paperback, first editions, illustrated books, fore-edge paintings, incunabula, maps, atlases, photographica, sets, newspapers.

General Subject Areas: African Studies, Americana, Arabic Studies, Bibles, Black History, Book Collecting, Bookbinding, Early Printed and Manuscript Books, Lexicography, Medicine, Occult, Pennsylvania, Printing, Urban Studies.

Specific Specialties: Samuel Johnson, William Shakespeare, Stephen James.

Author Specialties: Pennsylvania Authors: Benjamin Franklin, Henry W. Shoemaker, Herbert E. Stover.

Mail/Telephone Orders; Credit Cards: Both. No credit cards.

Business Hours: By appointment only.

Special Features: Appraisals.

Catalogue: Published 1 to 4 times per year.

Collections/Individual Items Purchased: Both.

Booksellers' Memberships: Antiquarian Booksellers Association of America, International League of Antiquarian Booksellers.

846
Gateway
Ferndale, Pennsylvania 18921   (215) 847-5644

The Gateway is exclusively mail order and specializes in occultism and mysticism. It is one of the oldest occult-metaphysical bookshops in the U.S., originally in New York City but since 1967 it has been in Ferndale, Pennsylvania.

Owner/Biography: Jeanne Urich Gorham.

Year Founded/History of Bookstore: 1930.

Number of Volumes: 10,000.

Types/Classifications: Hardbound, paperback, magazines, first editions, out-of-print, signed copies, presentation copies, limited editions.

General Subject Areas: Alchemy, Ancient Egypt, Astrology, Dowsing, Freemasonry, Hypnotism, Kabbalah, Magic, Medieval Mysticism, Metaphysics, Oriental Religions, Palmistry, Psychical Research, Rosicrucianism, Spiritualism, Tarot, Theosophy, Yoga, Zen.

Author Specialties: Nicholas Roerich, Aliester Crowley, G.I. Gurdjieff, Jacob Boehme, Agrippa, Joan Grant, Cheiro, Krishnamurti, Manly P. Hall, Noel Jaquin, Thomas Taylor, H.P. Blavatsky, Israel Regardie, John Dee, Plotinus, G.R.S. Mead, Franz Hartman, Charles Muses, MacGregor Mathers, Eliphas Levi, Algernon Blackwood.

Mail/Telephone Orders; Credit Cards: Mail orders exclusively. Write with request and specific information will be supplied. Telephone orders from established customers. No credit cards.

Business Hours: Mail order phone daily 10:00 AM - 5:00 PM.

Special Features: Search service.

Catalogue: Published 2 to 3 times per year.

Collections/Individual Items Purchased: Both.

847
George Hall, Jr. - Books
1441 Lincoln Way East
Chambersburg, Pennsylvania 17201   (717) 263-4388

The stock in this collection is eclectic and carefully selected. Visitors are welcome by appointment or chance during evenings and weekends.

How to Get There: The shop is located 1 mile east of I-81, Exit 6; on left.

Owner/Biography: George Hall, Jr.

Year Founded/History of Bookstore: 1975.

Number of Volumes: 3,000.

Types/Classifications: Hardbound, out-of-print, rare.

General Subject Areas: Americana, Fishing, Hunting, Military, New York City, Technology.

Mail/Telephone Orders; Credit Cards: Both. Cash with order including postage. No credit cards.
Business Hours: By appointment or chance, evenings and weekends.
Parking Facilities: Street parking.
Special Features: Search service.
Catalogue: Published annually.
Collections/Individual Items Purchased: Both.
Miscellaneous: Second location at Fayetteville Flea Market, 3 miles east of main store; open 7 days 9:00 AM - 5:00 PM.

848
Hillman Books
343 Hastings Street
Pittsburgh, Pennsylvania 15206 (412) 362-6472

Hillman Books is a rare book dealership specializing in the subjects of gastronomy, enology, and agriculture from the 15th to the 19th Centuries. The stock includes books and manuscripts in English, Italian, French, German, and Latin. An appointment is necessary.
Owner/Biography: Giampiero Zazzera and Liz Marcucci, Managers.
Year Founded/History of Bookstore: 1982.
Number of Volumes: 2,000.
Types/Classifications: Finely bound rare books as well as the occasional manifesto and manuscript; rare books from the 15th to 18th Centuries including some fine bindings, limited editions, and signed copies.
General Subject Areas: Agriculture, Enology, Gastronomy, Herbals.
Other Specialties: Books in English, Italian, French, German, and Latin.
Mail/Telephone Orders; Credit Cards: Both; telephone orders from regular clients. Cash with order if not already a Hillman Books customer. No credit cards.
Business Hours: Monday through Friday 10:00 AM - 5:00 PM; appointment necessary.
Parking Facilities: Street parking.
Catalogue: Published 2 times per year; lists also published 2 times per year.
Collections/Individual Items Purchased: Both.

849
Hobson's Choice Books
511 Runnymede Avenue
Jenkintown, Pennsylvania 19046 (215) 884-4853

Hobson's Choice Books carries hardbound books in fine condition, prints, and ephemera. It is located in a private residence and visits must be arranged by appointment.
How to Get There: The shop is 3 blocks from Route 611 on the Jenkintown N.E. line.
Owner/Biography: Jane Hobson Walker. Ms. Walker was employed by the Jenkintown Library for 25 years and did graduate library study at Drexel University.
Year Founded/History of Bookstore: 1979.
Number of Volumes: 1,200.
Types/Classifications: Hardbound, prints, ephemera, first editions, fine bindings, out-of-print, association copies, press books, signed copies, presentation copies, limited editions, color plate books, illustrated books.
General Subject Areas: Biography, Books About Books, Literature, Local History.
Author Specialties: Christopher Morley; Book Illustrators.
Mail/Telephone Orders; Credit Cards: Both. Check with order. No credit cards.
Business Hours: By appointment only.
Special Features: Search service.
Catalogue: Published 1 to 2 times per year.
Collections/Individual Items Purchased: Both.

850
J. Howard Woolmer - Rare Books
Marienstein Road
Revere, Pennsylvania 18953   (215) 847-5074

Mr. Woolmer specializes in twentieth century literature and operates from private premises. An appointment is imperative.

How to Get There: The premises are located one hour north of Philadelphia and two hours west of New York City. Call for precise directions.

Owner/Biography: J. Howard Woolmer. Mr. Woolmer opened his business in New York City in 1961. He later moved to upstate New York and in 1979 to Bucks County, Pennsylvania.

Year Founded/History of Bookstore: 1961.

Number of Volumes: Several thousand volumes, but varies.

Types/Classifications: First editions, presentation copies, fine bindings, out-of-print, association copies, press books, signed copies, limited editions.

General Subject Areas: Twentieth Century Literature.

Specific Specialties: Hogarth Press (London), Poetry Bookshop (London).

Mail/Telephone Orders; Credit Cards: Both. No credit cards.

Business Hours: Monday through Friday 9:00 AM - 5:00 PM by appointment.

Parking Facilities: Parking on premises.

Special Features: Appraisal service. Mr. Woolmer is also a bibliographer and publishes some poetry.

Catalogue: Published 3 to 4 times annually.

Collections/Individual Items Purchased: Both.

Booksellers' Memberships: Antiquarian Booksellers Association (London), Antiquarian Booksellers Association of America.

851
John F. Warren, Bookseller
1807 Chestnut Street
Philadelphia, Pennsylvania 19103   (215) 561-6422

This bookstore maintains probably the largest collection of books on the Fine Arts in Philadelphia, and one of the largest such collections in the country. Its strength lies in books on painting, sculpture, art history, art reference, antiques, and photography, with a particularly large selection of monographs on artists. In addition to the standard art reference books, the shop has an in-depth knowledge of and inventory in ephemera, exhibition catalogues, and original material pertaining to American art and artists of all periods.

How to Get There: The bookstore is located conveniently in the "Center City" Philadelphia, one block from Rittenhouse Square, in a cozy second floor space of about 400 square feet. Free coffee is offered.

Owner/Biography: John F. Warren, owner, had a background in American art before deciding to enter the antiquarian book trade. He proudly declares that he has no aspirations other than offering desirable art books in good condition at reasonable prices.

Year Founded/History of Bookstore: Founded in 1979, the bookstore has from the beginning specialized in art books with occasional forays into 19th Century color plate books and fine press books.

Number of Volumes: 5,000.

Types/Classifications: Used and Rare Art History and Monographs, Art Exhibition Catalogues, Rare Pamphlets on American Art, Fine Press Books, Illustrated Books, Artists Books.

General Subject Areas: Antiques, Art, Biography, Critical Studies, Graphic Arts, Painting, Photography, Sculpture.

Specific Specialties: American Painting, American Sculpture, American Graphic Arts of the 19th and Early 20th Centuries.

Mail/Telephone Orders; Credit Cards: Both; see below regarding mail order catalogues; no credit cards. The bookstore features an active mail order service.

Business Hours: Monday through Friday 10:00 AM - 5:00 PM.

Parking Facilities: Street parking (difficult); parking lot 1/2 block away on Chestnut Street.

Special Features: The bookstore publishes occasional monographs on 19th Century American Artists. A want list of client's book needs is maintained and checked regularly. The owner says: "Ours is a small, personalized service; no grumpy, disinterested sales clerks."

Catalogue: Mail order catalogues are issued 3 or 4 times a year on European, British, and American Art and Antiques; shorter lists are produced several times a year.
Collections/Individual Items Purchased: Both.

852
Last Hurrah Bookshop
937 Memorial Avenue
Williamsport, Pennsylvania 17701 (717) 327-9338

The bookstore is a general out-of-print shop, stocking titles in many fields. Its specialties include 20th Century American politics and modern fiction. Located in a residential area, the shop has a cozy, informal atmosphere, and contains approximately 600 square feet of space. Coffee is also a specialty.

How to Get There: Williamsport is located 18 miles north of I-80 on I-180. The motorist should take the Maynard Street exit and turn right. Go to the end of Maynard Street and turn left on 4th Street, then right at 5th Avenue, then the first right onto Memorial Avenue. The bookstore is the third house on the right.

Owner/Biography: Andrew and Linda Winiarczyk.

Year Founded/History of Bookstore: 1982.

Number of Volumes: 15,000.

Types/Classifications: Hardbound, paperback, uncorrected proofs, magazines, first editions, out-of-print, proof copies, signed books, color plate books.

General Subject Areas: American Politics, Biography, European History, Occult, Political Ephemera, Religion, Science Fiction and Fantasy, War History.

Specific Specialties: Kennedy Family, Kennedy Administration, Political Assassinations.

Mail/Telephone Orders; Credit Cards: Both; personal check with order; no credit cards.

Business Hours: Wednesday and Friday 9:00 AM - 6:00 PM, or by appointment.

Parking Facilities: Street, additional parking behind shop.

Special Features: Search service.

Collections/Individual Items Purchased: Both.

853
Liberty Bookshop
2 Liberty Avenue
Carlisle, Pennsylvania 17013 (717) 245-2933

The bookstore is located in historic Carlisle, Pennsylvania. The original Victorian store front welcomes bibliophiles and readers alike. The shop features a fine selection of used, out-of-print, and rare titles. Visitors are encouraged to "pull up a chair and make yourself at home." The shop contains 1,000 square feet of space.

How to Get There: The shop is situated near the main square, just off Hanover Street. Carlisle is 20 miles west of Harrisburg, just off the Pensylvania Turnpike (Exit 16), and Interstate 81.

Owner/Biography: Diane Kallmann.

Year Founded/History of Bookstore: The bookstore was founded in January 1983, and has doubled in size in a year.

Number of Volumes: 10,000.

Types/Classifications: Hardbound, paperback, ephemera, used, out-of-print, rare.

General Subject Areas: General.

Specific Specialties: History, Military History, Outdoors, Fly Fishing, Antiques, Architecture.

Mail/Telephone Orders; Credit Cards: Both; no credit cards.

Business Hours: Monday through Saturday 10:00 AM - 5:00 PM; Friday evening until 7:00 PM; other times, by appointment. Home telephone for appointments: (717) 245-0716.

Parking Facilities: Street, parking lots.

Catalogue: Occasionally.

Collections/Individual Items Purchased: Both.

854
Light of Parnell Bookshop
3511 Mercersburg Road
Mercersburg, Pennsylvania 17236   (717) 328-3478

The bookstore is located within sight of Mt. Parnell, the subject of a hard to obtain post-Civil War novel, "The Light of Parnell." The mountain is a picturesque knob of the Tuscarora Mountains, part of the Allegheny range. The area is rich in Indian lore, Pre-Revolutionary history, and Civil War battlefields. The shop contains 600 square feet of space.

How to Get There: The shop is located 4 miles north of Mercersburg, Pennsylvania on Rt. 416, near the village of Markes, and 12 miles west of Chambersburg. If driving Interstate 81, take Exit 3 (Greencastle) or Exit 6 (Chambersburg).

Owner/Biography: Nathan and Marian Heckman.

Year Founded/History of Bookstore: Founded in 1972, the bookstore grew out of a hobby and the owners' love of good old books.

Number of Volumes: Several thousand.

Types/Classifications: Hardbound, first editions, out-of-print, signed copies, color plate books.

General Subject Areas: American Indians, Americana, Biography, Civil War (U.S.), Early Pennsylvania History, Franklin County (PA) History.

Author Specialties: Jesse Stuart, Zane Grey, Gene Stratton Porter, Grace Livingston Hill, Jack London, Horatio Alger, L.M. Montgomery, Emma Southworth.

Mail/Telephone Orders; Credit Cards: Both; cash with order, postage extra; libraries billed; no credit cards.

Business Hours: Weekends and evenings, by appointment only.

Parking Facilities: Ample private parking.

Special Features: Search service.

Collections/Individual Items Purchased: Both.

Booksellers' Memberships: Chambersburg Area Booksellers Association.

855
Lincoln Way Books
136 Lincoln Way
Chambersburg, Pennsylvania 17201   (717) 264-7120

A general bookstore featuring used and out-of-print stock, it contains 560 square feet of space.

How to Get There: If driving, take I-81 to Exit 6 at Lincoln Way, west to the Square in Chambersburg; the shop is two blocks beyond the square.

Owner/Biography: William B. Earley.

Year Founded/History of Bookstore: 1977.

Number of Volumes: 20,000.

Types/Classifications: Hardbound, paperback, magazines, ephemera, autographs, maps, used, out-of-print, first editions, press books, limited editions, fine bindings, small press books.

General Subject Areas: Anthropology, Architecture, Art, Aviation, Biography, Boating, Children's Books, Cinema, Classics, Cookbooks, Eastern Religion, Fiction, Fishing, General Non-Fiction, History, Horror, Humor, Hunting, Industry, Literature, Medicine, Music, Mystery, Mysticism, Natural History, Philosophy, Photography, Poetry, Psychology, Reference, Science Fiction and Fantasy, Sports, Theater, Travel, War, Westerns.

Specific Specialties: Pennsylvania History, Modern Literature.

Author Specialties: Black Mountain Authors, "Beat" Authors.

Mail/Telephone Orders; Credit Cards: Both; cash with order plus postage due; the shop will pay insurance on orders of $25 or more; no credit cards,

Business Hours: Monday, Tuesday, Thursday 11:00 AM - 5:00 PM; Wednesday 11:00 AM - 2:00 PM; Friday 11:00 AM - 6:00 PM; Saturday 11:00 AM - 3:00 PM.

Parking Facilities: Street parking on both sides of Lincoln Way.

Special Features: Search service, appraisals.

Catalogue: List published once a year.

Collections/Individual Items Purchased: Both.

Booksellers' Memberships: Chambersburg Area Booksellers.
Miscellaneous: As a sideline, the shop carries used or out-of-print 33 1/3 and 45 RPM record albums.

856
Obsolescence
24 Chambersburg Street
Gettysburg, Pennsylvania 17325   (717) 334-8634

The bookstore, in historic downtown Gettysburg, Pennsylvania, offers a wide selection of antiquarian and out-of-print books. In addition to an extensive general line of out-of-print titles, there is a wide selection of Civil War books, Americana, Pennsylvania German literature, theological books, and ephemera. The store contains 3,400 square feet of space.

How to Get There: The shop is located on Route 30 in quaint downtown historic Gettysburg, just 1/2 block west of the town square.

Owner/Biography: Donald and Joan Hinks, owners, were raised in the Akron, Ohio area. Mr. Hinks received the Bachelor of Science degree in Mechanical Engineering from the University of Akron. Following several years as an engineer Mr. Hinks attended Grace Theological Seminary, receiving the Master of Divinity degree. Following a pastorate in Hanover, Pennsylvania, the Hinks moved to nearby Gettysburg and opened their business in 1972.

Year Founded/History of Bookstore: The antiquarian book trade for the owners began in 1972 as a small sideline to their Christian bookstore. Used and out-of-print religious books were made available to the pastors and religious scholars in the area. The purchase of 50,000 books from the estate of an antiquarian bookseller became the basis for a full line antiquarian bookstore, the only open shop of its type in south central Pennsylvania at that time. Steady growth over the years has made the bookstore one of the fine antiquarian bookstores in the Pennsylvania area.

Number of Volumes: 40,000.

Types/Classifications: Hardbound, magazines, autographs, ephemera, out-of-print, first editions, leather bound books, broadsides printed in America.

General Subject Areas: Abraham Lincoln, Civil War (U.S.), Fiction, Literature, Pennsylvania German Material, Religion.

Specific Specialties: Gettysburg (PA), German Language Books, Almanacs; Bretheren Church: History, Writings, and Hymn Books; Pennsylvania German Society Publications Pre-1840 German Imprints.

Author Specialties: Elsie Singmaster, Grace Livingston Hill, Helen Martin, Zane Grey.

Mail/Telephone Orders; Credit Cards: Both; no credit cards.

Business Hours: Monday through Thursday, Saturday 9:00 AM - 5:00 PM; Friday 9:00 AM - 8:00 PM; closed Sunday.

Parking Facilities: Street.

Special Features: Search service.

Catalogue: Yearly.

Collections/Individual Items Purchased: Both.

857
Palinurus Antiquarian Books
P.O. Box 15923
Philadelphia, Pennsylvania 19103   (215) 735-2970

Palinurus Antiquarian Books specializes in books printed before 1850 in science, medicine, and Americana plus literature and general books before 1800. Visits can be arranged by appointment only.

Owner/Biography: John Hellebrand.

Number of Volumes: 3,000.

Types/Classifications: First editions.

General Subject Areas: Americana, Medicine, Science.

Mail/Telephone Orders; Credit Cards: Both. No credit cards.

Business Hours: By appointment Monday through Friday 10:00 AM - 4:30 PM.

Catalogue: Published 3 times per year.
Collections/Individual Items Purchased: Both.
Booksellers' Memberships: Antiquarian Booksellers Association of America, International League of Antiquarian Booksellers.

858
Quadrant Book Mart
20 North Third Street
Easton, Pennsylvania 18042   (215) 252-1188

The bookstore is located in a restored brick building just off the main square of Easton, Pennsylvania. The stock is displayed on two floors. The premises also contain an intimate coffeehouse featuring espresso, cappuccino, and fine pastries.
How to Get There: Take the 4th Street Exit from Route 22; Easton is across the Delaware River from Phillipsburg, New Jersey and 16 miles east of Allentown, Pennsylvania.
Owner/Biography: Richard Epstein.
Year Founded/History of Bookstore: 1977.
Number of Volumes: 75,000.
Types/Classifications: Hardbound, out-of-print, rare, paperback, first editions.
General Subject Areas: Americana, Anthracite Mining, Biography, Canals, Fiction, New Jersey, Pennsylvania, World History.
Mail/Telephone Orders; Credit Cards: Both. Visa and Mastercard.
Business Hours: Monday, Wednesday, Thursday, Saturday 9:30 AM - 5:30 PM; Tuesday and Friday 9:30 AM - 9:00 PM; closed Sunday.
Parking Facilities: Business parking lot.
Collections/Individual Items Purchased: Both.

859
Ray Riling Arms Books Co.
6844 Gorsten Street
Philadelphia, Pennsylvania 19119   (215) 438-2456

This is a mail order business specializing in out-of-print, used, and rare books on firearms and hunting.
Owner/Biography: Joseph Riling.
Year Founded/History of Bookstore: 1945. Mr. Riling has been in business at the same location since its founding.
Number of Volumes: Over 10,000.
Types/Classifications: Hardbound, ephemera, first editions, fine bindings, out-of-print, association copies, press books, signed copies, presentation copies, limited editions, color plate books.
General Subject Areas: Firearms, Hunting.
Mail/Telephone Orders; Credit Cards: Both. No credit cards.
Business Hours: Monday through Friday 9:00 AM - 4:30 PM.
Parking Facilities: Street parking.
Catalogue: Published 4 times per year.
Collections/Individual Items Purchased: Both.

860
Rittenhouse Book Store
1706 Rittenhouse Square
Philadelphia, Pennsylvania 19103   (215) 545-6072

This bookstore specializes in medical and allied health books, both current and out-of-print. It occupies 900 square feet of space.
Owner/Biography: Richard W. Foster.

Year Founded/History of Bookstore: 1946.
Number of Volumes: 6,000.
Types/Classifications: Hardbound, paperback, current, out-of-print.
General Subject Areas: Allied Health, Medical.
Mail/Telephone Orders; Credit Cards: Both. Visa and Mastercard accepted.
Business Hours: Monday through Saturday 9:00 AM - 5:00 PM.
Catalogue: Catalogue published.
Collections/Individual Items Purchased: Both.

861
Robert F. Batchelder
1 West Butler Avenue
Ambler, Pennsylvania 19002   (215) 643-1430

Robert F. Batchelder specializes in American and European history. It is advisable to make an appointment for a visit.
How to Get There: Located in suburban Philadelphia, the shop is one block from the Ambler station of the Reading Railroad; near Exit 26 of the Pennsylvania Turnpike.
Owner/Biography: Robert F. Batchelder.
Types/Classifications: First editions, fine bindings, out-of-print, association copies, press books, inscribed books, limited editions.
General Subject Areas: American and European History.
Specific Specialties: Autograph letters, manuscripts, and documents in virtually all fields of interest throughout American and European history; included are statesmen and political figures, Presidents of the United States, signers of the Declaration of Independence; literary, musical, scientific, military, and other fields of interest.
Mail/Telephone Orders; Credit Cards: Both. No credit cards.
Business Hours: Daily 9:30 AM - 4:00 PM (advisable to have an appointment).
Parking Facilities: Public parking lot.
Catalogue: Published 5 times per year.
Collections/Individual Items Purchased: Both.
Booksellers' Memberships: Antiquarian Booksellers Association of America, Mansucript Society.

862
Schoyer's Books
1404 South Negley Avenue
Pittsburgh, Pennsylvania 15217   (412) 521-8464

Schoyer's is devoted almost entirely to out-of-print books. It occupies a first floor and basement in which volumes are arranged by a wide range of topics. Emphasis is on Americana with specialization on the unusual and hard-to-find. Notable collections located on the first floor are on Western Pennsylvania and the various states, fine editions, first editions plus the arts. Geography, fiction, U.S. wars, and many other topics are displayed downstairs. The store occupies 9,000 square feet of space.
How to Get There: The bookstore is located in the Squirrel Hill district in the eastern part of Pittsburgh. For the traveler it may be reached most easily by turning off the Parkway East at the Squirrel Hill exit. Parkway East may be reached by exiting the Pennsylvania Turnpike at Exit 6.
Owner/Biography: Maxine A. Schoyer and William T. Schoyer. Maxine and Will Schoyer both have had extensive careers in journalism, advertising, and public relations. They founded Schoyer's Books by purchasing an old store in downtown Pittsburgh more than 30 years ago.
Year Founded/History of Bookstore: 1953. Schoyer's Books was born when the Schoyer's purchased the old Seifert Bookstore which was in one of the few buildings in downtown Pittsburgh that survived the great fire of 1845. The extensive collection of Seifert books filled 3 floors. A large portion of the stock had to be abandoned in 1963 due to water damage from a fire next door. The building was so weakened it was torn down and the surviving stock was moved to Wilkensburg and some years later to the present Squirrel Hill location.

Number of Volumes: 30,000.

Types/Classifications: Hardbound only; some magazines, pamphlets, ephemera, postcards, trade cards, trade catalogs, almanacs, some manuscripts, some autographs and photographs, some related antiques and prints; first editions, fine bindings, special press books, many color plate books, early prints of various cities, out-of-print.

General Subject Areas: Americana, Architecture, Art, Biography, Children's Books, Civil War (U.S.), Classics, Cookbooks, Crafts, Gardening, History, Humor, Marine, Movies, Music, Mysteries, Poetry, Religion, Scholarly Works, School Books, Science Industry, Sports, Theater, Travel, True Crime, World Wars I and II.

Mail/Telephone Orders; Credit Cards: Both. No credit cards.

Business Hours: Monday, Tuesday, Thursday, Friday 11:00 AM - 4:00 PM; other days or hours by appointment.

Parking Facilities: Street parking.

Catalogue: Published irregularly.

Collections/Individual Items Purchased: Both.

863
Sessler's II
1310 Walnut Street
Philadelphia, Pennsylvania 19107   (215) 735-4434

Sessler's II began in 1980 as a table of used books outside the original Sessler's. The demand was so great that within the year it had opened an additional store with 1,200 square feet of space. With its overflowing shelves and tables, and comfortable antiques, it is a popular haunt for tourists, dealers, and booklovers. The shop features remainders, out-of-print, and rare volumes at competitive prices sold with the same personalized service long synonymous with the Sessler's name. See also: W. GRAHAM ARADER III, King of Prussia, Pennsylvania.

How to Get There: The bookstore is just a few blocks from any of the fine hotels in Center City Philadelphia. From City Hall it is three blocks south, one block east.

Owner/Biography: W. Graham Arader III.

Year Founded/History of Bookstore: Charles Sessler started his historic business in 1882 by selling Bibles. Over the years he built up a respected rare book business, specializing in Dickens material, among other interests. For many years the rare book department operated along with the new book department at 1308 Walnut Street, and even featured outside tables of used books beginning in 1980, but in July 1981 a new store was opened next door at 1310 Walnut to house used and rare books.

Number of Volumes: 20,000.

Types/Classifications: Hardbound, used, rare, out-of-print, selected used paperbacks, some noteworthy remainders. Occasionally prints, photographs, and autographs. First editions, fine bindings, limited editions, fine leather bindings, complete works.

General Subject Areas: American Adventure, Anthropology, Archaeology, Architecture, Art, Belles Lettres, Biography, Book Publishing, Books About Books, Children's Books, Classics in Original Languages and in Translations, Cookbooks, Crafts, Delaware History, Drama, Health, Humor, Military History, Music, Mysteries, Occult, Pennsylvania History, Performing Arts, Philadelphia History, Philosophy, Photography, Poetry, Reference, Religion, Science Fiction and Fantasy, Transportation, Travel, True Crime, War, World History.

Specific Specialties: Foreign Language Titles in German, French, Italian, Slavic.

Mail/Telephone Orders; Credit Cards: Both. Visa, Mastercard, American Express.

Business Hours: Monday through Friday 10:00 AM - 6:00 PM; Saturday 10:00 AM - 5:00 PM.

Parking Facilities: Street and nearby public parking lots and garages.

Special Features: Search service at $3 per title; hot spiced cider and home-baked cookies; browsing encouraged.

Catalogue: Published occasionally.

Collections/Individual Items Purchased: Both.

864
Tuckers
2236 Murray Avenue
Pittsburgh, Pennsylvania 15217   (412) 521-0249

The shop is a pleasant, old-worldly browsing bookstore, featuring good general stock, out-of-print, rare, and scholarly books. A carpeted floor, stools to sit on while browsing, and friendly assistance are available when (but only when) wanted. These features make the shop an oasis of quiet delight for booklovers.

How to Get There: Take Route 376 from Pittsburgh to the Squirrel Hill Exit; proceed north on Murray Avenue about half a block.

Owner/Biography: Esther J. Tucker, owner, was born in London, England. She received her B.S. from the University of Pittsburgh and M.S. from Purdue University. She is a sometimes speech and hearing therapist, occasional freelance writer and lecturer. A lifelong booklover, she has been a bookseller since 1972.

Year Founded/History of Bookstore: 1972.

Number of Volumes: 10,000.

Types/Classifications: Good general out-of-print and rare scholarly books, primarily hardbound; some graphics, much miscellaneous ephemera, illustrated books.

General Subject Areas: Adventure, American History, Anthropology, Art, Biography, Black Literature, Botany, Children's Books, Christian Religions, Collecting, Dance, Drama, Drink, Earth Sciences, Eastern Religions, Economics, Fishing, Food, Gardening, Hobbies, Home Arts, Humor, Hunting, Judaica, Law, Letters, Literature, Medicine, Music, Mysteries, Natural History, Outdoors, Philosophy, Poetry, Psychology, Regional Americana, Science Fiction and Fantasy, Social History, Sports, Swashbucklers, Technology, Transportation, Travel, Weapons, Westerns, Women's Studies, World History.

Specific Specialties: Pittsburgh, Western Pennsylvania.

Mail/Telephone Orders; Credit Cards: Both; no credit cards.

Business Hours: Daily 1:00 PM - 5:00 PM; Saturday 10:00 AM - 5:00 PM; other times by appointment.

Parking Facilities: Street, nearby public lot.

Special Features: Search service, appraisals.

Catalogue: Published occasionally by subject areas.

Collections/Individual Items Purchased: Individual items regularly, collections occasionally.

865
Used Book Store
474 West Main Street
Kutztown, Pennsylvania 19530   (215) 683-9055

The bookstore is a small white structure near the campus of Kutztown University of Pennsylvania. It contains 1,200 square feet of space plus 600 square feet of storage. The front room is primarily fiction paperbacks of all major categories. The next two rooms are non-fiction as are most of the rear stack areas. Books are arranged by category and alphabetically therein.

How to Get There: Kutztown is about midway between Allentown and Reading in eastern Pennsylvania. U.S. 78 (sometimes also labeled Route 22) is about six miles north of the city, running from New York through Harrisburg, Pennsylvania, and beyond. From 78 take Route 737 south at Krumsville. The bookstore is located at the west end of the borough of Kutztown, on Main Street, Route 222 (do not take the Kutztown bypass).

Owner/Biography: James H. Tinsman, owner, is a professor of anthropology at Kutztown University of Pennsylvania. A graduate of the Universities of Pennsylvania and Colorado, he has been a collector for years in the areas of anthropology, mystery-detective fiction, true crime, and antiquarian paperbacks. The store is a culmination of a lifetime of interest in books. The owner is planning to make the store a second career upon retirement.

Year Founded/History of Bookstore: The bookstore was opened in 1979 at the present location by the current owner. The area of the store was more than doubled in mid-1980.

Number of Volumes: 40,000.

Types/Classifications: Hardbound, paperback, some scholarly magazines, out-of-print, antiquarian paperbacks (pre-1960), paperback bestsellers.

General Subject Areas: Biography, Children's Books, Classics, Detective, Economics, History, Humor, Literature, Mystery, Philosophy, Poetry, Religion, Science Fiction and Fantasy, Social Sciences.

Mail/Telephone Orders; Credit Cards: Both. Require usual postage and handling charges; shipment to new customers after personal check clears. No credit cards.

Business Hours: Tuesday, Wednesday, Friday 2:00 PM - 6:00 PM; Saturday 10:00 AM - 5:00 PM.
Parking Facilities: Street parking without difficulty; small rear lot for loading.
Special Features: Will accept want lists.
Catalogue: Irregularly published.
Collections/Individual Items Purchased: Both.
Miscellaneous: Dealer discounts.

866
Valley Books
111 South Elmer Avenue
Sayre, Pennsylvania 18840   (717) 888-9785

The owner describes the shop as a "typical small town used and rare bookstore." The store carries a general stock of most all subjects, but specializes in art books; it contains 1,000 square feet of space.

How to Get There: The store is one mile south of Waverly, New York, off Route 17.
Owner/Biography: Lew Dabe, owner, has had as his sole occupation for the last 25 years the buying and selling of fine books, paintings, prints, and antiques.
Year Founded/History of Bookstore: Founded in New York City in 1960, the bookstore was moved to Sayre, Pennsylvania in 1979.
Number of Volumes: 10,000.
Types/Classifications: Hardbound, autographs, ephemera.
General Subject Areas: General.
Specific Specialties: Art Books.
Mail/Telephone Orders; Credit Cards: No mail or telephone orders; no credit cards.
Business Hours: Monday through Wednesday 10:00 AM - 5:00 PM; other days open by appointment.
Parking Facilities: Street.
Special Features: Ninety percent of the business is wholesale to other dealers.
Collections/Individual Items Purchased: Both.

867
W. Graham Arader III
c/o Charles Sessler, Inc.
1308 Walnut Street
Philadelphia, Pennsylvania 19107

See: W. GRAHAM ARADER III, King of Prussia, Pennsylvania.

868
W. Graham Arader III
1000 Boxwood Court
King of Prussia, Pennsylvania 19406   (215) 825-6570

Working out of seven branch locations in as many cities across the country, the business specializes in rare books, atlases, maps, and prints. The atlas collection in particular is perhaps the most extensive offering of this material in America. In addition to the rare books and atlases there is available to the visitor, in specially constructed cases and organized by subject, a collection of maps and prints that is probably unrivaled in America for depth and range of subject matter. In the field of natural history there are prints of birds, florals, animals, shells, trees, and fish. Maps range from the 15th through the 19 Century and cover every area of the world and all aspects of discovery and exploration. In addition, there are sailing prints, naval battles, Currier & Ives, an extensive collection of Western and American Indian prints, plus steamboat, railroad, and sporting prints. Browsing is encouraged. See below under MISCELLANEOUS for branch locations. The shop at King of Prussia is housed in a large, very old home. The original part of the house still remains, and was built in 1758. Several additions have been made throughout the years. The current name "Ballygomingo" was given to the house in 1821 along with an addition of a porticoed wing and columns, both name and architecture reflecting a Southern influence.

How to Get There: From the Pennsylvania Turnpike take the Valley Forge Exit 24, east on the Schuylkill Expressway (Route 76) to the Gulph Mills Exit 27. At the bottom of the ramp a sharp left to Route 320 north to Dechert Drive then right to the house.

Owner/Biography: W. Graham Arader III.

Types/Classifications: Hardbound books, maps, prints, color plate books.

General Subject Areas: Americana, Atlases, Books Related to Maps, Books Related to Prints, Natural History.

Mail/Telephone Orders; Credit Cards: Both. Visa, Mastercard.

Business Hours: Monday through Saturday 9:00 AM - 5:00 PM; other times by appointment.

Catalogue: Four to six times a year.

Collections/Individual Items Purchased: Both.

Miscellaneous: In addition to the main office in King of Prussia, Pennsylvania, branch locations, all under the name of W. Graham Arader III, are as follows: (1) 23 East 74th Street, Suite 5A, New York, NY 10021; (2) 2800 Virginia Street, Houston, TX 77098; (3) 1317 Berwick Avenue, Atlanta, GA 30306; (4) 110 East Delaware Place, Suite 1504, Chicago, IL 60601; (5) 560 Sutter Street, San Francisco, CA 94102; (6) Charles Sessler, Inc., 1308 Walnut Street, Philadelphia, PA 19107. (7) Sessler's II, 1310 Walnut Street, Philadelphia, PA 19107.

869
William H. Allen, Bookseller

2031 Walnut Street
Philadelphia, Pennsylvania 19103 (215) 563-3398

The bookstore is probably the largest used bookstore in the city of Philadelphia, and is located on three full floors of a 19th Century townhouse. It has the only full-time autographs and manuscripts department in the city, as well as a very wide variety of books. All items are catalogued and priced; the store is open for browsing. When planning to visit on the weekend it is urged that one call ahead to confirm that the department desired will be open.

How to Get There: The shop is in the heart of Philadelphia, just off Rittenhouse Square.

Owner/Biography: George Allen and David Szewczyk. Allen is a second generation bookseller, son of the founder of the company. He has been with the firm since 1940, and received the Presidential Citation while with the 101st Airborn in World War II. Szewczyk is an ex-Fulbright Scholar who was chief manuscripts cataloguer at the Rosenbach Foundation prior to joining the firm in 1979.

Year Founded/History of Bookstore: The firm was founded in 1918 in Temple, Pennsylvania, and moved to Philadelphia in 1920. Two other moves within the city occurred before assuming the present location in 1940.

Number of Volumes: 35,000 books, 800 manuscripts and autographs.

Types/Classifications: Hardbound, autographs, manuscripts, broadsides, first editions, signed copies, incunabula, very old books, association copies, rare books.

General Subject Areas: Africa, American History, American Literature, Americana, Books About Books, English History, English Literature, Greek Classics, Latin Americana, Latin Classics, Middle East, Modern European Languages, Orient, Seventeenth Century Books, Sixteenth Century Books, Travels, Voyages.

Mail/Telephone Orders; Credit Cards: Both. No credit cards.

Business Hours: Monday through Friday 8:30 AM - 5:00 PM; Saturday 8:30 AM - 1:00 PM.

Parking Facilities: Street, private lots nearby.

Special Features: The shop believes it is the largest browsing bookstore in the city of Philadelphia.

Catalogue: Five to six specialized catalogues a year.

Collections/Individual Items Purchased: Both.

Booksellers' Memberships: Antiquarian Booksellers Association of America, International League of Antiquarian Booksellers.

870
Young's Olde Book Shoppe
R.D. 5, Box 262
Ligonier, Pennsylvania 15658   (412) 238-7389

Located in a chalet in a pine woods near Fort Ligonier in southwestern Pennsylvania, the shop is surrounded by the ghosts of French and Indian warriors and Royal American and pioneer defenders. It specializes in American and Pennsylvanian history, with subject-arranged stock and a balcony overlooking pine trees.

How to Get There: The store is located off Route 30, then about 1/4 mile on Route 259. Turn left on Matson Road; the store is the first house on the right.

Owner/Biography: Wyatt M. and Nancy L. Young, owners, are native Western Pennsylvanians who trace their love affair with books back to a visit in 1960 with their Uncle Wyatt Martin, a distinguished book dealer in the town of Allen, Kentucky.

Year Founded/History of Bookstore: Founded in 1980, the bookstore is on the same property as the owners' home. Before being converted to a shop the chalet was rented as an apartment.

Number of Volumes: 6,000.

Types/Classifications: Hardbound in most all classifications, including sets.

General Subject Areas: Adventure, Americana, Autobiography, Biography, Birds, Cookbooks, Fiction, Gardening, Juvenile, Poetry, Sports, Travel.

Specific Specialties: Pittsburgh (Pennsylvania), Pennsylvania.

Mail/Telephone Orders; Credit Cards: Both. Cash with order. No credit cards.

Business Hours: Saturday and Sunday, 12:00 Noon - 5:00 PM; any other time by just phoning.

Parking Facilities: Business parking lot.

Special Features: The bookstore specializes in mail order service, and offers free listings. It also offers a free search service and free coffee.

Catalogue: Averages two or three times a year.

Collections/Individual Items Purchased: Individual items only.

RHODE ISLAND

871
Armchair Sailor
Lees Wharf
Newport, Rhode Island 02840   (401) 847-4252

The bookstore is a haven for nautical book lovers and has perhaps one of the largest collections of marine titles, professional texts, new and out-of-print books, in North America. The shop features a computerized book search of over 10,000 titles on two floors, charts and guides for the world, a 250-page bound annual, a self-published maritime bibliography/catalogue. The two floors contain 2,400 square feet of space.

How to Get There: The bookstore is located on Newport's historic waterfront, Lower Thames Street, near the Ark Restaurant and the America's Cup Bakery.

Owner/Biography: Ronald Barr and Jane Parfer, owners, have had an extensive past association with the sea, having spent over six years cruising both sides of the Atlantic. They have developed on-board instructional courses for adults in the subjects of whales, diving, birdlife, sea survival, navigation, etc., in conjunction with the University of Rhode Island, Earthwatch, Hampton Mariners Museum, and Outward Bound. Mark S. Tague is the used book sales manager.

Year Founded/History of Bookstore: 1979.

Number of Volumes: 12,000 in-print titles; 1,200 used and out-of-print books.

Types/Classifications: Hardbound, magazines, first editions, fine bindings, out-of-print, limited editions, color plate books.

General Subject Areas: Maritime, Nautical.

Specific Specialties: Yachting, America's Cup, Singlehanded Sailing, Small Craft Voyaging, Natural History, Sailing Instruction, Exploration, Maritime History, Boat Building, Boat Design, Navigation, Nautical Fiction, Marlinspike Seamanship, Steamboats, Ocean Racing.

Author Specialties: Uffa Fox, C.S. Forester, Sir Francis Chichester, Humphry Barton, Miles Smeeton, E. Keble Chatterton, Irving & Electra Johnson, Harry Pidgeon, C. Fox Smith, Robin Knox Johnston, Dougal Robertson, W.A. Robinson, William Smith, Joseph Conrad.

Other Specialties: Imported books from Australia, New Zealand, Italy, England, South Africa, Azores, Panama, West Indies.

Mail/Telephone Orders; Credit Cards: Both; the bookstore conducts an extensive mail order business throughout the world; Visa, Mastercard, American Express.

Business Hours: Monday through Saturday 10:00 AM - 6:00 PM.

Parking Facilities: Provided.

Special Features: The bookstore publishes a bibliography which is unique in that it is descriptive and very comprehensive for in-print English language marine offerings.

Catalogue: For used books, two times a year; the bibliography, once a year.

Collections/Individual Items Purchased: Both; the bookstore offers a trade-in service against new or used books.

872
Book & Tackle Shop
7 Bay Street
Watch Hill, Rhode Island 02891   (401) 596-0700

Book & Tackle Shop is a unique bookstore where one can buy fishing poles, fish hooks, and fishing lures as well as books on angling, sailing, and science. The shop has been in business for over thirty years and has an extraordinary collection of scarce and out-of-print books on all subjects.

How to Get There: The bookstore is 15 minutes from Interstate 95 at the Connecticut-Rhode Island border.

Owner/Biography: Bernard Ludwig Gordon. Mr. Gordon is the author of over 15 books including "Man and the Sea" and "Secret Lives of Fishes."

Year Founded/History of Bookstore: 1953. Mr. Gordon has been at the same summer location since the beginning of his business. His winter location is 29 Old Colony Road, Chestnut Hill, Massachusetts 02167.

Number of Volumes: 200,000.

Types/Classifications: Hardbound, paperback, postcards, prints, autographs, first editions, out-of-print, limited editions.

General Subject Areas: Angling, Cooking, Medicine, Music, Nature, Sea.

Specific Specialties: Rhode Island, New England.

Author Specialties: Local New England authors.

Mail/Telephone Orders; Credit Cards: Both. Visa accepted.

Business Hours: Summer 9:00 AM to 9:00 PM, seven days a week.

Parking Facilities: Street parking.

Special Features: Publisher of color postcards and 15 books.

Catalogue: Published occasionally.

Collections/Individual Items Purchased: Both.

Booksellers' Memberships: Antiquarian Booksellers Association of America, Massachusetts and Rhode Island Antiquarian Booksellers Association.

Miscellaneous: Appraisals of libraries, estates, and collections for heirs and institutions.

873
Corner Book Shop
418 Spring Street
Newport, Rhode Island 02840

(401) 846-1087

The Corner Book Shop has an interesting general stock of contemporary hardbound and paperback volumes plus a small stock of rare and out-of-print antiquarian material in any field as available.

How to Get There: The shop is located on the corner of Spring and Perry Streets.

Year Founded/History of Bookstore: 1962.

Number of Volumes: 5,000.

Types/Classifications: Hardbound, paperback, rare, out-of-print, first editions, fine bindings, association copies, press books, signed copies, presentation copies, limited editions, color plate books.

General Subject Areas: General.

Mail/Telephone Orders; Credit Cards: No mail or phone orders. No credit cards.

Business Hours: Monday through Saturday 1:00 PM - 5:00 PM and 6:30 PM - 9:00 PM.

Parking Facilities: Street parking.

Collections/Individual Items Purchased: Both.

874
Fortunate Finds Bookstore
16 West Natick Road
Warwick, Rhode Island 02886

(401) 737-8160

The store is the only building on a short part of the street. It has two floors and carries out-of-print hardbound books plus magazines, documents, sheet music, and ephemera.

How to Get There: The bookstore is located near the Warwick Mall.

Owner/Biography: Mildred E. Santille (Longo).

Year Founded/History of Bookstore: 1955.

Number of Volumes: 15,000.

Types/Classifications: Hardbound, magazines, broadsides, autographs, ephemera, documents, sheet music, out-of-print, first editions, illustrations, signed copies, presentation copies, color plate books, trade catalogues.

General Subject Areas: Americana, Biography, Children's Books, County Histories, Genealogy, History, Literature, Poetry.

Specific Specialties: Whaling, Sea Books.

Mail/Telephone Orders; Credit Cards: Both. No credit cards.
Business Hours: Friday and Saturday 9:00 AM - 5:00 PM and by appointment.
Parking Facilities: Ample parking available.
Special Features: Book appraisals; book sales for local libraries; book auctions.
Catalogue: Published 4 times per year.
Collections/Individual Items Purchased: Both.
Booksellers' Memberships: Ephemera Society, Rhode Island Historical Society.

875
Merlin's Closet
166 Valley Street
Providence, Rhode Island 02909   (401) 351-9272

The bookstore is located in what was the manager's office of a former mill/factory complex on Valley Street in the Olneyville section of Providence. A general used bookstore, it offers a wide selection of books for every interest, with specialties in science fiction and fantasy, H.P. Lovecraft, children's series, children's illustrated, religion, and the occult. The store is named after Merlin the Magician and Fibber McGee's fabulous hall closet ("if it's not here look in the closet").

How to Get There: The Olneyville section is the western gateway to Providence, Rhode Island. The shop is in the red brick building with the Coca Cola sign and the bookstore's sign in front, at the intersection of Helm and Valley Streets.

Owner/Biography: Faye Ringel, Elliot Shorter, Gail Eastwood-Stokes. Dr. Ringel earned her PhD. in Compararative Literature/Medieval Studies at Brown University; she brings a love of dark fantasy, H.P. Lovecraft, medieval song, dance, and poetry to the enterprise. Gail Eastwood-Stokes is a free-lance writer/editor and antiquarian book person; her interests lie in fine bindings and American firsts. Elliot Shorter is an ex-college bookstore manager and freelance science fiction book dealer. All three are united in a love of the Arthurian legends and like material.

Year Founded/History of Bookstore: The bookstore was opened in the Fall of 1979 in the Plantations Barn Building in Edward Sulzberger's Plantations Development in the old Port Area at the foot of College Hill, in Providence, Rhode Island. It was moved in March of 1983 to its present location in the center of the Old Mill Complex. The selling area contains 430 square feet of space.

Number of Volumes: 6,000.

Types/Classifications: Hardbound, paperback, most general classifications.

General Subject Areas: American Wars, Biography, Children's Books, Children's Series, Cooking, Crafts, Fiction, Folklore, History, Humor, Medieval Studies, Mysteries, Occult, Philosophy, Poetry, Regional History and Travel, Religion, Science Fiction and Fantasy, Sports, Theater, Westerns.

Specific Specialties: H.P. Lovecraft, Magic, Rhode Island History, Celtic Folklore, King Arthur.

Author Specialties: H.P. Lovecraft, Robert E. Howard, Isaac Asimov, Joseph Lincoln.

Mail/Telephone Orders; Credit Cards: Both; postage, to be paid by customer, must include $1 for the first book, 50 cents for each additional book; Ist Class, Airmail, UPS, Insurance, must be requested; excess costs will be billed; no credit cards.

Business Hours: Closed Monday; Tuesday and Wednesday hours vary; Thursday 6:00 PM - 11:00 PM; Friday and Saturday 10:00 AM - 8:00 PM; Sunday 12:00 Noon - 5:00 PM; best to call first, especially for Tuesday and Wednesday.

Parking Facilities: Business parking lot; street parking limit 2 hours.

Special Features: Search service; tours of Lovecraft country; publishing sideline being planned.

Catalogue: One to two times a year; lists occasionally.

Collections/Individual Items Purchased: Both.

Miscellaneous: Also for sale are Tarot decks and other paraphernalia, some original art and sculpture.

876
Rulon-Miller Books
P.O. Box 2536
Providence, Rhode Island 02906   (401) 351-6330

Rulon-Miller offers rare and fine books from diverse periods and and in diverse fields. Visitors are welcome by appointment.

Owner/Biography: Robert Rulon-Miller, Jr.

Year Founded/History of Bookstore: 1969. The company was founded under the name of The Current Company and was originally located in Bristol, Rhode Island. Mr. Rulon-Miller, Jr. purchased the business from his father in the fall of 1983 and the name was changed to Rulon-Miller Books. Barbara Walzer now operates this branch office in Providence, Rhode Island while the main offices are in Minneapolis, Minnesota.

Number of Volumes: 5,000.

Types/Classifications: Rare and fine books, first editions, fine bindings, association copies, press books, signed and presentation copies, limited editions, prints.

General Subject Areas: Americana, Letters, Literature, Manuscripts, Science, Yachting and Sporting.

Specific Specialties: America's Cup Races, Mountaineering, Polar Material, Rhode Island and Minnesota Material, American Literature (19th Century), Early American Science and Technology.

Author Specialties: Herman Melville, Henry David Thoreau, J.D. Salinger, John Fowles, Ian Fleming, Mark Twain, James Fenimore Cooper, Philip Freneau, John Gardner, Alan Brody.

Mail/Telephone Orders; Credit Cards: Both. Visa and Mastercard accepted.

Business Hours: By appointment only.

Parking Facilities: Street parking.

Catalogue: Published 6 times per year.

Collections/Individual Items Purchased: Both.

Booksellers' Memberships: Antiquarian Booksellers Association of America, International League of Antiquarian Booksellers, Manuscript Society.

877
Sewards' Folly, Books
139 Brook Street
Providence, Rhode Island 02906   (401) 272-4454

The bookstore is located on the ground floor of a fine old house in the College Hill Preservation District of Providence, Rhode Island. The shop contains 1,500 square feet of space.

How to Get There: The shop is about ten blocks from Brown University.

Owner/Biography: Schuyler and Peterkin Seward.

Year Founded/History of Bookstore: 1974.

Number of Volumes: 15,000.

Types/Classifications: Hardbound and paperback books only.

General Subject Areas: General.

Specific Specialties: Scholarly Books in any specialization.

Mail/Telephone Orders; Credit Cards: No credit cards.

Business Hours: Wednesday, Thursday, Friday 12:00 Noon - 8:00 PM; Saturday 9:00 AM - 8:00 PM; Sunday 12:00 Noon - 8:00 PM.

Parking Facilities: Street; is in residential area.

Special Features: Search service.

Collections/Individual Items Purchased: Both.

Booksellers' Memberships: Massachusetts and Rhode Island Antiquarian Booksellers Association.

878
Sign of the Unicorn Bookshop
604 Kingstown Road
Peace Dale, Rhode Island 02883   (401) 789-8912

The bookstore is housed in the 19th Century former office building of the mill owners, the Hazard family. The shop covers all subject areas. The owners describe their stock this way: " Our determining factor is if you can find it in supermarkets or ordinary bookstores, it won't be here." They describe the size as being "large enough to breathe, small enough to feel cozy."

How to Get There: The shop is located on Route 108 near the center of Wakefield, Rhode Island, off Route

1. The University of Rhode Island is three miles north on Route 108 and 138.

Owner/Biography: Mary Jo Munroe and John Romano. "M.J." Munroe is a librarian and appraiser; John Romano is a bookbinder who also runs the Hard Pressed Bindery.

Year Founded/History of Bookstore: Founded in December 1978, the bookstore is on its original site and has its original owners.

Number of Volumes: 16,000.

Types/Classifications: Generally hardbound, some trade paperbacks in specific areas, first editions, out-of-print, limited editions, color plate books.

General Subject Areas: General.

Specific Specialties: Rhode Island, Science Fiction and Fantasy.

Author Specialties: Illustrator Fritz Eichenberg.

Mail/Telephone Orders; Credit Cards: Both; cash with order. No credit cards.

Business Hours: Wednesday through Saturday 10:00 AM - 5:00 PM.

Parking Facilities: Parking lot on small town park.

Special Features: Search service.

Catalogue: Published irregularly.

Collections/Individual Items Purchased: Both.

Booksellers' Memberships: New England Archivists.

Miscellaneous: Appraisals featured. Presentations on binding and rare books available to libraries.

879
Tyson's Old & Rare Books
334 Westminster Street
Providence, Rhode Island 02903 (401) 421-3939

This is a small bookstore with general stock, but with an emphasis on American and British works.

How to Get There: Located in downtown Providence, Rhode Island, the bookstore is 5 minutes from Route I-95. From I-95 North take the Broadway Exit, bear right to Empire Street. From I-95 South take the Atwells Avenue ramp to downtown (left), and Empire Street. Westminster is the third left on Empire Street. The shop is one block east, on the second floor.

Owner/Biography: Mariette P. Bedard.

Year Founded/History of Bookstore: Founded in 1930 in downtown Providence, the bookstore was moved one block to its present location in 1979.

Types/Classifications: Mostly hardbound, broadsides, autographs, ephemera, magazines (usually hardbound magazines), first editions.

General Subject Areas: American Literature, Americana, English History, English Literature, General.

Specific Specialties: Rhode Island, Fall River Line (Old Steamship Line).

Mail/Telephone Orders; Credit Cards: Both. Cash with order; libraries will be billed. No credit cards.

Business Hours: Monday, Tuesday, Thursday, Friday 12:00 Noon - 4:30 PM; Saturday (Winter) 10:00 AM - 2:00 PM; Saturday (Summer) by appointment.

Parking Facilities: Public parking behind the building.

Special Features: Search service.

Catalogue: Published occasionally.

Collections/Individual Items Purchased: Both.

Booksellers' Memberships: Massachusetts and Rhode Island Antiquarian Booksellers Association.

SOUTH CAROLINA

880
Book Dispensary
Dentsville
7359 Two Notch Road
Columbia, South Carolina 29204   (803) 736-4033

See: BOOK DISPENSARY, Decatur (Atlanta), Georgia. This branch contains 4,000 square feet of space.
How to Get There: The bookstore is located between I-20 and Columbia Mall.
Business Hours: Monday through Saturday 10:00 AM - 9:00 PM; Sunday 12:00 Noon - 6:00 PM.

881
Book Dispensary
Boozer Shopping Center
1600 Broad River Road
Columbia, South Carolina 29210   (803) 798-4739

See: BOOK DISPENSARY, Decatur (Atlanta), Georgia. This branch contains 5,000 square feet of space.
Business Hours: Monday through Saturday 10:00 AM - 9:00 PM; Sunday 12:00 Noon - 6:00 PM.

882
Book Dispensary
Landmark Square Shopping Center
6800 Garners Ferry Road
Columbia, South Carolina 29209   (803) 783-4608

See: BOOK DISPENSARY, Decatur (Atlanta), Georgia. This branch contains 2,400 square feet of space.
How to Get There: The Landmark Shopping Center is located across from the VA Hospital.
Business Hours: Monday through Saturday 10:00 AM - 9:00 PM; Sunday 12:00 Noon - 6:00 PM.

883
DuPriest's Bookshop
1230 Pendleton Street
Columbia, South Carolina 29201   (803) 256-2756

This is a small shop with select stock located directly across from the University of South Carolina in the lobby of Cornell Arms Apartments.
Owner/Biography: Maggie DuPriest. Ms. DuPriest is a knowledgeable book dealer with 23 years in the trade.
Year Founded/History of Bookstore: 1961. The bookshop has been located previously in Miami, Florida and New York City.
Number of Volumes: 5,000.
Types/Classifications: Hardbound, scholarly out-of-print, rare, press books.
General Subject Areas: Art, Literature, Music, Southern History, Theater.
Mail/Telephone Orders; Credit Cards: Both. Visa and Mastercard accepted.

Business Hours: Tuesday through Friday 10:00 AM - 5:30 PM; Saturday 1:00 PM - 5:00 PM.
Parking Facilities: Street.
Catalogue: Published occasionally.
Collections/Individual Items Purchased: Both.
Booksellers' Memberships: Antiquarian Booksellers Association of America.

884
Norm Burleson, Bookseller
104 First Avenue
Spartanburg, South Carolina 29302   (803) 853-8845

Mr. Burleson operates a mail order only business dealing exclusively in religious books.
Owner/Biography: Norm Burleson. Mr. Burleson has 16 years' experience in religious bookselling.
Year Founded/History of Bookstore: 1979.
Types/Classifications: Out-of-print.
General Subject Areas: Religious Books.
Mail/Telephone Orders; Credit Cards: Both. No credit cards.
Business Hours: Not open for visitors; mail order only.
Catalogue: Catalogue published.
Collections/Individual Items Purchased: Both.
Booksellers' Memberships: Southeastern Bibliophile Society.

TENNESSEE

885
Andover Square Books
Kingston Pike Antique Mall
5404 Kingston Pike
Knoxville, Tennessee 37919

(615) 693-8984

The bookstore consists of two large booths at the Kingston Pike Antique Mall, for a total of 800 square feet of space. It features Americana and Tennessee materials, children's books, and 17th, 18th, and 19th Century items.

How to Get There: If driving, take the Bearden/Papermill exit from I-40/I-75W; exit to Kingston Pike and turn left heading east; after four blocks is the Mall on the right; look for a long one-story building.

Owner/Biography: G. A. and M. R. Yeomans, owners, are both college professors, former book collectors, and have worked in and with college libraries for years.

Year Founded/History of Bookstore: 1978.

Number of Volumes: 4,500.

Types/Classifications: Hardbound, magazines, pamphlets, newspapers, first editions, limited editions, color plate illustrated classics and children's books, press copies, signed copies, 17th and 18th Century items, leather bound.

General Subject Areas: American History, American Literature, Art, Biography, Children's Books, Classics, Detective, Drama, Early Americana, English Literature, European History, European Literature, Fiction, Homemaking, Law, Medicine, Philosophy, Poetry, Recreation, Religion, Sports, Travel.

Specific Specialties: Tennessee, Elbert Hubbard, George MacDonald, Abraham Lincoln, Presidential Biography.

Author Specialties: William Faulkner, Ernest Hemingway, Willa Cather, George MacDonald, Elbert Hubbard, James Whitcomb Riley, Harold Bell Wright, Pearl Buck, Kenneth Roberts, Edward Everett Hale, Thornton Wilder, Oscar Wilde, Robert Burns, George McCutcheon.

Other Specialties: Seventeenth and Eighteenth Century Classics, Eighteenth Century French and German Works.

Mail/Telephone Orders; Credit Cards: Both; personal check with orders, except for college or public libraries which may order by purchase order. The bookstore pays shipping costs. Visa, American Express, and Mastercard accepted at the bookstore only.

Business Hours: Monday through Saturday 10:00 AM - 6:00 PM; Sunday 1:00 PM - 6:00 PM.

Parking Facilities: Business parking lot; ample space.

Special Features: Free search service; sell through the mails.

Catalogue: Once a month.

Collections/Individual Items Purchased: Both.

Miscellaneous: Exhibit at one or two book fairs annually.

886
Battery Press, Inc.
2506 Franklin Road
Nashville, Tennessee 37204

(615) 298-1401

The Battery Press, Inc. occupies approximately 800 square feet of public-access area with new, reprint, and out-of-print books on military, aviation, and naval subjects.

How to Get There: Nearest interstate highway is I-65 South. To reach the shop, exit at Wedgewood Exit, turn towards west and then turn left at first light (Franklin Road). Travel south approximately 1 mile. The shop is on the second story of 2-story building, directly across from York Motel.

Owner/Biography: Richard S. Gardner.

Year Founded/History of Bookstore: 1976.
Number of Volumes: 2,000.
Types/Classifications: Hardbound, reprints.
General Subject Areas: Military (1900 to Present).
Specific Specialties: Military Unit Histories, Airborne/Elite Units, Vietnam War, Military Books (1900 to Present).
Mail/Telephone Orders; Credit Cards: Both. American Express, Visa and Mastercard.
Business Hours: Monday through Friday 9:00 AM to 4:00 PM. Weekends by appointment.
Parking Facilities: Business parking on site.
Special Features: Specialty publisher of unit histories, airborne books, and Vietnam material.
Catalogue: Published 3 times per year. Cost is $1.
Collections/Individual Items Purchased: Both.

887
Book Shelf
3765 Hillsdale Drive, N.E.
Cleveland, Tennessee 37311 (615) 472-8408

The Book Shelf is located in an enclosed carport at a private residence in northeast Cleveland. The stock occupies 600 square feet of space. Visits can be arranged by appointment only.
How to Get There: Take North Ocoee Street to Blythe Ferry Road, turn east and count five streets on the left, turn left and the store is the fifth house on the left.
Owner/Biography: William R. Snell. Mr. Snell is a history professor by vocation and a book dealer by avocation in what time he has available.
Year Founded/History of Bookstore: 1974. The store opened with a small stock of new and out-of-print material and grew slowly through the years.
Number of Volumes: 2,000.
Types/Classifications: Hardbound, paperback, some pamphlets and ephemera, first editions, out-of-print.
General Subject Areas: Alabama Authors, Alabama History, Civil War (U.S.), South (U.S.), Tennessee Authors, Tennessee History.
Specific Specialties: Civilian Conservation Corps, Tennessee Valley Authority, Cherokee Indians, Genealogy, Andrew Jackson, Andrew Johnson, James K. Polk.
Author Specialties: Harriet S. Arnow, Alfred L. Crabb, Charles E. Craddock, Harrison H. Kroll.
Mail/Telephone Orders; Credit Cards: Mail order only, no telephone orders. Check with order. No credit cards.
Business Hours: By appointment only.
Parking Facilities: Driveway parking at residence.
Special Features: Search service.
Catalogue: Published quarterly.
Collections/Individual Items Purchased: Both.

888
Burke's Book Store, Inc.
634 Poplar Avenue
Memphis, Tennessee 38105 (901) 527-7484

This bookstore carries hardbound stock only. It occupies 2,400 square feet of space.
How to Get There: The shop is located 7 blocks from Main Street.
Owner/Biography: Diana W. Crump, Philip H. W. Crump.
Year Founded/History of Bookstore: 1875. The bookstore was owned by three generations of the Burke family. It was sold in 1978 by the widow of William Burke to Diana W. Crump who incorporated the store with her son Philip and her husband Charles. The original site was sold to the city of Memphis and the present store was built seven blocks from the original site.
Number of Volumes: 20,000.

Types/Classifications: Hardbound, first editions, fine bindings, out-of-print, signed copies, limited editions, color plate books.

General Subject Areas: Civil War (U.S.), Regional History and Authors, Technical and Reference Books.

Specific Specialties: Tennessee History and Authors, Southern Authors, South (U.S.).

Mail/Telephone Orders; Credit Cards: Both. Check with order if individual; purchase order if dealer, institution, or company. No credit cards.

Business Hours: Monday, Tuesday, Wednesday, Friday 9:00 AM - 5:00 PM; Thursday 9:00 AM - 6:00 PM; Saturday 10:00 AM - 4:00 PM.

Parking Facilities: Business parking lot.

Special Features: Search service; special orders.

Collections/Individual Items Purchased: Both.

Booksellers' Memberships: Mid-South Booksellers Association.

889
Donaldson's Books
2711 Holbrook Drive
Knoxville, Tennessee 37918

(615) 687-8872

Donaldson's Books at the above address can be visited by appointment only (also for mail orders). The business has book booths at two Antique Malls: Bearden Antique Mall, 310 Mohican Street in Homberg Place and the Antique Merchants Mall, 2015 8th Avenue South in Nashville.

How to Get There: Holbrook Drive is in the heart of the Fountain City section of Knoxville and can be reached by Merchant's Road exit from I-75.

Owner/Biography: Ralph and Irene Donaldson. Ralph holds a Master of Fine Arts degree from the University of Iowa and Irene holds a BA in Art and Speech from Florida State.

Year Founded/History of Bookstore: 1977.

Number of Volumes: 10,000.

Types/Classifications: Hardbound, some magazines, autographs, ephemera, out-of-print.

General Subject Areas: Americana, Architecture, Art, Biography, Children's Literature, Dance, Literature, Music, Mysteries, Natural History, Philosophy, Photography, Reference, Self-Help, Southern Authors, Theatre, Travel.

Mail/Telephone Orders; Credit Cards: Both. Mail orders must be accompanied by a self-addressed stamped envelope for return of check in case book desired is sold; personal check with order; all books are sent by parcel post or UPS with a 10-day return privilege. No credit cards.

Business Hours: Daily 10:00 AM - 6:00 PM at the Malls; Sunday 1:00 PM - 6:00 PM (Bearden Mall); other times by appointment.

Parking Facilities: Free parking facilities.

Special Features: Search service.

Collections/Individual Items Purchased: Individual items; collections occasionally.

890
Elder's Book Store
2115 Elliston Place
Nashville, Tennessee 37203

(615) 327-1867

Elder's Bookstore is one of the great browsing bookstores in America. The store specializes in the South, the Civil War, and Tennessee and Nashville history. The books are arranged along the wall and in aisles in handsome antique oak lawyer's bookcases. The overflow items are neatly stacked and catalogued, and the fiction section is alphabetized by author.

How to Get There: From any Interstate entering Nashville, look for Exit 209 which is Church Street exit, turn away from town on Church and go 8 blocks to 22nd Avenue; the store is at the intersection of 22nd and Church.

Owner/Biography: Charles J. and John Randolph Elder.

Year Founded/History of Bookstore: 1951.

Number of Volumes: 27,000.

Types/Classifications: Hardbound, broadsides, autographs, first editions, fine bindings, out-of-print, association copies, press books, signed copies, fine leather bindings, signed literary and historical material, presentation copies, limited editions, color plate books.

General Subject Areas: Civil War (U.S.), South, Southern Literature, Tennessee.

Specific Specialties: Southern Authors, Vanderbilt Fugitive Poets, Civil War Regimentals.

Author Specialties: William Faulkner.

Mail/Telephone Orders; Credit Cards: Both. Cash with order including postage. No credit cards.

Business Hours: Monday through Friday 9:00 AM - 5:00 PM; Saturday 9:00 AM - 2:00 PM.

Parking Facilities: Street parking.

Special Features: Search service; publishing sideline.

Catalogue: Published 2 times per year.

Collections/Individual Items Purchased: Both.

891
Old Book Store
337 Second Avenue South
Nashville, Tennessee 37115   (615) 256-3512

The bookstore is housed in two rooms of a very old brick building on the corner of Franklin Street and Second Avenue South in Nashville. The owner's husband has his business in the same building. The two rooms of the shop are completely full of books and all kinds of other interesting items such as antiques, old letters, letterheads of early Nashville businesses, old photographs, postcards, and so forth.

Owner/Biography: Mrs. Richard B. Fox.

Year Founded/History of Bookstore: Founded in 1968, the bookstore was originally located in Old Hickory, Tennessee, and was moved to its present location in 1979.

Number of Volumes: 10,000.

Types/Classifications: A general bookstore, with a little bit of most everything; hardbound, magazines.

General Subject Areas: Americana, Children's Books, General, Sports.

Specific Specialties: Tennessee, South (U.S.).

Author Specialties: Southern Authors, Tennessee Authors.

Mail/Telephone Orders; Credit Cards: Both. No credit cards.

Business Hours: Open only on Tuesday 9:00 AM - 4:30 PM; at other times call (615) 868-2078.

Parking Facilities: The bookstore's own parking lot is at the corner of Second Avenue and Franklin Street.

Special Features: Search service.

Collections/Individual Items Purchased: Both.

892
Old South Books
352 Grandview
Memphis, Tennessee 38111   (901) 323-6585

Old South Books specializes in old, rare, and out-of-print books on medicine. Visits can be arranged by appointment.

Owner/Biography: Dr. D.J. Canale.

Year Founded/History of Bookstore: 1978.

Number of Volumes: 3,500.

Types/Classifications: Hardbound, rare, out-of-print.

General Subject Areas: Medicine.

Mail/Telephone Orders; Credit Cards: Both. No credit cards.

Business Hours: By appointment only.

Catalogue: Published quarterly.

Collections/Individual Items Purchased: Both.

893
Ollie's Books
3218 Boxdale Street
Memphis, Tennessee 38118   (901) 363-1996

Ollie's Books carries a general stock of hardbound out-of-print books and back issues of "Arizona Highways" magazines.
Owner/Biography: Ollie McGarrh.
Year Founded/History of Bookstore: 1966.
Number of Volumes: 5,000.
Types/Classifications: Hardbound, magazines, first editions, out-of-print, signed copies.
General Subject Areas: General.
Specific Specialties: Biography, Religion.
Mail/Telephone Orders; Credit Cards: Both. Cash with order; all books shipped postage paid. No credit cards.
Business Hours: Monday through Friday 4:00 PM - 8:00 PM; Saturdays 9:00 AM - 5:00 PM; other hours by appointment.
Parking Facilities: Street parking.
Special Features: Free search service.
Collections/Individual Items Purchased: Both.

894
R. R. Allen, Books
5300 Bluefield Road
Knoxville, Tennessee 37921   (615) 584-4487

R.R. Allen Books is essentially a mail order business. Viewing is available by pre-arranged appointment. The stock includes scarce, rare, and collectible books in a variety of fields.
How to Get There: Call for directions.
Owner/Biography: Ronald R. Allen.
Year Founded/History of Bookstore: 1964.
Number of Volumes: 5,000.
Types/Classifications: Hardbound, pamphlets, broadsides, ephemera, first editions, out-of-print, scarce, rare, prints, maps.
General Subject Areas: Americana, Juvenile Literature.
Specific Specialties: Rare Tennessee Books and Early Tennessee Imprints.
Mail/Telephone Orders; Credit Cards: Both. No credit cards.
Business Hours: By appointment (evenings or weekends best).
Catalogue: Published 2 to 3 times per year.
Collections/Individual Items Purchased: Both.

TEXAS

895
A Book Buyers Shop
711 Studewood
Houston, Texas 77007

(713) 868-3910

This is a general used book store, stocking nearly all types except textbooks. It is especially strong in fiction, biography, Texana, rare and collectible items, Christian theology.

How to Get There: The bookstore is located near downtown Houston in the Heights, six blocks north of I-10 West, Studemont exit. It is in a quiet residential neighborhood and contains 1,000 square feet of space.

Owner/Biography: Chester and Christine Doby, owners, have been in the book business in Houston, in one form or another, for over 20 years.

Year Founded/History of Bookstore: The current bookstore was founded in 1980; the owners sold two previously owned stores in Houston in 1979.

Number of Volumes: 20,000.

Types/Classifications: Hardbound, paperback, autographs, maps, current best-seller listings, first editions, signed copies, advance copies, limited editions, collectibles, rare, some dating back to the 1500's.

General Subject Areas: Biography, Books About Books, Fiction, History, Poetry.

Specific Specialties: Texas, Texas Maps, Texas Material in Wraps, Christian Theology, Mexican Conquest Era; the owners have few specialties, but favor the "odd and unusual books, the more bizarre the better."

Mail/Telephone Orders; Credit Cards: Both. Orders should be for specific titles. Visa and Mastercard accepted.

Business Hours: Monday through Thursday 11:00 AM - 8:00 PM; Friday through Sunday 11:00 AM - 6:00 PM.

Parking Facilities: Business parking lot and street.

Catalogue: On the Texas stock.

Collections/Individual Items Purchased: Both.

896
Antiquarian Book Mart & Annex
3127 Broadway
San Antonio, Texas 78209

(512) 828-4885

This book shop offers both hardbound and paperback books in contemporary U.S. and English fiction plus a specialty in Western Americana and Texana.

Owner/Biography: Dr. Frank Kellel, Jr.

Year Founded/History of Bookstore: 1971.

Number of Volumes: 500,000.

Types/Classifications: Hardbound, paperback, first editions.

General Subject Areas: Art Books, Contemporary American and English Fiction, Cookbooks, Military History, Natural History, Poetry, Texas, Western Americana.

Mail/Telephone Orders; Credit Cards: Telephone orders accepted. Visa and Mastercard accepted.

Business Hours: Monday through Saturday 10:00 AM - 6:00 PM.

Parking Facilities: Business parking lot.

Collections/Individual Items Purchased: Both.

897
Book Cellar
2 South Main Street
Temple, Texas 76501

(817) 773-7545

The name says it all - "Cellar." It is located below street level and stocks 3,000 square feet of both hardbound and paperback books.

Owner/Biography: Bob and Pat Jones.
Number of Volumes: 60,000.
Types/Classifications: Hardbound, paperback.
General Subject Areas: Comic Books (Collector's), General.
Mail/Telephone Orders; Credit Cards: No mail or telephone orders. Visa and Mastercard accepted for purchases at store.
Business Hours: Monday through Saturday 9:30 AM - 5:00 PM.
Parking Facilities: Street parking.
Special Features: Search service.
Collections/Individual Items Purchased: Both.

898
Bookshop
1808 North Main
Del Rio, Texas 78840

(512) 775-5935

The Bookshop is a small, compact office offering Texana, Southwest Studies, and books about Mexico. They also offer special ordering of new books with substantial discount, out-of-print books service, book search, research on authors and book related items, Spanish dictionaries, and language aids.

Owner/Biography: Jim and Sue Croom.
Year Founded/History of Bookstore: 1977. The Bookshop began in a 1,200 square foot store in a shopping center as a general bookstore. The owners eventually closed that store and entered the antiquarian field.
Number of Volumes: 5,000.
Types/Classifications: Hardbound, paperback, out-of-print, first editions.
General Subject Areas: Mexico, Pre-Columbian Studies, Regional Nature Books, Southwest Studies, Spanish Language Dictionaries and Language Aids, Texana.
Author Specialties: J. Frank Dobie.
Other Specialties: Spanish dictionaries and books to help individuals learn that language.
Mail/Telephone Orders; Credit Cards: Both. $1 charge per book, $.50 for each additional book. Visa and Mastercard accepted.
Business Hours: Irregular. Phone is on a recorder for 20-second message.
Parking Facilities: Street parking.
Special Features: Search service, special order for new books at a discount.
Collections/Individual Items Purchased: Both.
Booksellers' Memberships: American Booksellers Association, Central Texas Booksellers Association.

899
Crandall's Corner
5608 Pinemont Drive
Houston, Texas 77092

(713) 680-1870

Crandall's Corner is a general used and rare bookstore in northwest Houston designed for easy browsing. Books are arranged in over twenty categories with an extensive modern fiction collection including mysteries and science fiction. Biography, military, and cookery are other specialites.

How to Get There: Exit at Antoine off Highway 290 (Northwest Freeway), north on Antoine to Pinemont, right on Pinemont, shop is 1/4 block from the intersection of Antoine and Pinemont.
Owner/Biography: Dick and Judy Crandall. Dick is a publisher's representative in the Southwest. Judy's background includes 8 years as a reference librarian and 3 years as a publisher's representative. Both have

previous experience owning a "new" bookstore.

Year Founded/History of Bookstore: 1980. In 1980 the Crandall s opened for business in a small shopping center. In June 1981 the stock was moved to a larger store nearby, doubling their floor space to 2,600 square feet.

Number of Volumes: 50,000.

Types/Classifications: Hardbound, paperback, first editions, out-of-print.

General Subject Areas: Art, Biography, Children's Literature, Cookery, History, Military History, Music, Mysteries, Recreation, Religion, Science, Science Fiction and Fantasy, Southwestern History, Sports, Technology, Texana, Travel.

Mail/Telephone Orders; Credit Cards: Both. Visa and Mastercard accepted.

Business Hours: Tuesday through Friday 11:00 AM - 6:00 PM; Saturday 9:00 AM - 5:00 PM.

Parking Facilities: Business parking lot.

Special Features: Stamps and supplies for collectors.

Collections/Individual Items Purchased: Both.

900
Detering Book Gallery
2311 Bissonnet
Houston, Texas 77005   (713) 526-6974

The Detering Book Gallery specializes in literary first editions, illustrated books, private press books, fine printing, and fine bindings.

Owner/Biography: Herman E. Detering, III.

Types/Classifications: First editions, hardbound, illustrated books, fine printing, fine bindings, press books.

General Subject Areas: Literary First Editions.

Catalogue: Catalogues issued.

901
Fletcher's Books
Main Street
P.O. Box 65
Salado, Texas 76571   (817) 947-5414

Fletcher's Books is in a building built especially for the store. It is in early Texas style, rock and cedar, with a porch across the front. Inside there is a vaulted ceiling with hand rubbed walls and ceiling wood. The shop occupies 2,000 square feet of space.

How to Get There: Salado is on Highway 35 which bisects the state from north to south. In order to reach this historic village, one must take the exit less than a mile from Main Street.

Owner/Biography: Thelma R. Fletcher.

Year Founded/History of Bookstore: 1927. The business began in Houston and moved to Salado in 1954.

Number of Volumes: 30,000.

Types/Classifications: Hardbound, maps, autographs, first editions, out-of-print, association copies, press books, signed copies, presentation copies, limited editions, color plate books.

General Subject Areas: Americana, General, Texana.

Specific Specialties: Southwest Americana.

Author Specialties: Texas Authors.

Mail/Telephone Orders; Credit Cards: Both; from within the U.S. only. Visa and Mastercard accepted.

Business Hours: Weekdays 10:00 AM - 5:00 PM.

Parking Facilities: Business parking lot.

Special Features: Publishing sideline - Anson Jones Press.

Collections/Individual Items Purchased: Both.

Booksellers' Memberships: Texas Historical Association, Bell County Historical Commission, Salado Historical Society, American Society of Appraisers.

Miscellaneous: Appraisals.

902
Jenkins Company
7111 South I-Highway 35
P.O. Box 2085
Austin, Texas 78768   (512) 444-6616

This is a very large bookstore with a huge stock of Americana, Latin Americana, and 19th and 20th Century Literature, all housed in 20,000 square feet of space.

Owner/Biography: John H. Jenkins.
Year Founded/History of Bookstore: 1963.
Number of Volumes: 250,000.
Types/Classifications: Hardbound, paperback, broadsides, autographs, ephemera, rare books, scholarly books, manuscripts, documents, art, maps, prints, first editions, fine bindings, out-of-print, association copies, press books, signed copies, presentation copies, limited editions, color plate books.
General Subject Areas: American West, Americana of 17th through 20th Centuries, Black Americans, Civil War (U.S.), Economics, Latin Americana, Law, Literature of 19th and 20th Centuries, Mexico, Military, Politics, South (U.S.), Texas, Travels, Voyages.
Specific Specialties: Western Overlands, Books By and About Women, New England Romantic Authors, Confederate (U.S.) Imprints.
Mail/Telephone Orders; Credit Cards: Both; postage paid on order with personal check; Texas residents add 4% sales tax; no credit cards.
Business Hours: Monday through Friday 8:00 AM - 5:00 PM; call for appointment.
Parking Facilities: Business parking lot.
Special Features: Publishing sideline, preparation of bibliographies.
Catalogue: Six to eight times a year.
Collections/Individual Items Purchased: Both.
Booksellers' Memberships: Antiquarian Booksellers Association of America.

903
Limestone Hills Book Shop
P.O. Box 1125
Glen Rose, Texas 76043   (817) 897-4991

The bookstore welcomes telephone messages at any time and visitors by appointment. The location is a private residence and several separate bookrooms.

How to Get There: The bookstore sits on a bluff above the Paluxy River near the small town of Glen Rose, some 65 miles southwest of the Dallas-Fort Worth International Airport.
Owner/Biography: Aubyn and Lyle Harris Kendall, Jr.
Year Founded/History of Bookstore: 1975.
Number of Volumes: 10,000.
Types/Classifications: Hardbound, first editions, out-of-print, signed copies, literary periodicals, fine printing.
General Subject Areas: American Literature, Books About Books, Detective Fiction, English Literature, Eqyptology, Golf, Military, Mystery.
Specific Specialties: 19th and 20th Century English Literature, 19th and 20th Century American Literature, Pre-18th Century Medical Books.
Author Specialties: Thomas J. Wise, Frederick Locker-Lampson, C.S. Forester, David Garnett.
Mail/Telephone Orders; Credit Cards: Both; Visa, Mastercard.
Business Hours: By appointment only.
Special Features: International search service, appraisals.
Catalogue: Two times a year, in February and September.
Collections/Individual Items Purchased: Both.
Booksellers' Memberships: Antiquarian Booksellers Association of America, International League of Antiquarian Booksellers.

904
Maggie Lambeth, Booksearch
136 Princess Pass
San Antonio, Texas 78212   (512) 732-4551

Maggie Lambeth specializes in all areas related to Texas, Mexico, and the Southwest including maps, prints, and fine art with additional hardbound books in literature, biography, and non-fiction. The stock occupies 1,000 square feet of space, is housed in a private home and may be browsed by appointment or referral.

How to Get There: The bookstore is located near Trinity University between Shook and Mulberry. Call for precise directions when making an appointment.

Owner/Biography: Maggie Lambeth.

Year Founded/History of Bookstore: 1980. The shop was moved in the fall of 1983 from a location on the San Antonio River in the heart of downtown to a residential area in historic Monte Vista.

Number of Volumes: 3,000.

Types/Classifications: General used books, rare and out-of-print, maps, prints, fine art.

General Subject Areas: American and British Biography, American and British Literature, Mexico, Southwest, Texana.

Specific Specialties: Texas Presses, Cattle and Ranching, Genealogy related to Texas, Texas Town and County Histories; Early Views of Galveston, San Antonio, and Houston from the 19th Century; Mexican Revolution, Pancho Villa, Texas Republic.

Mail/Telephone Orders; Credit Cards: Both. No credit cards.

Business Hours: By appointment only.

Parking Facilities: Free parking available.

Special Features: Search service, research, collections built.

Catalogue: Published several times a year.

Collections/Individual Items Purchased: Both.

905
Montrose Book Shop
Box 66265
Houston, Texas 77006   (713) 522-1713

The Montrose Book Shop is not open to the public but operates by mail and telephone order.

Owner/Biography: Richard C. Palmer. Mr. Palmer is a former foreign correspondent for the International News Service.

Year Founded/History of Bookstore: 1968.

Number of Volumes: 5,000.

Types/Classifications: Hardbound, first editions, out-of-print, press books.

General Subject Areas: Cookbooks (Eighteenth and Nineteenth Centuries), Early and Unique Bibles, Eighteenth Century Drama, Johnson-Boswell and Circle, Seventeenth Century Drama, Sixteenth Century Drama.

Mail/Telephone Orders; Credit Cards: Both. No credit cards.

Business Hours: By appointment only.

Parking Facilities: Street parking.

Special Features: Search service.

Collections/Individual Items Purchased: Both

906
Old Bookshelf
2125 39th Street
Galveston, Texas 77550   (409) 763-8652

The bookstore is a small place (240 square feet) which has just recently changed ownership. Located in a residential area, the stock is general.

Owner/Biography: Roger Allen and Jeannine Coreil, owners, are a husband and wife team who came to

Texas three years ago and have just started in the business.

Year Founded/History of Bookstore: The bookstore was founded in 1967 by Dave Goodson and changed little during its history. In December 1983 the present owners took over.

Number of Volumes: 6,000.

Types/Classifications: Hardbound, paperback, magazines, prints, first editions, fine bindings, out-of-print, color plate books.

General Subject Areas: General.

Specific Specialties: Galveston (Texas), Texas, Sea, Civil War (U.S.), Literature.

Author Specialties: Larry McMurtry, Rudyard Kipling.

Mail/Telephone Orders; Credit Cards: Both. Mail orders require 10 percent down. No credit cards.

Business Hours: Monday, Tuesday, Wednesday, Friday 1:00 PM - 6:00 PM; Saturday 11:00 AM - 6:00 PM.

Parking Facilities: Street.

Special Features: The owners will be starting a search service in the near future.

Catalogue: A newsletter-catalogue is planned.

Collections/Individual Items Purchased: Both.

907
Sheldon Books
3136 Routh Street
Dallas, Texas 75201

(214) 521-6163

The bookstore features first editions of art books, archaeology, photobooks, and illustrated books. It contains 1,000 square feet of space.

How to Get There: The shop is located on Chelsea Square in Dallas, Texas.

Owner/Biography: Sheldon Rosen.

Year Founded/History of Bookstore: 1977.

Number of Volumes: 5,000.

Types/Classifications: Hardbound, first editions, fine bindings, out-of-print, association copies, press books, signed copies, presentation copies, limited editions, color plate books, photographs, broadsides, prints.

General Subject Areas: Archaeology, Art, History, Literature.

Mail/Telephone Orders; Credit Cards: Both. Visa, Diner's Club, American Express, Mastercard, Carte Blanche. Mailing address: P.O. Box 191284, Dallas, Texas 75219.

Business Hours: Daily 11:00 AM - 4:00 PM or by appointment.

Parking Facilities: Shopping Center.

Collections/Individual Items Purchased: Individual items only.

908
Trackside Books
8819 Mobud Drive
P.O. Box 770264
Houston, Texas 77215

(713) 772-8107

The bookstore is primarily a mail order business with customers in 43 states and 14 foreign countries. Retail sales from the base of operations, the owners' home, account for only 5 percent of the total. Visits are by appointment only. Any printed matter relating in any manner to the general subject of railroading is handled.

Owner/Biography: Lawrence E. and Kathleen M. Madole.

Year Founded/History of Bookstore: The bookstore began business in New York State in 1964 as a part time business by the present owners. The business had small steady growth, moving to Michigan and Illinois as the owners' careers required. In 1975 the shop was moved to Houston. Real growth started in Texas. The shop has always specialized in railroadiana but the move to Texas precipitated expansion in Texana and Western Americana material, which now accounts for 40 percent of retail sales.

Number of Volumes: 8,000.

General Subject Areas: Railroads, Texas, Western Americana.

Mail/Telephone Orders; Credit Cards: Both. No credit cards.

Business Hours: By appointment only.
Parking Facilities: Street.
Catalogue: Published Quarterly.

909
W. Graham Arader III
2800 Virginia Street
Houston, Texas 77098 (713) 527-8055

See: W. GRAHAM ARADER III, King of Prussia, Pennsylvania.

UTAH

910
Deseret Book Store
44 East South Temple
Salt Lake City, Utah 84111   (801) 328-8191

The main Deseret Book Store (there are currently 13 branch stores) deals in a wide variety of new books, both Mormon and general trade books. This particular description applies to the "Deseret Book Rare, Out-of-Print and Fine Books," a separate department within the store. It is a consolidation of two used and rare books operations which date back to 1977.
How to Get There: The bookstore is located 1/2 block east of Temple Square in downtown Salt Lake City. The rare book department is on the lower level.
Owner/Biography: Deseret Management Corporation.
Year Founded/History of Bookstore: 1866 (1977 for Rare and Out-of-Print Department). In 1977, one of Deseret Book's branch stores in Fashion Place Mall of Murray, Utah began a sideline of used and out-of-print books. Curt Bench began that sideline and has expanded the operaton to include 2 locations within the retail division of the company: the main store in downtown Salt Lake City and the Cottonwood Mall Store.
Number of Volumes: Over 25,000.
Types/Classifications: Hardbound, paperback, broadsides, autographs, ephemera, Mormon money and script, documents; first editions, fine bindings, out-of-print, association copies, press books, signed copies, presentation copies, limited editions, color plate books.
General Subject Areas: Americana, Nineteenth and Early Twentieth Century Literature, Western Americana.
Specific Specialties: Mormon Americana, Overland Narratives, Western Press Books.
Other Specialties: Mormon History and Biography.
Mail/Telephone Orders; Credit Cards: Both. Cash with order; institutions billed. American Express, Visa, Mastercard accepted.
Business Hours: Monday through Friday 10:00 AM - 9:00 PM; Saturday 10:00 AM - 6:00 PM.
Parking Facilities: Parking terrace for mall store.
Special Features: Search service; publishing of limited editions and fine press books is planned.
Catalogue: Published 3 to 6 times per year.
Collections/Individual Items Purchased: Both.

911
Sam Weller's Zion Book Store, Inc.
254 South Main Street
Salt Lake City, Utah 84101   (801) 328-2586

The mezzanine and basement of this large bookstore house the used books. First editions are displayed in a room off the mezzanine. Rare books are kept in a vault and USGS publications are on the third floor. The main floor is devoted to new books. The entire store occupies over 14,000 square feet of space.
How to Get There: The shop is located 2 1/2 blocks down the street from the Hotel Utah on the main street of Salt Lake City.
Owner/Biography: Sam Weller, Lila Weller, Tony Weller.
Year Founded/History of Bookstore: 1929. The store was begun by Gustave A. Weller, father of the current owner who took over in 1945.
Number of Volumes: Over 1,000,000.
Types/Classifications: Hardbound, paperback, new and used, first editions, rare, out-of-print.
General Subject Areas: Biography, Children's Boooks, Cookbooks, Crafts, Gardening, Geology, Health, History, Mining, Mormonism, Occult, Philosophy, Religion, Technical, Western Americana, Westerns.

Specific Specialties: Mormonism (Pro and Anti), Western History, Utah History.
Author Specialties: Jack London, Ernest Hemingway, Wallace Stegner, Vardis Fisher.
Other Specialties: USGS Publications.
Mail/Telephone Orders; Credit Cards: Both. Check or charge card number. American Express, Visa, Mastercard accepted.
Business Hours: Monday through Friday 9:30 AM - 6:00 PM; Monday and Friday Evening until 9:00 PM.
Parking Facilities: Undergound parking behind store, some street parking.
Special Features: Search service; want lists maintained; appraisals of private collections.
Catalogue: Published occasionally.
Collections/Individual Items Purchased: Both.
Booksellers' Memberships: Western Historians Association.

912
Walt West Books
1355 Riverside
Provo, Utah 84604   (801) 377-1298

This bookstore features general used and out-of-print books in the humanities. Emphasis is placed on the quality books with scholarly content. Carpeted floors and convenient chairs make for comfortable browsing in an area of 1,100 square feet of space. The owner's slogan is "if I don't have what you want you'll want what I have."

How to Get There: The shop is located near 1200 North and 500 West.
Owner/Biography: Walter R. West, Jr.
Year Founded/History of Bookstore: Founded in 1965, the bookstore has been in the same location since March 1981.
Number of Volumes: 20,000.
Types/Classifications: Hardbound scholarly classsics, many out-of-print; some paperbacks of the same type; first editions, signed copies.
General Subject Areas: Americana, Art, History, Literature, Music, Philosophy, Psychology, Religion.
Specific Specialties: Western Americana, Mormonism, Utah, Idaho.
Author Specialties: Aldous Huxley, Rufus Jones.
Mail/Telephone Orders; Credit Cards: Both. No credit cards.
Business Hours: Tuesday through Friday 11:00 AM - 5:30 PM; Saturday 1:00 PM - 5:00 PM; closed Sunday and Monday; other times by appointment.
Parking Facilities: Street, business parking lot.
Collections/Individual Items Purchased: Both.

VERMONT

913
Bear Bookshop
Butterfield Road
Marlboro, Vermont 05344

(802) 464-2260

The Bear Bookshop is a used and rare bookshop located in a large renovated cow barn on 120 acres in southern Vermont. The stock is comprised of all scholarly fields with particular emphasis on music, fine arts, antiques, illustrated books, and bibliographies. The shop occupies approximately 2,600 square feet of space.

How to Get There: The shop is located on the east side of a dirt road known locally as the Butterfield Road, 1/2 mile south of Route 9 from an intersection 1 mile east of the Hogback Mountain ski areas. There are state signs 1/2 mile from the intersection in both directions. Call if further assistance is needed.

Owner/Biography: John Greenberg.

Year Founded/History of Bookstore: 1975. The shop was started in the owner's apartment in downtown Brattleboro, Vermont and remained in that location from June 1, 1975 to June 1, 1976 when it moved to the farm in Marlboro. Until January 1983 the shop was operated from the house. Since then it has been in its present location in a renovated barn.

Number of Volumes: 25,000.

Types/Classifications: Hardbound, paperback, first edtions, fine bindings, out-of-print, association copies, press books, signed copies, presentation copies, limited editions, color plate books.

General Subject Areas: General.

Mail/Telephone Orders; Credit Cards: Both. Mail orders should be sent to The Bear Bookshop, R.D. No. 4, Box 219, West Brattleboro, Vermont 05301. No credit cards.

Business Hours: Appointment recommended, but generally 10:00 AM to 5:00 PM seven days a week. Hours from November to May can be sporadic.

Parking Facilities: Parking lot in front of store.

Special Features: Search service.

Catalogue: Catalogue published.

Collections/Individual Items Purchased: Both.

Booksellers' Memberships: Vermont Antiquarian Booksellers Association.

Miscellaneous: The owners state that there is no heat in the bookstore other than a small quartz heater.

914
Bradford Books
West Road
Bennington, Vermont 05201

(802) 447-0387

Bradford Books is located in a two room all pine-paneled building originally built as a dairy bar. Tables have been removed and bookcases built in each booth. There is ample light for the customer who can wander in and out of the booths, each filled with a different book category. An open fireplace burns for comfort on cool spring and fall days. It is a fine place for book browsers. The shop occupies 800 square feet of space.

How to Get There: The shop is 2 miles west of Bennington on Route 9 (main road to Albany and Troy).

Owner/Biography: Margaret L. and W. Bradford Craig.

Year Founded/History of Bookstore: 1973.

Number of Volumes: 10,000.

Types/Classifications: Hardbound, paperback, out-of-print, first editions.

General Subject Areas: Biography, Children's Literature, Drama, Fiction, History, Modern Library, Poetry.

Mail/Telephone Orders; Credit Cards: Both. No credit cards.

Business Hours: May to November: Wednesday through Saturday 11:00 AM - 5:00 PM; Sunday 1:00 PM - 5:00 PM; or by appointment.
Parking Facilities: Parking area available.
Special Features: Search service.
Collections/Individual Items Purchased: Individual items only.
Booksellers' Memberships: Vermont Antiquarian Booksellers Association.

915
Brickhouse Book Shop
Morristown Corners
Morrisville, Vermont 05661   (802) 888-4300

The Brickhouse Book Shop has three rooms full of books plus a book garage located in a 150 year old house at the four corners. A varied selection can be browsed and the shop is beginning to add prints and is considering adding a tea room.
How to Get There: Located on Route 100 between Morrisville and Stowe, the shop is approximately 2 miles from Morrisville and 7 miles from Stowe.
Owner/Biography: Alexandra Heller.
Year Founded/History of Bookstore: 1976.
Number of Volumes: 6,000.
Types/Classifications: Hardbound, paperback, broadsides, prints, first editions, fine bindings, out-of-print, signed copies, illustrated books.
General Subject Areas: Agriculture, Animal Husbandry, Art, Biography, Children's Literature, Cookbooks, Crafts, Fishing, Geology, Health, History, Horticulture, How-To, Humor, Hunting, Languages, Law, Medical, Music, Nature, New Englandiana, Occult, Philosophy, Poetry, Reference, Religion, Science Fiction and Fantasy, Sports, Theater, Travel, Vermontiana, War, Women.
Mail/Telephone Orders; Credit Cards: Both. No credit cards.
Business Hours: Daily 10:00 AM - 6:00 PM.
Parking Facilities: Business parking lot.
Special Features: Search service.
Collections/Individual Items Purchased: Both.
Booksellers' Memberships: Vermont Antiquarian Bookdealers Association.
Miscellaneous: The shop is near the Stowe ski resort; picnic tables are out front; located on a bike route.

916
Bygone Books
91 College Street
Burlington, Vermont 05401   (802) 862-4397

This former truck garage, with its own garden, has been attractively remodeled into a multi-level book shop. It occupies 800 square feet of space.
How to Get There: The bookstore is Located 2 blocks from Lake Champlain, between Pine and Champlain Streets; follow bookstore signs to offstreet doorway.
Owner/Biography: J. Soule, J. Tormey, E. VanBuren, B. Wadhams, P. Welsh.
Year Founded/History of Bookstore: 1978. Bygone Books has grown steadily in its original setting.
Number of Volumes: 10,000.
Types/Classifications: Hardbound, paperback, some magazines, ephemera, antique prints, first editions, fine bindings, out-of-print, association copies, press books, signed copies, presentation copies, limited editions, color plate books.
General Subject Areas: Americana, Art and Architecture, Biography, Children's Literature, Cinema, Criticism, Do-It-Yourself, Foreign Language, Humor, Literary History, Military, Music, Mysteries, Natural History, Poetry, Reference, Religion and Philosophy, Science Fiction and Fantasy, Social Science, Theater, Travel, U.S. West, Women.
Specific Specialties: Vermontiana.

Mail/Telephone Orders; Credit Cards: Both. Cash with order; institutions billed. Visa and Mastercard accepted.
Business Hours: Monday through Saturday 9:30 AM - 5:30 PM.
Parking Facilities: Public parking lot, street parking.
Special Features: Search service.
Collections/Individual Items Purchased: Both.
Booksellers' Memberships: Vermont Antiquarian Booksellers Association.

917
Fraser Publishing Co.
309 South Willard
Burlington, Vermont 05401 (802) 658-0322

Hardbound out-of-print books are available from this antiquarian dealer. Visitors are welcome by appointment.
How to Get There: Call for appointment and directions.
Owner/Biography: James L. Fraser. Mr. Fraser was born in Paris, France and educated in the U.S.
Year Founded/History of Bookstore: 1962. The business was established in Wells, Vermont and moved to Burlington in 1969.
Number of Volumes: 5,000.
Types/Classifications: Hardbound, paperback, magazines, periodicals, out-of-print.
General Subject Areas: Business Biography, Commmodities, Crowd Psychology, Financial History, Institutions, Speculation, Stock Market, Wall Street.
Mail/Telephone Orders; Credit Cards: Both. Include payment with order. Visa and Mastercard accepted.
Business Hours: Monday through Friday 8:30 AM - 4:30 PM.
Special Features: Search service; publishing.
Catalogue: Published once per year.
Collections/Individual Items Purchased: Both.
Booksellers' Memberships: Antiquarian Booksellers Association of America including New England Chapter.

918
Green Mountain Books and Prints
100 Broad Street
Lyndonville, Vermont 05851 (802) 626-5051

This bookstore has many odd corners and books are shelved in categories. The store has a large selection of remainders.
How to Get There: Take the Lyndonville Exit off Route 91 North and on to Route 5, go north for 2 miles. The store is located on the corner of Broad and Depot.
Owner/Biography: Corporation.
Year Founded/History of Bookstore: 1976.
Number of Volumes: 50,000.
Types/Classifications: Hardbound, paperback, out-of-print, first editions.
General Subject Areas: Antiques, Art, Drama, History, Literature, Music, Ships and the Sea.
Mail/Telephone Orders; Credit Cards: Both. No credit cards.
Business Hours: Monday through Thursday 10:00 AM - 4:00 PM; Friday 10:00 AM - 6:00 PM; Saturday 10:00 AM - 1:00 PM.
Parking Facilities: Street parking.
Special Features: Search service.
Catalogue: Published 4 times per year.
Collections/Individual Items Purchased: Both.
Booksellers' Memberships: Vermont Antiquarian Booksellers Association.

919
Haunted Mansion Bookshop
Route 103
Cuttingsville, Vermont 05738   (802) 492-3337

The Haunted Mansion Bookshop is a century-old Victorian mansion with two floors full of books. It is located across the road from a cemetery. The shop has an extensive collection of Vermontiana and Americana plus some appropriate antiques. The decor is maintained as it was when the house was built.

How to Get There: Located ten miles south of Rutland, the shop is on the main road through the country town.

Owner/Biography: Clint and Lucille Fiske. Clint has been in the book business over 40 years and was associated with C.E. Tuttle Co. before founding the bookstore. Both are native Vermonters.

Year Founded/History of Bookstore: 1968.

Number of Volumes: 65,000.

Types/Classifications: Hardbound, some paperpack, some magazines, broadsides, ephemera, first editions, press books, out-of-print, color plate books.

General Subject Areas: Africa, Agriculture, Alaska, Americana, Architecture, Arctic, Art, Asia, Astronomy, Biography, Business, Canadiana, Civil War (U.S.), Classics, Cookbooks, Economics, Education, England, Europe, Far East, Fiction, France, Germany, Great Wars, History, Humor, Indians, Ireland, Juvenile, Literature, Medical, Mysteries, Near East, New England, Philosophy, Poetry, Political Science, Psychology, Religion, Russia, Sailing and the Sea, Science, Science Fiction and Fantasy, Sociology, Technical, Travel, Vermontiana, Women.

Mail/Telephone Orders; Credit Cards: Both. No credit cards.

Business Hours: Daily.

Parking Facilities: Parking in yard.

Special Features: The bookstore also has a few antiques and some old bottles for browsers not addicted to books.

Collections/Individual Items Purchased: Both.

Booksellers' Memberships: Vermont Antiquarian Bookdealers Association (Founder).

920
John Johnson Natural History Books
R.D. 2
North Bennington, Vermont 05257   (802) 442-6738

The bookstore consists of a large stock of natural history books in the owners' home and two barns. It is not set up for browsing but issues catalogues several times a year.

Owner/Biography: John Johnson, owner, and wife Betty have operated as a husband-and-wife team specializing in natural history since 1948.

Year Founded/History of Bookstore: 1948.

Types/Classifications: Hardbound, out-of-print, rare.

General Subject Areas: Amphibians, Animals, Birds, Botany, Cryptograms, Darwin, Explorations, Fish, Insects, Invertebrates, Natural History, Paleontology, Reptiles, Snakes, Voyages.

Specific Specialties: Marine Mammals; Fossil: Birds, Mammals, Invertebrates, Reptiles, Plants; Poisonous: Plants, Fish, Reptiles, Insects; Venoms; Lewis and Clark Expedition; Naturalist Travels.

Author Specialties: Charles Darwin, Alfred Russel Wallace, Asa Gray.

Mail/Telephone Orders; Credit Cards: Both. Cash with order.

Business Hours: Daily 8:00 AM - 8:00 PM.

Special Features: Publishing sideline.

Catalogue: Three or four times a year.

Collections/Individual Items Purchased: Both.

Booksellers' Memberships: Antiquarian Booksellers Association of America (National and Mid-Atlantic Chapters), International League of Antiquarian Booksellers.

921
Johnny Appleseed Bookshop
Main Street
Manchester, Vermont 05254   (802) 362-2458

The bookstore has been providing the region with good books since 1930. Located in an 1832 bank building in the village of Manchester, the browser may find books from $.25 to several thousand dollars. The shop contains 1,250 square feet of space.

How to Get There: The shop is located in the village of Manchester on historic Route 7.

Owner/Biography: Frederic F. Taylor, sometime reviewer and columnist, has owned the shop since 1965. He attended Middlebury College and Columbia University.

Year Founded/History of Bookstore: The bookstore was founded in 1930 by the poet Walter Hard, his wife Margaret (also an author), and their daughter Ruth at the start of the Depression, in an apple orchard. It was moved in 1949 to an 1832 bank building. In 1965 the store was sold to its present owner.

Number of Volumes: 5,000.

Types/Classifications: Hardbound, paperback, ephemera, first editions, fine bindings, signed copies, presentation copies, limited editions, illustrated books, leatherbound, sets.

General Subject Areas: American Art, American History, Barre Press, Detective, Dogs, Fishing, Golf, Hunting, Imprint Society, Mystery, Sailing, Vermont.

Specific Specialties: Derrydale Press, Angler's Club, Sporting, books dealing with the solution to Dickens' "The Mystery of Edwin Drood," editions of "The Riddle of the Sands," books pertaining to Abraham Lincoln's Family, especially Robert Todd Lincoln.

Author Specialties: Vermont Writers, Walter Hard, Margaret Hard, Dorothy Canfield Fisher.

Other Specialties: Vermont Life Magazine.

Mail/Telephone Orders; Credit Cards: Both. Postage: $1.50 first book, $.50 per book thereafter. Visa, Mastercard.

Business Hours: Daily 9:30 AM - 5:00 PM.

Parking Facilities: Street.

Catalogue: Catalogue published.

Collections/Individual Items Purchased: Both.

Booksellers' Memberships: Vermont Antiquarian Booksellers Association.

Miscellaneous: A book was written about the bookstore: "A Memory of Vermont: Our Life in the Johnny Appleseed Bookshop 1930-1965," by Margaret Hard (N.Y., Harcourt Brace, 1967). Experiencing five printings, the book touches on the famous writers who spent time in the shop including Robert Frost, Sinclair Lewis, Carl Sandburg, Alexander Woollcott, and others.

922
Lilac Hedge Bookshop
Main Street
Norwich, Vermont 05055   (802) 649-2921

Located in the center of a traditional New England village, the shop occupies two large rooms (750 square feet of space) in a colonial home built in 1804. It is surrounded by gardens and a white picket fence. The 9,000 volumes cover all categories, with many in fiction, literature, and art. Modern first editions are a specialty. Browsing is encouraged by virtue of many stools and chairs throughout, as well as roomy aisles, good lighting, and a fire in the fireplace in winter.

How to Get There: The bookstore is located across from the Norwich Inn, and is only one mile from Hanover, New Hampshire, the home of Dartmouth College. When driving, take Exit 13 off Interstate 91, five miles north of the intersection of I-91 and I-89. These are the main routes to Boston, New York, Montreal, and Burlington, Vermont.

Owner/Biography: Katherine and Robert Ericson.

Year Founded/History of Bookstore: Founded in 1980, the bookstore began in the Ericson's home in Putney, Vermont. The new location so far has only one lilac bush, but the name was retained, not only because the first shop was known by that name, but also because the original lilac hedge was famous locally, having been planted by the state governor.

Number of Volumes: 9,000.

Types/Classifications: Hardbound, paperback, prints, first editions, fine bindings, association copies, out-of-print, press books, signed copies, presentation copies, limited editions, color plate books.

General Subject Areas: American Political Biography, Americana, Antiques, Architecture, Arctic Adventure, Art, Business, Children's Books, Cinema, Cookbooks, Economics, Education, Fiction, Fishing, Foreign Countries, Gardening, History, Humor, Hunting, Law, Literature, Medicine, Military, Music, Nature and Animals, Philosophy, Photography, Plays, Poetry, Printing, Psychology, Reference, Religion, Science, Sea, Ships, Sociology, Sports, Technology, Theater, Women.

Mail/Telephone Orders; Credit Cards: Mail orders; personal checks are welcomed and should be sent with orders; no credit cards.

Business Hours: Thursday through Sunday 10:00 AM - 5:00 PM; Monday through Wednesday by appointment only.

Parking Facilities: Ample street and on-property parking.

Special Features: Search service, appraisals, readings of works in progress by local authors.

Catalogue: One or two times a year.

Collections/Individual Items Purchased: Both.

Booksellers' Memberships: Vermont Antiquarian Book Association.

923
Old Book Store
Main Street
Chapman's Pharmacy
Fairlee, Vermont 05045 (802) 333-9709

The bookstore is located in a store which features a pharmacy, vintage clothing, antiques, and sporting goods.

How to Get There: The store is located on Route 5, one-half mile north of Exit 15 of Route I-91.

Owner/Biography: Adele Chapman, John Larson.

Year Founded/History of Bookstore: 1976.

Number of Volumes: 10,000.

Types/Classifications: General stock, postcards, ephemera.

General Subject Areas: General.

Mail/Telephone Orders; Credit Cards: Both. No credit cards. An additional telephone number is (802) 333-9107.

Business Hours: Monday through Saturday 9:00 AM - 6:00 PM; Summers: Sunday, too.

Booksellers' Memberships: Vermont Antiquarian Book Sellers Association.

924
Richard H. Adelson, Antiquarian Booksellers
North Pomfret, Vermont 05053 (802) 457-2608

These antiquarian booksellers carry a stock of old and rare books for serious collectors only. Their last two travel catalogues were on collections of books on the Pacific Basin and on African exploration. Very few of the titles were printed after 1900. Visits are by appointment only.

Owner/Biography: Jane and Richard Adelson.

Year Founded/History of Bookstore: 1971.

Number of Volumes: 3,000.

Types/Classifications: Old and rare only.

General Subject Areas: Travel and Exploration.

Specific Specialties: Voyages and Travels to: North America, South America, Africa, Middle East, Pacific, East Asia; Rare Children's Books; Illustrated Books.

Author Specialties: Richard Francis Burton, Frederick Courteney Selous, Henry R. Schoolcraft, Kate Greenaway, Walter Crane, Edmund Dulac, Arthur Rackham, Peter Newell, Charles Robinson, W. Heath Robinson, H. Willabeek Le Mair.

Mail/Telephone Orders; Credit Cards: Both. No credit cards.

Business Hours: By appointment only.
Catalogue: Published 2 to 3 times per year.
Collections/Individual Items Purchased: Both.
Booksellers' Memberships: Antiquarian Booksellers Association of America, Vermont Antiquarian Booksellers Association.
Miscellaneous: The Adelsons exhibit at the ABAA Book Fairs in Boston, New York, Los Angeles, and San Francisco.

925
Tuttle Antiquarian Books, Inc.
28 South Main Street
Rutland, Vermont 05701   (802) 773-8930

The bookstore features a general line of second hand books in dozens of subject categories. The rooms are well lighted, and the bargain basement offers sets and selected remainders. There is a mail order department for genealogies, town and country histories of all 50 states and Canada, and related material.
How to Get There: The bookstore is on U.S. Route 7 in Rutland, Vermont, on the east side of Main Street Park.
Owner/Biography: Charles E. Tuttle. The Tuttle name has been known in bookselling and publishing in Rutland since 1832.
Year Founded/History of Bookstore: Formerly the old and rare book department of Charles E. Tuttle Co., Tuttle Antiquarian Books is now a separate corporation, sharing offices with its sister firm.
Number of Volumes: 50,000.
Types/Classifications: Hardbound, some broadsides, and other ephemera.
General Subject Areas: General.
Specific Specialties: Genealogy, Vermont, State and Local History of all 50 States and Canada.
Mail/Telephone Orders; Credit Cards: Both. Payment must accompany orders. No credit cards.
Business Hours: Monday through Friday 8:00 AM - 5:00 PM; Saturday 9:00 AM - 4:00 PM.
Parking Facilities: Plenty of street and off-street parking available.
Special Features: Located next door are the display room and office of the store's sister firm, Charles E. Tuttle Co., Inc., publishers and distributors of books about Japan, the Far East, and other selected publishing interests.
Catalogue: Occasionally.
Collections/Individual Items Purchased: Both.
Booksellers' Memberships: Antiquarian Booksellers Association of America.

926
Unique Antique
Main Street
Putney, Vermont 05346   (802) 387-4488

The bookstore is the downstairs of a large Victorian house, with a total of 1,200 square feet of space. In addition to a large stock of select antiquarian volumes, there are photographs from the 19th Century, a large assortment of ephemera, original prints, drawings, and paintings. The owner describes the shop as "a browser's dream, a poker's delight."
How to Get There: Putney, Vermont is 8 miles north of Brattleboro, in the southeast corner of the state. The shop is near Exit 4 of Interstate 91.
Owner/Biography: Jonathan Flaccus.
Year Founded/History of Bookstore: 1977.
Number of Volumes: 6,000.
Types/Classifications: Hardbound, ephemera, photographs, original art; the following are all in the out-of-print category: first editions, fine bindings, association copies, press books, signed copies, presentation copies, limited editions, color plate books.
General Subject Areas: Americana, Biography, Children's Books, Science Fiction and Fantasy.

Mail/Telephone Orders; Credit Cards: Telephone orders only; no credit cards.
Business Hours: By appointment only: 9:00 AM - 6:00 PM.
Parking Facilities: Private parking on the side of the building.
Special Features: The shop features individual attention to the interests of every customer.
Collections/Individual Items Purchased: Both.
Booksellers' Memberships: Vermont Antiquarian Booksellers Association, Ephemera Society of America.

927
Vermont Book Shop Inc.
38 Main Street
Middlebury, Vermont 05753 (802) 388-2061

This large trade store features out-of-print books of Vermont interest and Robert Frost items, of which it has a good stock.
Year Founded/History of Bookstore: 1949.
General Subject Areas: General, Vermont.
Specific Specialties: Robert Frost.
Author Specialties: Robert Frost.
Mail/Telephone Orders; Credit Cards: Both. Visa, Mastercard.
Business Hours: Daily 8:30 AM - 5:30 PM.
Special Features: Publishing sideline.

VIRGINIA

928
Alexander Lauberts Books
1073 West Broad
Falls Church, Virginia 22046   (703) 533-1699

This is a general antiquarian bookstore.

Owner/Biography: Alexander Lauberts, owner, was born in Latvia in 1908 and came to the United States in 1927. He returned to Europe in 1931 as a foreign correspondent.

Year Founded/History of Bookstore: The business was founded in 1942; the original bookstore was in Riga, Latvia. The first shop in the United States was in Georgetown, Washington, DC, in 1959.

Number of Volumes: 40,000.

Types/Classifications: Hardbound only; rare and out-of-print.

General Subject Areas: Americana, Aviation, Books About Books, Foreign Language Books, World War I, World War II.

Specific Specialties: Non-fiction only.

Mail/Telephone Orders; Credit Cards: No mail or telephone orders; no credit cards.

Business Hours: Wednesday through Saturday 12:00 Noon - 5:00 PM.

Parking Facilities: Parking lot.

Collections/Individual Items Purchased: Both.

929
Allbooks
4341 Majestic Lane
Fairfax, Virginia 22033   (703) 968-7396

Allbooks is a small shop occupying 150 square feet of space in the owner's home. Visits are by appointment only.

How to Get There: The shop is six miles west of Fairfax. Take U.S. 50 west from Fairfax, turn left at traffic light and go one mile on Majestic Lane to 4341.

Owner/Biography: Charles J. Robinore.

Year Founded/History of Bookstore: 1979.

Number of Volumes: 3,000.

Types/Classifications: Hardbound, out-of-print, general stock.

General Subject Areas: American Indians, Science Fiction and Fantasy.

Mail/Telephone Orders; Credit Cards: Both. Cash with order. No credit cards.

Business Hours: Any time by appointment.

Parking Facilities: Street parking.

Special Features: Search service with stock.

Catalogue: Annual catalogue published.

Collections/Individual Items Purchased: Both.

930
Book Ends
2710 Washington Boulevard
Arlington, Virginia 22201   (703) 524-4976

Book Ends is a general stock used bookstore situated in an old house. The seven rooms contain 30,000 books in all subject areas occupying 1,200 square feet of space.

How to Get There: The store can be reached by taking exit 8-A off Interstate 395.

Owner/Biography: Janet and Mike Deatherage.

Year Founded/History of Bookstore: 1978.

Number of Volumes: 30,000.

Types/Classifications: Hardbound, paperback, out-of-print.

General Subject Areas: Americana, Children's Books, Cookbooks, Military Literature, Mystery Novels, Performing Arts, Science Fiction and Fantasy, Transportation, World History.

Mail/Telephone Orders; Credit Cards: Both. No credit cards.

Business Hours: Friday through Monday 12:00 Noon - 6:00 PM.

Parking Facilities: Business parking lot.

Collections/Individual Items Purchased: Both.

931
Book House
209-B North Boundary Street
Williamsburg, Virginia 23185   (804) 229-3603

The Book House has a general stock of out-of-print and used books. It is situated in a small house in an alley within 1-1/2 blocks of the restored area of Williamsburg. It occupies 360 square feet of space.

How to Get There: 1-1/2 blocks north of Wren Building at College of William and Mary.

Owner/Biography: Mary Lewis Chapman. Ms. Chapman has published "Literary Sketches," a monthly literary newsletter since 1961. She has organized biennial literary tours of England since 1977 and completed the 5th trip in 1983. She is the author of "Literary Landmarks - Guide to Homes of American Writers" (1974).

Year Founded/History of Bookstore: 1977. The Book House has been in the same location and under the same ownership since its inception.

Number of Volumes: 4,000.

Types/Classifications: Hardbound, some paperback, famous illustrators, unusual bindings, first editions.

General Subject Areas: American History, Art, Black History, Children's Books, Civil War (U.S.), Cookbooks, Fiction, Hobbies, Literature, Mysteries, Occult, Philosophy, Psychology, Religion, Science Fiction, Sports, Travel, Women's Biography, World History.

Specific Specialties: Virginiana.

Mail/Telephone Orders; Credit Cards: Both. No credit cards.

Business Hours: Tuesday through Friday 10:00 AM - 4:00 PM; Saturday 10:00 AM - 2:00 PM. Closed Sunday and Monday.

Parking Facilities: Street parking.

Special Features: Literary tours of England; monthly newsletter ("Literary Sketches").

Collections/Individual Items Purchased: Both.

Miscellaneous: Friendly management.

932
Bookhouse
805 North Emerson Street
Arlington, Virginia 22205   (703) 527-7797

The Bookhouse occupies an old house entirely filled with books. It covers 1,700 square feet of space.

How to Get There: The bookstore is located off the 5100 block of Wilson boulevard (Route 613).

Owner/Biography: Edward and Natalie Hughes.

Year Founded/History of Bookstore: 1970. The bookstore began on Irving Street. With the purchase of a commercial zoned house on North Emerson Street, the Bookhouse expanded to fill seven rooms, a couple of nooks, plus a garage with additional books shelved.

Number of Volumes: 40,000.

Types/Classifications: Hardbound, some prints, first editions, out-of-print, color plate books, illustrated books.

General Subject Areas: American Indians, Americana, Art, Children's Books, Civil War (U.S.), Natural History, Rivers of America, Travel, Virginiana, WPA Guides.

Mail/Telephone Orders; Credit Cards: Both. American Express, Visa, Mastercard accepted.

Business Hours: Tuesday and Thursday 11:00 AM - 7:00 PM; Wednesday, Friday, Saturday 11:00 AM - 5:00 PM; Sunday 1:00 PM - 5:00 PM.

Parking Facilities: Parking and entrance are at the back.

Catalogue: Published irregularly.

Collections/Individual Items Purchased: Both.

933
Bookstop
109 South Alfred
Alexandria, Virginia 22314 $\qquad$ (703) 548-6566

The Bookstop is located in a spacious townhouse in historic Old Town Alexandria. It carries a general stock of books and a large collection of sheet music and memorabilia. The shop occupies 2,000 square feet of space.

Owner/Biography: Toby Cedar.

Year Founded/History of Bookstore: 1981.

Number of Volumes: 10,000.

Types/Classifications: Hardbound, paperback, ephemera, sheet music, memorabilia, first editions, out-of-print.

General Subject Areas: General.

Mail/Telephone Orders; Credit Cards: Both. Cash with order. No credit cards.

Business Hours: Monday, Tuesday, Wednesday, Friday, Saturday 11:00 AM - 6:00 PM; Sunday 12:00 Noon - 5:00 PM; closed Thursday.

Parking Facilities: Street parking.

Special Features: Search service.

Catalogue: Published quarterly.

Collections/Individual Items Purchased: Both.

934
Camelot Books
7603 Mulberry Bottom Lane
Springfield, Virginia 22153 $\qquad$ (703) 455-9540

Camelot Books specializes in Eugene O'Neill first editions, signed copies, and ephemera and also Wyeth family books.

How to Get There: Call for directions.

Types/Classifications: First editions, signed copies, ephemera, out-of-print, pre-1940 literary magazines.

Author Specialties: Eugene O'Neill, Wyeth Family.

Mail/Telephone Orders; Credit Cards: Mail orders.

935
Collectors' Old Book Shop
15 South Fifth Street
Richmond, Virginia 23219 $\qquad$ (804) 644-2097

The Collectors' Old Book Shop occupies approximately 1,200 square feet of space and carries hardbound, rare, and out-of-print stock.

How to Get There: The shop is located at the corner of Fifth and Cary Streets.

Owner/Biography: Mary Clark Roane.

Year Founded/History of Bookstore: 1945. The shop moved from 26 North Seventh Street at 707 East Franklin Street and subsequently to its current address.

Number of Volumes: 15,000.

Types/Classifications: Hardbound, broadsides, autographs, ephemera, first editions, out-of-print, signed copies.
    General Subject Areas: Americana, Confederacy, Juveniles, Literature, Virginiana.
    Mail/Telephone Orders; Credit Cards: Mail orders. No credit cards.
    Business Hours: Monday through Friday 11:00 AM to 5:00 PM; Saturday 11:00 AM to 3:00 PM.
    Parking Facilities: Street parking.
    Special Features: Search service.
    Collections/Individual Items Purchased: Both.

936
Daedalus Bookshop
121 4th Street, N.E.
Charlottesville, Virginia 22901   (804) 293-7595

    This bookshop specializes in fiction and has over 90,000 books in all subjects and categories. The stock occupies three floors.
    Owner/Biography: Sandy and Donna McAdams. Sandy McAdams is also the owner of the C & O Restaurant at 515 East Water Street which was given a "Five Spoons" rating by PM Magazine, Channel 9, Washington, D.C.
    Year Founded/History of Bookstore: 1972.
    Number of Volumes: 90,000.
    Types/Classifications: Hardbound, paperback, magazines, broadsides, autographs, ephemera, first editions, fine bindings, out-of-print, association copies, press books, signed copies, presentation copies, limited editions, color plate books.
    General Subject Areas: General.
    Specific Specialties: Fiction.
    Mail/Telephone Orders; Credit Cards: Both. No credit cards.
    Business Hours: Monday through Saturday 10:00 AM - 5:00 PM.
    Parking Facilities: Public parking lot, street parking.
    Special Features: Search service.
    Collections/Individual Items Purchased: Collections only.

937
From Out of the Past
6440 Richmond Highway
Alexandria, Virginia 22306   (703) 768-7827

    From Out of the Past is a unique bookstore with over one million items in stock covering many subject areas. It has a full-range of material for the hardbound and paper collector, from the quite common to the very rare. Leisurely browsing through the open-stack sections is encouraged. Also included is an excellent selection of collector prints, both old and new, and a wide choice of original, classic, period advertising. The paperback book section contains both current and early collectible titles in many categories. The stock is well organized and much of what is in stock is catalogued and content referenced.
    How to Get There: Located 1 1/2 miles south of the Capital Beltway on Richmond Highway (Route 1), the shop is in the small shopping area just before the MEMCO store on the right-hand side of the street heading south.
    Owner/Biography: Barbara and Mike Keck.
    Year Founded/History of Bookstore: 1974.
    Number of Volumes: 200,000 hardbound; 500,000 magazines.
    Types/Classifications: Hardbound, magazines, ephemera, first editions, fine bindings, out-of-print, association copies, press copies, signed copies, presentation copies, limited editions, color plate books.
    General Subject Areas: Americana, General, Military, World History.
    Mail/Telephone Orders; Credit Cards: Both. Visa and Mastercard accepted.
    Business Hours: Tuesday through Saturday 11:00 AM - 6:00 PM.

Parking Facilities: Business parking lot.
Catalogue: Catalogue published.
Collections/Individual Items Purchased: Collections only.

938
Ghent Bookworm
1407 Colley Avenue
Norfolk, Virginia 23517 (804) 627-2267

The Ghent Bookworm occupies two rooms and a hallway in an old beauty shop plus two rooms in a converted garage. The shop is attached to an early 20th Century house. Primitive tools and household items are on display throughout the shop.

How to Get There: The shop is located in the Old Ghent area of Norfolk not far from the newly constructed Waterside Festival Place.
Owner/Biography: Bill Hudnall.
Year Founded/History of Bookstore: 1970.
Number of Volumes: 15,000.
Types/Classifications: Hardbound, paperback, ephemera, first editions, fine bindings, out-of-print, association copies, press books.
General Subject Areas: American and European History, American and World Literature, Art, Biography, Black History, Children's Books, Civil War (U.S.), Domestic Science, Languages, Maritime, Music, Natural History, Philosophy, Politics, Religion, Science Fiction and Fantasy, Sociology.
Mail/Telephone Orders; Credit Cards: Both. American Express, Visa, Mastercard accepted.
Business Hours: Tuesday through Friday 11:30 AM - 5:30 PM; Saturday 10:00 AM - 5:30 PM.
Parking Facilities: Street parking.
Special Features: Search service; appraisals; special orders.
Collections/Individual Items Purchased: Both.

939
Givens Books Inc.
2345 Lakeside Drive
Lynchburg, Virginia 24501 (804) 237-3440

Given Books has a general stock of hardbound and paperback used and out-of-print books. The store occupies 4,000 square feet of space.

How to Get There: The bookstore is on Route 221 just east of the intersection with the 291 Expressway.
Owner/Biography: George and Sylvia Givens.
Year Founded/History of Bookstore: 1975.
Number of Volumes: 50,000.
Types/Classifications: Hardbound, paperback, first editions, out-of-print, limited editions.
General Subject Areas: Americana, Biography, Children's Literature, Classics, Religion, Travel, World History.
Mail/Telephone Orders; Credit Cards: Both. Visa and Mastercard accepted.
Business Hours: Monday through Saturday 9:30 AM - 9:00 PM.
Parking Facilities: Business parking lot.
Collections/Individual Items Purchased: Both.

940
Heartwood Books
5 & 9 Elliewood Avenue
Charlottesville, Virginia 22903 (804) 295-7083

Heartwood Books has two shops next door to one another. The general used bookshop is at Number 5 Elliewood and features scholarly and popular books in most areas. Number 9 Elliewood houses a general antiquarian bookshop.

How to Get There: The shops are 1 block from the main grounds of the University of Virginia, just off University Avenue. There is a large tree painted on the side of Number 5 Elliewood.

Owner/Biography: Paul Collinge and Sher Joseph. Both owners are veterans of Washington, D.C.'s largest new book shop, Savile Books (now closed). They have been dealing exclusively in used and rare books since 1973.

Year Founded/History of Bookstore: 1975.

Number of Volumes: 40,000.

Types/Classifications: Hardbound, paperback, autographs, ephemera, pamphlets, leatherbound, first editions, fine bindings, out-of-print, association copies, press books, signed copies, presentation copies, limited editions.

General Subject Areas: Americana, Art, Cookbooks, English and American Literature, History, Scholarly Books, Social Sciences.

Specific Specialties: 19th Century English and American Literature, Virginiana, Civil War (U.S.), Thomas Jefferson.

Author Specialties: William Dean Howells, Max Beerbohm, Thomas Jefferson.

Other Specialties: Scholarly works in most fields.

Mail/Telephone Orders; Credit Cards: Both.

Business Hours: Monday through Friday 11:00 AM - 7:30 PM; Saturday 11:00 AM - 6:00 PM; Number 9 Elliewood open Monday through Saturday 11:00 AM - 6:00 PM.

Parking Facilities: 2 adjoining parking lots.

Special Features: Search service; appraisals for estate insurance; purchase and removal of books.

Catalogue: Published quarterly.

Collections/Individual Items Purchased: Both.

Booksellers' Memberships: Antiquarian Booksellers Association of America.

941

Jo Ann Reisler, Ltd.

360 Glyndon Street, N.E.

Vienna, Virginia 22180 (703) 938-2967

Jo Ann Reisler, Ltd. operates predominantly through catalogues and shows but has a warm welcome for clients visiting the Washington area who would like to stop by. It is requested that an appointment be made.

How to Get There: The bookstore is situated just 5 minutes from Washington via Capitol Beltway (Exit 11S).

Owner/Biography: Jo Ann and Donald Reisler.

Year Founded/History of Bookstore: 1972.

Number of Volumes: 4,000.

Types/Classifications: First editions, fine bindings, out-of-print, association copies, press books, signed copies, presentation copies, limited editions, color plate books, illustrated books.

General Subject Areas: Children's Books, Early Paper Dolls and Toys, Miniature Books, Original Illustrative Art (Contemporary and Antiquarian).

Specific Specialties: Victorian Color Plate (Greenaway, Crane, etc.), 20th Century Illustrators (Rackham, Dulac, etc.), Oziana, Alice in Wonderland, Contemporary Illustrative Art by Alice and Martin Provensen and Michael Hague.

Mail/Telephone Orders; Credit Cards: Both. No credit cards.

Business Hours: By appointment only.

Parking Facilities: Street parking.

Catalogue: Published 2 times per year.

Collections/Individual Items Purchased: Both.

Booksellers' Memberships: Antiquarian Booksellers Association of America.

942
Nelson Bond
4724 Easthill Drive
Roanoke, Virginia 24018

(703) 774-2674

The bookstore is located in a specially constructed, well lighted, well shelved bookroom annexed to the owner's private residence in the Roanoke suburbs. The bookroom is 45' by 25', but the stock necessarily spills over into adjacent rooms when large lots are purchased. The stock is principally literature, arranged alphabetically by authors, but with sections on such other fields as Virginiana, Science, and so forth. The main specialty is books by and about Virginia author James Branch Cabell. The owner probably buys and sells more Cabell items annually than any other ten book dealers combined. The shop is not open to the general public, but visiting bookpersons are welcome at all times.

How to Get There: If driving to Roanoke via Interstate 81, turn off at Exit 41, proceed south on Route 419 seven miles to a green and white sign: Sugar Loaf Farms. Turn right (only possible way) then immediately take left fork one block, and next left again one block to the intersection of Geiser Road and Easthill Drive. The shop is in a large house with four white two-story columns. The bookroom is at the rear; there are two driveways.

Owner/Biography: Nelson Bond, owner, has been a professional writer since the 1930's. He wrote and published more then 500 short stories in national magazines, 300 radio plays, 50 TV plays, several stage plays, and numerous books. Bond left Hollywood in the 1960's to enter his new profession of bookman, but is still being actively published in the U.S. and abroad. He also has a science fiction fan club named in his honor: The Nelson Bond Society.

Year Founded/History of Bookstore: Establishing his new business in 1967, Nelson Bond experienced the common transition from book collector to knowledgeable book scout, then gingerly adopted books as a full time profession about 1967. His first years were spent learning the business without great capital growth or expansion. The venture developed into a sturdy business about 1970, and has now become the proprietor's chief source of income.

Number of Volumes: 7,500.

Types/Classifications: Hardbound books only. Fine First Editions, Signed Copies, Limited Editions, Presentation Copies. The stock is principally literature, but there are other categories.

General Subject Areas: General.

Specific Specialties: Books by and about James Branch Cabell.

Author Specialties: James Branch Cabell, Ray Bradbury, Larry McMurtry.

Mail/Telephone Orders; Credit Cards: Both. No special requirements; cash with order is not required; prices include postage and insurance; no handling fee. No credit cards.

Business Hours: There are no specific business hours; the owner is available 24 hours a day. It is advisable to telephone ahead if planning to visit.

Parking Facilities: Ample parking in the double driveways and street.

Special Features: Mr. Bond features friendly relations with fellow bookmen; he says he "would rather give them a drink and talk to them than to sell to them."

Catalogue: Catalogues are published quarterly; lists are issued monthly.

Collections/Individual Items Purchased: Both.

Booksellers' Memberships: Antiquarian Booksellers Association of America, International League of Antiquarian Booksellers.

943
Old Favorites Bookshop
610 North Sheppard Street
Richmond, Virginia 23221

(804) 355-2279

The shop is a relatively new used and antiquarian bookstore located just outside Richmond's historic Fan District. Its modest collection of used books covers all fields, with an emphasis on the American Civil War and Science Fiction and Fantasy. The shop contains 630 square feet of space.

How to Get There: If driving Interstate 95 take the Boulevard Exit and proceed south for about 2 miles, turn right at Park Avenue, and go 2 blocks; left on Sheppard to the fourth shop on the right.

Owner/Biography: Gary O'Neal and Karen O'Neal.

Year Founded/History of Bookstore: 1982.
Number of Volumes: 15,000.
Types/Classifications: Hardbound, paperback, magazines, newspapers, first editions, limited editions, out-of-print.
General Subject Areas: Children's Books, Civil War (U.S.), Science Fiction and Fantasy, World War I, World War II.
Author Specialties: H.P. Lovecraft, Edgar Allan Poe, Bram Stoker, C. Dowdy, D.S. Freeman, Thomas Mann.
Other Specialties: Some German language books; the shop hopes to expand this area.
Mail/Telephone Orders; Credit Cards: Both. Cash with order except for institutions. Visa, Mastercard.
Business Hours: Monday through Friday 10:00 AM - 6:00 PM; Saturday 10:00 AM - 4:00 PM.
Parking Facilities: Street.
Special Features: Search service.
Catalogue: U.S. Civil War, 3 times a year; Science Fiction and Fantasy, several times a year.
Collections/Individual Items Purchased: Both.

944
Richmond Book Shop
808 West Broad Street
Richmond, Virginia 23220   (804) 644-9970

The Richmond Book Shop is in a two-story brick building and occupies 3,500 square feet of space.
How to Get There: The shop is one block from Route 1 and Route 301; if using I-95, take the Belvidere Exit to Broad Street.
Owner/Biography: V.T. Gilligan, President; Jean K. Gilligan, Vice President.
Year Founded/History of Bookstore: 1957. The owners originally took over Cooper's Old Book Shop, changed the name to its present one, and moved twice until the present location was chosen 15 years ago.
Number of Volumes: 25,000.
Types/Classifications: Hardbound, rare, remainders, paperback, back issues of magazines, first editions, out-of-print.
General Subject Areas: Adventure, Americana, Animals, Antiques, Art, Astrology, Astronomy, Automobiles, Aviation, Black Americans, Children's Books, Circus, Civil War and Confederacy, Cookbooks, Drama, Engineering, Erotica, Fishing, Genealogy, Guns and Hunting, Humor, Language, Literature, Military, Movies, Music, Mysteries, Natural History, Occult, Philosophy, Photography, Poetry, Politics, Railroads, Religion, Science Fiction and Fantasy, Sea, South (U.S.), Sports, Theater, Travel and Foreign, Westerns, Women, World Wars I and II.
Specific Specialties: Virginia.
Mail/Telephone Orders; Credit Cards: Both. Visa and Mastercard accepted.
Business Hours: Monday through Saturday 10:00 AM - 4:00 PM.
Parking Facilities: Street parking.
Collections/Individual Items Purchased: Both.

945
Royal Oak Bookshop
207 South Royal Avenue
Front Royal, Virginia 22630   (703) 635-7070

The Royal Oak carries new, used, and out-of-print material including paperbacks. The stock is general and covers most subject areas.
How to Get There: Located in the Shenandoah Valley, the shop is 1 mile from the Skyline Drive.
Owner/Biography: Nan Hathaway.
Year Founded/History of Bookstore: 1975.
Types/Classifications: Hardbound, paperback, magazines, broadsides, autographs, ephemera, first editions, out-of-print.
General Subject Areas: General.

Specific Specialties: Civil War (U.S.), Virginiana.
Author Specialties: May Sarton.
Mail/Telephone Orders; Credit Cards: Both. American Express, Visa, Mastercard accepted.
Business Hours: Monday through Saturday 9:00 AM - 6:00 PM; Sunday 12:00 Noon - 5:00 PM.
Parking Facilities: Business parking lot.
Special Features: Search service.
Collections/Individual Items Purchased: Both.

946
Samuel Yudkin & Associates
1125 King Street
Alexandria, Virginia 22314 (703) 549-9330

Samuel Yudkin & Associates is the "oldest bookshop - new or used - in Alexandria." The shop carries a large and extensive general stock of hardbound and paperback material. In addition to used books, the store has many new remainders, comics, magazines, postcards, and first day covers. The store occupies 4,000 square feet of space.
How to Get There: The store is on the main street of Alexandria in West Old Town, a few blocks from the Metro Subway. Alexandria is about 10 minutes from Washington National Airport.
Owner/Biography: Samuel Yudkin.
Year Founded/History of Bookstore: 1970.
Number of Volumes: 70,000.
Types/Classifications: Hardbound, paperback, magazines, postcards, press books, comics, documents, ephemera, out-of-print, first editions, color plate books, remainders.
General Subject Areas: General.
Specific Specialties: Civil War (U.S.), World War II, Naval, Americana.
Other Specialties: Science Fiction (Paperback).
Mail/Telephone Orders; Credit Cards: Both. Visa and Mastercard accepted.
Business Hours: Monday through Saturday 10:00 AM - 6:30 PM; Sunday 12:00 Noon - 5:00 PM.
Parking Facilities: Street parking (2 hour zone).
Special Features: Search service; listing charge $1 per title except for institutions.
Catalogue: Published occasionally.
Collections/Individual Items Purchased: Both.

947
Store, The
240 Main Street (Route 11)
Mt. Crawford, Virginia 22841 (703) 433-9388

The Store in Mt. Crawford is located in a Pre-Civil War building which until recently has always housed a general store. Now the shelves contain books and the center of the large room is filled with tables and cabinets which hold one of Virginia's largest collections of old prints and ephemera.
How to Get There: Mt. Crawford in is the heart of the Shenandoah Valley 7 miles south of Harrisonburg, Virginia. It can be reached via Route 11 or I-81.
Owner/Biography: Kay Hodge.
Year Founded/History of Bookstore: 1976.
Number of Volumes: 10,000.
Types/Classifications: Hardbound, magazines, ephemera, prints, postcards, some first editions, some signed copies, pamphlets, out-of-print.
General Subject Areas: Americana, Architecture, Art, Biography, Children's Literature, Fiction, History, Local and Confederate Imprints, Music, Poetry, Religious Short Stories, Theater.
Mail/Telephone Orders; Credit Cards: Both. Visa and Mastercard accepted.
Business Hours: By chance or appointment.
Parking Facilities: Parking lot across the street, street parking.

Special Features: Search service; kid's corner for browsing parents with small children.
Catalogue: Published occasionally.
Collections/Individual Items Purchased: Individual items; collections sometimes.

948
Waves Press & Bookshop
4040 MacArthur Avenue
Richmond, Virginia 23227 (804) 264-7276

Featuring a long and narrow storefront, the bookstore is located on a small, isolated commercial street in the midst of a pretty neighborhood. A small desk with a typewriter greets the customer, and beyond that are walls on shelves plus free-standing bookcases. Also on the walls are old etchings, prints, and pastels. In the center of the shop is an old Vandercook No. 4 proof press. The shop contains 400 square feet of space.

How to Get There: The shop is easily reached if driving on either of two interstates: from I-95 take the Virginia Museum Boulevard or 301 north, local traffic exits; from I-64 take the Laburnum Avenue Exit. In both cases one should ask directions.

Owner/Biography: Damon Persiani, owner, was born in Washington, D.C. and has a B.A. in English Literature and Philosophy; married in 1971, he is the father of a young son.

Year Founded/History of Bookstore: The bookstore was opened in 1973 as The Book Room at a nearby downtown location. After one year the stock was moved to the owner's home to issue catalogues. In 1977 the present location was rented.

Number of Volumes: 10,000.

Types/Classifications: Hardbound, limited stock of little magazines and vintage paperbacks, first editions, fine editions, leather sets, publisher's trade bindings, signed copies, fiction reprints in dust jackets (no later printings - firsts only), illustrated books, modern first editions.

General Subject Areas: Books About Books, Boxing, Detective Fiction, Fishing, Golf (Pre-1950), Hunting, Literature, Nineteenth Century Gardening and Landscape, Richmond (Virginia), Science Fiction and Fantasy, Sporting, Tennis (Pre-1950), Virginia.

Specific Specialties: Papermaking, Wood Engraving, Engravers, Marbling, Bookbinding, Letterpress Printing and Presswork, Bibliomysteries.

Author Specialties: Ellen Glasgow, Rex Stout, Erle Stanley Gardner, Havilah Babcock, W.A. Dwiggins, Edgar Allan Poe, Bram Stoker, Maurice Le Blanc, Gaston Leroux, Dashiell Hammett, Raymond Chandler, Fergus Hume, Arthur Conan Doyle, Melville Davisson Post, Dard Hunter, John Mason.

Mail/Telephone Orders; Credit Cards: Mail orders; cash with order if not known to the bookstore. Visa, Mastercard.

Business Hours: Monday through Friday 12:00 Noon - 5:00 PM; Saturday 12:00 Noon - 4:00 PM.

Parking Facilities: Street.

Special Features: Publisher of limited signed editions, especially mysteries. The owner says "there is beer in the 'fridge or scotch in the desk."

Catalogue: Two to four times per year.

Collections/Individual Items Purchased: Both.

Miscellaneous: Reciprocal 10 percent trade discount; reciprocal catalogue exchange; fellow booksellers welcome.

WASHINGTON

949
A Different Drummer
420 Broadway East
Seattle, Washington 98102 (206) 324-0525

The bookstore sells both new and used books. The back half of the shop is devoted to a large variety of first editions, out-of-print, and general used books. There are stepladders about, to make it easy for people to help themselves, and chairs and alcoves for serious browsers to sit in. It is a general bookstore, but features strong art, fiction, science fiction and fantasy, religion, and occult sections. It contains 1,600 square feet of space.

How to Get There: The bookstore is located in the heart of the Broadway shopping district on Capitol Hill, just northeast of downtown.
Owner/Biography: Bud and Hazel Tinsley.
Year Founded/History of Bookstore: 1970.
Number of Volumes: 28,000 used books; 20,000 new books.
Types/Classifications: Hardbound, paperpack.
General Subject Areas: Americana, Anthropology, Architecture, Art, Biography, Black Studies, Car Repair, Cinema, Cookbooks, Crafts, Drama, Eastern Religions, Economics, Education, Fiction, Foreign Languages, Games, Gardening, History, Home Repair, Humor, Indian Studies, Literary Criticism, Music, Nature, Occult, Outdoors, Philosophy, Photography, Poetry, Psychology, Reference, Science, Science Fiction and Fantasy, Sexuality, Sociology, Sports, Western Religions.
Specific Specialties: Pacific Northwest.
Mail/Telephone Orders; Credit Cards: Mail orders only; cash with order.
Business Hours: Weekdays 10:00 AM - 11:00 PM; Sunday Noon - 10:00 PM.
Parking Facilities: Street.
Special Features: Search service.
Collections/Individual Items Purchased: Both.

950
Book Store
108 East 4th Avenue
Olympia, Washington 98501 (206) 754-7470

The Book Store sells quality used and out-of-print books in all categories but emphasizes books on the Pacific Northwest and books by and about women. The women's section, recently expanded to an upstairs room, has a rapidly growing selection of titles. The shop occupies 900 square feet of space.

How to Get There: Centrally located in downtown Olympia.
Owner/Biography: Carol D. McKinley. A former English teacher, Ms. McKinley has been in the book business for seven years.
Year Founded/History of Bookstore: 1976. Originally The Book Store was located in Centralia, Washington and was operated by Carol McKinley and Carol Papworth. In 1978 the business moved to Olympia and in 1983 Carol McKinley became the sole proprietor.
Number of Volumes: 10,000.
Types/Classifications: Hardbound, some quality paperback, out-of-print.
General Subject Areas: Biography, Children's Literature, Games, History, Literature, Natural Science, Northwest Americana, Reference, Social Science, Sports, Technical, Women's History, Women's Literature.
Specific Specialties: Literary Women, Pacific Northwest History.
Mail/Telephone Orders; Credit Cards: Both. Cash with order. No credit cards.

Business Hours: Monday through Saturday 10:00 AM - 5:30 PM.
Parking Facilities: Street parking.
Special Features: Search service, special orders.
Catalogue: Published twice yearly.
Collections/Individual Items Purchased: Both.
Booksellers' Memberships: Book Club of Washington.

951
Brused Books
N. 105 Grand
Pullman, Washington 99163   (509) 334-7898

Brused Books is a general used bookstore with a little of everything arranged so one can find books of interest. It occupies 1,300 square feet of space.
How to Get There: Located in downtown Pullman at corner of Main and Grand.
Owner/Biography: Bruce Calkins.
Year Founded/History of Bookstore: 1981.
Number of Volumes: 17,000.
Types/Classifications: Hardbound, paperback, some magazines.
General Subject Areas: Animals, Anthropology, Biography, Children's Books, Cookbooks, History, How-To, Literature, Nature, Northwest History, Philosophy, Psychology, Religion, Science Fiction.
Mail/Telephone Orders; Credit Cards: Both. No credit cards.
Business Hours: Tuesday through Saturday 11:00 AM - 6:00 PM.
Parking Facilities: Street parking.
Special Features: Search service.
Collections/Individual Items Purchased: Both.

952
C.L. Easton, Books
1010 West Division
Mount Vernon, Washington 98273   (206) 424-4617

This bookshop has a general stock of used hardbound and paperback books including first editions, out-of-print, and scarce items. The shop occupies 1,200 square feet of space.
How to Get There: Mount Vernon is located 70 miles north of Seattle. The store is 1 mile from the Mt. Vernon-Kincaid Street Exit off Interstate 5 on the west side of the Skagit River.
Owner/Biography: Diana Cornelius.
Year Founded/History of Bookstore: 1976.
Number of Volumes: 25,000.
Types/Classifications: Hardbound, paperback, out-of-print, first editions, scarce.
General Subject Areas: Art, Biography, Boating, Children's Books, Classics, Cooking, History, Humor, Natural Science, Outdoors, Psychology, Religion, Sociology, Technical, Travel.
Specific Specialties: Pacific Northwest.
Mail/Telephone Orders; Credit Cards: Both. Check with order. No credit cards.
Business Hours: Tuesday through Saturday 10:30 AM - 5:00 PM.
Parking Facilities: Free parking in front of store.
Collections/Individual Items Purchased: Both.
Booksellers' Memberships: American Booksellers Association.

953
Clark's Old Book Store
318 West Sprague
Spokane, Washington 99204
                                                           (509) 624-1846

This bookstore carries mostly hardbound stock with some paperback and magazines. It is a family bookstore and occupies 1,100 square feet of space.

How to Get There: The shop is located in downtown Spokane.

Owner/Biography: James and Irene Simon.

Year Founded/History of Bookstore: 1910. Spokane's first and oldest used bookstore was established by a retired school teacher, Reba Knight, who soon sold to Mrs. John Clark in 1910. She and her family operated the store after the death of Mr. Clark in 1930. In 1950 Jerome and LaVerle Pettier purchased the store and maintained the name and location on West Main Street. A western art gallery was possible by a move to West Riverside. The current location was found in 1972 as Spokane prepared for Expo '74. James and Irene Simon became the third owners in 1978.

Number of Volumes: 15,000 hardbound, 5,000 paperback.

Types/Classifications: Hardbound, paperback, magazines, comics.

General Subject Areas: Americana, Ancient Cultures, Anthropology, Antiques, Art, Astrology, Astronomy, Automotive Repair, Aviation, Bibles, Biography, Children's Books, Civil War (U.S.), Classics, Cookbooks, Crafts, Criminology, Drama, Economics, Education, Fishing, Gardening, Genealogy, Health, Humor, Hunting, Mathematics, Medical, Mountaineering, Movies, Music, Mysteries, Nature, Needlecraft, Occult, Philosophy, Photography, Poetry, Psychology, Railroads, Reference, Religion, Science, Science Fiction, Self-Help, Sociology, Speech Arts, Sports, Travel, Trivia, U.S. History.

Specific Specialties: Northwest (U.S.)

Mail/Telephone Orders; Credit Cards: Both. Book cost and shipping (4th class) prepaid to U.S. only. No credit cards.

Business Hours: Tuesday through Saturday 10:00 AM - 5:00 PM.

Parking Facilities: Public parking lot within a block of store, street parking.

Special Features: Trade paperback fiction and magazines; maintenance of "want" file and will contact buyer when available.

Collections/Individual Items Purchased: Both; limited collections purchased.

954

Comstock's Bindery and Bookstore

7903 Rainier Avenue South

Seattle, Washington 98118 (206) 725-9531

The store is a modern block building with book stock tightly packed on shelving from floor to ceiling. The back file magazine stock is arranged by years in display boxes. Paperbacks are filed by author or subject. There is also a small custom hand bookbindery.

How to Get There: Near Lake Washington, the bookstore is 8 miles south of downtown Seattle and exactly 4 miles north of Renton at the corner of Rainier Avenue South and Kenyon Street.

Owner/Biography: David and Anita Comstock.

Year Founded/History of Bookstore: 1963. The business began with just the bindery, operating from the basement of the owners' home. In 1968 the owners moved into the present building and began the bookstore.

Number of Volumes: 30,000 hardbound plus 10,000 back file special interest magazines and 12,000 paperback.

Types/Classifications: Hardbound, paperback, magazines, out-of-print.

General Subject Areas: Alaska, Art, Automobile, Aviation, Books About Books, Cookery, History, Juveniles, Literature, Military, Mountaineering, Natural History, Nautical, Naval, Pacific Northwest Americana, Photography, Religion, Science, Technical, West (U.S.).

Specific Specialties: World War II, Pacific Northwest History.

Mail/Telephone Orders; Credit Cards: Both. Orders must be prepaid before shipping. Visa and Mastercard acepted.

Business Hours: Monday through Friday 10:00 AM - 6:00 PM; Sunday 12:00 Noon - 5:00 PM; closed Saturday.

Parking Facilities: Business parking lot.

Special Features: Custom hand book binding; search service for regular customers.

Collections/Individual Items Purchased: Both.

955
David Ishii, Bookseller
212 First Avenue South
Seattle, Washington 98104 (206) 622-4719

The bookstore is in the Grand Central On The Park Arcade south of downtown Seattle. The stock is a small collection of scarce and out-of-print used books. There is a carpeted balcony storing the literature, history, and poetry books and downstairs are the art, juveniles, and Northwest books. The bookstore occupies about 700 square feet of space including the balcony.

How to Get There: The bookstore is located in the historic Pioneer Square which was built after the 1889 fire. The Square now has a good selection of restaurants, shops, and several tours. The bookstore is only a few blocks from the Kingdome, home of the Seattle Mariner baseball team.

Owner/Biography: David Ishii.

Year Founded/History of Bookstore: 1972. Mr. Ishii put the store together along with Taylor Bowie in its present location. Taylor Bowie was only 19 years old when he did the buying for the store. Today he has his own store in Seattle.

Number of Volumes: 5,000.

Types/Classifications: Hardbound, pamphlets, out-of-print, fine printing, first editions, limited editions, fine press books.

General Subject Areas: American Art in the 1950's, Dance, Fly Fishing, Juveniles, Literature, Music, Theatre, Western Americana.

Specific Specialties: Asian Americana (Japanese, Chinese, Fillipinos in America).

Author Specialties: Roderick Haig-Brown.

Mail/Telephone Orders; Credit Cards: Both. Exact title and author needed. No credit cards.

Business Hours: Monday through Saturday 10:00 AM - 6:00 PM; Sunday 10:00 AM - 5:00 PM.

Parking Facilities: Public parking lots, street parking (do be careful not to park on some streets after 4:00 PM and watch for no parking signs on the Sundays the Seahawks play in the Kingdome).

Special Features: Search service for which a small fee is charged; appraisals.

Catalogue: Published infrequently.

Collections/Individual Items Purchased: Both.

Booksellers' Memberships: Book Club of Washington.

Miscellaneous: Always especially welcome to come in and chat are those interested in fly fishing, historic preservation, and the arts; the owner likes to keep in touch first-hand as to what is happening in other parts of the country on these subjects.

956
Fillipi Book & Record Shop
1351 East Olive Way
Seattle, Washington 98122

This bookshop features not only used hardbound books but old 78 and 33 1/3 RPM recordings.

How to Get There: The shop is located in downtown Seattle.

Owner/Biography: Mr. and Mrs. Fillipi.

Types/Classifications: Hardbound, out-of-print, first editions, phonograph records, artwork.

General Subject Areas: General.

Mail/Telephone Orders; Credit Cards: Both.

Business Hours: Daily.

Parking Facilities: Available.

Collections/Individual Items Purchased: Both.

957
Fouray Book Store
1306 First Avenue
Seattle, Washington 98101

The Fouray Book Store stocks a general line but has specialties in technical and how-to books.
How to Get There: The store is located in downtown Seattle.
Types/Classifications: Hardbound, paperback, out-of-print, first editions.
General Subject Areas: General, How-To, Technical.
Mail/Telephone Orders; Credit Cards: Mail orders.
Business Hours: Daily.
Parking Facilities: Available.
Collections/Individual Items Purchased: Both.

958
George H. Tweney - Books
16660 Marine View Drive S.W.
Seattle, Washington 98166 (206) 243-8243

This antiquarian bookstore is operated from a private residence by appointment only. It carries hardbound, out-of-print stock plus maps, manuscripts, and prints.
How to Get There: The location of the business is 3 miles due west from Henry M. Jackson International Airport; owner will meet planes to pick up clients by prior arrangement.
Owner/Biography: George H. and Maxine R. Tweney. Mr. Tweney has been a book collector for 50 years and has been a full-time antiquarian bookseller since 1972.
Year Founded/History of Bookstore: 1962.
Number of Volumes: 3,500.
Types/Classifications: Hardbound, out-of-print, maps, manuscripts, prints, first editions, fine bindings, association copies, press books, signed copies, presentation copies, limited editions, color plate books.
General Subject Areas: American Literature, Book Collecting, Books About Books, Eighteenth Century English Literature, Voyages and Travels, Western Americana.
Specific Specialties: Lewis and Clark, Boswell and Johnson.
Author Specialties: A. Edward Newton, Jack London, George Sterling, Frederick Manfred, Lawrence Clark Powell.
Mail/Telephone Orders; Credit Cards: Both. Cash with order except for established clients, libraries, and institutions; $1 per volume for mailing, packing, and insuring. No credit cards.
Business Hours: By appointment; telephone anytime.
Parking Facilities: Private driveway.
Special Features: Appraisal service of all kinds.
Catalogue: Published randomly.
Collections/Individual Items Purchased: Both.
Booksellers' Memberships: Antiquarian Booksellers Association of America, International League of Antiquarian Booksellers, American Antiquarian Society.

959
Glover-Hayes Books
720 Pike Street
Seattle, Washington 98101

This bookstore handles old and used hardbound material with an emphasis on the arts and the Pacific Northwest.
How to Get There: The shop is located in downtown Seattle.
Types/Classifications: Hardbound, out-of-print, first editions.
General Subject Areas: Art, General, Pacific Northwest.
Mail/Telephone Orders; Credit Cards: Mail orders.
Business Hours: Daily.
Parking Facilities: Ample parking available.

960
Golden Age Collectables
1501 Pike Place Market
401 Lower Level
Seattle, Washington 98101   (206) 622-9799

Golden Age Collectables is "the largest comic book and movie nostalgia store in the Northwest," according to the owner's description. The store occupies 2,000 square feet of space.
How to Get There: The store is located on the lower level of Seattle's historic Pike Place Market in downtown Seattle overlooking the waterfront.
Owner/Biography: Rod and Colleen Dyke.
Year Founded/History of Bookstore: 1979.
Number of Volumes: 1 million comics; thousands of books.
Types/Classifications: Rare and new comic books, movie posters, autographs, movie stills.
General Subject Areas: Comic Books.
Author Specialties: Stephen King (Firsts, signed, proofs).
Mail/Telephone Orders; Credit Cards: Both. Phone orders with credit card preferred. Visa and Mastercard accepted.
Business Hours: Monday through Saturday 10:00 AM - 5:30 PM.
Parking Facilities: Public parking lot, street parking.
Catalogue: Annual Catalogue of Comic Books only.
Collections/Individual Items Purchased: Both.

961
Jane's Books
12348 Lake City Way
Seattle, Washington 98125   (206) 362-1766

This is a small, general bookstore, with 350 square feet of space.
Owner/Biography: Jane Blackney.
Year Founded/History of Bookstore: 1972; still on its original site.
Number of Volumes: 25,000.
Types/Classifications: Hardbound, paperback.
General Subject Areas: Automotive, Children's Books, Cookbooks, How-To Books, Northwest (U.S.), Science Fiction and Fantasy.
Specific Specialties: Large collection of Cookbooks.
Mail/Telephone Orders; Credit Cards: Both; self-stamped envelope.
Business Hours: Monday through Saturday 11:00 AM - 4:00 PM.
Parking Facilities: Street.
Collections/Individual Items Purchased: Both.

962
M. Taylor Bowie, Bookseller
2613 Fifth Avenue
Seattle, Washington 98121   (206) 682-5363

The bookstore features old, rare, and unusual books in many fields, especially modern literary firsts, travel and exploration, illustrated, and books about books. The shop contains 550 square feet of space.
Owner/Biography: M. Taylor Bowie.
Year Founded/History of Bookstore: 1976.
Number of Volumes: 7,500.
Types/Classifications: Hardbound, collector material of all kinds, first editions, fine bindings, out-of-print, association copies, press books, signed copies, presentation copies, limited editions, color plate books, literary first editions (English and American), inscribed, association copies.
General Subject Areas: Alaska, Americana, Books About Books, Crime, Criticism, Exploration, Jazz,

Literature, Natural History, Pacific Northwest, Popular Music (Pre-1960), Printing, Travel, Unusual Subjects.
Author Specialties: Robert Nathan.
Mail/Telephone Orders; Credit Cards: Both. Visa and Mastercard accepted.
Business Hours: Monday through Saturday 11:00 AM - 5:00 PM, but appointment is advised.
Parking Facilities: Ample street parking.
Catalogue: Two to three times a year.
Collections/Individual Items Purchased: Both.
Booksellers' Memberships: Antiquarian Booksellers Association of America including the Northern California Chapter, International League of Antiquarian Booksellers.

963
Magus Books
1408 North East 42nd Street
Seattle, Washington 98105 (206) 633-1800

This is a general bookstore with 2,000 square feet of space.
How to Get There: The bookstore is located 1/2 block west of the University of Washington, on 42nd Street.
Owner/Biography: David L. Bell.
Year Founded/History of Bookstore: Founded in 1974, the shop originally sold new books about the occult. The ownership changed in 1978, and the shop was turned into a used bookstore.
Number of Volumes: 65,000.
Types/Classifications: Hardbound, paperback, magazines.
General Subject Areas: General, Scholarly Works.
Mail/Telephone Orders; Credit Cards: No mail orders. Telephone orders accepted. Visa and Mastercard accepted.
Business Hours: Monday through Wednesday 10:00 AM - 8:00 PM; Thursday and Friday 10:00 AM - 10:00 PM; Saturday 11:00 AM - 6:00 PM; Sunday 1:00 PM - 5:00 PM.
Parking Facilities: There is a public parking lot next door.
Collections/Individual Items Purchased: Both.
Booksellers' Memberships: Antiquarian Booksellers Association of America.

964
McDuffie's Old Books
North 618 Monroe
P.O. Box 596
Spokane, Washington 99210 (509) 325-9022

A general used bookstore containing mostly non-fiction, out-of-print, and old books in all fields. The stock is designed for the walk-in trade, and contains 2,500 square feet of space.
How to Get There: The shop is located in downtown Spokane, Washington.
Owner/Biography: McDuffie Owen.
Year Founded/History of Bookstore: Founded in 1953, the bookstore has moved several times. It is a family owned business.
Number of Volumes: 20,000.
Types/Classifications: Hardbound, broadsides, prints, paintings, postcards, ephemera, small antiques, out-of-print in all subjects since 1800.
General Subject Areas: Americana, Architecture, Art, Atomic Energy, Behavior, Geology, Literary Classics, Medicine, Mining, Neurology, Photography, Psychology, Science, Surgery, Technology.
Specific Specialties: Medical Classics (since 1800), Early Western US Pioneer Printing, History, Natural History of the Rocky Mountains, Frank Lloyd Wright, Idaho, Washington State, Montana, Alberta, Spokane History, Yellowstone National Park, Glacier National Park, Pre-Historical Art, Ice Age Art, Primitive Art, Art Reference, Automobiles, Locomotives, Airplanes.
Mail/Telephone Orders; Credit Cards: Both.
Business Hours: Monday through Saturday 10:00 AM - 4:00 PM, or by appointment; closed Sunday.

Special Features: Appraisals of libraries and individual titles; search service for out-of-print materials; historic paper memorabilia.

Catalogue: Four time a year.

Collections/Individual Items Purchased: Both.

Booksellers' Memberships: Antiquarian Booksellers Association of America.

965
Mostly Books
3126 Harborview Avenue
Gig Harbor, Washington 98335 (206) 851-3219

This is a small shop, owner operated, containing new, used, and out-of-print stock. There is a representation of these categories in the store, but the major stock is in the adjacent storeroom. The shop invites want lists and has a modest selection of collector type books. The store contains 700 square feet of space; the annex, 660.

How to Get There: Gig Harbor lies approximately 40 miles southwest of Seattle on Highway 16. The driver should take the Bremerton exit off I-5, cross the Tacoma Narrows Bridge, then take the first Gig Harbor exit.

Owner/Biography: Harry and Shirley Dearth. The store operation grew out of the owners' interest in and collecting of books.

Year Founded/History of Bookstore: The bookstore was opened in 1969 in the scenic waterfront area, originally a Yugoslavian fishing village. The store developed new-book business, but the owners still maintain a strong love for and involvement in used and out-of-print books. The stocks are good with many interesting items, but the shop makes no pretense of being a serious antiquarian.

Number of Volumes: 12,000.

Types/Classifications: Hardbound, paperback, first editions, fine bindings, out-of-print.

General Subject Areas: Aviation, Biography, Classics, General Popular Fiction, Marine Fiction, Pacific Northwest, Western Americana, World War II.

Author Specialties: Kathleen Norris, Stewart Edward White, Nevil Shute.

Mail/Telephone Orders; Credit Cards: Both; mail should be addressed to Box 428, rest of address same as above; Visa, Mastercard.

Business Hours: Monday through Saturday 10:00 AM - 5:30 PM; Sunday 1:00 PM - 4:00 PM during late Spring through December.

Parking Facilities: Business parking lot, adjacent street parking.

Special Features: Want lists invited.

Collections/Individual Items Purchased: Individual items only.

966
O'Leary's Books
4021 100th S.W.
Tacoma, Washington 98499 (206) 588-2503

O'Leary's Books carries a large stock of out-of-print hardbound and paperback books and also has 300,000 comics. The shop occupies 3,000 square feet of space.

Owner/Biography: Ron and Barbara Trimble.

Year Founded/History of Bookstore: 1976.

Number of Volumes: 10,000 hardbound; 50,000 paperback; 300,000 comics.

Types/Classifications: First editions, fine bindings, out-of-print.

General Subject Areas: Americana, Children's Literature, Military History, Science Fiction and Fantasy.

Mail/Telephone Orders; Credit Cards: Both. Visa and Mastercard accepted.

Business Hours: Seven days a week.

Parking Facilities: Business parking lot.

Collections/Individual Items Purchased: Both.

967
Ottenberg Books
717 Pike Street
Seattle, Washington 98101   (206) 682-5363

This is a spacious shop with a select stock of general hardbound books chosen for their good condition. It emphasizes American literature.
How to Get There: The shop is located in downtown Seattle.
Owner/Biography: M. Taylor Bowie.
Types/Classifications: Hardbound, out-of-print, first editions.
General Subject Areas: American Literature, Fine Arts, General, Graphic Arts, Literary Criticism, Mountaineering, Seattle, Washington.
Mail/Telephone Orders; Credit Cards: Mail orders.
Business Hours: Daily.
Parking Facilities: Ample parking available.
Collections/Individual Items Purchased: Both.

968
Peggatty Books, Inc.
609 Maple Street
Clarkston, Washington 99403   (509) 758-9517

This is a general bookstore with both new and used books and a paperback exhange arrangement. Its main interest is in rare, scarce, out-of-print hardbound books which are carefully hand selected. The store occupies 1,500 square feet of space.
Owner/Biography: Margaret H. Behrens.
Year Founded/History of Bookstore: 1975.
Number of Volumes: 18,000.
Types/Classifications: Hardbound, paperback, first editions, fine bindings, out-of-print, association copies, press books, signed copies, presentation copies, limited editions, color plate books.
General Subject Areas: General.
Specific Specialties: Pacific Northwest, American Indians, Hunting and Fishing, Nature, Art, Books About Books, Biography, Letters, Children's Books, Political History, Military History, Engineering, Technical, Medical.
Mail/Telephone Orders; Credit Cards: Both. Visa and Mastercard accepted.
Business Hours: Monday through Saturday 11:00 AM - 5:30 PM.
Parking Facilities: Business parking lot.
Special Features: Search service.
Collections/Individual Items Purchased: Both.

969
Raymer's Old Book Store
920 Third Avenue
Seattle, Washington 98104   (206) 622-0357

Raymer's carries a wide variety of subject areas and specializes in metaphysics. The shop occupies 750 square feet of space.
How to Get There: The store is in the heart of downtown Seattle. The 50-story blackwalled 1st National Bank Building is a hundred feet north of the bookstore and across the street facing Raymer's is the brand new 47-story First Interstate Bank Building.
Owner/Biography: R.M. Glazier.
Year Founded/History of Bookstore: 1885. Raymer's was founded originally in Minneapolis and moved to Spokane, then to Seattle. It has relocated several times, always between 1st and 3rd Avenues. It has been in the present location for approximately 40 years.
Number of Volumes: 40,000.

Types/Classifications: Hardbound, paperback, first editions, out-of-print.
General Subject Areas: Adventure, Autobiography, Biography, Health, History, Literature, Metaphysics, New Age Music (Records and Cassettes), Northwest History, Travel.
Specific Specialties: Pacific Northwest.
Mail/Telephone Orders; Credit Cards: Both. Payment with order, except for schools. No credit cards.
Business Hours: Daily 11:00 AM - 5:30 PM.
Parking Facilities: Limited street parking.
Special Features: Search service.
Collections/Individual Items Purchased: Both.

970
Robert W. Mattila Bookseller
115 South Jackson Street
Seattle, Washington 98101   (206) 622-9455

This small antiquarian bookshop has many rare books dealing mostly with Alaska and the Pacific Northwest.
How to Get There: The shop is located in downtown Seattle, Washington.
Owner/Biography: Robert Mattila.
Types/Classifications: Hardbound, rare, out-of-print, first editions, ephemera.
General Subject Areas: Alaska, Pacific Northwest.
Mail/Telephone Orders; Credit Cards: Mail orders.
Business Hours: Daily.
Parking Facilities: Ample parking available.
Collections/Individual Items Purchased: Both.

971
Shorey's Bookstore
110 Union Street
Seattle, Washington 98101   (206) 624-0221

Shorey's is reportedly "largest antiquarian bookstore" in the Northwest. It has over 1,250,000 new, used, and rare books in stock. The second floor holds the main sales area.
How to Get There: Located in downtown Seattle, Shorey's Bookstore also has a smaller second store in Pioneer Square at 119 South Jackson Street, Seattle.
Owner/Biography: J.W. Todd, Jr., Manager.
Year Founded/History of Bookstore: 1890.
Number of Volumes: Over 1,250,000.
Types/Classifications: Rare, scarce, out-of-print, limited editions, first editions, sets.
General Subject Areas: Alaska, American Indians, Arctic, Early Voyages, Natural History, Pacific Northwest, Western Americana.
Mail/Telephone Orders; Credit Cards: Mail orders.
Business Hours: Daily.
Parking Facilities: Ample parking.
Collections/Individual Items Purchased: Both.

972
Shorey's Bookstore - Pioneer Square
119 South Jackson Street
Seattle, Washington 98104   (206) 624-0221

See SHOREY'S BOOKSTORE, 110 Union Street, Seattle WA 98101.

WEST VIRGINIA

973
Appalachia Book Shop
1316 Pen Mar Avenue
Bluefield, West Virginia 24701   (304) 327-5493

This is a general used book shop stressing West Virginia and Virginia books and occupying 2,000 square feet of space.
How to Get There: The bookstore is two blocks west of the South Bluefield post office.
Owner/Biography: Arnold Porterfield.
Year Founded/History of Bookstore: 1972.
Number of Volumes: 20,000.
Types/Classifications: Hardbound, paperback, ephemera, first editions, fine bindings, out-of-print.
General Subject Areas: Genealogy, Virginia History, West Virginia History.
Specific Specialties: Civil War (U.S.), Americana.
Mail/Telephone Orders; Credit Cards: Both. A personal check must accompany an order. No credit cards.
Business Hours: Daily 12:00 Noon - 5:00 PM.
Parking Facilities: Street.
Special Features: Search service.
Catalogue: Sporadically.
Collections/Individual Items Purchased: Both.

974
Major's Book Store
221 Hale Street
Charleston, West Virginia 25301   (304) 344-3504

Though small in area, 950 square feet, the bookstore manages to include 26,000 volumes, specializing in West Virginia books and authors.
Owner/Biography: Kim Major.
Year Founded/History of Bookstore: 1918.
Number of Volumes: 26,000.
Types/Classifications: Hardbound, paperback, magazines.
General Subject Areas: Biography, Children's Books, Science Fiction and Fantasy.
Specific Specialties: West Virginia.
Author Specialties: West Virginia Authors.
Mail/Telephone Orders; Credit Cards: Both; Visa, Mastercard.
Business Hours: Monday 9:00 AM - 9:00 PM; Tuesday through Friday 9:00 AM - 5:30 PM; Saturday 9:00 AM - 5:00 PM.
Parking Facilities: Street, public parking lot.
Special Features: Special orders.

975
Wolf's Head Books
P.O. Box 1048
198 Foundry Street
Morgantown, West Virginia 26507   (304) 296-0706

The long, narrow store building houses books on two floors. The main floor is divided into three rooms each containing different subject matter: a fine arts room, a philosophy/political science room, and a large room with all other subjects except fiction. The latter is arranged in alphabetical rows in the downstairs. The shop is decorated with lawyer's stacks and other oak bookcases. Oriental scatter rugs cover the floors. The owners have created an atmosphere in which to browse. The shop contains 3,260 square feet of space.

How to Get There: The bookstore is adjacent to the downtown post office, just off I-79; 45 minutes from I-70 at Washington, Pennsylvania; just off I-48, Corridor E.

Owner/Biography: Barbara E. Nailler and Harvey J. Wolf. Barbara, a former professor of educational psychology, left teaching to open this bookstore. Harvey is an associate professor of public administration at West Virginia University. Both owners have collected authors for many years.

Year Founded/History of Bookstore: Founding the bookstore in 1977, the owners worked out of their home, wholesaling and doing book searches. In 1980 they opened the store full time.

Number of Volumes: 32,000.

Types/Classifications: Hardbound, paperback, bookends, prints, ephemera, magazines, rare, first editions, out-of-print, signed copies, presentation copies, fine bindings, limited editions, sets, illustrated editions, pamphlets, post cards.

General Subject Areas: Alaska, American Indians, Americana, Animals, Architecture, Art, Biography, Birds, Children's Books, Collecting, Cooking, Crafts, Drama, Education, Fishing, Gardening, Genealogy, Hawaii, History, How-To Books, Humor, Hunting, Literary Criticism, Math, Medicine, Mid-West (U.S.), Military, Music, Mysteries, Mythology, Nature, North America, Occult, Pennsylvania, Philosophy, Photography, Poetry, Political Science, Psychology, Radio, Railroads, Reference, Religion, Science, Science Fiction and Fantasy, Sociology, South America, South (U.S.), Sports, Technology, Television, Travel, West (U.S.), Westerns.

Specific Specialties: Civil War (U.S.), West Virginia, Appalachia, Americana, Fiction.

Author Specialties: Melville Davisson Post, Charles Ambler, James Callahan, John Caruso, Oscar Lambert, Howard Lee, Oren Morton, Ruth Ann Musick, Davis Grubb, Hobert Skidmore, Hubert Skidmore, Samuel T. Wiley.

Other Specialties: Many French Language paperbacks and sets.

Mail/Telephone Orders; Credit Cards: Both. Self addressed stamped envelope for return of personal check; telephone orders held one week for personal check. Visa, Mastercard, American Express.

Business Hours: Monday through Friday 11:00 AM - 7:00 PM; Saturday 11:00 AM - 5:00 PM.

Parking Facilities: Street; after 5:00 PM parking lot across the street.

Special Features: Search service.

Catalogue: Fifteen times a year.

Collections/Individual Items Purchased: Both.

470

WISCONSIN

976
Books, Then and Now
2137 University Avenue
Madison, Wisconsin 53705   (608) 233-7030

Books, Then and Now is a typical small bookstore which carries 90 percent hardbound stock. It occupies 800 square feet of space.

Owner/Biography: Carl A. Boedecker.
Year Founded/History of Bookstore: 1975.
Number of Volumes: 15,000.
Types/Classifications: Collections of books in all areas of interest.
General Subject Areas: General.
Mail/Telephone Orders; Credit Cards: Both. No credit cards.
Business Hours: Tuesday 10:00 AM - 9:00 PM; Monday through Saturday 10:00 AM - 5:30 PM.
Parking Facilities: Business parking lot, street parking.
Special Features: Search service.
Collections/Individual Items Purchased: Both.

977
Constant Reader Bookshop, Ltd.
1625-27 East Irving Place
Milwaukee, Wisconsin 53202   (414) 291-0452

This book shop has an extensive selection of hardbound fiction and non-fiction, wide aisles, and adequate lighting. Organization is the keystone of the shop. Collections are clearly labelled with books shelved alphabetically by author. A card file of titles currently in the store is maintained allowing the owners to quickly determine if a title is in stock. New stock is added daily and lists of books for sale are issued weekly.

How to Get There: From downtown Milwaukee follow Wisconsin Avenue east to Prospect and proceed north to Kane Place, at Kane Place turn left and go two blocks to Oakland, make a right and go one block to Irving Place.

Owner/Biography: John M. Esser and David W. Hurlbutt. Mr. Esser holds degrees in English and Library Science and for many years taught American literature. His special interests and collections include 19th Century American literature and books about books. Dr. Hurlbutt has taught at the University of Wisconsin and New York University. His interest and research include the reading behaviors and habits of urban Americans.

Year Founded/History of Bookstore: 1979. The Constant Reader is located on a tree lined street two blocks from Lake Michigan. Originally the store occupied one half of the two-story building. In 1981 the store expanded to occupy the entire building (6,000 square feet of space).

Number of Volumes: 14,000.

Types/Classifications: Hardbound, first editions, fine bindings, out-of-print, association copies, press books, signed copies, presentation copies, limited editions.

General Subject Areas: Aeronautics, Americana, Art, Automobiles, Books About Books, Children's Books, Cookery, European History, Folk Tales, Humor, Literary Biography, Literary Criticism, Military History, Mysteries, Natural History, Nature, Nautical, Occult, Philosophy, Plays, Poetry, Polar, Religion, Science, Science Fiction, Theater, True Crime, World History.

Specific Specialties: Americana: Colonial, New England, Easter, Midwest, Western Moguls, Wisconsin, Civil War, South; John F. Kennedy.

Author Specialties: Dorothy Parker, Hilaire Belloc, G. K. Chesterton, Lord Shaftesbury (Anthony Ashley Cooper).

471

Mail/Telephone Orders; Credit Cards: Both. No credit cards.
Business Hours: Monday through Saturday 11:00 AM - 8:00 PM; Sunday 12:00 Noon - 6:00 PM.
Parking Facilities: Street parking.
Catalogue: Weekly lists published.
Collections/Individual Items Purchased: Collections only.

978
Littlewoods Book House
200 East Park Avenue
Waukesha, Wisconsin 53186   (414) 549-1125

The bookstore is located in a 90 year old home in which the entire first floor has been converted to a bright, carpeted shop. The stock is general, with titles in almost every field of interest. The shop contains 1,400 square feet of space.
How to Get There: Waukesha is 17 miles west of Milwaukee, just south of Interstate I-94. The bookstore is on one corner of the central business district, at the intersection of Park and Barstow.
Owner/Biography: Wm. and Marion Littlewood.
Year Founded/History of Bookstore: 1979.
Number of Volumes: 20,000.
Types/Classifications: The stock is 90 percent hardbound, with a small paperback section, some pre-1940 magazines, all general classifications, fine sets, fine bindings.
General Subject Areas: Americana, Animals, Art, Books About Books, Business, Children's Books, Collectibles, Cookbooks, Crafts, Entertainment, Fiction, Fishing, Games, Humor, Hunting, Literature, Music, Mystery, Nature, Occult, Philosophy, Plants, Poetry, Reference, Religion, Science, Science Fiction and Fantasy, Sociology, Sports, Technical, Transportation, Travel, War, Westerns, Women.
Specific Specialties: Biography, Juvenile Series, Wisconsin.
Mail/Telephone Orders; Credit Cards: Both; no credit cards.
Business Hours: Friday and Saturday 11:00 AM - 5:00 PM; other times by appointment.
Parking Facilities: Street; front and rear of store.
Special Features: Search service.
Catalogue: Irregularly published.
Collections/Individual Items Purchased: Both.

979
Mystery Bookstore
2266 North Prospect Avenue
Suite 209
Milwaukee, Wisconsin 53202   (414) 277-8515

The present bookstore is a spinoff from The Bookstore, which was a general bookstore with a mystery specialty; now it stocks only mysteries. The stock is mainly new paperbacks and selected harcovers. There are some used mysteries in both paper and hardcover, and some first editions.
How to Get There: The shop is on the second floor of a professional building, The Prospect Building. Tucked away in a corner, Suite 209 can be found by making a right turn from the elevator; it contains 550 square feet of space.
Owner/Biography: Lenore Woolf, owner, is also a published writer. She has been a bookseller for ten years.
Year Founded/History of Bookstore: 1983.
Types/Classifications: Hardbound, paperback, first editions, out-of-print.
General Subject Areas: Mystery, Suspense.
Mail/Telephone Orders; Credit Cards: Both; mail orders: cash with order, credit card number, postage paid for each book, with insurance added if desired; Visa, Mastercard.
Business Hours: Monday through Friday 12:00 Noon - 6:00 PM; Saturday 11:00 AM - 5:00 PM; or by appointment.
Parking Facilities: Street parking and public parking lot.

Special Features: Tea served daily.
Collections/Individual Items Purchased: Only individual items.

980
Old Delavan Book Co., Inc.
67 East Walworth Avenue
Delavan, Wisconsin 53115   (414) 728-6988

The bookstore carries a large stock of out-of-print titles in most fields. However, many are in "rough storage," some unsorted and unpriced. Consequently, most of the business is wholesale to the trade rather than retail, though the shop allows retail buyers to browse. The shop is located in an 1840 "Temperance House" (National Register of Historic Places).

How to Get There: The bookstore is situated at the west end of the Delavan shopping area, at the corner of Walworth and Main. Delavan is five minutes from Lake Lawn Lodge, fifteen minutes from The Abbey in Fontana, and 45 minutes from Milwaukee off the Beloit Expressway, Route 15.

Owner/Biography: Dorothy and Ed Chesko, owners, describe themselves as "refugees from Illinois." Ed is a retired school teacher and administrator.

Year Founded/History of Bookstore: The business was founded in 1973 and operates out of the owners' home. Open by appointment only, the shop is mainly mail order. The stock continues to grow.

Number of Volumes: 100,000.

Types/Classifications: Hardbound, out-of-print, vintage paperbacks, comics, post cards.

General Subject Areas: Americana, Biography, Children's Books, General, Science Fiction and Fantasy.

Specific Specialties: Juvenile, Mysteries, Early Wisconsiana, Territorial Imprints.

Mail/Telephone Orders; Credit Cards: Both. Cash with order, postpaid. No credit cards.

Business Hours: By appointment only.

Parking Facilities: Street.

Catalogue: No catalogue, but occasional lists are supplied.

Collections/Individual Items Purchased: Both.

Booksellers' Memberships: Midwest Bookhunters, Wisconsin Early Printing History Association.

981
Sadlon's Limited
109 North Broadway
De Pere, Wisconsin 54115   (414) 336-6665

Sadlon's carries a general stock of hardbound used books. The shop occupies 2,900 square feet of space.

How to Get There: Located on the east side of the Fox River, the shop is 2 doors north of the bridge.

Owner/Biography: Ramona J. Sadlon.

Year Founded/History of Bookstore: 1981.

Number of Volumes: 700.

Types/Classifications: Hardbound, out-of-print.

General Subject Areas: General.

Specific Specialties: Children's Books, History, Exploration, Travel, Americana, Literary Firsts.

Mail/Telephone Orders; Credit Cards: Both. Visa and Mastercard accepted.

Business Hours: Tuesday through Thursday 10:00 AM - 5:00 PM; Friday 12:00 Noon - 8:00 PM; Saturday 10:00 AM - 4:00 PM.

Parking Facilities: Street parking.

Special Features: Antiquarian prints; restoration.

Catalogue: Published twice yearly.

Collections/Individual Items Purchased: Both.

982
Stony Hill Antiques
2140 Regent Street
Madison, Wisconsin 53705 (608) 231-1247

Stony Hill Antiques specializes in antiquarian material on Wisconsin, Midwest Americana, Wisconsin authors, and American first editions.
Owner/Biography: David Ward.
Year Founded/History of Bookstore: 1976.
Number of Volumes: 4,000.
Types/Classifications: Hardbound, first editions, fine bindings, out-of-print.
General Subject Areas: Western Americana, Wisconsin.
Mail/Telephone Orders; Credit Cards: Both. Visa and Mastercard accepted.
Business Hours: Tuesday through Saturday 10:00 AM - 5:15 PM.
Parking Facilities: Street.
Collections/Individual Items Purchased: Both.

983
T. S. Vandoros Rare Books
5827 Highland Terrace
Middleton, Wisconsin 53562 (608) 836-8254

This is mainly a mail order operation, but customers may visit by appointment. It contains 600 square feet of space.
Owner/Biography: Takis S. Vandoros.
Year Founded/History of Bookstore: Mr. Vandoros is a Greek national, naturalized U.S. citizen, and married. He received a degree in political Science from Athens, Greece, a masters degree in modern European history from UCLA, and has completed all the requirements except the dissertation for the Ph.D. in German history at University of Wisconsin.
Number of Volumes: August 1981.
Types/Classifications: Hardbound, nearly all are first editions, fine bindings, out-of-print, limited editions, signed copies, presentation copies, association copies, press books, color plate books.
General Subject Areas: English Literature.
Specific Specialties: The main stock is in 19th Century English Literature specializing in Byron and Dickens first editions, 20th Century English Literature, Illustrated Children's Books in English, German, and French, Victorian First Editions.
Author Specialties: Lord Byron, Charles Dickens.
Other Specialties: Some works in History.
Mail/Telephone Orders; Credit Cards: Mail orders; telephone orders only to put a hold on specific items. It is advised that even for mail orders the customer should put a hold by telephone. No credit cards.
Business Hours: Monday through Friday 9:00 AM - 2:00 PM by appointment only.
Special Features: Mail order.
Catalogue: One catalogue has been published; the owner is aiming at two substantial catalogues per year.
Collections/Individual Items Purchased: Both.

984
Twentieth Century Books
108 King Street
Madison, Wisconsin 53703 (608) 251-6226

Basically 20th Century Books is a general used bookstore with some specialization in mystery and science fiction and fantasy. It contains 1,500 square feet of space.
How to Get There: The bookstore is just off the capital square in Madison.
Owner/Biography: Hank Luttrell.

Year Founded/History of Bookstore: 1979.
Number of Volumes: 200,000.
Types/Classifications: Hardbound, paperback, magazines, first editions, and out-of-print.
General Subject Areas: Children's Literature, Cinema, Comics, Cookbooks, Detective, Mystery, Science Fiction and Fantasy, Vintage Paperbacks, Wisconsiniana.
Specific Specialties: Ace Science Fiction Paperbacks, Philip K. Dick.
Author Specialties: Philip K. Dick
Mail/Telephone Orders; Credit Cards: Both; no credit cards.
Business Hours: Monday through Saturday 10:30 AM - 5:30 PM; Sunday 1:00 PM - 4:00 PM.
Parking Facilities: Street parking, Doty Street ramp.
Catalogue: Two times a year.
Collections/Individual Items Purchased: Both.

985
W. Bruce Fye Antiquarian Medical Books
1607 North Wood Avenue
Marshfield, Wisconsin 54449   (715) 384-8128

This is a mail order bookstore dealing in out-of-print medical stock only. The shop contains 1,500 square feet of space.
Owner/Biography: W. Bruce Fye and Lois B. Fye. W. Bruce Fye has degrees in medicine and medical history, and began collecting books in 1961 while in medical school at Johns Hopkins. Subsequently he has combined his interests in medicine, medical history, and antiquarian books. He is a practicing cardiologist and holds an appointment in medical history at the University of Wisconsin. Since 1972 he has been a bookseller. His wife Lois is a retired nurse.
Year Founded/History of Bookstore: The business, which has always been mail order, was initiated in New York City in 1972. The location was moved to Baltimore for three years, and since 1978 has been located in Marshfield, Wisconsin. The stock has steadily grown and now numbers some 10,000 books, pamphlets, and related items. The stock is highly specialized and deals exclusively with medicine and the related life sciences.
Number of Volumes: 10,000.
Types/Classifications: Hardbound, pamphlets, author's offprints, autographs, manuscript material, prints, broadsides, out-of-print.
General Subject Areas: Medical Biography, Medical History, Medicine, Medicine Bibliography, Science Bibliography.
Specific Specialties: Cardiology, Plastic Surgery, Neurosciences. Not handled are home medical guides, self-help material, psychiatry, psychology, dentistry.
Author Specialties: William Osler, Harvey Cushing, S. Wier Mitchell, William Hammond, Oliver Wendell Holmes; all other important medical authors.
Mail/Telephone Orders; Credit Cards: Both. No credit cards.
Business Hours: By mail order only.
Catalogue: Six times per year.
Collections/Individual Items Purchased: Both.

986
Winsted Shop
140 South Winsted Street
Spring Green, Wisconsin 53588   (608) 588-2042

The bookstore prides itself in being different. It is in a renovated gas service station, originally constructed in the 1930's, with 1,700 square feet of space. It retails gifts, greeting cards, new books (hardbound and paperback), out-of-print books (hardbound and paperback), limited office supplies, and has a paperback book exchange service.
How to Get There: The bookstore is located in the village of Spring Green, Wisconsin, on Highway 23.
Owner/Biography: Virgil A. and Helen J. Steele.

Year Founded/History of Bookstore: The Steeles have owned and operated the bookstore since its founding in 1967.

Number of Volumes: 8,000.

Types/Classifications: Hardbound, paperback, out-of-print.

General Subject Areas: Americana.

Specific Specialties: Wisconsin.

Author Specialties: Frank Lloyd Wright, August Derleth.

Mail/Telephone Orders; Credit Cards: Both. Cash with order, self addressed stamped envelope. Visa, Mastercard.

Business Hours: Daily 8:30 AM - 5:30 PM.

Parking Facilities: Business parking lot.

Special Features: Search service, special order service.

Collections/Individual Items Purchased: Both.

Booksellers' Memberships: American Booksellers Association.

WYOMING

987
Backpocket Ranch Bookshop
364 Farrall Road
Sundance, Wyoming 82729   (307) 283-2665

For ease of remembrance, dial (307) 283-BOOK. The bookshop is located on a ranch, 20 miles from the nearest town. It is temporarily housed in a house trailer until a permanent log building can be built - this has required a somewhat original use of space to make total display coverage. There are regular customers and some drop-in customers, but most of the business is by mail order.

How to Get There: The store is located in a rural area 20 miles from Sundance. Take I-90 East from Sundance (or west from Spearfish, South Dakota) to the Aladdin exit (Higway 111). Take Highway 111 north for 4 miles, turn west toward Black Hills National Forest on Gravel County Road. Go 3.64 miles to old house on left.

Owner/Biography: Roy and Gaydell Collier. The Colliers lived on a ranch southwest of Laramie for many years before moving to the Sundance area. Roy is a rancher with a degree in Agricultural Economics from the University of Wyoming. Gaydell is a freelance writer. She has had two books published by Doubleday (with co-author Eleanor Prince) as well as having been published in a variety of magazines. She has reviewed for "Library Journal" for over 12 years and is a member of Western Writers of America and Wyoming Writers.

Year Founded/History of Bookstore: 1977. Although the Colliers are ranchers (raising Hereford cattle, Morgan horses, and some Jersey cows), the bookshop was started as a lifelong dream. They try to keep in stock those books that are needed by small farmers and ranchers as well as Wyoming books for readers in-state and everywhere around the country. Their mail order business has expanded to Europe and Australia.

Types/Classifications: Hardbound, paperback, general, out-of-print.

General Subject Areas: Books About Writing, Children's Books, Draft Horses, Horses, Quality Coloring Books, Small Farming/Rural Living, Western Americana, Wyoming, Wyoming Authors.

Author Specialties: Wyoming Writers, Regional Writers (Black Hills).

Other Specialties: Maps of Wyoming.

Mail/Telephone Orders; Credit Cards: Both. Visa and Mastercard accepted.

Business Hours: By appointment and by chance (the Colliers are usually around the ranch somewhere).

Parking Facilities: Ranch dooryard.

Special Features: Search service, free order service, coffee or milk in the house - or lunch, if you can stay.

Catalogue: Published 2 times per year.

Collections/Individual Items Purchased: Individual items only.

Miscellaneous: The Colliers state that one of their most important functions is to provide a central distribution outlet for Wyoming writers who have self-published or been published by small regional presses.

988
Corner Book Shop
250 East 15th Street
Casper, Wyoming 82601   (307) 266-6124

This is a small personal book shop specializing in ordering books that the big chains frequently ignore. It also has a staff that knows books. The shop occupies 500 square feet of space.

Owner/Biography: Dodie Stewart, Don and Dee MacQueen.

Year Founded/History of Bookstore: 1978.

Number of Volumes: 5,000.

Types/Classifications: Hardbound, paperback.

General Subject Areas: General.

Mail/Telephone Orders; Credit Cards: Both. Visa and Mastercard accepted.
Business Hours: Monday through Saturday 9:00 AM - 5:00 PM.
Parking Facilities: Street parking.
Special Features: Search service.
Collections/Individual Items Purchased: Neither.

989
E & S Summerhouse Books
715 Cemetary Road
Dayton, Wyoming 82836   (307) 655-2367

The bookstore is housed in a former summer dining hall near the residence on the grounds. It is in a wooded area near a stream.
How to Get There: The bookstore is located off Highway 14 at the foot of the Big Horn Mountains. Signs leading to the store are posted down the country lane.
Owner/Biography: Bonnie J. Switzer.
Year Founded/History of Bookstore: 1979.
Number of Volumes: 5,000.
Types/Classifications: Hardbound, paperback, magazines, ephemera, prints.
General Subject Areas: Agriculture, Americana, Art, Biography, Children's Literature, Cookbooks, Fishing, Gardening, Hunting, Literature, Nature, Religion, Western Americana.
Specific Specialties: Wyoming History.
Mail/Telephone Orders; Credit Cards: Both. No credit cards.
Business Hours: Summer months Monday through Saturday 9:00 AM - 5:00 PM; winter months by appointment.
Parking Facilities: Ample parking available.
Collections/Individual Items Purchased: Both.

Canada

ALBERTA

990
Tom Williams - Books
Box 4126 Stn. C
Calgary, Alberta T2T 5M9   (403) 264-1084

The bookstore features carefully selected hard cover books with an emphasis on Canadian material.
How to Get There: The shop is an eight minute walk from the central hotel area.
Owner/Biography: Tom Williams.
Year Founded/History of Bookstore: Opened in 1958 in what was called the "smallest building in the world," 4.5' X 16', the shop now occupies a location of over 1,000 square feet of space of floor to ceiling books.
Number of Volumes: 20,000.
Types/Classifications: Hardbound, prints, maps, photographs, pamphlets, ephemera, first editions, fine bindings, out-of-print, limited editions.
General Subject Areas: Arctic, Canada, Cattle, Cowboys, Mountaineering, Natural History, Petroleum, Royal Canadian Mounted Police.
Specific Specialties: Canadian Railroads, Canadian Immigration and Settlement, Klondike, Plains Indians, Eskimos, Canadian Art.
Author Specialties: Canadian Authors, G. A. Henty.
Mail/Telephone Orders; Credit Cards: Both. Cash with order. No credit cards.
Business Hours: By appointment only.
Parking Facilities: Street, business parking lot.
Special Features: Search service.
Catalogue: Published occasionally.
Collections/Individual Items Purchased: Both.
Booksellers' Memberships: Antiquarian Booksellers Association of Canada, Provincial Booksellers Association, National Archival Appraisal Board (Canada), Canadian Biographical Society.
Miscellaneous: Canadian Art, Good Coffee.

BRITISH COLUMBIA

991
Ahrens Book Shop
756 Davie Street
Vancouver, British Columbia V6Z 1B5   (604) 683-2014

The bookstore features a general stock of hardbound and quality paperback, both used and out-of-print. The shop contains 750 square feet of space.
How to Get There: The bookstore is situated on the southeast corner of Davie and Howe Streets in downtown Vancouver.
Owner/Biography: John F. Ahrens.
Year Founded/History of Bookstore: The bookstore was opened in 1950 by its present owner.
Number of Volumes: 30,000.
Types/Classifications: Hardbound, quality paperback, general stock.
General Subject Areas: Art, Biography, Drama, Economics, Fiction, History, Juvenile, Marine, Music, Occult, Pacific Northwest, Poetry, Science, Science Fiction and Fantasy, Sociology, Technical, Theology, Travel.
Mail/Telephone Orders; Credit Cards: Both. No credit cards.
Business Hours: Tuesday through Saturday 11:00 AM - 6:00 PM.
Parking Facilities: Street and public parking lot.
Collections/Individual Items Purchased: Both.

992
Ainslie Books
10640 Bridgeport Road
Vancouver, British Columbia V6X 1S7

A catalogue of holdings is available on request. The owner fulfills mail order requests only.
Owner/Biography: Ainslie Peach.
Year Founded/History of Bookstore: 1973.
Number of Volumes: Ainslie Books has been in the same location since 1973.
Types/Classifications: Hardbound, paperbacks, out-of-print.
General Subject Areas: Canadian Authors, Canadian History, Cookbooks, Family Humor.
Specific Specialties: Canadian Prairies, British Columbia, Arctic.
Mail/Telephone Orders; Credit Cards: Any book ordered must be listed in the Ainsley Books catalogue. No telephone orders. No credit cards.
Special Features: Interested book buyers may send name and address to receive a free copy of the Ainsley Books catalogue.
Catalogue: Catalogue published on variable dates.
Collections/Individual Items Purchased: Neither.

993
Haunted Bookshop
822 1/2 Fort Street
Victoria, British Columbia V8W 1H6   (604) 382-1427

The Haunted Bookshop has five rooms full of books arranged by subject with a parlor where one can sit and peruse one's selections. Customers are encouraged to discuss their favorite authors over coffee or tea.

How to Get There: The shop is situated on "Antique Row" within walking distance of Inner Harbour, not far from the museum. It is centrally located and close to other bookshops.
Owner/Biography: Mrs. Marina Gerwing.
Year Founded/History of Bookstore: 1947.
Number of Volumes: 20,000.
Types/Classifications: Hardbound, first editions, fine bindings, out-of-print.
General Subject Areas: Biography, Canadiana, Children's Literature, Fine Arts, History, Letters and Diaries, Maritime, Military, Natural History, Pacific Northwest Indians, Poetry, Travel.
Specific Specialties: British Columbia.
Mail/Telephone Orders; Credit Cards: Both. Visa accepted.
Business Hours: Monday through Saturday 10:00 AM - 5:00 PM.
Parking Facilities: Public parking lot behind the store as well as a couple of spots directly behind the store.
Special Features: Search sevice; publishing sideline; occasional literary soirees; appraisals.
Catalogue: Catalogue published.
Collections/Individual Items Purchased: Both.

994
Poor Richard's Books Ltd.
968 Balmoral Road
Victoria, British Columbia V8T 1A8 (604) 384-4411

Poor Richard's Books has a general stock of used, out-of-print, and antiquarian books. Browsers are welcome.
How to Get There: The shop is located at the corner of Vancouver Street and Balmoral Road, just 4 blocks from City Hall.
Owner/Biography: Barney and Joanna Hagar.
Types/Classifications: Rare, out-of-print, first editions, limited editions.
General Subject Areas: General.
Mail/Telephone Orders; Credit Cards: Mail orders.
Business Hours: Six days per week.
Parking Facilities: Ample parking.
Catalogue: Published occasionally.
Collections/Individual Items Purchased: Both.
Booksellers' Memberships: Antiquarian Booksellers Association of Canada.

995
William Hoffer, Bookseller, Limited
58-60 Powell Street
Vancouver, British Columbia V6A 1E7 (604) 683-3022

The bookstore specializes in rare books, modern literary first editions, Canadiana, and Pacifica. It contains 1,800 square feet of space.
Owner/Biography: William Hoffer.
Year Founded/History of Bookstore: 1969.
Number of Volumes: 40,000.
Types/Classifications: Hardbound, rare, first editions.
General Subject Areas: Canadiana, Pacifica.
Mail/Telephone Orders; Credit Cards: Both. Mail orders require references. Visa.
Business Hours: Monday through Saturday 9:00 AM - 5:00 PM.
Parking Facilities: Street.
Special Features: The bookstore is a publisher of bibliographies and limited editions of poetry and fiction.
Catalogue: Four times a year.
Collections/Individual Items Purchased: Both.
Booksellers' Memberships: Antiquarian Booksellers Association of Canada, Antiquarian Booksellers Association International, International League of Antiquarian Booksellers, National Archival Appraisal Board

of Canada.

996
Windhover Books
8491 Cartier Street
Vancouver, British Columbia V6P 4T7   (604) 266-2929

This is a mail order operation from the owner's residence. Visitors may make an appointment to view the stock.

Owner/Biography: R. Klarenbach.

Year Founded/History of Bookstore: 1978.

Number of Volumes: 1,500.

Types/Classifications: Hardbound, some periodicals, incunabula, literary first editions.

General Subject Areas: American Literature, British Literature, Canadian Literature, Plays, Poetry.

Author Specialties: Joseph Conrad, Joyce Cary, Arnold Bennett, Virginia Woolf, D.H. Lawrence, Charles Williams.

Mail/Telephone Orders; Credit Cards: Both. Quotes given, invoices issued, and books mailed upon payment. No credit cards.

Business Hours: By appointment only.

Catalogue: Published semi-annually.

Collections/Individual Items Purchased: Individual items only.

NEW BRUNSWICK

997
Pansy Patch
59 Carleton Street
St. Andrews, New Brunswick E0G 2X0   (506) 529-3834

Pansy Patch is a unique historic house in a beautiful setting on Passamaquody Bay. The entire lower floor is devoted to the book and print shop. It is furnished with antiques which are also for sale. The Pansy Patch also has four guest rooms.

How to Get There: St. Andrews is easily accessible from the Trans Canada Highway; it is 20 miles from Calais, Maine.

Owner/Biography: Kathleen and Michael Lazure. Kathleen is a life-long children's book collector.

Year Founded/History of Bookstore: 1980.

Number of Volumes: 10,000.

Types/Classifications: Hardbound, prints, paintings, antiques, first editions, out-of-print.

General Subject Areas: Americana, Art, Biography, Canadiana, Children's Books, Cookbooks, Exploration, Gardening, Natural History, Poetry, Travel.

Specific Specialties: 20th Century Wood Engravings.

Mail/Telephone Orders; Credit Cards: Both. American Express, Visa, Mastercard accepted.

Business Hours: May 15 to October 1: Monday through Saturday 9:00 AM - 6:00 PM; Sunday 1:00 PM - 6:00 PM.

Parking Facilities: Public parking, street parking.

Collections/Individual Items Purchased: Both.

Booksellers' Memberships: Antiquarian Booksellers Association of America.

Miscellaneous: The Lazures are active book dealers in Connecticut from October to May.

NOVA SCOTIA

998
House of Antique Books
1246 Hollis Street
Halifax, Nova Scotia

The House of Antique Books deals in antiquarian material relating to Canada, Bermuda, and Hebraica. Visits can be arranged by appointment.

Types/Classifications: First editions, out-of-print, rare, maps, prints, pamphlets, manuscripts.

General Subject Areas: Bermuda Before 1900, Eastern Canada Before 1900, Hebraica Before 1700, Jerusalem and the Holy Land Before 1860.

Specific Specialties: Nova Scotia, Cape Breton, New Brunswick, Prince Edward Island, Newfoundland, Labrador.

Mail/Telephone Orders; Credit Cards: Mail Orders.

Business Hours: By appointment only.

Parking Facilities: Available.

Collections/Individual Items Purchased: Both.

999
Nautica Booksellers
1579 Dresden Row
Halifax, Nova Scotia B3J 2K4   (902) 429-2741

The bookstore is situated in a delightful old heritage building in uptown Halifax, one of Canada's premier historic seaports. The owner reports that this is one of the few bookshops where rare old sherry and decent scotch are served to selected clients. The stock of books is exclusively nautical.

How to Get There: The shop is an easy walk from the main hotels, shops, and the business district.

Owner/Biography: John Holland, owner, is a former seaman, naval officer, yachtman, professional diver, and mariner; he is also a lifelong bookman. According to Mr. Holland himself, he tends to be somewhat eccentric, never erratic, and dotes on his clients, offering personalized service to discriminating book buyers. Fittingly, he says, he is married to a psychiatrist.

Year Founded/History of Bookstore: Founded in 1976, the business was started in the owner's home as a purely catalogue operation. Two years later it was moved to a warehouse, still as a catalogue operation, then in 1980 to the current premises as a store.

Number of Volumes: 10,000.

Types/Classifications: All classifications.

General Subject Areas: General.

Specific Specialties: Exclusively Nautical, including Naval, Merchant Marine, Yachting, Pirates, Whaling, Naval Arts, Ship Modeling, Polar Exploration, Travel, Voyages, Diving, Ocean Sciences, Marine Law, Maritime Technical.

Mail/Telephone Orders; Credit Cards: Both; no credit cards.

Business Hours: Generally, weekdays 9:00 AM - 5:30 PM; it is advisable to telephone first.

Parking Facilities: Street.

Special Features: Search service, appraisals.

Catalogue: Three times a year.

Collections/Individual Items Purchased: Both.

Booksellers' Memberships: Antiquarian Booksellers Association of Canada.

1000
Schooner Books
5378 Inglis Street
Halifax, Nova Scotia B3H 1J5　　　　　　　　　　　　　　(902) 423-8419

Schooner Books is situated in a 100 year old house. The stock has emphasis in scholarly material, rare books and books on the Atlantic Provinces of Canada.

How to Get There: The shop is located at the south end of Halifax.
Owner/Biography: John D. Townsend and Mary Lee MacDonald.
Types/Classifications: Hardbound, first editions, out-of-print.
General Subject Areas: General.
Specific Specialties: Canadian Atlantic Provinces.
Other Specialties: Scholarly Works.
Business Hours: Daily.

ONTARIO

1001
About Books
280 & 355 Queen Street West
Toronto, Ontario M5V 2A4   (416) 593-0792

The bookstore is composed of two shops directly across the street from one another on Toronto's main "book street." On the north side, it has a large general stock of used paperbacks and hard covers in all subjects, especially literature. On the south side, there are mostly out-of-print, scholarly, and specialized books, such as modern first editions, books about books, mountaineering books, and antiquarian books. A second telephone listing is (416) 591-9151.

How to Get There: The bookstores are on a main tram line and are an easy walk from City Hall.

Owner/Biography: L. A. Wallrioh, owner, has been a bookseller for over 30 years in the United States, Europe, the United Kingdom, and Canada.

Year Founded/History of Bookstore: 1956.

Number of Volumes: 30,000.

Types/Classifications: Hardbound, paperback, magazines, modern first editions, press books, out-of-print, scholarly.

General Subject Areas: General.

Specific Specialties: Books on Books, French Literature, Mountaineering, Dogs.

Mail/Telephone Orders; Credit Cards: Both. Visa and Mastercard accepted.

Business Hours: North Shop: Monday through Friday 10:00 AM - 9:00 PM; Saturday 10:00 AM - 6:00 PM; Sunday 11:00 AM - 6:00 PM. South Shop: Monday through Saturday 10:00 AM - 6:00 PM.

Parking Facilities: On the street 9:00 AM - 4:00 PM, and 6:00 PM - 7:00 PM; also, parking lots within a block.

Catalogue: Published sporadically.

Collections/Individual Items Purchased: Both.

Booksellers' Memberships: Antiquarian Booksellers Association (U.K.), Antiquarian Booksellers Association of Canada.

1002
Acadia Book Store
232 Queen Street East
Toronto, Ontario M5A 1S3   (416) 364-7368

The bookstore is one of Toronto's longest established antiquarian bookstores, specializing in art books and Canadiana but with a large general stock as well. A large collection of rare and out-of-print fine books is for sale by appointment. The shop contains 2,000 square feet of space.

How to Get There: The bookstore is located in downtown Toronto within easy walking or transit distance of the Queen Subway station. Car access is also simple with parking available on both sides of Queen Street.

Owner/Biography: Asher Joram.

Number of Volumes: 25,000.

Types/Classifications: Hardbound, paperback, first editions, fine bindings, out-of-print, association copies, press books, signed copies, presentation copies, limited editions, color plate books.

General Subject Areas: Art, Canadiana, Literature, Military History, Music, Natural History, Transportation, World History.

Mail/Telephone Orders; Credit Cards: No mail orders; telephone orders accepted. Visa accepted.

Business Hours: Monday through Saturday 10:00 AM - 6:00 PM.

Parking Facilities: On both sides of Queen Street.

Collections/Individual Items Purchased: Both.
Booksellers' Memberships: Antiquarian Booksellers Association of Canada.

1003
Alphabet Bookshop
656 Spadina Avenue
Toronto, Ontario M5S 2H9 (416) 924-4926

A general bookstore located near the University of Toronto, the shop carries a general used stock in the arts and humanities as well as modern literary first editions, some autographs, and 19th Century material. The bookstore contains 500 square feet of space.
Owner/Biography: Richard Shuh and Linda Woolley.
Year Founded/History of Bookstore: 1977.
Number of Volumes: 10,000.
Types/Classifications: Hardbound, paperback, broadsides, autographs, first editions, association copies, out-of-print, signed copies, presentation copies.
General Subject Areas: Literature in Translation, Mysteries, Nineteenth Century Literature, Science Fiction and Fantasy, Twentieth Century Literature.
Specific Specialties: Americana, British Literature, Canadian Literature.
Other Specialties: Scholarly books in the Humanities.
Mail/Telephone Orders; Credit Cards: Both; inquire first for specific mail order instructions. Visa and Mastercard accepted.
Business Hours: Monday through Saturday 10:00 AM - 6:00 PM; any other time (day or night), by appointment.
Parking Facilities: Public parking lot and street parking.
Special Features: Want lists given special attention.
Catalogue: Quarterly.
Collections/Individual Items Purchased: Both.
Booksellers' Memberships: Antiquarian Booksellers Association of Canada.

1004
Anne Sherlock Books
1600-A Bloor Street West
Toronto, Ontario M6P 1A7 (416) 533-3207

The bookstore is located in an apartment above Joseph Patrick Books, but has no connection with that establishment.
How to Get There: The location is a ten minute walk west from Yonge & Bloor on the Bloor-Danforth line of the subway.
Owner/Biography: Anne Sherlock.
Year Founded/History of Bookstore: Founded in 1973, the bookstore has remained in the same location.
Number of Volumes: 6,000.
Types/Classifications: Hardbound, paperback, autographs, ephemera, original art work, first editions, association copies, signed, limited editions.
General Subject Areas: Detective, Folklore, Mysteries, Science Fiction and Fantasy.
Specific Specialties: Dark Fantasy, which includes Ghosts, Horror, Incubus, Cruel, Weird, Supernatural, Vampires, Werewolves.
Mail/Telephone Orders; Credit Cards: Both; specific requirements for mail orders are listed in the catalogue; no credit cards.
Business Hours: Wednesday through Saturday 2:00 PM - 7:00 PM; or by appointment.
Parking Facilities: Metered street parking; public parking nearby.
Special Features: Wants searched.
Catalogue: Four times a year.
Collections/Individual Items Purchased: Both.

1005
Atticus Books
698 Spadina Avenue
Toronto, Ontario M5S 2J2 (416) 922-6045

The bookstore features scholarly books, both antiquarian and recent, in all languages. It occupies 1,000 square feet of space.

How to Get There: The shop is located one block south of Bloor Street, near the University of Toronto.
Owner/Biography: Michael Freedman, owner, has a PhD. in Sanskrit and Buddhist Studies.
Year Founded/History of Bookstore: 1979.
Number of Volumes: 20,000.
Types/Classifications: Hardbound, scholarly, antiquarian and recent, all languages.
General Subject Areas: Anthropology, Archaeology, Art, Classics, Criticism, History, History of Science, Linguistics, Literature, Philosophy, Religion, Science.
Specific Specialties: Philosophy, Classics.
Mail/Telephone Orders; Credit Cards: Both; cash with order. Visa accepted.
Business Hours: Daily 12:00 Noon - 6:00 PM.
Parking Facilities: Available.
Special Features: Mr. Freedman says, "We will go anywhere to purchase fine collections in our areas of interest. We will assist individuals to sell their collections."
Collections/Individual Items Purchased: Both.
Booksellers' Memberships: Antiquarian Booksellers Association of Canada.

1006
Bakka
282 Queen Street West
Toronto, Ontario M5V 2A1 (416) 596-8161

Bakka is a specialty store dealing in science fiction, fantasy, and horror exclusively with such related items as cards, posters, art items, and games (no comics!). The store occupies 1200 square feet of space.

How to Get There: Located in central Toronto and reachable by subway.
Owner/Biography: John Rose.
Year Founded/History of Bookstore: 1972. The bookstore began in 1972 and branched into comics in 1975 and mysteries in 1976. A second store opened in Toronto in 1977 but closed in 1978. The business was sold to the present owner in 1980 and is now Canada's oldest and largest science fiction specialty store.
Number of Volumes: 15,000.
Types/Classifications: Hardbound, paperback, magazines, broadsides, autographs, ephemera, first editions, fine bindings, out-of-print, association copies, press books, signed copies, presentation copies, limited editions, color plate books.
General Subject Areas: Science Fiction and Fantasy, Science Fiction and Fantasy (Films and TV Series), Science Fiction and Fantasy Magazines and Digests, Science Fiction and Fantasy Reference.
Mail/Telephone Orders; Credit Cards: Both. Prepaid with order. Visa and Master card accepted.
Business Hours: Monday through Thursday 10:00 AM - 6:00 PM; Friday 10:00 AM - 9:00 PM; Saturday 10:00 AM - 6:00 PM; Sunday 12:00 Noon - 6:00 PM.
Parking Facilities: Street Parking.
Catalogue: Published 6 times per year.
Collections/Individual Items Purchased: Both.
Booksellers' Memberships: Antiquarian Booksellers Association International, Canadian Booksellers Association.

1007
Blacks Rare Books & Prints
106-150 Metcalfe Street
Ottawa, Ontario K2P 1P1

Blacks is located in an old medical/dental building with 3 carpeted rooms full of rare books and prints. The shop occupies 1,200 square feet of space.

How to Get There: Five blocks south of the Canadian Parliament Buildings in the center of Ottawa, at the corner of Metcalfe Street and Laurier Avenue.

Owner/Biography: Henry V. Black. Mr. Black is interested in the book collectors of the late 1940's and dealers of the 1950's and 1960's in the Toronto, Hamilton, and Niagara areas. During those years, Mr. Black made trips to stores in New York, Albany, Cleveland, Detroit, and Chicago. He has received many catalogues from various American and British shops.

Year Founded/History of Bookstore: 1974. Mr. Black first opened on Eastbend Avenue in Hamilton, Ontario.

Number of Volumes: 10,000.

Types/Classifications: Hardbound, paperback, magazines, broadsides, autographs, ephemera, leather bound sets.

General Subject Areas: Canadian History, Confederacy, Exploration, Maritime Provinces, Newfoundland, Old City Directories, Quebec, Travel, Upper Canada, War of 1812.

Specific Specialties: First editions of some 17th Century writers.

Author Specialties: William Butler Yeats, Charles Dickens, Thomas Hardy, Leigh Hunt, Lewis Carroll, William Morris, George Cruikshank.

Mail/Telephone Orders; Credit Cards: Mail orders only. No credit cards.

Business Hours: Monday through Friday 4:00 PM - 6:30 PM; Saturday 1:00 PM to 6:00 PM.

Parking Facilities: Street parking (free on Saturday).

Special Features: Mr. Black will prepare lists for specific areas.

Catalogue: Odd sheets and lists published.

Collections/Individual Items Purchased: Both.

Booksellers' Memberships: Ottawa Antiquarian Booksellers Association.

1008
Book Bazaar
755 Bank Street
Ottawa, Ontario K1S 3V3   (613) 233-4380

The Book Bazaar is a well lit open shop on one of Ottawa's main streets. It occupies 1,000 square feet of space. The staff specializes in friendly service and all sections are well organized for browsers' pleasure.

Owner/Biography: Beryl McLeod.

Year Founded/History of Bookstore: 1974.

Number of Volumes: 10,000.

Types/Classifications: Hardbound, paperback, first editions, fine bindings, out-of-print, association copies, press books, signed copies, presentation copies, limited editions, color plate books, sheet music.

General Subject Areas: Art, Biography, Canadiana, Children's Books, Literature, Music, Philosophy, Travel.

Mail/Telephone Orders; Credit Cards: Both. Cash with order unless an established customer. No credit cards.

Business Hours: Tuesday through Sunday 10:00 AM - 5:30 PM; closed Monday.

Parking Facilities: Street parking, public parking lot.

Special Features: Search service.

Catalogue: Published infrequently.

Collections/Individual Items Purchased: Both.

Booksellers' Memberships: Ottawa Antiquarian Booksellers Association, Antiquarian Booksellers Association of Canada.

1009
Book Bin - Berry & Peterson Books
225 Princess Street
Kingston, Ontario K7L 1B3   (613) 548-4871

The Book Bin features general stock on 2 floors and occupies 10,000 square feet of space. The store features one of the largest selections in eastern Ontario with specialties in literary first editons, travel, and exploration.
How to Get There: The bookstore is on the main street of downtown Kingston.
Owner/Biography: Richard Peterson and John Berry.
Year Founded/History of Bookstore: 1972.
Number of Volumes: 50,000.
Types/Classifications: Hardbound, paperback.
General Subject Areas: Exploration, General, Literary First Editions, Travel.
Mail/Telephone Orders; Credit Cards: Both. Cash with order including postage. No credit cards.
Business Hours: Monday through Thursday 10:00 AM - 5:30 PM; Friday 10:00 AM - 9:00 PM.
Parking Facilities: Street parking, public lots.
Catalogue: Published once per year.
Collections/Individual Items Purchased: Both.
Booksellers' Memberships: Antiquarian Booksellers Association of Canada.

1010
Boudicca Books
P.O. Box 901, Station K
Toronto, Ontario M4P 2H2   (416) 483-2431

Boudicca Books is a mail order book service selling old, rare, and out-of-print books and specializing in books by and about women.
Owner/Biography: Elizabeth F. Nuse.
Year Founded/History of Bookstore: 1981.
Number of Volumes: 2,000.
Types/Classifications: Hardbound, paperback, magazines, broadsides, out-of-print (both collector's and reading copies).
General Subject Areas: Ancient Religions, Anthropology, Archaeology, Feminist Movement, Women Authors, Women's Biography, Women's History, Women's Suffrage.
Specific Specialties: Literary First Editions.
Mail/Telephone Orders; Credit Cards: Both. Pro-forma invoice to new customers; libraries and institutions billed. Visa accepted.
Business Hours: Telephone answered 24 hours a day.
Special Features: Search service; publication of biliographies in Women's Studies.
Catalogue: Published several times per year.
Collections/Individual Items Purchased: Both.

1011
D & E Lake Ltd.
106 Berfley Street
Toronto, Ontario M5A 2W7   (416) 863-9930

This book shop carries maps, prints, and books dating from before the 20th Century.
How to Get There: The bookstore is located 8 blocks east of Yonge Street and one block north of Queen Street.
Owner/Biography: Donald and Elaine Lake. Both of the Lakes have strong academic backgrounds.
Year Founded/History of Bookstore: 1977.
Number of Volumes: 6,000.
Types/Classifications: Hardbound, pamphlets, letters, maps, prints, water colours, first editions, out-of-print, fine bindings.
General Subject Areas: Americana, Canadiana, Social Sciences.
Mail/Telephone Orders; Credit Cards: Both. Visa accepted.
Business Hours: Monday through Saturday 9:00 AM - 6:00 PM.
Parking Facilities: Street parking.

Catalogue: Published 6 times per year.
Collections/Individual Items Purchased: Both.
Booksellers' Memberships: Antiquarian Booksellers Association of Canada, Canadian Antique Dealers Association.

1012
David Mason - Books
342 Queen Street West
Second Floor
Toronto, Ontario M5V 2A2   (416) 598-1015

David Mason - Books carries antiquarian books and specializes in the Victorian Period. The shop occupies 2,000 square feet of space.
How to Get There: David Mason.
Owner/Biography: The shop is located in downtown Toronto, easily reached via subway and surface transportation.
Year Founded/History of Bookstore: 1967.
Number of Volumes: 35,000.
Types/Classifications: Hardbound, rare, antiquarian, first editions, fine bindings, press books, out-of-print, association copies, signed copies, presentation copies, limited editions, color plate books.
General Subject Areas: Canadiana, Children's Books, English Literature (19th Century), History, Literature (U.S.), Modern First Editions, Mysteries, Science, Social Subjects.
Specific Specialties: Victorian Period.
Mail/Telephone Orders; Credit Cards: Both. Visa and Mastercard accepted.
Business Hours: Monday through Saturday 11:00 AM - 6:00 PM; Sunday 12:00 Noon - 6:00 PM.
Parking Facilities: Public parking lot, street parking.
Catalogue: "General Antiquarian Monthly Literature" published 3 to 4 times per year.
Collections/Individual Items Purchased: Both.
Booksellers' Memberships: Antiquarian Booksellers Association of Canada, International League of Antiquarian Booksellers.

1013
Gail Wilson Bookseller Inc.
198 Queen Street West
Toronto, Ontario M5V 1Z2   (416) 598-2024

Located in the heart of Toronto's well-known bookselling area, the shop has been in existence for over five years. Apart from the general stock in the many-alcoved shop, the back room has antiquarian material concentrating on agriculture, folklore, technology, and domestic science. The shop is popular with Torontonians who often drop in for a browse, a chat, and a welcome from the two resident dogs.
How to Get There: The shop is located 4 blocks west of City Hall.
Owner/Biography: Gail Wilson.
Year Founded/History of Bookstore: 1978.
Number of Volumes: 15,000.
Types/Classifications: Hardbound, paperback, first editions, out-of-print.
General Subject Areas: Agriculture, Domestic Science, Folklore, Technology.
Mail/Telephone Orders; Credit Cards: Both. Prepayment required unless customer is known to the owner. Visa accepted.
Business Hours: Monday through Friday 10:00 AM - 9:00 PM; Saturday 10:00 AM - 6:00 PM; Sunday 1:00 PM - 6:00 PM.
Parking Facilities: Street parking; 1 parking space at side of shop.
Catalogue: Published infrequently.
Collections/Individual Items Purchased: Both.
Booksellers' Memberships: Antiquarian Booksellers Association of Canada.

1014
Great Northwest Book Company
338 Jarvis Street
Toronto, Ontario M4Y 2G6   (416) 964-2089

The bookshop is located in a century-old Victorian house. The shop occupies the ground floor and the owners live upstairs.

Owner/Biography: D.V. Baker and Tamara Antonov. Tamara is a graduate of York University and is currently working on her M.A. in English at the University of Toronto. Vincent Baker is the former president of Phalanx Corporation, a graphic design firm in downtown Toronto.

Year Founded/History of Bookstore: 1977.

Number of Volumes: 20,000.

Types/Classifications: Hardbound, paperback, some magazines, ephemera, first editions, fine bindings, out-of-print, some new books.

General Subject Areas: Americana, Anthropology, Art, Aviation, Back-to-the-Land, Biography, Birds, Boating, Books About Books, Business, Canadiana, Children's Books, Cinema, Classics, Cookbooks, Corporate History, Crime, Dance, Dogs, Economics, Education, Electronics, Folklore, Games, Gardening, General Fiction, Geology, Health, Humor, Journalism, Law, Literary Criticism, Literature, Martial Arts, Medicine, Military History, Music, Mysteries, Native People, Nature, Occult, Outdoors, Philosophy, Poetry, Politics, Presidential History (U.S.), Psychology, Royalty, Science, Science Fiction and Fantasy, Sports, Theater, Travel, Western Frontier.

Other Specialties: Extensive Canadiana section.

Mail/Telephone Orders; Credit Cards: Both. Check with order.

Business Hours: Monday through Saturday 12:00 Noon - 6:00 PM; other times by appointment.

Parking Facilities: Street parking in the front, public parking lot close by.

Collections/Individual Items Purchased: Both.

1015
Hannelore Headley Old and Fine Books
71 Queen Street
St. Catharines, Ontario L2R 5G9   (416) 684-6145

The bookstore carries a wide selection of good general antiquarian stock with some rarities and finer items. It contains about 2,000 square feet of space.

Owner/Biography: Mrs. Hannelore Headley, owner, was born in Berlin, Germany, and spent the war years in Shanghai, China, where her father, Heinz Heinemann, a well-known book dealer, had a bookshop. She has been in the book business for 25 years.

Year Founded/History of Bookstore: September 1972.

Number of Volumes: 10,000.

Types/Classifications: Hardbound, paperback, first editions, fine bindings, out-of-print, association copies, press books, signed copies, presentation copies, limited editions, color plate books.

General Subject Areas: Art Books, Biography, Canadiana, Cookbooks, Drama, Fiction, History, Literary Criticism, Military, Mysteries, Occult, Philosophy, Poetry, Science Fiction and Fantasy, Technical, Theology, Travel.

Mail/Telephone Orders; Credit Cards: Both. Visa accepted.

Business Hours: Tuesday through Saturday 10:00 AM - 5:00 PM; Friday 11:00 AM - 6:00 PM; closed Monday.

Parking Facilities: Street.

Special Features: Search service; evaluations for insurance or estate purposes.

Collections/Individual Items Purchased: Both.

Booksellers' Memberships: Antiquarian Booksellers Association of Canada.

1016
Heritage Books
866 Palmerston Avenue
Toronto, Ontario M6G 2S2 (416) 533-6816

Heritage Books specializes in Canadiana only. Visits may be arranged by appointment only.
Owner/Biography: Robert M. Stamp.
Year Founded/History of Bookstore: 1978.
Number of Volumes: 5,000.
Types/Classifications: Hardbound, first editions, out-of-print.
General Subject Areas: Canadiana.
Specific Specialties: Western Canadiana, Fur Trade, Canadian Arctic, Canadian Native Peoples, Canadian Rocky Mountains, Royal Canadian Mounted Police, Canadian Military.
Mail/Telephone Orders; Credit Cards: Both. No credit cards.
Business Hours: By appointment only.
Catalogue: Published monthly.
Collections/Individual Items Purchased: Both.

1017
Hortulus
101 Scollard Street
Toronto, Ontario M5R 1G4 (416) 960-1775

Hortulus is located in an old house with a garden in Toronto's Yorkville area. Visits may be arranged by appointment.
Owner/Biography: Linda and Bruce Marshall.
Year Founded/History of Bookstore: 1978.
Number of Volumes: 2,000.
Types/Classifications: Out-of-print, some new.
General Subject Areas: Agriculture, Architecture, Botany, Garden History, Garden Lore, Gardens, Horticulture, Landscape Design, Plant Hunting, Wild Flowers.
Mail/Telephone Orders; Credit Cards: Both. Mastercard accepted.
Business Hours: By appointment only.
Parking Facilities: Public parking lot, street parking.
Catalogue: Published 3 to 4 times per year.
Collections/Individual Items Purchased: Both.

1018
Joseph Patrick Books
1600 Bloor Street West
Toronto, Ontario M6P 1A7 (416) 531-1891

This is a two floor bookstore. The basement contains stacks of general books; the first floor features a collection of Canadian paperbacks, prints, maps, and rare Canadiana. The shop contains 1,000 square feet of space.
How to Get There: By subway, the Bloor-Danforth line.
Owner/Biography: Mr. Sherlock.
Year Founded/History of Bookstore: The business started in 1958 as a Catholic book service. By 1960 the specialty was changed to Canadiana. Before remaining in its present location in 1971 the shop had moved 3 times.
Number of Volumes: 35,000.
Types/Classifications: Hardbound, paperback, magazines, broadsides, autographs, ephemera, maps, pamphlets, stereoscopic views, first editions, out-of-print, association copies, press books, signed copies, limited editions, presentation copies, unique manuscripts.
General Subject Areas: Arctic, Art of Canada, Canadian Indians, Canadiana, Catholic Church History,

Catholicism, Fur Trade, History of Canada.
   Specific Specialties: Ontario (Canada) History, Canadian Transportation, Emigration Guides, Canadian Folklore, Canadian Military History.
   Mail/Telephone Orders; Credit Cards: Both. Mail order requirements are listed in catalogue. Visa.
   Business Hours: Monday through Saturday 9:00 AM - 5:00 PM.
   Parking Facilities: Meters on street; public parking near by.
   Catalogue: Six times a year.
   Collections/Individual Items Purchased: Both.
   Booksellers' Memberships: Antiquarian Book Dealers Association of Canada.

1019
Madonna House Bookshop
Combermere, Ontario K0J 1L0   (613) 756-2252

   The bookstore is operated by the community of Catholic lay people called Madonna House. Founded in 1930 by Catherine de Hueck Doherty it has always lived by donations. Many of these donations are books, and the good and scarce ones end up in the bookshop to be sold. All profits are used for Third World projects.
   Owner/Biography: Madonna House, Inc.; Karen Van De Loop, Manager.
   Year Founded/History of Bookstore: 1970 for the bookstore.
   Number of Volumes: 20,000.
   Types/Classifications: Hardbound, paperback, ephemera, out-of-print, first editions.
   General Subject Areas: General.
   Specific Specialties: Catholic, Canadiana, Catholic Pre-Vatican II Classical Authors, Catholic Classical Spirituality.
   Mail/Telephone Orders; Credit Cards: Mail orders only; no credit cards.
   Business Hours: Summer: Daily 10:00 AM - 12:00 Noon, and 2:00 PM - 5:00 PM; closed Wednesday. Winter: Thursday through Saturday 2:00 PM - 5:00 PM.
   Parking Facilities: Parking lot.
   Special Features: Nice people; tourist area; fine antique shop is part of the operation.
   Catalogue: Three to four times a year.
   Miscellaneous: All books are donated; the proceeds are used for Third World projects.

1020
Old Favorites Book Shop Ltd.
250 Adelaide West
Toronto, Ontario M5H 1X8   (416) 977-2944

   This bookstore is known as the "old curiosity shop" of Toronto's antiquarian book trade. Located in a basement, it is often mistaken for a library, so large and general is its stock. It boasts a warehouse with an additional 150,000 titles. In addition to keeping requests on file until filled, the bookstore runs a search service for rare and out-of-print titles. The shop contains 2,000 square feet of space.
   Owner/Biography: Lou Morris, Ken Saunders.
   Year Founded/History of Bookstore: Founded in 1953, the bookstore has been in four different downtown Toronto locations, but maintained a continuous family ownership. Ken Saunders, the current president, is the son-in-law of the founder, Lou Morris.
   Number of Volumes: 250,000.
   Types/Classifications: All aspects of the out-of-print and antiquarian trade as well as a large stock of used books and magazines.
   General Subject Areas: Agriculture, Canadiana, General, Horses, Hunting, Literature, Science Fiction and Fantasy.
   Mail/Telephone Orders; Credit Cards: Both. Letter requests are answered upon receipt. If the book is in stock it will be quoted postpaid in American, English, or Canadian funds. Cash with order. Visa.
   Business Hours: Tuesday through Saturday 10:00 AM - 9:00 PM.
   Parking Facilities: Public parking lot.
   Special Features: Search service, auctions, catalogues.

Catalogue: Published annually.
Collections/Individual Items Purchased: Both.
Booksellers' Memberships: Canadian Association of Antiquarian Booksellers.

1021
Past and Present Shop
269 Dalhousie Street
Amherstburg, Ontario N9V 1W8   (519) 736-4123

The shop carries new children's books, Eskimo art, War of 1812 reprints, and other related gift items. The building was built in 1830 and is an historic site. Its several rooms are filled with used books on all general subjects and is a browser's delight.
How to Get There: Amherstburg is located 17 miles south of Winsdor and Detroit on the Detroit River; take Highway 18 from the Detroit-Windsor Bridge.
Owner/Biography: Betty and Bill Ransome.
Year Founded/History of Bookstore: 1973.
Number of Volumes: 10,000.
Types/Classifications: Hardbound, paperback, music, ephemera, out-of-print.
General Subject Areas: General.
Specific Specialties: Children's Literature, Juvenile, Canadiana, Border Area History.
Author Specialties: Jack London, R.M. Ballantyne.
Mail/Telephone Orders; Credit Cards: Both. Visa and Mastercard accepted.
Business Hours: Monday through Saturday 9:30 AM - 5:00 PM.
Parking Facilities: Public parking.
Collections/Individual Items Purchased: Both.

1022
Richard Simmins Books
245 1/2 Bank Street
Ottawa, Ontario K2P 1X2   (613) 237-0895

This bookstore carries a stock of used and rare books in most subject areas.
Owner/Biography: Richard Simmins.
Types/Classifications: Rare, out-of-print, first editions, used.
General Subject Areas: General.
Mail/Telephone Orders; Credit Cards: Mail orders.
Business Hours: Monday through Saturday 11:00 AM - 5:30 PM.
Parking Facilities: Available.
Collections/Individual Items Purchased: Both.

1023
Rising Trout Sporting Books
130 Country Club Drive
Guelph, Ontario N1H 6Z9   (519) 824-3551

Rising Trout Sporting Books is a small, specialist operation where friendliness, hospitality, and good coversation make up for lack of space. The owner is always ready to discuss fishing books, trout flies, Scotch whiskey, and similar vital topics. He always believes fish stories related to him by customers and knows, from personal experience, that the Big One always gets away.
How to Get There: Guelph is about 15 minutes north of the MacDonald-Cartier Freeway (Highway 401), approximately half way between Toronto and London, Ontario. It is about one hour from either Toronto International Airport or the Stratford Shakespearian Festival.
Owner/Biography: John A. Modlenhauer. Mr. Modlenhauer has been a fly fisherman for nearly thirty years and has been in the antiquarian book business for ten years.

Year Founded/History of Bookstore: 1974.
Number of Volumes: 3,000.
Types/Classifications: Hardbound, paperback, magazines, broadsides, autographs, ephemera, trade catalogues, first editions, fine bindings, out-of-print, association copies, press books, signed copies, presentation copies, limited editions, color plate books.
General Subject Areas: Canoeing, Field Sports, Fishing, Gun Collecting, Guns, Hunting, Shooting, Sporting.
Specific Specialties: Fly Fishing, Fly Tying, Trout, Salmon, Sporting Travel, Sporting Bibliography, Sporting Reference, British Angling, Canadian Angling, Specimen Books.
Author Specialties: F.M. Halford, G.E.M. Skues, A. Ronalds, I. Walton, R. Haig-Brown.
Other Specialties: Anything related to sport fishing from any period and in any language.
Mail/Telephone Orders; Credit Cards: Both. Payment with order. No credit cards.
Business Hours: By appointment only (seven days a week).
Parking Facilities: Ample free street parking.
Special Features: Want lists searched; appraisals and evaluations; commissions taken for any auction.
Catalogue: Published once per year.
Collections/Individual Items Purchased: Both.

1024
St. Nicholas Books
P.O. Box 863, Station F
Toronto, Ontario M4Y 2N7   (416) 922-9640

This is a mail order business primarily, open by appointment only.
How to Get There: Call for directions.
Owner/Biography: Yvonne Knight.
Year Founded/History of Bookstore: 1973.
Number of Volumes: 2,500.
Types/Classifications: Hardbound books, ephemera.
General Subject Areas: Children's Books, Children's Illustrated Books, Decorative Arts.
Specific Specialties: Advertising Ephemera which is mostly of a juvenile nature.
Mail/Telephone Orders; Credit Cards: Both. No credit cards.
Business Hours: By appointment only.
Parking Facilities: Private driveway.
Catalogue: Three or four times a year.
Collections/Individual Items Purchased: Individual items only.
Booksellers' Memberships: Antiquarian Booksellers Association of Canada.

1025
William Matthews, Bookseller
46 Gilmore Road
Fort Erie, Ontario L2A 2M1   (416) 871-7859

The bookstore is on the main floor of an old house in Fort Erie, Ontario, Canada. It contains 1,000 square feet of space. Fort Erie is on the Canada-United States border immediately across the Niagara River from Buffalo, New York, U.S.A.
How to Get There: Take the Peace Bridge from Buffalo, head north along the Niagara River, turn left onto Gilmore Road.
Owner/Biography: William Matthews, Ann Hall.
Year Founded/History of Bookstore: William Matthews opened the business in 1976 as "Star Treader Books," in Vancouver, British Columbia, Canada. It was there until 1980 when moved to Toronto for two years. The name was changed to its present one when the store was moved to Fort Erie in 1982.
Number of Volumes: 4,000.
Types/Classifications: Hardcover primarily, first editions, early editions, uncommon books.

General Subject Areas: Literature, Science Fiction and Fantasy.
Specific Specialties: Early Fantasy (18th and 19th Centuries), Lost Race, Interplanetary, Future Fiction, Utopian Fiction, Supernatural Fiction.
Author Specialties: William Hope Hodgson, John Collier, Lord Dunsany.
Mail/Telephone Orders; Credit Cards: Both. Visa.
Business Hours: By appointment only.
Parking Facilities: Driveway.
Special Features: Qualified appraisals for insurance or tax purposes.
Catalogue: Four times a year.
Collections/Individual Items Purchased: Both.
Booksellers' Memberships: Antiquarian Booksellers Association of Canada (Secretary).

1026
William Nelson Books
686 Richmond Street West
Toronto, Ontario M6J 1C3   (416) 361-0220

This bookstore stocks only Canadian literature. It contains 2,500 square feet of space.
Owner/Biography: Nelson Ball.
Year Founded/History of Bookstore: 1972.
Number of Volumes: 30,000.
Types/Classifications: All types and classifications including hardbound, out-of-print, first editions.
General Subject Areas: Canadian Literature.
Mail/Telephone Orders; Credit Cards: Both. No credit cards.
Business Hours: By appointment only.
Catalogue: Published quarterly.
Collections/Individual Items Purchased: Both.
Booksellers' Memberships: Antiquarian Booksellers Association of Canada.

QUEBEC

1027
Bibliography of the Dog
4170 Decarle Boulevard
Montreal, Quebec H4A 3K2
(514) 488-6279

This bookseller deals exclusively in books about dogs.
How to Get There: Call for instructions.
Types/Classifications: Out-of-print, rare.
General Subject Areas: Dogs.
Mail/Telephone Orders; Credit Cards: Mail order.
Business Hours: Phone for appointment and information.

1028
Librairie Jean Gagnon
764 St. Joseph E (402)
Quebec, Quebec G1R 4S2
(418) 523-6760

This book shop deals in out-of-print French and Canadian material and can be visited by appointment only. The stock occupies 1,200 square feet of space.
How to Get There: Call for appointment and directions.
Owner/Biography: Jean Gagnon.
Year Founded/History of Bookstore: 1955.
Number of Volumes: 15,000.
Types/Classifications: Hardbound, paperback, out-of-print.
General Subject Areas: Canadiana, French Literature.
Mail/Telephone Orders; Credit Cards: Both. No credit cards.
Business Hours: By appointment only.
Parking Facilities: Public parking lot.
Catalogue: Published 10 times per year.
Collections/Individual Items Purchased: Both.
Booksellers' Memberships: Antiquarian Booksellers Association of Canada.

SUBJECT INDEX

Number to right refers to numerical listing in text